Legal Issues of Services of General Interest

Series editors

Johan Willem van de Gronden
Markus Krajewski
Ulla Neergaard
Erika Szyszczak

More information about this series at http://www.springer.com/series/8900

Caroline Wehlander

Services of General Economic Interest as a Constitutional Concept of EU Law

ASSER PRESS

Springer

Caroline Wehlander
Stockholm
Sweden

Legal Issues of Services of General Interest
ISBN 978-94-6265-116-6 ISBN 978-94-6265-117-3 (eBook)
DOI 10.1007/978-94-6265-117-3

Library of Congress Control Number: 2016935209

Published by T.M.C. ASSER PRESS, The Hague, The Netherlands www.asserpress.nl
Produced and distributed for T.M.C. ASSER PRESS by Springer-Verlag Berlin Heidelberg

Printed on acid-free paper

This Springer imprint is published by Springer Nature
The registered company is Springer-Verlag GmbH Berlin Heidelberg

Series Information

The aim of the series *Legal Issues of Services of General Interest* is to sketch the framework for services of general interest in the EU and to explore the issues raised by developments related to these services. The Series encompasses, inter alia, analyses of EU internal market, competition law, legislation (such as the Services Directive), international economic law and national (economic) law from a comparative perspective. Sector-specific approaches will also be covered (health, social services). In essence, the present Series addresses the emergence of a European Social Model and will therefore raise issues of fundamental and theoretical interest in Europe and the global economy.

Series Editors

Ulla Neergaard
Faculty of Law
University of Copenhagen
Studiestræde 6
1455 Copenhagen K
Denmark
e-mail: ulla.neergaard@jur.ku.dk

Johan Willem van de Gronden
Faculty of Law
Radboud University
Comeniuslaan 4
6525 HP Nijmegen
The Netherlands
e-mail: j.vandeGronden@jur.ru.nl

Erika Szyszczak
Sussex Law School
University of Sussex
Brighton, BN1 9SP
UK
e-mail: E.Szyszczak@sussex.ac.uk

Markus Krajewski
Fachbereich Rechtswissenschaft
Universität Erlangen-Nürnberg
Schillerstraße 1
91054 Erlangen
Germany
e-mail: markus.krajewski@fau.de

Preface

During the years 2004–2010, I worked as a practitioner of Swedish public law on housing and waste treatment; this book was born out of that experience. As a legal advisor for local and regional authorities in Sweden, I faced the challenge of understanding what a service of general economic interest (SGEI) is and how the SGEI character of an activity affects the application of EU market rules to national measures affecting the activity. I was also able to witness the striking contrast between the intensity of the EU debate on services of general interest at an EU level and the loud silence on this topic in Sweden. Yet it was clear that in Sweden as anywhere else in the EU, market law implacably made its way into the Member States' regulation of social services, one of the most sensitive parts of national democracy. It was also clear that this evolution could explain the introduction of several new provisions on SGEI in the EU Treaties, first through the Treaty of Amsterdam 1997–1999 and a decade later through the Treaty of Lisbon 2007–2009.

This transformation of SGEI into a constitutional concept of EU law is the result of a political compromise and, unsurprisingly, the post-Lisbon Treaty framework on SGEI has not only brought up new legal issues but also left crucial legal questions unanswered. This book addresses some of the unsolved questions: in particular, what constitutes an economic activity for the purpose of EU market law and what is the legal meaning of the EU concept of SGEI? The debate on SGEI may not be particularly topical at the moment but it seems important to discuss the meaning and relevance of SGEI, especially because the EU Commission has a mandate to negotiate the international trade agreement between the Union and the USA. The book also proposes an analysis of the ambiguous relationship between the SGEI provisions in the FEU Treaty, as interpreted by the CJEU, and the EU procurement and state aid legislative package adopted within the frame of the Commission Communication on Services of General Interest 2012. Finally, in order to gain a better understanding of the strategic choices made in these legislative packages, the book focuses on the Swedish regulation of public social services in systems of choice and on the effects a strict application of the EU state aid rules would have on their liberalization.

The book would never have existed without enduring attention from Pr. Tom Madell and Pr. Ulla Neergaard, and precious guidance from Pr. Jörgen Hettne, Pr. Johan Lindholm, Pr. Gareth Davies, Pr. Johan van de Gronden and Pr. Erika Szyszczak. The cheering team was composed of Per Wehlander, my beloved husband, and my children, César and Lila. They have amply proved that they know what solidarity means.

Lucky and grateful.

Stockholm,
January 2016

Caroline Wehlander

Contents

Abbreviations

AC	Swedish Competition Act (Sw: *Konkurrenslagen* (2008:579))
AG	Advocate General
CJEU	Court of Justice of the European Union
EAGCP	Economic Advisory Group for Competition Policy
EC	European Community
ECJ	European Court of Justice
EEC	European Economic Community
EFTA	European Free Trade Association
EU	European Union
EUCFR	Charter of Fundamental Rights of the European Union
FAQ	Frequently Asked Question
GC	General Court (of the EU), formerly Court of First Instance
IG	The Instrument of Government (Regeringsformen 1974:152), one of the four fundamental laws comprised in the Swedish Constitution
LGA	Swedish Local Government Act (Sw: *Kommunallagen* (1991:900))
LOV	Act on Systems of Choice in the Public Sector (Sw: *Lag om Valfrihetssystem* (2008:962))
LRAs	Local and Regional Authorities in Sweden
NESGI	Non-Economic Services of General Interest
Nyr	Not yet reported
OECD	Organisation for Economic Co-operation and Development
OJ	Official Journal
PISA	Programme for International Student Assessment
PSO	Public Service Obligation
SALAR	Swedish Association of Local Authorities and Regions
SCA	Swedish Competition Authority
SEA	Single European Act
SGEI	Services of General Economic Interest
SGI	Services of General Interest
SPC	Social Protection Committee

SSGI	Social Services of General Interest
TEU	Treaty on the European Union
TFEU	Treaty on the Functioning of the European Union
USO	Universal Service Obligation

Part I
No Exit from EU Market Law for Public Services

Chapter 1
Introduction: The Constitutionalisation of the EU Concept of SGEI as a Story of Exit, Voice and Loyalty for Public Services in EU Law

Abstract This introductory chapter outlines the legal and political context which has led services of general economic interest to become a constitutional concept of EU law, and the regulatory developments in the field of social services in the Union. It introduces the main objective of the book which is to find out whether it is possible to understand SGEI as a constitutional EU concept relevant throughout the EU Treaties, and whether a transparent and loyal enforcement of the Treaty principles attached to SGEI can restrict the Member States' discretion to liberalize social services and the expansion of a European market for social services. In order to answer this main research question, three sub-questions are formulated and addressed in the three main parts of the book. The chapter outlines the theory and method used in the study, which includes a case study on Swedish regulation of social services in part III.

Contents

C. Wehlander, *Services of General Economic Interest as a Constitutional Concept of EU Law*, Legal Issues of Services of General Interest,
DOI 10.1007/978-94-6265-117-3_1

1.1 The Expansion of EU Law in the Field of Public Services, Including Social Services: Crucial Legal Issues Unsolved

In a letter addressed in 2014 to the Swedish State, the European Commission (hereinafter "the Commission") explained that it did not prioritize complaints alleging illegal state aid in the partial privatisation of municipal schools and primary healthcare entities to private owners.[1] The Commission closed the case on the motive that "the described measures, their beneficiaries and the markets involved seemed to be purely local".[2] Although independent schools—many of them run for-profit—are part of the Swedish education system, the Commission did simply not question their economic character. This is striking because national school systems have been regarded not only by the Member States, but also by the Commission, as a national "chasse gardée", consisting wholly of non-economic activities. This letter—not registered in its public database by the Commission—signals discreetly a major turn in EU law on public services: not only healthcare services but also other social services as politically sensitive as education in a national school system may in all the more cases be covered by EU rules on state aid and, more broadly, on competition.

While allowing for-profit schools in the education system is still a specifically Swedish experiment, liberalization of social services is a trend in many Member States, which gives rise to complaints from private competitors, for instance in Germany and the Netherlands about the financing of public long-term care providers.[3] A more visible part of this "legal iceberg" is the *IRIS-H* decision, where the Commission found that public hospitals in the Brussels region constituted undertakings in competition with publicly funded private hospitals, and that public

[1]The term "partial privatization" is used here as these entities, although privately owned, continue to be, for the most part, financed by public resources.

[2]See letter of the Head Section for Market and Competition Division at the Swedish Ministry of Enterprise, Energy and Communication, registered under reference COMP/H-2/BC—(2012)33624, dated 29.03.2012.

[3]Commission, "The Application of EU State Aid rules on Services of General Economic Interest since 2005 and the Outcome of the Public Consultation", SEC (2011) 397, p. 30. In this paper, the Commission evokes the decisions without reference to their numbers, but underlines that the public financing was found to comply with EU state aid rules.

funding of their public service tasks was therefore subject to the Treaty rules on state aid.[4] This evolution owes much to the development of "mixed systems" for the supply of welfare services in the Member States. However, the applicability of EU market rules to social services would have been impossible without the "functional" definition of "undertaking" developed by the CJEU for the purpose of EU competition rules, i.e. "every entity engaged in an economic activity, regardless of the legal status of the entity and the way in which it is financed".[5] In *IRIS-H*, the Belgian authorities were forced to justify this public funding by relying on Article 106(2) TFEU, which provides that the Treaty rules apply to undertakings entrusted with services of general economic interest (hereinafter "SGEIs"), but "in so far as the application of such rules does not obstruct the performance, in law or in fact, of the particular tasks assigned to them".

The "close encounter" between Member States' measures in the field of social services and EU law does not only take place in the field of state aid, where we find EU secondary law rules specifically designed for SGEI and even more specifically for social services, but today in all fields of EU market law[6]: in EU free movement law (the Patients' rights Directive[7]), and now in EU procurement law, as a new chapter on social services has been introduced in the 2014 procurement directives.[8] This Europeanisation of the legal framework for social services is striking, because it takes place in a field where the Member States have retained their policy competence. As observed by Krajewski, "autonomous domestic regulatory reforms and policy changes" explain this transformation, but it is undeniable that the CJEU's interpretation of EU market law "put[s] traditional models of supplying [public services] in particular on the basis of regional and local monopolies under enormous pressure". [9] The CJEU has played a major role in building the foundations allowing to integrate the internal market of public services, including social services, in particular through a very broad interpretation of Treaty notions such as "service", "good", "capital", "undertaking", and not least

---

[4]Commission Decision of 28 October 2009 on the public financing of Brussels public IRIS hospitals (Belgium) in case SA.19864 (ex NN54/2009)—2014/C. The first decision not to raise objections against the aid measures, annulled by the GC, is only available in Dutch and in French.

[5]Case C-41/90 *Höfner* [1991] ECR I-1979, para 21. In this study, the expression "competition rules" is meant "in a broad sense", in other words both EU competition rules (often improperly called "antitrust rules"), and EU state aid rules.

[6]By "EU market law" is meant here EU law on free movement, procurement, competition and state aid.

[7]Directive 2011/24/EU of the European Parliament and of the Council of 9 March 2011 on the application of patients' rights in cross-border healthcare (the Patients' rights Directive) [2011] OJ L88/45.

[8]In this study, the EU procurement directives adopted in February 2014 are referred to as "the 2014 procurement directives", while the EU procurement directive in force until April 2016 are referred to as "the EU procurement directives".

[9]Krajeswski 2009, p. 503.

"non-discrimination". The Court has multiplied free movement and competition based arguments which may be relied on to challenge Member States' statutory and administrative measures in the field of public services, and as observed by van de Gronden, the Court's approach is clearly also one of market opening.[10]

The CJEU's case law, and the Commission's decision practice, constitute the legal basis of the Europeanisation of public services—and now also social services –even if these decisions do not immediately have an impact on the Member States' systems. As noted by Sauter, the liberalizing pressure induced by the CJEU's broad interpretation of the notion of "economic activity"—inherent to the notions of "services", "goods" and "undertaking" in the Treaties—largely explains the growing importance of the notion of SGEI in the case law of the CJEU and in the European legal-political debate.[11]

1.1.1 The CJEU's Use of the EU Concept of SGEI in Article 106(2) TFEU to Address Member States' Concerns on the Expansion of EU Law in Their Fields of Competence

To be sure, the CJEU has not acted in a political vacuum, but rather accompanied the "public turn" of EU competition law launched by the Commission's 1992 Programme, where a major element was the integration of the Single Market through the elaboration of EU public procurement rules. This was followed by the adoption in 1986 of the Single European Act (SEA)[12] which, in Weiler's view, was not simply a programme removing barriers to free movement, but "a highly politicized choice of ethos, ideology, and political culture: the culture of 'the market'".[13] As Member States realized that this "eruption of significant proportions" would affect the demarcation of competences, the principle of subsidiarity was

[10]Van de Gronden holds that "the analysis of the CJEU's case law demonstrates that EU free movement law may force Member States to introduce elements of competition in their national schemes governing [social services of general interest (SSGI)]. Although it is for the Member States to regulate these services, the stance of EU law is not neutral in this respect; rather it is based on the view that competition should play some role in the national organisation and provision of SSGI." See van de Gronden 2013a, p. 156.

[11]Sauter 2008, p. 3.

[12]Commission, "Completing the Internal Market" (White Paper to the European Council, Milan: 28–29 June 1985) COM (85) 310 final. The SEA introduced Article 100a EEC (now Article 114 TFEU) allowing all measures for the establishment and functioning of the internal market to be adopted by a qualified majority through Article 100a, which was described as "the most important of the Act's internal market provisions, being probably more far- reaching in its implications than any other provision in the entire Act", see Ehlerman 1987, p. 381.

[13]Weiler has explained that, for different reasons, the European Parliament and the Commission were "far from thrilled" with the SEA, which in particular led Margaret Thatcher to characterize it as "a modest step forward". See Weiler 1991, p. 2455, 2459 and 2477.

introduced in EU primary law in 1992 through the Treaty of Maastricht.[14] Many of them expressed growing concerns that the *negative* integration of the internal market—driven judicially on the basis of proportionality assessments—restricted the exercise of their powers under the EU principle of conferral.[15] Relying inadequately on the argument of "subsidiarity"—a principle which is hardly helpful in relation to *negative* integration—they used their "voice" against the CJEU's expansive interpretation of EU primary and secondary law on free movement, procurement and competition.

Faced with the worries caused by its expansion of EU market law's scope in the field of public services, the CJEU has shown loyalty to the "masters of the Treaties" in several ways. Firstly, the Court has built up from the 1990s onwards, a case law applying the exemption rule for "services of general economic interest" (SGEIs) in Article 106(2) TFEU. In a series of seminal rulings, including *Corbeau,*[16] *Almelo,*[17] the so called "electricity cases",[18] *Altmark*[19] and more recently *BUPA,*[20] the Court has established that the SGEI-character of an activity constitutes a legitimate ground for state (or EU) intervention in the public sector, and developed a specific "soft test" under Article 106(2) TFEU, to assess measures such as authorization schemes, exclusive rights, public financing, and cross-subsidization of services in the public sector. By relaxing the tensions between market interests and general interests, this case law has facilitated the adoption of EU law in the sectors of energy, telecommunications, postal services and transport, aimed at market harmonisation and therefore based on Article 114 TFEU, but at the same allowing the imposition of public service obligations justified explicitly or implicitly on Article 106(2) TFEU.[21]

Although Article 106(2) TFEU has also been found applicable outside the field of competition law, in particular to justify statutory exclusive rights, its relevance

---

[14]As noted by Weiler, the Member States' urge for a clearer demarcation of competences was already clear from the Resolution of Parliament of July 12, 1990 (PE 143.504). See Weiler 1991, p. 2463 not 173.

[15]Integration theories distinguish between positive and negative integration. Positive integration implies that common rules are adopted by a higher authority to remove regional differences, while negative integration refers to the removal of barriers between countries. Weiler 2005.

[16]Case C-320/91 *Corbeau,* [1993] ECR 1-2563.

[17]Case C-393/92 *Almelo* [1994] ECR I-1477.

[18]Case C-157/94 *Commission v Netherlands* [1997] ECR I-5699; Case C-158/94 *Commission v Italy* [1997] ECR I-5789; Case C-159/94 *Commission v France* [1997] ECR I-5815.

[19]Case C-280/00, *Altmark* [2003] ECR I –7747.

[20]Case T-289/03 *BUPA* [2008] ECR II-81.

[21]By contrast, large areas of the public sector in the Member States, although clearly or increasingly economic in character, are not subject to EU *sector* law clarifying the principles and conditions of public intervention—justified by objectives of general interest—in the *economy* of these sectors. This is for instance the case concerning waste and water management, covered by EU sector law of administrative nature not primarily aiming at harmonizing the internal market and/ or ensuring undistorted competition.

to mitigate public procurement rules is both legally uncertain and politically controversial. However, the CJEU has found it appropriate to limit the scope of EU procurement rules (which it had contributed to expand), by formulating conditions allowing public authorities to provide services and goods with their own resources (the *Teckal* doctrine), and more recently, conditions allowing public authorities to cooperate, even on the basis of contracts, in the achievement of common "*public service tasks*", a term also used by the CJEU as synonym of SGEI *tasks*.[22]

There are today many judgments where EU free movement and/or competition rules have been found applicable to social services. In particular, the CJEU's very extensive interpretation of the notion of "remuneration" in Article 57 TFEU has led to find EU free movement rules applicable to cross-border healthcare provision, para-medical services and university courses. However, in those fields the Court has considered it appropriate to examine measures motivated by certain types of "overriding reasons related to the general interest" under a relaxed test which departs from its standard proportionality test in the field of free movement, and seems to transpose the test it commonly applies under Article 106(2) TFEU. This case law has allowed the adoption of the Patients' Rights Directive, a very rare example of sector-specific EU legislation in the field of social services.[23]

For Member States worrying about the expanding applicability of EU law in their fields of competence, it was important that the Court formulated in *Humbel* a doctrine exempting courses in national education systems from the scope of EU law.[24] Also, it could be comforting that the Court has developed a doctrine based on its *Poucet and Pistre* ruling, exempting the operation of social security services based exclusively on the principle of solidarity from the scope of EU competition rules.[25] Nevertheless, in many cases, the latter doctrine has not kept the Court from finding EU competition rules applicable to measures related to social security schemes despite the fact that they included many solidarity elements.

Cases on social services other than social security services are scarce in the field of competition, but as the notion of undertaking must be interpreted functionally in EU competition law, it must be expected that their provision will be seen as economic in national systems of supply "where there is an interplay between public and private", and in such mixed market systems, the SGEI character of the service constitutes an important ground to justify State intervention.[26] With the growth of markets in the sector of social services, the tension between internal market interest and social interests must be resolved in a special manner, which explains the importance of the Treaty rules on SGEIs in the development of EU procurement and state aid law applying to such services.

---

[22]Case C-480/06 *Commission v. Germany* [2009] ECR I-4747.

[23]One exception is the Patients Rights Directive.

[24]Case 263/86 *Humbel* [1988] ECR I-5365.

[25]Joined Cases C-159/91 and C-160/91 *Poucet and Pistre* [1993] ECR I-00637.

[26]De Vries 2011, p. 462.

1.1.2 The Progressive and (Too?) Subtle Approach of the CJEU: Two Important Legal Questions

As market mechanisms and markets develop in the field of public services, Member States must in more and more sectors explicitly or implicitly rely on the EU framework on SGEIs to motivate measures allowing them to conduct social and environmental policies in the frame of their powers. This picture emerges not only from the case-law of the CJEU but also from EU market law.[27] To secure the legality of their horizontal or sector-specific public service regulation, the Member States should be able to answer the two following questions:

a. What criteria determine that an activity in their public sector is covered by EU free movement rules and/or by EU competition rules?
b. Which margins of discretion does EU market law give them as legislators, and their public authorities as regulators and administrators, to secure the achievement of public service tasks defined statutory or administratively in the frame of their national legal system? In other words, is the fact that SGEI missions exist in national law relevant only to enable *market operators* to achieve public service tasks on the market, or is it also relevant to enable *public authorities* to achieve public service tasks on the market?

Regarding question (a), Davies has observed that, "for *convenience*, services falling within free movement and competition law are conventionally referred to as 'economic' services, while 'non-economic' services fall without".[28] This "convention" is undeniable but makes it very difficult to understand the scope of the Treaty market rules. In the Treaties, neither the free movement rules nor the competition rules contain the word "economic", as their scope is instead delineated by the notions of goods, service, capital, and undertaking. Indeed, the CJEU has established that an undertaking is any entity conducting an "economic activity", but the Court does not use the notion of "economic activity" (or the notion of "market") as an element in the definition of services or goods for the purpose of EU free movement and procurement rules. In fact, the Court seems to *avoid* the notion of "economic activity" to assess the applicability of the internal market rules to public services.

Thus, in evaluating the national legislators or administrators' freedom to intervene on general interest grounds in certain fields of activity, the "conventional question" is "whether it is an economic activity", although free movement rules can apply to activities which are non-economic in a Member State. From a democratic perspective, the "convenient convention" is problematical because it blurs

[27] Thus, healthcare and other social services are excluded from the scope of Directive 2006/123/EC of the European Parliament and of the Council of 12 December 2006 on services in the internal market (the "Services Directive") [2006] OJ L 376/36 , while all SGEIs—regardless of the sector at issue—are excluded from Article 16 in the Services Directive.

[28] Davies 2006, p. 16.

the legal political grounds for the applicability of EU principles of free movement to activities which are not—or cannot be—offered on the market in a Member State. In other words, the "convention" may conceal a mechanism which is welcomed by the "masters of the Treaties",[29] but also an *inconvenient* truth on the limits of their prerogatives in relation to "market powers" in the field of social services. From a rule of law perspective, the use of this convention is also problematic, because it implies that an "economic service" can be two things (one in the field of competition and another in the field of free movement), and logically also that a "non-economic service" can be one thing in the field of competition and another thing in the field of free movement. Under such circumstances, the Member States may certainly wonder what sense they can make of the following EU rules:

- Article 2 of the SGI Protocol providing that "[t]he provisions of the Treaties do not affect in any way the competence of Member States to provide, commission and organise non-economic services of general interest"
- The assertions made in the 2014 procurement directives that Member States "are free to organise the provision of compulsory social services or of other services such as postal services either as services of general economic interest or as non-economic services of general interest or as a mixture thereof", and the clarification (!) that "non-economic services of general interest should not fall within the scope of this Directive".

It is important to be aware that question (a) above - what does "economic activity" mean in EU law—is profoundly related to the notion of SGEI in two ways. First, because the economic character of the activity may trigger a necessity to rely on the SGEI tasks attached to this activity in order to justify state intervention. Second, because depending on the relation of the word "economic" in SG(E)I to the notion of "economic activity", the answer to question (b) above ("what is the meaning of the concept of SGEI") may differ. In other words, clarifying what an "economic activity" is, may have an impact on the meaning that the concept of SGEI should have, and on the derogations from a strict application of the Treaty-based rules which SGEIs should be able to motivate. As a result, a clarification of the meaning of the EU notion of "economic activity" is simply crucial for certain Member States' wish to obtain a broad public service exception, allowing them to retain more powers in the organisation of public services, and more particularly of publicly financed social services. Their wish that SGEI obtains a broad understanding is confronted to the Commission's determination "to avoid opening a Pandora's Box that could threaten the application of the market freedoms".[30]

The persistence of this uncertainty, and of a scholarly debate, is made possible by the CJEU's subtle use of the notion of "economic activity", never spelling out clearly which precise "generic" criteria make an activity "economic" (regardless

[29]This term is borrowed from Roth, see Roth 2011, p. 77.

[30]Sauter 2008, p. 1.

of the type of activity considered) and what relevance (if any) the economic character of an activity has for the applicability of the different Treaty market rules. The Court tends, instead, to focus on the "economic relevance" of the specific measures or transactions brought to its jurisdiction, in particular in the fields of free movement and procurement. By this approach, the Court has given itself a legal-technical space to expand the scope of the free movement, competition and procurement rules in accordance with the signals of political acceptance—or lack of acceptance—sent by the Member States for letting EU market rules constrain public intervention in public services.[31] Likewise, the tests used by the Court to allow exemptions from Treaty provisions and Treaty-based rules on free movement and procurement have so far been formulated in a manner that makes it very difficult to discern how it understands the EU concept of SGEI, although it is difficult to deny that SGEI is a concept of EU law.

The casuistic character and the "subtlety" of the CJEU's approach are arguably related to the Court's awareness of the *political* implications of having expanded the scope of EU market law, and of spelling too clearly how the EU concept of SGEI may be understood. When deciding if, and how, the Treaty market rules apply to public services, in particular social services, the Court must clarify essential questions left unsolved by the Member States, and does probably not always find appropriate to say what it does. As a result, what the Court means by "economic activity" and how it understands the EU concept of SGEI is still difficult to put in intelligible words.

1.1.3 SGEI: EU Debate and Constitutionalisation Through the Treaty of Lisbon 2007/2009

Acknowledging the existence of "worries about the future of [general interest services] accompanied by concerns over employment and economic and social cohesion", the Commission published in 1996 its first Communication on the European future of what it chose to call "services of general interest" (SGIs), and defined as "market and non-market services which the public authorities class as being of general interest and subject to specific public service obligations".[32] This was followed by half a dozen other Communications, whereby the Commission added to its conceptual arsenal the term of "non-economic services of general interest" (NESGIs). In this conceptual architecture, services of general interest (SGIs) seemed to constitute the sum of SGEIs and NESGIs.

---

[31]Such signals could be found in Treaty modifications, in the Commission's "public turn" in the field of competition, but also in EU legislation, for instance the procurement directives adopted on the basis of the White paper of 1985 (as an example of acceptance)—or the Services Directive (as an example of non-acceptance).

[32]Commission, "Services of General Interest in Europe" (Communication) 96/C 281/03.

During the consultation exercise for the Green Paper on SGIs, the actors of the social sector (local public authorities, service providers, representatives of the providers) expressed concerns about the lack of legal certainty as to whether social services were to be seen as economic or non-economic, which could imply the applicability of a different body of EU rules. In response, in it its White Paper of 2004, the Commission gave assurances that it would clarify the framework in which they operated, but could only come up in 2006 with a shallow Communication on "Social Services of General Interest" (SSGIs).[33] This Communication did not bring much of a legal clarification, but launched the neutral and non-legal notion concept of SSGI, which has been and still is a political key in the process of Europeanization of social services, as it builds on the neutral and generic concept of SGIs that overall has been a useful vehicle to develop a soft law discourse on the controversial concept of the European Social Model.[34] Also, given the complexity of the case law and given the considerable lack of certainty on what makes an SSGI "economic" (SGEI) or non-economic (NESGI), the notion of SSGI has served as a powerful support of communication on the issue of how the Member States can shield social services in their welfare systems from the full impact of EU market law.

This succession of communications has allowed the Commission to orchestrate a debate underpinned by the "big questions", in particular the welfare state v smaller state, and the national state's relevance in a European Social Model that for reasons not developed here must arguably be market-based. Although this debate was embedded in the neutral project to "clarify EU rules applying to SGEIs", its political dimension is evident. Very simplified, the debate is related to the confrontation between two socio-economic "models" for public services: a more liberal-oriented model, and a more solidarity-based model. The political dimension of the debate on SGEIs became fully visible when some Member States exercised pressure to introduce through the Treaty of Amsterdam 1997, "a general, rather than legally specific" Treaty objective for SGEIs, under Article 16 EC.[35] It was reaffirmed during the legislative process for the adoption of the Directive on services in the internal market (hereafter the "Services Directive"),[36] when SGEIs were partly left out and NESGIs wholly left out from its scope, a change of direction

---

[33]Bauby 2013, p. 26.

[34]This is the convincing explanation of Szyszczak who has shown how, in spite of the fact that policy competence has mostly not been conferred onto the EU in the field of social services, the Commission has since the 2000s, and very rapidly since the 2006 Communication on Social Services of General Interest in the European Union (COM 2006) 177 final), developed a new governance competence and capacity in the form of soft law and soft governance processes in that field of activities. Launching the term "social services of general interest" has been a very important step. See Szyszczak 2013, pp. 317–345.

[35]Bauby 2011, p. 27.

[36]Directive 2006/123/EC of the European Parliament and of the Council of 12 December 2006 on services in the internal market.

from the Commission's proposal which according to Neergaard was initiated by the Member States, but supported at an early stage by the European Parliament.[37]

While the Commission announced it would clarify the case law of the CJEU, its Communications do not really offer any pedagogic systematization, as its three consecutive "SGEI Guides" have taken the form of "Frequently asked questions".[38] Regarding the criteria determining that an activity is covered by EU free movement and/or EU competition rules, these guides are as casuistic as the case law they refer to. The "convenient" convention is upheld that only "economic activities" can be covered by the market rules of the Treaties.[39]

The EU debate on SGEIs had begun maturing when the draft Constitutional Treaty was rejected by French and Dutch voters in 2005.[40] The political re-negoti-

---

[37]See Neergaard 2008, pp. 97–98, where the author gives a detailed account of the approach to SGEIs in the context of the Services Directive, and explains the carving out of SGEIs and NESGIs by "tensions between what /…/ could be referred to as a more liberal point of view, situated mainly at the Commission, against a more protectionist point of view, situated at some of the Member States" which in her view have existed ever since the birth of the Community".

[38]The first Guide issued in 2007 was replaced by the Commission "Guide to the application of the European Union rules on state aid, public procurement and the internal market to services of general economic interest, and in particular to social services of general interest "SEC(2010) 1545 final (hereinafter the "2010 SGEI Guide"), itself replaced in 2013 by the Commission "Guide to the application of the European Union rules on state aid, public procurement and the internal market to services of general economic interest, and in particular to social services of general interest SWD(2013) 53 final/2 (hereinafter the "2013 SGEI Guide").

[39]The Commission issued two FAQs documents in 2007, see Commission, "Frequently asked questions in relation with Commission Decision of 28 November on the application of the EC Treaty to State aid in the form of public service compensation granted to certain undertakings entrusted with the operation of services of general economic interest, and of the Community Framework for State aid in the form of public service compensation" COM (2007) 1516; and Commission, "Frequently asked questions concerning the application of public procurement rules to social services of general interest" COM (2007) 1514. The second guide (hereinafter the "2010 SGEI Guide) was issued in 2010, see Commission, "Guide to the application of the European Union rules on state aid, public procurement and the internal market to services of general economic interest, and in particular to social services of general interest" SEC(2010) 1545 final. The third guide (hereinafter "2013 SGEI Guide) was issued in 2013, see Commission, "Guide to the application of the European Union rules on state aid, public procurement and the internal market to services of general economic interest, and in particular to social services of general interest" SWD(2013) 53 final/2. In the "2013 SGEI Guide" it is explained that "[g]enerally speaking, only services constituting 'economic activities' are covered by the Treaty rules on the internal market (Articles 49 and 56 TFEU) and the Services Directive", see point 223. Also, wishing to clarify the concepts of undertaking and economic activity, the Commission recalled in its 2011 Communication that "[b]ased on Article 107(1) of the Treaty, the State aid rules generally only apply where the recipient is an 'undertaking'" and that "[t]he only relevant criterion in this respect is whether it carries out an economic activity", see point 8 and point 9 para 2 of the 2013 SGEI Guide.

[40]"Constitutional Treaty" is the name usually given to the Treaty establishing a Constitution for Europe, signed on 29 October 2004 by representatives of the then 25 Member States. The rejection of the document by French and Dutch voters in May and June 2005 brought the ratification process to an end.

ation which followed led to the adoption of several new provisions on SGEIs through the Lisbon Treaty:

- Article 14 TFEU modifying Article 16 EC, imposing on the Union and the Member States to take care that SGEIs operate under principles and rules which enable them to achieve their missions, and introducing a legal ground for the adoption of such principles and rules.
- Protocol Nr 26 on Services of general interest (hereinafter the "SGI Protocol"), adopted under the pressure of the Netherlands and France.[41]
- Article 36 of the EU Charter on Fundamental Rights (EUCFR) which became binding on the Union through Article 6(1) TEU.

In Neergaard's words, these provisions were "almost desperately" wished for by some Member States. Others consented to them, seeing perhaps possibilities to relativize their effect on the liberalisation of public services, including social services. Indeed, some scholars have argued that the new provisions did not imply anything new, and on this premise, Vedder wondered "when and to what extent legal rules and judicial bodies become captured by politics".[42] However, Treaty modifications are evidence that politics have always been at the very heart of EU law. In the nuclear core of the negotiation of the Treaty of Lisbon 2007/09, we find some Member States' concern that public services based on national solidarity models may be rendered unmanageable by the integration of markets for public services—and social services. The legitimacy of this concern is highlighted by Dougan's observation, with reference to the *Commission v Austria* ruling which concerned Union Citizens' equal access to higher education in Austrian establishments, that once Community welfare policies that are "largely the resulting of elite choices" are superimposed on the national solidarity systems, they are "almost impossible to remove by any Member State unilaterally".[43]

The CJEU, entrusted with the exclusive prerogative to interpret the Treaties, is constantly forced to translate their political content into legal language, has certainly not understood Article 14 TFEU as "business as usual" but instead as "the promise of a shift in focus" of EU law. Why this "promise" had to be made, what it implies for the understanding of the EU concept of SGEI, and how EU institutions, in particular the Commission, integrate the signals sent by the CJEU on its understanding of the evolving Treaty framework related to public services, are the questions essentially addressed by this book. It is truly a challenge to analyse a legal transformation that takes place here and now, and is far from ended, but a premise is that the Court has many reasons not to address Article 14 TFEU as "nothing new". The main one is perhaps its own essential contribution to place

[41]On this element of negotiation, see Sauter 2014, p. 68.

[42]See Vedder 2008, p. 25. Vedder's view was that like Article 16 EC "[t]he Protocol on Services of General Interest attached to the Treaty of Lisbon has a similar political character without actually changing the legal framework". On the same path, see Jääskinen 2011, p. 599.

[43]Case C-147/03 *Commission v Austria* [2005] ECR I-5969.

public services in a legal paradigm which is miles away from what Member States and their peoples could imagine in 1957, or even in 1986 when the SEA was adopted. Of all EU Institutions, the Court should be the most aware that asking to introduce in the Treaties a welfare concept, apt to carry the "idea of the State" in the European construction, was certainly not welcomed by some State *members* of the Union, but not an illegitimate request from other States that are also *Members* of this Union.

If the CJEU takes responsibility for the political cohesion of the Union, it must read the compromise enshrined in the Treaties, and in Weatherill's words, "breathe life" in the new provisions on SGEIs.[44] As Article 14 TFEU converts SGEIs from a derogation into an obligation, the CJEU must in relevant cases be expected to give—be it implicitly—its understanding on the normative effect of Article 14 TFEU, and thereby contribute to shape the EU concept of SGEI. In relevant cases, the Court may also have to clarify the role of Article 106(2) TFEU in the post-Lisbon configuration, in particular whether the principle of proportionality, present in Article 106(2) TFEU but not in Article 14 TFEU, has a role to play in liberalised public services.[45] Finally, with the emergence of SGEI as an important constitutional EU concept, the question of the definition of non-economic services of general interest (NESGIs) will probably sooner or later have to be clarified by the Court.[46] The clearer and the more explicitly the CJEU delivers its interpretation of the Treaty SGEI provisions, the more it will constrain the EU legislator in its approach of public services' harmonisation, which is now "en marche" in the field of social services.

1.1.4 Emerging EU Governance of Social Services in EU Procurement and State Aid Rules: The Unclear Relation Between the Quality Framework for SGI and the Treaty Framework on SGEI

Although SGEIs are considered by the EU as so "important" that they deserve a specific legislative basis, the Commission considers that legislation on the basis of Article 14 TFEU is not an immediate priority, and has instead embraced what it characterizes as a sector approach, framed in the 2011 Communication "A Quality Framework for Services of General Interest".[47] In substance, the SGI Quality Framework builds mainly on the reform of the state aid rules for SGEIs (a new

---

[44]Weatherill 1995, p. 185.

[45]Ross 2000.

[46]Van de Gronden 2013b, p. 283.

[47]Commission, "A Quality Framework for Services of General Interest in Europe" (Communication) COM (2011) 900 final, hereinafter called "the SGI Quality Framework".

package adopted in 2011/2012) and the 2014 procurement directives which include a Directive on concessions.[48] Importantly, the document refers to the voluntary "European Quality Framework for social services".[49] Also, the Commission connects the SGI Quality Framework to its "Social Business Initiative", adopted under the Europe 2020 strategy, and supporting the development of "new and socially innovative ways of doing business and providing services".[50] The SGI Quality Framework addresses SGIs in general but it has a particular focus on social services of general interest (SSGIs), thereby addressing both economic and non-economic SSGIs.

The SGI Quality Framework constitutes the first EU overall policy for public services in Europe. The Commission has clearly launched a new phase in their Europeanisation, emphasizing that in times of financial and economic crisis, budget constraints in the Member States "make it necessary to ensure that high-quality services are provided as efficiently and cost-effectively as possible".[51] However, it is unclear how the path taken is related to the EU constitutional framework on SGEIs, in particular regarding social services. Thus, in the Decision on state aid in the form of public service to undertakings entrusted with SGEIs, adopted by the Commission in 2011, Member States are relieved from the duty to notify aid not only in the field of social housing and hospitals, but also of a number of other social services, on the argument that these services are local and that their public financing does not affect trade.[52] As a consequence, the *ex-ante* compliance control is decentralized to the Member States. In practice, Member States funding social services should perhaps not feel strong pressure to clearly and transparently characterize them as SGEIs, even if the exemption from notification is precisely motivated by the SGEI-character of the tasks funded. More generally, and surprisingly, the Commission has introduced the notion of "genuine SGEIs" in the latest package on state aid rules applying to SGEIs, adopted in 2011.

---

[48]Directive 2014/23/EU of the European Parliament and of the Council of 26 February 2014 on the award of concession contracts (hereinafter called "the 2014 Concessions Directive") [2014] OJ L94/1, and Directive 2014/24/EU of the European Parliament and of the Council of 26 February 2014 on public procurement (hereinafter called "the 2014 Public Sector Directive") [2014] OJ L94/65 and Directive 2014/25/EU of the European Parliament and of the Council of 26 February 2014 on procurement by entities operating in the water, energy, transport and postal services sectors and repealing Directive 2004/17/EC [2014] OJ L 94/243 (hereinafter called "the 2014 Utilities Directive").

[49]Social Protection Committee, "A Voluntary European Quality Framework for Social Services" SPC/2010/10/8 final.

[50]Ibid, p. 14. See Commission Communication "Social Business Initiative—Creating a favourable climate for social enterprises, key stakeholders in the social economy and innovation" COM (2011) 682 final of 25 October 2011, {SEC (2011) 1278 final}.

[51]Ibid, p. 2.

[52]Commission Decision 2005/842/EC of 28 November 2005 on the application of Article 86(2) of the EC Treaty to State aid in the form of public service compensation granted to certain undertakings entrusted with the operation of services of general economic interest, [2005] OJ L 312/67, hereinafter the "2005 SGEI Decision".

Regarding the new procurement directives, a novelty is that above certain thresholds, social services contracts and social services concessions must be opened to competition, and therefore are subject to a prior notice obligation. At the same time, Member States are required to adopt procurement rules allowing their public authorities to respect the "special needs of social services". Although these "special needs" are reminiscent of Article 1 in the SGI Protocol, and although Article 14 TFEU is mentioned in the directives' recitals, the connection between Article 14 and the Directives is unclear. More generally, it is underlined that the directives do not apply to non-economic services of general interest, but this notion is left undefined. And importantly, the notion of procurement is defined and excludes systems of choice and voucher systems.

Against this background, it appears that the EU legislator, and the Commission, wish to show that social services in mixed systems of supply may indeed be covered by EU state aid rules, that their public funding may indeed be compatible with the Treaties on the basis of their SGEI character, but clearly avoid connecting too explicitly their "particular treatment" in these frameworks to their SGEI character, which may indicate that certain principles related to SGEIs are not welcome on board.

1.1.5 Systems of Choice for Social Services: Showing the Way?

In the decentralized model designed by the Commission for state aid control in the field of social services, including health care and housing, it must be expected that—under a certain conception of the rule of law and in particular when the welfare systems are market-based but not procured—public authorities in the Member States can correctly answer the following questions

- Is the activity pursued by the operator economic?
- Is the funding justified by "genuine SGEI tasks"?
- Are those tasks designed, funded and entrusted in a manner that excludes state aid?

It is however highly questionable whether it is expected that Member States can answer these questions correctly, and in this respect the case of Sweden is illustrative. That Member State, known for its generous welfare services, and often cited as a good example for their modernization,[53] has liberalised welfare services with

[53]Former President of the European Commission J-M. Barroso stated 21 November 2011: "Sweden has very much shown the lead. In Sweden we are clearly seeing the fruits of previous ambitious reforms, both in terms of fiscal and structural reforms." Statement by President Barroso ahead of the meeting with Swedish Prime Minister Fredrik Reinfeldt, Speech 11/781. See also economist Jean Tirole's views addressed to Members of the French Senate: "The French public services must be quality services. We are all very fond of it, but it must be rendered

in the frame of decentralisation and "consumer empowerment" policies. Although still broadly regulated and largely financed by public resources, the supply of all welfare services, including school education, is nowadays open to private operators for-profit, for a good part in systems of choice. Local and regional authorities (LRAs) fund, commission and coordinate these systems and are essential actors in this model, inspired by the concept of New Public Management. In this phase of liberalisation, the focus of the Swedish autonomous competition rules is not so much on undistorted competition between all operators, but rather on competition *neutrality*—by which is meant that on the quasi-markets created by mixed systems of supply, the public operators should not receive selective advantages. Thus, competition rules applying to public authorities acting as providers of services and goods have been introduced in sector laws and in the Swedish Competition Act.[54]

So far, the Swedish legislator has been reluctant to address on a broad cross-sector basis the issue of the applicability of EU market rules to social services under LRAs' competence, and there are strikingly few explicit SGEI-characterizations of services in Swedish law. Where the question of the de facto existence of SGEIs in Swedish law or the possibility to define SGEI tasks has arisen, several arguments have been put forward in documents reflecting the views of the Swedish State or of the Swedish legislator.

A first argument invoked is that *tax-financed services cannot be regarded as economic for the purpose of EU law* and are therefore not covered by EU economic law.[55] However, since *Höfner*, it seems difficult to argue that services, social or not, supplied by private actors or not, are excluded from the scope of EU

Footnote 53 (continued)

sustainable, and to that purpose reforms must be conducted. I will take the example of four countries, Germany, Sweden, Australia and Canada. /…/ they have all maintained their social models, while conducting reforms, and downsizing the State. Sweden did it after the crisis of 1991, as Canada and Australia. /…/ all the reforms have been conducted by socialists, and the right has retained them when it returned to power." It is interesting to notice that Tirole's view of "who did what" in Sweden is somewhat mistaken, hopefully unintentionally. Own translation of the French version of the Minutes of the audition of Jean Tirole (winner of The Sveriges Riksbank Prize in Economic Sciences in Memory of Alfred Nobel for 2014) by the Commission of Economic Affairs at the French Senate, 19 November 2014, available at http://www.senat.fr/compte-rendu-commissions/20141117/afeco.html#toc10.

[54]These rules are autonomous from EU law, the first ones constituting a "competence restriction" rule introduced in a number of sectors to radically avoid the risk of municipal undertakings being conducted in "anti-competitive" ways, the second one—in the Swedish Competition Act - being a horizontal "balancing rule", commonly called the "conflict-solving rule" and aimed at securing competition neutrality between public and private undertakings in sectors within the competence of local and regional authorities.

[55]See Sweden's report to the European Commission on the application of Commission's decision of 28 December 2005 on the application of Article 86(2) of the EC Treaty to State aid in the form of public service compensation granted to certain undertakings entrusted with the operation of services of general economic interest, C(2005) 2673, N2008/5126 p. 2. See also the report of the commission of inquiry on LRAs' competence "Kommunal kompetens i utveckling" SOU 2007:72, p. 113 and 116.

competition law on the sole ground that they are tax-financed, and the legality of public intervention in those sectors may therefore require that they be justified by the services' SGEI-character.[56]

A second argument invoked is that *there is no need for SGEI in sectors where the use of procurement excludes the occurrence of state aid.*[57] This relates to *Altmark* where the CJEU laid down conditions excluding over-compensation of public service obligations and state aid in the meaning of Article 107(1) TFEU.[58] However, social services are not only externalized on the basis of Swedish rules implementing EU procurement rules,[59] but also on the basis of the Swedish Act on Systems of Choice in the Public Sector adopted in 2008 (Sw: *Lag (2008:962) om valfrihetssystem*, hereinafter "LOV"),[60] in which there is no competition on price. As to the system of free choice of school education, it builds on authorizations delivered by state authorities to entities financed by local authorities. In such systems, the occurrence of state aid with some effect on trade does not seem excluded, and may have to be justified on the basis of the rules in the Almunia package on state aid to SGEIs.

A third argument is that there are *no clear SGEI missions or tasks in the sectors at issue*. This argument was unconvincingly put forward concerning household waste management, where EU secondary law does impose public service tasks on public authorities, which explains that in *Commission v Germany* the CJEU connected these obligations to an exemption from EU procurement rules, thereby

[56]Case C-41/90 *Höfner* [1991] ECR I-1979. In *Höfner*, the CJEU considered the tax-financed activities of the German Federal Office of Employment to be economic. This aspect of the *Höfner* ruling is underlined by Buendia Sierra, see Buendia Sierra J. L., 1999, p. 59. Van de Gronden holds that "the ECJ almost automatically regards health care providers as undertakings within the meaning of European competition law. In other words, these providers cannot escape from the competition rules." See van de Gronden 2009b, p. 10.

[57]This argument has been raised in the frame of the reform of national rules on rental housing, liberalized since 2011. The Commission of inquiry on municipal housing companies stressed that neither housing supply in general nor LRAs' responsibility for housing supply to any part ought to be characterized as SGEI, as local authorities willing to entrust tasks that are not economically profitable would apply the procurement rules. See the report of the ministry publication on municipal housing companies "Allmännyttiga kommunala bostadsaktiebolag - övervägande och förslag" Ds 2009:60, p. 90 ff.

[58]It was raised in general terms in the Swedish report on the application of the 2005 SGEI Decision. See the Swedish report to the European Commission on the application of Commission's decision of 28 December 2005 on the application of Article 86(2) of the EC Treaty to State aid in the form of public service compensation granted to certain undertakings entrusted with the operation of services of general economic interest, C(2005) 2673, N2008/5126 p. 2.

[59]Thus LRAs must comply with national provisions imposing procurement procedures for so-called B-services and contracts under EU-threshold values which go beyond the directives it builds on.

[60]At present, the Act on Systems of Choice is mandatory only for the procurement of primary healthcare and voluntary for the other services covered by the Act.

opening for a broader understanding of the SGEI concept.[61] The argument that SGEI missions are not needed has also been raised in the government Bill which led to an extensive liberalization of rental housing in 2011.[62] The view that neither housing supply in general nor LRAs' responsibility for specific housing supply ought to be characterized as SGEIs,[63] as economically non-profitable tasks would be entrusted under the procurement rules, was apparently not shared by the Swedish National Board of Housing, Building and Planning.[64] Also, several experts, inside and outside Sweden, contested the view of the Commission of inquiry preparing this Bill that the Swedish regulation in force at the time did not include SGEI missions.

A fourth argument, difficult to deny, is that the SGEI concept and rules are subject to legal uncertainty.[65] As a whole, these arguments shed an interesting light on the Commission's supposition that authorities in the Member States know what is an economic activity in EU law, know what the EU concept of SGEI means, and can correctly construct, supervise and report their funding of social services, an assumption underpinning the 2011 state aid package.

Another problem is that, as Swedish systems of choice do not include a competition on price, and as the performance of many different operators is difficult

---

[61]EU secondary law on waste management is mostly based on Article 192 TFEU and has environmental protection (not market harmonization) as primary objective. The legislation adopted on this basis leaves to judicial interpretation crucial issues on the legal instruments which the Member States—and public authorities in the Member States in charge with the environmental protection at issue—may rely on to fulfil their obligations without illegally breaching against the Treaty imperatives of free movement and competition. Although the Commission has underlined that SGEIs exist in those areas, there is much controversy in Sweden as to whether local authorities may invoke environmental principles governing waste management as justifying exemptions from EU market rules.

[62]The reform process was pushed forward by two complaints filed to the Commission in 2002 and 2005 by the Swedish Property Federation, arguing that municipal housing companies were granted illegal state aid from the State respectively from their owning municipalities. The first complaint concerned a government Bill proposing a temporary scheme of aid to restructuring of municipal housing companies and was filed 1 July 2002. The second complaint concerning aid to municipal housing companies was filed 30 May 2005. Both complaints have been filed under the number CP115/02. These object and arguments of these complaints will be presented at more length in Chap. 2.

[63]See government Bill on municipal housing companies, *Allmännyttiga kommunala bostadsaktiebolag och reformerade hyressättningsregler*, proposition 2009/10:185, p. 27.

[64]In a report commissioned by the Swedish Social Ministry, the Swedish National Board of Housing, Building and Planning has taken the view that it is necessary to strengthen local authorities' capacity to fulfil their missions, in particular on markets where demand is weak (which is the case in many parts of Sweden), or when LRAs try to achieve social and/or environmental objectives through housing measures. The Board proposes that LRAs' missions concerning housing supply be specified and that certain objectives may be invoked to entrust SGEI tasks to housing companies—municipal or not. See the report of the Swedish National Board of Housing, Building and Planning *Boverkets översyn av bostadsförsörjningslagen*, rapport 2012:12, p. 26.

[65]See the report of the commission of inquiry on municipal housing companies "EU, allmännyttan och hyrorna" SOU 2008:38, p. 36 and 419–421.

to specify and supervise, the risk of over-compensation is not excluded. One way to try excluding it can be to *under-compensate* provision, which is another expression of non-proportionality evidently capable to affect the quality of the services, but which does not seem clearly addressed by EU law. EU constitutional principles related to SGEI may be relevant at a normative level, in particular the Union and the Member States' duty, according to Article 14 TFEU, to take care that SGEIs operate under principles and conditions, in particular economic and financial conditions, enabling them to achieve their missions, and the Union's duty to respect the right of access to SGEIs protected by Article 36 EUCFR. However, the scope and meaning of these principles are not yet clarified by the CJEU, which so far leaves a wide space of policy freedom to the EU legislator.

Under such circumstances, it may be questioned whether the legal acts adopted in the frame of the SGI Quality Framework under the motto of simplification and flexibility, provide reliable guidance on the two important questions "what is an economic activity?" and "what is SGEI?". It must be remembered that the Commission is both a legislative and a political actor in the EU, and makes no secret of its policy vision on services of general interest. In "Europe 2020", the Commission reconfirmed the need to develop new services, delivered both physically and on-line, that generate growth and create jobs, which can include innovative services of general interest".[66] In this vision, it seems that social services are seen as potential growth sectors, but the Commission is certainly aware that in the EU, this growth still depends on public financing, which can constitute a threat to the EU objective of undistorted competition.

To let the market for social services grow, two ways seem possible. One way is to liberalize social services "top-down" through regulations based on Article 14 TFEU, but the Member States do not seem to agree on what they want from SGEI. Another slower but possibly surer option, allowing markets to grow in the Member States, may be the option favoured by the Commission. It explains (1) that the Commission has not opened any broad public discussion on the market integration of social services and (2) its legal approach in the frame of the SGI Quality Framework. On the one side, transferring the up-front *ex-ante* control of SGEI-compensation to the Member States gives them much leeway, as they reported problems in applying the Commission's first state aid package on SGEIs adopted in 2005. On the other side, the new EU procurement directives introduce an obligation to publish *ex-ante* notice of contracts for social services over a certain threshold.[67] Thus, *some* competition is introduced for the market to grow. What emerges from this ambiguous approach is that justifying the funding of tasks by explicitly relying on their SGEI-character may not only be perceived as problematic by some Member States, but also by the Commission itself.

---

[66]Commission, "A Quality Framework for Services of General Interest in Europe" (Communication) COM (2011) 900 final, p. 2, referring to Commission, "Europe 2020: A Strategy for smart, sustainable and inclusive growth" (Communication) COM (2010) 2020).

[67]Regarding social services, the threshold is at present set at EUR 750 000 for public service contracts and at EUR 5 186 000 for service concession.

1.2 Aims and Structure of the Book

Against this background, the aim of the book is to answer the following main question

> Is it possible to understand SGEI as a constitutional EU concept relevant throughout the EU Treaties, and can a transparent and loyal enforcement of the Treaty principles attached to SGEI restrict the Member States' discretion to liberalize social services and the expansion of a European market for social services?

This question addresses two legal problems. First, the constitutional relevance of the post-Lisbon Treaty provisions on SGEI—in other words, their place in the foundational principles of the Treaties—seems today obvious, but the legal meaning of the EU concept of SGEI, in particular the (E) in SGEI, is still very unclear. Second, the harmonization of social services in the SGI Quality Framework has an ambiguous relation to the Treaty principles on SGEIs. In the book, these legal issues are addressed in their political context. In a legal-theoretical perspective, the aim is to identify the constitutional meaning of the concept of SGEI, and to shed light on the complex relation between the EU legislator's use of this concept and its open intention to integrate public services, in particular social services, in the dominating EU paradigm of the internal market. In a legal-political perspective, the purpose is to examine how the introduction of new SGEI related provisions in the Treaties implies a constitutionalisation of the concept of SGEI, and contributes to transform Europe into a polity level in the governance of social services.

A normative element of the book must be acknowledged here. By its interpretation of EU market rules, the CJEU has accelerated the encounter of national welfare regulation—which often includes concrete elements of solidarity—and EU's "culture of the market". This interpretation of the notions of is often qualified as *functional*, but the Court has not been willing to delineate more explicitly and precisely the *legal-political* notions of "service", "undertaking", "economic activity", and SGEI. This owes much to the fact that, while its guiding star continues being the "integration" element, the CJEU is aware that political acceptance to the left and to the right is necessary for its interpretations to be accepted as valid law in the Member States. To ensure such acceptance, the integration element is often kept incremental and discreet in judgments addressing public service regulations, in particular in the sensitive field of social services.

Indeed, EU integration of public services develops in the language of EU law principles and rules, on the basis of concepts which often divert from the concepts of national law, which is difficult to apprehend in a democratic debate. In this process of integration through law, legal-conceptual confusion may therefore not be entertained by EU institutions without raising serious democratic issues. As the CJEU has largely contributed to the Europeanisation of social services, it would secure its legitimacy by spelling pedagogically its settled meaning of Treaty concepts, allowing to bridge the conceptual discrepancies between EU and national law, and easing a democratic conversation between EU institutions and the Member States. If the Court understands the concepts of "service", "undertaking" and "economic activity" clearly, it should explain them readily, unless *political* reasons, for instance a certain mistrust of open democratic debates, hold it from doing so. Habermas, warning that "postponing democracy is a dangerous move", says it best:

> [C]onceptions of the European Union and ideas of its future development have remained diffuse among the general population. Informed opinions and articulated positions are for the most part the monopoly of professional politicians, economic elites, and scholars with relevant interests; not even public intellectuals who generally participate in debates on burning issues have made this issue their own.[68]

On this normative premise, and in order to address the main research question, three sub-questions have been formulated:

1. *Can the case law of the CJEU on the definition and the relevance of the notion of "economic activity" explain the necessity of a constitutional public service concept in the post-Lisbon Treaties?*
2. *Can SGEI be regarded as an EU constitutional concept imposing public service principles in all fields of EU market law?*
3. *What place does the EU legislator give to the Treaty principles on SGEIs in EU legislation harmonizing the market for social services and how can it affect the liberalization of these services in the Member States?*

To help answering these questions, Hirschman's economic theory on "exit, voice and loyalty" is utilized.[69] Hirschman identifies two "countervailing forces" that can reverse the decline of firms or organisations: "exit", when unsatisfied customers leave a firm—or members leave an organisation, and "voice", when they choose instead to complain or protest. Exit loses its character of rational behaviour and can be perceived as desertion and treason in the presence of "loyalty" to a firm or organization. Loyalty can thus raise the price of exit and make it a less reasonable option, but can also stifle voice because "the effectiveness of the voice mechanism is strengthened by the possibility of exit". According to Hirschmann, an organisation strongly promoting loyalty can repress feedback in the form of both exit and voice, and deprive itself from "recuperation mechanisms" preventing its decline.

Thus essentially, the book proposes a legal understanding of the notion of SGEI thriving at identifying valid law, but through the prism of Hirschman's theory, used at a non-expert level, it considers its controversial political nature, and sheds light on the legal-political transformation of the framework for services of general interest taking place here and now in Europe. As a result, the study consists of three parts addressing the three research sub-questions, and the legal answers proposed to each sub-question constitute an element in the analysis of the EU *political* process of exit, voice and loyalty which is argued to take place through EU law at the moment. The focus of part I is on the EU notion of economic activity and its relevance for the applicability of the Treaty principles on free movement and competition, part II analyses the constitutional substance of the EU concept of SGEI, and part III examines the EU legislator's ambiguous approach of the concept of SGEI in the 2014 procurement directives and in the Almunia package on state aid, with a special focus

[68]Habermas 2013.

[69]Hirschman 1970.

on social services. To propose some explanation to this ambiguity, part III includes also a case study on Swedish systems of choice for social services under local and regional authorities. The case law of the CJEU is taken into account to June 2015.

1.2.1 Part I: No Exit from EU Market Law for Public Services

Part I—composed only of Chap. 2—addresses the first research sub-question, whether the CJEU's case law on the definition and the relevance of the notion of "economic activity" can explain the necessity of a constitutional public service concept in the post-Lisbon Treaties. The focus in Chap. 2 is on proposing:

(a) A coherent understanding of the relation—and the difference—between the notion of "economic activity" and the Treaty concepts of goods, services, establishment, and capital. In this understanding, an activity does not have to be economic in a specific Member State for this Member State's regulation of this activity to be subject to EU free movement rules.
(b) An analysis of the criteria considered by the CJEU as decisive for an activity to be *in casu* economic for the purpose of competition law respectively free movement law.
(c) An analysis of the relevance of the notion of "economic activity" for the applicability of EU procurement rules, which may help understanding the relationship between the notion of "economic activity" and the concept of "service" in the meaning of the Treaties.

Chapter 2 submits that there is a *legal and unitary* interpretation of the notion of "economic activity" for the purpose of EU rules on competition, free movement, and procurement. Thus, the fact that the Treaty's free movement rules and competition rules have different scopes does not simply follow from the fact that they have different primary addressees (the Member States under free movement rules, undertakings under competition rules), but also from the fact that the notions of services and goods in the field of free movement go beyond the *legal* notion of "economic activity". Also, Chap. 2 shows that, although the "surface language" of the CJEU's interpretation of the notions of "economic activity", "goods", "services" "capital" and "establishment" is complicated arguably due to its "consensus model",[70] the

[70]The distinction between a rights and a consensus model, made by Groussot, has been summarized by Neergaard and Nielsen as follows: "[A] judge following a rights model is inspired by Dworkin's theory of law and focuses on securing individual's rights in accordance with justice and fairness. A judge following a consensus model focuses on delivering judgments that can be expected to be accepted by the community he/she functions in as representing its values." see Groussot 2005, p. 186ff. To refer to this less explicit element in the Court's interpretative approach of the criteria of applicability of EU market rules in sensitive cases, the notion of "acceptance" is used several times in Chap. 2.

"deep structure" of its case law displays a certain degree of conceptual coherence and convergence between the different fields of EU market law and between the different activities at issue.[71]

Obviously, no interpretation of the Court's understanding of the notion of "economic activity" and of its relationship to the concepts of entry to the Treaty market rules will be perfectly convincing unless confirmed by the Court itself. However, the interest of proposing an understanding of these concepts on the basis of a thorough analysis of the Court's case law and of its "deep structure" is threefold.

First, it shows how the CJEU's case law on the criteria of applicability of the Treaty market rules, supporting of the Commission's public turn, may be seen as a major *cause* of the development of the Treaty framework on public services. The Court's approach involves that, even in the field of social services and even in the absence of positive harmonisation, a Member State cannot escape *by its own decision* the domino effects of the liberalisation conducted by other Member States. From a legal point of view, this situation rendered the legitimacy of EU market law applicable to public services problematic in the pre-Lisbon constitutional frame. From a political point of view, such a situation may be characterized, in accordance with Hirschman's theory, as precluding "exit" from the paradigm of the internal market in the realm of social services, enhancing the need for, and the legitimacy of "voice". Thus, searching for the meaning of the notion of economic activity and finding out that it may be only indirectly relevant for the applicability of EU market rules can explain that it may have been *politically* necessary to transform the Treaties, by introducing horizontal provisions and a legal ground specifically devoted to public services.

Second, the analysis in Chap. 2 constitutes an essential pre-requisite to an analysis of SGEI as a constitutional concept of EU law in the post-Lisbon Treaties, as its meaning cannot be apprehended outside its legal-political relation to the expansion of the scope of EU market law. Indeed, the stronger the CJEU lets EU fundamental freedoms exercise pressure on public service systems to be open for competition, the stronger the pressure to give to the EU concept of SGEI a *broad* interpretation should expected to be, especially from Member States desiring to retain their powers of economic policy in the field of social services. Chapter 2 shows that the CJEU is highly aware of the limits of EU powers in the frame of the Treaties and of the limits of political acceptance for its interpretations, and sheds light on

a. The rationale of the Court's relatively lenient approach in the application of EU market rules in the field of public services, even in fields where some academics had not expected it to take such a stance.
b. The relationship between this lenient approach and the Treaty principles and rules on SGEI.

Third, analysing the Court's approach of the notion of "economic activity" and of its relevance for the applicability of the Treaty market rules, paves the way for answering sub-question (2), centred on the meaning of the concept of SGEI in the new Treaty framework, as it will allow reasoning on how the word "economic" in

[71] See Wehlander 2015.

SG(E)I may be understood. In fact, Article 106(2) TFEU on services of general *economic* interest has been found relevant by the CJEU in the field of free movement law, and so the term "economic" must in some way have *legal* relevance in that field too, especially as Article 2 of the SGI Protocol provides that the provisions of the Treaties *do not affect in any way* the competence of the Member States to provide, commission and organise *non-economic* services of general interest.

1.2.2 Part II: SGEI as a Constitutional Voice for Public Services in EU Law

Part II builds on the conclusions of part I and aims to answer the second research sub-question of this book, namely whether SGEI be regarded as an EU constitutional concept imposing public service principles in all fields of EU market law. Given the expansion of EU market law, Member States must expect that their regulatory and administrative measures, even measures related to social services, are "inexorably exposed to market forces".[72] Such measures can namely easily come into conflict with Treaty rules on competition and free movement, as the Court has multiplied the possibilities to challenge them:

- The competition law instrument: the Court has established that Article 107(1) TFEU, and Article 106(1) TFEU in combination with Article 101 or Article 102 TFEU, allow challenging the public funding or the grant of exclusive or special rights to undertakings supplying public services.
- The free movement instrument: the Court has established that even non-discriminatory public service regulation restricting the attraction of cross-border trade may be challenged.
- The procurement instrument: basic EU procurement rules follow directly from the Treaty principle of non-discrimination as interpreted by the Court, in particular concessions contracts and contracts for values below the thresholds set by EU legislation.

As Member States and undertakings in charge of public services have claimed that the measures challenged were aimed at fulfilling services of general interest, the CJEU has been led to apply Article 106(2) TFEU. This case law has facilitated the introduction of a "principle of protection of SGEI missions" in former Article 16 EC through the Treaty of Amsterdam 1997, a provision which, as already mentioned, was replaced by Article 14 TFEU and completed by other important provisions on SGEIs in the Lisbon Treaty. As a result, a strong "voice" on public services has emerged in the post-Lisbon Treaties, largely articulated on the core notion of SGEI, but also of the new notions of SGI and NESGI. Part II—consisting of Chaps. 3 to 6—proposes a *legal*

---

[72] The quotations are borrowed from van de Gronden and Sauter. See their conclusions in Sauter and van de Gronden 2010, p. 45.

understanding of the Treaty concept of SGEI, but does so in the context of EU's political transformation through primary and secondary EU law.

Chapter 3 examines the legal-political outcome of the expansion of EU law in the field of public services, as reflected in the post-Lisbon framework on SGEIs. It shows how this framework essentially relates to the Union's "foundational principles" in the post-Lisbon Treaties, acknowledges the multilevel governance of public services in the Union, and puts EU institutions face to face with the Article 14 TFEU injunction to adopt regulations on the principles and conditions allowing SGEIs to fulfil their missions. As this would force the Commission and the EU legislator to take a clear stance on public services the European Social Model, the Commission has unsurprisingly found that legislation based on Article 14 TFEU "is not an immediate priority".[73] In this context, Chap. 3 asks whether the principle formulated in Article 14 TFEU completes Article 106(2) TFEU, and implies that the interests of achieving public service tasks and of market integration *should* be balanced, even in the field of EU free movement and procurement law. This supposes that Articles 14 and 106 TFEU together shape SGEI as a concept of a "public service" in EU primary law which is broader than tasks entrusted to undertakings and makes room for public authorities' public service missions.

The validity of this understanding is tested in Chap. 4, which shows first how the CJEU has shaped principles and conditions for the application of EU market rules to public services in its case law directly related to Article 106(2) TFEU, and developed under this provision a "balancing test" where financial and economic conditions allowing public service missions to be achieved may be taken into consideration. The second part of Chap. 4 shows how the Court has transposed its "Article 106(2) TFEU balancing test" to free movement and procurement cases, which gives a "horizontal dimension" to this balancing and implicitly leads to a broad understanding of the EU concept of SGEI. Indeed, whilst overriding reasons related to the general interest may in principle not be economic, the Court has recognized the risk of seriously undermining the *financial* balance of a social security system to constitute an overriding reason related to the general interest capable of justifying an obstacle to the freedom to provide services.[74] It is also shown that, by connecting exemptions from procurement rules related to in-house provision or public-public cooperation to public authorities' explicit or implicit "public service tasks", the CJEU gives de facto a "horizontal" understanding of the EU concept of SGEI overarching Article 14 TFEU and Article 106(2) TFEU. Chapter 4 concludes that, albeit discreetly, the CJEU does not consider the first sentence of Article 14 TFEU—and the SGI Protocol interpreting it—as declaratory but spells a principle which is normative for all EU market law.

Based on the results of Chaps. 3 and 4, Chap. 5 proposes a legal understanding of the EU concept of SGEI, trying to identify what is the meaning of "economic"

[73]Commission, "A Quality Framework for Services of General Interest in Europe" (Communication) COM (2011) 900, p. 5.

[74]Case C-372/04 *Watts*, para 103, *Kohll*, para 41; *Smits and Peerbooms*, para 72; and *Müller-Fauré and van Riet*, para 73.

in SGEI and what the core elements of the concept in EU law can be in the present Treaty frame. An essential submission in that chapter is that the notion of "*entrustment* to an undertaking", repeatedly included as a central element in the Commission's tentative definitions of the notion of SGEI, is not part of the core elements of the EU concept of SGEI, whereas the notion of obligation/task is. Another important argument is that the "E" in SGEI refers to the fact that the public service regulation is of economic interest, in the sense that it can affect the economic conditions for the exercise of an activity which *can be* economic at EU level, i.e. *is* economic in some Member State(s), but not necessarily in the Member State imposing that regulation.

General conclusions of part II are drawn in Chap. 6. First, the relatively deferential approach by the CJEU of Member States' measures to define, regulate and organise public service tasks cannot simply be categorized as a move to achieve the *Union's* general social and environmental objectives, but rather as a sign that the Court finds itself forced—by the foundational principles, in particular Article 14 TFEU on SGEIs—to respect the retained competence of Member States. Second, if the veil of the CJEU's terminological subtleties is lifted, SGEI emerges as a broad constitutional concept of EU law—certainly broader that the Commission's ideas so far –, allowing Member States to benefit from exemptions from strict state aid, procurement and free movement rules. However, the Court's understanding of SGEI is still ambiguous, and quite unclear on whether the transparency and proportionality principles embedded in Article 106(2) TFEU still have autonomous relevance for the application of the Treaty competition rules, in particular for the application of the Treaty rules on state aid to SSGIs. As the Court has not either clarified pedagogically the important difference between "economic activity" and "economic rule/measure" for the applicability of EU market rules, the *market powers* embedded in the (E) word in the EU concept of SGEI are kept unclear, and the scope of Article 14 TFEU is kept unclear. As a result of this legal-conceptual confusion, public services, and now also social services, are Europeanised without a true democratic process, and in particular without a discussion on the role solidarity should play in this integration. In this process, EU Institutions—in particular the Member States' governments in the Council—are not forced to account on whether and how EU legislation on procurement and state aid applying to public services, including social services, integrate the Treaty principles specifically related to SGEIs loyally and coherently, but may instead rely on a "pick and choose" approach.

1.2.3 Part III: Cost of Loyalty, the Relationship Between EU Procurement and State Aid Legislation on Social Services and the Treaty Rules on SGEI, with a Case Study on Swedish Systems of Choice

Part III—consisting of Chaps. 7 to 10—addresses the book's third research subquestion, namely what place the EU legislator gives to the Treaty principles on

SGEIs in EU legislation harmonizing the market for social services and how this can affect the liberalization of these services in the Member States.

Since the financial crisis in 2008, the EU governance of social services funded to a large extent by the Member States, has increased significantly. One sign is that several States, that are members of the Eurozone, have been enjoined to cut their welfare budgets, another is the new legislative basis in Article 14 TFEU, which sends to all Member States a signal that EU Institutions may decide how social services should be framed by EU law in order to achieve their missions. Adopting legislation based on Article 14 TFEU would be one way of concretising EU's new "social market economy" principle in the Lisbon Treaty, but the Commission has instead found a "sector-based" harmonisation more appropriate, and capable in its view to address the strained economic situation in Europe, and develop new services that generate growth and create jobs.[75] It is evident that the procurement directives adopted in 2014 (to be implemented in the Member States by March 2016) and the 2011 Package on state aid to SGEIs, must respect the principle laid down in Article 14 TFEU, that the Union and the Member States must take care that SGEIs, notably in the sector of social services, operate under conditions, in particular economic and financial, enabling them to achieve their missions, without prejudice of the Treaty state aid rules applicable to SGEIs.

Part III has its focus on a legal analysis of the relationship between EU legislation on social services to the understanding of the SGEI concept and the Treaty principles on SGEIs emerging from the CJEU's case law studied in part II. However, the analysis is conducted in the prism of Hirschman's theory, with a view to shedding light on the ambiguous relation between the "tailor-made" sector-based approach in the field of social services and the principles and rules on SGEIs following from the Treaties, and to provide some explanation to this ambiguity. In other words, part III questions the loyalty of EU legislation towards the Treaty principles on SGEIs, and proposes that some answer may be found in the political costs of such a loyalty. It proceeds as follows.

Chapter 7 examines, with a special focus on social services, how the 2014 procurement directives and the Commission's 2011 SGEI Package relate to the Treaty principles and rules on SGIs, including SGEIs and NESGIs. First, although lighter or inexistent procurement rules for social services must, in an EU constitutional perspective, be justified by their character of services of general interest, which implies that their EU market regulation is covered by Article 14 TFEU on SGEIs and the SGI Protocol, Chap. 7 points at the ambivalence of the 2014 procurement directives. Indeed, the EU legislator avoids justifying social services' procurement rules by their SGEI missions by using the notion of "special service" instead, but at the same time stresses the necessity to respect Article 14 TFEU and the SGI Protocol, and in fact implicitly relies on the SGEI character of public-funded and externalized social services to impose on the Member States an *obligation* to

[75]Commission, "A Quality Framework for Services of General Interest in Europe" (Communication) COM (2011) 900, p. 5.

ensure that contracting authorities *may* take into account the need to ensure their quality, continuity, etc. By (1) not acknowledging that, in certain national legal systems, contracting authorities have an *obligation*, imposed by law, to ensure quality, continuity, etc., and in such cases have *compulsory public service tasks that can affect economic activities*, i.e. SGEI missions in the meaning of Article 14 TFEU, and (2) stressing that provisions on NESGI in the SGI Protocol but making no attempt to clarify the meaning of "E" in SG(E)I—and of "NE" in (NE)SGI, Chap. 7 finds that the EU legislator thrives at maintaining an understanding of SGEI that is narrower than the CJEU's discreet but discernible understanding of SGEI as a broad concept of EU law.

Second, Chap. 7 finds it striking that, as the light or inexistent procurement constraints on social service contracts do not exclude the presence of state aid in social service contracts and even less in systems of choice, the Commission's decision to decentralize the control of state aid to social services de facto eases the pressure on Member States to identify the SGEI tasks that they compensate in that field, and to adapt their systems to the substantial requirements of the 2011 SGEI Package aimed at ensuring the transparency and proportionality of public funding to social services' substantial requirements. This reinforces the impression that the EU legislator avoids forcing the Member States to formulate clearly the SGEIs existing in their system. Thus, this package may be regarded as a significant step towards an EU approach to social services, of great interest for national social welfare states,[76] but its impact depends on whether its rules are applied loyally, and through them the principles of transparency and proportionality of SGEI measures in Article 106(2) TFEU.

Chapter 7 concludes that the Commission is apparently not so preoccupied by the proportionality of public service compensation of social services, which is at odds with Article 106(2) TFEU, and its own statement that what must be achieved in times of budget constraints is "quality services /…/ provided as efficiently and cost-effectively as possible").[77] In particular, systems of choice and voucher systems are exempted from both the procurement directives and state aid notification. When such systems are neither procured, nor compensated on the basis of the comparison with efficient undertakings in accordance with the fourth *Altmark* criteria, they must comply with the state aid rules now applicable to SGEIs in the field of social services rules. This requires that national rules underpinning these systems prevent their over-compensation by ensuring a transparent and precise definition of SGEI tasks, but as such requirements may render systems of choice less attractive for private investors and counteract their development, Chap. 7

---

[76]Van de Gronden and Rusu 2013, pp. 185–186.

[77]The Commission acknowledges distortions of competition can occur in in the field of social services, but considers that such funding, even with large sums, will have only limited and acceptable effects on competition. See Commission Decision 2012/21/EU of 20 December 2011 on the application of Article 106(2) of the Treaty on the Functioning of the European Union to State aid in the form of public service compensation granted to certain undertakings entrusted with the operation of services of general economic interest [2012] OJ L7/3, para 11.

concludes that the de facto leeway consented for systems of choice may be meant to support their development. In a policy perspective, this would be logical because systems of choice allow a production cost "per service unit" to emerge, thereby facilitating cross-border trade of services, which is the aim of pursued by the SGI Quality Framework. In a legal perspective, this legislative bias for systems of choice for social services may come into conflict with the "Union's interest" that EU institutions and Member States show loyalty to the Treaty principles related to SGEIs, and to the state aid rules enforcing those principles.

Examining the case of Swedish systems of choice for social services allows testing this hypothesis. Whilst for-profit provision of school education is allowed in the public system, the Swedish legislator is reluctant to acknowledge the economic character of its social services and has argued, not so convincingly, that systems of choice fulfil the fourth *Altmark* criterion, which indicates that EU state aid rules applying to SG(E)Is under Article 106(2) TFEU are perceived as problematic for the systems' design and the policy pursued. Chapter 9 looks into the regulation, organisation and public funding of elderly home care in Swedish contract-based systems of choice and school education in Swedish authorisation-based systems of choice. These systems, based on a procurement model that promotes competition but not based on price, fall outside the 2014 directives' definition of procurement and their present design does not appear to fit the concept of SGEI addressed by the regulatory model of the Commission's state aid rules. Chapter 9 draws some conclusions on the relation between the lack of clear SGEI tasks and issues of service quality, service continuity, under-compensation and over-compensation, which have occurred in these fields, and on how EU procurement and state aid rules applicable to SGEIs would probably have been fatal for Swedish systems of choice, had it not been for the leeway which these systems enjoy in the recently adopted EU legislation.

Chapter 9 is introduced by Chap. 8 which places the case study in its broader legal context. It examines in particular whether Swedish public and competition law governing activities under LRAs' competence is conceptually apt to "receive" EU state aid rules applying to social services, and allows relating the cases studied in Chap. 9 to the broader question of the decentralised and increasingly individualised model of welfare services in Sweden. Chapter 10 draws conclusions on part III in relation to the third research sub-question, and pulls together these strands with the results of parts I and II in Chaps. 2 and 6 in order to propose answers to the main research question of this study, and includes a short final reflection on the Europeanisation of social services in a democracy perspective.

References

Bauby P (2011) From Rome to Lisbon: SGIs in primary law, in developments. In: Szyszczak E et al (eds) Services of general interest. T.M.C Asser Press, The Hague

Bauby P (2013) Unity and diversity of SSGIs in the European Union. In: Neergaard U et al (eds) Social services of general interest in the EU. T.M.C Asser Press, The Hague

Davies G (2006) The process and side-effects of harmonisation of European welfare states. Jean Monnet working paper 02/06

De Vries SA (2011) Services of general economic interest in the interplay between public and private in Europa after Lisbon: the search for more coherence. Europarättslig Tidskrift Nr 3(2011):462–482

Ehlerman CD (1987) The internal market following the single European Act. Common Mark Law Rev 24(3):361–409

Habermas J (2013) Democracy, solidarity and the European crisis, lecture delivered by Professor Jürgen Habermas on 26 April 2013 in Leuven, http://www.kuleuven.be/communicatie/evenementen/evenementen/jurgen-habermas/ democracy-solidarity-and-the -european-crisis. Accessed 10 Sept 2013

Hirschman AO (1970) Exit, voice, and loyalty: responses to decline in firms, organisations, and states. Harvard University Press, Cambridge

Jääskinen N (2011) The new rules on SGEI. EStAL 4/2011

Krajewski M (2009) Conclusion. In: Krajewski M et al (eds) The changing legal framework for services of general interest in Europe: between competition and solidarity. T.M.C Asser Press, The Hague

Neergaard U (2008) Services of general (economic) interest and the services directive. In: Nergaard U, Nielsen R, Roseberry L (eds) The services directive—consequences for the welfare state and the European social model. DJØF Publishing, Copenhagen

Ross M (2000) Article 16 E.C. and services of general interest: from derogation to obligation? Euro Law Rev 25(1):22–38

Roth WH (2011) The importance of the instruments provided for in the treaties for developing a European legal method. In: Neergaard U, Nielsen R, Roseberry L (eds) European legal method—paradoxes and revitalisation. DJØF Publishing, Copenhagen

Sauter W (2008) Services of general economic interest and universal service in EU Law. http://ssrn.com/abstract=1136105

Sauter W (2014) Public services in EU law. Cambridge University Press, Cambridge

Sauter W, van de Gronden JW (2010) Taking the temperature: a survey of the EU law on competition and state aid in the healthcare sector. TILEC discussion paper 2010-038, http://ssrn.com/abstract=1702832

Szyszczak E (2013) Soft law and safe havens. In: Neergaard et al (eds) Social services of general interest in the EU. T.M.C. Asser Press, The Hague

Van de Gronden JW (2013a) Transnational competition law and public services. In: Hermann C, Krajewski M, Terhechte JP (eds) European yearbook of international economic law. Springer, Heidelberg, pp 109–146

Van de Gronden JW (2013b) Free movement of services and the right of establishment: does EU internal market law transform the provision of SSGI? In: Neergaard et al (eds) Social services of general interest in the EU. T.M.C. Asser Press, The Hague

Van de Gronden JW, Rusu CS (2013) The Altmark update and social services. In: Szyszczak E, van de Gronden JW (eds) Financing services of general economic interest, reform and modernization. T.M.C Asser Press, The Hague

Vedder H (2008) The constitutionality of competition—EC internal market law and the fine line between markets, public interests and (self-)regulation in a changing constitutional setting, http://papers.ssrn.com/sol3/papers.cfm?abstract_id=1282035

Weatherill S (1995) Law and integration in the European Union. Clarendon Press, Oxford

Wehlander C (2015) Who is afraid of SGEI—services of general economic interest in EU Law with a special study on Swedish systems of choice. Skrifter från Juridiska Institutionen i Umeå, Nr. 32, Umeå

Weiler JHH (1991) The Transformation of Europe. Yale Law J 100(8):2403–2483

Weiler JHH (2005) Mutual recognition, functional equivalence and harmonization in the evolution of the European common market and the WTO. In: Kostoris F, Schioppa P (eds) The principle of mutual recognition in the European integration process. Palgrave Macmillan, Basingstoke

Part II
SGEI as a Constitutional Voice for Public Services in EU Law

Chapter 2
"Economic Activity": Criteria and Relevance in the Fields of EU Internal Market Law, Competition Law and Procurement Law

Abstract This chapter analyses the legal meaning of the notion of "economic activity" and the relevance of this notion for the applicability of EU free movement, competition and procurement rules. It shows that the CJEU makes a distinction between an activity which at an EU level *can be* economic, and therefore constitutes services, goods or capital in the meaning of the Treaties, and an activity which in a specific case (under a national regulation or in a specific transaction) *is* economic. It finds that a *legal and unitary* interpretation of the notion of "economic activity" for the purpose of EU rules on competition, free movement, and procurement emerges from the Court's case law. It also finds that in a case by case approach, the Court determines that an activity *is* economic on the basis of two criteria of agreement and remuneration, both easily fulfilled. The Court's approach implies that an activity does not have to be economic in a Member State for this Member State's regulation of this activity to be subject to EU market rules. Once the CJEU has established that public services, including social services, *can be* economic at a Union level, the Court finds that the Member States' regulatory and administrative measures affecting these services are covered by EU market rules. The chapter concludes that the Court's approach explains the development of its case law on public services, with a relatively lenient approach in the application of EU market rules. It also concludes that these judicial developments made it legally and politically necessary to transform the Treaties, and constitute a major cause of the emergence of SGEI as a constitutional public service concept in the post-Lisbon Treaties.

C. Wehlander, *Services of General Economic Interest as a Constitutional Concept of EU Law*, Legal Issues of Services of General Interest,
DOI 10.1007/978-94-6265-117-3_2

Contents

This chapter is devoted to examining the first sub-question of the book, which should be recalled here:

> *Can the CJEU's case law on the definition and the relevance of the notion of "economic activity" explain the necessity of a constitutional public service concept in the post-Lisbon Treaties?*

To make sense of the complex case law on the criteria of applicability of EU market rules to public services, in particular social services, it seems helpful to follow Hatzopoulos advice, and to distinguish the concept of economic activity from the scope of application of the Treaty and secondary law market rules.[1] Based on an in-depth study of the case law of the CJEU conducted elsewhere,[2] this chapter has therefore its focus on identifying the legal meaning of the notion of economic activity for the purpose of the Treaty rules on free movement, competition and public procurement and on the relationship between this notion and the concepts of entry to these rules.

The first section briefly recalls important elements in the CJEU's approach to determine the applicability of the Treaty market rules, and addresses critically the

[1]Hatzopoulos holds the view that the concept is unitary and has the same content under both internal market and competition law. See Hatzopoulos 2011, p. 4–6.

[2]See Wehlander 2015, pp. 37–187.

thesis that there may be a dual meaning of the notion of economic activity. The relevance of the notion of "economic activity" for the applicability of the Treaty market rules and the criteria determining that an activity is economic are then examined for the purpose of the Treaty rules on free movement in Sect. 2.1, on competition rules in Sect. 2.3, and on procurement in Sect. 2.4. The last section concludes on the question addressed by part I.

2.1 "Economic Activity": "One Test" Determining the Applicability of the Treaty Market Rules to Activities in the Public Sector?

Let us begin here by recalling that the notion of "economic activity" was present in old Articles 2 EEC and 2 EC, suggesting that the economic character of an activity constituted a legal limit to the applicability of EU law. The notion has disappeared in Article 3 TEU, not only because Treaty modifications have led EU law to cover certain activities regardless of their economic character, but also because the CJEU's basic test to determine whether a Member State's legislative or administrative measure is covered by EU market rules is not possible to contain in a horizontal legal criterion of "economic activity".

Taking the Union's mission to establish an internal market very seriously, the CJEU has namely delineated the scope of the Treaty market rules in what is often called a functional manner. The Court has in particular established that certain inherent or regulatory elements of activities in the Member States' public sector may be able to mitigate the application of EU market rules, but do not in themselves limit their scope. Thus, the fact that the activity lies within the policy powers of the Member States, in accordance with the principle of conferral, can never be invoked to exclude the applicability of the Treaty market rules to public services. As the Treaties in no way prejudice the rules governing the system of property ownership in the Member States—a principle laid down in Article 345 TFEU—the existence of markets in the public sector is initially a question for each Member State. However, one Member State cannot prevent another Member State from liberalizing activities in the public sector, and therefore cannot deny the existence in that Member State of commercial interests which may be protected by EU law.

Also, the CJEU has found that the special nature of certain services is not enough to exclude the applicability of the fundamental freedom of movement and the application of Articles 56 and 57 TFEU,[3] even if it is settled case law that "Community law does not detract from the powers of the Member States to organize their social security systems".[4] Regarding the Treaty rules on competition in a

[3]Case C-157/99, *Smits and. Peerbooms* [2001] ECR I-05473, paras 44–45.

[4]This was first laid down in *Duphar*, see Case C-238/82 *Duphar* [1984] ECR I-00523, para 16.

broad meaning (i.e. including state aid rules), the Court has not been as explicit, but by establishing in *Höfner* that "every entity engaged in an economic activity, regardless of the legal status of the entity and the way in which it is financed", it opened for a very broad application of these rules, including to public bodies destined to fulfil social and environmental policy.[5] As a result, the fact that a service is related to social or environment objectives cannot *per se* suffice to claim the inapplicability of the Treaty competition rules to this service, and in *AG2R*, the Court of Justice could reiterate its earlier made statement that "the social aim of an insurance scheme is not in itself sufficient to preclude the activity in question from being classified as an economic activity (for the purpose of Article 102 TFEU, precision added)".[6]

Some authors argue that the notion of "economic activity", defined for the purpose of EU competition rules as "any activity consisting in offering goods and services on a given market"[7] has different meanings for the purpose of the free movement rules respectively the competition rules, which would explain their different scopes.[8] They usually invoke the Court of Justice's approach in *Meca-Medina,*[9] but it is argued here that this ruling does not support their thesis. Indeed, having found that the rules of the International Olympic Committee (IOC) rules were subject to competition rules, the Court never said that the reason why the IOC rules fell outside the free movement rules was that the athletes at issue did not conduct an economic activity for the purpose of the free movement rules. Thus the Court did establish that the economic relevance of one and the same regulatory measure may vary in the two fields of law, but not the criteria determining the economic character of the activity affected.

AG Poiares Maduro's Opinion in *FENIN* has also been invoked to argue that the notion of "economic activity" would have a dual meaning in EU law, but does not either make a good case for this thesis.[10] The AG's statement that "there is no doubt that the provision of health care free of charge is an economic activity for the purpose of Article 49 EC" can be seen as his own practical manner to express

---

[5]Case C-41/90 *Höfner and Elser* [1991] ECR I-1979, para 21. The challenging element in the ruling in *Höfner* was arguably the irrelevance of the form of the activity's financing, as the Court, in *Commission* v *Italy*, had established not only the irrelevance of the legal form for determining the existence of a public undertaking, but also, long before the ruling in Cases C-180/98 to C-184/98 *Pavlov and Others* [2000] ECR I-6451, that the State may act either by exercising public powers or *by carrying on economic activities of an industrial or commercial nature by offering goods and services on the market* (see Case C-118/85, *Commission* v *Italy* [1987] ECR 2599, paras 10 and 7).

[6]Case C-437/09 *AG2R* [2011] ECR I-973, para 45, where the Court refers to the same statement in several earlier cases.

[7]See Cases C-180/98 to C-184/98 *Pavlov and Others* [2000] ECR I-6451, para 75.

[8]See in particular Odudu 2009, p. 226.

[9]Case C-519/04 P *Meca-Medina* [2006] ECR I-6991.

[10]Opinion of AG Poiares Maduro in Case C-205/03 P *FENIN v. Commission* ECR [2006] I-6295, para 51.

that any national rule related to healthcare services is regarded by the CJEU as covered by Article 56 TFEU, rather than a view that the activity *is* economic in the Member State upholding such a rule.

2.2 "Economic Activity" in the Field of Internal Market Law: Relevance and Criteria

This section analyses first how the CJEU's understanding of the concepts of "goods", "services", "establishment", and "capital"[11] that determine the applicability of the Treaty provisions on free movement relates to the notion of economic activity, and second the substantial criteria determining case by case that an activity *is* economic in the meaning of EU free movement law.

2.2.1 The Relationship Between the Notion of "Economic Activity" and the Concepts of Entry of the Treaty Rules on Free Movement

It is important to observe that the CJEU actually avoids the terminology of "economic activity" when reasoning on the applicability of the fundamental freedoms to Member States' measures related to public services, and in particular social services regarding for which this question is particularly sensitive.[12] In order to determine that Articles 30, 56 or 63 TFEU apply to the measure at issue, the Court normally questions instead whether it affects goods, services, or capital in the meaning of these rules, which it finds to be the case if "they may be subject to economic transactions". This interpretation of the concepts of entry to the free movement rules allows the Court to maximize their capacity to liberalise activities in the public sector, without having to state that the activity *is* economic in every Member State, which in the present state of EU law on social services is not possible. The Court has also maximized the effet utile of the free movement principles by reading in Article 56 TFEU both an active right for persons established in a Member State to offer services in another Member State, and a passive right for persons established in a Member State to go to another Member State and receive a service there.

However, the Court does make a distinction between on the one side finding that an activity *is* economic in the meaning of the free movement principes (and

[11] For the sake of simplicity, the free movement of workers and of EU-citizens has been left outside the scope of the study conducted in this chapter.

[12] Although to a lesser extent, this is true even in cases relating to the freedom of establishment.

therefore allows its provider or recipient to benefit from their fundamental freedoms), and on the other side an activity that in general *can be* economic (regardless of the regulatory context of a particular Member State) and therefore relates to goods, services, or capital.[13] This distinction appears to underpin all freedoms, but is clearest in the field of services, where the Court makes the following distinction:

(a) A service activity *is* economic if it is *actually* provided for remuneration in the frame of a specific transaction or in the frame of a specific regulation. This test, determining whether a fundamental freedom may be claimed in relation to a given provider, and based on the direct effect of the Treaty provisions ensuring its respect, was explicitly applied in *Freskot*.[14] In the Greek compulsory insurance scheme at issue, the Court found clear that the insurance against natural risks provided by the public body to Greek farmers could *in that specific case* not be regarded as services within the meaning of Articles 56 and 57 TFEU, because the contribution by the Greek farmers did not constitute *economic* consideration for the benefits provided by the public body managing the compulsory insurance scheme.
(b) A service activity *can be* economic if it is *normally* provided for remuneration. It is namely submitted that the CJEU interprets the word "normally" in the definition of services in Article 57 TFEU, as meaning that the service *can be* provided for remuneration. This "basic test" determines that a national rule which can affect the supply of such a service is an "economic rule" covered by the Treaty rules on free movement, even if the service is *actually* pursued as an economic activity only in other Member States and not in the Member State of the rule at issue.

While test (a) has to be made case by case, test (b) is made once and for all. Once it is established that a service is "normally" provided for remuneration, any national rule related to this service is a priori an "economic rule", which implies that it must by principle and *ex-ante* be adapted to the fundamental freedoms, *both the freedom to provide services and the freedom of establishment*. This does not mean that national rules related to that service would not be compatible with EU law, but involves that they must be justified by the Member State as necessary in

[13]See in-depth study in Wehlander 2015, pp. 57–105.

[14]Case C-355/00 *Freskot* [2003] ECR I-05263, paras 52–59. As to the freedom of establishment, it is explicitly characterized by the Court as a right to pursue an "economic activity", see for instance Case C-221/89 *Factortame II* [1991] ECR I-3905, para 20, and regarding service activities, the Court defines an economic activity for the purpose of the freedom of establishment as services "provided for remuneration", see Case C-268/99 *Jany* [2001] ECR I-8615, para 48. However, by contrast with by AG Bot, the Court is obviously careful to justify the applicability of the Treaty provision to national rules restricting social services, by invoking their character of "service in the meaning of the Treaties" and not by characterizing them as an "economic activity". Examples of this approach can be found in Joined Cases C-171/07 and C-172/07 *Apothekerkammer des Saarlandes* [2009] ECR I-4171, para 18. In this paragraph, the Court refers to Case C-372/04 *Watts* [2006] ECR I-4325, paras 92 and 146 and to Case C-169/07 *Hartlauer* [2009] ECR I-1721, para 29, see Wehlander 2015, pp. 71–78.

order to attain legitimate objectives. The CJEU has found that hospital, medical and paramedical services, elderly care, manpower, university courses, and education in schools essentially financed by private funds fulfilled *in casu* the (a) test. This implies that the (b) test is from then on automatically fulfilled, and also that the free movement of services and the freedom of establishment have a normative effect on national legislative and administrative measures related to these social services.

The term "normally" in Article 57 TFEU seems to be understood by the CJEU as a broad notion, which is quite in line with the CJEU's very restrictive interpretation of the notion of "activities connected, even occasionally, with the exercise of official authority" in Article 52 TFEU, requiring that such activities are conducted by entities with a high degree of decisional autonomy in exercising official authority. Although even such services could be argued to be at least *in theory* possible to provide for remuneration, it is submitted that the strong derogation allows a legally strong presumption that they are not. This is why, regarding public services (or in EU words, services of general interest), "activities connected, even occasionally, with the exercise of official authority" constitute arguably the "surest" form of non-economic services of general interest.

The distinction between tests (a) and (b) above has several implications.

First it explains how relying on the ambiguity of the word "normally" in Article 57 TFEU allows the CJEU avoiding the notion "economic activity" in the field of service activities, thereby sparing many feelings. The Court does not have to state explicitly that whereas Member State A may organise a service through rules that imply that the activity *is* non-economic in its territory, fundamental freedoms may anyway challenge these rules as soon as the same activity *is* economic in some other Member State, and possibly impose reforms which implacably lead the activity to become economic in Member State A. It does not either have to state, in relevant cases, that an activity constitutes a service in the meaning of the Treaty rules on free movement, but as pursued under the rules of a specific Member State, *is not* economic for the purpose of free movement law", which would entertain the perception that there can be some possibility for Member States to withdraw a service from both EU competition rules *and* EU free movement rules. However, by its ambiguous use of the term "service in the meaning of Article 57 TFEU" and its reluctance to clarify that the notion term "economic activity" in the field of free movement law can only refer to a specific activity in a specific regulatory frame, the Court maintains confusion.

Second, it explains the different scopes of EU free movement rules and EU competition rules. While a Member State's rules rendering non-economic the activity of the provider in that Member State cannot be challenged by economic rights based on EU competition law, they can be challenged on the basis of the fundamental freedoms if the activity (for instance a social service) is economic in at least one other Member State, which implies that, *in an EU market perspective*—the activity *can be* economic.

Third, although it does not demonstrate that the criteria determining that a specific activity (as pursued in a given regulatory context) *is* economic are the same in the fields of competition and free movement, it supports the thesis that these criteria can be identical.

And fourth, it sheds new light on the word "economic" in the concept of service of general economic interest and on the CJEU's approach of this notion and of its relevance for the application of free movement law to welfare services, in particular social services. This issue is developed in Chap. 5.

2.2.2 The Meaning of the Notion of "Economic Activity" for the Purposes of the Treaty Rules on Free Movement

Let us now look closer at the criteria used by the CJEU to determine that an activity *is* economic in the frame of a specific type of transaction or of a regulatory scheme, in other words that the service *is* provided for remuneration, test (a) above.

In *Humbel*, the Court has defined the notion of remuneration by stating that its essential characteristic lies in the fact that it constitutes "consideration for the service in question, and is normally agreed between the provider and the recipient of the service in question".[15] In that ruling, the Court considered that teaching or enrolment fees which pupils or their parents must sometimes pay in order to make a certain contribution to the operating expenses of courses provided under the national education system could not be seen as remuneration as

- The State, in establishing and maintaining the system, is not seeking to engage in gainful activity but fulfils social, cultural, educational duties towards its population and
- The system is as a general rule funded by public purse and not by parents/pupils.[16]

As a result of this approach, the Court concluded that courses taught in a technical institute which form part of the secondary education provided under the national education system cannot be regarded as services for the purpose of Article 59 EEC (now Article 56 TFEU).[17] The *Humbel* ruling has led some Member States to hope that services provided in the frame of publicly funded welfare systems *never* would be regarded as services in the meaning of the Treaties. However, in the field of public services, the CJEU normally discards the "system approach" of *Humbel*, and uses instead a case by case "economic provider's approach". In that approach, remuneration can exist even when the service is not paid for by those for whom it is performed, as what is relevant is *whether payments received by the specific*

[15]Case C-263/86 *Humbel* [1988] ECR 5365, para 17.

[16]Case C-263/86 *Humbel*, para 18.

[17]Case C-263/86 *Humbel*, para 20.

service operator may be regarded as economic compensation in this provider's perspective, which supposes that two basic conditions are fulfilled:

1. The provider receives a compensation amount but the provision does not have to be for-profit (the "compensation criterion").
2. The economic compensation received can be seen as a market price for the service, as it is comparable to remuneration normally *agreed* between the provider and the recipient of the service (the "agreement criterion").

Indeed, in *Freskot*, the activity of the body providing the insurance service was non-economic in the meaning of free movement (and of competition law), because Greek farmers' financial contribution could not be seen as an *economic* compensation for the service in question. The benefit provided was not a service for the purpose of Article 56 FEUF and the public body providing this benefit was not an undertaking for the same reason: there was some compensation from farmers but it was not *agreed* by the public body, which had no control over the nature and level of the benefits, and could not either decide the characteristics and rate of the contribution, as all these elements were set by law.[18]

Regarding the compensation criterion, the Court has taken the view in *Jundt* that remuneration may exist as soon as the service is "not for nothing", which suggests that the compensation does not even have to cover all costs incurred to provide the service.[19] As to the agreement criterion, it is arguably regarded as fulfilled by the CJEU as soon as the operator can be regarded as having *in some way* agreed *ex-ante* to provide the service in question for a certain compensation amount, as a sign that the provider controls its financial risk for providing the service. This view emerges discreetly from judgments as *Smits and Peerbooms* and *Watts*, where the Court carried weight on the fact that treatment received from an operator in a Member State by patients from another Member State, had been paid directly by the patients.[20] It also emerges from an *obiter dictum* in *Smits and Peerbooms*, where the Court took the view that public hospitals which provided free of charge health care and received flat-rates payments from Dutch sickness insurance funds under *contractual arrangements*, unquestionably received remuneration (compensation for the service in question, i.e. the first part of the *Humbel* definition of remuneration) and were therefore, in the conduct of their intrastate transactions, engaged in an "activity of an economic character".[21] As this view

[18]Case C-355/00 *Freskot* [2003] ECR I-05263, paras 56–59 and 78–79. The contribution was essentially a charge imposed by law equally to all operators and levied by the tax authority.

[19]Case C-281/06 *Jundt* [2007] ECR I-12231, para 33.

[20]Case C-157/99 *Smits and Peerbooms* [2001] ECR I-5473, para 55.

[21]Case C-157/99 *Smits and Peerbooms* [2001] ECR I-5473, para 58. The Court's statement signals also that "consideration for the service in question" may cover the total volume of service provided under a period rather than per service unit, and can be agreed upon between the provider and the financer of the service, rather than "as normally on a market" between the provider and the recipient.

was specified to be "in the present cases" and "under the contractual arrangements" provided for by Dutch law in force at the time of the judgment, the Court did obviously not mean that providing health care free of charge is *under any circumstances* an economic activity in the meaning of free movement.

As clear from the above, the Court gives a wide interpretation of both the "compensation criterion" and the "agreement criterion", which involves that remuneration is easily found and that test (a) above, determining whether an activity *is* economic in a specific transaction or scheme—a service actually provided for remuneration—is very easily fulfilled. However, to understand the extent of the liberalization of welfare services, in particular social services, which the Court's case law can lead to, it is essential to be aware of the relation between tests (a) and (b). As soon as the Court finds in the frame of a dispute brought to its jurisdiction that a cross-border transaction on social services fulfils test (a), the Court does not merely establish that this specific type of transaction may not be restricted by national rules without being justified under the principle of proportionality. It also demonstrates that the service fulfils test (b) and *can be* provided for remuneration, that it is "a service *normally* provided for remuneration".

Apart from the notion of "activities connected with the exercise of official authority", there is no constitutional limit to which services may be deemed to be "normally" provided for remuneration. In fact, it is seriously doubted here that courses in national systems of education may be seen as non-economic services of general interest in the sense that they *cannot* be subject to economic transactions. The "economic provider's approach" has not only excluded the *Humbel* formula in the sector of healthcare, but also considerably weakened the *Humbel* formula in the field of education. Indeed, the *Schwarz* and *Jundt* cases show that national rules governing the national education system may be seen as "economic rules" and be challenged on the basis of both the passive and the active freedoms to provide services. Besides, if publicly-funded but for-profit school services develop in the Member States, relying on *Humbel* to exclude the applicability of EU free movement rules to education provided in the frame of systems established, maintained and essentially funded by the State, looks increasingly as a weak legal shield.

The above does not only confirm that there is "no nucleus of sovereignty that the Member States can invoke, as such, against the Community",[22] but also shows that there is *almost* no nucleus of sovereignty that the Member States can invoke to claim that their national rules organising welfare services escape EU market law. Some may argue that the CJEU's case law simply expresses what the Treaties have always meant, but things are not that simple. AG Stix-Hackl's questioning of the consequences of the Court's choice allowing "a way out of closed systems of national solidarity" suggests that there has been a debate within the Court on the

[22]This radical statement was made 25 years ago by Judge Koen Lenaerts, see Lenaerts 1990, *Constitutionalism and the many faces of federalism*, 38 American Journal of Comparative Law 205 (1990) at 220.

meaning of the principle of solidarity in national welfare systems and on whether other EU foundational principles do not exclude a judicially driven liberalization of social services.[23] At any rate, the Court has discreetly but resolutely established a mechanism of tests with minimal criteria and broad effects, which closes the possibility for national rules to "exit" from EU free movement law.

This considerable expansion of the scope of the fundamental freedoms may easily lead to far-reaching liberalisation requirements on social services, not only on the demand side, but also on the supply side of social services. In particular, given the limited "bite" of the EU state action doctrine, it may be tempting for economic operators to rely on the freedom of establishment, which requires no effect on trade to apply, in order to challenge national rules affecting their opportunities of business in the field of social services. When such disputes are brought under its jurisdiction, Judge Lenaerts has explained that the Court takes a nuanced approach aimed at "striking a fair balance between the general interest pursued by such services and the effectiveness of the relevant Treaty provisions governing the internal market".[24] Indeed, in the absence of EU legislation in the sector of social welfare, the CJEU faces not only a risk of rejection from the Member States (a political issue), but also a competence problem (a constitutional issue), and its "nuanced" approach includes the following key elements.

First, it must be underlined that the Court considers certain rules to be non-economic in nature, and for that reason not covered by the economic rights to free movement. As in *Keck,*[25] the CJEU's doctrine in *Meca-Medina*[26] implies that rules governing strictly non-economic aspects of an otherwise commercial activity may escape from the scope of the fundamental freedoms, even where the activity *can be* economic.

Second, the Court's *Humbel* doctrine may be understood so that a *theoretical* possibility for a service to be provided for remuneration does not suffice for a service to be seen as "normally" provided for remuneration in the meaning of Article 57 TFEU. In other words, "normally" requires that the service is actually provided for remuneration *in at least one* Member State. If this interpretation is correct, the Court requires economic rights to free movement to *actually* exist somewhere in the EU, which is excluded as long as no Member State allows that providers in a welfare system objectively have another aim than the State—an economic purpose—in providing the service.[27] Accordingly, although the thesis that "state edu-

[23]Opinion of AG Stix-Hackl in C-76/05 *Schwarz* [2007] ECR I-6849, paras 39–40: the creation of a way out' of closed systems of national solidarity, accompanying the possibility of exercising the fundamental freedoms laid down in the EC Treaty/.../ is in itself detrimental at least to the idea of national solidarity, because the spreading of risk is restricted".

[24]Lenaerts 2012, p. 1249.

[25]Joined Cases C-267 and C-268/91 *Keck and Mithouard* [1993] ECR I-6097.

[26]Case C-519/04 P *Meca-Medina* [2006] ECR I-6991.

[27]Another thing is of course that non-economic EU rights, such as the right to move and reside freely within the EU in accordance with Article 20(2) TFEU, may not unjustified be restricted by the national legislators.

cation is special" still finds support,[28] it seems reasonable to expect that the CJEU will regard courses in national education systems as services *normally* provided for remuneration when confronted with the fact that a Member State allows private providers in the national system to have an aim of profit instead of the State's aim to serve its population, as is now the case in Sweden. How long the *Humbel* doctrine can stand the test of reality and of legal coherence remains thus to be seen, in particular as there is pressure for "modernizing school" in several Member States.

Third, the Court's approach in *Sodemare* is submitted to mean that even when the provision of a service is externalized to private entities, a Member State withholds the power to deny solidarity funding of for-profit activity without infringing the freedom of establishment.[29] The *Sodemare* ruling may be interpreted as acknowledging the Member States' retained powers not only as regulators but also as financers of social services. Where neither the societal objectives nor the modes of supply are harmonized, the legislator of a Member State may—on the basis of a democratic mandate—define precisely the service it finds important to finance on the basis of solidarity and decide that solidarity funding does not remunerate capital.

This understanding gets support from the recent ruling in *San Lorenzo*. In this ruling, the Court found first that national legislation imposing on local authorities to entrust the provision of ambulance services to non-profit associations with priority and by direct award (financing the costs incurred for providing the service and certain fixed costs necessary to fulfil the task) was covered by Articles 49 and 56 TFEU, provided that the national court could establish the existence of a certain cross-border interest.[30] However, the Court confirmed its stance in *Sodemare* that these provisions (1) do not preclude that a Member State, in the exercise of its retained powers to organize social security systems, decides the social aims of welfare services and (2) considers that recourse to non-profit associations is consistent with these aims and may help to control costs relating to those services, provided that this preferential regime actually contributes to the social purpose and the pursuit of the objectives of the good of the community and budgetary efficiency on which the system is based.[31]

[28]See Lenaerts 2012, p. 1251.

[29]Case C-70/95 *Sodemare* [1997] ECR I-3495, where the Court found that the Italian regulation imposing a not-for-profit condition to admit operators in the public-funded welfare system for old peoples' homes in Italy was compatible with the right of establishment of a profit-making company established in Luxemburg which had set up for-profit old peoples' homes in Italy.

[30]Case C-113/13 *San Lorenzo* [decided on 11 December 2014, nyr], para 50.

[31]Ibid, paras 59–60. The Court emphasized that this freedom is subject to several conditions, in particular that the associations do not pursue objectives other than the good of the community and budgetary efficiency, do not make any profit as a result of their services, apart from the reimbursement of the variable, fixed and on-going expenditure necessary to provide them, and do not procure any profit for their members, see paras 61–63.

It will be seen in Chap. 9 that as a result of the Swedish policy on public education, the *Sodemare* approach may constitute the only manner for other Member States to claim their powers to impose a not-for-profit condition for subsidizing courses provided by private entities, which allows guessing that this approach is difficult to overrule, and important to confirm.

2.3 "Economic Activity" in the Field of Competition: Relevance and Criteria

In order to determine the applicability of the Treaty rules on competition, the CJEU has elaborated an intricate body of definitions and tests, and thereby forced the principle of competition into the core of national welfare services.[32] This section sheds first light on the difference between tests determining whether an activity which *can be* economic (the so called "comparative test" in *Höfner* and the doctrine on activities related to the exercise of public authority in the *Eurocontrol* line of case law) and others determining whether an activity *is* economic in the specific case (the market participation test in *Pavlov* and the doctrine on activities fulfilling an exclusively social function in the *Poucet and Pistre* line of case law). The second part of the section examines the criteria determining that an activity *is* economic for the purpose of EU competition law, and compares them with the corresponding criteria in EU free movement law. This should allow answering the questions whether the notion of "service" has the same meaning for the purpose of EU competition rules and EU free movement rules, and what the CJEU means with the notion "on a market".

2.3.1 Relevance of the Fact that an Activity Can Be *Economic for the Applicability of the Treaty Competition Rules*

The CJEU established in *Commission v Italy* that the State may act either by *exercising public powers* or by carrying on economic activities of an industrial or commercial nature by *offering goods and services on the market.*[33] One must therefore consider *case by case* the activities exercised by the State and determine the category to which those activities belong.[34] In line with this basic axiom, the Court later defined in *Höfner*—now settled law—the notion of

[32]According to Semmelmann, the CJEU's interpretation of the Treaty competition rules pursues the same overarching goal as its interpretation of EU free movement rules, "namely to abolish obstacles to cross-border trade". See Semmelmann 2010, p. 521.

[33]Case C-118/85 *Commission v Italy* [1987] ECR 2599, para 7.

[34]Ibid.

"undertaking"—constituting the concept of entry to the Treaty competition rules—as "every entity engaged in an economic activity, regardless of the legal status of the entity and the way in which it is financed". The "undertaking" character of an entity is thus determined solely by the economic character of its activity *under the rules it is subject to*, and consequently competition rules can apply even to (1) entities conducting activities directly or indirectly funded by the State or with State resources and (2) public entities that are not organized as private law entities.

The *Höfner* definition of an undertaking is generally qualified as functional but leaves unsaid what an economic activity is. In *Höfner* the CJEU found relevant for the applicability of the Treaty competition rules that "the activity is not necessarily, and has not always been, conducted by public entities".[35] It is obviously incorrect to understand this comparative formula as a definition of an "economic activity" for the purpose of the Treaty competition rules. The Court produced namely in *Pavlov* the pivotal definition of an "economic activity" for the purpose of EU competition rules as "any activity consisting in offering goods and services on a given market".[36]

The meaning of the comparative formula launched in *Höfner* and later also used in *Glöckner*, is not explicit in the Court's case law, but in these two cases, where it was difficult to show that the activity pursued by a specific entity *was* economic, this "comparative test" was clearly used by the Court to establish that it *could be* economic, in other words that there is some market for the activities in question. It is therefore submitted that the comparative test is an inherent part of the definition of an undertaking formulated in *Höfner* and of the definition of an economic activity in *Pavlov*, and has the following meaning:

- It allows determining whether the activity *can be* economic. Thus, a service activity which fulfils the comparative test has "a potential market" in a Member State, as it could (in theory) be conducted by private entities for-profit. This capacity of a given service to be subject to commercial transactions is precisely what is meant by "service *normally* provided for remuneration" in Article 57 TFEU. Hence, the comparative test in the field of competition law seems to correspond in substance to the notion of "service" in Article 57 TFEU and "goods" for the purpose of the Treaties.
- Where it is found that the activity *can be* economic, it may be presumed that the absence of effective competition for the activity in a specific case is due to the Member State's own regulatory or administrative measures. That the activity *can be* economic does not mean that the activity as conducted under the scheme of a Member State *is* economic, but that EU competition law "may have a role to play".

In this understanding, the comparative test, construed as a basic test, is made once and for all in the Union for a given activity, and is therefore not explicitly formulated each time the CJEU refers to *Höfner*.

As this test can be fulfilled by virtually any activity, the Court has been forced to give substance to its own axiom that the State may in certain cases be seen as

[35]Case C-41/90 *Höfner* [1991] ECR I-1979.

[36]See Cases C-180/98 to C-184/98 *Pavlov and Others* [2000] ECR I-6451, para 75.

not offering goods or services on a market, and to formulate criteria determining that the State acts instead by "exercising public powers". The Court has done so in a line of case law including the *Eurocontrol* ruling on navigation control activities conducted by an organization which also established and collected route charges from airlines, and the *Cali* ruling on charges levied by a company entrusted with anti-pollution surveillance in the port of Genoa.[37] In this doctrine, the Court has established that an activity which by its nature, its aim and the rules it is subject to, involves powers which are typical of a public authority, consists in the exercise of public powers. For the purpose of determining whether an activity amounts to the exercise of public powers, the comparative test is totally irrelevant, because the Court defers instead to the *Member State's own assessment* that the activity *cannot* be economic due to its aim and nature, and necessitates instead that the entity entrusted with its conduct relies on powers derogating from ordinary law and typical of the prerogatives of the State.

If an activity constitutes the exercise of public powers, the Member State may be accountable at national and/or international level for fulfilling the general interest missions pursued by the activity, but the activity is not affected by EU competition law and most probably not either by EU free movement law. The correspondence between the doctrine on the exercise of public powers and the free movement derogation in Article 52 TFEU is rather obvious, as they both address the "exercise of public powers", are both very potent, and are both interpreted by the Court very restrictively. Thus, by developing this doctrine, the CJEU has undeniably increased, in the field of services, the symmetry between the criteria of applicability of the Treaty rules on free movement rules and on competition.[38]

---

[37]In Case C-364/92 *Eurocontrol* [1994] ECR I-43 and Case C-343/95 *Diego Cali* [1997] ECR I-1547, the Court concluded that the activities at issue constituted the exercise of public powers, and came to the opposite conclusion regarding the provision of airline facilities against fees freely set by the airport management company in Case C-82/01 P *Aéroports de Paris* [2002] ECR I-09297. For a more in-depth analysis, see Wehlander 2015, pp. 121–128.

[38]In this respect, it is interesting to note the Commission Decision finding that the electronic procurement platform (TenderNed) supplied in-house by the Dutch Ministry of Economic Affairs, Agriculture and Innovation must be een as the exercise of public powers. Therefore, and Although a market exists in the Netherlands for the supply of electronic procurement platforms, the Commission concluded that the supply of this platform is a non-economic activity. The Commission reasoning is challenging, as it argues in particular that supplying such a platform is not an "inherent economic activity, but rather a service of general interest, which can be commercially exploited only so long as the State fails to offer the service itself" and thus can be an economic activity as conducted by private operators, see Commission's Decision of 18 December 2014 on The Netherlands E-procurement platform TenderNed SA.34646 (2014/NN) (ex 2012/CP), point 68. Unsurprisingly, this Decision has been contested and brought to the General Court, see Case T-138/15 *Aanbestedingskalender a.o. v Commission*. The Commission's approach regarding TenderNed does not seem to fit well with its own reasoning in its Decision 2012/485/EU of 25 April 2012 on the aid to the Zweckverband Tierkorperbeseitigung in Rheinland-Pfalz, im Saarland, im Rheingau-Taunus-Kreis und im Landkreis Limburg-Weilburg (ZT) SA.25051 (C 19/10), supported by the General Court, see Case T-309/12 *ZT* EU:T:2014:676. On these decisions, see Szyszczak 2015, p. 684.

As to the relationship between the comparative test and the *Pavlov* definition of an economic activity ("an offer of *services* or *goods* on the market"), it is submitted that the comparative criterion allows establishing that the activity examined is related to "goods or services" in the meaning of the *Pavlov* definition. Thus, in the presence of a service activity, the comparative test allows determining that it is a "service *normally* provided for remuneration". When this is established, it remains to examine whether the activity at issue consists in offering these goods or services on a market, which the comparative test cannot tell. Thus, in spite of the confusing terminology used by some Advocates General,[39] it seems clear that the comparative test alone is not meant to determine whether a specific activity in the specific case *is* economic under national rules, as the Court does not consider that an activity fulfilling the comparative criterion *is* economic unless it also fulfils the condition "offered on the market" laid down in the *Pavlov* definition.

Finding that a non-harmonised social service fulfils the comparative test and thus constitutes a "service" in the meaning of the Treaties, legitimates that EU competition law has the upper hand and that the policy powers of the Member States are constrained by the objectives of the Treaties, with the following legal effects:

- As the activity involves the provision of "services" or "goods" in the meaning of the Treaties, the interpretation of the notion of "offer on the market" in the *Pavlov* definition is made under EU law and not under national law.
- National rules restricting or eliminating competition are put "under EU competition law control". The CJEU applies a "principle of competition" from which it derives a "duty of consistency" on the Member States' regulation and organisation of the activity on their territory. This was the case in *Ambulance Glöckner*, where awarding to non-profit organisations exclusive rights to conduct emergency and ambulance transport was acceptable only if the operators were not manifestly unable to satisfy demand.[40]

2.3.2 Criteria Determining that an Activity Is *Economic for the Purpose of the Treaty Competition Rules*

The CJEU considers obviously that most activities, unless they are characterized by the exercise of public powers, *can be* economic, either by reference to situations in the past, or to their organisation in some Member States. This implies,

---

[39] In particular AG Jacobs characterized an activity that could at least in principle be carried on by a private undertaking in order to make profits as "economic in character", which is a somewhat confusing term for an activity only fulfilling the "comparative test", see Opinion of AG Jacobs in Joined Cases C-264/01, C-306/01, C-354/01 and C-355/01 *AOK* [2004] ECR I-2493, para 28.

[40] As seen above, such a "duty of consistency" has also emerged in *San Lorenzo* regarding not-for-profit conditions in public service systems restricting the freedom of establishment, see Case C-113/13 *San Lorenzo* [decided on 11 December 2014, nyr].

if the interpretation of the term "normally" in Article 57 TFEU proposed above is correct, that the Court regards most public services, including social services, as "services" both in the meaning of Article 57 TFEU and for the purpose of its *Pavlov* definition of an economic activity ("services" offered on a market). Under such circumstances, the CJEU's criteria determining whether the services or goods are "offered on a market" are entirely decisive to determine whether the specific entity's activity *is* economic and whether its operator *is* an undertaking. Concerning these criteria, the following elements emerge from the CJEU's case law.

First, while repeating that certain characteristics are *not* in themselves decisive to exclude that services or goods are "offered on a market" (see above Sect. 2.1), the Court has clarified that it takes an "offer" to make an "economic activity" for the purpose of EU competition rules. The *FENIN* ruling established namely that unless contracting authorities' purchasing activity is directly related to *their* offer of goods or services on a market, this purchasing activity is not an economic activity.[41]

Second, the CJEU's case law suggests that the Court considers remuneration, *in some sense*, as relevant in determining whether an activity is economic for the purpose of the Treaty rules on competition. Thus, the criterion of remuneration, related to a risk for the service provider, must be fulfilled for self-employed persons to constitute undertakings.[42] Also, in *Aéroports de Paris*, the airport management company was regarded as conducting an economic activity, because it provided airport facilities to airlines and other service providers *for a fee at a rate which the company fixed freely*.[43] Even in *Höfner* and in *Glöckner*, where the CJEU has launched the comparative criterion and thereby gone furthest in widening the applicability of the Treaty rules on competition, it has not discarded the requirement that the entity examined must actually provide goods or services for remuneration. Thus, the element of compensation for the service offered appears relevant to find that it is offered on a market, as is the case to find that an activity *is* economic in the meaning of free movement law.

Third, starting with *Poucet and Pistre*, the Court has elaborated a doctrine so far only applied in the field of social security, involving that the social security activity considered in a specific case may constitute services or goods in the meaning of the Treaties, but *is* not economic for the purpose of EU competition rules if it is regulated so that it fulfils an exclusively social function. This approach seems binary: goods or services are either "offered on the market" or provided to fulfil

[41]Case C-205/03 P *FENIN* [2006] ECR I-6295, para 26, confirmed in Case C-113/07 P *SELEX* [2009] ECR I-2207, paras 102 and 114.

[42]See Case C-35/96 *Commission* v *Italy* [1998] ECR 1-3851, para 37; Joined Cases C-180/98 to C-184/98 *Pavlov* [2000] ECR I-5481, para 76; Case C-309/99 *Wouters* [2002] ECR I-1577, para 48.

[43]Case C-82/01 P *Aéroports de Paris* [2002] ECR I-9297, para 78. In that case the issue was rather that a distinction had to be made between the non-economic and economic activities conducted by the airport management company.

an exclusively social function. If this understanding is correct, the factor implying that the activity does not exclusively fulfil a social function should be relevant to determine that it consists in offering goods or services "on the market". In the field of social security, the Court has found an activity is non-economic if it pursues social objectives, is organised predominantly under the principle of solidarity, and is conducted under state control. The Court has thus signalled that its social objectives and its solidarity elements are important but not *per se* decisive, as what also counts is that providers enjoy a degree of autonomy allowing them to influence the economic conditions for providing the service. This element of "autonomous agreement" to provide fits well with the Court's approach of an economic activity for the purpose of the Treaty free movement rules examined above.

Competition rulings on social services are scarce and the CJEU has never clarified what in substance distinguishes the *Pavlov* definition from the comparative test, in other words it has not spelled out which criteria determine that an activity in a specific situation is "offered on the market", and thus *is* (as opposed to *can be*) economic for the purpose of EU competition rules.[44] In that situation of uncertainty, AG Poiares Maduro argued in *FENIN* that to determine the applicability of EU competition rules, healthcare provision must be assessed separately from the social security elements of a national healthcare system. Referring to the *obiter dictum* in *Smits and Peerbooms* the Advocate General proposed that the provision of healthcare under a scheme characterized by a high degree of solidarity *is* economic if the State has not reserved the activity exclusively to State bodies guided solely by considerations of solidarity.[45] His approach is discussed below but supports the view submitted in Sect. 2.3 that by entities *actually* providing *for remuneration*, the CJEU spelled the *legal* definition of an economic activity "in free movement law terms". And indeed, the Commission and the High Surveillance Authority have also used the *obiter dictum* in *Smits and Peerbooms* in state aid decisions in the fields of hospital services, tertiary education, school education and primary healthcare, an approach which was validated by the GC in *CBI*.[46]

AG Poiares Maduro's statement may be understood as meaning that public bodies offer services on a market as soon as the State allows, be it only in fact, that some entities provide a *similar* service for remuneration, *regardless of whether these public bodies enjoy a minimum degree of autonomy allowing them to influence the economic conditions of their own service provision.* As "similarity" may be quite far from identity, this understanding would imply that public funding of

---

[44]By "positive criterion" is meant here a criterion which specifically can be found in an economic activity, by contrast with an approach finding that an economic activity can be found even in the absence of certain criteria.

[45]Opinion of AG Poiares Maduro in Case C-205/03 P *FENIN* [2006] ECR I-6295, paras 47 and 52.

[46]Case T-137/10 *CBI*, Judgement of 7 November 2012, para 91, refereing to Commission decision of 28 October 2009 Financement des hôpitaux publics du réseau IRIS de la Région Bruxelles-Capitale (Belgique), NN 54/2009—C (2009) 8120 final.

public bodies is considered as remuneration, even if this funding does not cover the costs of providing the service under the conditions imposed on them by the State. Would such an interpretation be compatible with the principle that Member States may decide the level of social protection in their welfare services, and would it fit with the Court's finding in *Freskot* that the public provider is not an undertaking if it lacks control over the characteristics of the service and the compensation received?

In fact, in *Smits and Peerbooms* and in *CBI*, both private and public entities were allowed to provide similar hospital services, but both did so in the frame of *contractual arrangements* implying that both received payments from public authorities giving them powers to influence the financial conditions of service provision. In the Dutch system and in the Belgian schemes at issue in those cases, the public hospitals seemed to enjoy an economic autonomy allowing them to influence the risk of providing hospital services, and could be argued to provide hospital services for remuneration. And in *Glöckner*, the not-for-profit organisations providing ambulance services enjoyed some economic autonomy allowing them to cover their costs. *Höfner* emerges as the only case where the activity of a publicly funded not-for-profit public body was found economic in the meaning of EU competition rules without this body's economic autonomy or lack of economic autonomy being at least evoked as a fact in the case. Thus, at this stage in the development of the CJEU's case law, it seems possible to argue that the requirement that services or goods are "offered on a market" by an entity implies that the two following criteria are fulfilled:

1. The entity does not provide goods/services for free (compensation criterion).
2. The entity can influence the economic conditions of its own service provision (agreement criterion).

2.4 EU Procurement Law: The Concepts of "Service" and "Undertaking" Meet in the Notion of "Economic Transaction"

Hatzopoulos holds as "indisputable" that at as soon as activities, even what he calls "genuinely non-economic activities", are to be awarded to some non-state actor, EU rules and principles on public procurement become applicable.[47] In that case, should we expect that even school education services are subject to EU

[47]Hatzopoulos 2011, p. 2: "some authors strive to demonstrate that certain Treaty rules also apply in the absence of an economic activity". In a similarly pragmatic manner, van de Gronden states that "[i]f a public authority externalises the provision of SSGI, the Directive for the award of public works contracts, public supply contracts and public service contracts comes into play, see van de Gronden 2013b, p. 150–151.

procurement law when their provision is entrusted against remuneration to non-state actors? To elude this troublesome question, some may put their thrust in *Humbel*, where the CJEU found that the provision of courses in national education systems is not a service in the meaning of the Treaties decision, or in the fact that school education services are not "prioritized" in EU procurement legislation. However, it is nowadays well-known that the CJEU's appreciation of whether an activity constitutes a service in the meaning of the Treaties may evolve, subject to policy and economic facts in the Member States, and that the Treaty principles imply procurement rules of primary law that the EU legislator must respect when adopting secondary law on procurement.

Against this background, this section examines the criteria determining that a transaction falls within the scope of EU procurement law. Hatzopoulos' assertion is taken as a premise, and it is therefore assumed that *something* must happen *in the process of planning the award of a non-economic activity to a non-state actor*, which transforms the activity into an activity that at least *can be* economic, as otherwise Article 2 in the SGI Protocol, providing that the provisions of the Treaties *do not affect in any way the competence of the Member States to commission and organise non-economic services of general interest,* does not make any sense. This section draws upon (1) the constitutionalisation of EU procurement law resulting from the CJEU's case law, (2) the Court's broad interpretation of the notion of "public contract" triggering the applicability of the procurement directives, which allows identifying the essential elements of procurement as an "economic transaction", and (3) the "certain cross-border interest", "in-house" and "public-public cooperation" doctrines, introduced by a CJEU aware that its interpretation of EU procurement rules may build "a bridge too far" and calls for limitations.[48]

The CJEU has established that, when organising the provision of public services, Member States must not only respect EU procurement directives, but also procurement rules based directly on the EU Treaties. By finding in particular that an obligation of prior publication for the award of certain contracts follows directly from a duty of transparency concomitant to a duty of equal treatment, the Court has elevated the dignity of "equal treatment" from an *objective* of EU procurement legislation to a *principle* directly deriving from the fundamental freedoms in Articles 49 and 56 TFEU.[49] The Court has justified its approach by a will to open up public contracts to the widest possible *undistorted* competition. Some authors claim that the Court's approach is justified by a principle of free competition that would *always* have formed a basic part of EU procurement rules.[50]

However, by grafting the principle of undistorted competition—a competition law principle—onto EU free movement principles, the Court has arguably

[48]These are the terms used by Hordjik and Meulenbelt to criticise the CJEU's approach, see Hordijk and Meulenbelt 2005, p. 126.

[49]See for instance Case C-324/98 *Telaustria AG* [2000] ECR I-10793, paras 60–62; Case C-458/03 *Parking Brixen* [2005] ECR I-8585, para 50 and Case C-410/04 *ANAV* [2006] ECR I-3303, para 22.

[50]For instance, Sánchez Graells 2011, p. 195.

established the principle of competition as one of the fundamental principles of Community law on the award of public contracts.[51] As this approach has shaped a quasi-constitutional right to *equal* access to "public procurement", the delineation of this notion is decisive for the scope of EU procurement law, and for the Member States' freedom to organise public services, in particular social services. As "procurement" is not defined in the Treaties, and as EU primary law on procurement can evidently not apply unless certain *legal* criteria are fulfilled, an attempt to identify what essential elements a planned transaction must include to be covered by any EU procurement law, be it primary and secondary law, may be made by inferring these elements from the CJEU's case law

1. Interpreting the notion of "public contract" that triggers the applicability of the procurement directives and is defined therein
2. Exempting from EU procurement law transactions regarded as "in-house", lacking a certain cross-border interest, or public-public cooperation to achieve public service tasks.

Let us focus for the sake of simplicity on the definition of "public contract" in the Public Sector Directive as (1) a contract, (2) for pecuniary interest, (3) in writing, (4) between contracting authorities and economic operators, and (5) having as its object services, goods or works.[52] These basic criteria delineate procurement as an *economic transaction* between public authorities (or bodies governed by public law) and *economic* operators. It should be underlined here that the requirement that contracting authorities must have a "pecuniary interest" in this economic transaction does not per se entail that they conduct an economic activity, as follows from *FENIN*. Also, the requirement that the contract is "in writing" appears as a formal one, and may be construed by the Court as proving rather than constituting the existence of a contractual situation. From a detailed analysis of the CJEU's case law,[53] the following two elements emerge as essential for a planned transaction to be caught by EU procurement law:

(a) An *agreement between two autonomous wills*, finding a specific expression in the Directive's requirement of a contract (an agreement criterion). The CJEU appears to interpret this criterion functionally rather than formally, for instance when the authority's autonomy does not include the choice of the provider, or when the provider's autonomy is limited by the fact that the agreement is governed by public law and is concluded with authorities in their exercise of public power.[54]

[51]This argument was made by AG Stix-Hackl in her Opinion to Case C-247/02 *Sintesi* [2004] ECR I-9215, para 33.

[52]See Article 1(2) (a) Directive 2004/18/EC.

[53]See for instance Wehlander 2015, p. 167–178.

[54]Case C-399/98, *La Scala* [2001] ECR I-5409, para 73.

(b) An *offer of remuneration in exchange for services/goods/works*, finding a specific expression in the Directive's requirement of a pecuniary interest (a compensation criterion). This criterion supposes providers' economic interest but also contracting authorities' of gaining access, for themselves or third persons, to services, goods or works having economic value. In the Court's view, the fact that remuneration remains limited to reimbursement of the expenditure incurred to provide the agreed service does not exclude a contract's pecuniary interest, and does not exclude that it may constitute a public contract.[55] Also, the requirement that the object of the transaction must be "services" or "goods" is fulfilled as soon as the authority plans to offer remuneration for the services/goods in question, because this very planning shows that the services/goods at issue can be subject to an economic transaction.

In light of these criteria, determining the existence of "public contract" and by inference, of "public procurement", it is submitted that EU procurement rules (secondary or primary law rules) apply only inasmuch as, in the frame and under the conditions of the contract *planned*, the transaction is economic both in the meaning of free movement law and in the meaning of competition law. In the frame of an economic transaction covered by EU procurement law, operators must provide de facto for remuneration, and thus be "*economic* operators". In *CoNISMa* the CJEU has defined the notion of "economic operator" in a manner that is strikingly similar to the definition of the notion of "undertaking" in the field of EU competition law.[56] It emerges namely that "economic operator" in the meaning of the procurement directives is "any natural or legal person or public entity or group of such persons and/or bodies, regardless of whether it is governed by public law or private law, whether it is active as a matter of course on the market or only on an occasional basis and whether or not it is subsidised by public funds, which offers on the market, respectively, the execution of works and/or a work, products or services".[57]

As a result of this definition of "economic operator", it is submitted that in *CoNISMa* the CJEU has enlarged eligibility to take part to tendering procedures to the point where *in fact* it recognizes a freedom for any *potential* undertaking to compete for contracts covered or partly covered by the directives, which triggers a duty of transparency enabling to ensure equal access to the award procedure. This approach was confirmed in *Lecce* (Grand Chamber), where the Court also reaffirmed that Member States may regulate non-profit public entities "and inter alia authorise or not authorise them to operate on the market, taking into account their objectives as an institution", but that "if and to the extent that [non-profit] entities

[55]Case C-159/11 *Lecce*, [decided by the Grand Chamber on 19 December 2012, nyr], para 29. This approach is quite in line with the Court's interpretation of the notion of "remuneration" for the purpose of the fundamental freedoms.

[56]Case C-305/08 *CoNISMa* [2009] ECR I-12129.

[57]Ibid., see paras 28 to 30 read in combination.

are entitled to offer certain services on the market, they may not be prevented from participating in a tendering procedure for the services concerned".[58] Thus, in public procurement transactions, the economic character of the activity can be equivalently characterized in free movement terms "provided (actually) for remuneration" or in competition law terms "offered on a market".

The CJEU has certainly been aware that it challenged the acceptance of the masters of the Treaty by its "purposive approach",[59] where the basic criteria of applicability of EU procurement rules, identified above, entail that a wide range of transactions are covered by EU primary law on procurement and that a wide range of operators must be given access to such transactions. This explains doubtlessly the derogations it has opened for in its case law, as these derogations seem to fit well with the understanding proposed above of what triggers the applicability of any rule of EU procurement law. However, these derogations have been formulated in terms which are so nuanced that they create new uncertainties.

In *Teckal*, the CJEU established that a contract between a public authority and a person legally distinct from that authority falls outside EU procurement directives if it is "in-house", which is the case if the two following criteria are fulfilled:

(a) The authority exercises over the person at issue a control similar to the control it exercises over its own departments (the "control criterion")
(b) This entity carries out the essential part of its activities with the authority or authorities that control it (the "activity criterion").[60]

In *Parking Brixen* the Court found that these considerations could be transposed to service concessions only covered by primary EU procurement law as

> the principle of equal treatment and the specific expressions of that principle, namely the prohibition on discrimination on grounds of nationality and Articles 43 EC and 49 EC, are to be applied in cases where a public authority *entrusts the supply of economic activities to a third party*. By contrast, it is *not appropriate* to apply the Community rules on public procurement or public service concessions *in cases where a public authority performs tasks in the public interest* for which it is responsible by its own administrative, technical and other means, without calling upon external entities.[61]

Through this "nuanced" reasoning, the Court tells us arguably that in-house transactions may derogate from EU procurement principles,

- Not because the operator's activity is not economic (it may offer some of its services/goods on a market), but
- Because public authorities' prerogatives are essentially founded on their mandate to act in the public interest, and hence forbidding that they perform their

---

[58]Case C-159/11 *Lecce*, [decided by the Grand Chamber on 19 December 2012, nyr], para 27. This implies perhaps that the benefit of an advertising obligation is not only for operators whose activity was economic before they tendered.

[59]See Arrowsmith et al. 2011, p. 37.

[60]Case C-107/98 *Teckal* [1999] ECR I-8121, para 50.

[61]Case C-458/03 *Parking Brixen* [2005] ECR I-8585, para 61, emphasis added.

public interest tasks by using entities which *to a sufficient degree* must share their motivation to act in the public interest (and not to offer services/goods on a market) would be *inappropriate*.

The in-house doctrine reflects the Court's insight that, as long as "procurement" is not a well-defined constitutional concept of EU law, it is constitutionally "inappropriate" to extend the impact of pro-competitive EU procurement law on Member States' *administration* of services for which they have retained competence.

The CJEU's will to limit the impact of its approach—placing free competition at the heart of EU primary law on procurement—is also clear from *An Post* where it established that publication obligations following directly from the principle of equal treatment and the concomitant duty of transparency apply only to contracts having "a *certain* cross-border interest", in other words the transaction is economic but has not enough impact on EU's economic activities.[62] The Court regards objective criteria such as the contract's value and the place where it is carried out as relevant to assess this interest. In the Court's view, indications on such criteria may be laid down in national or regional regulation, but contracting authorities/entities must examine case by case whether a cross-border interest exists or not, and their appreciation is judicially reviewable, which supposes that the fundamental freedoms are normative whatever the case. Thus, the criterion "no certain cross-border interest" is not a truly "safe" exemption rule, even if the 2014 procurement directives try to take the lead by establishing an assumption that social services under a certain threshold are not of cross-border interest and need not be published *ex ante*.

In *Commission v Germany* there was no "in-house situation" and the cross-border interest was clear, the contract at issue concerning the continuous delivery of household waste by some municipalities to the municipality of Hamburg.[63] The Court could not justify a derogation by the transaction's lack of economic impact, and had to point explicitly at another decisive criterion, which the Court in that ruling chose to name "public service tasks" rather than "services of general interest". The relevance of the concept of SGEI for this derogation is studied in detail in Chap. 4.

It should finally be stressed that the concrete impact of the fundamental freedoms on the Member States welfare systems has grown not only as a consequence of the CJEU's interpretation of EU procurement law, but also because the Court tends to submit any public measures generating business opportunities on their territories—such as schemes combining authorizations and public funding—to principles of EU administrative law which coincide with "general principles of EU procurement law". A case in point is *Hartlauer*, where the Court found that Austrian rules which did not submit *all* private entities providing dental care to a requirement of authorization, did not pursue its social objectives consistently and systematically. It also found that the authorization system was not based on objective, non-discriminatory criteria known in advance, and adequately circumscribing the exercise by the national authorities of their discretion. By combining the

[62]Case C-507/03 *Commission v Ireland ("An Post")* [2007] ECR I-9777, para 29.

[63]Case C-480/06 *Commission* v *Germany* [2009] ECR I-04747.

Court's arguments, it appears that the authorization system was incompatible with the freedom of establishment, because it did not respect the principles of non-discrimination, equal treatment and transparency, which is exactly the same combination of principles as those governing procurement.[64] However, by contrast with procurement measures, systems of public funding through authorizations such as in *Hartlauer* are not submitted to any obligation of prior *publication*, which explains that the EU legislator introduced definitions of "procurement" and "concession" in the 2014 procurement directives, as seen in more detail in Chap. 7.

2.5 Conclusions: Closure of "Exit" from EU Law for Public Services Enhances the Need of Member States' "Voice"

2.5.1 Legal Meaning of "Economic Activity" as a Unitary Notion of EU Market Law

The analysis above allows submitting the following conclusions.

Firstly, the CJEU appears to make, in the three fields of Treaty market rules—free movement, competition, and procurement, a distinction between an "economic activity"/"economic transaction" and an activity/transaction that *can be* economic exists in the three fields or EU market law.

(a) An activity can be economic in the meaning of EU free movement rules if it consists in the provision of goods or services that *normally* (in the EU generally but not necessarily in the case considered) are provided for remuneration. An activity can be economic in the meaning of EU competition rules if it consists in providing services or goods that *can be* offered on the market (it fulfils the comparative test in *Höfner*).

(b) An activity *is* economic in the meaning of free movement law and as such entitled to free movement rights if it *actually* (in the specific case considered) consists in providing goods or services for remuneration. An activity *is* economic in the meaning of EU competition rules if it *actually* (in the specific case considered) consists in offering goods or services on the market (it fulfils the definition in *Pavlov*).

(a) and (b) interact through a "domino effect", as

- The fact that an activity *is* economic in one Member State or in cross-border transactions, shows that the activity *can be* economic at EU level in general, and
- The fact that the activity *can be* economic (is about services or goods which can be subject to economic transactions) shows that there is market potential, allowing to examine whether national rules constitute the cause of an absence of competition.

[64]Case C-169/07 *Hartlauer* [2009] ECR I-1721.

Second, regarding case (b) above, two criteria emerge as essential to determine that an activity *is* economic for the purpose of EU free movement law, competition law and procurement law:

1. A remuneration criterion: the entity at issue receives remuneration for providing the services/goods. Remuneration exists as soon as provision is not for free, and provision does not have to be for-profit. This criterion finds a specific expression in the procurement directives' requirement that the planned transaction has a pecuniary interest.
2. An agreement criterion: the remuneration can be seen as a market price for the provision, in the sense that the operator can agree *ex-ante* to provide the services/goods in question for this amount. This criterion finds a specific expression in the procurement directives' requirement of a contract.

In all fields of EU market law, the CJEU has widened the scope of what is an "economic activity"/"economic transaction" by a functional approach of the two criteria. It is therefore submitted that, at this stage in the development of the CJEU's case law, the notion of economic activity/transaction has a unitary meaning in EU market law, and that its definition in the field of free movement—provision of services/goods for remuneration—is equivalent to its definition in the field of competition—offer of services/goods on the market. Thus, the fact that an activity in a specific transaction/regulation is regarded as an economic activity for the purpose of EU free movement means that it is in that specific case also an economic activity for the purpose of EU competition rules, and vice versa. As will be seen in more detail in Chap. 7, this seems to be the Commission's point of departure in its state aid decision-practice.

Third, it emerges that the CJEU considers as "procurement" the planning of an *economic transaction* between contracting authorities and economic operators. The very *planning* of such an economic transaction shows that the activity *can be* economic, which involves per se that its object constitutes services or goods in the meaning of the Treaties. This explains Hatzopoulos' view, evoked above, that even "genuinely non-economic activities" covered by EU rules and principles on public procurement become applicable, as soon as they are to be awarded to some non-state actor.

2.5.2 Relevance of the Economic Character of an Activity/Transaction for the Applicability of EU Rules on Free Movement and Competition

The CJEU's tests and doctrines analysed in Sects. 2.2 and 2.3 entail that EU market law affects national rules related to public services depending on three basic alternatives:

- If the activity of public service *cannot be economic*, neither the free movement nor the competition rules can apply. Therefore national rules governing the

public service are not "economic rules" and not constrained by the EU rules. This is the case of activities related to the exercise of public authority, which the Court seems to understand as an activity that *cannot be a service* (Articles 51 and 62 TFEU), and *cannot be offered on a/the market* (*Eurocontrol*, *Diego Cali*). However, EU procurement rules may apply to such activities, as soon as public authorities plan to award them to non-state actors against *remuneration*.
- If the activity of public service *can be economic but is not economic* in the specific case, EU competition rules are normally not applicable, but EU free movement rules are applicable to national rules related to the public service. This is the situation in *Freskot* where the public service was regarded as neither provided for remuneration nor offered on the national market due to the fact that it was regulated by national rules based on the principle of solidarity, but where it overlapped at least to a certain extent with services *normally* provided for remuneration. In this alternative, the national rules related to the public service are "economic rules" and must *accommodate* the fundamental freedoms related to services/goods which they affect. This "accommodation" may be regarded as setting lighter pressure on national rules than a strict duty of "compliance", but they can force a Member State to open a public service for competition.
- If the activity of public service in general *can be economic and is economic* in the specific case, the national rules affecting this activity must *comply with* both EU free movement rules and competition.

It is easy to see that the Court has developed a sophisticated tool box to integrate and facilitate the opening of national markets in the field of public services, in particular social services. Indeed, while the test that an activity is economic has to be made case by case, the test of whether it can be economic is made once and for all. Once it is established that a service is "normally" provided for remuneration (for instance because it is so in one Member State), national rules related to this service are a priori "economic rules" and must "make some place" for the fundamental freedoms which they affect. This does not mean that national rules related to that service would not be compatible with EU, but that they must be justified by the Member State as necessary to achieve missions or objectives of general interest. Also, in order to adapt to free movement imperatives, the national rules must normally be reformed, with the probable effect that the activity will become economic in that Member State too, as the criteria of market autonomy and remuneration are fulfilled on very tenuous grounds, according to the CJEU's case law.

2.5.3 Exit from EU Law Closed for Public Services Within Member States: An EU Constitutional Issue of Competence

These propositions may not seem so surprising. According to Azoulai, the fact that "EU law, in some of its provisions, has a practically unlimited field of application" is "nothing that the generalists of EU law do not already know".[65] However, the analysis conducted in this chapter shows that the CJEU's implacable determination not to let the argument of solidarity stand in the way of EU integration through market law, leads to a situation where neither the solidarity doctrine in the field of competition law nor the *Humbel* doctrine in the field of free movement law can effectively shield national rules governing social services from being challenged under EU law.

In a legal perspective, this situation implies that there is simply no way for Member States to keep their welfare legislation and administration totally "outside" from EU market law, be it on policy grounds. If Hirschman's theory on "voice" and "exit" is applied to the Member States' political situation, it is easy to see that, as members of the Union, they cannot choose "exit" to lead their welfare systems to a desirable result for their community, and it should surprise no one that they have felt a pressing need to have their "voice" heard in EU law, in particular in the field of social services where they have repeatedly emphasized their wish to retain policy powers.

It may be argued that the CJEU has understood the legitimacy of this "voice" before other EU institutions, and that this understanding explains that the Court activated the Member States' possibility to invoke the SGEI rule in Article 106(2) TFEU. Azoulai submits that the Court has recognized the Member States' legitimate claim to retain their powers, in particular in the field of social services, through the "formula of retained powers" formulated first in *Duphar* and developed in *Schumacker* as follows:

> Although, as Community law stands at present, direct taxation does not as such fall within the purview of the Community, the powers retained by the Member States must nevertheless be exercised consistently with Community law.[66]

Azoulai argues that the formula's recurrence in the CJEU's case law amounts to the emergence of a new "total law doctrine", based on (1) the recognition of the Member States' essential own capacities within the EU and (2) the requirement to include certain under-protected interests and situations in the manner national authorities usually use to think and to act.[67] In his view, the formula of retained powers is related to Weiler's theory on "absorption"—illustrated by the *Casagrande* ruling—as one of four categories of mutation operated by the CJEU in the division of competences between the Community and the Member States, as both build on a distinction between the *existence* of Member States' competence

[65] Azoulai 2011, p. 192–219.

[66] Case C-279/93, *Schumacker* [1995] ECR I-225, para 21.

[67] Azoulai 2011, p. 211.

and their *exercise* of this competence.[68] However, Azoulai believes that the formula on retained powers goes further than absorption, and signals a new phase in the transformation of Europe, where the CJEU acknowledges the "raison d' être" of the Member States' retained powers in the European construction, which supposes that these powers can be exercised.

One may wonder what happened between Weiler's "absorption" and Azoulai's "totalization", and the explanation is arguably to be found in the Commission's White Paper of 1985, the Single European Act (SEA) and the Treaty of Maastricht, which all opened for market integration and not for social regulation. The Commission's dramatic shift of emphasis in competition law toward the problem of government interference with the competitive process was based on the view that "Community-wide liberalization of public procurement in the field of public services [was] vital for the future of the Community economy".[69] As noted by Gerber, this "public turn" had procurement law as the main "motor" and aimed at integrating the market in public sector activities, with a focus on state aid as a competition concern.[70]

In the pre-Lisbon Treaty absence of enumerated powers and in the name of market integration, the CJEU has effectively supported the Commission's public turn. However, the Court has also signalled that its determination to pursue market integration and apply the principle of EU law's supremacy did not mean that in "areas of reserved competence", the market objectives of EU law had a higher dignity than their own societal objectives. In other words, the CJEU, knowing that its

[68]In his classic essay on the transformation of the European Community between 1957 and 1991, Weiler argued that under a period of political stagnation, from 1973 to the mid-1980s, when the Treaty itself did not precisely define the material limits of Community jurisdiction, the Court's case law constituted evidence of a substantial change in the distribution of competences without resort to Treaty amendments. In his view, this had taken place through jurisdictional mutations in the concept of enumeration, which Weiler divided in four categories of mutation in the Court's case law, which he called extension, absorption, incorporation and expansion. He illustrated "absorption" by the *Casagrande* ruling. In that case, and on the basis of Regulation (EEC) No 1612/68 of the Council of 15 October 1968 on freedom of movement for workers within the Community [1968] OJ L 257/2, Casagrande had requested annulment of a German law entitling children satisfying a means test to a monthly educational grant, but which excluded from entitlement non-Germans except stateless people and residents under a right of asylum. In a two-phase reasoning the Court stated that: "*Although educational and training policy is not as such included in the spheres which the treaty has entrusted to the Community institutions, it does not follow that the exercise of powers transferred to the Community is in some way limited if it is of such a nature as to affect the measures taken in the execution of a policy such as that of education and training; Chapters 1 and 2 of Title III of Part Two of the Treaty in particular contain several provisions the application of which could affect this policy.*" Weiler held that in this reasoning, it was not the Community policy that encroached on national education policy, but instead the national educational policy that was impinging on Community free-movement policy and thus had to give way. See Weiler 1991, p. 2440, with reference to Case 9/74 *Casagrande* [1974] 773.

[69]Commission, "Completing the Internal Market: White Paper from the Commission to the European Council (Milan, 28–29 June 1985)" COM (85) 310, point 87.

[70]Gerber 1994, p. 137.

case law had closed "exit" from EU law for very sensitive areas of Member States' competence, was aware that it had to enhance Member States' capacity to have their "voice" heard if they were expected to remain loyal to the project of EU integration.[71] It is submitted that this is an essential explanation of the remarkable development of the Court's pre-Lisbon case law on based on Article 106(2) TFEU, as SGEIs have a good potential to clarify what a State wants to achieve through regulation, in particular through public funding of social services.

There is no doubt that some Member States have demanded a constitutionalisation of this case law in exchange for their adherence to the Lisbon Treaty, and thus, it may be concluded that indeed, the CJEU's case law on the definition and the relevance of the notion of "economic activity" can explain the necessity of a constitutional public service concept in the post-Lisbon Treaties.

References

Azoulai L (2011) The 'Retained Powers' Formula in the Case Law of the European Court of Justice: EU Law as Total Law? Eur J Legal Stud 4(2)

Arrowsmith S et al (2011) EU Public Procurement Law: an Introduction, Arrowsmith S (ed). Asia Link Europe Aid

Gerber DJ (1994) The transformation of European Community competition law. Harvard Univ Law J 35(1)

Hatzopoulos V (2011) The concept of "economic activity" in the EU Treaty: from ideological dead-ends to workable judicial concepts. Research Papers in Law 06/2011, College of Europe

Hordijk P, Meulenbelt M (2005) A bridge too far: why the European Commission's attempts to construct an obligation to tender outside the scope of the Public Procurement directives should be dismissed. Public Procurement Law Review, p 123

Lenaerts K (1990) Constitutionalism and the many faces of federalism. Am J Comp Law 38:205–220

Lenaerts K (2012) Defining the concept of "Services of General Interest" in Light of the "Checks and Balances" set out in the EU Treaties. Jurisprudencija/Jurisprudence 2012, 19 (4):1247–1267

Odudu O (2009) Economic activity as a limit to EU law. In: Barnard C, Odudu O (eds) The outer limits of European Union Law. Hart Publishing, Oxford/Portland

Sanchez-Graells A (2011) Public procurement and the EU competition rules. Hart Publishing, Oxford/Portland

Semmelmann C (2010) The European Union's economic constitution under the Lisbon Treaty: soulsearching among lawyers shifts the focus to procedure. ELRev 35:516–541

Szyszczak E (2015) Services of general economic interest and State Measures affecting competition. J Eur Competition Law Prac 6(9)

[71]In Azoulai's words, the question arises "how to safeguard the "essential functions" of Member States without undermining the "core" of EU integration? This indefinite oscillatory motion will repeat in the case law." Azoulai relates this "oscillatory motion" to the political and social context of distrust towards further integration and federalization of Europe, See Azoulai 2011, p. 206, footnotes omitted.

Van de Gronden JW (2013b) Free movement of services and the right of establishment: does EU internal market law transform the provision of SSGI? In Neergaard et al (eds) Social services of general interest in the EU. T.M.C. Asser Press, The Hague

Wehlander C (2015) Who is afraid of SGEI—services of general economic interest in EU law with a special study on Swedish Systems of Choice. Skrifter från Juridiska Institutionen i Umeå, Nr. 32, Umeå

Weiler JHH (1991) The transformation of Europe. Yale Law J 100(8):2403–2483

Chapter 3
The Importance of SGEI in the Post-Lisbon Treaties

Abstract This chapter examines the EU constitutional framework on public services, as reflected in the post-Lisbon framework on SGEI. It looks first on Article 106(2) TFEU as a Treaty provision allowing Member States to retain powers, and second on the other Treaty rules on SGEI which have emerged from the political debate between 1997 and 2007. A general analysis of these rules shows that they open for an Europeanisation of public services, and promote the concept of SGEI has a Treaty "voice" for public service regulation. Article 14 TFEU is the prominent element of this framework as it contains both a principle on the protection of SGEI missions and a legal ground for EU law on SGEIs. Both the place of Article 14 TFEU in the Treaties and its wording suggest that the interests of achieving public service tasks and of market integration *should* be balanced, even in the field of EU free movement and procurement law. The chapter further examines the relationship between this framework and the Union's "foundational principles" in the post-Lisbon Treaties, in particular the values of the Union, the respect for human rights, of democracy and of the identity of the Member States, and the promotion of social and territorial cohesion. Based on these analyses, it is concluded that Article 14 TFEU forces the CJEU to take a stance on whether SGEI may be understood as a broad concept of "public service" in EU primary law.

Contents

C. Wehlander, *Services of General Economic Interest as a Constitutional Concept of EU Law*, Legal Issues of Services of General Interest,
DOI 10.1007/978-94-6265-117-3_3

The overall purpose of this chapter is to shed light on the constitutionalisation of the concept of SGEI into a broad exemption for public services, as a reaction to the broad application of EU market rules to public services. Indeed, the Court's expansionist approach has enhanced the need of what Azoulai calls a form of "pluralism", giving specific activities a "special—more relaxed—regime of justification".[1]

The first part of the chapter examines how the notion of SGEI has grown from what was considered as a strict derogation rule in Article 106(2) TFEU, to become the cornerstone of the debate on a special regime for public services in the Treaties, and now the cornerstone of several new Treaty provisions governing the Union's approach to public services. In that part, the approach is historical, as it outlines firstly the debate which has preceded and led to the introduction of these new provisions, in order to shed light on the ideological and political tensions which may still nourish and inform their interpretation. Some attention is given to the introduction of the notion of non-economic services of general interest in Article 2 of the Protocol 26 on SGI ("SGI Protocol"), which *prima facie* appears to provide for a strong derogation for some public services within the Member States' competence, but can well turn out to be a very weak shield against the Europeanization of public services.

The second part of the chapter looks closer at what *in the Treaties* can justify that SGEIs are declared to be "important" in the SGI Protocol. The focus is mainly on analysing and systematizing the normative synchronization in the "quasi-constitutional" post-Lisbon Treaties, between the principles attached to SGEIs and the Union's values and aims formulated in the Treaties "foundational principles" (understood here as the provisions under Title I TEU). This allows appraising the place Article 14 TFEU may be expected to receive in EU law and case law, and confronting such expectations with the fact that no EU legislation with Article 14 TFEU as an *explicit* legal basis has been so far proposed.

All the EU law principles studied in that part constitute *valid* Treaty *law*, and the analysis is in essence legal in the sense that it thrives at shedding light on their *legal-political* normative significance. Indeed, *all* EU foundational values and missions formulated by the Treaties are taken seriously, by which is meant that they are *all* taken to have a normative substance which must be coherent with specific elements of the Treaties such as the provisions on SGEIs. This approach is based on a view that the EU Treaties constitute an essential product of European democracy. They

[1]Azoulai 2011.

reflect the political deliberation which most authoritatively governs the CJEU's judicial law-making, and contain tangible terms of understanding between the Union and its peoples, through their respective States.[2] To reduce the risk of arbitrary interpretation, non-legal material is used, such as Commission views on the relation between SGEIs and values enumerated in Article 2 TEU, and statements from experts entrusted by EU Institutions to comment on draft versions of the late Constitutional Treaty. This material is either of legal-political nature, or simply political in the case of the Commission's statements. As Dann foresaw, historical interpretation, long seen as impermissible in Union law, may play a role in the present case.[3] Certain documents may be considered as *travaux préparatoires* to the Treaties as they stand, and inasmuch as they provide relevant elements of interpretation, are therefore given significance in the discussion in that part of the chapter.

The second part discusses also the new locution "highly competitive social market economy" in Article 3(3) TEU. The ambition is not to develop any elaborate views on whether its introduction can change the direction of the EU project, but simply to shed light on the lack of scholarly consensus on its legal-political meaning. It is argued that any specific direction for the Union's approach of welfare services is difficult to predict on the basis of this extremely open-ended norm, and that its normative substance depends decisively on which use is made of Article 14 TFEU.

The last part of this chapter concludes on these analyses and discusses the consequence of EU institutions' decision not to legislate on SGEIs on the basis of Article 14 TFEU, which leaves to the CJEU a prominent role in the interpretation of the SGEI principles expressed in Article 14 TFEU, the SGI Protocol and Article 36 EUCFR.

3.1 The Concept of SGEI Promoted as a Treaty "Voice" for Public Services

The development of a Treaty "voice" on SGEIs, examined in Sect. 3.1.3, is argued to be due to the particularities of the exemption rule for undertakings entrusted with SGEI tasks in Article 106(2) TFEU, evoked in Sect. 3.1.1, and to the legal-political doctrine which the Commission has elaborated on the basis of this Treaty notion, outlined in Sect. 3.1.2.

---

[2]On this path, Pernice states: "the conclusion and earlier revisions of the Treaties, but also the attempt to substitute them by the Treaty establishing a Constitution for Europe and the (sic) finally the submission of the Treaty of Lisbon to ratification and, under some new conditions, to a second Irish referendum are certainly steps of the "constitutional process" by which the European peoples, having learned from horrible experiences of the past centuries and, in particular from World-War II are trying to find a legal framework for better organizing their common future (footnotes omitted)" See Pernice 2009, p. 57.

[3]Dann 2006, p. 1463.

3.1.1 Article 106(2) TFEU: Comparative Advantages of a Provision Allowing Member States to Retain Powers

To justify regulatory or administrative measures affecting competition and free trade in public sector activities—public funding of supply, exclusive rights, in house provision, public-public cooperation, compulsory affiliation to welfare systems, requirement of prior authorization for establishment of service operators, or requirement of prior authorization to receive services from operators which are not part to the national welfare system—Member States may adopt different legal strategies, briefly outlined here.

They may first put their faith in claiming that the activity *cannot* be economic and is not at all constrained by EU law. As shown in Chap. 2, this strategy runs a very high risk to fail even regarding publicly funded social services. The Court's decision in *Humbel*, withdrawing courses provided under national education systems from the scope of EU free movement law, can clearly not anymore be perceived by the Member States as shielding publicly funded social services from EU market law. Besides, Sweden's "experiment" shows that even publicly funded school education *can be* provided by means of an economic activity. Member States may also try to claim that a measure complies with EU market law because it is related to an activity which they consider as not economic as regulated in their legal system. Indeed, this can be for instance the case of social security services provided in a solidarity-based scheme subject to state control, and thus fulfilling the conditions established in the *Poucet and Pistre* case law.

However, even if they have established solidarity-based schemes for social services, Member States will often find it impossible to deny the existence of a market on their territory: Van de Gronden notes that, in the sensitive and politically complex field of social services of general interest, the national legislature is often forced to make compromises between the interests of different stakeholders, with the result that even where the general intention is to exclude market mechanisms, the activity is partly on the market anyway.[4] And even if they succeed in claiming that the activity *is* not economic in their territory because of its regulation in their legal system, it may anyway be difficult to uphold these rules if they restrict fundamental freedoms and are challenged judicially. This is clear for instance from *Freskot* or from the *Schwarz* cases where a measure was claimed to infringe both free movement and competition rules in the Treaties.[5] As observed by Azoulai, even apparently minor requirements to respect fundamental freedoms are overarching, and thus, even regarding activities in the frame of their competence, "Member States are exposed to the encroachment of EU law that they cannot withstand other than by adapting their law".[6]

[4]Van De Gronden 2013, p. 147.

[5]Case C-355/00 *Freskot* [2003] ECR I-05263, Case C-76/05 *Schwarz* [2007] ECR I- 6849 and Case C-318/05 *Commission v Germany* [2007] ECR I-6957.

[6]Azoulai 2011, p. 211.

In the field of procurement, Member States may claim that EU principles governing public procurement do not apply in a specific field of activity, based on their own perception that contracts will typically have no certain cross-border interest. Yet, as underlined in Sect. 2.4, this assessment is made at the contracting authorities' own risk and is judicially reviewable. In periods of poor economic climate, cross-border interest can arise at lower values than the thresholds established in EU legislation. Regarding anticompetitive measures, they may also claim that the activity affected is pursued on local markets and not subject to cross-border trade—in which case EU competition and state aid rules will not "bite". Regarding state aid to social services, they may put their hope in the Commission's de minimis rules, but as emphasized by Szyszczak, the Court has repeatedly stated that *de minimis* does not exclude state aid.[7]. The exemption from the duty of notification of state aid to social services, social housing and hospital care provided for by Commission Decision COM (2011) 9380 does not exclude complaints alleging that an aid scheme does not fulfil the Decision's conditions and therefore is illegal, in which case the Commission might impose its revision.[8] Thus, it is unsure to what extent the thresholds and exceptions rules in secondary law constitute "safe havens", in particular because secondary law evolves with developments on the internal market.

To justify the compatibility with the Treaties of their regulatory and administrative measures, Member States may invoke the Treaty-based justifications in Articles 36, 51, 52 and 62 TFEU. These justifications, which may apply to discriminatory measures, are traditionally interpreted by the Court in a very restrictive manner, although Hatzopoulos observes that the Court has expanded the scope of the public health justification, in particular in the "patients' mobility cases".[9] Member States may instead invoke that their regulatory or administrative measures are motivated by mandatory requirements or overriding reasons related to the general interest. These exceptions to the free movement rules, often referred to as "the rule of reason", were invented by the CJEU in *Van Binsbergen* and formulated more explicitly in *Cassis de Dijon*.[10] It appears uncertain whether the Court sees

[7]Szyszczak refers to Case C-280/00 *Altmark* [2003] ECR I-7747, para 81 and Joined Cases C-34/01 to C-38/01 *Enirisorse* [2003] ECR I-14243, para 28, where the CJEU's position seems indeed quite clear. See Szyszczak 2013, p. 330. This is also acknowledged by the Communication from the Commission, Draft Commission Notice on the notion of State aid pursuant to Article 107(1) TFEU, available at http://ec.europa.eu/competition/consultations/2014_state_aid_notion/draft_guidance_en.pdf.

[8]If that is not the case, the measure will be assessed in accordance with the principles contained in the Commission Communication on a framework for State aid in the form of public service compensation. See Recital 26 in the Commission Decision 2012/21/EU of 20 December 2011 on the application of Article 106(2) of the Treaty on the Functioning of the European Union to State aid in the form of public service compensation granted to certain undertakings entrusted with the operation of services of general economic interest.

[9]Hatzopoulos 2012, p. 148.

[10]Hatzopoulos 2012, p. 151. The "patients' mobility cases" include in particular Case C-157/99 *Smits and Peerbooms*, and Case C-372/04 *Watts* [2006] ECR I-4325.

all overriding reasons related to the general interest as exception grounds, or in certain cases as objectives involving that a measure is *ex-ante* justified and not labelled as "*restriction* of free movement" in the first place.[11]

Importantly, overriding reasons related to the general interest may not only justify regulatory measures but also procurement measures, although they cannot justify discriminatory restrictions on fundamental freedoms.[12] Also, it was originally understood that overriding reasons related to the general interest could not be of economic nature[13] and that they were examined by the Court under a strict proportionality test.[14] These understandings call nowadays evidently for qualification. First, the Court tends to apply a lenient proportionality test to certain grounds of general interest, which Hatzopoulos identifies as morality and solidarity in the field of social services. This view is shared here, as in the field of social services, the Court's proportionality test is indeed rather concerned with "the concrete manifestations of solidarity" and whether they exclude all market forces.[15] Second, the Court has admitted that certain overriding reasons related to the general interest may address economic considerations, notably in the field of health care services. As argued by some authors, this incoherence is only apparent, and its relation to the normative power of the concept of SGEI is discussed under Sect. 4.2.

The notion of overriding reason related to the general interest can be perceived as palliative for the fact that even non-discriminatory measures may contravene free movement rules,[16] but this notion was clearly not appropriate to mitigate certain effects of the "public turn" in EU competition case law, constructed around the following provision, now found in Article 106(1) TFEU:

[11]Ibid., p. 151.

[12]See Case C-153/08 *Commission* v *Spain* [2009] ECR I-9735, para 36.

[13]This perception was based in particular on the Court's position in *Bond van Adverteerders* that a restriction on the free movement of services could not be justified by a concern to secure for a national public TV foundation all the revenue from the advertising destined for the public of that Member State, see Case 352/85 *Bond van Adverteerders* [1988] ECR 2085, para 34; also, in Case C-398/95 *SETTG v Ypourgos Ergasias* [1997] ECR I-3091, para 23, the Court considered that "maintaining industrial peace as a means of bringing a collective labor dispute to an end and thereby preventing any adverse effects on an economic sector, and consequently on the economy of the State, must be regarded as an economic aim which cannot constitute a reason relating to the general interest that justifies a restriction of a fundamental freedom guaranteed by the Treaty". For a list of cases where this stance has been confirmed, see Bekkedal 2011, p. 65 footnote 65.

[14]The restrictions must be suitable for securing the attainment of the objective which they pursue, and they must not go beyond what is necessary in order to attain it, see for instance Case C-288/89 *Gouda and Others* [1991] ECR 1-407, paras 13–15; Case C-19/92 *Kraus* [1993] ECR 1-1663, para 32, and Case C-55/94 *Gebhard* [1995] ECR 1-4165, para 37.

[15]In Hatzopoulos' view, it is clear that the Court question neither Member States' definition of morality nor their definition of the scope of social services and the extent to which solidarity applies to them. See Hatzopoulos 2012, p. 151, 160 and 161.

[16]Ibid., p. 157.

> In the case of public undertakings and undertakings to which Member States grant special or exclusive rights, Member States shall neither enact nor maintain in force any measure contrary to the rules contained in the Treaties, in particular to those rules provided for in Article 18 and Articles 101 to 109.

The CJEU has namely optimized the "effet utile" of the Treaty competition rules by combining this provision with Articles 101 or 102 TFEU, and as a result requiring that Member States do not place public undertakings and undertakings to which they have granted special or exclusive rights in a position to infringe EU competition rules without acceptable motives.[17] In *Corbeau*, the Court implicitly ruled that any grant of exclusive rights is contrary to Article 106(1) TFEU, thereby going very far in its crusade against "the sacrosanct and inviolable character of exclusive rights".[18] It found timely to compensate this encroachment in the Member States' exercise of their competence, by ruling also that they were permitted only to the extent that they came under the exception in Article 106(2) TFEU, which reads:

> Undertakings entrusted with the operation of services of general economic interest or having the character of a revenue-producing monopoly shall be subject to the rules contained in the Treaties, in particular to the rules on competition, in so far as the application of such rules does not obstruct the performance, in law or in fact, of the particular tasks assigned to them. The development of trade must not be affected to such an extent as would be contrary to the interests of the Union.

In *Corbeau*, the CJEU "explained" that this provision "permits the Member States to confer on undertakings to which they entrust the operation of services of general economic interest, exclusive rights which may hinder the application of the rules of the Treaty on competition in so far as restrictions on competition, or even the exclusion of all competition, by other economic operators are necessary to ensure the performance of the particular tasks assigned to the undertakings possessed of the exclusive rights.[19] The crucial element in the Court's SGEI-based approach was its view that a restriction on competition—in that case the exclusion of all competition from other economic operators—could be justified by the necessity to allow the holder of the exclusive right to perform its task of general interest, and to do so "under economically acceptable conditions".[20] The legitimacy of ensuring "economically acceptable conditions" was confirmed in *Almelo*.[21]

---

[17]Exclusive rights have been called the "State measure par excellence among those contemplated in Article [106(1) TFEU]", see Buendia Sierra 1999, p. 134. The CJEU's useful effect doctrine has allowed the Commission to engage, in the late 1980s, the liberalization of the telecommunications sector on the basis of Article 106(3) TFEU. This provision enjoins the Commission, where necessary, to address appropriate directives or decisions to Member States, in order to ensure the application of the provisions of Article 106(1) and (2) TFEU.

[18]Ibid., p. 163.

[19]Case C-320/91 *Corbeau* [1993] ECR 1-2563, para 14. The Court's approach in *Corbeau* has been called by the participants to the XVI FIDE Conference "the limited competition approach", as opposed to "the limited sovereignty approach", see Buendia Sierra 1999, p. 189.

[20]Ibid., para 16.

[21]Case C-393/92 *Almelo* [1994] ECR I-1477.

Arguably this development helped the Court in finding acceptance for making exclusive rights a priori contrary to Articles 106(1) and 102 TFEU. At the same time, it made clear that SGEI tasks in a field of activity could lead to a more lenient proportionality test than overriding reasons related to the general interest, as such *tasks* could justify state measures not only aiming at pursuing certain missions of general interest, but also at securing financial conditions allowing them to be fulfilled *in fact*.

In spite of the wording of Article 106(2) TFEU, it was not evident that the Court would apply Article 106(2) TFEU and not overriding reasons related to the general interest to justify certain state measures restricting the fundamental freedoms. For instance, the Court could have chosen to examine exclusive rights in the fields of electricity as restrictions of the fundamental freedoms possible to justify on the basis of overriding reasons related to the general interest, subject to a strict proportionality test. It did not, and this choice was arguably dictated by the necessity to maintain its legal-political authority in a context where its case law had irreversibly eroded the principle of enumeration. The Court had to reassure Member States that EU law allowed them to retain relatively strong policy powers in areas of competence that they obviously were not ready to confer onto the Union. Besides, in cases where exclusive rights were challenged, the Court could not easily disregard Member States' claim that such rights were justified by the necessity to secure the fulfilment of SGEI tasks.

In fact, until the entry into force of the Treaty of Amsterdam in 1997, the provision in Article 106(2) TFEU was the *only horizontal Treaty provision*, borne out of an EU democratic process (slightly more democratic than the judge-made overriding reasons related to the general interest) and explicitly

- Referring to the notion of general interest in another meaning than "the general interest of the Union", in other words general interests that can be conceived and decided by the Member States and their own citizens (or by the Member States as masters of the Treaties).
- Legitimating that public service tasks are used *as a point of departure* to evaluate the necessity to derogate from the Treaty market rules.[22]
- Having a potential to be applicable "horizontally", for derogation from *any* Treaty rule. This can imply that Article 106(2) TFEU could be relevant in relation to EU procurement rules, a very controversial issue.

These features alone explain that the Court *had to* consider SGEI-based arguments and to respect the constitutional importance of SGEIs latently signalled by Article 106(2) TFEU. The necessity to dispose of efficient legal instruments to regulate certain markets became obvious when public service obligations were introduced in EU legislation on energy, telecommunications and transport. The dignity of public service missions and tasks in relation to the Treaty principles of free

[22]Case 67/96 *Albany* [1999] ECR I-5751.

movement and undistorted competition is simply difficult to question per se. In the absence of EU legislation primarily addressing the principles and rules governing public service missions, the issue for the Court has instead been which proportionality test it would apply to conflicts between the public service missions and the Treaty principles protecting free movement and free competition.

To assess the compliance with the Treaties of restrictions of free movement of goods following from exclusive rights in the form of State monopolies in the meaning of Article 37 TFEU, it was technically possible for the Court to apply Article 106(2) TFEU "directly", as the restriction was operated by the State, but through an *undertaking*. By contrast, regarding state measures restricting the free movement of services but not operated through an undertaking, for instance regulatory barriers to entry or exit from national social service systems, the Court cannot not easily apply Article 106(2) TFEU "directly" as a justification, but may instead have to "transpose" the public service logic of Article 106(2) TFEU. The reason is that it is often primarily not undertakings', but rather the *public authorities*' necessity to achieve their public service missions—for instance securing access to social services—which justifies the restrictive regulation—for instance a solidarity-based system of supply.

In any case, the Member States have grown aware that, as long as they did not legislate on these issues, the Court would continue strike a balance case by case, and sent a first "signal" through the Treaty of Amsterdam 1997, in the form of Article 16 EC on SGEIs, which was commented on by Ole Due in the following terms: "A new Article 7d introduces a curious provision in the EC Treaty, requiring the Community and the Member States to take care that services of general economic interest operate on the basis of principles and conditions which enable them to fulfil their missions. The Article itself provides that this must be done "without prejudice to Articles 77, 90, and 92. Nevertheless, it has been found necessary to annex a Declaration, according to which the Article shall be implemented" with full respect for the jurisprudence of the Court of Justice, *inter alia* as regards the principles of equality of treatment, quality, and continuity of such services. Both the Article and the Declaration reflects the ongoing confrontation between liberalist states and states where public services used to be synonymous with public undertakings. It seems doubtful what impact, if any, such an amendment will have on the case law of the Community Courts."[23]

Arguably, this "curious provision" had more than no impact on the Court's case law. It is possible, as suggested by Due's doubts that Article 16 EC would change anything in the CJEU's approach, that the Court had "not waited for" Article 16 EC to acknowledge the "latent" normative signal in Article 106(2) TFEU, namely the high "dignity" of SGEIs in relation to EU market law. However, it is interesting to note that the Court's first clear acknowledgement of Article 106(2) TFEU's normative signal was arguably made in the "electricity cases", decided 21 days

[23] Due 1998, p. 70.

after the adoption of the Treaty of Amsterdam 1997. It is argued—and developed in Chap. 4—that it was in those cases the Court took the decisive step to explain the telos of its lenient proportionality test under Article 106(2) TFEU, thereby replacing the perception of Article 106(2) as a derogation rule to a perception of Article 106(2) TFEU as a balancing rule.[24] Thus, the introduction of Article 16 EC did not say what the "masters of the Treaty" want from SGEIs, but forced the Court to take loyal account of the evident political divergence on the future of public services in Europe and therefore on their liberalization through EU law. After the Treaty of Amsterdam, the Court did not *choose* a "nuanced" approach, it was rather *forced* to it.[25] The "importance" of SGEIs had not been emphasized by the Court before the Amsterdam Treaty and certainly not before it delivered its judgments in *Corbeau* and *Almelo*.

In the period between the adoption of the Treaty of Amsterdam and of the Lisbon Treaty (from 1997 to 2007), the debate on services of general interest in Europe, which the Commission tried to orchestrate under the neutral theme of "need of legal certainty", evidenced the confrontation of an ordo-liberal approach and a "welfare state approach" of public services, in particular during the legislative process preceding the adoption of the Services Directive. This open confrontation has probably reinforced the Court's obligation to reflect on what the concept of SGEI and Article 106(2) TFEU *should* mean to remain coherent with the Treaties, and to give more precision to its views on these issues. In this "dialogue" going on between the Member States and the CJEU through successive Treaty modifications, the Lisbon Treaty signals arguably a new constitutional compromise regarding EU law in the field of public services, not only but particularly by introducing new provisions directly related to SGEIs (Article 14 TFEU, SGI Protocol and Article 36 in the EU Charter of Fundamental Rights). Two important decisions, the *BUPA* judgment in the field of state aid, and the *Commission v Germany* judgment in the field of public procurement, were taken *after* the adoption of the Lisbon Treaty. In both cases, the existence of *statutory* public service tasks seems to have played a particular role in public authorities' margin of discretion, and mirror possibly the emergence of a Court's doctrine on SGEIs.

---

[24]See in particular Case C-157/94 *Commission v Netherlands* [1997] ECR I-5699, paras 38–40. This aspect of the CJEU's case law is studied in detail in Chap. 4.

[25]Indeed, Article 16 EC did not go unnoticed by the Court. In 2001, AG Alber referred to "the newly promulgated Article 16 EC and Article 36 of the Charter of Fundamental Rights of the European Union" as underlining the importance of Article 86(2) EC (now Article 106(2) TFEU) as an expression of a fundamental value judgment of Community law. Some months later AG Jacobs started his reasoning in *Ambulanz Glöckner*, on the premise that "services of general economic interest have a special importance in the Community, as is /…/ emphasized by Article 16 EC".

3.1.2 *From Amsterdam to Lisbon: 10 Years of Debate and a Compromise on SGEI in the Treaties*

As early as 1986, Delors was aware that the SEA and the 1992 programme would intensify EU's pressure on the welfare systems in the Member States, and addressed the "masters of the Treaties" in the following terms:

> .../the more competitive countries would be greatly mistaken if they thought they could have the large market without paying the price of cohesion. Is the price merely to be paid from the budget? No, what is needed is Community spirit, otherwise the Europe of Twelve will fall apart. We must therefore prevent incidents such as these through our resolute commitment to both economic and social cohesion in the Community.[26]

Thus, the Delors Commission acknowledged that EU law's expansion enhanced the need to address at EU level the challenge of very diverse social and welfare systems in the Member States. Indeed, the European Council of June 1995 reported that "the importance of general interest services [had been] brought out by the Heads of State and Government, who acknowledged them as part of the set of values shared by all our countries that helps define Europe." [27] Thus, the concept of "services of general interest" was probably considered as an appropriate platform for agreeing on what a European "voice" on public services would say, in particular because it was close to the notion of SGEI which already existed in the Treaty. However, by crystallizing the debate on the future of public services in Europe on the notion of SGEI, the future of public services in Europe could not be conducted as a broad public debate. Instead it was canalized in the expert and technocratic term "SGEI", which explains that the problematic lack of consensus on the future of public services in Europe could be formulated by Sauter as the Member States' incapacity to say "what they want from SGEI".[28]

The Commission inaugurated officially the debate on services of general interest in 1996, when the 1996 Intergovernmental conference prepared a review of the Treaties preparing in particular the Union's enlargement. The Commission was of course aware that some Member States and stakeholders perceived EU market law's pressure on public services as a threat, while others could perceive it as an opportunity. It is therefore interesting to note its declaration, very much evoking the compromise finally reached in the Treaty of Lisbon:

> Europe is built on a set of values shared by all its societies and combines the characteristics of democracy—human rights and institutions based on the rule of law—with those of an open economy underpinned by market forces, internal solidarity and cohesion. These

[26]Delors 1986, p. 22–37.

[27]Cannes European Council 26–27 June 1995, Conclusions of the Presidency SN 211/95 point A.I.1.7. It is striking to see that the declaration of SGI's "importance" was finally introduced in the SGI-protocol.

[28]To be sure, there is still no chance to conduct a debate on the future of public services in Europe in national parliaments or in the Member States' public opinion under the parole "what is it we want from SGEI?".

values include access for all members of society to universal services or to services of general benefit, thus contributing to solidarity and equal treatment.[29]

The first Communication issued in 1996 was followed by the Laeken Declaration (2001), the Green Paper on SGI (2003), the White Paper on SGI (2004), the Communication on Social Services of General Interest (2006) and the Communication on Services of General Interest, including Social Services, in 2007, perceived by the Commission as "closing the debate".[30] These Communications focused increasingly on social services, when it became clear that the trend towards marketization of these services, in particular health care, was there to stay, and that national measures restricting the free movement of social services were successfully challenged in processes brought to the CJEU. By then, it was impossible for the Member States to believe that they could retain powers by defining "legislative priorities". While it was their initiative to point out energy, post and telecommunications were as "priority action sectors" in the Spaak Report, and later "A-services" as priority services in the procurement directives,[31] they were losing the upper hand in the field of social services. By not legislating on the balance between free movement and competition of social services and the necessity to maintain welfare systems to secure objectives of solidarity, it became clear that the CJEU would decide in their place. As a logic of "voluntary integration" through legislation let the place to "integration under judicial pressure", Member States did simply not any more *openly decide* which sectors EU integration would prioritize.[32]

In the course of the open "SGI debate"—from 1996 to 2007—some Member States, particularly concerned with EU law pressure on their systems of welfare, exercised pressure to introduce the provision in Article 16 EC, later modified by Article 14 TFEU, enhancing the dignity of SGEIs and pushing forward the idea

---

[29]Commission, "Reinforcing political union and preparing for enlargement" (Opinion for the Intergovernmental Conference) COM (96)90 final, p. 1.

[30]Commission, "Services of General Interest in Europe" (Communication) EJ C 281, 26.9.1996; Commission, "Report to the Laeken European Council—Services of general interest" COM(2001)598 final; Commission, Services of general interest (Green paper) COM(2003) 270 final; Commission, Services of general interest (White paper) COM(2004) 374 final; Commission, "Implementing the Community Lisbon program: Social services of general interest of the European Union" COM(2006) 177 final; Commission, "Services of general interest, including social services of general interest: a new European commitment" COM(2007) 725 final and the accompanying Commission Staff working documents, published in the context of Commission "A single market for 21st century Europe" COM(2007) 724 final.

[31]Report to the Ministers of Foreign Affairs on the General Common Market, drafted by the Intergovernmental Committee headed by Henri Spaak ("Spaak Report"), Brussels, 21 April 1956. p. 126–135.

[32]In this regard, it was certainly frustrating for the German government that in *Germany v Commission* the General Court deemed that the Commission's Interpretative Communication on the Community law applicable to contract awards not or not fully subject to the provisions of the Public Procurement Directives (2006/C 179/02) rightly transposed the case law of the CJEU on public service concessions, to contracts below the thresholds and to non-prioritized contracts. See Case T-258/06 *Germany v Commission* [2010] ECR II-2027, paras 74–84.

that Article 106(2) TFEU had to be perceived not as a derogation rule, but rather as a rule balancing two equally legitimate interests, (1) public service objectives and tasks democratically decided by Member States in the frame of their competence, and (2) the Union's interests (principally an internal market interest before the Lisbon Treaty entered into force). That the notion of SGEI could convey the claim to retain national powers in the field of public services was most obvious in the debate on the Services Directive. This claim was also evident in the process of adopting the Lisbon Treaty, and explains the final drafting of Article 14 TFEU and the introduction of the SGI-protocol. It seems thus clear that the outcome of the debate is the introduction of a distinct "voice" on SGEIs in the Treaties. Mario Monti's report made no mistake on the enhanced constitutional dignity of SGEIs, declaring that "[s]ervices of general economic interest are considered to be a key sphere for broad social policy, at the national, regional and local level."[33]

Yet, this "voice" on SGEIs is eminently heterogeneous and there is evidence of the persisting tension between holders of a broad special regime for public services, including EU procurement rules, and holders of an EU procurement regime which holds tight the Member States' discretion in order to free market forces. It is for instance clear from the following declaration of the European Economic and Social Committee in the debate preceding the adoption of the new procurement directives: "[a]fter a long debate on services of general interest (SGIs), it was concluded that these are *not public contracts in the true sense of the term*, but services provided by authorities or on their behalf. The EESC reiterates that contracting authorities are free to carry out all or some of their functions themselves or to outsource those tasks which they deem appropriate. Account must also be taken of the systems of the Member States which respect the principles of equal treatment, non-discrimination and transparency laid down in EU primary law and which provide a general right of access to the provision of services. SGIs themselves should not, therefore, come within the scope of the directive, although any outsourcing or contract related thereto awarded by the contracting authorities or on their behalf should be clearly subject to the directive".[34] The view was evidently—but controversially—that Member States' prerogatives to freely organise the supply of certain services, including by choosing in-house provision, must be regarded as essentially following from the character of these services as "services of general interest". In other words, the EESC regarded the concept of SGI—including

[33]Report of Mario Monti to the President of the European Commission José Manuel Barroso, 9 May 2010, "A New Strategy for the Single Market—At the service of Europe's economy and society".

[34]European Economic and Social Committee, "Opinion on the Proposal for a Directive of the European Parliament and of the Council on procurement by entities operating in the water, energy, transport and postal services sectors COM(2011) 895 final—2011/0439 (COD) Proposal for a Directive of the European Parliament and of the Council on public procurement COM(2011) 896 final—2011/0438 (COD) Proposal for a Directive of the European Parliament and of the Council on the award of concession contracts COM(2011) 897 final—2011/0437 (COD)", point 4.6, emphasis added.

SGEI—as a broad concept justifying *per se* the freedom to conclude "in-house agreements" and a "balance" with the interest of free movement of services in the public sector.

In fact, the debate on the future of public services, fundamentally related to the place of the state in a European market including public services, can simply not end with the adoption of new constitutional provisions on SGEIs in the Treaty of Lisbon. The reason is that this political "deal" on SGEIs is based on legal provisions formulated in the typical "Treaty coded language" and leaves much room to combine and use these provisions. The debate continues less officially in the interpretation, combination and use of Treaty provisions related to SGEIs, a particular issue being whether the notion of "SGEI" is given explicit or implicit relevance in the field of free movement law and in the field of procurement law.

3.1.3 New Framework on SGEI in the Post-Lisbon Treaties: SGEI "Voice"

3.1.3.1 Article 14 TFEU: Public Services at the Heart of EU Law, and a Challenge for the Coherence of EU Law on Public Services

Article 14 TFEU is a dual provision, comprising both a policy declaration (first sentence) and a legal basis (second sentence). Let us here focus on the first sentence that almost exactly reproduces former Article 16 EC, completed through the Treaty of Lisbon by words emphasized in the following text

> Without prejudice to Article 4 of the Treaty on European Union or to Articles 93, 106 and 107 of this Treaty, and given the place occupied by services of general economic interest in the shared values of the Union as well as their role in promoting social and territorial cohesion, the Union and the Member States, each within their respective powers and within the scope of application of the Treaties, shall take care that such services operate on the basis of principles and conditions, *particularly economic and financial conditions*, which enable them to fulfil their missions.[35]

When Article 16 EC was introduced through the Amsterdam Treaty 1997, Ole Due was not the only person who considered that it was a "curious provision". Most of those who commented on the provision—which at the time did not contain the words "particularly economic and financial conditions" were perfectly aware of its political genesis. Duff observed for instance that Article 16 EC was "probably the clearest exposure in the Treaty of the division between those who wish to regulate to protect public utilities and the like and those who which to make them competitive".[36] Buendia Sierra evoked that some Member States

---

[35]Emphasis added.

[36]Duff 1997, p. 84.

wished to include a reference to "economically acceptable conditions" for undertakings entrusted with SGEI missions, and considered that, given the absence of such a reference in the final text of Article 16 EC, the new provision did not modify the balance of the Treaty as it "only repeated in a more diluted way the very principle contained in Article 86(2) [EC]", left unchanged the scope of Articles 73, 86 and 87 (now Articles 93, 106 and 107 TFEU) and did not solve the question as to how Article 86(2) (now Article 106(2) TFEU) should be interpreted.[37] In his view, the text of Article 16 EC suggested less flexibility than the rule of Article 86(2) EC, that exempts application of Treaty rules obstructing *in law or in fact* the fulfilment of the SGEI tasks. Regarding the normative significance of Article 16 EC, views diverged profoundly. While Edwardsson held that Article 16 EC was a pure declaration lacking any legal significance,[38] Prosser believed that Article 16 EC contributed to change the general attitude to SGEIs from an unwelcome obstacle for the realization of the internal market to a positive policy element. He held that "[t]he objective is no longer only to limit their scope but to improve their delivery through applying principles of good governance, including (but not limited to) the use of competitive markets".[39]

These analyses must arguably be read in a new context, as the first sentence of Article 14 TFEU modifies former Article 16 EC by requiring that the Union and the Member States take care in particular that SGEIs operate on the basis of "economic and financial conditions" enabling them to fulfil their missions, and as Article 14 TFEU now also includes a second sentence reading:

> The European Parliament and the Council, acting by means of regulations in accordance with the ordinary legislative procedure, shall establish these principles and set these conditions without prejudice to the competence of Member States, in compliance with the Treaties, to provide, to commission and to fund such services.

The meaning of Article 14 TFEU is difficult to be sure of, and it may seem uncertain how it should be enforced, but it is today difficult to find authors doubting that Article 14 TFEU has normative effect. Ross expresses what seems to be a dominant perception, namely that Article 14 TFEU represents a "critical step", upgrading services of general interest into positive horizontal policy-shaping considerations for both Member States and the Community institutions.[40] In fact, some elements in this provision are perhaps not so ambiguous. First SGEIs have now constitutional dignity in EU law, on the explicit motive of their importance for the Union "shared values" and their role in promoting cohesion, both social and territorial. Second, it is clear that Article 14 TFEU imposes a norm on the Union and the Member States, a "duty to take care" that the principles and

[37]Buendia Sierra 1999, p. 333.

[38]Edwardsson 2003, p. 122–123. Edwardsson refers to Buendia Sierra's argument and concludes that Article 16 EC had no legal significance and has not altered the legal situation for SGEIs.

[39]Prosser 2005, p. 123.

[40]Ross 2009, p. 92.

conditions on which SGEI operate allow them to fulfil their missions. The incertainty on the enforcement of Article 14 TFEU is rather related to the following elements:

a. The relationship between Article 14 TFEU and Articles 4, 106 and 107 TFEU requires clarification.
b. Article 14 TFEU does not define SGEI, but it reinforces its status as an *EU law* concept and suggests strongly that this concept is relevant "transversally" in EU constitutional law. If SGEI is a transversal notion of EU law, it may arguably not be limited to SGEI tasks—or "public service obligations" (PSO)—entrusted to undertakings. There must simply be more to SGEI than tasks entrusted to undertakings. This emerges in particular from the fact that Article 14 TFEU imposes a "duty" on the Union and the Member States affecting—even if not exclusively—the exercise of their legislative and regulatory powers. In the field of public services, these legislative and regulatory powers are more often than not used to impose obligations on public authorities rather than on undertakings. The SGEI tasks are often entrusted to undertakings by public authorities which are themselves under an obligation to secure access to certain services or infrastructures.
c. Article 14 TFEU suggests that SGEIs may enjoy a specific EU law regime to fulfil their missions. It does specify that this special regime may include economic and financial conditions, but to get a more concrete notion of what may be meant by such common principles and conditions, one must look at the "SGEI shared values" of Article 1 of the SGI Protocol. Also, as emphasized by de Witte et al., in this legislative basis, the second part seems intended to restrict the scope of the first part of the sentence.[41]
d. The obligation to "take care" can obviously be understood as addressed to the Union and Member States as legislators, but it may also be understood as addressed to any EU institution, in particular the CJEU, and to public authorities as parts of the State in a broad meaning. This raises the question of how Article 14 TFEU relates to Article 106(2) TFEU, in particular whether Article 14 TFEU implies that Article 106(2) TFEU has some relevance to justify derogations from EU procurement law.

A particular issue is that the EU legislator's new competence to decide on principles and conditions enabling SGEIs to fulfil their missions, appears to be interpreted in quite different ways. It is expressed as an obligation to legislate on the basis of regulations, but so far, SGEIs are only regulated through decisions, frameworks and directives. At the same time, it appears that in the absence of EU

[41]De Witte et al. 2010, p. 40. The authors explain that the provision's complicated drafting may be the cause of its ambiguity. They consider "contradictory to state, on the one hand, that the EU will have the competence to lay down the main principles and conditions for the operation of the SGEIs, but on the other hand, that this leaves untouched the Member State competence to provide, organise and finance these services".

legislation explicitly deciding on SGEI principles and conditions in the meaning of Article 14 TFEU, the CJEU is led to define them in case law, and as a result also to define the notion of SGEI for the purpose of this provision.

Given the marketization of welfare supply in the Member States and the wide interpretation of the notion of economic activity both for the purpose of free movement and competition rules, the national rules of welfare might increasingly find themselves "within the scope of EU law". Of course EU law must respect the principle of subsidiarity but, as observed by Sharpf, the supremacy doctrine postulated by the CJEU has given it the status of a constitutional court in the relationship between the EU and the Member States. In Scharpf's view, this implies that the case law does not recognize any sphere of national autonomy in which purposes of public policy and the measures through which these are to be realized should be chosen by democratically legitimated political processes.[42] Davies holds that the principle of subsidiarity was actually not meant to limit the Court's judicial interpretation of Treaty based liberties.[43] As a matter of fact, the Court has so far never invoked the principle of subsidiarity to restrain from balancing national rules, including rules governing the definition, organisation and financing of SGEI, against free movement rights. It may be questioned whether the second sentence of Article 14 TFEU has a potential to alter this situation.

In any case, it may also be questioned whether the CJEU has begun applying the first sentence of Article 14 TFEU, more or less explicitly. This issue is evoked in more detail in Sect. 3.3 and is at the heart of the case law analysis in Chap. 4.

3.1.3.2 Protocol 26 on SGI

The EU framework on SGEI has been fleshed out through the Protocol (No 26) on Services of General Interest or "SGI Protocol", which was adopted by the Heads of States and Heads of Government at the June 2007 European Council on the initiative of the Netherlands who, with the support of Germany and France, made its insertion in the final Reform Treaty to a condition for adoption.[44] The SGI Protocol adopts the architecture elaborated by the Commission and centred on the concept of SGI. As early as 1996 the Commission had launched the term "Services of General Interest" which at that time was absent from the Treaties, and explained that it covered "both market and non-market services which the public authorities class as being of general interest and subject to specific public service obligations".[45] In the

[42]Scharpf 2009, p. 17 and 21.

[43]Davies 2006a.

[44]The origin of this proposal is related to a disagreement between the Commission and the Netherlands concerning the application of the doctrine of manifest error when the public financing of measures for housing purpose was claimed by the Netherlands as justified by an SGEI mission. The Prime Minister of the Netherlands had in particular the support of Germany and France.

[45]Commission, "Services of General Interest in Europe" (Communication) EJ C 281, 26.9.1996, p. 2.

later communications of the Commission on SGI a ramification was consistently reaffirmed, "services of general interest" covering both "services of general *economic* interest" and "*non-economic* services of general interest". Clearly building on this ramification, the Protocol attached to the Treaties and forming an integral form thereof, as provided in Article 51 TEU, reads:

The High Contracting Parties,
Wishing to emphasize the importance of services of general interest,
Have agreed upon the following interpretative provisions, which shall be annexed to the Treaty on European and to the Treaty on the Functioning of the European Union

Article 1
The shared values of the Union in respect of services of general economic interest within the meaning of Article 14 of the Treaty on the Functioning of the European Union include in particular:

- the essential role and the wide discretion of national, regional and local authorities in providing, commissioning and organising services of general economic interest as closely as possible to the needs of the users;
- the diversity between various services of general economic interest and the differences in the needs and preferences of users that may result from different geographical, social or cultural situations;
- a high level of quality, safety and affordability, equal treatment and the promotion of universal access and of user rights.

Article 2
The provisions of the Treaties do not affect in any way the competence of Member States to provide, commission and organise non-economic services of general interest.

Regarding the expression "shared values" in the SGI Protocol, although Article 14 TFEU evokes SGEIs' place in the Union's "shared values", the interpretative elements formulated in the Protocol may rather be seen as legal-political principles.[46]

As to the notions of SGI and NESGI in the SGI Protocol, they consolidate the terminology of categories developed by the Commission in its Communications. Due to their presence in the SGI Protocol, the notions of SGI and NESGI are now *legal* notions, but as the notion of SGEI, they are not defined, and the relationship between the three notions is not explicitly formulated in EU law. It seems clear

---

[46]This point was aptly made by the European Economic and Social Committee, see Analysis of the implications of the Lisbon Treaty on Services of General Interest and proposals for implementation, *Discussion paper drawn up by European experts,* European Economic and Social Committee, March 2008, p. 46. The Protocol came very late in the process of adopting a Reform Treaty, and its formulation was probably not as thought-out as other elements in the Lisbon Treaty.

that the Protocol reflects the Commission's views on the relationship between the three notions, with a "mother notion" and two "daughter notions", making of SGI a pivotal legal notion of EU primary law. At any rate, this is the perception of many legal authors. For instance, Neergaard describes the notions of SGEI, SGI, NESGI and SSGI as "the relatives in the conceptual family".[47] Regarding the relationship between the three legal notions in the SGI Protocol, Neergaard's view, based on the Communications of the Commission, is that SGIs may be viewed as including both SGEIs and NESGIs. This perception of "SGI" as a "general" concept comprising the two sub-groups SGEI and NESGI is shared by Lenaerts, who also refers to the Commission' understanding of the expression "SGI".[48] Indeed, the symmetry between Article 1 on SGEI and Article 2 on NESGI, which are the only provisions contained by the SGI Protocol suggests strongly that SGI must be seen as the sum of the two categories SGEI and NESGI.

In its Communication on SGIs of 2007 the Commission considered that the Protocol constitutes "a decisive step towards establishing a transparent and reliable EU framework" and affirmed that "[b]y spelling out the role of the Union, the Protocol brings *the necessary clarity* and certainty to EU rules."[49] Rodrigues underlines that the Protocol is not intended to be merely a declaration of principle, but instead takes "an operational stance, as an "interpretative" guide to the Treaties and a real set of instructions on how to implement Article 14 and 106(2) TFEU for both the EU and the Member States".[50] Presented by Damjanovic and De Witte as "the final layer of the Lisbon edifice" relating to SGEIs, the Protocol may actually be seen as the *bottom* layer of this edifice as it provides a broad orientation platform:

a. Establishing fundamental concepts of public service in EU law
b. Providing elements to identify SGEI
c. Providing principles completing Article 14 TFEU for EU legislation on SGEI
d. Providing principles completing Articles 14 and 106(2) TFEU for the application of EU market rules to SGEI
e. Providing principles for the application of EU law to NESGI

As an interpretative tool, the Protocol must arguably itself be interpreted against the background of Treaty provisions which it is profoundly related to, in particular Articles 2–6 TEU. Indeed, Article 1 of the SGI Protocol contains normative elements that are related to the Union's foundational values and principles, and are therefore directly relevant to explain SGEI's enhanced dignity in the Treaties. This relation is addressed in Sect. 3.2.1, especially in Sect. 3.2.1.4. As to Article 2 of

[47]Neergaard 2013, p. 207.

[48]Lenaerts 2012, p. 1250.

[49]Commission, "Services of general interest, including social services of general interest: a new European commitment" (Communication) COM (2007) 725 final, p. 3, emphasis added.

[50]Rodrigues 2009, p. 263.

the SGI Protocol, it excludes any EU law constraint on the exercise of Member States' discretion to exercise their competence to provide, commission and organise NESGI. The lack of certainty on the concepts of SGI and NESGI is obviously a problem to delineate the scope of Article 2, and is examined in the two following sub-sections.

3.1.3.2.1 SGI Not Defined in EU Law, Only Defined in the Commission's Communications

As SGI is not defined in EU law, guidance on the concept can only be found in the Commission's Communications on SGIs. The Commission's definition and political stance on services of general interest seems to have evolved between 1996 and 2007, parallel with the evolution of the Commission's "working definitions" of SGEI between 2004 and 2010. This appears from a comparison between the way the Commission presented the notion of SGI when it launched the concept on its own initiative in 1996 and ten years later in 2007.

In the SGEI Communication of 2007, the Commission gives its own definition and understanding of SGIs, in the following terms:

> Although their scope and organisation vary significantly according to histories and cultures of state intervention, they can be defined as the services, both economic and non-economic, which the public authorities classify as being of general interest and subject to specific public service obligations. This means that it is essentially the responsibility of public authorities, at the relevant level, to decide on the nature and scope of a service of general interest. Public authorities can decide to carry out the services themselves or they can decide to entrust them to other entities, which can be public or private, and can act either for profit or not for profit.[51]

In 1996, the Commission was perhaps more inspired by Durkheim's theories in explicitly connecting SGIs to their importance for social cohesion[52] and in a more diffuse way by Duguit's idea that securing certain services indispensable for social cohesion require State intervention, "serving the public" being the very fundament

[51]Communication from the Commission to the European Parliament, the Council, the European Economic and Social Committee and the Committee of the Regions of 20 November 2007 "Services of general interest, including social services of general interest: a new European commitment" COM (2007) 725 final, Section 2.

[52]The issue of social cohesion in modern societies is central in the works of Durkheim, who believed that modern societies tend to achieve cohesion through "organic solidarity" rather than "mechanic solidarity". In his view social cohesion was indispensable to a society's sustainability, as "For if society lacks the unity that derives from the fact that the relationships between its parts are exactly regulated, that unity resulting from the harmonious articulation of its various functions assured by effective discipline and if, in addition, society lacks the unity based upon the commitment of men's wills to a common objective, then it is no more than a pile of sand that the least jolt or the slightest puff will suffice to scatter.", see the re-publication of the English version of Emile Durkheim's book Education morale, Durkheim E. 2002, *Moral Education,* Courier Dover Publications, p. 102.

of State legitimacy.[53] This appears rather clearly in the following quotation from the Commission's Communication on SGI of 1996:

> European societies are committed to the general interest services they have created which meet basic needs. These services play an important role as *social cement over and above simple practical considerations*. They also have a symbolic value, reflecting a sense of community that people can identify with/…/The roles assigned to general interest services and the special rights that they may ensue reflect considerations inherent in the concept of *serving the public*, such as ensuring that needs are met, protecting the environment, economic and social cohesion, land-use planning and promotion of consumer interests"/…/ Central to all these issues are the *interest of the public*, which *in our societies* involves *guaranteed access to essential services, and the pursuit of priority objectives*. General interest services are meant to *serve a society as a whole and therefore all those living in it*. The same applies in the Community to the universal service concept.[54]

This French sociological and legal heritage, still influential under the Delors Commission, was toned down by the Barroso Commission, as appears from the way the Commission justifies SGIs in its Communication of 2007:

> These services are *essential for the daily life of citizens and enterprises*, and reflect Europe's model of society. They play a major role in ensuring social, economic and territorial cohesion throughout the Union and are vital for the sustainable development of the EU in terms of *higher levels of employment, social inclusion, economic growth and environmental quality*.[55]

In the 2007 approach, the Commission gives a more technical conception of the EU concept of SGI, which might have contributed in making their final entry into the Treaties more acceptable by Member States under liberal governance. Importantly, it underlines that SGIs—which at the left of the political spectrum still constitute a fundamental element of state legitimacy—"can vary through histories and cultures of state intervention".

Be it as it may with the varying "culture of state intervention", SGIs are consistently defined by the Commission as "both market and non-market services which the public authorities class as being of general interest and subject to specific public service obligations".[56] In the present state of EU law, there is no material provision specifically applying to the legal notion of SGIs. Consequently its raison d'être must be understood to establish a *legal* conceptual link between SGEIs and NESGIs, both characterized in the introductory sentence of the Protocol as having a particular *political* importance. From a legal-political point of view this goes beyond the rhetoric of Article 14 TFEU. By declaring the

[53]In the view of Léon Duguit the State was legitimated not by public authority but by its capacity to organise society to serve the general interest, see in particular Duguit 1923, p. 55.

[54]Commission, "Services of General Interest in Europe" (Communication) [1996] OJ C281/03, p. 4, emphasis added.

[55]Commission, "Services of general interest, including social services of general interest: a new European commitment" (Communication) COM (2007) 725 final, p. 3, emphasis added.

[56]Ibid., p. 6–7.

importance of the wider notion of "services of general interest", the Member States express explicitly for the Union, including themselves, that the very concept of "general interest" has become part of EU's political project.[57] It seems thus that an important political page has been turned, which the Commission apparently acknowledged by entitling its Communication of 2007 on SGI "a new European Commitment".[58] It is worth remembering how the Commission already 2003 envisaged *some* broader European political concept of general interest, as it considered that "the future of non-economic services of general interest, whether they are related to prerogatives of the State or linked to such sensitive sectors as culture, education, health or social services, *raises issues on a European scale, such as the content of the European model of society*"[59] and raised the question of which role the Community should have regarding NESGIs.[60]

3.1.3.2.2 NESGI Not Defined in EU Law: Considerable Uncertainty on the Scope of Article 2 of the SGI Protocol

It is clear from the SGI Protocol that even NESGIs are considered as "important", which justifies the presence of Article 2 stating that the provisions of the Treaty do not in any way affect *the competence of Member States to provide, commission and organise NESGIs*. Through this wording, Article 2 affirms that Member States and their authorities retain strong powers regarding NESGIs within their competence, but the effect of this derogation is restricted for two main reasons.

First, by carving out exhaustively which specific powers (provide, commission and organise) are withdrawn from EU law's constraint, Article 2 suggests that EU law may affect Member States' discretion to *regulate* NESGIs.[61] The provision may be seen as implicitly consolidating the CJEU's case law applying to national rules on certain social services the principle of non-discrimination in Article 18 TFEU or the principle of the free movement of persons, and the rights associated with EU-citizenship. Indeed, it is perhaps easier to interpret Article 2 of the SGI Protocol if it is understood as some Member States' attempt to prevent the erosion of their discretion to take measures related to public service activities which for

[57]See Recital 13 of the Preamble to the Treaty on European Union.

[58]Communication from the Commission to the European Parliament, the Council, the European Economic and Social Committee and the Committee of the Regions of 20 November 2007 "Services of general interest, including social services of general interest: a new European commitment" COM (2007) 725 final.

[59]See Commission Green Paper of 21 May 2003 on services of general interest [2004] OJ C76/ (COM (2003)270 final), point 47.

[60]Ibid., point 48.

[61]In the 2013 SGEI Guide, the Commission takes the view that NESGIs are not covered by the internal market and competition rules of the Treaty, but that some aspects of how these services are organized may be subject to other general Treaty rules, such as the principle of non-discrimination. See the 2013 SGEI Guide, p. 21.

the time being are *normally not* conducted by market operators, in reaction to rulings where the CJEU has applied certain Treaty provisions to activities in the public sector, without considering whether the activity at issue was economic or not. An early case in point is *Gravier*.[62]

The CJEU understands the *Gravier* ruling as meaning that the prohibition of discrimination on grounds of nationality "always applies to vocational training, *whatever the circumstances*".[63] In *Gravier* the circumstances were that fees for access to courses in strip cartoon art were imposed on nationals on other Member States and not to students who were nationals of the host Member State. The national court wished to know whether this rule infringed the Treaty and if so on which ground. Referring to *Forcheri*, the national court had found no clear answer to the question whether students should be considered as persons to whom services are provided, and even if the answer to that question was in the negative, whether access to education lies outside the scope of the Treaty.[64] The Court of Justice decided to "define precisely the nature of the problem", and found first that the questions referred concerned neither the organisation of education nor even its financing, but rather the establishment of a financial barrier to *access to education* for foreign students only, and second that they concerned "a particular type of education", referred to as "vocational training".[65]

In *Gravier*, the Court underlined also that, while education was to a large extent not a Community competence, the Community had begun using its Treaty-based policy competence in the field of vocational training. It considered that vocational training, by enabling persons to obtain a professional qualification in the Member State where they intend to work, was particularly likely to promote the Community's objectives of free movement of persons, mobility of labour and improvement of the living standards of workers. On these grounds the Court established that *access* to vocational training fell within the scope of the Treaty, and concluded that the disputed rule infringed the principle of non-discrimination.[66] The Court gave no relevance to the argument that Member States have "special responsibilities" toward their own population in the area of education—in particular ensuring access to education, scholarships, grants, and other social facilities for students—and therefore should not be prevented from treating their own nationals more favourably.[67] In other words, the SGI character of the activity could "what-

[62]Case 293/83 *Gravier* [1985] ECR I-593.

[63]This was explained in Case 263/86 *Humbel* [1988] ECR I-5365, para 23.

[64]Case 293/83 *Gravier* [1985] ECR I-593, para 10, referring to Case 152/82 *Forcheri* [1983] ECR 2323.

[65]Ibid., para 18.

[66]Ibid., paras 19–25. When the judgment was delivered, the Community competence in the field of vocational training was based on Article 128 EEC, now Article 166 TFEU. The principle of non-discrimination was then based on Article 7 EEC, now Article 18 TFEU.

[67]Ibid., para 16. The argument was raised by the Danish Government and the United Kingdom intervening in the case.

ever the circumstances"—including possibly the circumstance that the SGI was a NESGI—not exclude the applicability of the principle of non-discrimination to the national rules.[68]

The second reason limiting the significance of Article 2 of the SGI Protocol for the Member States' freedom to govern public services, is the very restricted scope of the notion of NESGI which the rule itself supposes, by stating that the provision, commission and organisation of NESGI is not at all affected by EU law. This very restrictive interpretation is namely indispensable to reconcile Article 2 of the SGI Protocol with the CJEU's case law on the application of free movement rules to social services. As seen in Chap. 2, the CJEU made it rather clear in *Freskot* that it makes a distinction between "economic activity" and "economic rule", as it found that an activity could be non-economic for the purpose of EU free movement rules, but that its regulation was economic for the purpose of these rules.[69] In that case, the compulsory agricultural insurance activity could be argued to constitute a service of general interest, and as defined and provided under the Greek rules, was found non-economic for the purpose of both competition and free movement rules. However, the Greek rules restricted the free movement of economic services available in other Member States, and in order to comply with the Treaty, this restriction had to be proportional to its social objective, or otherwise be modified.[70] Accordingly, the Greek rules—and as a consequence probably also the organisation of the non-economic social service—were affected by EU free movement rules.

On this background, it is submitted that for Article 2 of the SGI Protocol to make sense, the notion of NESGI must be understood as a service of general interest which *cannot* be subject to economic activity—at least not in the present state of affairs in the Member States and in EU law—and is therefore covered neither by EU competition rules nor by EU free movement rules. If this understanding is correct, it is not sufficient that an activity *is* non-economic as defined and regulated in a specific Member State to constitute a NESGI in the meaning of Article 2 of the SGI Protocol.

---

[68]In Humbel the Court explained that "the judgment in the Gravier case /.../ means that the prohibition of discrimination on grounds of nationality/.../always applies to vocational training, *whatever the circumstances* (emphasis added)". This suggests that prohibition of discrimination constrains even national rules implying that the service is non-economic in the frame of these rules. See Case 263/86 *Humbel* [1988] ECR I-5365, para 23.

[69]Case C-355/00 *Freskot* [2003] ECR I-05263.

[70]The CJEU concluded that the national court would have to examine whether the financing of the state-owned organization and its primarily social objective, would be compromised if the scheme to some extent was liberalized. The liberalization in question would allow Greek farmers taking out insurance policies with private insurers in respect of certain risks covered by the compulsory insurance scheme and made exempt from paying the contribution to a corresponding extent. Interestingly, AG Stix-Hackl also found that the body managing the compulsory insurance scheme did not carry out an economic activity, but evoked the possibility to examine the disputed service monopoly under Article 106(2) TFEU, which applies to services of general *economic* interest. See Opinion of AG Stix-Hackl in Case C-355/00 *Freskot*, para 6.

In the absence of CJEU case law clarifying this issue, it is interesting to be aware of the Commission's understanding of the notion of NESGI. In the 2013 SGEI Guide, it reiterated its view that it is useless to establish a list of non-economic services, as such a list evolves with time, but provided examples of "non-economic activities for the purpose of the competition rules" and of "non-economic activities for the purpose of EU rules", based on the CJEU's case law.[71] This may involve that the Commission envisages two categories of NESGIs, one for the purpose of EU competition rules and one for the purpose of EU free movement rules. Yet, as the Commission also states that NESGIs are not subject to specific EU legislation and are not covered by the internal market and competition rules of the Treaty, it seems possible that it considers instead NESGIs to be activities that are non-economic for the purpose of both EU competition and EU internal market rules. The latter understanding seems more reasonable.

The lack of certainty on the limits of the notion of NESGI may appear as unproblematic as the Commission holds the view that "the vast majority of services can be considered as "economic activities" within the meaning of EC Treaty rules on the internal market".[72] Yet it is submitted that Article 2 of the SGI Protocol is a challenging provision, and that the incertitude on its scope and effect in practice reveals the excessively sophisticated character of the CJEU's case law.

3.1.3.3 Article 36 EUCFR and the Principle of Respect of Access to SGEI

In 1999, the Council of Cologne saw a need to establish the EU Charter on Fundamental Rights (EUCFR, hereafter referred to as "the Charter") in order to make fundamental rights' importance and relevance more visible to the Union's citizens, underlining that protecting fundamental rights had become a prerequisite for the Union's legitimacy.[73] Making the Charter binding on EU law, with the same legal value as the Treaties, pursuant to Article 6(1) TFEU, was a central

[71]See points 27 and 224 of the SGEI Guide 2013.

[72]Commission, "Services of general interest, including social services of general interest: a new European commitment" (Communication) COM (2007) 725 final, p. 5.

[73]See Conclusions of the Presidency, Cologne European Council 3–4 June 1999, point 45, and Annex IV containing the European Council decision on the drawing up of a Charter of Fundamental Rights of the European Union, available at: http://www.europarl.europa.eu/summits/kol2_en.htm. One may wonder what made this reaching out to the citizens of the Union so "needed" just then. A key explanation is argued to be that—in the same document—the Council considered overall economic stability and growth to require "a growth-oriented taxation policy, in particular a decrease in the fiscal and social security burden on the labour factor, and an employment-oriented wage policy by the parties to collective wage agreements". As some unpopular messages had to be delivered to citizens of the EU, it was urgent to signal that the Union took social and environmental claims seriously. That the Charter should articulate a coherent system of rules connecting the national, European and international levels of fundamental rights was in that context a secondary task.

element of the Lisbon political "new deal". This will have legal consequences many of which are difficult to foresee,[74] but it is submitted that this shift implies that fundamental rights recognized by the Charter are now part of the "interests of the Union" in Article 106(2) TFEU.

The Charter includes (1) freedoms and rights traditionally present in the democratic constitutions of the Member States, (2) social-economic rights inspired from the European Social Charter and inherited welfare models existing in the Member States and (3) the *European* market freedoms and citizens' rights introduced by the Treaties. The Charter is addressed to both Union institutions/organs *and* to the Member States "only when they are implementing EU law", and subordinates the legality of their respective acts to the respect of the freedoms, rights and principles recognized by the Charter.[75] Also, the Charter makes a distinction between rights—including the rights to free movement and all provisions corresponding to rights protected by the ECHR—and principles—such as social rights under Title IV on solidarity. By contrast with rights, principles are judicially cognisable only in the interpretation of acts implementing them, and in the ruling of their legality.[76]

Article 36 EUCFR is said to be what is left of a more ambitious French proposal, and reads:

> The Union recognises and respects access to services of general economic interest as provided for in national laws and practices, in accordance with the Treaties, in order to promote the social and territorial cohesion of the Union.

As doubts were raised as to whether this principle could be a matter of fundamental rights, it has been introduced in the Charter as a compromise. The right of access to SGEIs belongs to the category "principles" of the Charter and thus does not found any individual opposable right. The effects of Article 36 EUCFR are still unclear, but its scope is limited by Article 51 EUCFR, providing that the

[74]There are concerns over the Charter opening for judicial activism and leading to a "federal" interpretation by the Court of Justice. Groussot, Pech and Petursson argue that nothing in Article 51 EUCFR allows the CJEU to submit Member States to the EU fundamental rights outside the scope of EU law and to enforce common standards applicable right across the EU regardless of whether national measures fall within or outside the scope of application of EU law They regard as virtually impossible an American evolution "à la Gitlow" whereby the Charter could have federalizing effect through judicial activism and on the basis of its primary law status. See Groussot et al. 2011, p. 18, where a short review of *Gitlow v. New York*, 268 U.S. 652 (1925) is also made.

[75]See Article 51(1) EUCFR. Groussot, Pech and Petursson show convincingly how the wording of Article 51(1) may be an "inadvertent omission", as in the pre-Lisbon case law Member States have been held to be bound by EU fundamental rights not only when implementing or applying EU law, but more generally whenever they act *within the scope of EU law*, which—as established in *ERT*—includes situations where the Member States seek to justify national measures derogating from EU law by reasons of public interest. See Groussot et al. 2011, p. 20, referring to Jacobs F. G., 2001, p. 338. As the authors point out, their view is shared by Craig and de Búrca, see Craig and de Búrca 2008, p. 395.

[76]Article 52(5) EUCFR.

principle is addressed to EU institutions and bodies with due regard for the principle of subsidiarity, and to Member States only when implementing EU law. As all other rights and principles of the Charter, the principle in Article 36 EUCFR is not absolute, and therefore its application can be restricted subject to conditions formulated in Article 52(1) EUCFR. In particular the essence of the principle must be respected, and its limitation be proportional to objectives of general interest recognized by the Union, or to the need to protect the rights and freedoms of others.

In the explanations to the Charter, it is underlined that Article 36 "merely sets out the principle of respect by the Union for the access to services of general economic interest as provided for by national provisions, when those provisions are compatible with Community legislation".[77] Thus, to found rights based on Article 36 EUCFR, SGEI must be compatible with the rules on free movement and competition. If national measures enabling their performance restrict free movement and competition, they will have to be assessed under the principle of proportionality.[78] In particular, if their performance is publicly funded, EU state aid rules applying to SGEI and largely based on the *Altmark* ruling will apply. One may certainly wonder whether a strict application of these rules cannot endanger the principle's essence, for instance if it is found that a service operator is over-compensated.

AG Jääskinen has expressed the view that the principle that EU law respect access to SGEI as provided in national laws may necessitate a "light competition" approach of the fourth *Altmark* criterion.[79] Regarding locally provided social, educational, housing or health services, he found less evident that excessive SGEI compensations may distort competition and affect trade between Member States, and that successful second-guessing of the appropriate cost level is perhaps of less importance. He considered that in such fields, the approach should be "one of solidarity", as Article 36 EUCFR in his view evidently excludes the termination of the provision of a SGEI only because authorities miscalculated.[80]

In Article 36 EUCFR, it is also important to note the words "provided for in national laws and practices", suggesting that even in cases where public service tasks are not formally characterized as SGEIs in national law, it is sufficient that they exist de facto to be recognized and respected by EU law. Thus, a flexible

[77]Text of the explanations relating to the complete text of the Charter of Fundamental Rights of the European Union as set out in CHARTE 4487/00 CONVENT 50, p. 33.

[78]As underlined by Szyszczak, Article 36 EUCFR—apparently a safeguard for the Member States' competence in the area of access to SGEI - sits uneasily with the moves to Europeanize SGEI over the last two decades, in particular with the reference in Article 14 TFEU to observance and compatibility with Articles 4, 93, 106 and 107 TFEU acting as a major constraint upon Article 36 EUCFR, see Szyszczak 2014, p. 978 and 980.

[79]Jääskinen 2011, p. 600. The *Altmark* ruling has laid down four cumulative criteria preventing state funding of public services provision to constitute aid in the meaning of Article 107(1) TFEU, the fourth criterion referring to two alternative procedures allowing to avoid over-compensation, namely the use of procurement procedures or the comparison of the amount received by an undertaking with the costs of a well-run company providing a similar service.

[80]Ibid.

application of the fourth *Altmark* criterion may indeed be required by Article 36 EUCFR. However, Article 36 EUCFR may support arguments against a too relaxed application of state aid rules in the field of publicly-funded social services, as such an application may instead contribute to deprive users from their rights. Indeed, if the SGEI is compensated but not clearly defined, neither EU institutions nor users have a chance to know which service—or rather which service conditions—Article 36 EUCFR protects access to.

Besides, it may be questioned whether social services are as local in nature as they often are depicted. While it is true that they tend to be provided and used locally, certain social services, such as elderly care or health care can generate considerable cross-border commercial activity. Indeed, in the process of welfare marketization, social services constitute an attractive investment sector. This business reality is well known by EU institutions, and part of the social entrepreneurship which is actively promoted by the Union. Article 36 EUCFR enjoins EU institutions to recognize and respect access to SGEI rights as fundamental rights of EU citizens. This recognition implies a certain deference to the relation established between the Member States and their peoples, but it does arguably not allow to hide behind the local character of social services to relax EU competition requirements based on Article 106(2) TFEU, because these requirements can actually promote access to the SGEI rights.

The EU network of independent experts on fundamental rights held a few years ago that the EU courts' case law on SGEIs had not yet touched on the right of access to SGEIs but essentially on aid granted to providers as a compensation for the costs incurred by public service obligations.[81] However, in the field of health care, it appears that the CJEU has in fact widened the national conditions of access to an SGEI, by requiring that Member States finance SGEI provided in other Member States. It is namely argued, and shown in Chap. 4, that *Smits and Peerbooms, Kohl* and *Watts* can also be read as concerning the access of citizens from certain Member States to an SGEI supplied by service providers established in other Member States. This confirms that to be recognized and respected, access to SGEI must be based on national rules respecting EU rules on free movement, and that Article 36 EUCFR cannot oblige the CJEU to unconditionally recognize and respect national conditions of access to SGEIs which restrict free movement.

Another question, not discussed here, is whether the principle laid down in Article 36 EUCFR may have some relevance in litigation between SGEI-users and undertakings entrusted with SGEI tasks.[82]

---

[81]Network of Independent Experts on Fundamental Rights, *Commentary of the Charter of Fundamental Rights of the European Union*, June 2006, p. 313. This network was set up by the European Commission, upon request of the European Parliament and coordinated by Olivier De Schutter, with the assistance of Valérie Van Goethem.
Available at: http://ec.europa.eu/justice/fundamental-rights/files/networkcommentaryfinal_en.pdf

[82]For some analysis of this issue and also on the role of Article 36 EUCFR as a teleological tool but also as a principle that may allow challenging EU legislative interferences with national SGEI, see Szyszczak 2014, p. 979.

3.2 The Political Importance of SGEI for the Foundational Principles of the EU

The legal-political motives of SGEIs' dignity in EU constitutional law is signalled by several connections between the Treaty framework on SGEIs, including Article 36 EUCFR, and certain Treaty "foundational principles", by which is meant here Articles 2–6 TEU. This section examines first the relation between the Treaty framework on SGEIs and EU's values and objectives, and second the relation between the Treaty framework on SGEIs and the principles of conferral, respect of the national identity and local self-government.

3.2.1 Relationship Between the Treaty Framework on SGEIs and the Values and Objectives of the EU

The SGI Protocol declares that SGIs, obviously including SGEIs, are "important" for the Union. This term indicates that SGEIs achieve a high dignity in EU law, which according to Article 14 TFEU is related to the place they occupy in the shared values of the Union, and to their role in promoting social and territorial cohesion. Accordingly, it appears that the Union's values and missions constitute the legal-political foundation, and that SGEIs are seen as playing an important function in giving substance to these values and missions in the daily life of EU peoples.

3.2.1.1 SGEI and the Shared Values of the Union

The term "values" appears in several provisions of the Treaties, but first and foremost in Article 2 TEU, which reads:

> The Union is founded on the values of respect for human dignity, freedom, democracy, equality, the rule of law and respect for human rights, including the rights of persons belonging to minorities. These values are common to the Member States in a society in which pluralism, non-discrimination, tolerance, justice, solidarity and equality between women and men prevail.

Are these values in Article 2 TEU equivalent to the "shared values of the Union" mentioned in Article 14 TFEU, or are they related in some other way? Some light on this question is shed by comments of a group of experts, nominated by the Legal Services of the European Parliament, the Council and the Commission, on the draft text of the Constitutional Treaty. In a report annexed to notes addressed by the Secretariat of the European Convention to the Members of the Convention, the expert group considered the use of the term "shared values" in the draft amendments to ex Article 16 EC (now the first sentence of Article 14 TFEU) as problematic when "values", in Article 2 of the draft text of the Treaty

Articles establishing a Constitution for Europe, were defined in terms of human rights values. They suggested finding another term.[83] The wording of Article 2 in the draft text of the Constitutional Treaty was actually quite close to the provision now enforced in Article 2 TEU and read as follows:

> The Union is founded on the values of respect for human dignity, liberty, democracy, the rule of law and respect for human rights, values which are common to the Member States. Its aim is a society at peace, through the practice of tolerance, justice and solidarity.[84]

Thus, it seems possible to deduce from the expert group's view that "values" in Article 2 TEU and "shared values of the Union" in Article 14 TFEU are not meant as the same thing. This does not exclude that they are related. Indeed, the Praesidium of the European Convention explained how other ethical elements in the late Constitution would relate to the values of the Union listed in Article 2 of the Draft text:

> That does not, of course, prevent the Constitution from mentioning additional, more detailed elements which are part of the Union's "ethic" in other places, such as, for instance, in the Preamble, in Article 3 on the general objectives of the Union, in the Charter of Fundamental Rights (which, unlike this Article, does not, however, apply to autonomous action by the Member States), in Title VI on "The democratic life of the Union" and in the provisions enshrining the specific objectives of the various policies.[85]

This distinction between "core values" and "additional, more detailed elements of the Union's ethic", may help in understanding SGEIs' "place" in the Union's shared values. It is argued that SGEIs have a place in EU's shared values inasmuch as they convey elements of ethic which are more detailed than, but in line with, the core values enunciated in Article 2 TEU.[86] To get a better sense of this relation, let us take a closer look at Article 2 TEU.

---

[83]The experts group was mandated with a view to making technical adjustments to EC and EU Treaty provisions for insertion into Part Two of the Constitutional Treaty and its report was attached to Note (CONV 618/03) addressed by the Secretariat of the European Convention to the Members of the Convention and dated 19th March 2003, p. 1, http://register.consilium.europa.eu/pdf/en/03/cv00/cv00618.en03.pdf, accessed 27 February 2015. See footnote to clause 3 under the title "The Union's values". Clause 3 reads: "This concept of "shared values" is questionable when "values" are defined in the draft Article in Part One entitled "The Union's values" (Article 2 CONV 528/03) in terms of human rights values.

[84]See Note (CONV 528/03) from the Praesidium of the European Convention to the Members of the Convention including a draft text of the Articles of the Treaty establishing a Constitution for Europe, p. 2.

[85]The Praesidium consisted of the Convention Chairman and Vice-Chairmen and nine members drawn from the Convention: the representatives of all the governments holding the Presidency of the Union during the Convention (Spain, Denmark and Greece), two national parliament representatives, two European Parliament representatives and two Commission representatives.

[86]This proposition seems supported by the following statement made by the Commission in 1996: "Europe is built on a set of values shared by all its societies, and combines the characteristics of democracy - human rights and institutions based on the rule of law - with those of an open economy underpinned by market forces, internal solidarity and cohesion. These values include the access for all members of society to universal services or to services of general benefit, thus contributing to solidarity and equal treatment." See Commission, "Reinforcing political union and preparing for enlargement" (Opinion) COM (96) 90 final.

Although the Treaties are not formally a constitution, von Bogdandy considers the concepts listed in Article 2 as legal norms constituting "founding principles" of EU law, and expressing a constitutive—as opposed to restrictive—constitutionalism in EU positive law.[87] This view is in line with the explanation of the provision's "early draft version" in the late Constitutional Treaty, given by the Praesidium of the European Convention, emphasizing the extraordinary powers related to the adhesion to or breach of these values:

> This Article concentrates on the essentials—a short list of fundamental European values. Further justification for this is that a manifest risk of serious breach of one of those values by a Member State would be sufficient to initiate the procedure for alerting and sanctioning the Member State [see Article 7(2) TEU], even if the breach took place in the field of the Member State's autonomous action (not affected by Union law). This Article can thus only contain a hard core of values meeting two criteria at once: on the one hand, they must be so fundamental that they lie at the very heart of a peaceful society practising tolerance, justice and solidarity; on the other hand, they must have a clear non-controversial legal basis so that the Member States can discern the obligations resulting therefrom which are subject to sanction.[88]

The list of values in the first sentence of Article 2 is exhaustive and includes concepts present in the preamble to the EU Treaty, but there named "universal values" (second recital) alternatively "principles" (fourth recital). Article 2 TEU includes also a second sentence providing that these values are "common to Member States in a society in which pluralism, non-discrimination, tolerance, justice, solidarity and equality between women and men prevail". This wording suggests that these latter notions, expected to *prevail* in the European society, do not constitute "values" of the same dignity as those on which the Union is *founded*.[89] The Praesidium's explanation cited above appears to support this interpretation of Article 2, "slicing" the concepts it refers into (1) characteristics of European societies which are part of the social contract and illustrating what is meant with (2) the non-negotiable "core".

Micklitz holds that Article 2 TEU deals with "the Social" in line with a concept of *shared responsibility* between the Union and the Member States, the Union upholding "access justice", leaving to the Member States the responsibility to achieve social justice.[90] To Pernice, Article 2 TEU evokes a social contract, and

[87]Von Bogdandy 2010, p. 106.

[88]See Article 2 of the draft text of the Articles of the Treaty establishing a Constitution for Europe.

[89]According to Von Bogdandy, "the obscure normative function of the second sentence" illustrates the remaining uncertainties concerning the identification of European founding principles, see Von Bogdandy 2010, p. 106–107. Whether the notions named in the second sentence of Article 2 may be considered "values referred to in Article 2" may have significance for the hopefully rare application of Article 7(2) TEU.

[90]Micklitz 2010, p. 3 and 7. Micklitz borrows the term "the Social" from Kennedy in Kennedy D., 2006, p. 19–73.

this view is shared here, given the similitude between the values enumerated in that provision and a number of fundamental rights recognized by the EU Charter. However it is argued that this "social contract" includes also Article 3(1) TEU, which declares that EU's aim is to promote peace, EU's values and the well-being of its peoples.[91] The EU may be seen as bound to EU citizens through its foundational values and aims, and also bound to do so on the basis of more specific missions and objectives enumerated in Article 3(2–5) TEU.[92] The mission to establish an internal market is cardinal but completed by societal and environmental objectives—full employment, social progress, high level of protection and improvement of the quality of the environment, social justice and protection, equality between women and men, protection of the rights of the child—which must be pursued loyally by the Union.[93]

Obviously, the particular "shared value" consisting for services of general economic interest in "a high level of quality, safety and affordability, equal treatment and the promotion of universal access and of user rights"[94] seems to promote the Union's values of human dignity, equality and respect for human rights, and the well-being of the peoples of Europe. This specific SGEI value seems also apt to promote social justice and combat social exclusion and discrimination.

3.2.1.2 SGEI and Human Rights

According to Rossi, Article 2 TEU includes a new list of fundamental values of the EU, which is broader than Article 6 of the former EU Treaty, and is equally

[91]To Pernice, Article 2 TEU evokes a social contract, "which, through diverse new provisions on solidarity among the Member States, would embrace citizens individually as well as their respective countries". See Pernice 2009, p. 41, who underlines this element of contract between the Union and "its" citizens. Thus he points out that the protection of citizens is mentioned among the aims of the Treaty in Article 3(3) and (5) TEU, and that Article 13 TEU states that the institutional framework shall serve not only the interests of the Union and its Member States, but also those of its citizens.

[92]Von Bogdandy is critical of the use of the term *values* in the Treaty, as he believes that "value discourses can easily acquire a paternalistic dimension", see Von Bogdandy 2010, p. 104. While he advocates a legal doctrine of principles based on a better foundation than "sociological assumptions regarding normative dispositions of EU citizens", it may be argued that the Treaty is not only written for legal scholars. The fact that certain principles are dignified in the Treaty as "values", was arguably decisive for public adhesion to the almost constitutional Lisbon Treaty in the first place, and a popular expression of this dignity was probably crucial from a democratic point of view. The Council may according to Article 42(5) TEU entrust the execution of a common security and defence task, within the Union framework, to a group of Member States, in order to protect the Union's *values*. The concept of "value" conveys a more profound adhesion of citizens to the common project, which the Union has been given legal powers to appeal to. Is anybody ready to die for "founding principles"?.

[93]Pursuant to Article 7 TFEU, the EU must also ensure the consistency of its policies and activities.

[94]Pursuant to Article 1 third dash of the SGI Protocol.

binding for the EU and Member States, a sort of "mini-catalogue" of the values and principles promoted by the EUCFR.[95] Indeed, the semantic or logical connection between the titles of the EUCFR and the values enunciated in the first sentence of Article 2 TEU is obvious—with the important exception of title IV on "solidarity", a concept which is only present in the second sentence of Article 2 TEU.[96] By formulating "more detailed ethic elements", Article 14 TFEU, aimed at protecting the fulfilment of SGEI missions, and Article 36 EUCFR, aimed at supporting access to SGEI, play an important function in ensuring that the Union can pursue its aim to promote the respect for human dignity and the respect for human rights, and fulfil its mission to combat exclusion and discrimination, solidarity between generations and protection of the rights of the child.[97] To be sure, SGEIs and public service obligations related thereto are generally introduced to ensure rights recognized by the Charter, in particular the right to education, the rights of the elderly, the right of access to placement services, family rights in particular to paid maternity leave, social security and social assistance, health care.[98]

A Working Paper elaborated in 1999 by the Directorate General for Research of the European Parliament explains that fundamental social rights in the context of the EUCFR are "the rights to which the individual is entitled as a member of a group and which can be made effective only if the State takes action to safeguard the individual's environment. They do not give effect to freedom from the State but to freedom with the State's assistance".[99] In many social fields, where it lacks both policy powers and powers to levy taxes, the EU depends heavily on the Member States' social policies to take action, give assistance to its peoples, and give substance to the social rights recognized by the Charter.

These social rights do not constitute individual rights or rights that can be enforced through litigation, but they are cognisable, although according to Article 52(5) EUCFR, only in the *interpretation* of EU legislative and executive acts—and national measures implementing EU law. Such a legality review does not exclude that social rights are limited, but as already seen, any limitation must respect the essence of the social rights protected. The "essence" of social rights, protected by Article 52 EUCFR can be particularly tricky to define, in particular because its

---

[95]Rossi 2008, p. 81.

[96]Indeed, each value enunciated in the first sentence of Article 2 TEU seems to correspond to one of the titles of the Charter: title I for "dignity", title II for "freedoms", title III for "equality, title V for "citizens' rights, title VI for "the rule of law".

[97]The aim follows from Article 3(1) TEU and the missions from Article 3(3) TEU.

[98]See Articles 14, 25, 28, 33, 34, 35 EUCFR.

[99]This definition is proposed in *Fundamental Rights in Europe*, European Parliament, Directorate General for Research, Working Paper, Social Affairs Series, 3 PE 168.629, 2009, authors: Butt ME, Kubert J and Schultz CA, Editor: Bauer L, Division for Social, Legal and Cultural Affairs, Directorate General for Research. It is based on a definition made by Wipfelder, in Wipfelder 1986, p. 140.

definition is generally related to costs.[100] In other words, the binding status of the social principles recognized by the Charter does not say much of which "essence" they guarantee. In specific cases, it may be possible to argue that this essence is in particular found in public service tasks assigned on the basis of democratic mandates to public authorities in the Member States. Hence, the Union's duty to recognise and respect access to SGEI pursuant to Article 36 EUCFR may play an important legal-technical role in ensuring that EU law respects social rights, thereby fulfilling its objectives and respecting it core values.

3.2.1.3 SGEI and Social and Territorial Cohesion

The Union must establish an internal market, pursuant to Article 3(2) TEU, but it has also a mission to promote social and territorial cohesion and solidarity among Member States according, pursuant to Article 3(3) TEU. These missions are both instrumental for the Union's aim to promote peace, which is still a concrete issue today in a Europe where racism and militant nationalism have not been eradicated.[101] The idea that market interaction and social cohesion are important for peace appears related to theories developed—in quite different ways—by Comte, Spencer and Durkheim.[102] By declaring that they play a role for social and territorial cohesion, Article 14 TFEU characterizes SGEIs as beneficial to the Unions' fundamental

[100]The term "essence" appears to be as open-ended as the Court's ruling in *Karlsson* which, according to the explanations of the Charter, it is based on, see explanations of the Charter, p. 48 referring to Case C-292/97 *Kjell Karlsson* [2000] ECR I-02737. In *Karlsson* the Court examined a right to non-discrimination on the basis of nationality claimed by milk producers against EC fixed milk-quotas. Under para 45, the Court declares that EU law allows restrictions on the exercise of fundamental rights, in particular in the context of a common organization of the market, provided that those restrictions in fact correspond to objectives of general interest pursued by the Community and do not constitute, with regard to the aim pursued, disproportionate and *unreasonable* interference undermining the very substance of those rights. In *Karlsson* the Court referred to *Wachauf* which prohibited restrictions entailing "a disproportionate and *intolerable* interference, impairing the very substance" of fundamental rights, se Case C-5/88 *Hubert Wachauf* [1989] ECR 02609, para 18.

[101]The heads of States declare in the TEU preamble their desire to deepen the solidarity between their peoples and in the TFEU preamble intend to confirm the solidarity which binds Europe and the overseas countries and express their resolution, "by thus pooling their resources, to preserve and strengthen peace and liberty".

[102]See for instance Durkheim 1893. Durkheim analysed the specialization of labor and its relation to social cohesion. Lack of cohesion was found at both individual/psychological level and from a societal perspective to constitute a source of depression and misery. Together, organic interdependence and common ethical values are found to be factors of social cohesion and integration of social systems. Long before Durkheim, Auguste Comte had also acknowledged the fundamental role played by the division of labor in the structure of modern societies which he saw as a threat to feelings of community and togetherness. By contrast with this so called "moral communalist" approach, other philosophers, like Herbert Spencer, contributed to theories on cohesion with a more liberal approach, based on a "law of equal freedom" leading to a recognition of individual rights.

missions, which enhances their dignity. This declaration is important, because as seen in Sect. 3.1.2, SGEIs are perceived by some Member States as problematic in the liberalization of public services, depending on how they are defined and regulated in EU market law. Yet, the relation between SGEIs and the EU objective of social cohesion is still very complex, in particular because SGEIs defined by Member States and provided on the basis of national rules, tend to promote national solidarity, which is arguably different from the meaning of the concept of solidarity at EU level.

In the Commission Communication on Services of General Interest of 1996, the Commission theorized on "the European model of society" and formulated the relationship between SGIs—economic or non-economic—and the Union's objectives in the following words:

> Solidarity and equal treatment within an open and dynamic market economy are fundamental European Community objectives; objectives which are furthered by services of general interest. Europeans have come to expect high quality services at affordable prices. Many of them even view general interest services as social rights that make an important contribution to economic and social cohesion. This is why general interest services are at the heart of the European model of society, as acknowledged by the Commission in its recent report on the reform of the European Treaties.[103]

While referring to the notions of solidarity and equal treatment, this "European model of society" evoked discreetly but surely two different visions of SGIs. The first vision is one where SGIs consist of market services for which particular conditions of quality and affordability should be secured (which may not necessarily require solidarity), whereas in the other vision SGIs correspond to social rights supposing a direct welfare relation between the State and its people (normally based on solidarity). In the face of these two different visions, it may appear that the Treaties are neutral, as Article 14 TFEU emphasizes SGEI's role for social cohesion, not their role for solidarity.

Although the notion of solidarity is present in Article 2 TEU (as a value prevailing in the Member States) and in the Charter (as the title for several social rights), it is thus probable that its meaning in these contexts is specific for EU law and differs from the meaning that this notion can have—implicitly or explicitly—in the national welfare systems. As argued by Micklitz, the upgrading of solidarity in the Treaty Lisbon 2007/9 requires an understanding of what is behind the concept of solidarity at the European level and to what extent it complies with the particular national understanding.[104] His contention that national solidarity concepts can be disintegrated by European integration gets support from the CJEU's approach in the health care cases, evoked in Chap. 2, and in cases where Member States denying or restricting access to their social services for citizens from other Member States were found to infringe the EU principles of non-discrimination or free movement.[105]

---

[103]Commission, "Services of General Interest in Europe" (Communication) 96/C 281/03, point 1.

[104]Micklitz 2010, p. 5.

[105]See in particular Case C-184/99 *Grzelczyk* [2001] ECR I-6193 and Case C-209/03 *Bidar* [2005] ECR I-2119.

Micklitz' view that the autonomous meaning of solidarity will play a crucial role in the dialectic of European integration and national disintegration is shared here. However, the "totalization" of EU law—and the closure of "exit" from EU market rules for social services—has arguably faced EU institutions, and the masters of the Treaties, with the challenge of upholding EU law as a *legitimate* legal order. This may imply that EU law respects the expression of social contracts uniting EU citizens to their respective States, as the latter unquestionably enjoy, in Weiler words, a "constitutional demos".[106] Indeed, it seems that Article 1 third indent of the SGI Protocol establishes a framework of compatibility between the EU understanding and the national understandings of solidarity, by laying down as "SGEI shared values" a high level of quality, safety, and affordability, equal treatment and the promotion of universal access and of user rights. Where solidarity-based measures are found appropriate and necessary to secure these shared values as expressed by an SGEI, it may be difficult for EU institutions to submit these measures to strict proportionality tests under EU market rules, as Article 14 TFEU imposes on the Union to take care that such SGEI must enjoy conditions, in particular economic and financial, enabling them to achieve their missions as defined by Member States, and *their* expression of solidarity.

According to Article 14 TFEU, SGEIs play also a role for territorial cohesion, which is an EU mission, arguably related to the core value of equality in Article 2 TEU. As communities of persons, territories need cohesion with one another, which is promoted when they receive equal assistance from the State, for instance in the form of infrastructure, or from EU in the form of funds.[107]

3.2.1.4 SGEI and Democracy

Article 14 TFEU emphasizes that the shared responsibility to take care that SGEIs can achieve their missions is assigned to the Union and the Member States, "each within their respective powers and within the scope of application of the Treaties", which reflects the principle of conferred powers provided for by Article 5(1) and (2) TEU, and the principle under Article 4(1) TEU that competences not conferred on the Union remain with the Member States. This delimitation of competence under the principle of conferral is not the only price that the Union has to pay for democracy, as the Union has also committed itself under Article 4(2) TEU to respect the national identities of Member States, inherent in their fundamental structures, political and constitutional, inclusive of regional and local self-government.[108]

[106]Weiler 2001, p. 6.

[107]See for instance Case C-205/99 *Analir* [2001] ECR I-1271, para 27, where the objective of territorial continuity was seen as a legitimate public interest.

[108]Lenaerts underlines that "Article 14 TFEU states that, when laying down the general principles and conditions underpinning the operation of SGEI, the EU legislator must comply with Article 4(2) TEU, which states that '[t]he Union shall respect the equality of Member States before the Treaties as well as their national identities'." See Lenaerts 2012, p. 1258.

In relation to SGEIs, respect for national identity was already mirrored in the CJEU's stance in the electricity cases that in view of the Member States interest to use certain undertakings as instruments of their economic policy, in particular in the public sector, they cannot be precluded, when defining the services of general economic interest which they entrust to certain undertakings, from taking account of objectives pertaining to their national policy or from endeavouring to attain them by means of obligations and constraints which they impose on such undertakings.[109]

Also, the principles enunciated in Articles 4 and 5 TEU are mirrored in Article 1 indent 1 of the SGI Protocol, which declares that national, regional and local authorities have a wide discretion in providing, commissioning and organising SGEIs. In that provision, their discretion is related to their essential role for SGEIs, but also to its exercise "as closely as possible to the needs of the users". This locution can be interpreted as suggesting that users' needs must conduct the SGEI's definition in order to legitimate the wide discretion permitted by EU law. If this understanding is correct, it is the local self-government's capacity to come close to the "general interest" which justifies that not only national, but also regional and local authorities enjoy a wide discretion. Also, in Article 1 dash 2 of the SGI Protocol, the Union characterizes as a "shared value" the diversity between various SGEIs and the differences in the needs and preferences of users that may result from different geographical, social or cultural situations, which may be seen as an illustration of its respect for the national identity of Member States.

This analysis shows that Article 14 TFEU and Article 1 indents 1 and 2 of the SGEI Protocol constitute a particular expression, related to SGEIs, of the EU's aim to promote democracy, and its obligation to respect the limits of its conferred powers, respect national identity, and local self-government. By spelling which powers Member States retain in relation to SGIs covered by EU rules on free movement and competition (SGEIs), Article 1 of the SGI Protocol mirrors the divide between competence and exercise of competence made by the CJEU in the formula of retained powers, already evoked in Sect. 2.5. The exercise of Member States' competence—as framed in the SGI Protocol—should allow them to achieve the SGEI missions resulting from a democratic bargain between them and their citizens.

3.2.2 SGEI: An Appropriate Instrument to Develop Public Services in a "Highly Competitive Social Market Economy"?

Given the constitutional links between SGEI and the Union's values and principles exposed above, regulations on the basis of Article 14 TFEU may *prima facie* be

[109]Case C-157/94 *Commission v Netherlands* [1997] ECR I-5699, para 40. It may be argued that this approach was developed in Case T-17/02 *Fred Olsen* v *Commission* [2005] ECR II-2031, para 216 and Case T-289/03 *BUPA* [2008] ECR II-81, para 66.

considered as "appropriate instruments commensurate with powers conferred on it by the Treaties" in the meaning of Article 3(6) TEU.[110] This could be argued to reflect that the concept of "market economy" in the former EC Treaty has been replaced by concept of "social market economy" in the post-Lisbon Treaties. Pursuant to Article 3(3) TEU, the Union must however establish the internal market on the basis of a *highly competitive* social market economy, and there is much incertitude on the role this concept will play for the evolution of EU law affecting welfare services in the Member States.

Neergaard and Nielsen hold that the concept of "social market economy" is related to the concept of "European Social Model" that was applied for the first time by the Commission in 1994, and had a predominant place in the Lisbon strategy formulated in 2000 as a compromise between the neo-liberal and the more socially-oriented governments of Member States. Unsurprisingly, given the considerable political, sociological and environmental mutations inside and outside the Member States, they find a lack of consensus among scholars on how the concept of "European Social Model" should be understood or defined.[111] As to what a world in a social market economy could be, it seems that there is not either any common or clear picture.[112]

Joerges and Rödl doubt that the Treaty concept of "social market economy" can bring about a social model at all. They remind us that the concept of a social market economy, ascribed to the German economist Alfred Müller-Armack, is deeply interwoven with ordo-liberalism, and they acknowledge that this model aims at infusing market economy with "social fabric". However, the concept of "social market economy" might, in their view, have been misunderstood by those who supported its introduction in the Treaties and might have regarded it as a constitutional principle imposing a "social Europe".[113] They contend namely that the model can only be realized in the counterfactual framework of state-like federalist competencies, and therefore they believe that "we won't get anything social out at all" of social market economy.[114] In contrast with such views, Neergaard believes that the concept of a social market economy has a potential to play an explicit and significant role in the future.[115] Also, Hettne considers the introduction of this

[110]It seems that Szyszczak reasons on a similar line, finding extraordinary that Article 14 TFEU confers a non-exclusive legislative competence on the Union in the field of SGEI although Article 4 TFEU does not mention SGEI as an area where the Union and Member States share competence. She notes however that indirectly there is shared competence in areas where SGEI may *contribute to Union policies* such as the internal market, social policy, the environment, etc., see Szyszczak 2014, p. 973.

[111]Neergaard and Nielsen 2010, p. 15–16.

[112]See Joerges and Rödl 2004, p. 11–12.

[113]Ibid., p. 15–16.

[114]Ibid., p. 21. The authors believed that "the socially engaged conventionists were victims of their own trap: omitting a reference to an equivalent of a European "social State", they choose "social market economy"—"to get "at least something social in".

[115]Neergaard 2013, p. 217.

concept to give renewed arguments justifying national rules and decisions restricting the freedoms promoted by the EU Treaties.[116] On a similar path, Jääskinen holds that the Treaty of Lisbon 2007/9 makes a social market economy an objective of the European Union.[117]

To assess the potential role of the concept, it seems important to place its introduction in the context of the European development, especially the decade 2000–2010. In view of the political turbulence accompanying the process of ratification of the Constitutional Treaty and the adoption of the Services Directive,[118] the drafters of the Treaty of Lisbon 2007/9 had arguably sensed the Member States' "market fatigue" before it was diagnosed by Mario Monti.[119] In order to rescue a broad adhesion to the European project, they may arguably have seen a need to distance the Union from the philosophy of the Single European Act 1986, when—in the lyrical words of AG Colomer—"competition was installed as the new deity on 'the altar of political ideas' and "public service has become an obstacle to be overcome in the name of a liberalisation on which all hopes were pinned".[120] It is difficult to ascertain whether this distancing was meant as a matter of rhetoric, or, of substance. De Vries holds that the concept of social market economy alludes to the fact that the European economic integration process should, at least, not be perceived as a "neo-liberal project".[121] As to Neergaard and Nielsen, they hold that "the importance of the European Social Model and the Social Market Economy primarily lies in the function of indicating that Europe is now heading in a different direction than what it originally did".[122] They also hold that the social dimension of the EU will make the European project more acceptable to some than when it was primarily defined as an economic project.

Neergaard and Nielsen seem to have very few doubts over the fact that the concept of a social market economy will change the direction of the EU project, which unavoidably implies a larger impact and at times limitations on the national organisation of welfare. They expect negative reactions, due to the uneven and

---

[116]Hettne considers that the Treaty of Lisbon, in particular through the social concerns its preamble expresses, provides new support for such argumentation. He underlines nevertheless that such argumentation must be conducted in the right contexts and in all available fora, both political and legal. He does not call for reinforcing judicialisation of politics, but instead a better understanding for EU's legal construction and a strategic adaptation to this construction. See Hettne 2011 p. 39.

[117]Jääskinen 2011, p. 599.

[118]Directive 2006/123/EC on services in the internal market.

[119]See Report of Mario Monti to the President of the European Commission José Manuel Barroso, 9 May 2010, "A New Strategy for the Single Market—At the service of Europe's economy and society", p. 6.

[120]See Opinion of AG Ruiz-Jalabo Colomer in Case C-265/08 *Federutility* [2010] ECR I-3377, para 2.

[121]De Vries 2013.

[122]Neergaard and Nielsen 2010, p. 15–16.

disputed legitimacy of EU to deal with welfare services.[123] In fact, it is submitted here that the expansion of EU law has already begun changing the direction of the EU project. The welfare systems of many Member States are already affected by EU law, and every Member State's social model is to some extent Europeanized, mainly under the impact of EU procurement and state aid rules. If this is agreed, the introduction of the concept of a "highly competitive social market economy" may be seen to a large extent as an acknowledgement of the fact that EU market law applies to national welfare systems, including social services, although the latter still are in the policy competence of the Member States. The concept may indicate that EU market law applying to social services has a special telos, but what this telos must be is unsaid.

There are indeed many shades of social fabric in a market economy, and the paradigm of a "highly competitive social market economy" is so open-ended that it can probably be used to justify varied models of regulation of welfare service markets including any of those shades.

In this regard it is interesting to quote Mario Monti's view in his Report to the former president of the Commission Manuel Barroso: "The single market today is less popular than ever, while Europe needs it more than ever".[124] Building partly on this Report, the Single Market Act 2011 adopted by the Commission underlines that the internal market is based on a "highly competitive social market economy", which reflects "the trend towards inclusive, socially fairer and environmentally sustainable growth". As a token of such a trend, the Commission takes that "[n]ew business models are being used, in which these societal concerns are taking precedence over the exclusive objective of financial profit".[125] While the existence of a trend for business pursuing, according to its *legal* statutes, societal concerns before profit-maximization needs empirical support, it seems that in Brussels the winds of the Single European Act 1986 still blow in the Single Market Act 2011, promoting a "social entrepreneurship" which in several Member States supposes a liberalization and privatization of welfare services. Also, as a part of its Social Business Initiative, the Commission has proposed a Regulation on European Social Entrepreneurship Funds, promoting the development of private funding of undertakings providing housing, healthcare, assistance for elderly or disabled persons, child care, access to employment and training as well as dependency management

[123]Neergaard and Nielsen 2010. Regarding EU's legitimacy to deal with welfare services, Neergaard and Nielsen refer to views put forward by Damjanovic and de Witte, see Damjanovic and de Witte 2009.

[124]See Report of Mario Monti to the President of the European Commission José Manuel Barroso, 9 May 2010, "A New Strategy for the Single Market—At the service of Europe's economy and society", p. 6.

[125]Communication from the Commission to the European Parliament, the Council, the Economic and Social Committee and the Committee of the Regions, Single Market Act, Twelve levers to boost growth and strengthen confidence, "Working together to create new growth" COM(2011)206 final, p. 14 (social entrepreneurship), p. 15.

on the market for investment funds.[126] In this approach, "social servicing" is seen as a vector for new undertaking and for growth, rather than primarily as a vector for cohesion and democratic self-determination. Thus, the initiatives elaborated by the Barroso Commission in the field of social services reflect already a certain vision of the European Social Model based on a "highly competitive social market economy", which promotes the development of welfare service markets, in particular social service markets.

In the absence of EU legislation specific to social services, the telos of applying EU market law to social services is undetermined. The EU concept of "highly competitive social market economy" may not be seen as determining this telos, because for these services, the policy powers (the primary "telos") are retained by the Member States. Therefore, a crucial factor in the process of précising the telos of EU market rules applied to social services may instead depend on the use made, or not made, by Member States and EU legislative and judicial institutions of the EU framework on SGEI. In other words, to know where the European Social Model is heading in the field of social services, it may be more enlightening to study what use Member States, the EU legislator and the CJEU make of Article 14 TFEU.

Evoking public consultations and an on-going dialogue with stakeholders, the Commission has signalled in the Communication on a SGI Quality Framework that it will continue to examine the need for legislation based on Article 14 TFEU, but that "the consensus at this stage seems to be that this not an immediate priority".[127] Also, the Commission explains that it finds more appropriate a sector approach, where tailor-made solutions can be found to concrete and specific problems in different sectors, and refers in this regard to its 2011 Package on state aid to SGEIs. This reference denotes that the Commission understands as a true imperative the need to legislate with regard to the Union's duty under Article 14 TFEU, requiring that the Union respects the Member States' retained powers and takes care that SGEIs *existing* in their legal systems operate on the basis of principles and conditions enabling them to fulfil their missions. The reference suggests also that the Commission regards the specific regime for social services in its 2011 state aid package as *related to* its duties under Article 14 TFEU. What is sure is that neither the injunction to adopt regulations on the basis of Article 14 TFEU nor the injunction to establish an internal market on the basis of a highly competitive social market economy model have lead EU institutions to legislate *explicitly* on the basis of Article 14 TFEU.

---

[126]See the Communication of the European Commission "Social Business Initiative—Creating a favourable climate for social enterprises, key stakeholders in the social economy and innovation", COM (2011) 682. This initiative has resulted in the proposal, not yet adopted, to lay down a common framework of rules imposed to investment funds wishing to use the designation "European Social Entrepreneurship Fund", see 2011/0418 (COD). It has also resulted in a proposal to reorient structural funds towards social enterprising.

[127]Commission, "A Quality Framework for Services of General Interest in Europe" (Communication to the European Parliament, the Council, the European Economic and Social Committee and the Committee of the Regions" COM(2011) 900 final, p. 5.

3.2.3 Conclusions

In this chapter, it has been shown how the debate urged by the absorption of national welfare systems by EU law has led to a new Treaty framework on SGEIs, consolidating and building on elements of the CJEU's case law, linked not only to the EU's fundamental values and missions, but also to a paradigm of multilevel governance, opening for pluralism in national welfare systems, in the respect of Member States' retained powers. The Treaty framework on SGEIs emerges rather evidently as a particular expression of the Union's foundational principles in Articles 2–6 TEU, which appear to establish a kind of social contract between the Union and its peoples. This appears to imply that, in the field of social services within the Member States' competence, the Union's legislative and judicial action must be guided by the values and principles of Articles 2 and 3 TEU, but also by the respect of social rights recognized by the EU Charter, of the limits of conferred competences, and of the national identity of the Member States, including local self-government.

The introduction of this strong "SGEI voice" in the post-Lisbon Treaties, with its core in Article 14 TFEU combining values of cohesion and a respect of Member States' retained competence, has installed the controversy on the development of the European Social Model at the heart of EU constitutional law. Consequently, although the EU has committed to a social market economy, and although Member States and the Union must, pursuant to Article 14 TFEU, adopt regulations providing for principles and conditions, in particular economic and financial, enabling SGEIs to achieve their missions, no such project seems envisaged for the time being, neither by the Commission nor by the Member States. Instead we have, in the frame of the SGI Quality Framework, a revised state aid package which excludes social services from the duty of prior notification, and revised procurement directives, including more substantive provisions on social services. There are also signs that social services are seen by the Commission as not only important for social cohesion but as a potential growth sector.

Yet Article 14 TFEU, as interpreted by the SGI Protocol, seems here to stay as a Treaty provision having horizontal relevance. Its normative value, already clear from the 2001 Laeken's declaration on the future of the Union,[128] cannot reasonably be denied, and as expressed by Ross, the first sentence of Article 14 TFEU is "a yardstick by which other measures and acts can be judged".[129] Even if the Union does not adopt regulations as intended by Article 14 TFEU, it has to address its normative message in its legislative, administrative and judicial practice. This became very clear when the Commission had to introduce exemptions for SGEIs and specific social services in the Services Directive, not only under pressure from

[128]SN 300/1/01 REV 1, Annex I, see in particular under the title "A better division and definition of competence in the European Union".

[129]Ross 2007, p. 1073.

a majority of the European Parliament members, but arguably also because Article 16 EC (now the first sentence of Article 14 TFEU) gave legal support to their claim that Member States' competence should be respected by the Union.[130] At the same time the Commission seems determined to keep control over the notion of SGEI for the purpose of the state aid rules, as evidenced by its use of the notion of "genuine SGEI" in the 2011 Package on state aid to SGEI, to delineate public service obligations that Member States may in its view attach to certain activities.[131]

Against this background, and unsurprisingly, it is to a large extent for the CJEU to show the way and clarify how EU law can "take care" that SGEIs can achieve their missions, in the respect of the Union's and the Member States' respective competence. Article 14 TFEU is a tricky yardstick to use, for several reasons. First, it is no secret that many political and economic experts, in particular in the Commission, favour a narrow understanding of the notion of SGEI, confined to its relevance for the Treaty rules on competition and state aid. The CJEU may have reasons to support this approach, but in Article 14 TFEU the notion of SGEI seems horizontal, in particular as Article 14 TFEU is a provision having general application. This may imply that SGEI must be understood as a *broad* EU concept, capable to have relevance in any part of EU law, in particular EU market law. The CJEU's approach of the concept is crucial for the present and future normative influence of Article 14 TFEU, and Chaps. 4 and 5 are devoted to analyse how the Court has shaped the concept, and as a consequence how it may be understood.

It appears that the meaning of the EU concept of SGEI is directly related to the type of test applied by the Court to assess the proportionality of national measures claimed to be necessary for the achievement of public service missions. Indeed, the lenient proportionality test applied by the Court in certain free movement cases related to social services, not requiring the least restrictive measure and not excluding that economic considerations are weighed in the test, is often an indication of its acknowledgment that SGEI missions are at hand. This test is examined in the next chapter.

Explicitly or not, the CJEU must interpret and enforce the normative elements of Article 14 TFEU, as it is its duty under the rule of law and the principle of sincere cooperation.[132] However, when it strives at loyally implementing the first sentence of Article 14 TFEU in its case law, the Court goes on a very tight rope. If it is too explicit in shaping the contours of the concept of SGEI, it may satisfy certain Member States but at the same time deeply frustrate others. Also, if the Court does not leave the concept of SGEI in the shadows of uncertainty, it may render very divisive the other EU institutions' approach of Article 14 TFEU in EU legislation.

---

[130]See European Parliament legislative resolution P6_TA (2006) 0061 on the proposal for a directive of the European Parliament and of the Council on services in the internal market (2004/0001(COD).

[131]Communication from the Commission, European Union Framework for State aid in the form of public service compensation (2011) 2012/C 8/03, para 13. More on this in section 11.2.2.3.

[132]Pursuant to Article 4(3) TEU.

Finally, as legislation on SGEI principles and rules is supposed to take place in the form of regulations,[133] a risk, if the Court develops principles and conditions for the application of EU rules on free movement and procurement too explicitly motivated by the existence of SGEI missions, is that the process of legislative developments made necessary by its case law become politically conflictual, and perhaps hampered. It will be seen in chapter 11 that, with the support of the Court's "nuanced approach", the Commission and the EU legislator have been able to incorporate "Article 14 TFEU-rules" (by which is meant rules motivated by the norm promulgated in this Article), in the revised procurement rules in a discreet manner, which allows maintaining the lock on the Pandora's box of the application of Article 106(2) TFEU to procurement.

References

Azoulai L (2011) The 'Retained Powers' formula in the case law of the European Court of Justice: EU Law as Total Law? Eur J Legal Stud 4(2)

Bekkedal T (2011) Article 106 TFEU is dead. Long live Article 106! In: Szyszczak E et al (eds) Developments in services of general interest. T.M.C. Asser Press, The Hague

Buendia Sierra JL (1999) Exclusive rights and state monopolies under EC law. Oxford University Press, Oxford

Craig P, De Búrca G (2008) EU law text, cases and materials, 4th edn. Oxford University Press, Oxford

Damjanovic D, de Witte B (2009) Welfare integration through EU law: the overall picture in the light of the Lisbon Treaty. In: Neergaard U, Nielsen R, Roseberry L (eds) Integrating welfare functions into EU law—from Rome to Lisbon. DJØF Publishing, Copenhagen

Dann P (2006) Thoughts on a methodology of European constitutional law. German Law J 06(11)

Davies G (2006a) Subsidiarity: the wrong idea, in the wrong place, at the wrong time. (2006) 43 C.M.L.Rev. 63, 63

Delors J (1986) The single act and Europe: a moment of truth. Office for Official Publications of the European Communities, Luxembourg

De Vries SA (2013) The protection of fundamental rights within Europe's internal market after Lisbon—An endeavour for more harmony. In: de Vries S, Bernitz U, Weatherill S (eds) The protection of fundamental rights in the EU after Lisbon. Bloomsbury Publishing, London

De Witte B et al (2010) Legislation after Lisbon, New Opportunities for the European Parliament, EUI paper. http://www.eui.eu/Projects/EUDO/Documents/EUDO-LegislatingafterLisbon(SD).pdf

Due O (1998) The impact of the Amsterdam treaty upon the court of justice. Fordham Int Law J 22(6) Article 4

Duff A (1997) The treaty of Amsterdam. The Federal Trust, Sweet and Maxwell, London

Duguit L (1923) Traité de droit constitutionnel, tome 2. Sirey, Paris

Durkheim E (1893) De la division du travail: Etude sur l'Organisation des Sociétés Supérieures, Livre I-III Division of labor in society: A Study of the Organisation of Advanced Societies, 1997, Halls WD (trans), Coser LA (introd). Free Press, New York

Edwardsson E (2003) Konkurrenslagen och konkurrensbegränsande offentliga regleringar. Uppsala universitet

[133]Pursuant to the second sentence of Article 14 TFEU.

Groussot X, Pech L, Peturson GT (2011) The Scope of Application of Fundamental Rights on Member States Action: in search of Certainty in EU Adjudication. Eric Stein Working Paper 1/2011

Hatzopoulos V (2012) Regulating services in the European Union. Oxford University Press, Oxford

Hettne J (2011) Kan Lissabonfördraget minska EU:s sociala underskott? In: Bertola G, Hettne J, Scharpf FW and Tarschys D (eds) Är EU en social marknadsekonomi, Sociala Europa – en antologi, Svenska Institutet for Europapolitiska Studier (SIEPS) 2011:2, pp 21–38

Joerges C, Rödl F (2004) "Social Market Economy" as Europe's Social Model. EUI Working Paper Law 2004/8. European University Institute, Florence

Jääskinen N (2011) The New Rules on SGEI. EStAL 4/2011

Lenaerts K (2012) Defining the concept of "Services of General Interest" in Light of the "Checks and Balances" set out in the EU Treaties. Jurisprudencija/Jurisprudence 2012, 19 (4):1247–1267

Micklitz HW (2010) Failure or ideological preconceptions—thoughts on two grand projects: the European constitution and the European Civil Code. EUI Working Papers Law 2010/04. European University Institute, Florence

Neergaard U (2013) The concept of SSGI and the asymmetries between free movement and competition law. In: Neergaard et al (eds) Social services of general interest in the EU. T.M.C. Asser Press, The Hague

Neergaard U, Nielsen R (2010) Blurring boundaries: from the Danish welfare state to the European social model? http://ssrn.com/abstract=1618758S. Accessed 31 Dec 2015

Pernice I (2009) The treaty of Lisbon: multilevel constitutionalism in action. Walter Hallstein Institut für Europäisches Verfassungsrecht, Paper 2/09. Humboldt-Universität, Berlin

Prosser T (2005) The limits of competition law: markets and public services. Oxford University Press, Oxford

Rodrigues S (2009) Towards a general EC framework instrument related to SGEI? In: Krajewski M, Neergaard U, van de Gronden JW (eds) The changing legal framework for services of general interest in europe, between competition and solidarity. T.M.C. Asser Press, The Hague

Ross M (2007) Promoting solidarity: from public services to a European model of competition? Common Market Law Rev 44(4):1057–1080

Ross M (2009) A healthy approach to services of general economic interest? The BUPA judgment of the Court of First Instance. European Law Review, February 2009, pp 127–140

Rossi LS (2008) How fundamental are fundamental principles? Primacy and fundamental rights after Lisbon. Oxford J Yearb Eur Law 27(1):65–87

Scharpf FW (2009) The double asymmetry of European integration or: why the EU cannot be a social market economy max planck institute for the study of societies. MPlfG Working Paper 09/12

Szyszczak E (2013) Soft law and safe havens. In: Neergaard et al (eds) Social services of general interest in the EU. T.M.C. Asser Press, The Hague

Szyszczak E (2014) Article 36: access to services of general economic interest. In: Steve P et al (eds) The EU charter of fundamental rights: a commentary. CH Beck Hart Nomos, Oxford, pp 969–982

Van de Gronden JW (2013) Free movement of services and the right of establishment: does EU internal market law transform the provision of SSGI? In Neergaard et al (eds) Social services of general interest in the EU. T.M.C. Asser Press, The Hague

Von Bogdandy A (2010) Founding principles of EU law: a theoretical and doctrinal sketch. European Law J 16(2)

Weiler JHH (2001) Federalism and Constitutionalism: Europe's Sonderweg. In: Nicolaidis K, Howse R (eds) The federal vision: legitimacy and levels of governance in the US and the EU. Oxford University Press, Oxford

Wipfelder HJ (1986) Die verfassungsrechtliche Kodifizierung sozialer Grundrechte. Zeitschrift für Rechtspolitik 1986(19):140–149

Chapter 4
SGEI as a Ground for a Special Regime in the Case Law of the CJEU Related to Public Services

Abstract This chapter studies the CJEU's understanding of the EU concept of SGEI. It examines first how the Court has shaped principles and conditions for the application of EU market rules to public services in its case law directly related to Article 106(2) TFEU, and developed under this provision a "balancing test" where financial and economic conditions allowing public service missions to be achieved may be taken into consideration. The second part of this chapter shows how the Court has transposed its "Article 106(2) TFEU balancing test" to free movement and procurement cases, which gives a "horizontal dimension" to this test. This analysis shows that the CJEU understands the first sentence of Article 14 TFEU—and the SGI Protocol interpreting it—as spelling a principle which is normative for all EU market law. It is concluded that the Court, albeit discreetly, has begun shaping the EU concept of SGEI as a broad concept of EU constitutional law, overarching Article 14 TFEU and Article 106(2) TFEU.

Contents

C. Wehlander, *Services of General Economic Interest as a Constitutional Concept of EU Law*, Legal Issues of Services of General Interest,
DOI 10.1007/978-94-6265-117-3_4

This chapter builds on the conclusions in Chap. 3 that Article 14 TFEU, compared to the objective of "highly competitive social market economy", constitutes a more concrete and substantial obligation for the Union, that this obligation has a high dignity in relation to the obligation to establish the internal market because of the many links between SGEI principles and foundational principles of the Union, and that Article 14 TFEU, although its relation to Article 106(2) TFEU has to be clarified, suggests that SGEI is a broad EU concept, which makes EU's mission to take care of SGEI missions relevant in any part of EU law.

On this basis, the present chapter addresses two legal issues which very much seem to be related. The first one is the scope of the SGEI rule in Article 106(2) TFEU. The provision has been applied to justify restrictions of the rights to free movement, but it is uncertain whether Article 106(2) TFEU applies, and technically can apply, to EU procurement rules. The second issue is what motivates the Court to decide that SGEIs' proportionate public funding needs no derogation from state aid rules under Article 106(2) TFEU, or to modify its standard test for overriding reasons related to the general interest, with characteristic elements of the lenient test it has developed under Article 106(2) TFEU, when it examines whether national measures restricting fundamental freedoms may be justified by their role for the achievement of Member States' public service missions.[1] These judicial steps seem to signal that "public service obligations" (the Court's less politically sensitive term for SGEI tasks) enjoy a higher dignity than mere "imperative reasons of general interest" in the balance with any Treaty market rule, including the rules protecting the freedom of trade, because they express a particularly strong commitment of Member States to their policy objectives, and because this commitment is seen as legitimate in EU law. The overall question addressed by this chapter is whether the Court's approach of deference to Member States' definition, organisation and financing of public service obligations may be regarded as the Court's interpretation and application of Article 14 TFEU on SGEI, formerly Article 16 EC.

The general approach chosen is to put in parallel the CJEU's test under Article 106(2) TFEU and cases where the Court explicitly or implicitly deems the activity at issue to be subject to public service obligations and at the same time shows

---

[1]It is important to be aware that these legal issues have legal-political significance: at surface level opinions may diverge on the scope of Article 106(2) TFEU, while at a deeper level, they may diverge on which relevance a relaxed proportionality test *should* have for conflicts between national measures and the fundamental freedoms. See for instance, Bekkedal 2011.

a particularly deferential approach of Member States', or their public authorities' appreciation of which measure is needed to achieve the general interest objective, called here its "SGEI-related case law".

Section 4.1 examines the characteristic features of the CJEU's interpretation of what it still calls "the derogation rule" for SGEI in Article 106(2) TFEU, showing that it gives a wide discretion to Member States' definition of SGEIs, and conducts in many cases a lenient test to review national measures, reflecting a *reconciliation* of economic and non-economic interests rather than a *derogation* from EU market rules interpreted restrictively. It also looks at the de facto scope of Article 106(2) TFEU and at the requirement of entrustment of the SGEI tasks protected by this provision. The purpose is not only to show how "Article 106(2) TFEU works", but also that the CJEU has found this derogation/reconciliation rule appropriate for very varied fields of activity and policy objectives, and applicable outside EU competition law. The material studied is the CJEU's case law actualizing the application of Article 106(2) TFEU, and the purpose being to describe valid law, an EU legal method is used.

Section 4.2 examines a number of "SGEI-related cases" where the Court has not applied Article 106(2) TFEU, but explicitly or implicitly transposed its normative elements into the definition of EU market law concepts such as "public contract" or "state aid", or into the proportionality test applied under the rule of reason. The method is primarily legal in the sense that it strives at identifying valid EU law. It does so on the basis of the CJEU's case law, as it is in practice the decisive source of law concerning the standards of review affecting national measures related to public services. The intention is not to conduct an exhaustive analysis of all relevant cases, but instead to gather cases capable of illustrating how, in the fields of state aid, free movement and procurement law, the Court seems to combine characteristic features of its test under Article 106(2) TFEU—namely the relevance of acceptable economic conditions and/or a lighter proportionality test—and the existence in the case of "public service obligations" incumbent on undertakings or public authorities, arguably a corollary of SGEIs.[2] In some cases, it is indicated whether the judgment was delivered post Treaty of Amsterdam 1997 or post Treaty of Lisbon 2007/9, in order to show that the Court's approach may be related to the introduction of Article 16 EC, and later of a more comprehensive framework on SGEIs centred on Article 14 TFEU.

The approach in Sect. 4.2 is normative, in the sense that it is based on a view that legal scholarship is not bound by the Court's motives to avoid being too clear on what the EU notion of SGEI may mean, in particular because SGEIs have now a central place in the EU legal system's approach to public service systems in the

[2]This observation does not seem new. Thus, commenting on the Court's relaxed proportionality test in *Freskot* an in *Kattner Stahlbau*, Van de Gronden observes that the CJEU has apparently transplanted its "*Corbeau* approach" of Article 106(2) TFEU into its case law on free movement and social security and related this approach to the role played by solidarity in the financial sustainability of social security schemes. See Van de Gronden 2013a, p. 142.

Member States. As the Court is often in the difficult position to decide on the compliance with EU law of national measures related to activities under Member States' competence, it is not questioned here that it may have legitimate reasons to be cautious and avoid saying openly what it is doing. Indeed, delineating the concept of SGEI is a controversial political act which does not ideally belong to the judicial sphere, as an openly broad delineation of the concept may probably have effects on the integration of the internal market and on the process of disintegration of national welfare systems. Therefore, it may arguably be convenient for the Court to use the language of "public service tasks" instead of the term SGEI to fulfil the duty to respect Article 14 TFEU in applying the Treaty market rules to public services.[3]

Legal scholarship does not have to follow this cautious path and may instead contribute to place the Treaties in a more open democratic light. Interestingly, it seems that the Commission perceives the CJEU's decisions on in-house procurement and public-public cooperation as part of the "SGEI acquis", as it provides explanations on these lines of case law in its 2013 SGEI Guide.[765] Thus, although these decisions neither mention Article 106(2) TFEU nor the concept of SGEI, the Commission appears to see them as relevant for the achievement of SGEI missions, although it remains to be *explained why and how, which this study may provide some answers.*

4.1 The Case Law of the CJEU Directly Based on Article 106(2) TFEU

The provision in what is now Article 106(2) TFEU raises passion in legal literature. Davies describes Article 106 TFEU as "a messy article, full of ambiguities, which has become redundant, and is positively malignant", "an unnecessary Cassandra, promising protection from threats that do not exist", that "adds nothing to what is already inherent to economic law itself".[4] In his view, "[t]he Treaty, and society, would be better if it was gone".[5] In sharp contrast with Davies, Wernicke contests the view that Article 106(2) TFEU is superfluous, and underlines that both this provision and Article 14 TFEU are regularly used in practice, offering "unique guidance for both the Commission and the Court in the solution of conflicts between competition aims and social demands without requiring any innate hierarchy between these fields".[6] This section examines judgments of the CJEU directly founded on the application of Article 106(2) TFEU, and focuses on the following aspects:

- The tasks which the CJEU has admitted to constitute SGEI tasks in the meaning of Article 106(2) TFEU

[3]As observed by Davies, there is more going on in the case law than judges choose to say. See Davies 2010, p. 120.

[4]Davies 2009, pp. 51, 58, and 67.

[5]Davies 2009, p. 67.

[6]Wernicke 2009, p. 70.

- The scope of Article 106(2) TFEU, i.e. the Treaty principles and rules in relation to which restrictions necessitated by SGEI tasks can be justified
- The CJEU's standard in reviewing whether a measure infringing a Treaty market rule may be justified by SGEI tasks and finally
- The form and the function of the requirement of "entrustment" of SGEI tasks in Article 106(2) TFEU.

4.1.1 SGEI in the Meaning of Article 106(2) TFEU: Only Control of Manifest Error

The EU concept of SGEI tasks is not defined in EU law but only subject to a control of manifest error by the Commission or the Court, and thus the only guidance on what SGEIs may be is found in the casuistic law making of the Court, which shows that they may be found in many activities, starting with public infrastructure. In the field of postal services, the Court considered in *Corbeau* that "the obligation to collect, carry and distribute mail on behalf of all users throughout the territory of the Member State concerned, at uniform tariffs and on similar quality conditions, irrespective of the specific situations or the degree of economic profitability of each operation" constituted an SGEI. In *Deutsche Post*, the Belgian state-owned La Poste was not only universal postal service operator, but also responsible for numerous "tasks of public interest, including basic banking activities open to all, the delivery of press materials at reduced rates, the delivery of printed electoral materials, the payment of pensions at home, the sale of fishing licences and the receipt of administrative fines".[7]

In the field of energy, the CJEU admitted in *Almelo* that an undertaking had to fulfil SGEI tasks when obliged to ensure, for all the territory it had been granted a concession for, that "all consumers, whether local distributors or end-users, receive uninterrupted supplies of electricity in sufficient quantities to meet demand at any given time, at uniform tariff rates and on terms which may not vary save in accordance with objective criteria applicable to all customers".[8] In the so called "electricity cases" the Court regarded as SGEI tasks

- To contribute, through the planning for which it is responsible, to the proper functioning of a national system for electricity supply on the basis of costs that are as low as possible and in a socially responsible manner,[9]
- To supply energy on the basis of cost and price containment such as to guarantee the balanced economic development of the country,[10]

[7]Case T-388/03 *Deutsche Post* [2009] ECR II-199, para 3. It is unsure whether these "tasks of public interest", accompanying the universal postal service, were seen by the GC as SGEI tasks.

[8]Case C-393/92 *Almelo* [1994] ECR I-01477 paras 48–49.

[9]Case C-157/94 *Commission v Netherlands* [1997] ECR I-05699, para 55.

[10]Case C-158/94 *Commission v Italy* [1997] ECR I-5789, paras 51 and 60.

- To supply all customers, in the case of [the electricity provider] throughout the national territory and, in the case of [the gas provider], in the areas served; ensuring continuity of supply; and observing equal treatment between customers.[11]

Regarding public service TV broadcasting, the CJEU recognized in *Sacchi* that Member States could legitimately define a broadcasting SGEI task to include the broadcast of full-spectrum programming.[12] This was reaffirmed in *SIC v Commission* by the General Court, interpreting the statement in the Amsterdam Protocol 1997 that 'the system of public broadcasting in the Member States is directly related to the democratic, social and cultural needs of each society and to the need to preserve media pluralism',[13] as a direct reference made by the Member States to public service broadcasting systems introduced by them and entrusted with broadcasting full-spectrum television programmes for the benefit of the entire population of those States.[14] In *TV2* the General Court allowed a wide and qualitative definition of the public service mission, such as to "provide the entire Danish population with varied programming that satisfies the requirements of quality, versatility and diversity".[15]

SGEI tasks exist in the field of water services and waste management, which is underlined in the Services Directive.[16] In these fields, many tasks of general interest are imposed by EU law on the Member States in EU secondary law enacted on the basis of Article 192 TFEU. In *FFAD* the CJEU stated that the management of particular waste may properly be considered to be capable of forming the subject of a service of general economic interest, *particularly* where the service is designed to deal with an environmental problem.[17] The Court held that "the task of processing building waste produced in that municipality and of receiving and

[11]Case C-159/94 *Commission v France* [1997] ECR I-5815, para 61 compared with para 83. The considerations put forward by the French Government did not support the conclusion that the state-owned EDF was under an obligation to seek to secure the most competitive tariffs and the lowest costs for the community. It seems that the Court implicitly drew the conclusion that the latter tasks could therefore not be seen as SGEI missions in the meaning of Article 90(2). As this question is connected to the requirement of entrustment in Article 106(2) TFEU, it is further discussed under Sect. 8.1.4.

[12]Case 155/73 *Sacchi* [1974] ECR 409, final ruling point 1, where the exclusive right granted by a Member State to an undertaking to make all kinds of television transmissions, even for advertising purposes, could breach the rules of competition and be incompatible with the Treaties unless justified under Article 90(2) (now Article 106(2) TFEU).

[13]The Amsterdam Protocol was introduced by the Treaty of Amsterdam as an annex to the EC Treaty OJ 1997 C 340, p. 109.

[14]Case T-442/03, *SIC v Commission* [2008] ECR II-1161, para 201.

[15]Joined Cases T-309/04, T-317/04, T-329/04 and T-336/04, *TV 2/Danmark A/S and Others v Commission* [2008] ECR II-2935, paras 122–124.

[16]See Article 17(1) (d-e) of Directive 2006/123/EC of the European Parliament and of the Council of 12 December 2006 on Services in the Internal Market [2006] OJ L 376/36.

[17]Case C-209/98 *Sydhavnens Grus och Sten*, [2000] ECR I-3743, para 76.

processing that waste so that it can be reused as far as possible" constituted an SGEI task. In *ZT*, the General Court seemed unsure as to whether the obligation to maintain a spare capacity if an epidemic broke out constituted an SGEI entrusted to a German public law association in charge of collecting and disposing of dead animals (*ZT*).[18]

SGEI tasks can be found in the field of maritime infrastructure, for instance the task of ensuring the navigability of a State's important waterway[19] or as in *Corsica Ferries,* the obligation for mooring groups to provide at any time and to any user a universal mooring service.[20] The Court has, however, underlined that commercial ports do not operate SGEIs if they are not imposed with any public service tasks.[21]

The Court has recognized SGEIs in several social sectors. In *Glöckner* the Court regarded as an SGEI task the "obligation to provide a permanent standby service of transporting sick or injured persons in emergencies throughout the territory concerned, at uniform rates and on similar quality conditions, without regard to the particular situations or to the degree of economic profitability of each individual operation".[22] In *Hanner* the Court did not question that "to contribute to the protection of public health by guaranteeing access for the Swedish population to medicinal products" could constitute an SGEI task.[23] In *Ferring*, the Court regarded as SGEI tasks the pharmaceuticals wholesalers' obligation, according to French law, to "keep in stock a range of medicines comprising at least nine tenths of all forms of medicines currently sold in France" and to be able in particular to (a) to satisfy at all times the needs of its regular customers for a period of at least two weeks and (b) to deliver any medicine in its range within 24 h of receipt of the relevant order.[24] In *Höfner* the Court considered as an SGEI task the activity of "bringing prospective employees into contact with employers and administering unemployment benefits, the general aim of this activity being to achieve and maintain a high level of employment, constantly to improve job distribution and thus to promote economic growth".[25]

[18]Case T-309/12, Zweckverband Tierkorperbeseitigung in Rheinland-Pfalz v Commission, EU:T:2014:676, paras 118-125 compared to para 127.

[19]Case 10/71 *Muller and Others* [1971] ECR 723, para 11.

[20]Case C-266/96 *Corsica Ferries* [1998] ECR I-3949, para 45.

[21]Case C-242/95 *GT-Link* [1997] ECR I-4449, para 52.

[22]Case C-475/99 *Ambulanz Glöckner* [2001] ECR I-8089, para 55.

[23]See Opinion of AG Léger in Case C-438/02 *Krister Hanner* [2005] ECR I-04551, paras 148 and 150. The Advocate General reminded that the Court had accepted that the need to guarantee that medicinal products are widely available and sufficient to meet the requirements of the population constitutes a public interest aim pursuant to Article 30 EC, referring in particular to Case C-322/01 *Deutscher Apothekerverband* [2003] ECR I-14887, paras 106 and 107.

[24]Case C-53/00 *Ferring* [2001] ECR I-9067, paras 7 and 33.

[25]See Case C-41/90 *Höfner* [1991] ECR I-1979, paras 3 and 24. A similar activity of "intermediate between supply of and demand for paid employment was considered as a SGEI in Case C-55/96 *Job Center II* [1997] ECR I-07119, paras 4 and 26.

In *BUPA* the General Court held that Member States have a wide discretion to determine the nature and scope of an SGEI mission in areas where EU has no, or only limited, competence, and where the Member States retain their competence. This prerogative was confirmed by

1. The fact that Member States definition of SGEIs can be questioned by the Commission only in the event of a manifest error, as clear from *Fred Olsen* v *Commission*[26]
2. The absence of any competence specially attributed to the Commission
3. The absence of a precise and complete definition of the concept of SGEI in Community law
4. The "division of powers" emphasized in Article 16 EC (now first sentence of Article 14 TFEU).[27]

The principle of conferral and the EU's restricted powers in the field of health care pursuant to Article 152(1) EC, imply that the Community can only engage in not legally binding action in that sector. The Court underlined that the Member States govern the organisation and provision of health services and medical care, and may also, at least *primarily*, define SGEI obligations in that sector. The Court found admissible the Commission's view that obligations imposed on all insurers active on the Irish private medical insurance (PMI) market, designed "to ensure that all persons living in Ireland would receive a minimum level of PMI services at an affordable price and on similar quality conditions" constituted SGEI tasks in the meaning of Article 106(2) TFEU.[28] To be authorized to offer PMI in Ireland, operators had an open enrolment obligation, a lifetime cover obligation, a community rating obligation and an obligation to provide minimum benefits.[29] Member States' wide discretion to define SGEIs in their areas of competence was reaffirmed by the GC in *TV2*.[30] It is important to note that Article 1 first indent of the SGI Protocol does not mention a wide discretion to *define* SGEIs. This is arguably due to the fact that, in areas where the EU has been conferred powers, this freedom is potentially or de facto restricted.

In *BUPA*, the General Court had two important points of departure. First, it made a distinction between the general interest "in a broad sense" and SGEIs in the meaning of Article 106(2) TFEU, considering that "[t]he mere fact that the national legislature, acting in the general interest in the broad sense, imposes certain rules of authorisation, of functioning or of control on all the operators in a particular

[26]Case T-17/02 *Fred Olsen* v *Commission* [2005] ECR II-2031, para 216 and case-law there cited.

[27]Case T-289/03 *BUPA* [2008] ECR II-81, paras 166–169.

[28]Ibid., para 41.

[29]PMI insurers were obliged to offer a PMI contract to any person requesting such a contract, not to reject the policy-holders when they became sick or old, to apply the same premium to all policy-holders for the same type of product, irrespective of their health status, age or sex, and to offer PMI products respecting certain minimum quality standards, although they were free to design their insurance products[789].

[30]Case T-309/04 *TV2* [2008] ECR II-2935, paras 113 *et seq.*

sector does not in principle mean that there is an SGEI mission".[31] Second, the GC held that the existence of SGEI tasks is not precluded because all providers of a given service are subject to certain obligations determined by law.[32] This involves arguably that the Court made a distinction between the question of the objective existence of an SGEI task and the question of its *individual* entrustment.

The GC found that the Irish legislation at issue could not be regarded as a regulation or authorisation of PMI insurers' activity, but constituted an act of public authority defining a specific *mission* consisting in the provision of PMI services in compliance with the PMI obligations. The reason was that it "define[d] in detail the PMI obligations, such as community rating, open enrolment, lifetime cover and minimum benefits, to which all PMI insurers within the meaning of that legislation [were] subject" and that these PMI obligations "restrict[ed] the commercial freedom of the PMI insurers to an extent going considerably beyond ordinary conditions of authorisation to exercise an activity in a specific sector", with the general interest objective to allow (at the time) about half of the Irish population to benefit from alternative cover for certain health care, in particular hospital care.[33]

4.1.2 Standard of Review Under Article 106(2) TFEU: From Derogation to Balance

The CJEU's application of the proportionality test under Article 106(2) TFEU has been described by Buendia Sierra as "one of the most controversial areas of Community law", and is subject to abundant analysis in legal literature.[34] In this regard, Article 106(2) TFEU can be seen as consisting of three affirmations:

a. Undertakings entrusted with SGEI are, as other undertakings, "subject to the rules contained in the Treaties, in particular the rules on competition".

---

[31]Case T-289/03 *BUPA* [2008] ECR II-81, para 178.

[32]Ibid., para 180.

[33]Ibid., para 182.

[34]Buendia-Sierra delivered in 1999 a particularly extensive review of the evolution of the application and perception of the proportionality test, whose interpretation has in his opinion constituted "the main legal-political battleground in the field of Article 86" (now Article 106 TFEU), see Buendia Sierra 1999, pp. 300–355. Sauter observes that what he calls a "mild test" (manifestly disproportionate) has often been applied by the CJEU under Article 106(2) but that the more traditional "strict test" (least restrictive means) seems relevant in the presence of a common policy, see Sauter 2008, pp. 186–188. The Court's test under Article 106(2) TFEU has been described as "flexible enough to allow the Court to identify illegitimate uses of Article 86(2), while being less intrusive than that of proportionality" by Baquero-Cruz, who also held that "[a] single test should apply to all these situations once it is clear that an undertaking has been entrusted with a task of general economic interest", a view which does not really fit with the findings of the present section, see Baquero-Cruz 2005, pp. 197–198; see also Stergiou 2008, p. 183; and Lenaerts, who observes that, in the absence of harmonizing measures, the CJEU applies a soft version of the principle of proportionality, while it applies a rather strict version of the principle of proportionality, where the EU legislator has adopted harmonizing measures, see Lenaerts 2012, p. 1259.

b. The Treaty rules, in particular the competition rules, apply only inasmuch as they do not obstruct the fulfilment of the SGEI tasks entrusted.
c. This balancing is constrained, as "the development of trade must not be affected to an extent that would be contrary to the interests of the Union".

The Court has generally qualified Article 106(2) TFEU as a *derogation* rule[35] and there is a perception in scholarly literature that this provision must normally be interpreted restrictively.[36] Indeed, the CJEU has underlined that Member States have the burden of proof for the existence of SGEIs which they rely on to justify derogations from EU market rules. However, this *strict* approach seems necessary to objectify the existence of a public service *obligation* which EU institutions are not in a position to know about, rather than a sign that Article 106(2) TFEU should be interpreted *restrictively*. In fact, the CJEU's rhetoric on the derogatory character of Article 106(2) TFEU is subtle. In *Commission v Netherlands* the Court stated both that the provision must, as a derogation from the Treaties, be interpreted *strictly*, and that "exemptions to the Treaty rules are permitted provided that they are necessary for performance of the particular tasks assigned to an undertaking entrusted with the operation of a service of general economic interest".[37] The Court went further in *Commission v France* and stated that "[i]n allowing derogations to be made from the general rules of the Treaty on certain conditions, [Article 106(2) TFEU] seeks to reconcile the Member States' interest in using certain undertakings, in particular in the public sector, as an instrument of economic or fiscal policy with the Community's interest in ensuring compliance with the rules on competition and the preservation of the unity of the Common Market."[38]

In *Commission v Netherlands*, the Court added that "[t]he Member States' interest being so defined, they cannot be precluded, when defining the services of general economic interest which they entrust to certain undertakings, from taking account of objectives pertaining to their national policy or from endeavouring to attain them by means of obligations and constraints which they impose on such undertakings". [39] Thus, in *Commission v Netherlands*, the Court maintained the derogation rhetoric—implying a *strict* approach regarding in particular the burden of proof on the existence of an SGEI task—but introduced the idea that the

[35]See for instance Case C-159/94 *Commission v France* [1997] I-5815, para 12; Case C-393/92 *Almelo* [1994] ECR I-1477, para 26; Case C-67/96 *Albany* [1999] ECR I-5751, para 103, Case C-209/98 *FFAD* [2000] ECR I-3743, para 31.

[36]Sauter 2008, p. 26.

[37]Case 157/94 *Commission v Netherlands*, [1997] ECR I-5699, paras 37–38. In para 31, the Court held that the provision lays down the conditions in which undertakings entrusted with the operation of SGEI may *exceptionally* not be subject to the Treaty rules.

[38]Case C-202/88 *France v Commission* [1991] ECR I-1223, para 12. Later this reference was often made by the Court, see for instance Case C-242/10 *Enel Produzione* [2011] ECR I-13665, para 41.

[39]Case C-157/94 *Commission v Netherlands* [1997] ECR I-5699, paras 39–40.

provision in Article 106(2) EU is *not a restrictive* derogation rule, as it aims at *reconciling two legitimate interests*, the definition of SGEI tasks and their entrustment to certain undertakings being a legitimate manner for Member States to pursue national policy objectives within their competence. It is argued here that the derogatory character of Article 106(2) TFEU is expressed by the constraint in element (c) above: the development of trade must not be affected to an extent that would be contrary to the interests of the Union, a constraint which seems open-ended and gives EU institutions much discretion. Also, the constraint's effect may depend on how the Union's trade interests are defined in the Treaties. At any rate, the Court's test under Article 106(2) TFEU shows two specific features.

First, it seems settled law that proportional exemptions from the application of Treaty rules may be justified to secure the fulfilment of SGEI tasks under "economically acceptable conditions".[40] This position was first formulated in *Corbeau*, and retained later.[41] The Court clarified in *Albany* that a measure may be seen as necessary if, in the absence of the measure at issue, it would not be possible for the undertaking to perform the particular tasks entrusted to it, under economically acceptable conditions; thus, it is not necessary that the financial balance or economic viability of the undertaking entrusted with the operation of a service of general economic interest is threatened.[42] In *Glöckner*, the Court of Justice admitted that to perform its obligation in conditions of economic equilibrium, the undertaking entrusted with an SGEI task can offset profitable sectors against the profitable sectors, which justifies a restriction of competition from individual undertakings in economically profitable sectors (cross-subsidization), justified under Article 106(2) TFEU.[43]

In *Almelo*, the Court went further and stated that restrictions on competition from other economic operators *must be* allowed if they are necessary to enable the undertaking entrusted with an SGEI task to perform it. In that regard, insisted the Court, "it is necessary to take into consideration the economic conditions in which the undertaking operates, in particular the costs which it has to bear and the legislation, particularly concerning the environment, to which it is subject".[44] This wording suggests that "economically acceptable conditions" is not seen as a derogation, but rather as an inherent part of what market-based supply of services of general interest normally requires. Thus, this wording in *Almelo* is arguably close to the wording of the first sentence of Article 14 TFEU (former Article 16 EC), which allows an argument that its "spirit" was in fact consolidated in Article 16 EC, and later clarified by the addition of the words "particularly economic and financial conditions" in the first sentence of Article 14 TFEU. Besides being an

---

[40]Case C-320/91 *Corbeau* [1993] ECR I-2533, para 16.

[41]Ibid., paras 14–16.

[42]Case C-67/96 *Albany* [1999] ECR I-5751, para 107.

[43]Case C-475/99 *Ambulanz Glöckner* [2001] ECR I-8089, para 57.

[44]Case C-393/92 *Almelo* [1994] ECR I-1477, para 49.

interesting case of reciprocal influence of Treaty-based law and judge-made law, this supports the view that the first sentence of Article 14 TFEU contains a normative element which constitutionally affects the interpretation to give to the provision in Article 106(2) TFEU. The explicit reference to "economically and financial conditions" in Article 14 TFEU confirms that to take into consideration such conditions is not a derogation but a duty for EU institutions, even when they apply Article 106(2) TFEU.

The doctrine of "economically acceptable conditions" explains also the CJEU's view, summarized in *Altmark*, that where a State measure must be regarded as compensation for the services provided by the recipient undertakings in order to discharge public service obligations, it does not put them in a more favourable position than competitors, and does not constitute state aid for the purpose of Article 107(1) TFEU.[45] A measure allowing undertakings to deliver SGEI tasks under acceptable economic conditions is not only seen as in principle "the right thing to do". The Court considers also that such conditions may include a margin of reasonable profit for undertakings providing SGEIs. It is important to notice that Recitals 1 and 2 of Commission Decision 2012/21/EU on state aid to SGEIs address this doctrine as a principle of EU law flowing from Article 14 TFEU. Recital 1 states that EU institutions have a duty to take care that such financial support is allowed under EU law, pursuant to Article 14 TFEU, and Recital 2 states that for certain SGEIs to operate on the basis of principles and under conditions which enable them to fulfil their missions, "financial support from the State may prove necessary". The Commission considers that these duties do not prejudice its powers to enforce EU competition and state aid rules according to Articles 93, 106 and 107 TFEU.[46]

The second specific feature of the Court's test under Article 106(2) TFEU, is that it is "softer" than the three-pronged proportionality test formulated in *Gebhard*, i.e. that the measure examined serves an objective of general interest (general interest objective), is necessary to attain this objective (necessity) and is the least trade restrictive measure enabling to achieve it (strict proportionality).[47] The bottom line seems to be that Article 106(2) TFEU is interpreted by the CJEU as a "rather strict" necessity test. In *Höfner*, the Court ruled that Article 106(2) TFEU cannot justify a prerogative to limit demand for a service (employment service). In *Corbeau*, it found that cross-subsidization can be justified by the necessity to ensure that the operator can fulfil its SGEI task under financial equilibrium, but that services that are dissociable from the SGEI services must be opened to competition if that does not compromise the economic equilibrium of the SGEI operation.

[45]Case C-280/00 *Altmark* [2003] ECR I-7747, para 87.

[46]Recitals 1 and 2 of Commission Decision 2012/21/EU of 20.12.2011 on the application of Article 106(2) of the Treaty on the Functioning of the European Union to State aid in the form of public service compensation granted to certain undertakings entrusted with the operation of services of general economic interest [2012] OJ L7/3.

[47]Baquero-Cruz 2005, pp. 187–197.

However, the Court's test under Article 106(2) TFEU is satisfied if the measure at issue is appropriate and necessary to secure the SGEI's fulfilment, and does not require that the measure at issue is the most efficient, which is illustrated by the judgment in *Commission v Netherlands*, where the risk of "cherry-picking" was considered as undeniable.[48] The Court stated that, while a Member State must demonstrate in detail why removing a contested measure would satisfy the Treaty market rules but jeopardize the performance, under economically acceptable conditions, of the SGEI tasks which it has entrusted to an undertaking, Article 106(2) TFEU does not impose any duty to "prove, positively, that no other conceivable measure, which by definition would be hypothetical, could enable those tasks to be performed under the same conditions".[49] In other words, if a Member State makes a reasonable case that SGEI tasks are at risk if the measure is obstructed, the burden of proof of the contrary is on the part contesting this risk. In *Commission v Italy*, another of the three "electricity cases", the Court found that the Commission had not fulfilled this "secondary" burden of proof, as in challenging the exclusive rights, it had neither taken account of the particular features of the national system of electricity supply, nor specifically pointed at alternative measures enabling the operator to fulfil the SGEI tasks under economically acceptable conditions.[50]

In the field of social services, the judgment in *Albany* provides a good illustration of the CJEU's application of the proportionality principle under Article 106(2) TFEU. First, the Court acknowledged that securing access to the supplementary pension scheme at issue was an SGEI mission, given the low levels of statutory pension in the Dutch pensions system.[51] Considering the risk of cherry-picking as evident if the funds' exclusive right to manage the supplementary pension scheme for all workers in a given sector was removed, the Court considered that public intervention was justified. Second, the Court agreed that removing the exclusive right would lead to the supplementary pension fund losing "good risks" to its

[48]The Dutch State argued that if the national electricity distributor's exclusive import rights were removed, customers and distribution companies would be able to buy electricity from suppliers in other Member States at lower prices than those charged by the exclusive right holder in their Member State. The Court underlined that it would be the main advantage of opening up the market, but at the same time it would affect the national supply system, in particular the national distributor's ability to fulfil its planning obligation and its SGEI tasks. See Case C-157/94 *Commission v Netherlands* [1997] ECR I-5699, paras 53–57.

[49]Case C-157/94 *Commission v Netherlands* [1997] ECR I-5699, para 58.

[50]Case C-158/94 *Commission v Italy* [1997] ECR I-5789, paras 52–53. Since the exclusive import rights were found contrary to Article 37 TFEU, the Court considered that it was unnecessary to consider whether they were contrary to Article 34 TFEU or, consequently, whether they could be justified under Article 36 TFEU.

[51]Case C-67/96 *Albany* [1999] ECR I-5751, para 105. Under para 106, the Court referred also to Council Directive 98/49/EC of 29 June 1998 on safeguarding the supplementary pension rights of employed and self-employed persons moving within the Community [1998] OJ L209/46.

competitors and being left with an increasing share of 'bad' risks, which would increasing the cost of pensions for workers, and prevent the fund from offering pensions at an acceptable cost, particularly as it offered pensions with a high level of solidarity. Consequently, the exclusive right was necessary for the fund to perform the task of general economic interest it was entrusted.[52]

Regarding the nature and predictability of the Court's approach under Article 106(2) TFEU, the scholarly analyses do not diverge so much. Baquero-Cruz holds that the CJEU has consistently construed Article 106(2) as a reconciliation test rather than a true proportionality test, and applied a 'suitability' test with some added force from the 'necessity' element.[53] Lenaerts holds that Article 106(2) TFEU must be read in light of the principle of proportionality, as the CJEU must strike "a balance between, on the one hand, guaranteeing the effectiveness of EU [competition] law and, on the other hand, safeguarding the general interest pursued by national authorities".[54]

Sauter distinguishes two proportionality tests: (a) the "not manifestly disproportionate" ("mild" test), only requiring that measures imposed are *prima facie* suitable to achieving the task at hand and (b) the least restrictive means ("strict" test), imposing that, out of all imaginable measures, the one chosen is the least restrictive of market freedoms. He argues that the mild test (a) is used by the CJEU when examining a measure in the light of Article 106(2) TFEU, and involves steps 1–2 below, while the strict test (b) includes steps 1–3 below:

1. the measure is motivated by the pursuit of a general interest objective
2. the restrictions caused by the measure are balanced by the benefits obtained in terms of the general interest
3. the objective cannot be achieved by less restrictive means[55]

In Sauter's view, shared here, the Court' approach in the electricity cases, easing the Member States' burden to prove the necessity of exclusive rights, involves that in the absence of EU sector law, the Court will choose the mild test, as it "will not consider itself bound to judge on the feasibility of alternative regulatory solutions, even if these may theoretically be more consistent with EU law".[56] The Court may

[52]Ibid., paras 108–111.

[53]Baquero-Cruz 2005, pp. 169–212. Bekkedal adheres to Baquero Cruz's submission that the test induced by Article 106(2) TFEU cannot be regarded as a "proportionality test", understood in the traditional sense of this notion Bekkedal questions the very legitimacy of employing what he calls the "seemingly softer test entailed by Article 106(2) TFEU" to Member State regulation intended to ensure the provision of SGEIs which encroaches upon the rules on the four freedoms, as it will not be unconstitutional to employ the traditional notion of proportionality. See Bekkedal 2011, p. 68.

[54]Lenaerts 2012, p. 1256.

[55]Sauter 2008, p. 29.

[56]Ibid., pp. 28–29.

arguably consider that where Member States have retained powers, it is *bound not to judge on the feasibility of alternative regulatory solutions*. Arguably *Albany* supports the understanding that the Court sees as its own constitutional duty not to let EU law trespass on the Member States' powers. It explicitly included in the "retained powers" the power to evaluate whether less restrictive measures can guarantee the objective of general interest, in the following terms:

> Finally, as regards Albany's argument that an adequate level of pension for workers could be assured by laying down minimum requirements to be met by pensions offered by insurance companies, it must be emphasised that, in view of the social function of supplementary pension schemes and the margin of appreciation enjoyed, according to settled case-law, by the Member States in organising their social security systems [references to *Duphar*, *Poucet and Pistre*, and *Sodemare*[57]], it is incumbent on each Member State to consider whether, in view of the particular features of its national pension system, laying down minimum requirements would still enable it to ensure the level of pension which it seeks to guarantee in a sector by compulsory affiliation to a pension fund.[58]

Thus, in the field of social services, the "interests of the Union" do not command a balancing favoring the least trade restrictive solution, but rather a balancing that is clearly consistent with, and proportional to, the welfare objective, and at the same time defers to Member States' prerogative to make the economic and political "risk assessment", i.e. the choice of objectives of general interest, and the balance between these objectives and the interest of free trade and undistorted competition. This prerogative can be pre-empted by EU legislation, which explains the Court's strict proportionality test in *Dusseldorp*, where the Court examined national rules requiring undertakings to deliver their dangerous waste for recovery to a national undertaking on which the state had conferred the exclusive right to incinerate dangerous waste, unless the processing of their waste in another Member State was superior to that performed by that undertaking.[59] Regarding these rules' compatibility with Article 106 TFEU, in conjunction with Article 102 TFEU, the Court stated that

> Even if the task conferred on that undertaking could constitute a task of general economic interest, however, it is for the Netherlands Government, as the Advocate General points out at paragraph 108 of his Opinion, to show to the satisfaction of the national court that that objective *cannot be achieved equally well by other means*. Article 90(2) of the Treaty can thus apply only if it is shown that, without the contested measure, the undertaking in question would be *unable* to carry out the task assigned to it.[60]

---

[57]Case 238/82 *Duphar* [1984] ECR 523, para 16; Case C-160/91 *Poucet and Pistre* [1993] ECR I-637, para 6; and Case C-70/95 *Sodemare* [1997] ECR I-3395, para 27.

[58]Case C-67/96 *Albany* [1999] ECR I-5751, para 122.

[59]In order to implement the objective of ensuring the best possible method of disposal of dangerous waste, the Netherlands had attributed to a national undertaking, AVR Chemie CV, the responsibility for dangerous waste management. AVR Chemie was thus designated as the sole end-processor for the incineration of dangerous waste in a high-performance rotary furnace.

[60]Case C-203/96 *Dusseldorp* [1998] ECR I-4075, para 67, emphasis added.

The Court required a strict proportionality test, as the exclusive right was acceptable only if it was the *least restrictive efficient* instrument to attain the objective. In *Dusseldorp*, the Court relied on its view in *Corbeau* and *Commission v France* rulings, that Article 106(2) TFEU may be relied upon to justify exclusive rights contrary to Article 102 TFEU "if that measure is necessary to enable the undertaking to perform the particular task assigned to it and if it does not affect the development of trade in a manner contrary to the interest of the Community".[61] In *Dusseldorp*, the Court did not refer to the element of "economically acceptable conditions" for the exclusive right holder, which was prominent in *Corbeau* and *Commission v France*. The latter argument was arguably not acceptable in a regulatory context where free trade is meant to solve both the environment and the financial challenges. To ensure the recovery of used oil filters, the EU legislator has pointed to a well-functioning internal market as the solution, which supposes that some economic operators will find it economically feasible to offer this service without an exclusive right, and that dangerous waste will find its way to these operators through cross-border transport. Only in the face of an observable market failure—evidence of insufficient offer of environmentally optimal end-processing of dangerous waste—could this assumption be questionable.

That exclusive rights in the field of waste management may require a tangible market failure to be justifiable under Article 106(2) TFEU is shown by the *FFAD* ruling.[62] The CJEU made the finding that *measures less restrictive than an exclusive right* had not necessarily ensured that the waste produced in the municipality had been recycled, which amounts to a strict test. As in *Dusseldorp*, the strict test in *FFAD* was arguably motivated by the Court's interpretation of "the interests of the Union" in the field of waste management. Compared to non-harmonized sectors, where the "interests of the Union" for the purpose of Article 106(2) TFEU are less clear and normative, the EU has clarified its policy objectives and instruments in the field of waste management. The abundant EU legislation based on Articles 191 and 192 TFEU, known as "minima-regulation", involves that the Member States may decide higher protection standards than those agreed, but must be loyal to the policy elements and premises underpinning this EU legislation.[63] EU waste law builds at present on the policy options that recovery is better than disposal, and that market integration will solve the huge infrastructure deficit in the EU and promote recovery both in quality and quantity. To support this policy, which downplays the problem of CO_2 emissions caused by waste transport,

[61] Ibid., para 65. The Court referred "only" to para 14 in Case C-320/91 *Paul Corbeau* [1993] ECR 1-2533, and para 49 in Case C-159/94 *Commission v France* [1997] ECR 1-5815.

[62] Case C-209/98 *FFAD* [2000] ECR I-3743.

[63] By "loyal" is not meant here that the Member States may not question the existing EU policy and seek to amend both this policy, and the EU legislation which is meant to implement it.

free movement for recovery—and shipments for recovery—may not be restricted as easily as free movement for disposal—and shipments for disposal.[64]

Thus, in the field of waste management, the "interests of the Union" give added weight to market freedoms, and explain the strict proportionality test. In contrast with *Dusseldorp*, the CJEU in *FFAD* gave relevance to the municipality of Copenhagen's argument that exclusive rights were necessary to safeguard the performance of the SGEI task *under economically acceptable conditions*.[65] There was a "serious environmental problem", as most building waste was not recycled, due to the lack of processing capacity, and the exclusive rights, limited to a period allowing investments to be written off and to the boundaries of the municipality, were necessary to attract investment in treatment infrastructure, but guaranteeing them a flow of waste.[66] Thus, the exclusive right fulfilled the requirement of strict proportionality, given the evident lack of solutions provided by the *European* market.

In sum, it seems that the test is mild where the Member States have retained powers, as for social services, but strict in fields of activity where EU public service objectives and missions have been formulated and/or the economic approach to fulfil them has been harmonized, at least partly, at EU level. It is submitted that this asymmetry explains that the Court continues to call Article 106(2) TFEU a derogation rule.

4.1.3 Horizontal Scope of Article 106(2) TFEU

The formulation of the provision under Article 106(2) TFEU does not exclude that it is invoked by Member States, and Member States' possibility to invoke this provision is

---

[64]This is particularly clear from the substantial differences between the conditions under which a Member State may object to shipments of waste regarding waste shipments destined for disposal respectively for recovery, see Articles 11 and 12 in Regulation (EC) No 1013/2006 of the European Parliament and of the Council of 14 June 2006 on shipments of waste [2006] OJ L190/1. Evidence that EU-intern transport of non-hazardous waste for recovery is not regarded as an environmental and health problem in the present EU policy on waste is arguably clear from the Sixth Environment Action Programme of the European Community 2002–2012, stating that "preference should be given to recovery and especially to recycling; the quantity of waste for disposal should be minimized and should be safely disposed of; waste intended for disposal should be treated as closely as possible to the place of its generation, to the extent that this does not lead to a decrease in the efficiency in waste treatment operations", but designating no such preference for recycling waste as closely as possible to the place of generation. It is only where pest meets cholera that the EU policy is clearly against waste transport is clear: when waste is transported on long distances for *disposal*, nuisance is exponential and transport is hardly possible to motivate by any gain of not purely economic nature.

[65]Case C-209/98 *FFAD* [2000] ECR I-3743, para 77, where the Court referred not only to para 14 but also to para 16 in the *Corbeau* ruling.

[66]Ibid., paras 78–80.

nowadays not controversial in the legal literature.[67] While the scope of this provision is still uncertain, Lenaerts underlines that its formulation, allowing Member States to derogate from "the rules contained in the Treaties", must be considered and involves that the derogation rule may also be relied upon to justify derogation from the Treaty principles on free movement. Indeed, the CJEU's case law shows that Article 106(2) has been applied in cases involving measures infringing these principles.[68]

4.1.3.1 Article 106(2) TFEU and EU Competition Rules

The question brought to the Court in *Corbeau* was whether exclusive rights *granted by law* to the Belgian public body Régie des Postes for both profitable and unprofitable postal activities, were compatible with the Treaty provision prohibiting abuse of dominant position. As already mentioned, the Court found that cross-subsidization, allowing the operator to offset the costs incurred for the unprofitable postal SGEI tasks by profitable postal activities, could be justified under Article 106(2) TFEU by the necessity to secure that SGEI tasks are operated under "economically acceptable conditions". However, it also emphasized that exclusive rights for services dissociable from the SGEI task could be granted only if opening them to other operators could jeopardize the operator's fulfilment of the SGEI task in financial equilibrium.[69]

The Court's approach implied that the application of Article 106(1) TFEU (imposing on the Member States a duty of loyalty when granting exclusive or special rights to undertakings) in combination with the rule in Article 102 TFEU could obstruct the fulfilment of SGEI tasks because it excluded the granting of exclusive rights. As observed by Buendia Sierra, by founding the compatibility of the exclusive rights on Article 106(2) TFEU, without first determining whether they necessarily led the undertaking to abuse the dominant position it was granted, the Court implicitly held that exclusive rights were per se prohibited by the Treaties, and justifiable only if they were objectively necessary to guarantee the effective fulfilment of SGEI tasks.[70] After *Corbeau*—called by Bekkedal the most

[67]The view defended by Bekkedal, and regarded by other authors as radical, is rather that the exception in Article 106(2) TFEU cannot be invoked by the Member States to justify *barriers to free movement*, with reference to the CJEU's approach of this provision's scope in *Campus Oil*, which to many others, arguably the Court itself, has later been rejected. Bekkedal 2011, p. 65.

[68]Lenaerts 2012, pp. 1255–1256. Lenaerts refers in particular to the electricity case C-157/94 *Commission v Netherlands* [1997] ECR I-5699 and Case C-266/96 *Corsica Ferries France* [1998] ECR I-3949.

[69]Case C-320/91 *Corbeau* [1993] ECR I-02533, paras 16–19.

[70]Ibid., paras 11–13. This approach in *Corbeau*, already evoked in Sect. 3.1.1, was called by Buendia Sierra "a doctrine of automatic abuse" and holds that the ruling, by enlarging the scope of the prohibition under Article 86(1) EC (now Article 106(1) TFEU) in combination with Article 82 EC (now Article 102 TFEU) and by radically reversing the burden of proof for the legality of exclusive rights, made the application of the exception rule in Article 106(2) TFEU decisive for the rise of Article 106(2) TFEU. See Buendia Sierra 1999, p. 176.

expansive and famous interpretation of the provision in Article 106(1) TFEU[71]—the Court went back to a milder "behaviour approach" implying that exclusive rights are not presumed to be illegal, and infringe Article 102 TFEU read in combination with Article 106(1) TFEU only if they lead the undertaking enjoying them to abuse its dominant position.[72]

In *Glöckner*, the CJEU found that granting statutory exclusive rights to operate profitable non-emergency patient transport, to non-profit bodies entrusted with the task of supplying non-profitable emergency transport, infringed Article 106(1) TFEU in combination with Article 102 TFEU. The exclusive rights did extend these entities' dominant position in the ambulance sector, but could be motivated under Article 106(2) if they enabled the operator to fulfil the SGEI task (emergency transport) under conditions of economic equilibrium, and as long as this operator was not manifestly unable to satisfy the demand for emergency transport and patient transport services, regarded by the Court as two non-dissociable activities.[73] It may be noted that Hatzopoulos sees the *Glöckner* ruling as a case of derogation from EU public procurement rules, which is evoked in more detail below.

In *Almelo* the Court found that a regional electricity distributor's purchasing clause prohibiting local distributors from importing electricity for public supply purposes, infringed Articles 101 and 102 TFEU, as it affected trade between Member States. However, the undertaking could justify its exclusivity clause under Article 106(2) TFEU, if it could show that it was necessary to perform its SGEI task.[74]

In *FFAD*, the undertaking Sydhavnens Sten & Grus had brought an action in a national court against the Municipality of Copenhagen, which had refused its request to receive and process non-hazardous building waste in the frame of the municipality's collection system. The CJEU found that contracts with only three specific undertakings for receiving and processing such waste produced within its boundaries, concluded in the frame of municipal rules, constituted exclusive rights in the meaning of Article 106(1) TFEU.[75] The national court was left with the task of determining the relevant market and whether these exclusive rights created a dominant position, but the CJEU underlined that these rights did not seem to necessarily lead to abuse infringing Article 106(1) TFEU in combination with Article 102

---

[71] Bekkedal 2011, p. 79.

[72] On the divide between the "effet utile approach" and "the behaviour approach" in the CJEU's interpretation of Article 106(1) TFEU in combination with Article 102 TFEU, both illustrating the Court's so called "competition approach", see Buendia Sierra's illuminating analysis of the CJEU's case law in Buendia Sierra 1999, p. 173180.

[73] Case C-475/99 *Ambulanz Glöckner* [2001] ECR I-8089, paras 60–62.

[74] Case C-393/92 *Almelo* [1994] ECR I-01477 paras 48–49.

[75] Case C-209/98 *FFAD* [2000] ECR I-3743, paras 53–54.

TFEU, and even if was found to be the case, that this infringement could be justified under Article 106(2) TFEU to address "a serious environmental problem".[76]

The CJEU's interest in examining exclusive rights in the light of Article 106(1) TFEU in combination with Article 102 TFEU resurfaced in *Commission v DEI*.[77] The Court took the view that exclusive rights conferred by the Greek government to a public undertaking generating and supplying electricity infringed these rules in combination as soon as it was liable to lead to "a potential or actual anti-competitive consequence".[78] Szyszczak notes that, in stating that "it is sufficient to show that that potential or actual anti-competitive consequence is liable to result from the State measure at issue", the Court departed from earlier case law focussing on exclusive rights' effect on the behaviour of public undertakings. This approach left in her view little room to examine the social motives for organizing the electricity market in that manner.[79] As a matter of fact, the Greek government had not argued that the measure was intended to protect an SGEI but more vaguely that it was relevant for the interests of consumers.

4.1.3.2 Article 106(2) TFEU and the Free Movement of Goods

In the three electricity cases the Commission alleged that, by granting to a single operator exclusive rights for import of electricity, the Netherlands, Italy and France, infringed Articles 30, 34 and 37 EC, now Articles 34, 35 and 37 TFEU.[80] The CJEU held that by its wording, the provision now in Article 106(1) TFEU necessarily implies that the Member States may grant exclusive rights to certain

[76]Ibid., paras 66–81.

[77]Case C-553/12 P *European Commission v Dimosia Epicheirisi Ilektrismou AE (DEI)*, EU:C:2014:2083.

[78]Ibid., para 47. In a situation where DEI had a dominant position on the wholesale electricity market in Greece, the Greek State had decided to grant DEI an exclusive licence to explore and exploit lignite in Greece. In the contested decision, the Commission had found that the grant and maintenance of those rights was contrary to Article 86(1) EC, read together with Article 82 EC, since it created a situation of inequality of opportunity between economic operators as regards access to primary fuels for the purposes of generating electricity and allowed DEI to maintain or reinforce its dominant position on the Greek wholesale electricity market by excluding or hindering any new entrants. Ibid., paras 7–8.

[79]Szyszczak 2015, pp. 684–686.

[80]As explained by AG Cosmas, the Commission sought a ruling that the Member States were *obliged by the Treaty* itself to repeal national legislation granting exclusive rights to import electricity and natural gas, as contrary to the prohibition of State monopolies nowadays provided for by Article 37(1) TFEU. It had proposed directives introducing a right of access for producers, distributors and final users to the transmission and distribution systems of each Member State, as a prerequisite for conditions for effective competition in the electricity and natural gas sector, and met resistance in the Council.

undertakings and thereby grant them a monopoly, but found that the national import monopolies were discriminatory, and thus obviously infringed Article 37 TFEU.[81]

The Commission argued that Article 106(2) TFEU could be invoked to justify State measures incompatible with the free movement of goods,[82] referring to the Court's statement in *Campus Oil* that Article 106(2) TFEU does not exempt a Member State which has entrusted the operation of an SGEI task to an undertaking from the prohibition on adopting, in favour of that undertaking and with a view to protecting its activity, measures that restrict imports from other Member States contrary to Article 34 TFEU.[83]

AG Cosmas's view was that the Court's position in *Campus Oil* seemed contradicted by later decisions in *France* v *Commission*, *Porto di Genova*, *Corbeau*, and *Almelo*.[84] Although naming none of these cases, nor *Campus Oil*, the Court came to the same conclusion as the Advocate General, namely that Article 106(2) TFEU was applicable to Article 37 TFEU. It explained that Article 106(1) TFEU must be interpreted as "being intended to ensure that the Member States do not take advantage of their relations with those undertakings in order to evade the prohibitions laid down by other Treaty rules addressed directly to them, such as those in Articles 30, 34 and 37, by obliging or encouraging those undertakings to engage in conduct which, if engaged in by the Member States, would be contrary to those rules".[85] With regard to the scope thus attributed to Article 106(1) TFEU, and to its combined effect with Article 106(2) TFEU, the Court held that *a Member State* may rely on 106(2) TFEU to justify that it grants to an undertaking entrusted with SGEIs, exclusive rights contrary *in particular* to Article 37 TFEU.[86]

The electricity rulings seem to contradict Bekkedal's assertion that in all cases where the Court has applied Article 106(2) TFEU to infringements of the four

[81]Case C-157/94 *Commission v Netherlands* [1997] ECR I-5699, para 23; Case C-158/94 *Commission v Italy* [1997] ECR I-5789 para 32; Case C-159/94 *Commission v France* [1997] ECR I-5815, para 40. In the three cases, the Court referred to Case 59/75 *Pubblico Ministero* v *Manghera* [1976] ECR 91, para 12, and Case C-347/88 *Commission* v *Greece* [1990] ECR I-4747, para 44, where it held that exclusive import rights give rise to discrimination prohibited by Article 37(1) against exporters established in other Member States. In *Manghera*, the Court also underlined that, in order to attain the objective of Article 37(1) TFEU in a Member State where a commercial monopoly exists, the free movement of goods from other Member States comparable to those with which the national monopoly is concerned must be ensured.

[82]Case C-157/94 Commission v Netherlands [1997] ECR I-5699, para 26; Case C-158/94 Commission v Italy, para 35; Case C-159/94 *Commission v France*, para 43. All referred above.

[83]Case 72/83 *Campus Oil* [1984] ECR 2727, para 19.

[84]See Opinion AG Cosmas in C-157/94 *Commission v Netherlands*, referred above, paras 87 and 89, referring to Case C-202/88 *France* v *Commission* [1991] ECR 1-1223; Case C-320/91 *Corbeau* [1993] ECR 1-2533, para 14; and Case C-393/92 *Almelo* [1994] ECR I-1477, para 46.

[85]Case C-157/94 *Commission v Netherlands* [1997] ECR I-5699, paras 29–30.

[86]Ibid., paras 31–32.

freedoms, the Member State was held responsible for violating both the competition rules and the Treaty rules on the four freedoms.[87] In these cases, the Commission's action was solely based on Articles 34 and 37 TFEU.[88] The Court did reason on Article 106 TFEU, but only to delineate the scope of Article 106(2) TFEU as a derogation rule and to underline that Article 106(1) TFEU actually shows that the Member States may grant exclusive rights to undertakings.

In *Hanner*, the CJEU confirmed its view that Member States may rely on Article 106(2) TFEU to justify exclusive rights infringing Article 37(1) TFEU.[89] The Court held that Article 106(2) TFEU could in principle be relied upon to justify the State monopoly for the retail trade of medicinal preparations. This monopoly was granted to Apoteket AB, which was also assigned the SGEI task to contribute to the protection of public health by guaranteeing access for the Swedish population to medicinal products.[90] Nevertheless, the Court concluded that the regulatory scheme did not fulfil all the conditions imposed by Article 106(2) TFEU to justify a derogation from Article 37 TFEU, as it did not exclude discrimination against medicinal preparations from other Member States.[91]

4.1.3.3 Article 106(2) TFEU and the Free Movement of Services

In *Corsica Ferries,* the Court found that Italian legislation requiring vessels owned by shipping companies established in other Member States and making stops in Italian ports to use the services of local mooring groups operating on the basis of exclusive rights, for a charge higher than the actual cost of the service provided, had so negligible effect on imports of goods that it did not breach Article 34 TFEU.[92] The Court recalled that exclusive rights do not infringe Article 102 TFEU in combination with Article 106(1) TFEU, if the undertaking to which they are granted is not led to abuse its dominant position merely by exercising these rights, and if the rights do not create a situation in which the undertaking is led to commit such abuses.[93] As mooring groups were entrusted a universal mooring service for reasons of safety in port waters, an SGEI task in the meaning of Article 106(2) TFEU, the Court considered that it could be regarded as necessary, on grounds of public security, to confer on local groups of operators the exclusive right to provide the service, to include in the price of the service a component designed to cover the supplementary cost of maintaining a universal mooring service, and to

[87]Bekkedal 2011, p. 71.

[88]To that purpose, see Case C-157/94 *Commission v Netherlands* [1997] ECR I-5699, para 1.

[89]Case C-438/02 *Krister Hanner* [2005] ECR I-04551.

[90]Ibid., para 47.

[91]Ibid., para 48.

[92]Case C-266/96 *Corsica Ferries* [1998] ECR I-3949.

[93]Ibid., paras 40–41.

lay down for that service different tariffs on the basis of the particular characteristics of each port.[94] On the facts of the case, the Court also excluded that anticompetitive agreements had taken place between the mooring groups.[95]

With regard to the scope of Article 106(2) TFEU, the Court's assessment of the effect of the obligation to use the mooring groups' services on the freedom to provide services is of particular interest. Concerning firstly the exclusive right's restriction of the freedom for operators from other Member States to provide mooring services, the Court held that "such an impediment, if it exists, is not contrary to Article 59 of the Treaty [now Article 56 TFEU] since the conditions for application of Article 90(2) [now Article 106(2) TFEU] are satisfied".[96] In other words, the universal service task justified the exclusive right, and therefore justified also that the freedom of other operators to provide the service be restricted. Concerning secondly the exclusive right's possible restriction of the freedom for economic operators to provide maritime transport services (transport service operators using, as consumers, the service of port waters' security), the Court observed that the mooring service was essential to the maintenance of safety in port waters and that it had "the characteristics of a public service", which the Court held to be universality, continuity, satisfaction of public interest requirements, regulation and supervision by the public authorities. Hence, even if it could restrict the freedom to provide maritime transport services, the obligation to use the local mooring service could be justified by the interest of public security under Article 52 TFEU.

Provided that the price supplement in relation to the actual cost of the service indeed truly corresponded to the mooring groups' additional cost of fulfilling the universal service function, the objective of the service and its public service character in the national legislation motivated a restriction of the freedom to provide maritime transport services.[97] Thus, *Corsica Ferries* shows that the *same general interest*—in that case public security in port waters—can justify at the same time

- An obligation to provide a service under specific conditions, an SGEI task
- An obligation to receive the service under these specific conditions, an overriding reason related to the general interest.

These specific conditions—in that case the public service of universal mooring service—laid down in national law, may justify both a restriction of competition and a restriction of fundamental freedoms, both in the field of the regulated service and in other fields of activity related.

---

[94]Ibid., paras 45–46. In each of the ports concerned the tariffs for mooring services were fixed by the local maritime authority, on the basis of a general formula determined at national level by the public authorities.

[95]Ibid., para 53.

[96]Ibid., para 59, precisions added.

[97]Ibid., para 60.

4.1.3.4 Article 106(2) TFEU and EU Procurement Rules: Why not?

The applicability of Article 106(2) TFEU to EU procurement rules is a very contentious issue. Let us formulate the question in the following terms: why would Article 106(2) TFEU apply to restrictions from the fundamental freedoms but not from EU procurement principles and rules?

In her Opinion in *Commission v Ireland*, AG Stix-Hackl took a courageous bite into this poisonous issue. The contentious issue was that the Eastern Regional Health Authority in Ireland permitted emergency ambulance services to be provided by Dublin City Council (DCC) without the Eastern Regional Health Authority undertaking any prior advertising, which the Commission claimed to infringe the Treaty based rules on public procurement. Understanding the Court's case law as indicating that the very grant of exclusive rights falls within Article 106(1) TFEU in combination with Article 102 TFEU, the AG held that the exclusive rights' compatibility with the Treaties could be determined under Article 106(2) EC, "because of the lead time involved and the period to be specified for the submission of tenders, the carrying out of an award procedure entailing a call for tenders can in certain cases obstruct the performance of tasks". When this Opinion was delivered, the CJEU had begun interpreting the Treaties as requiring that certain contracts not covered by the directives should be published *ex ante*. According to the Advocate General, this raised the issue of finding for such contracts a Treaty provision allowing an exemption for exclusive rights corresponding to the exemption for exclusive rights provided by the procurement directives.[98] For contracts not covered by EU procurement directives, and challenged on the basis of Article 106(1) TFEU, the provision in Article 106(2) TFEU was arguably the only Treaty-based instrument offering a solution.

On these premises, the AG examined whether a partial or total restriction of competition was necessary to enable the holder of the exclusive right to perform its SGEI task under economically acceptable conditions, and concluded that the Irish state had not been able to demonstrate this.[99] Importantly, the AG's view was that Article 106(2) TFEU had relevance *only in relation to the conduct of the bodies which have been granted exclusive rights*.[100] The Court did not follow the AG's approach based on a reading of the situation as an exclusive right possibly justifiable by an SGEI task. It chose to analyse the case as a public-public arrangement which was not necessarily to be regarded as public procurement covered by EU procurement rules. It found that the Commission had not demonstrated the existence of a public contract, since it was conceivable that DCC provided emergency ambulance services based on statutory powers. Besides, the existence of funding

---

[98]Article 11(3) of Directive 92/50 and Article 31 of the 2004 Public Sector Directive. See Opinion of AG Stix-Hackl, cited above, para 111.

[99]Ibid., paras 103–106.

[100]Opinion Stix-Hackl in Case C-532/03 *Commission v Ireland* [2007] ECR I-11353, paras 100–101.

agreements in respect of "such services" between two public bodies did not necessarily constitute an award of a public contract to be assessed in the light of the Treaty fundamental rules.[101]

In *Germany v Commission*, the legal-political necessity to ensure that the Court's elaboration of procurement principles directly stemming from the Treaty would not restrict Member States' powers more than they had consented to in EU procurement legislation was also relevant for the General Court's reasoning. In this ruling, the GC examined Germany' arguments to seek annulment of the Commission Communication on EU law applicable to contracts not or not fully subject to the procurement directives (hereunder "the Communication").[102] At issue was in particular the Commission's view that the procurement directives' derogations may be applied to the award of contracts not covered by the Directives and that consequently, contracting entities may award such contracts without publishing a prior advertising, provided they meet the conditions laid down in the Directives for one of the derogation.[103] The General Court emphasized that the Communication did not in any way exclude the possibility of other derogations from the obligation of prior publication. It held that if the Member State or the contracting authority can rely on a provision of the EC Treaty providing for a general exemption from the application of primary law, *such as Article 86(2) EC (now Article 106(2) TFEU),* or Articles 296 EC or 297 EC, the principles of the EC Treaty are not affected. The General Court concluded that "in such cases, the obligation of prior publication laid down in the Communication and flowing from the principles of the EC Treaty does not apply to the award of a public contract".[104] It seems thus that the General Court does not exclude the applicability of Article 106(2) TFEU to the obligation of prior publication derived directly from the Treaties principles applicable to public procurement.

According to Hatzopoulos, *Glöckner* constitutes the (only) example of a case where the CJEU has accepted an exemption from procurement on the basis of Article 106(2) TFEU. In this ruling, the Court accepted the argument that the emergency transport services, which require costly investments in equipment and qualified personnel may only be financially viable if its operator also enjoys special rights to non-emergency transport. In Hatzopoulos' view, this was an implicit acknowledgement that, in exceptional circumstances, not only is it impossible to

[101]Case C-532/03 *Commission v Ireland* [2007] ECR I-11353, para 37. This reasoning augured arguably the reasoning in Case C-480/06 *Commission v Germany* [2009] ECR I-04747.

[102]Case T-258/06 *Germany v Commission* [2010] ECR II-2027.

[103]Ibid., para 138, referring to Sect. 2.1.4 of the Communication on '[p]rocedures without prior publication of an advertisement', the most important cases concern situations of extreme urgency due to unforeseeable events and contracts which may, for technical or artistic reasons or for reasons connected with the protection of exclusive rights, be executed only by one particular economic operator.[859] Ibid., para 139, referring to Sect. 2.1.4 of the Communication.

[104]Case T-258/06 *Germany v Commission* [2010] ECR II-2027, para 140. See, for an overriding reason relating to the general interest, Case C-158/03 *Commission* v *Spain*, para 35 and the case law cited.

have competition in the market, but also competition for the market—and thus competition is *altogether excluded*.[105] Hatzopoulos emphasizes that the Court had not developed the Treaty-based public procurement principles when *Glöckner* was decided, which explains that Article 106(2) TFEU in that case was successfully pleaded in order to avoid the application of the procurement rules, but he also believes that this is likely to remain an isolated occurrence.

Against this background, the question raised above must be re-formulated: if it is not excluded that Article 106(2) TFEU is relevant to justify derogations from the Treaty-based procurement principles, why *should* it be irrelevant as a derogation from procurement rules in EU secondary law? Hatzopoulos is one of the few scholars to give an (elliptic) answer to that question, holding that, given that public procurement rules and principles specifically apply to "public" services, not provided within normal market conditions, Article 106(2) TFEU *should* in principle not allow for exceptions from them. Let us quote him for more clarity:

> Indeed, the *special nature* of the activity is already taken into account when an entity qualifies as a "contracting authority", thus making the procurement rules applicable in the first place. It would seem redundant or even counterproductive, that this same element be considered again in order to set aside the procurement rules.[106]

If rightly understood, Hatzopoulos holds that Article 106(2) TFEU allows the "special nature of the activity" to be taken into account in the application of the Treaty rules. By claiming that this special nature is already considered in EU procurement rules, by giving to an entity the special status of "contracting authority", he suggests strongly that the essence of Article 106(2) TFEU is already *incorporated* in EU procurement rules. In these rules, the balance between the strict application of the Treaty rules on free movement and competition and public authorities' interests to achieve their public service missions is already made. For that reason, the balance *should* not be made a second time, as it would be counter-productive (by which he probably means for the opening of competition). Does this entail that EU procurement directives are meant to "lay down principles and conditions, in particular economic and financial conditions", meant to enable SGEIs to fulfil their missions for the purpose of Article 14 TFEU? The answer is perhaps in the question. If the "Article 106(2) TFEU balance" is already present within EU procurement rules, it seems quite arguable that they establish principles and set conditions to provide, to commission and to fund such services, even if they *also* cover public acquisition in fields which are not of "a special nature", such as pens and tables for schools.

4.1.3.5 Article 106(2) TFEU and State Aid Rules

As is clear from Part I, neither the fiscal character, nor the social aim, nor the general objectives of a measure can exclude its characterization as aid within the

[105]Hatzopoulos 2012, pp. 90–91, emphasis added.

[106]Ibid., p. 90.

meaning of Article 107(1) TFEU.[107] In *Altmark*, AG Léger was very much in favour of the view that the Court would reverse its "compensation approach" in *Ferring*. He recommended taking the "state aid approach", implying that the financing measure constitutes aid prohibited by Article 107(1) TFEU, but is possible to justify under the exemption for undertakings entrusted with SGEI tasks under Article 106(2) TFEU. The Court decided against the Advocate General and definitively adopted the "compensation approach", whereby funding of public service obligations is not state aid in the meaning of Article 107(1) TFEU, if the undertaking receives compensation strictly proportionate to the costs incurred by the task imposed.[108] The Court formulated four cumulative conditions (known as "the *Altmark* criteria") under which public service compensation does not constitute state aid:

- first, the recipient undertaking is actually required to discharge public service obligations and those obligations have been clearly defined
- second, the parameters on the basis of which the compensation is calculated have been established beforehand in an objective and transparent manner
- third, the compensation does not exceed what is necessary to cover all or part of the costs incurred in discharging the public service obligations, taking into account the relevant receipts and a reasonable profit for discharging those obligations
- fourth, where the undertaking which is to discharge public service obligations is not chosen in a public procurement procedure, the level of compensation needed has been determined on the basis of an analysis of the costs which a typical undertaking, well run and adequately provided with means of transport so as to be able to meet the necessary public service requirements, would have incurred in discharging those obligations, taking into account the relevant receipts and a reasonable profit for discharging the obligations.[109]

Altmark is a Gordian knot in the EU legal system, because it establishes public procurement as a procedure giving equal market access *and* excluding state aid. In that ruling, the Court has not applied Article 106(2) TFEU, but it has incorporated the concept of SGEI *tasks* in the very definition of state aid, using the synonym notion of "public service obligations". Thus, *Altmark* has provided the Commission with a model to test the proportionality of state aid compensating SGEI tasks, and the Commission rules on state aid rules applying to SGEIs (adopted firs in 2005 and revised in 2011) are based on the *Altmark* criteria. However, the *Altmark* criteria, formulated in a case concerned with transport services, constitute a rather rigid test, and the *Altmark* ruling leaves unsaid how measures that did not fulfil these four criteria could comply with the Treaties by

[107] See also the Opinion of AG Léger in Case C-290/00 *Altmark* [2003] ECR I –7747, para 77.

[108] Case C-280/00 *Altmark*.

[109] Ibid., para 95.

application of the exemption rule in Article 106(2) TFEU.[110] The question was, therefore, how the Court would approach the need of flexibility in the conditions of public service compensation in other fields, in particular regarding social services. Some answer to this question is provided by the rulings in *BUPA* and *CBI*.[111]

In *BUPA* the General Court found that the Commission had been right in not raising objections against a risk equalization scheme (RES) established by Irish law to ensure that all persons living in Ireland would receive a minimum level of private medical insurance (PMI) at an affordable price and on similar quality conditions. PMI insurers were found subject to SGEI tasks, and the RES aimed at securing these tasks by neutralizing differential in risk between all PMI insurers on the Irish market. The RES was found compatible with the *Altmark* criteria and therefore did not involve state aid for the purpose of Article 107(1) TFEU[112] Having underlined that the scopes of the *Altmark* criteria and of Article 106(2) TFEU overlap, the GC found appropriate not to apply the *Altmark* criteria strictly, but rather "in accordance with the spirit and the purpose which prevailed when they were laid down", and with adjustments to the particular SGEI scheme at hand.[113]

Regarding the first and the second criteria, the Court affirmed Member States' wide discretion to define SGEI tasks, but also that its corollary is a wide discretion in the setting of compensation parameters, the complex economic facts underpinning the choice of parameters being subject to only restricted control by the Community institutions.[114] However, the Court emphasized that this very discretion motivates that the parameters must be objective and transparent, and in particular defined in such a way as to preclude any abusive recourse to the concept of an SGEI on the part of the Member State.[115]

The General Court considered it appropriate not to apply strictly the third criterion requiring that compensation is proportional to the SGEI-costs, as the RES did not compensate the cost of supplying a PMI service, but instead the *risk* of providing PMI to "too many unhealthy and expensive customers".[116] Considering that

[110]See for instance Szyszczak 2004, p. 991, and De Vries 2011, p. 302.

[111]Case T-289/03 *BUPA* [2008] ECR II-81 and Case T-137/10 *CBI*, Judgment of 7 November 2012.

[112]Indeed, the General Court explained that the judgment in *Altmark* was not limited in time, which implied that it had to examine the *BUPA* facts by the *Altmark* standard, although this standard did not exist when the Commission adopted the contested decision by BUPA. The GC also found that RES was justified under Article 106(2) TFEU, see paras 258 and 305.

[113]Case T-289/03 *BUPA* [2008] ECR II-81, paras 158–160.

[114]To support the view that Member States have a wide discretion to define SGEI missions, the GC felt confident that it could refer to its own case law and to the 2001 Communication on SGEI, as it was consolidated in protocol 26 to the Lisbon Treaty and already adopted when the ruling was delivered, see Case T-289/03 *BUPA*, para 166.

[115]Case T-289/03 *BUPA*, cited above, para 214.

[116]Case T-289/03 *BUPA*, paras 239–240.

the third criterion's purpose coincides broadly with the criterion of proportionality established by the case-law on the application of Article 106(2) TFEU, the GC considered that neither this purpose nor the spirit of the third Altmark criterion required that receipts be taken into account in a system of compensation which operates independently of receipts.[117] On these premises, the GC found (1) that PMI insurers' SGEI tasks made compensation necessary, (2) that the RES mechanism was not a manifestly inappropriate means of compensation and (3) that the calculation method provided for by the RES, limited payments between PMI insurers to the level strictly necessary to neutralise the differential between their risk profiles.[118] For the same reasons (the specificity of the scheme), the Court considered inappropriate to apply the fourth *Altmark* criterion (efficiency) strictly, and was satisfied that compensation was regulated in a manner which excluded compensation of inefficiencies.[119]

The "*Altmark*-light" criteria in *BUPA* have been abundantly commented by legal scholars; to Ross, *BUPA* shows that the Court does not regard the *Altmark* criteria as a one-size-fits-all test for SGEIs.[120] It is important to note that *BUPA* was delivered three months after the adoption of Article 14 TFEU through the Treaty of Lisbon 2007/9, and the GC may have thrived for an approach respecting the evolution of EU constitutional law. Indeed, the ruling's first paragraph refers to Article 16 EC, held under paragraph 167 to reflect "generally" the division of powers between the Union and the Member States.[121] Importantly, the GC used the term SGEI *mission* (used in Article 14 TFEU) and underlined the absence of a clear and precise regulatory definition of this concept, and of an established *precise legal concept definitively fixing the conditions that must be satisfied* before a Member State can properly invoke the existence and protection of an SGEI mission in the meaning of the first *Altmark* condition or of Article 106(1) TFEU.[122]

De Vries has underlined the discrepancy between, on the one side, the economic approach in *Altmark* and in the Commission's 2005 state aid action plan, and on the other side, what he called the "jurisdictional approach" in *BUPA*, where the GC made no in-depth economic assessment of whether the public service mission was discharged in a proportionate manner, and did not clarify how precise the definition of SGEI tasks must be to exclude the applicability of Article 107(1)

[117]Ibid., para 224, para 246, referring to para 92 of the *Altmark* ruling, and para 241.

[118]Ibid., paras 232–238.

[119]Ibid., paras 247–248.

[120]See Sauter 2014, p. 15; Ross 2009, pp. 127–140, p. 138; Baquero-Cruz 2005, p. 308.

[121]*BUPA* was delivered after the adoption of the Treaty of Lisbon in December 2007 and before its entry into force in December 2009.

[122]Case T-289/03 *BUPA* [2008] ECR II-81, para 165. What the Court signalled was arguably that the *regulatory function* of the EU concept of SGEI is not clear and precise, but also that there is as yet not much case law from the Court of Justice on the test to be used to assess whether measures protecting the invoked SGEI mission are compatible with the Treaty.

TFEU to their public funding.[123] However, although Article 14 TFEU and Article 36 EUCFR were not yet in force, they had been introduced in EU primary law when *BUPA* was decided, and the Court chose to introduce its decision with references not only to the freedom of establishment and the freedom to provide services, but also to the duty to protect SGEI missions enuntiated in Article 16 EC. In De Vries' view, *BUPA* should not be seen as a case "captured by politics", but rather as implying a recognition of the evolution of the Treaties, and of a competition model including social concerns.[124]

In contrast with *BUPA*, the *CBI* ruling indicates that the General Court does not interpret the post-Lisbon constitutional framework on SGEI as systematically allowing a "light touch" in the application of the *Altmark* criteria. At issue in *CBI* was the Commission's *IRIS-H* decision taken in 2005.[125] Two associations of Brussels private hospitals had alleged that unlawful state aid had been granted since 1995 to the five public general hospitals existing in the Brussels Capital Region and grouped into the IRIS network in 1996. In particular they argued that financing measures covered their deficits, and not the deficits of the Brussels private hospitals. The Belgian authorities put forward the argument that apart from the basic hospital missions fulfilled by both public and private hospitals in Belgium, and equally financed by public authorities, the public IRIS hospitals performed additional SGEI missions, which entailed special costs compensated through the deficit financing. Without opening a formal procedure, but after a rather extensive analysis, the Commission found that the funding measures were compatible with the Commission's rules on the application of Article 106(2) TFEU to state aid compensating SGEI tasks. The association of private hospitals contested the Commission's decision and brought the case to the General Court, in what is known as the *CBI* case.[126]

In *CBI*, the GC held that "although the conditions stated in the *Altmark* judgment and in the SGEI Package concern all sectors of the economy without distinction, their application must take into account the specific nature of the sector in question". Noting that *Altmark* concerned the transport sector, it held that its criteria could not be applied as strictly to the hospital sector, "which does not necessarily have such a competitive and commercial dimension".[127] On these premises, and regarding the first *Altmark* criterion (SGEI mandate), the GC found serious doubts as to the existence of a clearly defined public service mandate relating to

---

[123]De Vries 2011, pp. 303 and 314. De Vries saw a lack of coherence between the Commission's intention to apply a refined economic approach and the GC's approach in *BUPA*, and also in *TV2 Denmark*, see pp. 305–308.

[124]Ibid., p. 314.

[125]Commission Decision of 28 October 2009 on the financing of public hospitals of the IRIS-network of the region Brussels-capitale (Belgium) in case SA.19864 (ex NN54/2009)—C (2009) 8120 final.

[126]T-137/10 *CBI*, Judgment of 7 November 2012, para 85.

[127]Ibid., para 89.

the specific hospital missions of the IRIS hospitals. To the Court, the very fact that the Commission had not been able to carry out a comprehensive and consistent assessment of the content of the official acts relating to these missions indicated the existence of serious difficulties.[128] Also concerning the non-hospital public service missions of the IRIS hospitals, the Court found that the Commission had not dispelled doubts as to whether their nature and content was defined with sufficient clarity.[129]

Regarding the second *Altmark* criterion (prior compensation parameters), the GC recalled first its view in *BUPA* that Member States have a wide discretion not only when defining an SGEI mission but also when determining the compensation for the costs connected with the SGEIs (the national legislature may even grant national authorities a certain discretion to determine this compensation). A condition of this discretion is however that the compensation *parameters* are established in advance in an objective and transparent manner, to preclude any abusive recourse to the concept of SGEI.[130] In assessing the compensation parameters of the hospital missions, the GC observed that the Commission had not separated the parameters relating to measures of advance funding and the parameters relating to the measures of deficit financing, although they could be described as different aid measures, and concluded therefore that doubts existed as to the fulfilment of the second *Altmark* criterion. The GC found that the Commission had not either dispelled doubts as to whether the public financing of the hospitals missions and social missions of the IRIS hospitals fulfilled the third *Altmark* criterion relating to the existence of procedures for avoiding overcompensation and ensuring its repayment.[131] The GC considered the breadth and complexity of the Commission's assessment of compensation proportionality as in itself a sign of serious difficulties.[132]

Regarding the fourth *Altmark* criterion (analysis of costs in relation to a typical, well run and adequately provided undertaking), the GC pointed out that it did not have to be fulfilled, as Decision 2005/842/EC was applicable in the case.[133] Considering that the criteria in the *Altmark* judgment were laid down not to assess whether state aid is compatible with the internal market but in order to assess the existence of state aid, the GC referred also to earlier decisions where it found the fourth Altmark criterion irrelevant for assessing the compatibility of aid measures

---

[128]Ibid., paras 168–169–70.

[129]Ibid., paras 187–188.

[130]Ibid., paras 189–191. The Court underlined that Commission Decision 2005/842 similarly required that official acts entrusting the administration of the SGEI specify 'the parameters for calculating, controlling and reviewing the compensation'. The CG referred to Case T-289/03 *BUPA and Others* v *Commission* [2008] ECR II-81, para 214.

[131]Ibid., paras 265 and 278.

[132]Ibid., para 288.

[133]Ibid., para 291. Public service compensation to hospital was already exempted from notification according to Article 2(1)(b) of Commission Decision 2005/842.

under Article 106(2) EC.[134] The GC concluded that "as EU law now stands, the criterion linked to the economic efficiency of an undertaking in supplying the SGEI is unconnected with the assessment of the compatibility of State aid in the light of Article 86(2) EC", and thus the national authorities' choice relating to the economic efficiency of the public operator providing the SGEI could not be challenged on the basis of the fourth *Altmark* criterion.[135] Finally, The GC annulled the Commission's decision, finding that there were serious difficulties in the preliminary examination of the scheme and that the Commission had failed in not initiating the formal investigation procedure. As a result, the Commission has opened an in-depth investigation in October 2014.[136]

In sum, *Altmark*

- Provides a "proportionality recipe" for public funding of SGEI tasks, which is highly similar to the logic of the rules in EU procurement legislation, as the first three criteria must be fulfilled even if the SGEI task is funded through procurement.
- Offers an opportunity for the Member States, and the EU legislator, to dilute the proportionality calculus inherent to Article 106(2) TFEU in EU procurement rules. Translating the notion of SGEI by the notion of "public service obligation" facilitates this dilution, erasing the idea that procurement rules may, unless taken care of, obstruct the fulfilment of SGEI tasks in Article 106(2) TFEU.

Given the limited scope of the EU procurement directives, and the limited capacity of certain EU procurement procedures to fulfil the first three *Altmark* criteria, Member States remain relatively free to organise social services according to autonomous procedures, but they must comply with EU state aid rules, which implies that the SGEI-character of the services remains the *visible* EU constitutional frame for their funding measures. Thus, their freedom to organise social services is counterbalanced by constraints on the legitimacy and the proportionality of their funding measures. In this respect, the *Altmark* test displays two problematic features:

a. It imposes strict proportionality between funding and SGEI-costs.
b. It is a rigid model in the sense that it supposes that public authorities can calculate compensation of SGEI tasks in terms of costs and receipts, which risks restricting Member States' freedom to organise SGEIs.

In *BUPA*, the Court consented to a wide definition of the SGEI objectives and of the SGEI tasks, and on that basis was ready to depart from the rigid model of the

---

[134] Ibid., para 292, referring to Case T-354/05 *TF1* v *Commission* [2009] ECR II-471, paras 129–140, and order of 25 November 2009 in Case T-87/09 *Jørgen Andersen v Commission*, [2009] ECR II-225, para 57.

[135] Ibid., para 300.

[136] Commission Decision of 1 October 2014 on the public financing of Brussels public IRIS hospitals (Belgium) in case SA.19864 (2014/C) (ex NN54/2009)—C (2014) 6833 final.

third and fourth Altmark criteria. This approach seems in line with the SGI Protocol, giving in principle a wide freedom to organise SGEIs (which can be limited by EU procurement law or EU sector law). Some may argue that the freedom to fund SGEIs without prior notification allowed by *Altmark* should not be restricted by an obligation to organise them in an overly rigid transparency and proportionality model, but in Ross' view, a very light touch in the application of the third *Altmark* criterion can negate the "revitalization" of Article 106(2) TFEU in the future, because it would not be seen as an acceptable rule to balance.[137] This concern explains perhaps that in *CBI*, a case also dealing with social services in the frame of Member States' competence, the GC required that the Commission applies more strictly its own rules on the application of Article 106(2) TFEU to public service compensation which constitutes state aid.[138] Thus, while the GC relaxed the rigidity of the *Altmark* test to accommodate a model where SGEI compensation was based on "financial solidarity" between market operators, it required a stricter observation of the *Altmark* test in the case of a model where SGEI compensation was based on direct State funding. The fact that state aid cases are normally decided by the General Court, implies that the *BUPA* case and the *CBI* case are important but may be perceived as not conclusive regarding the CJEU's reasoned approach. As underlined by Sauter, so far we do not have the CJEU's own view: neither of the Commission's approach nor of the General Court's approach.[139]

4.1.4 Entrustment

The provision in Article 106(2) TFEU can be relied on in the presence of undertakings *entrusted* with SGEIs. The Court of Justice explained in *BRT* that undertakings may come under that provision, provided that they are entrusted with the operation of SGEIs by an act of a public authority.[140] This act allows *proving* that particular and specific SGEI tasks are binding on them, and can play a central role in assessing the proportionality of certain measures motivated by the tasks and affecting competition and trade. This explains the particular importance of entrustment in the field of state aid, the requirement of entrustment being in particular found in the first of the four criteria formulated by the CJEU in *Altmark* to exclude that compensation of SGEI tasks is considered as state aid in the meaning of Article 1(1) TFEU, and correspondingly also in Commission Decision 2012/21/EU exempting from prior notification certain aid measures of SGEI compensation.

---

[137]Ross 2009, pp. 138–139.

[138]Sauter seems also to perceive that the General Court's critical review of the Commission's preliminary assessment of the financing of the IRIS-hospitals in *CBI*, suggests that it may have tightened its approach as compared to *BUPA*. See Sauter 2014, p. 15.

[139]Ibid.

[140]Case 127/73 *BRT II* [1974] ECR 318, paras 20–22.

It is important not to confuse (1) the existence of SGEI tasks, (2) the requirement that undertakings are entrusted with SGEI tasks objectively and transparently, and (3) the instruments which may be used to allow that such SGEI tasks are fulfilled under acceptable economic conditions. Entrustment has essentially a function of *proof* that the undertakings subject to measures derogating from the Treaty rules are actually *bound* to discharge certain SGEI tasks. Entrustment is fundamentally a procedure and should not be confused with instruments such as exclusive rights or public funding, allowing SGEI tasks to be fulfilled under acceptable economic conditions by undertakings. The use of such instruments in a specific field of activity can constitute a signal of the existence of SGEI tasks, but is not constitutive of these tasks, and does not either per se constitute an entrustment. The role of entrustment in relation to the concept of SGEI is further discussed in Chap. 5.

The CJEU has taken a flexible approach to the modes of entrustment, admitting that SGEI tasks may be entrusted by law, legislative decrees and administrative decisions (*Servizi Ausiliari*[141]), by contract (*FFAD*[142]), and contrary to the Commission's view expressed in the 2013 SGEI Guide, also by prior administrative authorization.[143] It appears namely from *Analir* that the CJEU does not exclude prior administrative authorisations as a mode of entrustment of SGEI tasks in the meaning of Article 106(2) TFEU, requiring that "the nature and the scope of the public service obligations to be imposed by means of a prior administrative authorisation scheme must be specified in advance to the undertakings concerned".[144]

Another question is whether there has to be "an individual and formal entrustment" to a specific undertaking, or a specific group of undertakings, in law or in any other act, for an SGEI regulation to exist in national law. The General Court established in *BUPA* that there could be no requirement that each of the operators subject to the public service obligations be separately entrusted with that mission by an individual act or mandate. The regulation chosen by Ireland did not provide for the grant of exclusive or special rights, but for the achievement of the mission by all operators active on the Irish market for private medical insurance, which—according to the Court—is a choice open to the Member States.[145]

By contrast with this flexible approach regarding the mode of entrustment, more precise conditions are required by the Commission package on the application of state aid rules to aid compensating SGEI tasks entrusted to undertakings. In particular, it is explained in Recital 14 of Commission Decision 2012/21/EU that in order to ensure that the criteria set out in Article 106(2) of the Treaty are met, the act of entrustment should specify, at least, (1) the undertakings concerned, (2) the precise content and duration of and, where appropriate, the territory concerned by

[141] Case C-451/03 *Servizi Ausiliari* [2006] ECR I-2941.

[142] Case C-209/98 *FFAD* [2000] ECR I-3743, paras 26 and 76.

[143] SGEI Guide 2013, point 47.

[144] Case C-205/99 *Analir* [2001] ECR I-1271, para 38.

[145] Case T-289/03 *BUPA* [2008] ECR II-81, para 183.

the public service obligations imposed, (3) the granting of any exclusive or special rights, and (4) the compensation mechanism and the parameters for determining the compensation and avoiding and recovering any possible overcompensation.[146] It is thus clear that for the purpose of state aid control, the entrustment act has been regulated by the Commission in order to simplify the control of proportionality of the measures affecting competition and trade for that type of activity.

To combine a flexible approach to the modes of entrustment, with requirements that SGEI tasks are defined with sufficient precision to allow controlling the proportionality of measures motivated by these tasks but affecting competition and trade, is a particular challenge for EU institutions. In market-based models of supply of social services, Member States may wish to signal their commitment to welfare services by defining both SGEI objectives and missions in rather general terms in law, while defining with more precision the tasks and the financial mechanisms covering their costs in legal instruments allowing more flexibility to adapt to changing needs, public finances and market offer at local or regional level. This can render more difficult a systematic and transparent assessment of the proportionality of measures claimed to be necessary to secure public service compensation.

4.2 The Case Law of the CJEU Transposed from Article 106(2) TFEU

Bekkedal argues that the CJEU regards Article 106(2) TFEU as a special exception rather than as a general exception.[147] From a formal point of view this seems correct. However it appears that the CJEU gives normative weight to the explicit or implicit existence of SGEIs in cases where Article 106(2) is not applied. In the following sections, a number of cases are studied, in order to shed light on how the concept of SGEI is actually relevant in virtually all fields of EU market law, and how it affects a strict interpretation of these rules in different ways.

4.2.1 Altmark: No State Aid for Proportional Compensation of Public Service Obligations

By providing substantial criteria allowing public funding of SGEIs not to be regarded as aid in the meaning of Article 107(1) TFEU, the *Altmark* ruling,

[146]In order to ensure transparency in relation to the application of this Decision, the act of entrustment should also include a reference to it. See Article 4 of Commission Decision 2012/21/EU.

[147]Bekkedal 2011, p. 65.

already evoked above, has important implications. Instead of applying Article 106(2) TFEU, it seems clear that the Court has "incorporated" the notion of SGEI tasks in the very notion of state aid. However, it is important to note that in *Altmark*, the term SGEI does not appear at all, as the Court exclusively uses the language of "public service obligations". This is all too normal, because the questions referred to the Court of Justice were related to aid to transport, subject to Article 77 EC (now Article 93 TFEU) which is formulated in the language of public service obligations.[148] In *BUPA*, the GC connected the notion of "public service obligations" to the concept of SGEI in the following terms:

> It is common ground between the parties that the concept of public service obligation referred to in that judgment corresponds to that of the SGEI as designated by the contested decision and that it does not differ from that referred to in Article 86(2) EC.[149]

This connection is ambiguous, because it suggests that the equivalence between "public service obligations" and SGEI is not established by the Court itself but only *agreed* by the *parties*. Nevertheless, the profound relation between the two notions is widely admitted, to the effect that the funding of SGEI tasks as framed by the *Altmark* criteria is not derogatory but instead corresponds implicitly to the normal exercise of public authorities' powers in the frame of their competence.

A remarkable effect of *Altmark* is that the tension between the Union's interest of developing trade, and the duty not to obstruct SGEI missions, tangible in Article 106(2) TFEU, is translated into the neutral language of public service obligations and the apparently simple recipe of four criteria. As public procurement procedures are supposed to be able to exclude over-compensation (fourth criterion), *Altmark* contributes to promote what is basically a free movement instrument—EU procurement rules—as an instrument of EU competition law constraining public funding.[150] Also, *Altmark* seems to offer an opportunity to dilute Article 106(2) TFEU in EU procurement legislation, which becomes EU's convenient "all-in-one solution" to address internal market and competition concerns in the public sector.

4.2.2 Public Service Tasks (or SGEI Tasks?) and Exemptions from EU Procurement Rules

We have seen above under Sect. 4.1.3.4 how Hatzopoulos seems to discreetly suggest that the special character of SGEIs is already incorporated in EU procurement rules. At the same time, anyone having followed the debate on EU public

[148]Aids shall be compatible with the Treaties if they meet the needs of coordination of transport or if they represent reimbursement for the discharge of certain obligations inherent in the concept of a public service.

[149]Case T-289/03 *BUPA* [2008] ECR II-81, para 162.

[150]On this path, see De Cecco 2013.

procurement rules in the last decade knows that many Member States—but also many members of the EU Parliament—have exercised pressure for their relaxation, in particular to allow more say in the definition of tasks commissioned. On this premise, it may be easier to understand the articulation between EU law on procurement and the CJEU's case law on in-house procurement and on public-public cooperation, already touched on in Sect. 2.4.

It may be recalled here how the Court in *Parking Brixen* considered it was "not appropriate" to apply the EU rules on public procurement or public service concessions in cases where a public authority performs *tasks in the public interest for which it is responsible* by its own means.[151] Thus, the Court has related the in-house exemption to the existence of general interest services that public authorities are in some manner obliged to supply, and chosen to incorporate the in-house exemption in the very definition of "contract for the purpose of procurement". This incorporation of the notion of public service task in the "concept of entry" of EU procurement rules reminds of the approach in *Altmark* concerning state aid, studied in the precedent section. In practice, the effect of the in-house exemption is to widen public authorities' discretion in providing and commissioning tasks in the general interest, which seems to have been consolidated in Article 1 of the SGI Protocol.

The *Coditel* ruling supports this understanding of the *Teckal* case law as evidently an "SGEI related case law". Although the judgment does not contain any direct reference to the notion of SGEI, the entrustment of *public service broadcasting tasks* played an important role for the application the in-house exemption in that case.[152] By application of the *Teckal* criteria, a local authority's award of a concession for the management of its cable television network to an inter-municipal cooperative it owned together with a number of other municipalities, was found not to be covered by Articles 12 EC, 43 EC and 49 EC. Regarding the so called "control-criterion", the Court expressed that "where a number of public authorities own a concessionaire to which they entrust the performance of one of their *public service tasks*, the control which those public authorities exercise over that entity may be exercised jointly".[153] This ruling indicates that a flexible approach of the so called "control criterion" as formulated in *Teckal* must typically be adopted in consideration of the fact that the tasks entrusted are just "public service tasks", the word task suggesting that the municipality is *obliged* to provide a service of general interest. As a matter of fact it seems there was indeed such a public service *obligation* for the cable operators owned by municipalities in the Brussels region, as appears from the *UPC* case discussed in Sect. 4.2.3.[154]

In *Coditel*, the relation between the in-house exemption and the public authorities "public service tasks" is thus made by the Court itself. Its legal-political

[151] Case C-458/03 *Parking Brixen* [2005] ECR I-8585, para 61.

[152] Case C-107/98 *Teckal* [1999] ECR I-8121.

[153] Case C-324/07 *Coditel Brabant* [2008] ECR I-8457, para 47.

[154] Case C 250/06 *UPC* [2007] ECR I-11135.

motive is arguably to allow that public authorities retain a freedom to organise the tasks they are by law responsible for, which includes a possibility to *provide* certain services with their own resources, thereby withdrawing the task from the market. This freedom is based on the Union's obligation to respect local and regional authorities' right to self-government, as now clear from Article 4(2) TEU. The Union's duty to respect this right, enshrined in the European Charter on Local Self-Government drawn up within the framework of the Council of Europe, signed by all EU Member States and ratified by most of them, had already been emphasized by AG Kokott in *Parking Brixen*[155] and by AG Trstenjak in *Coditel.*[156] In AG Trstenjak's view, the first *Teckal* criterion was not to be construed too narrowly, as doing so "would be to attach disproportionate weight to competition-law objectives at the same time as interfering too much with the municipalities' right to self-government and with it in the competences of the Member States." AG Trstenjak underlined finally that "heed is to be paid" to the role of regional and local self-government for the relevant national identity protected by Article 4(2) TFEU.

The General Court went even further in *SIC v Commission*, by explicitly relating the SGEI status of a service and the need of flexible application of procurement rules, in particular of the in-house exemption. It held that the specific status for public service broadcasting is the basis for the freedom accorded by the Amsterdam Protocol to Member States in the award of broadcasting SGEIs. According to the GC, this specific status explained and justified the fact that a Member State cannot be required to have recourse to competitive tendering for the award of such an SGEI, at least where it decides to ensure that public service itself through a public company.[157]

It seems thus clear that the *Teckal* doctrine has its legal-political ground in the SGEI character of the services *before they are commissioned*, under the pre-procurement phase. This seems to be confirmed by Article 1 of the SGI Protocol, recognizing as an EU shared value the essential role and the wide discretion of national, regional and local authorities in *providing* SGEIs. If their discretion to *provide* SGEIs themselves is recognized, it seems to imply that the SGEI exists

---

[155]AG Kokott held that applying the procurement rules also to transactions between contracting authorities and their wholly-owned subsidiaries would constitute an extensive interference in the organizational sovereignty of Member States and, in particular, in the self-government of many municipalities be — even from the point of view of the market-opening function of procurement law — entirely unnecessary, as "[a]fter all, the purpose of procurement law is to ensure that contractors are selected in a transparent and non-discriminatory manner in all cases where a public body has decided to use third parties to perform certain tasks. However, the spirit and purpose of procurement law is not also to bring about, '*through the back door*', the privatization of those public tasks which the public body would like to continue to perform by using its own resources. This would require specific liberalisation measures on the part of the legislature (footnotes omitted)." See Opinion of AG Kokott in Case C-458/03 *Parking Brixen* [2005] ECR I-8585, paras 70–71.

[156]Opinion of AG Trstenjak in Case C-324/07 *Coditel Brabant* [2008] ECR I-8457, paras 84–85.

[157]Case T 442/03 *SIC* v *Commission* [2008] ECR II-1161, para 154.

regardless of whether they decide to commission it, and more often than not due to their statutory *obligation* to supply SGEIs (a "public service task"). In the field of public procurement, the role of national, regional and local authorities is necessarily double: as public authorities and as contracting authorities. The functional approach of their activity for the purpose of EU competition rules, formulated in *Commission v Italy*, and operating a dichotomy between their *exercise of public powers* from their *offer of goods and services on the market,*[158] seems in the field of public procurement to give way to a more "formal" approach, as public authorities are expected to act on the basis of their competence in national law even when they organise the supply of services within this competence. In other words, their societal missions must be expected, and allowed, to affect their purchasing strategies, normally funded through tax.[159]

Likewise, the exemptions consented to by the CJEU for public-public cooperation under certain conditions are connected by the Court itself to the existence of public service tasks devolved to public authorities, and justifying enhanced discretion in the organisation of service provision and commission. In *Commission v Germany* the Court found that procurement rules did not apply to a contract providing for "waste pooling" and mutual assistance between the municipality of Hamburg and four smaller municipalities in the same region.[160] This conclusion rested mostly on the argument that the objective of the municipalities when entering this contract was to cooperate in fulfilling their public service task, and to establish the frame of Hamburg's future procurement for the construction of an incineration facility offering sufficient treatment capacity. Several authors have questioned the relationship between this ruling and the *Teckal* case law respectively the *Coditel* doctrine.[161]

Indeed, in *Commission v Germany* the Court established connections with both *Teckal* and *Coditel* but opened a new line of reasoning. While the Court of Justice did not use the term SGEI, it emphasized first that the four smaller municipalities

---

[158]Case 118/85 *Commission v Italy* [1987] ECR 2599, para 7.

[159]In a paper where he firmly criticizes what he calls a neo-liberal approach of public procurement, Kunzlik holds that the marketization of public services has intensified the ideological importance of the regulation of public procurement, because as government activities are increasingly outsourced and delivered through contracts, the discretion of public bodies is increasingly controlled by public procurement law. He relates the ideological meaning of this regulation to Daintith's observation in the 1970s, that government can exercise two kinds of power: "imperium" (powers to prohibit and sanction conduct of which it disapproves, resulting from the state's monopoly on the use of force) and "dominium" (the power to pursue policy objectives by deploying the state's wealth, for example, by awarding or withholding public contracts). Kunzlik insists that "the very fact that public purchasers are indeed public bodies having public functions means that they may seek to pursue "non-market" goals in their procurement so that their decisions may produce "inefficient" outcomes in the sense that they differ from the outcomes to be expected from the normal working of the free (private) market". This opinion is shared here. See Kunzlik P., p. 311.

[160]Case C-480/06 *Commission v Germany* [2009] ECR I-04747.

[161]See Naundrup Olesen 2011, and Steinicke 2011.

and the municipality of Hamburg had agreed, by the contract in dispute, on mutual commitments directly related to "public service objectives" and on mutual assistance to perform their "legal obligations to dispose of waste"; the contract was therefore seen as the "basis and the legal framework" in order *at a later stage* to contract out the performance of a "public service, namely thermal combustion of waste".[162] It is therefore submitted that the red thread of the judgment is the discretion for municipalities to *refine* the definition of the task of general economic interest, *before* they procure it on the market. Under their obligation to plan and ensure treatment, the municipalities were simply seen as organising the service through waste flow optimization. Hence the Court considered that procurement rules should not deprive the public authorities from the right to fulfil their mission better and cheaper. By pooling their needs in form of a *contract*, as a basis for Hamburg's future contract to be established through lawful procurement, they did not bereave the market of anything.[163] As in *Coditel*, the approach in *Commission v Germany* was clearly motivated by the municipalities' own public service tasks, recognized as legitimate by the Court, in line both with Article 1 of the SGI Protocol and with the Union's duty to respect local self-government pursuant to Article 4(2) TEU.

In *Lecce*, the Court of Justice summarized the criteria exempting municipal cooperation from the scope of procurement law as follows. "European Union rules on public procurement *are not applicable* in so far as,

a. The public entities establish their cooperation with the aim of ensuring that a public task that they all *have to* perform is carried out
b. Contracts are concluded exclusively by public entities, without the participation of a private party
c. No private provider of services is placed in a position of advantage vis-à-vis competitors
d. Implementation of that cooperation is governed solely by considerations and requirements relating to the pursuit of objectives in the public interest".[164]

Condition (a) is that the public entities have an *obligation* to *perform a task of general interest.* The Court does not only mean that the activity is covered by the authority's competence and the principle of self-government, which must be respected by EU law. It seems clear that the Court refers to a *legal obligation* to supply a service of general interest (SGI). Condition (d) is that the cooperation's sole aim is the pursuit of the objective of general interest, and evokes the Member

[162]Case C 480/06 *Commission v Germany* [2009] ECR I-04747, paras 41, 42 and 44.

[163]Importantly this contract implied only financial transfers from the four small municipalities to the municipality of Hamburg, covering their part of the charges paid by Hamburg to the operator of the facilities. There was thus no direct "remuneration for the provision of a service" from the small municipalities to the municipality of Hamburg. See Case C-480/06 *Commission v Germany,* para 43.

[164]Case C-159/11 *Lecce* (CJEU 19 December 2012), paras 34–35, referring to Case C-480/06 *Commission* v *Germany* [2009] ECR I-04747, paras 44 and 47, emphasis added.

States' duty, provided for by Article 14 TFEU, to take care that SGEIs are operated under conditions which enable them to achieve their missions, in particular economic and financial conditions. Public-public cooperation may from an economic point of view be precisely a manner to fulfil this duty, and the CJEU's view is arguably that, under the strict conditions formulated in *Lecce*, the exemption from the application of EU procurement for such agreements (even in the form of contract) is constitutionally needed.

Thus, regarding both the in-house exemption and the public-public cooperation exemption, the Court establishes a direct link between the exemption from EU procurement rules and the existence of general interest tasks which public authorities are under an obligation to supply. This link is not so visible regarding the in-house exemption, because the CJEU has entwined it in the notion of contract in the meaning of EU procurement rules. By contrast, the public-public exemption could not be "incorporated" in the definition of contract for the purpose of EU procurement rules, and this exemption gives therefore more visibility to the existence of a public service task as a fundamental criterion. It must be emphasized here that the notions of "public service obligations" and "public service tasks" have been used by the Court in *Altmark* in a way perceived by the General Court in *BUPA* as in principle synonym with SGEI tasks.[165] Hence it is submitted that in *Commission v Germany*, the CJEU has (discreetly) opened Pandora's Box: it has explicitly found a derogation from EU procurement rules to be necessary, under its duty as an EU institution to take care that SGEI missions can be achieved, a principle established by Article 14 TFEU, and also expressed by Article 106(2) TFEU. This time, the SGEI mission was on the public authorities.[166]

To attribute such a clear meaning to *Commission v Germany* and to *Lecce* may certainly be feared for its implications. For instance, Wiggen admits that *Commission v Germany* has broadened public authorities' margin of discretion. Also, she agrees with Karayigit that the CJEU's judgment seems to be in line with Article 14 TFEU and even envisages that the cooperation at issue, could possibly be regarded as concerning an SGEI.[167] However, she denies that this in itself could be the deciding factor, on the following arguments. She considers that a contracting authority will virtually always be acting to secure the fulfilment of what she calls its "public interest tasks". However, in *Commission v Germany*, the exemption was admissible due to the existence of a "*public service* task", not a "public interest task". She also argues that in previous cases concerning cooperation between public sector entities, the fact that the service at issue could be considered

[165]See discussion in Sect. 7.2.3.5.

[166]Naundrup Olesen has evoked the possibility that the Court used in *Commission v Germany* the "ideas" contained in Article 16 EC (now Article 14 TFEU), but considered that more case law would be needed to conclude that the general interest plays an important role for the issue of compliance with the procurement rules, and perhaps more broadly EU Internal market rules. See Naundrup Olesen 2011, pp. 254–258.

[167]Wiggen 2011, p. 162. Regarding Wiggen's reference to Karayigit, see Karayigit 2010, p. 190.

of general economic interest had not been sufficient to prevent the application of the procurement rules. This is an interesting but inconclusive argument. The fact is that *Commission v Germany* was decided by the Grand Chamber, signalling the importance of the case, and arguably also that the Court deferred to its duty to take care that SGEIs achieve their missions, under Article 14 TFEU. The SGEI missions at issue in *Commission v Germany* were hardly deniable as they were imposed by the EU legislator itself.

Wiggen's last argument is that granting an exception from the Directive's scope of application on SGEI motives would undermine the objectives of the public procurement rules. Although respectable, this is a political argument, not legal. Besides, the Court does not exactly make it easy to invoke the derogation, as the SGEI at issue legitimates public-public cooperation subject to conditions which may be regarded as a proportionality test.

Fiedziuk has noted that Article 106(2) TFEU has, so far, not played any significant role in the application of EU public procurement rules, but holds that "the reliance on its provisions is becoming a necessity".[168] On the same path, Damjanovic notes that, so far, an exception from this regime has never been justified on the basis of Article 106(2) TFEU, but refers to *Commission v Germany* as a case showing that Article 106(2) TFEU might also be invoked in relation to the application of secondary law on public procurement, even though she underlines that it is not easy to argue for an exception from the application of the Public Procurement Directive on the basis of Article 106(2) TFEU.[169] In fact, in the field of public procurement, it seems arguable that Article 14 TFEU may play a role which Article 106(2) TFEU cannot easily play because it has its focus on *undertakings'* conditions to fulfil SGEI tasks.

4.2.3 A Lenient Review of Restrictions of the Free Movement of Services Justified by Public Service Tasks

Outside the field of social services, it seems worth mentioning here the *UPC* ruling, where the CJEU examined Belgian legislation requiring cable operators providing services in the Brussels-region to broadcast TV programmes transmitted by broadcasters designated by Belgian authorities.[170] This "must-carry-obligation"

---

[168]Fiedziuk 2013, p. 113.

[169]Damjanovic 2013, p. 1711. In contrast with Fiedziuk, Damjanovic finds the Court's restrictive approach in allowing SGEI tasks to allow derogations from EU procurement rules "understandable against the background of the effect of these rules on the Member States' welfare regimes: they do not oblige the Member States to contract out (i.e. to privatize), nor do they have any other market-opening effect, but merely oblige the Member States when they have already taken the crucial decision to contract out to do so in a transparent and fair manner, by awarding the contracts in a competitive procedure."

[170]Case C-250/06 *UPC* [2007] ECR I-11135.

regime was part of a national policy designed to enable television viewers to have access to both private broadcasters assuming public service obligations (public service TV programs) and public service broadcasters.[171] The Court found that the must-carry-obligation restricted the freedom to provide services,[172] but that it was appropriate to achieve the general interest of preserving the pluralist character of the television programmes available in that bilingual territory.[173] The obligation was *not disproportionate* in relation to that objective, if it was applied subject to a transparent procedure based on objective non-discriminatory criteria known in advance.[174] This test was evidently softer than the standard *Gebhard* test, which requires that measures restricting the freedom of establishment do not go beyond what is strictly necessary in order to attain the objective of general interest pursued.[175]

In fact, the TV-broadcasters enjoying "a right to be carried" by cable operators had themselves public service obligations to develop local TV and to broadcast local news aimed at the local public. The must-carry-obligation was thus necessary to secure the achievement of their SGEI task, and therefore it is difficult not to see an analogy the Court's test in *UPC* and the mild test applied by the Court when it applies Article 106(2) TFEU to measures aimed at securing the fulfilment of SGEI tasks.

In a line of health care cases, the CJEU considered that although the objective of a balanced medical and hospital service open to all is *intrinsically* linked to the method of financing the social security system, it may constitute an overriding reason related to the general interest.[176] As the financing system was an intrinsic instrument to achieve the objective of balanced hospital health care, the Court found that "to prevent the possible risk of *seriously* undermining a social security system's financial balance" constituted per se an overriding reason related to the general interest.[177] On these premises, the Court found that national rules requiring prior authorization for the reimbursement of costs of medical treatment provided in another Member State by a non-contracted care provider, could under

---

[171]For instance owned by local authorities, as in *Coditel*, evoked above in 8.2.2.

[172]Case C-250/06 *UPC* [2007] ECR I-11135, para 38.

[173]Ibid., para 43. The Court held that this legislation sought to harmonize the audio-visual landscape in Belgium in order to safeguard the maintenance of the pluralism connected with freedom of expression, protected by Article 10 of the European Convention on Human Rights and Fundamental Freedoms, see paras 40–41.

[174]Ibid., para 51.

[175]Case C-55/94 *Gebhard* [1995] ECR I-4165, para 39.

[176]Case C-158/96 *Kohll* [1998] ECR I-1931, para 50, and Case C-157/99 *Smits and Peerbooms* [2001] ECR I-5473, para 73.

[177]This was first asserted in Case C-120/95 *Decker* [1998] ECR I-1831, para 39, and confirmed in Case C-158/96 *Kohll,* para 41, Case C-157/99 *Smits and Peerbooms*, para 72, Case C-385/99 *Müller-Fauré* [2003] ECR I-4509, para 73, Case C-372/04 *Watts* [2006] ECR I-4325, para 103, and Case C-444/05 *Stamatelaki* [2007] ECR I-3185, para 30.

certain conditions be justified as necessary to prevent the risk of *seriously* undermining a social security system's financial balance. The Court admitted that giving insured persons full liberty to use the services of hospitals situated in the State where they are insured or in another Member State, with which their sickness insurance fund has no contractual arrangements, could jeopardize the planning of a Member State's hospital care. The Court admitted also that such planning was necessary for a rationalised, stable, balanced and accessible supply of hospital services, in terms of number of hospitals, their geographical distribution, and even the nature of the medical services which they are able to offer.[178]

Called by Bekkedal a "fiction under the mandatory requirements doctrine", the Court's approach in those cases consisted in overlooking that the measures at issue were most probably connected to the maintenance of systems pursuing SGEI missions (generally established by law) and SGEI tasks (entrusted through contracts or arrangements). In this fiction, Bekkedal argues, the Court upheld its doctrinal stance that overriding reasons related to the general interest cannot be of economic nature, but allowed economic aims exceptionally "when they are of imperative importance".[179] Bekkedal's view that the Court's approach involved a fiction is shared here, but his view that "economic aims are undoubtedly accepted under the exception in Article 106(2) TFEU" is worth discussing.[180] In cases where Article 106(2) has been invoked by Member States, it is rather the term "acceptable economic *conditions*" which has been used by the Court. While such conditions may be an aim for undertakings entrusted with SGEIs, public authorities consider them as an *instrument* in the fulfilment of their missions (in particular to secure continuity and security). It is therefore argued here that "preserving the financial balance of the social security system" is not an independent economic *aim*, but rather an *economic principle*—to be respected—for the achievement of the mission to supply balanced hospital care open to all.

Bekkedal considers that the Court's approach does not take anything from the Member States, because it does not follow from the wording of Article 106(2) TFEU that it can be brought forward by the Member States in four freedom cases at all. However, it has been shown in Sect. 4.1.3 that this provision has a horizontal scope and has been successfully brought forward, for instance in *Corsica Ferries*, to justify national legislation restricting free movement, a view shared by several authors.[181] Although Article 106(2) TFEU evokes *undertakings*' tasks, the Court has consented exemptions under Article 106(2) for state measures, with regard in particular to its understanding of the scope of Article 106(1) TFEU, and of the fact that the protection of SGEI tasks provided by Article 106(2) TFEU does not primarily serve undertakings, but instead the interests of the Member States entrusting them.

---

[178]Case C-157/99 *Smits and Peerbooms*, paras 76 and 81.

[179]See Bekkedal 2011 p. 75.

[180]Ibid.

[181]Case C-266/96 *Corsica Ferries*, [1998] ECR I-3949. Among many authors supporting this view, we find Szyszczak 2007, p. 217 and Lenaerts 2012, p. 1255.

Yet, it is undeniable that the focus of Article 106(2) TFEU on the SGEI tasks of undertakings does not fit legal-technically with invoking public authorities' SGEI missions, which arguably explains the need of a "fiction", implying that the test of Article 106(2) TFEU is applied to justify restrictions of the free movement of services, but that the notion of SGEI is not used. The interesting question is why the Court would do that. Well, even if the CJEU may not be argued to "keep Article 106(2) TFEU in the dark", to use Bekkedal's words, it has some reason to keep the notion of SGEI itself in the dark if it wishes to conduct what Lenaerts calls an approach "open to nuances". Under this approach, it keeps a margin to design the balance between the system interest and the free movement interest in a manner that may find acceptance in all Member States, both holders of national welfare systems and holders of a more market-based policy on public services. In addition to this "political reason", it is argued that another very legal reason also explains the tests used in the cases evoked here. It is submitted that the Court saw itself obliged, as an EU institution, to respect SGEI missions in the meaning of Article 16 EC, which existed and expressed a normative signal when these rulings were delivered. It is submitted that what the Court did was to apply the principle of Article 14 TFEU, before it was explicitly formulated through the Lisbon Treaty. In so doing, the Court delineated, not least for itself, the contours of the EU concept of SGEI.

It is true that the Court has applied a softer test to national measures related to "infrastructure conditions" necessary to maintain SGEI missions. Indeed, the Court has so far always allowed that Member States upholding a requirement of prior authorization to reimburse patients receiving health care from operators outside the public funded system, without demanding that these Member States give evidence that removing this requirement implies a risk of *seriously* undermining a social security system's financial balance.[182] In that sense, and using Bekkedal's words, it may seem that the Court "does not take away anything from the Member States". However, it appears that by disregarding from the SGEI character of the missions and the tasks, the Court frees itself from reasoning in terms of "economic pressure on the undertakings entrusted with SGEI tasks", and allows itself to reason instead in terms of "financial pressure which the national social service system must tolerate". It looks as if the Court trades EU law's deference to Member States' assessment that a procedure of prior authorization is appropriate and necessary to protect the financial balance of the social security's system, against EU law's imposition of conditions on:

a. The risk standard for the social security's system and
b. The governance of the procedure of prior authorization.

Regarding (a), the Court sets a standard of "risk of seriously undermining" the system's financial balance, which may seem strict but at the same time is rather

[182]This has been underlined by Hancher and Sauter, see Hancher and Sauter 2009, p. 17.

open-ended. Regarding (b), van de Gronden explains that the Court's case law on hospital care evoked above forces Member States to take account of the interests of patients in managing their systems, as the Court sets standards for reimbursement rates, waiting lists, and prior authorization procedures on a case-by-case basis, which inevitably leads to the harmonization of several aspects of the organisation of national health care systems.[183] Thus, the Court transposes an element characteristic of the case law under Article 106(2) TFEU (i.e. the relevance of economic and financial conditions in the balance between fundamental market freedoms and the sustainability of national systems aimed at securing universal access to social services), while keeping in the dark the SGEI-character of the regulation at issue. The Court's fiction is to make believe that it does not regulate the economic conditions for the achievement of SGEI missions, although it does in fact decide what economic "good governance" involves in Europeanized social services. What may legitimize the Court's step is that it is left alone to decide how free movement law will "domino-affect" national welfare systems, as long as the Member States do not proceed to develop the rules in a more democratic manner.

Thus, in *Kattner Stahlbau* the CJEU found that a body providing insurance against accidents at work and occupational diseases did not constitute an undertaking, as it fulfilled an exclusively social objective, but also that the national rules governing its activity were subject to the freedom to provide services, because they covered services which at least partly could be provided for remuneration in other Member States.[184] The Court found that the national rule imposing compulsory affiliation to the insurance body did restrict the freedom to provide services for insurers established in other Member States, but held that ensuring the financial balance of that branch of social security could constitute an overriding reason related to the general interest, and that compulsory affiliation could be a suitable means to achieve this objective.[185] The Court found that the statutory insurance scheme did not go beyond what was necessary to achieve its objective of general interest, as it held that there was a high risk of cherry-picking, as the scheme was based on solidarity and offered only minimal cover, allowing undertakings to top up their cover by taking supplementary insurance possibly available on the market.[186]

Here again, it is argued that the implicit SGEI-character of the mission entrusted to the entity at issue in *Kattner Stahlbau* was decisive when the Court decided to bifurcate from the doctrine that overriding reasons related to the general interest cannot be related to economic conditions. In its assessment of the compulsory affiliation rule, the Court did neither deprive the Member State from the possibility to invoke the financial sustainability of its welfare system, nor forced it to prove that solidarity was the least restrictive solution to secure access

[183] Van de Gronden 2009, p. 758.

[184] Case C-350/07 *Kattner Stahlbau* [2009] ECR I-1513.

[185] Ibid., para 85 and 88.

[186] Ibid., para 89–90.

to the type of insurance at issue in the case. However, to be proportional to its restriction of free movement, the solidarity system had to be kept to a minimal cover—a "core welfare"—that allowed undertakings covered by the scheme to take out supplementary insurance available on the market: a "top up welfare". The Court was cautious in its liberalizing approach, stating that the restriction to a minimal cover would *militate* in favour of the proportionality of compulsory affiliation, and that it was for the national court to assess how the balance would be struck. If the Court had approached the scheme as based on SGEI missions defined by a Member State, it would have been obliged to explain why Member States must define "*core* SGEIs" instead of enjoying a wide discretion in defining SGEI missions in their areas of competence.

4.2.4 Lenient Review of Restrictions of the Freedom of Establishment Justified by Public Service Tasks: Hartlauer

In *Hartlauer*, the Court of Justice assessed the compatibility with the freedom of establishment of Austrian rules requiring authorisation to set up a private independent outpatient clinic for dental medicine. These rules involved that authorisation must be refused if needs were covered by already established dentists, doctors and establishments contracted to or owned by sickness funds. The Austrian government did not contest that these rules restricted the freedom of establishment, but argued that the system ensured a medical service of high quality, balanced and accessible to all, and that the rules ensured the financial balance of the social security system in that they enabled social security institutions to control expenditure by adapting it to planned needs.[187] This system consisted primarily of a system of benefits in kind, and in addition of a system of reimbursement by social security institutions of costs incurred by insured persons having recourse to non-contractual practitioners.[188]

To justify the authorization requirement and the fulfilment of certain conditions to receive an authorization, the Austrian government claimed first that uncontrolled establishment of new independent outpatient dental clinics could jeopardize the possibility for contractual practitioners to offer their services under acceptable economic conditions, and in turn for patients' access to the medical services they provided throughout national territory. Second, the Austrian government argued that in the public health sector, an increase in supply tends to lead to an increase in the volume of services supplied at constant prices, and therefore an uncontrolled

[187]Case C-169/07 *Hartlauer* [2009] ECR I-1721, para 41.

[188]Ibid., paras 16–17. Reimbursement of costs incurred by persons consulting a doctor who was not a contractual practitioner was up to a ceiling which is generally 80 % of the sum which would have been charged if the treatment had been entrusted to a contractual practitioner.

growth in the number of providers of medical services could impose uncontrollable burdens on the social security institutions. Even if these institutions did not offer contracts to the new service providers, the rules on reimbursement of costs paid by the person insured would oblige them to spend sums substantially the same as those spent in the context of the system of benefits in kind.[189]

Having noted that the system of authorization applied without discrimination on grounds of nationality, the Court recalled that, in accordance with the CJEU's case law, the protection of public health under Article 52 TFEU may specifically justify (1) the objective of maintaining a balanced high-quality medical service open to all[190] and (2) preventing the risk of serious harm to the financial balance of the social security system.[191] The Court admitted that planning could be necessary to supply not only hospital care but also outpatient care, and that prior authorisation could prove indispensable "to ensure medical care which is adapted to the needs of the population, covers the entire territory and takes account of geographically isolated or otherwise disadvantaged regions".[192] It also admitted that the system of benefits in kind could have priority in this planning, in order to secure easy access to the services of contractual practitioners throughout the national territory.[193] However, the Court found that the national rules were incompatible with the Treaties, as they (a) submitted to a system of prior authorisation new outpatient dental clinics but not new group practices, although those two categories of providers were comparable in service features, number of practitioners and service volume and (b) allowed certain Austrian provinces to assess needs according to non-objective criteria.

Thus, although the Austrian rules fell on their lack of consistency, the Court did neither reject the Austrian arguments supporting the need of an authorization scheme nor examine with great care whether less restrictive means were available.[194] Hancher and Sauter see a striking contrast between the soft standard of review in establishment cases such as *Hartlauer* and *German hospital pharmacies*, and the strict standard of review (a form of mutual recognition) in the free movement of service case *French laboratories*.[195] The latter case concerned French rules requiring that bio-medical laboratories had their place of business in France and barring reimbursement of analyses carried out in other Member States. The Court held that, in the absence of harmonisation, this restriction of the freedom to

---

[189]Ibid., para 43.

[190]Ibid., para 48. Article 52 TFEU allowing the Member States, in particular, to restrict the freedom to provide medical and hospital services in so far as the maintenance of treatment capacity or medical competence on national territory is essential for the public health, and even the survival, of the population.

[191]Ibid., para 49.

[192]Ibid., para 51–52.

[193]Ibid., para 53.

[194]See Van de Gronden 2013a, p. 146.

[195]Case C-496/01 *French Laboratories* [2004] ECR I-2351; Case C-141/07 *German Hospital Pharmacies* [2008] ECR I-6935. See Hancher and Sauter 2009, p. 17.

provide services could be justified by the aim of maintaining the quality of medical services, covered by the derogations for public health in Article 52 TFEU, in so far as it contributed to the attainment of a high level of health protection.[196] However, as similar requirements existed in the Member State of establishment, and considering that monitoring the service in that State was possible and less restrictive, the Court concluded that the French rules were non-proportional and contrary to Article 56 TFEU. To Hancher and Sauter, this could suggest that the freedom to provide services is applied more strictly than the freedom of establishment, or that regulation of activities in state-run or "mixed" system enjoys a more lenient review than simple regulation of market-based provision of services.

It is submitted here that the difference in the standards of review may rather have to do with the implicit acknowledgement that the national rules set conditions for the achievement of SGEI missions in the meaning of Article 16 EC (now modified in Article 14 TFEU). In this regard, it is important to recall the GC's view in *BUPA*, already evoked above, that the fact that the national legislature, acting in the general interest in the broad sense, imposes certain rules of authorisation, of functioning or of control on all the operators in a particular sector does not in principle mean that there is an SGEI mission. The French laboratories were subject to functioning rules, but apparently not to SGEI tasks.

By contrast, it seems that in *Hartlauer*, the Court implicitly acknowledged the implementation of the objectives pursued by the national Austrian authorization scheme as motivated by the national legislator's intention to secure patients' access to an SGEI, and which the Court's conditions may not obstruct. It is submitted here that this implicit acknowledgement explains the softer proportionality in *Hartlauer*, and the Court's admission that a welfare system's economic conditions may justify a restriction of the freedom of establishment, both transposed from the Court's test under Article 106(2) TFEU in areas where the Member States retain policy competence, as in the field of social services. This is not contradicted by Hancher and Sauter's observation that in *Hartlauer* and in other cases where a more lenient proportionality test is applied, the Court invoked the Member States' powers in the field of health care and their freedom to determine the desired level or health protection.[197] As seen in Chap. 3, the respect of national identity lies at the core of SGEIs' values.

4.2.5 *Libert*: Lenient Review of Restriction of the Free Movement of Capital Justified by Public Service Obligations

The *Libert* case sheds particularly interesting light on how the CJEU seems to consider that undertakings' SGEI tasks may motivate public service compensation and

[196] Case C-496/01 *French Laboratories*, cited above, para 66.

[197] Hancher and Sauter 2009, p. 17.

at the same time that a restriction of fundamental freedoms may be justified by the objective pursued by these SGEI tasks. In that case, the Court had to examine two rules laid down in a Flemish Decree, both aiming at securing access to housing in Flemish communes: the first rule prevented persons without a "sufficient connection" from purchasing land or buildings in certain target communes, the second rule required from land subdividers or developers, as a condition for the grant of a building or land subdivision authorisation, to discharge a social obligation consisting in either devoting part of their building project to the development of social housing units, or paying a financial contribution to the commune in which that project was developed (Fig. 4.1).

The second rule imposing a "social obligation" on undertakings was relevant both as a free movement issue and in connection to a state aid issue.[198] The Court assessed the requirement of "social obligation" in the light of the free movement of capital.[199] It found that the obligation to devote a part of land development projects to develop social housing units or instead contribute financially to a social housing project developed by the commune they seek authorization from, constituted a restriction of the free movement of capital in accordance with settled case law.[200] The Court recalled that the fundamental freedoms could lawfully be restricted by an objective to guarantee sufficient housing for the low-income or otherwise disadvantaged sections of the local population, as this objective had been held to constitute an overriding reason related to the general interest relating to social housing policy in a Member State.[201]

Thus, the "social obligation" at issue in *Libert* could be compatible with Article 63 TFEU, if it was justified by the objective of guaranteeing sufficient housing for the low-income or otherwise disadvantaged sections of the local population, and if it was assessed and found by the national court to be appropriate and necessary to attain this objective.[202] This proportionality test of the authorization condition contains no requirement of least restrictive measure, and seems thus "softer" than the "standard Gebhard test" applied to restrictions justified by overriding reasons related to the general interest. This is important, because by contrast, the Court used a strict proportionality test regarding the other requirement at issue in the case, namely a requirement of "sufficient connection" with the target commune in the Flemish Decree. As none of the conditions for establishing a sufficient connection reflected the socio-economic aspects relating to the objective put forward by the

[198]Joined Cases C-197/11 and C-203/11 *Libert* (CJEU 8 May 2013), para 65.

[199]Observing that the restriction of the freedom of establishment and the freedom to provide services was an inevitable consequence of the restriction of the free movement of capital, the Court considered unjustified to examine the legislation at issue in the light of Articles 49 and 56 TFEU. See C-197/11 and C-203/11 *Libert*, para 62.

[200]Cases C-197/11 and C-203/11 *Libert*, paras 64–66, with reference to Case C-567/07 *Sint Servatius*, [2009] ECR I-9021 paras 21–22.

[201]Ibid., para 67, with reference to *Sint Servatius*, paras 29–30, and Case C-400/08 *Commission* v *Spain* [2011] ECR I-1915, para 74.

[202]Ibid., paras 67–69.

Flemish Government, and as the conditions of sufficient connection could also be met by persons with no specific need for social protection on the property market, the CJEU considered that the requirement went beyond what was necessary to achieve the goal pursued, and moreover, argued that there were other means of pursuing it, for instance by "subsidies for purchase or other subsidy mechanisms specifically designed to assist less affluent persons".[203]

Nicolaides found puzzling the CJEU's approach, leaving to the national court the task of evaluating whether the social obligation was appropriate and necessary to attain its objective.[204] It is proposed here that these two elements (1) the lenient proportionality test of the social obligation and (2) leaving the assessment to the national court are explained by the Court of Justice's view that the social obligation could constitute an SGEI task. The Court held namely one of the referred questions to be "in essence" whether the tax incentives and subsidy mechanisms granted to operators fulfilling the conditions for authorization, had to be classified as state aid to be notified *read in conjunction with the SGEI Decision*. It is unclear from the case whether the argument that these advantages could constitute the compensation of an SGEI task had been raised by the parties or the intervening parties to the case.[205] In any case, the Court, which in the free movement assessment had chosen the cautious and neutral term of "social obligation", held that it was not "inconceivable" that the social obligation could be regarded as a "public service".[206] Based on this view, the Court answered to the national court that it would first have to assess, on the basis of the four *Altmark* criteria, whether the public service compensation measures constituted state aid in the meaning of Article 107(1) TFEU, and if so, that it would have to ascertain whether the SGEI Decision was applicable to the Flemish Decree providing for that compensation.[207]

In light of the above, the following approach emerges arguably from the *Libert* ruling. The CJEU considered that the national rule, imposing a social obligation on operators applying for building/developing authorizations, could be conceived as an SGEI task. It therefore enjoined the national court to assess the national rule providing for an economic compensation of this obligation, as public service compensation subject to a lenient test under Article 106(2) TFEU (if the fourth *Altmark* criterion was not fulfilled). It is proposed that the Court also conceived the State's compensation measure not only as an economic condition necessary for operators to be interested to build in those communes, but also as a *qualified* commitment of the State, different from "a standard overriding reason related to the general interest". Assessed in the light of the Treaty rules on free movement, the

---

[203]See Cases C-197/11 and C-203/11 *Libert*, paras 55–56.

[204]See his analysis of the case in Nicolaides 2014, pp. 151–156.

[205]AG Mazàk *understood* the question referred as "seeking, in essence, to obtain clarification of the case-law within the meaning of which, where a State measure must be regarded as compensation for the services provided by the recipient undertakings in order to discharge public service obligations". See Opinion of AG Mazàk in Joined Cases C-197/11 and C-203/11 *Libert*, para 49.

[206]Cases C-197/11 and C-203/11 *Libert*, para 88.

[207]Ibid., paras 89–102.

rule imposing a social obligation (an SGEI task) was subject to a soft proportionality test, arguably because it transformed the overriding reason related to the general interest from a simple objective, into *a concrete financial commitment from the State*, engaging State resources, in other words, into an SGEI *mission* in the meaning of Article 14 TFEU. The approach in Libert may be visualised as follows:

Objective of rules 1 and 2

= guarantee sufficient housing for the low income and otherwise disadvantaged sections of local population (social housing)

Rule 1 = undertakings seeking authorization for building or land subdivision operations in a Flemish commune must discharge a **social housing obligation** which may be discharged in two alternative forms:

a. Contribute financially to local social housing project or

b. Conduct own social housing project in that commune

Rule 2 = Additional costs for operators are compensated by tax incentives & subsidy mechanisms

Rule 2 may distort competition but compatible with EU state aid rules

- If seen as compensating an SGEI task
- If appropriate and necessary for the fulfilment of this SGEI task

↓

Soft test for rule 2 (no RLM)

Rule 1 can be seen as an SGEI task in the meaning of Article 106(2) TFEU or *Altmark*, because Member States have a wide discretion to define SGEI

Rule 2: the State must compensate SGEI costs incurred by operators "SGEI mission" pursued by State →

Rule 1 restricts free movement but compatible with Article 67 TFEU

- If seen as based on an overriding reasons related to the general interest
- If appropriate and necessary for the fulfilment of the overriding reason related to the general interest

Soft test for rule 1 (no RLM)

↑

The "standard test for overriding reason related to the general interest" is not applied

↑

"Qualified overriding reasons related to the general interest" in this case

Fig. 4.1 The CJEU's approach in Libert

4.3 Conclusions

The study in Sect. 4.1 shows that the CJEU has used Article 106(2) TFEU mostly to justify exclusive rights to providers of services in the public sector infringing Treaty rules on competition or on free movement, and now also to justify public service funding measures constituting state aid. The standard of review under Article 106(2) TFEU emerges as heterogeneous, being in certain cases a "reconciliation rule", and in others a "derogatory rule" to be interpreted strictly. In a majority of cases, the Court applies a "soft proportionality test", which only requires that measures infringing the Treaty market rules are appropriate and necessary to enable undertakings entrusted with SGEIs to fulfil their tasks under economic acceptable conditions. By contrast, *Dusseldorp* and *FFAD* show that the review under Article 106(2) TFEU is stricter (requiring that the measure is the least restrictive) concerning SGEIs attached to activities covered by EU law harmonizing the objectives pursued in that field, and/or the measures which Member States may resort to in order to promote them. Also, the Court seems to require under Article 106(2) TFEU a control of strict proportionality between undertakings' SGEI-costs and their direct public funding. This emerges from *CBI* and is important for social services. In sum, these characteristics of the test under Article 106(2) TFEU seem coherent with the SGEI principle laid down in Article 14 TFEU, the SGI Protocol and the right of access to SGEIs in Article 36 EUCFR.

The analysis in Sect. 4.2 shows that the CJEU has applied essential elements of its soft proportionality test under Article 106(2) TFEU without applying Article 106(2) TFEU. It is submitted that this "SGEI-related case law" includes two main approaches.

The first approach, represented clearest by *Altmark* but also by *Teckal*, is one of "incorporation" of the notion of SGEI, *through the equivalent notion of public service task*, in the concepts of entry of the Treaty-based market rules. In this approach, inherently using the softer proportionality test typical of Article 106(2) TFEU, the CJEU finds that certain SGEI-justified measures do not have to be derogatory, because the derogation is incorporated in a concept decisive for the application of the market rule, "state aid" in Article 107(1) TFEU or "contract" in EU procurement rules. In *Altmark*, the CJEU used the notion of "public service obligation" as a synonym of SGEI tasks, and established that strictly proportional compensation of these tasks excludes the existence of "state aid in the meaning of Article 107(1) TFEU". In the *Teckal* doctrine, the CJEU has established that the contracting authorities' provision of "public service tasks" with their own resources excludes the existence of a "contract in the meaning of EU procurement law".

The second approach, clear from *Hartlauer* (freedom of establishment), *Kattner Stahlbau* (free movement of services), and *Libert* (free movement of capital) is one of "transposition". It implies that the soft proportionality test, typical of Article 106(2) TFEU in fields which belong to Member States' competence, is used to assess measures restricting the fundamental freedoms, and that their justification could be characterized as SGEI missions, but is instead approached by the Court as overriding reasons related to the general interest. This approach is eased by the overlap between overriding reasons related to the general interest and SGEIs recognized in EU law, this overlap being related to the Court's "formula of retained powers" and more fundamentally explained by the Treaty rules introduced by the Treaty of Lisbon 2007/9 and necessitating that Member States' competence and national identity are respected by the Union. Under this approach, the Court finds compatible with the Treaties certain measures restricting fundamental freedoms, such as requirements of prior authorization for service providers or service recipients, without requiring that they are proven to constitute the least restrictive measures, and admits that they may also be justified by economic concerns. This approach builds on a "fiction" in two respects:

- The measure supports overriding reasons related to the general interest which, when they consist in a State's qualified commitment to securing access to certain services, evidently are *very particular types of* overriding reasons, evoking rather SGEI missions in the meaning of Article 14 TFEU.
- The measure is presented by the Court as supporting a second "financial overriding reason related to the general interest", worded by the Court as consisting in "preventing the possible risk of seriously undermining a social security *system*'s financial balance". This second overriding reason related to the general interest is also very particular, as it amounts to an acknowledgement of the Member State's freedom to organise their task to supply welfare services in the frame of a solidarity-based *system*, and of their need to maintain this system under economic and financial conditions enabling them to achieve their tasks. This second overriding reason related to the general interest, the necessity of a system and of its financial balance, evokes very much the "conditions, in particular economic and financial conditions", for the operation of SGEIs in the meaning of Article 14 TFEU.

In this "transposition approach", the CJEU's spirit appears arguably to consist in taking care, by allowing a "financial overriding reason related to the general interest", that other "very particular types of overriding reasons related to the general interest", which evoke very much SGEI missions, operate under acceptable economic and financial conditions. Thus, both the transposition and the incorporation approaches seem underpinned by the Court's recognition that SGEIs exist not only at the level of undertakings but also at the level of public authorities, and that they must at both levels operate under conditions, in particular economic and financial conditions, enabling the SGEI missions to be achieved. Consequently, it is submitted that the Court's transposition and incorporation approaches mirror the Court's implicit application of Article 14 TFEU, and its interpretation of the notion of SGEI for the purpose of that provision. If this understanding of the CJEU's case law is correct, it explains its heterogeneous standard of review of restrictions of the fundamental freedoms.

This understanding is supported by the important ruling in *Commission v Germany*. In this case, the *Teckal* doctrine was not applicable, and incorporation barred because there was no concept the exemption could be incorporated into. The notion of "public contract" cannot be re-defined each time an exemption from EU procurement rules seems appropriate to accommodate EU principles related to public services, in particular the respect of Member States' competence. The application of Article 106(2) TFEU was also barred: even if the Court had wanted to apply the provision, which is quite improbable, and even though it can be, and has been, applied to justify restrictions of free movement, it is not worded in a manner that allows to address public authorities' own tasks related to SGEIs. Consequently, if the CJEU wanted to find the municipal cooperation at issue compatible with EU procurement law, it had to specify *why* a contract between two autonomous parts was not covered by EU procurement rules. The Court declared explicitly that the decisive reason was to enable the achievement of *public authorities'* public service tasks.

It is therefore proposed that, compared to the more ambiguous approach in *Teckal*, the CJEU crossed the Rubicon in *Commission v Germany*, establishing discreetly, but surely, that there is more to SGEI than tasks entrusted to undertakings, that SGEI tasks may exist at the level of public authorities, and that it may motivate *exemptions* from EU procurement rules for public-public cooperation. To justify an exemption from EU procurement rules, the Court used the notion of public service task, which can hardly be doubted to constitute a part of the EU concept of SGEI, because in *Altmark* the Court used the notion of public service obligations as an equivalent of SGEI tasks, and also because in *Commission v Germany*, the Court transposed the proportionality test under Article 106(2) TFEU into the field of EU procurement law, giving the Member States discretion to organise the public service task, in order to secure that the tasks could be achieved. The Court acknowledged public-public cooperation as a principle which can be necessary to enable that SGEIs achieve their missions, as an organisation form which allows public authorities to control the economic and financial frames of their public service tasks. If the Court took that path, which was confirmed in *Lecce*, it was not under the effect of a political whim. It is submitted that it saw it as its duty under Article 14 TFEU, which it interpreted and applied.

In sum, the CJEU does not seem to interpret Article 14 TFEU as simply consolidating an essential element of the acquis under Article 106(2) TFEU that in the frame of their retained powers Member States have a wide discretion to define policy objectives and to pursue them, define SGEI tasks, entrust them to undertakings and compensate them for. It goes further and, under the Treaty principle of conferral and EU's duty to respect national identity and local self-government, recognizes that Member States have not only a wide discretion to define policy objectives, but also to commit themselves to these objectives by imposing public service tasks on themselves or their public authorities (SGEIs in the meaning of Article 14 TFEU), on the basis of which public service tasks may be entrusted to undertakings (SGEI tasks in the meaning of Article 106(2) TFEU). In the frame of such public service tasks, it emerges from the case law studied that they are recognized a prerogative to do so under "acceptable conditions", including financial and economic conditions.

References

Baquero-Cruz J (2005) Beyond competition: services of general interest and European community law. In: De Búrca G (ed) EU law and the welfare state. Oxford University Press, Oxford
Bekkedal T (2011) Article 106 TFEU is dead. long live Article 106! In: Szyszczak E et al (eds) Developments in services of general interest. T.M.C. Asser Press, The Hague
Buendia Sierra JL (1999) Exclusive rights and state Monopolies under EC law. Oxford University Press, Oxford
Damjanovic D (2013) The EU market rules as social market rules: why the EU can be a social market economy. Common Market Law Rev 6:1685–1717
Davies G (2009) What does article 86 actually do? In: Krajewski M, Neergaard U, van de Gronden JW (eds) The changing legal framework for services of general interest in Europe. T.M.C. Asser Press, The Hague
Davies G (2010) The price of letting courts value solidarity: the judicial role in liberalizing welfare. In: Ross M, Borgmann-Prebil Y (eds) Promoting solidarity in the European Union. Oxford University Press, Oxford
De Cecco F (2013) State aid and the European Economic Constitution. Hart Publishing, Oxford, Portland
De Vries SA (2011) BUPA: a healthy case, in the light of a changing constitutional setting in Europe? In: van de Gronden JW et al (eds) Health care and EU law. T.M.C. Asser Press, The Hague
Fiedziuk NA (2013) Putting services of general economic interest up for tender: reflections on applicable EU rules. Common Market Law Rev 50:87–114
Hancher L, Sauter W (2009) One foot in the grave or one step beyond? From Sodemare to DocMorris: the EU's freedom of establishment case law concerning healthcare. http://ssrn.com/abstract=1429315. Accessed 31 Dec 2015
Hatzopoulos V (2012) Regulating services in the European Union. Oxford University Press, Oxford
Karayigit M (2010) A new type of exemption from the EU rules on public procurement established: "in thy neighbour's house" provision of public interest tasks. Public Procurement Law Rev 6:183–198
Lenaerts K (2012) Defining the concept of "Services of General Interest" in Light of the "Checks and Balances" set out in the EU treaties. Jurisprudencija/Jurisprudence 19(4):1247–1267
Naundrup OK (2011) Formål af almen interesse som element i EU-retten. In: Madell T, Bekkedal T, Neergaard U (eds) Den nordiska välfärden och marknaden: Nordiska erfarenheter av tjänster av allmänt intresse i en EU-rättslig kontext. Iustus förlag, Uppsala
Nicolaides P (2014) State aid uncovered: a critical analysis of developments in state aid 2014. Lexxion, Berlin
Ross M (2009) A healthy approach to services of general economic interest? The BUPA judgment of the court of first instance. European Law Rev 127–140
Sauter W (2008) Services of general economic interest and universal service in EU law. http://ssrn.com/abstract=1136105
Sauter W (2014) The criterion of advantage in state aid: Altmark and services of general economic interest. TILEC Discussion Paper 2014–2015. http://ssrn.com/abstract=2426230
Steinicke M (2011) In house-kontrakter eller administrative aftaler. In: Madell T, Bekkedal T, Neergaard U (eds) Den nordiska välfärden och marknaden – Nordiska erfarenheter av tjänster av allmänt intresse i en EU-rättslig Kontext. Iustus Förlag, Uppsala
Stergiou HM (2008) The increasing influence of primary EU law and EU public procurement law: must a concession to provide services of general economic interest be tendered? In: van de Gronden JW (ed) EU and WTO law on services: limits to the realization of general interest policies within the services market. Kluwer, Alphen aan den Rijn
Szyszczak E (2004) Financing services of general interest. Modern Law Rev 67(6):982–992

Szyszczak E (2007) The regulation of the state in competitive markets in the EU. Hart Publishing, Oxford, Portland

Szyszczak E (2015) Services of general economic interest and state measures affeting competition. J Eur Competition Law Practice 6(9)

Van de Gronden JW (2009) Cross-border health care in the EU and the organisation of the national health care systems of the member states: the dynamics resulting from the European court of Justice's decisions on free movement and competition law. Wisconsin Int Law J 26:705–760

Van de Gronden JW (2013a) Transnational competition law and public services. In: Hermann C, Krajewski M, Terhechte JP (eds) European yearbook of international economic law. Springer, Heidelberg, pp 109–146

Wernicke S (2009) Taking stock: the EU institutions and SGEI. In: Krajewski M, Neergaard U, van de JW (eds) The changing legal framework for services of general interest in Europe. T.M.C. Asser Press, The Hague

Wiggen J (2011) Public procurement rules and cooperation between public sector entities: the limits of the in-house doctrine under EU procurement law. Public Procurement Law Rev 2011(20):157–172

[illegible] (2020) [illegible] of [illegible] competition [illegible] markets in the EU. [illegible]

[illegible] general economic interest and [illegible]

[illegible]

[illegible]

[illegible]

Chapter 5
Meaning of the EU Concept of SGEI Emerging from the CJEU Case Law

Abstract Based on the results of Chaps. 3 and 4, this chapter proposes a legal understanding of the EU concept of SGEI, trying to identify what the meaning of "economic" is in SGEI and what the core elements of the concept in EU law can be in the present Treaty frame. An essential submission in that chapter is that the notion of "*entrustment* to an undertaking", repeatedly included as a central element in the Commission's tentative definitions of the notion of SGEI, is not part of the core elements of the EU concept of SGEI, whereas the notion of obligation/task is. Another important argument is that the "E" in SGEI refers to the fact that the public service regulation is of economic interest, in the sense that it can affect the economic conditions for the exercise of an activity which *can be* economic at an EU level, i.e. *is* economic in some Member State(s), but not necessarily in the Member State imposing that regulation.

Contents

C. Wehlander, *Services of General Economic Interest as a Constitutional Concept of EU Law*, Legal Issues of Services of General Interest,
DOI 10.1007/978-94-6265-117-3_5

It appears that in order to comply with Article 14 TFEU (and its earlier version Article 16 EC), the CJEU has proceeded to delineate the meaning of the concept of SGEI, even if it advances under the cover of "overriding reasons related to the general interest" and "public service obligations/tasks" deserving a "special" proportionality test under EU free movement and procurement rules. The Court seems to understand the EU notion of SGEI as including both undertakings' "public service obligations" *and* public authorities "public service tasks" which are part of the "chain of responsibilities" necessary for SGEIs to achieve their missions. This understanding supposes that public authorities, due to their public service tasks, have to be governed by principles and conditions allowing the SGEI missions to be achieved. On this basis, the purpose of this chapter is to examine whether it is possible to enumerate the core elements of the EU concept of SGEI. A major difficulty in such an enterprise is the multi-faceted character of the concept that is related to values, to a principle of joint responsibility (Article 14 TFEU), to a derogation/balance rule (Article 106(2) TFEU), and to a right of access (Article 36 EUCFR). Another difficulty is to render justice to the fact that SGEI is an EU notion—which legitimates EU's control of manifest error—while Member States have a wide discretion to define SGEI tasks, at least in the frame of their retained competence. Under such circumstances, the concept can arguably not be defined too precisely and lends itself better for an understanding.

A premise here is that the concept's meaning is already contained in the Treaties adopted by the Member States, which implies that it is not within their competence to define it, no more than it is for the Member States to define Treaty concepts such as "services" or "goods". A postulate founding the quasi-constitutional authority of the EU legal system is namely that the Member States know what they agree on when their governments sign new Treaties and later have them ratified. This fiction has to be accepted although of course they—and we—know that they fundamentally do not agree on certain elements. Also, while the existence of a "right of access to SGEIs" is an important element to integrate in the understanding of the concept, it is not in focus for this chapter. In focus here is that the understanding of the EU concept must be coherent for the purposes of Article 14 TFEU *and* Article 106(2) TFEU. Article 106(2) TFEU spells a proportionality rule allowing to derogate from any Treaty provision and not only from the competition rules, but it is inflexibly formulated to address SGEI tasks *entrusted to undertakings*. Article 14 TFEU requires that SGEIs operate under principles and conditions enabling them to achieve their missions, and thereby does not exclude that other entities than undertakings may need such specific principles and conditions, but contains no proportionality requirement. Therefore, it seems that the two provisions are meant to complement each other, Article 14 TFEU enouncing a principle that SGEIs deserve special principles and conditions to achieve their important missions, and Article 106(2) TFEU requiring a proportionality assessment, where the interests of the Union—including market integration—may not be affected.

The approach in this chapter is to set the understanding of the EU concept of SGEI emerging from the CJEU's case law in relation to the understanding emerging from "definitions" in soft law and EU secondary law.[1] Thus, the Court's understanding of the EU concept of SGEI does not land in a political vacuum.[2] In Sect. 5.1, these contextual elements are charted, with a historical approach of the Commission's "definitions" of SGEIs, mirroring both the political evolution of the Commission's approach and its persistent lack of legal clarity and comprehensiveness. Lastly, section 1 looks at the doctrinal search for a comprehensive understanding of the concept and sums up the section's findings.

Section 5.2 elaborates a tentative understanding of the notion of SGEI, inspired by Tuori's theory that envisages law as consisting of at least three dynamically interconnected layers, the surface level, the legal culture layer and the deep structure of law.[3] Thus, the understanding proposed is based on an analysis of the CJEU's case law studied in Chap. 4, but in this analysis, the approach consists in looking "through" or "under the surface" of the CJEU's confusing use of the terms "public service obligations" (PSO) and "public service tasks" (PST), and of its special standard of review for national measures related to social services in their competence. The notion of "entrustment" in Article 106(2) TFEU, which appears to constitute a formal rather than a substantial element of the SGEI concept, is studied particularly. The relevance of this approach is supported by the fact that the Court is arguably in a quite tricky situation, where it has some reasons not to say what it is doing. In openly delineating the meaning of the EU concept of SGEI as including more than tasks entrusted to market operators, the Court may regard that it fulfils its duty to respect Article 14 TFEU, but at the same time it is exposed to the worries of frustrating the more liberal Member States, of having to clarify the telos it serves in applying the Treaty market provisions to the Member States' regulation, organisation and financing of social services, and perhaps also of opening the Pandora's box of the relationship between SGEIs and EU procurement rules. At the same time, if the CJEU delineates the EU concept of SGEI without saying so, it denies that it clarifies the legal-political substance of Article 14 TFEU, delivering important rulings in a "what without a why manner", i.e. a style criticised by Weiler as communicating in essence "[i]t is so, because we say it so. And what it means—well you will find out."[4]

---

[1]SGEIs have been defined for the purpose of Directive on Services 2006/123/EC of the European Parliament and of the Council of 12 December 2006 on services on the internal market (hereinafter "the Services Directive").

[2]Rather to the contrary, as proposing a clear understanding of the meaning of the EU concept of SGEI may be compared to walking on a minefield.

[3]Tuori's critical positivist theory, based on a vision of law as a "multi-layered normative phenomenon"—the *surface* of individual statutes, decisions and scholarly interventions (the "will") being underpinned by *sub-surface cultural elements* of law such as general legal concepts and principles, legal theories or doctrines, and patterns of argumentation (the "reason"). Tuori professes that legal science is dual by nature, being a combination of legal practice and scientific practice. As a scientific practice legal science looks both at law as legal practices (which it is a part of) and as a legal normative order (which it considers from an observer's perspective). See Tuori 2002.

[4]Weiler 2013, p. 249. At page 238 of this paper, Weiler asks rhetorically: "The ECJ never crossed the line between law and politics? Transparent, non-cryptic, soundly reasoned decisions?"

5.1 Clear Understanding of the EU Concept of SGEI in Soft Law and Secondary Law?

The Commission's understanding of the EU notion of SGEI can be expected to transpire from its many Communications on services of general interest between 1996 and 2007, and its SGEI Guides (so far 2010 and 2013). Although it should not be forgotten that the Commission and the EU legislator are political institutions and that these documents are not legally binding, the understanding they convey is important because their ambition is a priori to be more comprehensive than —although based on—the CJEU's case law. Therefore their "vision" of the concept may differ from the CJEU's more or less implicit understanding, especially if the latter is too cryptic to take over EU Institutions' visions of what the EU concept of SGEI should mean.[5] In this regard it is important to look at the EU legislator's approach of the concept in the Services Directive. The following analysis focuses on the "definitions" of SGIs and of SGEIs.

5.1.1 The Commission's Understanding of the Concepts of SGI and SGEI

Neergaard has explained how the Commission's strategy has included continuous attempts to connect SGEIs to the European Social Model, which in her view could be regarded as an attempt, in particular through its Communications on SGIs (including SGEIs), to make regulation of services of general interest at EU level more acceptable.[6] In this strategy, an important step has been to propose a "third way" in the debate going back to the 1960s between the holders of a "national approach" (that Member States were free to choose which public services they intended to secure for their citizens and that the ends of these public services were always compatible with the Treaties) and the holders of a "Community approach", arguing instead that Community institutions had powers to control and sanction the genuine character of the general interest claimed.[7] In this "third way", the Commission formulated a compromise stating that Member States have a wide

[5]Syszczak has shown how the Commission's agenda for the modernization of social services of general interest and the Member States in the Council seeking justifications and exemptions for these services in secondary law on state aid, procurement and free movement have led to the deployment of soft law and safe havens. She found that the casuistic development of this soft law and these safe has produced an inconsistent terminology and inconsistent approaches to social services of general interest. See Szyszczak 2013.

[6]Neergaard 2008, p. 104–106.

[7]For a more detailed account of this discussion, see Buendia Sierra 1999, p. 279–283.

discretion to define what they regard as SGEIs,[8] a view nowadays firmly held by the Court of Justice.[9]

Another important step has been to introduce what is called here "working definitions" of the EU concepts of SGI and SGEI. As evoked in Chap. 3, the Commission's "definition" of SGI has evolved over time, from what Neergaard calls the "grand words" of the SGI Communication of 1996 to the SGEI Communication of 2007.[10] As to the EU concept of SGEI, which the Commission was also under pressure from the Council and the EU-Parliament to clarify the meaning and EU regulation of, the 2001 Communication provided the following understanding:

> Services of general economic interest are different from ordinary services in that public authorities consider that they need to be provided even where the market may not have sufficient incentives to do so. /…/[I]f the public authorities consider that certain services are in the general interest and market forces may not result in a satisfactory provision, they can lay down a number of specific service provisions to meet these needs in the form of service of general interest obligations./…/The classical case is the universal service obligation /…/[that is to say] the obligation to provide a certain service throughout the territory at affordable tariffs and on similar quality conditions, irrespective of the profitability of individual operations.[11]

This was the first "working definition" of the concept of SGEI formulated by the Commission, and it is important to note that it presents SGEIs as "altogether" a specific category of services that

- public authorities (undefined at which level—EU, national, regional or local) consider must be provided even when not commercially profitable
- due to a criterion of "general interest" and a *risk*, assessed *by public authorities*, that the service cannot be provided satisfactorily (arguably for reasons of quality in a broad sense, or of price)
- USOs are an example of SGEIs, presented by the Commission as the "classical case", which may raise the question of whether it is also the Commission's "preferred case".

It may be noted that in *BUPA*, a case which dealt with a risk-based SGEI compensation, the General Court chose to quote this early "working definition", although when the judgment was delivered in 2008, the Commission had had the time to give out new tentative definitions in the frame of its Communications.[12] But more importantly, this "definition" is puzzling. It includes public authorities' decision to "lay

[8]Commission, "Services of general interest in Europe" COM (2000) 580 final, point 22.

[9]Case T-106/95 *FFSA* [1997] ECR II-229, para 99; Case T-17/02 *Fred Olsen* [2005] ECR II-2031, para 216; Case T-289/03 *BUPA* [2008] ECR II-81, paras 166–169; Case T-442/03 *SIC* para 195; Case T-309/04 *TV2* [2008] ECR II-2935, paras 113 *et seq.*

[10]Regarding the "grand words" and their meaning, see Neergaard 2008, p. 105, referring to Freedland 1998.

[11]Commission, "Services of general interest in Europe" (Communication) 2001/C 17/04, point 14.

[12]See Case T-289/03 *BUPA* [2008] ECR II-81, para 10.

down specific service *provisions*", which suggests that SGEIs can be laid down as statutory rules, by the—EU or national—legislator. These SGEIs are said to meet general interest needs in the form of "service of general interest obligations", a term not used later by the Commission. In the frame of its Green and White Papers on SGIs, the Commission proposed namely other "working definitions" of SGEIs, presented as reflecting "Community Practice" and later "Union practice".[13]

Thus, in the 2003 Green Paper the Commission wrote simply that

> In Community practice there is broad agreement that the term [SGEI] refers to services of an economic nature which the Member States or the Community subject to specific public service obligations by virtue of a general interest criterion.[14]

This definition was completed in the White Paper of 2004 by the following "clarification":

> The concept of services of general economic interest thus covers in particular certain services provided by the big network industries such as transport, postal services, energy and communications. However, the term also extends to any other economic activity subject to public service obligations.[15]

It may be noted that in the "definitions" in the Green Paper and the White Paper, the Commission replaces the term "service of general interest obligation" in the 2001 Communication by the notion of "public service obligation" (PSO)—a term introduced by the CJEU in *Altmark*. Thus, PSOs are held to be a central element of the concept of SGEI, but it is unclear whether what the CJEU calls "public service tasks" (PSTs) in *Commission v Germany* are included too, either as "a particular kind of PSO" (public service obligations not imposed through entrustment on undertaking, but imposed on public authorities themselves), or simply as an element of the concept of SGEI together with PSO (where SGEI may in principle include PST and PSO).[16]

In its 2010 SGEI Guide, the Commission gave yet another "working definition", reading:

> In Union practice, the term refers in general to services of an economic nature that the public authorities in the Member States at national, regional or local level, depending on the allocation of powers between them under national law, subject to specific public service obligations through an act of entrustment/…/on the basis of a general interest criterion and in order to ensure that the services are provided under conditions which are not necessarily the same as prevailing market conditions. The Court has established that SGEIs are services that exhibit special characteristics as compared with those of other economic activities. [17]

[13]Some authors call it "clarification", see Sauter and Schepel 2007, p. 154.

[14]Commission, "Services of general interest" (Green Paper) COM (2003)270 final, p. 7.

[15]Commission, "Services of General Interest" (White Paper) COM (2004) 374 final, p. 22.

[16]See Case C-280/00 *Altmark* [2003] ECR I-7747 and Case C-480/06 *Commission v Germany* [2009] ECR I-4747 and Case 202/88 *France v Commission* [1991] ECR I-1223.

[17]2010 SGEI Guide, p. 15–16, emphasis added.

This new definition mirrored a typically "narrow" understanding of the EU concept of SGEI, in the sense that it only involved PSOs based on an act of entrustment, i.e. *undertakings*' SGEI tasks in the meaning of Article 106(2) TFEU. This was remarkable in a context where the Commission's guide addressed in particular "social services of general interest" (SSGIs), and explained how not only state aid rules, but also procurement and internal market rules apply to SSGIs. The impression is that the Commission had to give guidance on the application of procurement and internal market rules to SSGIs, but wished to avoid relating exemptions from these market rules to the SGEI-character of SSGIs. As a result, it is still unclear whether the Commission understands the procurement and free movement exemptions to be motivated by (1) the SGI-character of SSGIs, or (2) the SGEI-character of SSGIs implying that their EU regulation is covered by the principle formulated in Article 14 TFEU.

The Commission was perhaps not itself at ease with the narrow "definition" of the 2010 SGEI Guide. On the website of DG competition per September 2011, it preferred a wider definition:

> Services of general economic interest (SGEIs) are economic activities that *public authorities identify as being of particular importance to citizens* and that would not be supplied (or would be supplied under different conditions) if there were no public intervention. Examples are transport networks, postal services and social services.

Compared to the 2010 SGEI Guide, this "definition" lays emphasis both on the State's responsibility for SGEIs and on the democratic justification of the public intervention. Indeed, there is a striking difference between on the one hand the "democratic/functional" emphasis in this last definition and the definition of the Green Paper, and on the other hand the "competition/functional" emphasis of the 2010 SGEI Guide.

In its 2013 SGEI Guide, the Commission adjusted again the "definitions" of SGIs and SGEIs. It asserted that it had clarified the concept in its SGI Quality Framework, holding there that they are services that public authorities of the Member States at national, regional or local level classify as being of general interest and, *therefore*, subject to specific public service obligations (PSOs). In this understanding, it seems that the imposition of SGEI tasks in the meaning of Article 106(2) TFEU (if seen as equivalent to PSOs), *follows from* the fact that the service is classified as SGI by public authorities in Member States. As to SGEIs, the Commission put forward the following definition:

> SGEIs are economic activities which deliver outcomes in the overall public good that would not be supplied (or would be supplied under different conditions in terms of objective quality, safety, affordability, equal treatment or universal access) by the market without public intervention. A PSO is imposed on the provider by way of an entrustment and on the basis of a general interest criterion which ensures that the service is provided under conditions allowing it to fulfil its mission.[18]

This definition raises the following remarks here. First, the legal-economic notion of "overall public good" dominates, and it is interesting to note the

[18] 2013 SGEI Guide, p. 21.

assertive wording: "SGEIs *are*", suggesting that the Commission sets out to define rather than explain. Second, SGEIs are called "activities", although it is not clear whether the Commission means a whole field of activity (for instance social security) or a specific service as regulated by a Member State or by the EU (for instance private medical insurance). The activity must be "economic", although it is not clear what the Commission means by that, for instance whether it considers as economic for the purpose of the concept of SGEI an activity which is covered by the Treaty rules on free movement because it "can be" economic in some Member States. Third, the relation between SGEIs and PSOs is perhaps even more unclear than in previous definitions, and there is an obvious redundancy "obligation/imposed", raising the question whether there may be some *obligation before entrustment* takes place, and if so whom it engages. And fourth, it seems that the only SGEI missions envisaged are the undertakings' PSOs. In this understanding, public authorities have no operative "SGEI missions", only a role in defining SGIs and in "intervening" by defining PSOs entrusted to undertakings. Also, it is unsaid which authorities may define PSOs.[19]

Thus, it appears that the Commission's definition of SGEIs in the 2013 SGEI Guide, which, in spite of its wording, is of course *not* a legal definition, raises more questions than it brings answers. After all these years, the evolution of the Commission's "working definitions" has not brought about a clear and comprehensive vision of what SGEIs are about. Some important questions eluded by these many "definitions" of the concepts of SGI and SGEI by the Commission, are submitted to be:

- Are PSOs a synonym of SGEI tasks, and does the Commission see SGEI tasks as consecutive of a service's classification as SGI by national/regional/local authorities?
- Is the Commission's understanding that public authorities' public service tasks (PSTs) are part of SGIs and not of SGEIs, and does it imply that the Union and the Member States have no duty to care that PSTs may be conducted under principles, in particular economic and financial conditions, allowing them to fulfil the SGEI missions? This last question is related to the interpretation that may be made of the CJEU's ruling in *Commission v Germany*, an interpretation which the Commission does not seem eager to propose.[20]

[19]In the 2010 SGEI Guide, the Commission specified that SGEIs are economic services subject to public service obligations imposed by national, regional or local authorities, depending on the allocation of powers under national law, and did not name PSOs imposed by the EU, although the Green Paper on SGI presented SGEI as covering in particular "certain services provided by the big network industries such as transport, postal services, energy and communications". It was unsaid why the Community – without being replaced by the Union – was left out as one of the governance levels establishing specific public service obligations. In the 2013 SGEI Guide, it seems that PSOs are meant as a "public intervention", where it is unsaid which institutions are meant to intervene and impose obligations.

[20]Case C-480/06 *Commission v Germany* [2009] ECR I-04747.

5.1.2 *SGEI's Definition in the Services Directive, A(nother) Source of Confusion to Understand the EU Concept of SGEI*

The view that the concept of SGEI is relevant for the purpose of competition and state aid rules and not in the field of free movement is not only challenged by CJEU's case law but also by the presence of specific provisions on SGEI in the Services Directive. The point of departure in the Services Directive is that it generally applies to SGEIs, with the exemption for the freedom to provide services.[21] Also, a number of social services—which certainly can be deemed to be largely subject to SGEI regulation in the Member States—have been altogether exempted from its scope. As Neergaard observes, the formulations regarding SGEIs in the Services Directive are cryptic and "not very coherent".[22] Thus, the provisions related to the freedom of establishment apply to SGEIs on the condition that this should force the Member States neither to liberalise SGEIs, nor to privatise public bodies which provide such services, nor to abolish existing monopolies for other activities or certain distribution services.[23] Neergaard holds that the Directive seems anyway applicable to SGEIs as regards provisions on the right of service recipients (free movement of services), and as regards the quality of services.[24] Healthcare and social services as defined in the Directive are totally exempted from the scope of the Directive. Therefore, it has been assumed that the potential effects of the Directive on SGEIs are very limited.

Against this background, it is interesting that the EU notion of SGEI has a specific definition for the purpose of the Services Directive, reading as follows:

> For the purposes of this Directive, and *without prejudice to Article 16 of the Treaty*, services may be considered to be services of general economic interest only if they are provided in application of a special task in the public interest entrusted to the provider by the Member State concerned. This assignment should be made by way of one or more acts, the form of which is determined by the Member State concerned, and should specify the precise nature of the special task.[25]

This definition may restrict the scope of provisions specifically pertaining to SGEIs in the Directive by focusing on SGEIs *entrusted* to undertakings. It seems for instance to imply that only waste treatment *provided in application of a special task entrusted by the Member State to the provider by way of an act précising the task* is exempted from Article 16 on the basis of Article 17. In this definition, the mention "without prejudice to Article 16 of the Treaty" suggests that restricting

[21]Articles 16 and 17(1) of the Services Directive.

[22]Neergaard 2008, p. 74–75.

[23]See Recital 8 of the Services Directive.

[24]See Section 2 Chapter IV respectively Chapter V of the Directive on Services 2006/123/EC of the European Parliament and of the Council of 12 December 2006 on services on the internal market.

[25]See Recital 70 of the Services Directive, emphasis added.

SGEIs to SGEI tasks *entrusted* has a potential to affect the purposes of Article 16 EC (now Article 14 TFEU). This could in particular be the case if the definition in the Services Directive only covers a part of what is meant by SGEIs in Article 14 TFEU, a meaning which itself has not been clarified explicitly by the CJEU. SGEI "elements" which may be covered by Article 14 TFEU but are not covered by the definition in the Service Directive would thus be the object of the liberalization test in Article 16 of the Services Directive. The question is therefore whether the definition of SGEIs in the Services Directive excludes elements of SGEIs in the meaning of Article 14 TFEU and which elements this may be.

As a matter of fact, there is an asymmetry between the Directive's definition of SGEIs—focusing on entrusted SGEI tasks—and the open wording (not mentioning "entrustment") of Article 17(1) providing for a derogation from the rules on free movement of services for SGEIs such as services within the postal, electricity and gas sectors, water distribution and supply services and waste water services and treatment of waste.[26] This asymmetry mirrors the uncertainty as to whether

a. There is one EU concept of SGEI for the purpose of EU law, or
b. There is one understanding of SGEIs for the purpose of Article 14 TFEU and another for the purpose of Article 106(2) TFEU.

In *BUPA* the General Court touched on the issue of which elements SGEIs may be composed of. It found that in the contested state aid decision, the Commission had implicitly accepted that private medical insurance (PMI) services as regulated in Irish law had per se SGEI character. The Court considered that because of "the indissoluble link" between the obligations imposed to PMI insurers and the PMI services, it was impossible for the Commission to limit its assessment solely to the PMI obligations without also taking into account the PMI services forming the subject-matter of those obligations and the provision of which was dependent on compliance with those obligations. Therefore the Commission recognised that the PMI obligations constituted SGEI tasks and at the same time that the PMI services formed part of a more *general* SGEI mission defined by the Irish legislator. As interpreted by the GC, the Commission had thus seen (1) the obligations imposed on insurance companies *and* (2) the national public service mission in private medical insurance served by these obligations as *both* having SGEI character.[27]

The asymmetry between the Directive's definition of SGEIs and the open wording (not mentioning "entrustment") of Article 17(1) contributes to create confusion on the meaning of the EU concept of SGEI. This, together with several other elements in the Directive's drafting, has led Snell to declare that the Services Directive may in some cases be detrimental to legal certainty.[28]

---

[26]See Article 17(1).

[27]Case T-289/03 *BUPA and Others* v *Commission* [2008] ECR II-81, p. 175–176. Interestingly the General Court presents the view of the Commission without clearly expressing its support to this view. The word "recognizes" seems to indicate that the Commission's appreciation in that part is viewed by the Court as in principle binding.

[28]Snell 2008, p. 191.

5.1.3 Academic Approaches of the Notion of SGEI

A few years ago, Neergaard questioned whether the absence of exact definition is acceptable, considering that at least from a legal point of view this situation creates major problems.[29] In her view, a "rethinking of the terminology" seemed needed, along different possible lines. One was to focus on the nature of the service in what constitutes an SGEI, rather than who provides it or how it is financed, another being to develop the link between the concepts of SGI/SGEI/NESGI and the economic terms "public goods" and "private goods", and yet another to decide explicitly which services should be retained under national competence and which at EU level.[30] It may seem that, regarding social services, the EU legislator has partly followed the proposed path of connecting a specific legal treatment in EU state aid law and EU procurement law to the "special" nature of these services rather than to their SGEI-character.

Buendia Sierra has given his own comprehensive understanding of the EU concept of SGEI, as

> a service of an economic nature whose provision to the general public is considered to be essential. This character justifies a degree of State intervention in order to make sure that the service is actually supplied and to control the conditions under which it is supplied.[31]

This "definition" includes two elements in the concept of SGEI: a concrete service and a state intervention. Indeed, the element of "concrete service" seems crucial to understand the principle recognizing the right of access to SGEI, as it would make no sense to be recognized access to a *regulation*, while it seems that what is protected as a fundamental right is precisely access to a specific *service* secured (in Buendia Sierra's words "made sure") by the intervention of the State. Second, Buendia Sierra's "definition" supposes that state powers legitimate some degree of intervention in an economic activity. It leaves open the question of which government level has such powers and on which mandate. It also leaves open the question of which market actor is affected by this intervention, allowing the case where SGEI imposes constraints on the public authorities themselves, on the undertakings which are entrusted tasks in the framework of the SGEI, and possibly also on users in their choice of provider, which together form "multi-layered obligations implied by an SGEI". Thus it does cover the possibility of entrusting missions to undertakings ("market missions") but does not limit the notion of SGEI to such "market missions", as it leaves outside the word "entrustment".

In Buendia Sierra's understanding, the EU concept of SGEI allows state intervention making sure that a service—of an economic nature—can be "provided to the general public". This element may be understood as excluding neither SGEI provision wholly funded by the state (for instance in the field of social services), nor

[29] Neergaard 2008, p. 35.

[30] Ibid., p. 49.

[31] Buendia Sierra 2008, p. 192. In spite of negligible differences, this is the same definition he submitted 1999, see Buendia Sierra 1999, p. 277.

environmental services which the Commission has approved as SGEI, such as subsidised acquisition of land for sustainable nature conservation, where state intervention allows the economic service of sustainable nature management to be provided not to individuals but instead to the general public, including future generations.[32] It is namely easy to "explain" the EU concept of SGEI in a manner that is overly restrictive of Member States' discretion. One such misunderstanding was arguably found in the report of the Commission of inquiry on the Swedish national rules relevant for the internal market for goods and services,[33] considering that the existence of SGEI requires a service to be (1) important for consumers, (2) open to all consumers and (3) supplied on homogeneous conditions. The European Commission has namely seen no manifest error in classifying as SGEI an environmental service that is not "important for consumers", but rather "important for citizens".[34]

Buendia Sierra's approach shows arguably that it is worth trying to explain the EU concept of SGEI without defining it. Compared to the Commission's approach, he leaves outside the notion of entrustment, which may bring more coherence to the Treaty framework on SGEIs, as discussed in Sect. 5.2. At any rate, it is submitted here that at this stage of the development of EU law, the terminology of the Treaties cannot be rethought. The SGI/SGEI/NESGI terminology cannot easily be discarded on Neergaard's argument that it is a "conceptual disaster", first because the disaster reflects a political tension that should be addressed, and second because the EU concept of SGEI is not simply the Treaties' expression of a "social touch" in the European social model. It is the bearer of a fundamental principle recognized by the EU Charter of fundamental rights, and of a right for citizens to use their democratic and economic powers to govern certain services on the European and the global market. Last, but not least, the EU concept of SGEI is so far the only Treaty concept capable of legitimating that Member States fund social services regarded in EU law as market services, without following detailed procurement procedures and without notifying the Commission. It is certainly worth understanding the meaning of such a concept. It is also worth questioning whether looking away from it in applying EU market rules to social services necessarily leads to better law in that field in the Member States.

5.1.4 Some Signs of Conceptual Confusion on the Core Elements of the SGEI Concept

SGEI is developing into a concept of EU constitutional law, standing for checks and balances, but also for principles of *governance*—in particular the promotion

[32]See Commission Decision of 2 July 2009 on nature conservation areas (Germany) in case NN8/2009 – C(2009) 5080 final, and Commission Decision of 13 July 2011 on subsidy scheme for acquisition of land for nature conservation (Netherlands) in case SA.31243 (ex N308/2010) – C(2011)4945 fina.

[33]Report of the commission of inquiry on the Internal market "EU, Sverige och den inre marknaden – En översyn av horisontella bestämmelser inom varu- och tjänsteområdet" SOU 2009:71, p. 151.

[34]See Commission's Decision of 13 July 2011 on subsidy scheme for acquisition of land for nature conservation (Netherlands) in case SA.31243 (N 308/2010) – C (2011)4945 final, point 13.

of social cohesion, human dignity, equality and democracy—the respect of which EU Institutions and the Member States are politically accountable for in accordance with Article 14 TFEU, the SGI Protocol and Article 36 EUCFR. In the post-Lisbon Treaty framework on SGEI, the concept does not seem impossible to understand, but its legal definition may imply crucial political choices. Seen against this background, the confusion arising from the Commission's successive explanations and definitions of SGEI is not accidental. Depending on the period and the Commission's political agenda, the successive definitions of SGEI reflect profound ideological differences on the State's role in defining and securing rights to access to essential services.

What emerges is that SGEIs, which have been defined restrictively in the Services Directive (as only SGEIs which have been entrusted), are also all the more narrowly defined in the latest communications of the Commission. This development does not only cause confusion on what SGEIs are or may be, but risks limiting Member States' powers recognized by the Treaties and public authorities' capacity to achieve social and environmental missions considered as important or essential by citizens in the Member States. As a preliminary step towards a more correct approach of the notion, let us look at some confusing elements in the Commission's approach, and at the incoherence they may lead to.

In the 2010 SGEI Guide the Commission specifies that SGEIs are economic services subject to public service obligations imposed by national, regional or local authorities, depending on the allocation of powers under national law, through an act of entrustment. This definition, as the definition in the 2013 SGEI Guide, has its focus on SGEI tasks imposed by *public authorities* on *undertakings* through *entrustment*. It does not highlight the fact that SGEI missions may be imposed by the legislator—the national or the EU legislator—and that they may be imposed on undertakings but also on public authorities. While the Green Paper on SGIs presented SGEIs as covering in particular "certain services provided by the big network industries such as transport, postal services, energy and communications", the 2010 and 2013 Guides leave out the national legislator and the EU legislator as institutions which de facto have defined SGEIs.

By insisting on entrustment and by not mentioning Member States or the Union as institutions susceptible to define SGEI missions, the Commission's recent definitions suggest that SGEIs only exist through entrustment to undertakings and not at the stage of their definition as a democratically decided mission to be implemented at different levels in a market context.[35] This focus on entrustment as a constitutive element of SGEIs is also found in legal doctrine, as Sauter affirms that "a service of general economic interest in principle requires an explicit act of entrustment: this can be seen as a constitutive act (i.e. creating the SGEI where there was none previously)".[36]

The General Court's stance in *BUPA* that SGEIs may be entrusted to undertakings through law, confirmed also the essential perception that SGEI missions may

[35] 2010 SGEI Guide, SEC (2010)1545 (final), point 2.2.

[36] Sauter 2008, p. 184.

constitute a legislative commitment from the State. A good example is electricity, for which the core public service missions are defined in the Electricity Directive, and constitute the first level of governance of this SGEI.[37] The universal service obligation imposed by the Directive creates SGEI rights which the Member States are obliged to secure.[38] The SGEI mission existed most arguably at the very moment the Electricity Directive entered into force, before any measures were taken at national level to implement the Directive, and independently of its specific entrustment to any operator. Indeed, the achievement of the SGEI mission in the field of electricity supply (a universal service obligation) does not simply rest on the operators' willingness to respect the universal service obligation, but also on the Member States' obligation to ensure that operators' behaviour allows the mission to be achieved.[39] The Member States have not only an obligation to implement the Directive, but also to ensure the realization of universal service by intervening, if necessary for ensuring households' access to electricity, through regulatory, supervisory or other measures. The universal service obligation is not only directed at undertakings, but is also a commitment from the EU legislator and a duty for the national legislators.

The view here is that entrustment need not—or rather may not—be part of the *definition* of the EU concept of SGEI. Entrustment constitutes one possible element in the chain of implementation of an SGEI, a specific element allowing to control the proportionality of public measures towards specific undertakings, for instance exclusive rights, funding or authorisations. Entrustment—in law or otherwise—can be necessary to prove the existence of an SGEI task at the level of specific undertakings, but it cannot be a general condition for the existence of an SGEI, because SGEIs, which promote access to social or environmental fundamental rights, are not simply tasks for undertakings entrusted with their provision, but also missions imposed on public authorities by legislative or administrative decisions. The acknowledgement of a legal linkage between public authorities' missions and market operators' tasks may be crucial for the efficiency and the coherence of public intervention in certain fields of activity.

---

[37]This analysis of SGEIs as a multi-level responsibility appears to be reflected by the expression "*projects* of general economic interest" used by Buendia Sierra 1999, p. 176.

[38]Article 3(3) of Directive 2003/54/EC provides that "Member States shall ensure that all household customers, and, where Member States deem it appropriate, small enterprises, (namely enterprises with fewer than 50 occupied persons and an annual turnover or balance sheet not exceeding EUR 10 million), enjoy universal service, that is the right to be supplied with electricity of a specified quality within their territory at reasonable, easily and clearly comparable and transparent prices."

[39]That the Electricity Directive creates an SGEI is expressed in recital 26 of the Electricity Directive: "The respect of the public service requirements is a fundamental requirement of this Directive, and it is important that common minimum standards, respected by all Member States, are specified in this Directive, which take into account the objectives of common protection, security of supply, environmental protection and equivalent levels of competition in all Member States." The recital clarifies further that the SGEI thus defined must be "refined" at national level: "It is important that the public service requirements can be interpreted on a national basis, taking into account national circumstances and subject to the respect of Community law."

This *public* service dimension of the EU concept of SGEI, the idea that the obligation is imposed on market provision in a manner that restricts market freedom and at the same time expresses political power is perhaps the most "persistent irritant". In this regard, it is symptomatic that precisely when the CJEU sends a signal in *Commission v Germany* that SGEIs in the post-Lisbon Treaty framework should be understood as a "broad concept", the Commission has taken the bold step of introducing in its 2011 state aid Package on SGEIs its own "narrow concept" of what SGEIs may be. This is commented further in Chap. 7.

There is arguably, in the space created by the Treaty principles of conferral, subsidiarity and national identity, a wide freedom of the Union's peoples to decide through their elected representatives that certain objectives of societal nature which cannot or not fully be translated into service markets, constitute SGEI *missions* that public authorities at national, regional or local level are responsible to ensure throughout varying market circumstances. Their prerogative to *govern* public authorities' intervention on markets for services and goods related to fundamental rights recognized by the Charter may arguably not be restricted by the Commission, be it with the tacit ascent of Member States' governments. Restricting such prerogatives would require a democratic process.

The CJEU's case law on exemptions from EU procurement rules is now evidently related to the existence of public service tasks (PSTs) imposed on public authorities, for instance by the EU legislator. This relation, clearest established in *Commission v Germany*, is neither explained nor problematized in the many soft law documents of the Commission, as if its existence did not play a fundamental role in the debate on EU rules applying to SGEIs.[40] It all seems as if the Commission, and governments in the Member States, are satisfied with the CJEU's very discreet approach of the issue of whether public authorities' general interest tasks (public service tasks) are included in the EU concept of SGEI. As long as the CJEU is not crystal clear on that matter, the Commission may be excused of its unclear and confusing approach. This can go on *ad vitam eternam*.

To ensure a democratic development of the European social model, in which SGEIs are declared to play an important role, it is submitted that the concepts of SGI and SGEI must *really* be clarified.[41] Member States' elected representatives must know what is in the concept of SGEI, in order to make sense of their duties and prerogatives according to the Treaties. Not clarifying EU concepts is simply proof of a profound distrust in the political institutions of the Member States, and it is difficult to see how a robust European democracy can be built on such sad sands. The following section proposes an understanding of the EU concept of SGEI which hopefully can contribute to reduce confusion.

---

[40]See Case C-480/06 *Commission v Germany*, cited above.

[41]Szyszczak considered that a legislative framework on SGEI from the Commission would allow for the definition and clarification of the concepts of SGI and SGEIs. She believed that the legal base for the Internal market (Article 114 TFEU) could be used for measures relating to SGEIs. See Szyszczak 2009, p. 301.

5.2 Out of Confusion: Core Elements of the SGEI Concept

The case law studied in Chap. 4 shows that the CJEU has not only recognized explicitly the existence of SGEIs in applying Article 106(2) TFEU, but also implicitly admitted the SGEI-character of a service, particularly in the field of social services, by choosing a specific proportionality test to examine the compliance of state measures with free movement and procurement rules. In *Commission v Germany*, the Court admitted that public service tasks *devoluted to public authorities* can justify a derogation from *existing* EU procurement rules, in order to achieve their missions under acceptable economic and financial conditions.[42] Hence, it is submitted that the CJEU has not only identified SGEIs in a large variety of sectors (social services, environmental services), but also acknowledged the relevance of the SGEI-character of a regulation to allow many types of state intervention (regulation, organisation, commission, funding, provision). This broad interpretation of the EU concept of SGEI is supported by its present status of *horizontal* Treaty concept, and it is in that spirit that the three following elements are argued to be inherent to the EU concept of SGEI and constitute its "core":

1. Economic relevance of the service (the "E" in SGEI)
2. General interest of the service (the "GI" in SGEI)
3. Obligation/right (the "S" in SGEI)

It is analysed how these elements may be identified in national law or EU regulation, on the basis of the CJEU's case law studied in Chap. 4. The approach is normative in the sense that it seeks coherence between the derogation in Article 106(2) TFEU and the principle expressed in Article 14 TFEU, by considering that they both fundamentally aim at enabling missions and tasks related to services of general interest to be achieved. This approach implies that the notion of entrustment which is specific to the particular purposes of Article 106(2) TFEU is not seen as a core element of the concept.

5.2.1 SG(E)I: It Is Enough that the Activity Can Be *Economic*

Whereas SGEIs are covered by the Treaty rules by virtue of their economic character, it is generally held that the economic character of the service is difficult to assess. An important question is whether the (E) in SG(E)I means that the activity has economic relevance or whether the general interest is of economic character.

It has been submitted that the Court, in *Commission v Germany*, based implicitly its argument on the SGI character of the municipalities' task (a public service task), which raises the following question. If the SGI which public authorities

[42]Case C-160/08 *Commission v Germany* [2010] ECR I-03713.

have to perform was considered non-economic, the CJEU's approach, which puts strict conditions on public authorities' cooperation, would be in direct conflict with Article 2 in the SGI Protocol, which declares that the Treaties do not affect in any way the competence of Member States to provide, commission and organise non-economic services of general interest. The reason allowing the CJEU to impose conditions on municipal cooperation (and on in-house) is that such public service cooperation has a potential to affect an activity which is not necessarily economic in the Member State where the cooperation or the in-house transaction takes place, but that *can be* economic at EU level, and is *therefore* covered by EU free movement and procurement rules. In other words, the Court's regulation of the conditions under which public authorities' public service tasks (services of general interest) may derogate from procurement procedures implies that the term "economic" in SGEI must be understood as "*can be* economic" (or some would say "economic in the meaning of EU free movement law).

This understanding finds support in *MOTOE* where the Court found that granting authorizations to organise motor cycling events constitutes an act of public authority, and therefore cannot constitute a "service of general economic interest" within the meaning of Article 106(2) EC.[43] To be an SGEI, a public service task must be attached to an activity which at least *can be* economic. As seen in Chap. 2, the exercise of public authority *cannot* be economic, and is therefore neither covered by EU competition law nor by EU free movement law.

While the notion of "general interest" in the SGEI concept is analysed under Sect. 5.2.3, it is necessary to evoke here the locution "general economic interest", which is argued to cause confusion. In a very early case, *Port de Mertert*, AG Dutheillet stated that SGEIs "must be of interest to the general economic activity of society".[44] Much later, Advocate General Léger characterized in *Hanner* the adequate supply of medicinal products on uniform terms throughout Sweden as "a general economic interest exhibiting special characteristics as compared with the general economic interest of other economic activities".[45] The locution "general economic interest" is also found in scholarly literature. For instance Buendia Sierra held that, by contrast with Article 36 TFEU and overriding reasons related to the general interest, the exception for SGEIs in Article 106(2) TFEU can justify

[43]Case C-49/07 *MOTOE* [2008] ECR I-4863, paras 46–47.

[44]Buendia Sierra 2008, p. 207. In *Port de Mertert* Advocate General Dutheillet de Lamothe held that running a river port could constitute a service of general economic interest entrusted to an undertaking, when two conditions are fulfilled: first that the port should be for the public and, unless in exceptional cases, not a port reserved for the needs of one or more undertakings; second that the traffic using the port should be involved in a general economic activity. Thus, AG Dutheillet rather evoked a "general economic activity" than a "general economic interest". See Opinion of Advocate General Dutheillet de Lamothe in Case 10/71 *Port of Mertert* [1971] ECR 739.

[45]See Opinion of AG Léger in Case C-438/02 *Krister Hanner* [2005] ECR I-04551, para 150, where AG Léger uses exactly the formulation used in Case C-179/90 *Merci Convenzionali* [1991] ECR I-05889, para 27 and Case C-266/96 *Corsica Ferries* [1998] ECR I-03949, para 45.

objectives of an economic nature, as this provision "was especially conceived to protect objectives of general economic interest".

First it must be underlined that, in contrast with this view and, as seen in Chap. 4, the Court has actually admitted economic considerations, in particular in cases where an SGEI-based national system was arguably in the picture, using the fiction of "overriding reasons related to the general interest". But the point here is rather Buendia Sierra's submission that an economic objective may be part of an SGEI, as "an instrumental objective, directed at guaranteeing the achievement of one of the non-economic objectives", which seems difficult to reconcile with his view that the general interest pursued must be of a non-economic nature to ground a valid SGEI in the meaning of Article 106(2) TFEU.[46] It is unfortunately difficult to find any explicit assessment on this issue in the CJEU's case law, but the Court has in several rulings referred to its statement in *Sacchi* that considerations of public interest *of a non-economic nature* (and not some "general economic interest") may justify that Member States remove certain services from competition by granting exclusive rights.[47]

It seems thus rather clear that the CJEU assumes the general interest motivating an SGEI in the meaning of Article 106(2) TFEU to be non-economic, which should surprise no one. The general interest in the concept of SGEI is defined by legislators and public authorities on the behalf of citizens. It is precisely this public prerogative—and not a commercial purpose—which justifies that public authorities may use solidarity-based funding mechanisms, and to this purpose levy tax or charge fees to finance certain activities seen by the peoples they represent as essential, often on the basis of constitutional values and rights. The general interest of an SGI does not become economic simply because it is pursued in a market environment, or indeed in cooperation with market operators who have their own economic paradigm. What becomes economic under such circumstances is argued to be the service tasks, and as *economic* tasks, they will have to be defined, devolved, entrusted and funded in the knowledge of the market paradigm, but also constrained by market freedoms protected by EU law (as the activity affected is or at least *can be* economic). Another thing is that the exercise of these market freedoms must allow the general interest task to be operated under conditions, in particular economic and financial conditions, which allow authorities and providers to achieve the missions in cooperation. In many cases, SGEI-related measures are based on the analysis of the effects free competition can in specific circumstances be expected to have on the possibility to fulfil the tasks (economic calculus). It is also true that public authorities may rely on economic considerations, in particular the necessity to hold their budgets and to remunerate undertakings to which they

[46]Buendia Sierra 1999, p. 216 and 278.

[47]Case 155/73 *Sacchi* [1974] ECR 409, para 14. This statement was referred to in several other cases, for instance Case C-320/91 *Corbeau*, para 9, Case C-260/89 *ERT* [1991] ECR I-2925, paras 10–12 and 20, Joined Cases T-309/04, T-317/04, T-329/04 and T-336/04, *TV 2* [2007] ECR II-00491, para 103.

entrust SGEI tasks, but the primary general interest that legitimates the missions/tasks does not thereby become economic.[48]

Against this background, it appears that the locution "general economic interest" may lead one to assume that a general interest in the notion of SGEI can be of economic nature. However, it is submitted that in the EU concept of SGEI the term "economic" relates instead to the word "service", and implies simply that the service characterized as SGEI is conducted with a general interest but has market relevance. The terminological combinations "general interest" and "economic service" reflect in a clearer manner the tension—inherent to SGEIs—between *societal* general interests and the interest of free trade and undistorted competition, and also mirror the difference between the interest of public authorities in entrusting SGEI tasks and the interest of the undertakings entrusted with such tasks, which generally is to make profits. Besides, the introduction of the legal notions of service of general interest and non-economic service of general interest seems to confirm that the term "economic" must be dissociated from the notion "general interest" in the concept of SGEI.

It must also be mentioned here that in *CBI*, the General Court explained that in the application of Article 106(2) TFEU, it is necessary to take into consideration the lack of a commercial dimension to the public service in question, and that its classification as an SGEI is explained more by its impact on the competitive and commercial sector.[49] In *SIC v Commission*, the General Court stated that "although the public service of broadcasting is considered to be an SGEI and not a service of general non-economic interest, it must none the less be pointed out that that classification as an SGEI is explained more by the actual impact of public service broadcasting on the otherwise competitive and commercial broadcasting sector, than by an alleged commercial dimension to broadcasting".[50] Thus, although it uses the weird locution "service of general non-economic interest", the General Court appears to hold that the activity impacted must be economic, not the general interest.

In sum, although it is used in some EU legislation—for instance in the Electricity Directive—the locution "general economic interest" is problematic in trying to explain the meaning of the concept of SGEI.[51] It is argued that the term "services of general economic interest" may be seen as a rather unlucky terminological choice, which need not be taken so seriously as after all, the Treaties have never been perfect. SGEI could as well have been called economic services of general interest (ESGI).

---

[48]This involves that the control of manifest error does not only concern the Member States' definition of SGEI missions, but also their implementation of these missions, in particular because the costs related to the missions can call for the assessment of complex economic facts.

[49]Case T-137/10 *CBI*, [decided on 7 November 2012, nyr], para 88.

[50]Case T-442/03 *SIC* v *Commission* [2008] ECR II-1161, para 153.

[51]See Article 3(2) of Directive 2009/72/EC of the European Parliament and of the Council of 13 July 2009 concerning common rules for the internal market in electricity and repealing Directive 2003/54/EC [2009] OJ 211/55.

5.2.2 "Obligation" Rather Than "Entrustment" as a Core Part of the SGEI Concept

In *Enirisorse* the Court of Justice observed that "[it was] not clear from the documents /…/that public-service duties have been entrusted to the Aziende, and still less therefore that such duties have been clearly defined".[52] This denotes the necessity of distinguishing the definition of the obligation from its entrustment, in other words

- The larger concept of SGEI-obligation, imposed on bodies acting within the frame of their State prerogatives and/or on market operators
- The concept of entrustment in the meaning of Article 106(2) TFEU.

In this respect, it seems that the Court shows, most clearly in *Commission v Germany*, but also much earlier, in *France v Commission*, that the concept of SGEI must be treated with respect for its function.[53] While 106(2) TFEU should in principle, as an exemption from the rules of the Treaties, be interpreted *strictly*, the notion of SGEI itself as a task or mission defined to achieve social or environmental goals should not automatically be interpreted restrictively, and certainly not narrower than what the principles of subsidiarity and respect of the national identity of the Member States, inclusive of self-government, require.

On this background, it seems that the terminology of Article 106(2) TFEU cannot be used to define the very notion of SGEI. It is submitted that the use of the word "entrustment" implies confusion between the *condition* necessary for the application of Article 106(2) and the functional *task* or *mission* characterizing an SGEI. The "tasks assigned" to undertakings entrusted with SGEIs in the meaning of Article 106(2) as well as the "missions" of SGEIs in the meaning of Article 14 TFEU are functional notions. Both are obligations potentially affecting the conditions for a given market, the difference between tasks and missions being the degree of precision necessary in the definition of the specific tasks which are entrusted to undertakings and therefore can imply compensatory mechanisms of particular importance to competition. Another question is that such obligations will only have to be examined according to Article 106(2) TFEU if the need for an exemption from the Treaty rules is or could be necessary. Entrustment, as already suggested, fulfils a function of proof (of the obligation) and of support for control of the exemption's proportionality. This function of entrustment as a control instrument is well expressed by the Court in *Commission v France*, stating that "it is appropriate to examine the necessity of maintaining EDF's and GDF's exclusive import and export rights, but only in relation to the public-service obligations of

---

[52]Joined Cases C-34/01 to C-38/01 *Enirisorse* [2003] ECR I-14243 para 34.

[53]See Case C-480/06 *Commission v Germany* [2009] ECR I-4747 and Case 202/88 *France v Commission* [1991] ECR I-1223, para 12.

which the French Government *has proved the existence*, namely the obligations of supply, continuity of supply and equal treatment between customers or consumers."[54]

The case law shows that the CJEU makes a distinction between the two following aspects of an SGEI:

- A phase when the Union, the Member States or their national/regional/local authorities define the public service objective and a public service task, in the knowledge that there is or might be a market for some tasks of this mission but that the market alone can fail to fulfil the public service objective
- A phase when they refer to this task—or mission—to motivate an exception from competition and/or internal market rules.

This was particularly clear in the General Court's following statement in *BUPA*:

> even though the Member State has a wide discretion when determining what it regards as an SGEI, that does not mean that it is not required, when it relies on the existence of and the need to protect an SGEI mission, to ensure that that mission satisfies certain minimum criteria common to every SGEI mission within the meaning of the EC Treaty, as explained in the case law, and to demonstrate that those criteria are indeed satisfied in the particular case.[55]

Thus, the GC underlined that a Member State has a wide discretion *when determining what it regards as an SGEI.* It is at the moment it relies on the existence of and the need to protect an SGEI mission that a Member State is required to prove that certain criteria are fulfilled, which requires that the public service mission/task is legally objectifiable.[56] The Commission expressed arguably a similar meaning in its Communication on the application of State aid rules to public service broadcasting, when it underlines that "[t]he question of the definition of the public service remit must not be confused with the question of the financing mechanism chosen to provide these services".[57] Much earlier, in *Merci convenzionali Porto di Genova*, the Court had already indicated how the reasoning should be conducted:

> In that respect it must be held that it does not appear either from the documents supplied by the national court or from the observations submitted to the Court of Justice that dock work is of a general economic interest exhibiting special characteristics as compared with the general economic interest of other economic activities or, *even if it were*, that the application of the rules of the Treaty, in particular those relating to competition and freedom of movement, would be such as to obstruct the performance of such a task.[58]

---

[54] 159/94 *Commission v France* [1997] ECR I-5815, para 89.

[55] Case T-289/03 *BUPA* [2008] ECR II-81, para 166, see also Case T-17/02 *Fred Olsen* [2005] ECR II-2031, para 216 and the case law cited under that paragraph. The definition of such services by a Member State can be questioned by the Commission only in the event of manifest error.

[56] Ibid., para 172.

[57] Commission, "Communication on the application of State aid rules to public service broadcasting" 2009/C 257/01, para 49.

[58] 179/90 *Merci convenzionali* [1991] ECR I-5889, para 27.

The Court stated thus that the key element in the identification of an SGEI is its "*special characteristics* compared with the general economic interest of other economic activities". These characteristics, normally based on what a given society at a given time regards as fundamental needs, will then be assessed when the rules of the Treaties are relied on to justify a proportional exception from the rules of the market to secure those needs. Apparently these "special characteristics" had not been clarified in *Merci convenzionali Porto di Genova.*

In this respect some valuable clarification was given in *Corsica Ferries France*, which is also worth quoting:

> It is evident from the file on the case in the main proceedings that mooring operations are of general economic interest, such interest having special characteristics, in relation to those of other economic activities, which is capable of bringing them within the scope of Article 90(2) of the Treaty. Mooring groups are *obliged to provide at any time and to any user a universal mooring service, for reasons of safety in port waters*. At all events, the Italian Republic could properly have considered that it was necessary, on grounds of public security, to confer on local groups of operators the exclusive right to provide a universal mooring service.[59]

The Court does not use here the term "entrustment" to determine the presence of special characteristics which can bring an economic activity in the scope of Article 106(2), but instead the word "obligation", also present in "public service obligations", often used by the Court as a synonym for SGEIs. This approach seemed already to show that what makes an SGEI is not the formal entrustment of an undertaking but its intrinsic characteristics, including

- A legal *obligation*, for instance on Member States to ensure the conditions of existence of a service, on municipalities to ensure access to a service or on undertakings to perform a service): "how"
- A concrete mission for this obligation in the form of a service in a wide sense (a social or environmental "function") and specific conditions in the provision of this service (for instance universal provision at any time to any user, environmentally sound treatment of waste at a facility close to the source of waste, a certain nature and level of healthcare to any person in need of it within a given territory): "what"
- A plausible contribution of this mission to the realization of a general (economic) interest (safety, environmental protection, social protection): "why"

It is the *politically decided* objective to ensure, in a market context, the supply of a service in the general interest which is at the heart of the concept of SGEI. The same objective of general interest can therefore many times have to be analysed from different perspectives, as it can imply obligations for public authorities as well as for the undertaking(s) which many times will be entrusted with the performance of specific tasks within the frame of the SGEI. In some cases the objective of general interest at the core of an SGEI will be relevant to define the freedom of

[59]Case C-266/96 *Corsica Ferries* [1998] ECR I-3949, para 45; see also Case C-242/95 *GT-Link* [1997] ECR I-4449, paras 52–53, emphasis added.

national, regional or local authorities legally responsible for securing the service to organise it in a particular way (for instance through public-public partnerships as in *Commission v Germany*).[60] In other situations—normally pure competition issues—the objective of general interest inherent to the SGEI can be relevant as a reference for what the undertaking entrusted with specific obligations must achieve and which exemptions from internal market and competition rules may be justified, as for instance in *Commission v France.*[61]

This understanding of the EU concept of SGEI finds support in the reasoning of the Court of Justice in *Commission v Germany*, in which the Court builds its solution by reference to a law-based chain of responsibility from the EU-legislator to municipalities to ensure the achievement of SGEI missions related to environment protection. In its reasoning the Court starts by referring to the *obligation* for Member States, imposed by the Framework Waste Directive, to draw up plans for waste management.[62] These plans must provide for 'appropriate measures to encourage rationalisation of the collection, sorting and treatment of waste', one of the most important of such measures being to ensure that waste be treated in the nearest possible installation.[63] This can be seen as a first link in the chain of responsibility, where the Union imposes on Member States an *obligation to take state measures* by virtue of a general interest. The second link of responsibility identified by the Court is an obligation for all municipalities, on the basis of national German law, to ensure that waste treatment capacity is available in accordance with the Directive requirement of proximity, an obligation which the Court qualifies as a "public interest task".[64] The third link of responsibility is evoked as the future construction and operation of a facility intended to *perform* a "public service, namely thermal incineration of waste".[65]

---

[60]Case C-480/06 *Commission v Germany* [2009] ECR I-4747.

[61]See Case C-159/94 *Commission v France* [1997] ECR I-05815. Under para 71 the Court underlined that "[i]t should nevertheless be borne in mind that it is clear from the case law of the Court (see *Almelo/…/* para 49) that such obligations or constraints may be taken into consideration for the purpose of considering to what extent derogations from the Treaty rules which it is sought to justify are necessary in order to enable the undertaking in question to perform the tasks of general interest entrusted to it." Reference to case C-393/92 *Almelo* [1994] ECR I-1477.

[62]Case C-480/06 *Commission v Germany* [2009] ECR I-4747 para 37, referring to Council Directive 75/442/EEC of 15 July 1975 on waste [1975] OJ L194/39.

[63]This task was pursuant to Article 5(2) of Council Directive 91/156/EEC of 18 March 1991, amending Directive 75/442 [1991] OJ L 78/32. A similar task is now provided by Article 16(1) and (3) of Directive 2008/98/EC of the European Parliament and of the Council of 19 November 2008 on waste and repealing certain Directives, among which Directive 91/156/EEC (as consolidated by Directive 2006/12/EC on waste) [2008] OJ L312/3.

[64]Thus, by referring to the EU principle of proximity for the treatment of municipal waste, imposing on public authorities to plan this treatment in a manner that ensures that municipal waste is treated as close as possible from the place where it has been produced, the Court did clarify, although quite shortly, what the general economic task consisted in, contrary to Steinicke's view. See Steinicke 2011, p. 270.

[65]Case C-480/06 *Commission v Germany* [2009] ECR I-4747, para 44.

The obligation to perform tasks forming part of the SGEI (construction and operation of the waste treatment facilities) is made through acts of entrustment creating obligations for market actors.[66] Entrustment constitutes thus only the act stating and proving the transfer of specific SGEI obligations to the third link of responsibility. Obviously, in *Commission v Germany*, SGI obligations are considered to exist already in the frame of the second link of responsibility, *before entrustment*. It is in consideration of these obligations that the Court, under certain conditions, is ready to allow that procurement procedures normally required in presence of a contract for pecuniary interest are not applied. The question arises however whether the Court considers that

a. The obligation imposed to the municipalities is a non-economic task of public interest which leads them to entrust SGEI tasks or
b. The obligations resting by the local authorities to ensure access—in good economic conditions—to the service of general interest are an integral part of the SGEI or "public service" consisting in thermal incineration of waste, as well as the tasks which will later be entrusted to market operators.

It is submitted that the answer given by the Court may be taken to be (b), as the Court stresses the fact that there was no indication in the case that the local authorities at issue were contriving to circumvent the rules on public procurement. In other words the municipalities gave clear signs that they were aware of waste treatment being an economic activity (both in Germany and everywhere else in the EU), of their duty to procure some tasks and seemed ready to use the procurement rules. There is thus no doubt that the measures taken by the EU-legislator, the national legislator and the public authorities in charge with ensuring the service all had been adopted in the knowledge that they had a potential to affect trade and competition, and that their legality, based on the common objective to ensure that waste will be treated in adequate installations in accordance with the principle of proximity and the waste treatment hierarchy, could have to be examined in the light of competition and internal market rules.

The compulsory character of the public service task was in *Commission v Germany* thoroughly underlined by the Court. By contrast, the relevance for the conditions of application of Treaty principles of equal treatment, non-discrimination and transparency and/or procurement rules, of the *compulsory* character of the public authorities' public service task, is not clear in the *Teckal* to *Coditel* "in-house" case law. The Court asserted namely in *Coditel* that a public authority has the possibility of performing the *public interest tasks conferred on it* by using its own resources, and that it may do so in cooperation with other public authorities. It is nevertheless unsure whether the Court meant by the terms "tasks" and "conferred" that the possibilities named by the Court depend on public authorities being imposed an *obligation* to ensure the performance of a public interest task, and if so from which legal sources and in which form the obligation originates. A

[66] As already mentioned the Court has at several occasions used the term "public service" as a synonym for SGEI.

particularly interesting question is whether public authorities, on the base of general powers to act in the general interest, may impose on themselves obligations to ensure a public service task.

In a case actualizing a failure to apply the principle of transparency in procuring ambulance transport services, the CJEU made an explicit distinction between on the one hand the categorization of a service as SGEI—which it simply considered as unquestionable in the view of the judgment in *Ambulanz Glöckner*—and on the other hand the Member State's argument that Article 86(2) EC (now Article 106(2) TFEU) could justify an exemption from procurement rules—which implies for the Member State an obligation to show that all the conditions for application of that provision are fulfilled.[67] This seems to confirm that, contrary to the Commission's understanding emerging from its soft law documents, an SGEI can exist independently from any specific entrustment.

5.2.3 A General Interest of "Public Service"

As seen in Chap. 4, the CJEU transposes elements of its test under Article 106(2) TFEU to measures justified by the economic sustainability of welfare systems pursuing general interest missions, calling these missions overriding reasons related to the general interest instead of services of general interest missions. This transposition is facilitated by the fact that the Court uses synonymously the notions of general interest and of public interest, as shown by the following assertion of the General Court in *BUPA*.

> In the first place, as the case law shows, the provision of the service in question must, by definition, assume a general or public interest/.../In addition, as the applicants claim, the general or public interest on which the Member State relies must not be reduced to the need to subject the market concerned to certain rules or the commercial activity of the operators concerned to authorisation by the State.[68]

By characterizing public service obligations which in national welfare systems can exist both at the level of public authorities and at the level of undertakings often publicly financed—as overriding reasons related to the general interest instead of SGI or SGEI, the CJEU can open such systems (some authors call this a "disintegration") to both more service recipients and more service providers than they have been designed for. In the field of social services, this bifurcation from the SGI/SGEI terminology gives the Court a possibility to *redefine* the service of general interest underpinned by the national system, and to include conditions that Member States had not counted with. This bifurcated approach is important in several ways:

[67]Case C-160/08 *Commission v Germany* [2010] ECR I-03713, paras 125–126.

[68]Case T-289/03 *BUPA* [2008] ECR II-81, para 178.

- It dispenses the Court from deciding whether the service of general interest underpinned by the system is an SGEI or a NESGI.
- It leaves the Court *formally* unbound by its own case law, studied in Chap. 4, affirming that Member States retain a wide discretion to determine the nature and the scope of SGEI missions, especially in fields outside the Union's.[69]
- It allows to tone down welfare systems' role in the relation between Member States and "their peoples", which gives more elasticity to the notion of solidarity-based systems.

The CJEU's case law studied in Chap. 4 shows the CJEU's readiness—and in many cases the Commission's too—to easily admit the general interest ratios invoked by Member States as a justification to their intervention on certain markets, and focus instead on the proportionality of its intervention. However, the Court has made clear that the discretion of Member States is limited by the control of manifest error and in *BUPA* the GC emphasized that a Member State "must indicate the reasons why it considers that the service in question, because of its specific nature, deserves to be characterised as an SGEI and to be distinguished from other economic activities".[70] In the absence of such reasons, even a marginal review by the Community institutions on the basis of both the first *Altmark* condition and Article 86(2) EC with respect to the existence of a manifest error by the Member State in the context of its discretion would not be possible.

It is important to distinguish between the issue of the legitimacy to attach public service missions to an activity and the issue of whether certain entities—public authorities or undertakings—may invoke public service missions to justify measures infringing Treaty rules. In *BRT II*, the Court of Justice denied copyright management the character of service of general interest in the meaning of Article 106(2) TFEU, not because the service could intrinsically not be in the general interest, but rather because the undertaking invoking a derogation from competition rules had not been entrusted any such task by the State—at any relevant governance level.[71]

The CJEU distinguishes services in the general interest and services in the private interest. In *Züchner* the Court explained that although cross-border transfer of customers' funds constitutes an operation falling within the special tasks of banks, that was not sufficient to make them undertakings within the meaning of Article 106(2) TFEU unless it could be established that in performing such transfers, banks were operating an SGEI entrusted by a measure adopted by public authorities.[72] Likewise, in *GVL*, a company offering copyright and performing rights management services denied that it had abused its dominant position by refusing

[69]Ibid., paras 12 and 166, referring to para 22 of the Communication on SGEIs and to the case law of the Court of First Instance (now general Court).

[70]See Cases C-170/90 *Merci Convenzionali* [1991] ECR I-5889 para 27, C-38/01 *Enirisorse* [2003] ECR I-14243, at I-14247 paras 33–34 and T-289/03 *BUPA* [2008] ECR II-81, para 172.

[71]Case 127/73 *BRT II* [1974] ECR 318, paras 22–23.

[72]Case 172/80 *Züchner* [1981] ECR 2021, para 7.

to conclude management contracts with performing artists who were neither German nationals nor resident in the Federal Republic of Germany, and claimed that it was entrusted with an SGEI. The Court recognized that the German legislation on monitoring of this activity went further than the public supervision of many other undertakings. This showed that the activity was regarded as important, but was not sufficient for GVL to constitute an undertaking entrusted with SGEI in the meaning of Article 106(2).[73]

In *BUPA*, the GC referred to *GVL* and *Züchner*, pointing out that SGEIs must be distinguished from *services in the private interest*, notwithstanding the fact that a private interest may be more or less collective or be recognized by the State as legitimate or beneficial.[74] It further reminded that the mere fact that the national legislature, acting in the general interest in the broad sense, imposes certain rules of authorisation, of functioning or of control on all the operators in a particular sector does not in principle mean that there is an SGEI mission.[75] The Court found that an SGEI mission may consist in an obligation imposed on a large number of, or indeed on all, operators active on the same market.[76] Characteristic for an SGEI was a public authority's act creating and defining a specific mission consisting in the provision of a service in compliance with the service obligations.[77] It emphasized that, with the stated object of serving the general interest by allowing approximately half of the Irish population to benefit from alternative cover for certain health care, in particular hospital care, the private medical insurance obligations at issue restricted the commercial freedom of the insurers to an extent going considerably beyond ordinary conditions of authorisation to exercise an activity in a specific sector.

Thus, serving the public by ensuring access to essential services and goods is a core value in SGEI matters.[78] The general interest as understood in the concept of SGEI is not limited to serving individuals, but can reside in serving society as a whole. In *SIC v Commission*, the General Court referred to a resolution of the Council stating that public service broadcasting has a vital significance for ensuring democracy, pluralism, social cohesion, cultural and linguistic diversity, and must be able to continue to provide a wide range of programming, for "society as a whole".[79]

---

[73]Case 7/82 *GVL v Commission* [1983] ECR 483, paras 31–32.

[74]Case T-289/03 *BUPA* [2008] ECR II-81, para 178.

[75]Ibid., para 178.

[76]Ibid., para 179.

[77]Ibid., para 182.

[78]See van de Gronden 2013, p. 8.

[79]Case T-442/03 *SIC* v *Commission* [2008] ECR II-1161, para 153. The GC referred to the Resolution of the Council and of the Member States of 25 January 1999 concerning broadcasting, OJ 1999 C 30, p. 1 (recital B and point 7 of the Resolution).

5.2.4 Relationship Between SGEIs and Universal Service Obligations (USO)

It seems important to say some words here on USO-regulation of services in the public sector, which has been the model adopted for EU harmonizing of several important services in the public sector. The concept of universal service obligation (USO), said to have its origin in the United Kingdom, made its entrance in the EU legal-political sphere in the 1980s and has played a major role in the Europeanization of electricity, gas, postal and telecommunications services.[80] In the EU legislation harmonizing the markets for these services, universal service access is pursued through private law based solutions, replacing earlier public law-based citizen-state relationships in many Member States. The concept of USO varies according to legislation in different sectors but the Commission proposed a general understanding in the White Paper on SGI:

> It establishes the right of everyone to access certain services considered as essential and imposes obligations on service providers to offer defined services according to specified conditions including complete territorial coverage and at an affordable price.[81]

A more precise understanding may be gained by considering the Member States' universal service obligation according to the Electricity Market Directive to secure all household customers (and where Member States deem it appropriate, small enterprises), "the right to be supplied with electricity of a specified quality within their territory at reasonable, easily and clearly comparable and transparent prices".[82] To secure this right, the Directive requires that Member States impose on electricity distribution companies an obligation to connect customers to their grid under terms, conditions and tariffs set in accordance with a procedure laid down in the Directive, and it allows Member States to appoint a supplier of last resort to ensure the provision of universal service.[83] Thus, the Electricity Directive does not put obligations directly on service providers but instead requires that the Member States put certain minimum obligations on providers in order to secure users rights. Several authors have pointed to the fact that USO-based EU legislation on public services requires specific policy objectives and public intervention to achieve concrete welfare objectives. For instance, *Sauter* emphasizes that universal service obligations are rather pointless if they are not linked to other public

[80]See Prosser 2005, p. 177–181. Davies and Szyszczak note that whereas a Member State has a wide competence to define a SGEI, this is no longer the case when a USO is found in liberalising legislation. The see an expanding role for the concept of USOs in the future development of the EU, see their charting of USOs' development in Davies and Szyszczak 2011.

[81]Commission, "Services of General Interest in Europe" (Communication) COM (96) 443 final, p. 2.

[82]Article 3(3) of Directive 2009/72/EC of the European Parliament and of the Council of 13 July 2009 concerning common rules for the internal market in electricity and repealing Directive 2003/54/EC [2009] OJ 211/55.

[83]Ibid.

policy objectives as quality and continuity in order to achieve a worthwhile universal service guarantee in a particular case.[84]

Regarding more specifically the Electricity Directive, Roth points out that the user rights created by the Member States constitute a "minimum service standard", harmonized at EU level, and emphasizes that affordability is closely linked to the right of access to services.[85] As a matter of fact, the Electricity Directive allows Member States to "top-up" the regulatory pressure in order to reinforce its efficiency. Thus, Member States may impose public service obligations on market operators related to a limited number of specific general interests listed in the Directive, including affordability of the service.[86] These regulatory powers are crucial, because the Electricity Directive imposes only that "reasonable" prices are offered, while the imperative of affordability is clearer in the USOs laid down in the Directives on postal services and on electronic telecommunications.[87] As it is reckoned that USO-regulation of liberalized electricity markets does not exclude that prices for services covered by USOs remain in certain cases too high for many users, the responsibility to ensure these services' affordability is left primarily on Member States.[88] They must determine criteria for determining affordable prices, and the Court of Justice has recognized in *Enel* that, in the interest of the end consumer and of ensuring the security of the electricity system, they may impose price limitations on operators owning installations considered essential for this security.[89]

The *Enel* case, and the closely related *Federutility* case in the field of gas services, shed light on the important issue in terms of liability if the service provider entrusted with universal service obligations fails to fulfil universal service obligations. As emphasized by Rott, the vagueness of many aspects of USOs makes it

---

[84]Sauter 2008, p. 14. *Sauter* explains that "imposing full national coverage for free at zero quality would obviously be pointless".

[85]Rott 2009, p. 226.

[86]Article 3(2) the Electricity Directive.

[87]See Article 3(1) of Directive 2002/22/EC of the European Parliament and of the Council of 7 March 2002 on universal service and users' rights relating to electronic communications networks and services (Universal Service Directive) [2002] OJ L108/51: "Member States shall ensure that the services set out in this Chapter are made available at the quality specified to all end-users in their territory, independently of geographical location, and, in the light of specific national conditions, at an *affordable price*"; Article 3(1) of Directive 97/67/EC: "Member States shall ensure that users enjoy the right to a universal service involving the permanent provision of a postal service of specified quality at all points in their territory at *affordable prices* for all users."

[88]Rott 2009, p. 215–232. To justify these measures, these Member States had to rely on public service obligations in accordance with Article 106(2) TFEU, allowing a strong state commitment on the market.

[89]See Case C-242/10 *Enel* [2011] ECR I-13665.

unlikely that citizens deprived of access to the service would succeed in claiming a right of access against their state. This may explain that the CJEU has in those cases admitted Member States' claim for the appropriateness and necessity of price control measures—generally held as very intrusive in a market economy—compensating their weak liability for the "rights" created by EU legislation.[90] Also, the fact that EU Institutions must respect the right of access to SGEI, as follows from Article 36 EUCFR, may have played a role in the CJEU's deferential approach in these cases.[91]

5.2.5 Summing Up: The Relationship Between SGEI Missions, Tasks and Obligations

To a large extent "because of *Altmark*", the notion of "public service obligation" (PSO) has developed into a cornerstone element of the CJEU's understanding of the EU concept of SGEI and is predominant in the legal understanding of SGEIs.[92] It is present in the Treaties, as Article 93 TFEU declares compatible with the Treaties aid meeting the needs of transport coordination or representing reimbursement for the discharge of certain obligations inherent in the concept of public service. In Article 93 TFEU, the obligations reimbursed are said to be "inherent" to the concept of public service. This suggests that the concept of public service as understood in that provision contains more than "public service obligations" to be funded by state resources. In the light of the analysis conducted so far, the question in focus in this section is therefore whether there is nothing more to SGEIs than PSOs imposed on undertakings.

It is strongly questionable whether such a narrow understanding of the EU concept of SGEI—where all there is to SGEI is PSOs imposed on undertakings—can be upheld convincingly, because it does not seem to fit with the CJEU's case law in general, but most evidently not with the *BUPA* ruling. As observed by van de Gronden, a novelty in *BUPA* was that the GC regarded *all* undertakings operating in a given market as entrusted with a special task within the meaning of Article 106(2) TFEU, in a manner similar to the Commission Decision on the Dutch health-care insurance system that concerned state financial measures.[93]

[90]Rott 2009, p. 232. On the issue of how far Article 36 of the EU Charter could protect an individual fundamental right, when a USO are defined a minima to be attractive to private providers, see Szyszczak 2014, p. 978.

[91]This explanation gets support from Szyszczak's understanding of the role which Article 36 of the EU Charter could have where a Member State creates regulation and policy for an SGEI, see Szyszczak 2014, p. 978.

[92]Case C-280/00 *Altmark* [2003] ECR I-7747, para 89.

[93]Van de Gronden 2009, p. 238–239. This author noted that prior to *BUPA*, the provision now in Article 106(2) TFEU had only been applied to cases where only one or a limited number of undertakings were entrusted with SGEI tasks.

Commenting the GC's approach deriving a public service obligation from the general requirements laid down in the national legislation, van de Gronden proposed that "a SGEI mission may only be derived from general obligations that amount to the performance of tasks in favour of citizens or enterprises."[94] Not only is this view shared, but it is moreover argued here that it may precisely be such missions of "securing public access to certain services" which explain that the CJEU found national measures related to welfare services as justified by overriding reasons related to the general interest, but based on a proportionality test that looked very much like the test applied by the Court under Article 106(2) TFEU.

This said, van de Gronden held that "SGEI and public service obligations are concepts that are alike in that both concern special tasks that state bodies impose on undertakings", but it is argued here that in *BUPA*, the General Court made clear that it did not understand PSO and the concept of SGEI as synonyms.[95] Indeed, the Court admitted as common ground between the parties "that the concept of public service obligation referred to in [the *Altmark* judgment]/.../does not differ from that referred to in Article 86(2) EC".[96] However, having underlined that the services submitted to the PSO (private medical insurance, PMI) should be distinguished from the PSO imposed on all PMI providers (the PMI *obligations*), the GC considered the link between the PMI obligations and the PMI services as "indissoluble".[97] Subsequently, the GC regarded the obligations as SGEI tasks and at the same time considered that "the PMI services have *as such* an *SGEI character*".[98] What the Court exactly meant by an indissoluble link is not so clear, but by considering the service itself as a part of the SGEI, the GC's approach in *BUPA* gave sense to the principle in Article 36 EUCFR that the Union respects access to SGEIs as provided for in national laws and practice. As mentioned in Sect. 5.1.4 above, it makes little sense that EU should respect the right of access to public service obligations, if the service they secure is not a part of the SGEI.

In *Altmark*, were public funding of PSOs imposed on undertakings was at issue, the Court of Justice appears to also have admitted that in such circumstances, the concept of SGEI may encompass the service itself. The Court found

---

[94]Ibid., p. 237–239.

[95]Ibid., p. 236. In *ZT*, the General Court holds that the notion of PSO in *Altmark* corresponds to the notion of SGEI in Article 106(2) TFEU, see Case T-309/12 *TZ*, EU:T:2014:676, para 132. Contrary to Szyszczak's understanding, the Court did however not say that the notion of PSO in *Altmark* and the notion SGEI in the Treaties (i.e. not only in Article 106(2) TFEU but also in Article 14 TFEU) are synonyms, see Szyszczak 2015, p. 686.

[96]Case T-289/03 *BUPA* [2008] ECR II-81, para 162.

[97]Ibid., para 175. Remember that the obligations imposed on PMI insurers were open enrolment, community rating, lifetime cover and minimum benefits. The Court held that this "indissoluble link" implied that the Commission could not limit its state aid assessment to the obligations without also taking into account the services forming the subject-matter of those obligations and the provision of which was dependent on compliance with those obligations.

[98]Ibid., para 176, emphasis added.

that public subsidies intended to enable the operation of certain transport services were not caught by Article 107(1) TFEU "where such subsidies are to be regarded as compensation for the *services* provided by the recipient undertakings in order to discharge public service obligations".[99] In this landmark ruling constituting the ground of all state aid rules applying to SGEIs, the compensation is connected to the services provided, and not only to the PSOs discharged by the service providers.

In light of the above, it is submitted that, based on the Treaties framework on SGEIs, the CJEU sees more in the EU concept of SGEI than PSOs imposed on undertakings. Thus,

$$\text{SGEI} = \text{PSOs imposed on undertakings} + \text{X}$$

In this equation, (X) is everything that is not PSOs imposed on undertakings but is part of the EU concept of SGEI. Answering the question "what may (X) be?" is fundamentally related to two issues: (1) who imposes PSOs on undertakings (or SGEI tasks in the meaning of Article 106(2) TFEU) and (2) on which mandates/criteria.

Regarding the "who" (1), it is important to remind that public authorities—national, regional and local—are ensured by the SGI Protocol a wide discretion to organise, commission and provide SGEIs. This supposes that SGEIs may exist *before they are entrusted to undertakings*. In other words, the SGI Protocol supposes that public service tasks may exist at the level of public authorities. This may well be the Commission's understanding too. Indeed, in its Communication on the application of state aid rules to SGEI compensation, the Commission states that:

> The first *Altmark* criterion requires the definition of an SGEI task. This requirement coincides with that of Article 106(2) of the Treaty. It transpires from Article 106(2) of the Treaty that undertakings entrusted with the operation of SGEIs are undertakings entrusted with 'a particular task'. Generally speaking, the entrustment of a 'particular public service task' implies the supply of services which, if it were considering its own commercial interest, an undertaking would not assume or would not assume to the same extent or under the same conditions. Applying a general interest criterion, Member States or the Union may attach specific obligations to such services.[100]

Firstly, it is important to note that the Commission Communication uses here the term "public service task" (PST) as synonym for "public service obligation" (PSO). The term "public service task" is used by the CJEU (Grand Chamber) in *Commission v Germany* and *Lecce* regarding *public authorities*' obligation to secure the supply of certain services, and this obligation is regarded as a decisive condition for an important derogation from EU procurement rules. This semantic

[99]Case C-280/00 *Altmark*, [2003] ECR I-7747, para 95, emphasis added.

[100]Communication from the Commission on the application of the European Union State aid rules to compensation granted for the provision of services of general economic interest, 2012/C 8/02, points 47, footnotes omitted.

overlap seems to indicate that (1) PSO and PST are seen as comparable notions, and (2) that PST imposed on public authorities may be part of the SGEI concept, both in the Court's and the Commission's "deep layer's" understanding. If the notion of entrustment, specific to Article 106(2) TFEU, is understood as a proof of the obligation rather than its substance, there is a strong commonality between PSOs—the term generally used for public service tasks which undertakings are imposed—and PSTs—the term used by the CJEU for public service tasks which public authorities are imposed.

This understanding appears to give sense to the strong prerogatives which state authorities enjoy in relation to public service tasks according to the SGI Protocol and according to the CJEU's approach in *Altmark*, in *Teckal* and *Commission v Germany*. In a model where the legislator does not exclude the entrustment of SGEI tasks to undertakings, but imposes first on public authorities (at national, regional or local level) to secure the performance of these tasks, it is submitted that public authorities' public service tasks are inherent to the achievement of the SGEI missions, and thus are part of the SGEI. The public prerogatives are strong because the public obligations may also be strong, especially when they are not "simple" overriding reasons related to the general interest but instead amount to "the performance of tasks in favour of citizens or enterprises".[101]

Second, the Commission holds that PSOs are imposed on undertakings by application of "a general interest criterion". This "general interest criterion" is a very vague term. In fact, PSOs are often imposed on undertakings on the basis of public authorities' own public service tasks (PSTs). PSTs *imposed* on public authorities reflect a particularly strong commitment of the State (through national or EU legislation) to secure the performance of specific tasks in favour of citizens or enterprises. This commitment is particularly strong when the State is not simply engaged in regulating and supervising market performance, but also in defining the conditions of service provision, and in supplying the service to the public by securing its organisation and funding. In this strong commitment, public authorities do not act on the basis of general objectives, but on the basis of compulsory missions, based on democratic mandates.

Hence, when the reason for imposing SGEI tasks on undertakings is directly related to public authorities' own public service tasks, the "general interest criterion" to secure access to essential services is a mission depending on the capacity of both public authorities and undertakings to fulfil their respective tasks. It is submitted that in such a regulatory model, both PSO and PST are part of the SGEI and contribute to an SGEI mission in the meaning of Article 14 TFEU, broader than the SGEI tasks addressed by Article 106(2) TFEU.

[101]This refers to van de Gronden's understanding of SGEI missions, already evoked above, see van de Gronden 2009, p. 239.

5.3 Conclusions

In sum, looking at the Commission's Communications and Guides between 1996 and 2013 shows not only an evolution towards a more technocratic description of the EU concept of SGEI, but remarkably also an increasing sense of confusion. In the field of social services, this never ending succession of "clarifications" send a signal that the SGI or the SGEI character of social services plays an important role for the application of EU free movement and procurement rules to social services in the public sector of the Member States. Yet, this signal is clouded by a bifurcation from the concepts of SGI and SGEI to the notions of PSO and PST, used as synonyms by the Commission in the meaning "undertakings' SGEI tasks" without consideration for the fact that the CJEU has connected the notion of PST to *public authorities*' public service tasks, and found that such tasks may justify important derogations from EU procurement rules, most clearly so far in *Commission v Germany*.

In light of the study so far, it seems unreasonable to let this confusion stand in the way of attempts to propose an updated understanding of the EU concept of SGEI, based on the case law of the CJEU and more coherently connected to the post-Lisbon Treaty framework on SGEI. In that spirit, it is proposed that the notion of entrustment has a specific function for the purpose of Article 106(2) TFEU, but falls outside the core of the concept of SGEI, and that this core includes the following elements:

1. The SGEI mission involves public service obligations/tasks which may be imposed by the legislator directly on undertakings (model (a) of the *BUPA* case), or imposed by the legislator on public authorities, which then have a wide discretion to provide the SGEI, organise the SGEI and commission the SGEI, although this discretion can be constrained by national rules (model (b) of the *Commission v Germany* case).
2. The general interest is not in itself economic, but consists in serving the public by ensuring access to essential services and goods. The general interest as understood in the concept of SGEI is not limited to serving individuals, but can reside in serving society as a whole. It is the final mission which is addressed by Article 14 TFEU, not only the tasks imposed on undertakings in the meaning of Article 106(2) TFEU. Depending on the regulatory model at issue, both PSO/PST imposed on undertakings and/or on public authorities, contribute to the achievement of SGEI missions, and must operate under conditions, in particular economic and financial conditions, enabling the SGEI missions to be achieved.
3. The activity affected by an SGEI mission is not necessarily economic in the Member State defining this mission, but at the EU level *can be* economic. This explains that the definition of an SGEI mission can be relevant both in a competition perspective and in a free movement (including procurement) perspective. In certain models, PSOs imposed on undertakings may necessitate measures which can have to be reconciled with the Treaty competition rules

under Article 106(2) TFEU. In other models of SGEI-regulation, not only PSOs imposed on undertakings but also PSTs imposed on public authorities may necessitate measures which must be reconciled with the free movement and procurement rules following from the Treaties.[102]

In this understanding, which is argued to get at least implicit support from the CJEU's case law, the EU concept of SGEI constitutes a broad concept, allowing us to address both the vertical and the horizontal principles of EU law affecting public service tasks, and a functional concept comprising the missions, the tasks and the rights created by the missions. This understanding seems coherent with Article 14 TFEU and Article 36 EUCFR, but also with Article 106(2) TFEU, which requires that measures adopted to secure that undertakings fulfil their SGEI tasks do not derogate more than necessary from EU market principles and rules, and thereby that the "interests of the Union" are respected, especially in fields where the balance non-economic and economic interests has been harmonized. Hence, the Union's duty to take care that SGEIs operate according to conditions, in particular financial and economic conditions, enabling them to achieve their missions, implies also that free movement and procurement rules capable to obstruct the fulfilment of any public service tasks related to the SGEI mission, be it public authorities or undertakings.

References

Buendia Sierra JL (1999) Exclusive rights and state Monopolies under EC Law. Oxford University Press, Oxford

Buendia Sierra JL (2008) Finding the right balance: state aid and services of general economic interest. In: EC state aid law: Liber Amicorum Francisco Santaolalla. Kluwer, Alphen aan den. RijnFreedland M (1998) Law, public services, and citizenship—new domains, new regime, in public services and citizenship. In: Freedland M, Sciarra S (eds) European law. Public and labour law perspectives. Clarendon Press, Oxford

Davies J, Szyszczak E (2011) Universal service obligations: fulfilling new generations of services of general economic interest. In: Szyszczak E et al (eds) Developments in services of general interest. T.M.C. Asser Press, The Hague

Neergaard U (2008) Services of general (economic) interest and the services directive. In: Nergaard U, Nielsen R, Roseberry L (eds) The services directive—consequences for the welfare state and the European social model. DJØF Publishing, Copenhagen

Prosser T (2005) The limits of competition law: markets and public services. Oxford University Press, Oxford

Rott P (2009) The user-provider relationship: informed choice and user protection through private law. In: Krajewski M, Neergaard U, van de Gronden JW (eds) The changing legal framework for services of general interest in Europe, between competition and solidarity. T.M.C. Asser Press, The Hague

[102]Although it is difficult to say whether the Court makes a clear and consistent use of the terms PSO and PST in its case law, it appears that it has so far generally used the term public service obligation regarding undertakings and public service task regarding public authority.

Sauter W (2008) Services of general economic interest and universal service in EU Law. http://ssrn.com/abstract=1136105
Sauter W, Schepel H (2007) "State" and "market" in the competition and free movement case law of the EU courts. TILEC Discussion Paper 2007-024, http://ssrn.com/abstract=1010075
Snell J (2008) Freedom to provide services in the case law and in the services directive: problems, solutions, and institutions. In: Neergaard U, Nielsen R, Roseberry L (eds) The services directive—consequences for the welfare state and the European social model. DJØF Publishing, Copenhagen
Steinicke M (2011) In house-kontrakter eller administrative aftaler. In: Madell T, Bekkedal T, Neergaard U (eds) Den nordiska välfärden och marknaden – Nordiska erfarenheter av tjänster av allmänt intresse i en EU-rättslig Kontext. Iustus Förlag, Uppsala
Szyszczak E (2009) Legal tools in the liberalization of welfare markets. In: Neergaard U, Nielsen R, Roseberry L (eds) Integrating welfare functions into EU law—from Rome to Lisbon. DJØF Publishing, Copenhagen
Szyszczak E (2013) Soft law and safe havens. In: Neergaard UB et al (eds) Social services of general interest in the EU. T.M.C. Asser Press, The Hague
Szyszczak E (2014) Article 36: access to services of general economic interest. In: Peers S et al (eds) The EU charter of fundamental rights: a commentary. CH Beck Hart Nomos, Oxford, pp 969–982
Szyszczak E (2015) Services of General economic interest and state measures affeting competition. J Eur Compet Law Practice 6(9)
Tuori K (2002) Critical legal positivism. Ashgate, Aldershot
Van de Gronden JW (2009) The services directive and SG(E)I. In: Krajewski M, Neergaard U, van de Gronden JW (eds) The changing legal framework for services of general interest in Europe. T.M.C. Asser Press, The Hague
Van de Gronden JW (2013) Transnational competition law and public services European yearbook of international economic law
Weiler JHH (2013) Epilogue: judging the judges—apology and critique. In: Adams M et al (eds) Judging Europe's judges: the legitimacy of the case law of the European court of justice. Hart Publishing, Oxford

Chapter 6
Conclusions of Part II: SGEI Emerges as a Broad "Voice" in EU Constitutional Law

Abstract This chapter draws general conclusions on the concept of SGEI based on the analysis conducted in part II. If the veil of the CJEU's terminological subtleties is lifted, SGEI emerges as a broad constitutional concept of EU law, allowing Member States to benefit from exemptions from strict state aid, procurement and free movement rules. However, the Court's understanding of SGEI is still ambiguous, and the case law of the Court is quite unclear on whether the transparency and proportionality principles embedded in Article 106(2) TFEU still have autonomous relevance for the application of the Treaty competition rules, in particular for the application of the Treaty rules on state aid to social services of general interest. As the Court has not clarified pedagogically the important difference between "economic activity" and "economic rule/measure" for the applicability of EU market rules to SGEI, the scope of Article 14 TFEU remains unclear. As a result of this legal-conceptual confusion, public services, and now also social services, are Europeanised without a true democratic process, and in particular without a discussion on the role solidarity should play in this integration. In this process, EU institutions – in particular the Member States' governments in the Council – are not forced to account on whether and how EU legislation on procurement and state aid applying to public services, including social services, integrate the Treaty principles specifically related to SGEIs loyally and coherently, but may instead rely on a "pick and choose" approach.

Contents

C. Wehlander, *Services of General Economic Interest as a Constitutional Concept of EU Law*, Legal Issues of Services of General Interest,
DOI 10.1007/978-94-6265-117-3_6

The purpose of this chapter is to provide a comprehensive answer to the second sub-question of this study, namely:

> Can SGEI be regarded as an EU constitutional concept imposing public service principles in all fields of EU market law?

Section 6.1 recapitulates and concludes on the main results of part II. Section 6.2 discusses critically Judge Lenaerts's view that the meaning of the concept of SGEI is still for the Member States to decide. Section 6.3 draws on some effects which may take place if the CJEU took a less "nuanced" approach, and was more open on its "deep layer" understanding of the EU concept of SGEI. Given the CJEU's transposition and incorporation of the balance rule in Article 106(2) TFEU outside the field of EU competition law, the last section questions, at a very general level, the role of this provision in the post-Lisbon Treaty framework on SGEIs.

6.1 The EU Concept SGEI Emerges as a Broad Constitutional Concept

It has been shown in Chap. 3 that, in reaction to the Court's closure of "exit" from EU market rules for public service regulation in the Member States, the Treaty of Lisbon 2007/2009 creates a "voice" for public services based on the concept of SGEI present in Article 106(2) TFEU, but with its normative core in Article 14 TFEU, interpreted by a specific Protocol, and reinforced by a specific fundamental principle recognized by the EU Charter of Fundamental Rights. As the SGEI "voice" stands for a flexible application of EU market rules to public service regulation, there is unsurprisingly no political agreement on whether the concept of SGEI should be interpreted broadly or narrowly. However, it has been shown in Chap. 3 that the Treaty provisions on SGEIs constitute a strong "voice" for public service regulation, related to several foundational Treaties principles and to the new paradigm of "social market economy". Therefore it cannot be ignored, which is complicated because respecting the principle expressed by Article 14 TFEU requires that the notion of SGEI founding this principle is understood. The heterogeneity of political views on what SGEI *should* mean explains that no legislation has been adopted on the basis of Article 14 TFEU, although the Union and the Member States are enjoined to use the legal ground introduced in this provision to regulate the principles and conditions applying to SGEIs. Meanwhile, the CJEU must apply the principle contained in article 14 TFEU to relevant cases and thereby interpret that provision in coherence with the Treaties, in particular other provisions on SGEIs.

In this very problematic task, the CJEU takes a "nuanced" approach and its application of the Treaty market rules to SGEIs, analysed in Chap. 4, has led to the following findings. The Court does apply Article 106(2) TFEU to justify measures infringing free movement rules, but then mostly in relation to exclusive rights. In applying Article 106(2), the Court applies in fact a heterogeneous test under Article 106(2) TFEU, amounting to a soft "reconciliation test" in a majority of cases, and to a stricter "exemption test" in cases related to harmonized activities. Also, the analysis of the Court's case law has shown that without applying Article 106(2) TFEU, the Court applies essential elements of its soft proportionality test under Article 106(2) TFEU to certain measures justified by the need to achieve SGEI missions restricting the exercise of the fundamental freedoms, under two main approaches called here "incorporation" and "transposition".

First, the Court has "incorporated" the notion of SGEI in the concepts of entry of EU market rules, "state aid" in Article 107(1) TFEU and "contract" in EU procurement rules. Essentially, these cases imply that, due to their democratic mandates to secure SGEIs and under specific conditions, Member States may fund SGEI tasks (*Altmark*) and may provide SGEI-regulated services with their own resources (*Teckal*). This incorporation is realized by the Court *through the notion of public service task*. Second, it has been found that the Court "transposes" its soft test under Article 106(2) TFEU to measures motivated by "public service tasks" but restricting the exercise of the fundamental freedoms. In particular, regarding public services wholly or partly funded by a Member State, the Court considers that such measures may be motivated by a "financial overriding reason related to the general interest" connected to overriding reasons related to the general interest which very much look like SGEI missions. This approach is illustrated in the health care cases, where the fundamental freedoms could be restricted by measures aimed at securing the management of a welfare *systems* under financial conditions allowing the *systems* to achieve their missions. Transposition is also used in procurement cases such as *Commission v Germany* and *Lecce*, where incorporation is legal-technically not feasible: a soft test is used to allow a derogation from EU procurement rules for contracts allowing public authorities to achieve under acceptable financial conditions their common public service tasks though cooperation.

Thus, both the transposition and the incorporation approaches emerge as a judicial expression of the Union's duty to take care that SGEIs operate according to principles (freedom to organise SGEIs, for instance in solidarity-based systems maintained by public authorities) and conditions (economic and financial conditions, for the system and the providers in the system) enabling SGEIs to achieve their missions. This leads to conclude that the CJEU has in fact been applying and interpreting Article 16 EC, and now Article 14 TFEU, be it discreetly and through a terminological bifurcation, whereby the term "public service tasks" replaces the notion of "SGEI tasks", and the notion of overriding reason related to the general interest is expanded and articulated in a manner that avoids explicitly connecting exemptions from free movement rules and procurement rules to the existence of SGEI regulation.

If the veil of these terminological "nuances" is lifted, which is done in Chap. 5, it is submitted that the CJEU's case law establishes the EU concept of SGEI as a broad concept of EU law, implying that public service tasks imposed on undertakings and on public authorities have an indisputable place in EU's social market economy. Looking through the CJEU's ambiguous terminology based on public service tasks/obligations instead of SGEI tasks, and on economic and systemic overriding reasons related to the general interest instead of SGEI missions, it appears that SGEI missions as defined by Member States may justify the allocation of public resources to undertakings (*Altmark*), certain exemptions from the applicability of EU procurement rules (subject to conditions, *Teckal*, *Commission v Germany*), and the organisation of welfare services in national systems securing that their financial balance is not "seriously" undermined by the exercise of fundamental freedoms. At any rate, the Court's approach of the concept of public service tasks, which can be imposed on undertakings but also on public authorities, depending on the regulatory model, is at odds with the Commission's understanding. Chap. 5 concludes that the notion of entrustment in Article 106(2) TFEU is not a core element of the EU concept of SGEI in the Court's approach, but instead a functional element necessary to control the existence, the nature and the costs of the public service *obligations* affecting undertakings on a given market.

6.2 SGEI Is Approached by the CJEU All the More as an EU Constitutional (Legal) Concept and All the Less as a "National" Political Concept

The author of this book submits that the proposed understanding of the EU concept of SGEI is legally arguable, but is quite aware that this interpretation is not explicit in the Court's case law. The reason of this lack of clarity is argued to be that the Court approaches the notion all the more as a constitutional (legal) notion, but at the same time is aware that it is a highly politicised notion.[1] If the Court looks at SGEI as a *political* notion, it has to agree with everybody that the Member States disagree on the meaning it *should* have, and that the Court is probably not the EU-institution supposed to decide which meaning must take over. If the Court looks at SGEI as a *legal* notion, it has to acknowledge that it is now part of *four* important Treaty provisions, which may have to be respected *coherently* by the Court itself in its judicial activity. In applying the Treaty market rules to service regulation – explicitly characterized as SGEI or not in the cases at issue – the Court is forced to respect the essence of the Treaty provisions on SGEI, which inevitably leads it to interpret the concept of SGEI.

In a paper of 2012, Judge Lenaerts held that the notion of SGI may be examined under two competing socio-economic models, from an ordoliberal perspective as derogation from the Treaty provisions on competition to be interpreted restrictively, or from the perspective of a "second socio-economic model", as the symbol of the European social model, in accordance with which EU institutions

[1]In Vedder's view, "from a strictly legal perspective nothing has changed", and like Article 16 EC "[t]he Protocol on Services of General Interest attached to the Treaty of Lisbon has a similar political character without actually changing the legal framework". On such premises, and in the light of what he called "political fireworks", the question became "when and to what extent legal rules and judicial bodies become captured by politics". See Vedder 2008, p. 25.

must strive to protect SGIs from any threat which may impair their proper functioning. Lenaerts considered that

> a constructive debate on SGI must be open to nuances, because the EU must not really choose between those two competing socio-economic models, as the role of SGI in the EU legal order is being defined by striking a fair balance between the general interest pursued by such services and the effectiveness of the relevant Treaty provisions governing the internal market. It is only by striking the said balance that one may portray the role of SGI in the EU legal order accurately. When interpreting primary EU law, it will be for the ECJ to set out the basic elements that must be included in such balance. When the EU legislator has adopted measures, the ECJ will interpret and apply them in ways consistent with that same balance.[2]

This view is quoted here at length because it contains several elements important for this study. A first remark is that Lenaerts's approach does not only demonstrate what Weiler calls wittingly his "harmonising skills" but seems to set the scene for an institutional dialogue between the CJEU and the Union legislator, in a manner which Dougan holds to exist regarding EU citizenship.[3] Another remark is that Lenaerts appears to consider the notion of SGI as the non-economic policy element of the notions of SGEI and NESGI, which seems in line with the analysis of the concept of SGEI made in Chap. 5.

Regarding the EU concept of SGEI, Lenaerts points at the principle of conferral guaranteeing that, when interpreting the EU concept of "SGEI", the CJEU and, as the case may be, the EU legislator, must respect the competences retained by the Member States and their wide discretion to define what they regard as SGEI missions. At the same time, Lenaerts holds the following view, which also deserves being quoted:

> If, in accordance with Article 14 TFEU, the EU legislator ever decides to provide a general definition of SGEI, such a definition would have to incorporate the principles and conditions listed in Protocol (No 26). It would also have to be compatible with Article 36 of the Charter in so far as it must guarantee access to SGEI. Most importantly, such a general definition must comply with the principle of conferral and with the principle of institutional balance.[4]

This appears as a problematic view, as it implies that a concept of EU primary law, which as underlined by Neergaard, "is normally considered a Community concept" and "has from the very beginning been thought of as such", may be defined by the Member States in secondary law.[5] But why would the judicial autonomy of the Court be more restricted regarding Article 14 TFEU, introduced in the Treaties as a result of EU law's expansion brought about by the Court's judicial autonomy regarding the basic concepts contained in Articles 28, 49, 56 and 63 TFEU (goods, persons, services, capital)? The concept of SGEI is *in* Article 14 TFEU and *in* Article 106(2) TFEU, and constitutes there the basis for obligations addressed to the Union, the Member States, and undertakings. It is not at all disputed here that, as expressed by Lenaerts, "[n]either the ECJ nor the EU legislator

[2]Lenaerts 2012, p. 1249.

[3]Weiler 2013, p. 237, and Dougan M., 2013.

[4]Lenaerts 2012, pp. 1257–1258, footnote omitted.

[5]Neergaard 2008, p. 22.

are entitled to second-guess the determinations made by national authorities as to whether a service is of general interest, unless the latter commit a manifest error of assessment".[6] However, the very existence of this control power (strongest in harmonised fields but not absent in others), involves that the EU concept of SGEI is not "whatever the Member States decide it to be". Besides, what Article 14 TFEU leaves open for legislation are the principles and rules enabling SGEIs to fulfil their missions, and *not the definition of the EU concept of SGEI*.

Lenaerts' view that it is for the Member States to define the EU concept of SGEI is thus problematic in a constitutional perspective, and it is argued here that it does not fit with the results of the analysis of the CJEU's case law conducted in Chap. 4. In fact, Lenaerts' view rather reinforces the impression that the Court's strategy has so far been to respect the substance of the SGEI provisions in the Treaties, in particular Article 14 TFEU, while at the same time keeping a low profile on the understanding of the EU concept of SGEI which its respect of Article 14 TFEU implies.[7] Lenaerts' view can also be read as formulating the "recipe" used by the Court to address the SGEI provisions and which shapes its understanding of the concept, and to be followed by the EU legislator, when it is ready to use it. If it ever uses the "recipe", this may lead the EU legislator to define the concept in general terms in a manner which will happen to be in line with the Court's case law, because it would consolidate an understanding which the Court all along applies implicitly but restrains from spelling clearly. The point here is not to discuss the Court's strategy, only that its existence must be held as very probable in its tense political context.

Thus, the CJEU is forced to give judicial effect to the principle spelled in Article 14 TFEU, whereby it appears that the Court delineates the EU concept of SGEI broadly, which arguably was so far clearest in *Commission v Germany*. If this understanding of the CJEU's law is correct, a legitimate question is whether avoiding an open recognition of this understanding may be explained *only* by a concern to let democracy take (at least formally) the lead. In fact, another explanation is argued to be that the Court's approach, keeping the relation between Article 14 TFEU and EU free movement and procurement rules in the shadows of overriding reasons related to the general interest and of "public service tasks", provides the Court itself, but also EU institutions, with more discretion in the balance between non-market and market interests regarding activities in the Member States' competence. This explanation emerges from asking what the consequences would be if the Court, in its SGEI related case law, ever decided to clearly say what it does, and using "transparent, non-cryptic, soundly reasoned decisions" explained why and how it has "crossed the line between law and politics".[8]

[6] Lenaerts 2012, p. 1258.

[7] The author of this book does not here take a polemic.

[8] These words are borrowed from Weiler in a book where Weiler and several other distinguished scholars have given their views on the legitimacy of the CJEU's case law. In the final chapter, Weiler has chosen to focus on a critical commentary of Lenaerts' views developed in the book's first chapter. See Weiler 2013, p. 237–238.

6.3 Some Risks if the CJEU Is Too Clear on Its Understanding of the EU Concept of SGEI

If the Court did not bifurcate through the terminology of "public service tasks" and its case law on "special overriding reasons related to the general interest", and instead spelled out that the SGEI-character of the service at issue is decisive for its soft test of certain measures restricting free movement or derogating from EU procurement rules, some effects may arguably incur.

First, the Court would have to clarify why it applies a soft test to services which *can* be economic, but which are not covered by EU competition rules because the activity *is* non-economic in the Member State applying this measure. If the Court considers that such services constitute NESGIs, which is unsure (see the discussion in Sect. 3.1.3.2.2 above), it cannot motivate a soft test by the principle formulated in Article 14 TFEU, because this principle is only valid for *SG(E)I*. This may explain that Lenaerts draws attention to Article 9 TFEU, as one of the new provisions introduced by the Lisbon Treaty "highlighting the 'social aspects' of the European integration project", which states that:

> In defining and implementing its policies and activities, the Union shall take into account requirements linked to the promotion of a high level of employment, the guarantee of adequate social protection, the fight against social exclusion, and a high level of education, training and protection of human health.

Lenaerts underlines that, compared to its predecessor Article 127(2) EC, Article 9 TFEU goes beyond macroeconomic employment issues and holds that it could be seen, if the Court agreed with AG Cruz Villalón's view in *de Santos Palhota*, as 'a "cross-cutting" social protection clause' allowing to argue that non-discriminatory national measures which are not covered by EU competition rules because the service is non-economic under the law of the Member State at issue, but which restrict free movement, may be examined under a soft version of the principle of proportionality.[9] In other words, non-discriminatory rules related to NESGIs would be on par with the fundamental freedoms, not because they are defined by the Member States and as such important for cohesion and EUs values, but

[9]Lenaerts 2012, p. 1261. Reference to Opinion of AG Cruz Villalón in Case C-515/08 *de Santos Palhota and Others* (CJEU 7 October 2010), para 51: "The Advocate General relied on that provision (as well as on Article 31 of the Charter) with a view to arguing that '[a]s a result of the entry into force of the Lisbon Treaty, when working conditions constitute an overriding reason relating to the general interest justifying a derogation from the freedom to provide services, they must no longer be interpreted strictly. In so far as the protection of workers is a matter which warrants protection under the Treaties themselves, it is not a simple derogation from a freedom, still less an unwritten exception inferred from case-law. To the extent that the new primary law framework provides for a mandatory high level of social protection, it authorizes the Member States, for the purpose of safeguarding a certain level of social protection, to restrict a freedom, and to do so without European Union law's regarding it as something exceptional and, therefore, as warranting a strict interpretation. That view, [...] is expressed in practical terms by applying the principle of proportionality."

inasmuch as they are compatible with an EU standard of social protection (a standard that is uncertain, may be decided judicially, and – if the activity is seen as NESGI – is not protected by the EU Charter of Fundamental Rights).

A case in point is *Kattner Stahlbau*, where the compulsory affiliation rule was seen as motivated by the overriding reason related to the general interest consisting in "ensuring the financial equilibrium of a branch of social security". The Court's soft test of this restriction is difficult to justify by Article 9 TFEU, which was not in force when the judgment was delivered, and as already argued, the test evoked rather an SG(E)I test under Article 14 TFEU. Evoking Article 9 TFEU as justifying a soft test of a measure under the free movement rules appears as an after construction intended to legitimate that measures motivated by a non-economic SGI are submitted to the free movement rules, but as *NESGI*, with a weaker constitutional safeguard than SGEIs under Article 14 TFEU, Article 1 of the SGI Protocol and Article 36 EUCFR. It would be far more convincing intellectually if the Court recognized that the "E" in SGEI does not mean that the activity is economic but that it *can be* economic, which would have the merit of clarity and of legal certainty, even if it would display the very restricted scope of Article 2 of the SGI Protocol.

Second, not using the terminology of "public service tasks" would make definitively clear that, while EU procurement rules cannot easily be covered by Article 106(2) TFEU, they are covered by Article 14 TFEU, because they affect the conditions, in particular the financial and economic conditions, under which SGEIs are organized and provided. This would raise the question why the new EU rules harmonizing – albeit lightly – the procurement procedures of social services – are laid down in directives and not in regulations as provided for by Article 14 TFEU. This would also raise the question of what policy objectives the new rules seek to achieve. Indeed, Szyszczak has pointed out that Article 14 TFEU provides a legal base for Union legislation, whilst the post-Lisbon Treaties do not confer competence upon the Union to regulate SGEIs. She also found paradoxical the Commission's announcement that as a result of the SGI Protocol there was no need for Union legislation on SGEIs.[10] In fact, an alternative manner to understand the Commission's statement is that it sees no need of *new* EU legislation specifically addressing SGEIs, because there is *already* Union legislation establishing certain principles and conditions applying to SGEIs – namely in procurement and state aid legislation. The Commission may very well see things that way, but would hardly say it overtly.

The problem is that if the procurement directives were explicitly described by the Commission as regulating SGEI conditions, the EU legislator would have to explain what its policy objectives are with the new procurement rules, not only in market opening terms, but also in "SGEI terms", which would in particular require that the notion of SGEI be defined. Another problem would be that it would shed

[10] Szyszczak 2009, p. 295, referring to Commission, Working Document on progress made since the 2004 White Paper on SGIs (SEC(2007)1514).

brutal light on the fact that in adopting the 2014 procurement directives, the Member States have agreed to forget the Treaty injunction to adopt regulations on SGEI principles and conditions, but at the same time discreetly but surely begun transferring powers on the Union to decide on such principles and conditions in the field of social services, although social services *are still outside EU's policy competence*, and although they do not expose in clear and democratically assessable terms the common policy objectives with this competence transfer. By way of comparison, the EU Treaties *spell openly for the peoples of the Union* that environment legislation based on Article 192 TFEU is meant to achieve EU policy objectives laid down in Article 191 TFEU.

As long as the Court does not make crystal clear how it understands the EU concept of SGEI and *how* Article 14 TFEU constrains EU procurement law, the EU legislator will not have to explain how EU procurement rules are meant to allow SGEI missions to be achieved, and can avoid an overt competence issue in the field of social services.

In such a situation, it may be questioned whether Article 9 TFEU could fill in the competence gap. Barnard and De Baere note that the CJEU's reference to Article 9 TFEU in *Deutsches Weintor* would appear to imply that any of the goals in Article 9 TFEU, including the guarantee of adequate social protection, the fight against social exclusion, and a high level of education and training, could potentially constitute an objective of general interest justifying, where appropriate, a restriction of a fundamental freedom.[11] As with Lenaerts, they refer to AG Cruz Villalón's view, and conclude that the main relevance of Article 9 TFEU is its potential to require that EU measures do not affect in a disproportionate manner the social objectives listed in it.[12] However, they consider that Article 9 TFEU does not constitute a new conferral of competences and also obvious that it cannot be used as a legal basis for any EU act.[13] As their view is shared here, it seems that the competence issue remains unsolved.

Third, acknowledging that EU procurement rules are in principle constrained by Article 14 TFEU could raise concerns that positive market integration be compromised. Indeed, as seen in chaps. 3 and 4, this Treaty provision, together with the SGI Protocol and Article 36 EUCFR, constitutionalises EU law's respect of

---

[11]In Case C-544/10 *Deutsches Weintor* (CJEU 6 September 2012), para 49, the Court held that "the protection of public health constitutes, as follows also from Article 9 TFEU, an objective of general interest justifying, where appropriate, a restriction of a fundamental freedom". See Barnard and De Baere 2014, p. 36–37.

[12]Barnard and de Baere 2014, p. 36–37. According to these authors, "[a] key tool for systematically ensuring that the EU's common social objectives are mainstreamed in all relevant EU policy areas is the social impact assessment within the Commission's general Impact Assessment System (IAS), and the European Economic and Social Committee has advocated further strengthening of it".

[13]De Witte et al. 2010, p. 34. The authors hold that Article 9 TFEU cannot be used as a legal base for the establishment of a pro-active and comprehensive EU social policy, covering all the domains mentioned in that provision.

Member States' retained powers, which according to Azoulai are "the collective goods the State is supposed to protect so as to ensure the social cohesion of its own population in its territory". Azoulai's view is that, by recognizing retained powers, the Court recognizes that "Member States have a primordial (rather than exclusive) power in the organisation of a subject area that is considered to be essential to social integration" and that they are "autonomous political actors fulfilling their duties as guarantor of the cohesion of the European populations".[14] It is certainly arguable that the Court, under the pressure of Treaty modifications and of reality, acknowledges that Member States have a primordial responsibility in giving access to public services, and therefore should have more say in their definition and funding.[15] At this stage in the development of EU law, the problem is rather at which stage – legislative or judicial – their say should be allowed to be given some weight.

In the field of procurement, Fiedziuk seems to advocate more flexibility at the derogation stage. She holds the view that Article 106(2) TFEU could become an alternative to the rigid in-house exemption test in the application of EU public procurement rules, as "the currently changing legal trends evolving towards more restrictive rules on public spending call for more flexible derogatory tests". [16] To suggest that market-based provision can in certain cases be argued to be too expensive for Member States that must balance their budgets, was rather heretic before 2008 and the beginning of the long-lived economic crisis. By contrast, Davies considers that "[t]he more that general interest considerations are shunted off to Article 86(2), the less they will be internalised in the competition rules themselves, and the less these rules will come to be economically realistic and responsible. That will lead to bad, inefficient and incoherent policy."[17] It is noted here that Davies uses the vague formula of "general interest considerations" (compared to SGEIs imposed in order to secure the achievement of service missions), but if his reasoning is correctly understood, the SGEI character of services is best taken hand at the legislative stage.[18]

---

[14]Azoulai 2011, p. 207.

[15]In *Sodemare* it is submitted that the CJEU acknowledged that in fields where Member States have retained most policy powers, they may not only decide policy objectives but they retain also economic powers. When adjudicating in the field of social services, the central constitutional issue appears to be which powers, in particular *economic powers*, the Member States retain in the exercise of their retained competence in the social sphere.

[16]Fiedziuk 2013a, p. 108. According to Fiedziuk, the in-house exemption plays the role of *sui generis* Article 106(2) TFEU general exemption in the field of procurement law. However, she underlines that unlike the in-house exemption, Article 106(2) TFEU allows undertakings providing SGEIs to operate in parallel on the open market carrying out activities of a commercial nature, the only limitation being that their internal accounts must show separately the costs and revenues associated with the SGEI from those of the other services.

[17]Davies 2009, p. 330.

[18]Rules that are "economically realistic and responsible" should not dispense from transparent and precise SGEI tasks, secured by proportionate economic and financial conditions, because as will be argued in part IV, transparency and proportionality are necessary for a democratic governance of quality services in the public sector.

Fourth, if the CJEU acknowledged that by combining two welfare overriding reasons related to the general interest – for instance (1) secure balanced medical and hospital service open to all and (2) prevent the possible risk of *seriously* undermining a social security system's financial balance" – it fulfils its duty to take care that public welfare systems operate under financial conditions enabling them to fulfil their SGEI mission, the Court would have to explain why it makes a different interpretation of "economic and financial conditions" regarding SGEI tasks entrusted to undertakings (acceptable economic conditions, including a reasonable profit) and regarding SGEI missions in national welfare systems (not seriously undermining the financial balance).

6.4 Concluding with a Burning Issue: Which Normative Role Is Left for Article 106(2) TFEU in the European Framework Governing Public Services?

Certain of the elements evoked in the precedent section may explain the CJEU's discreet approach of the Treaty provisions on SGEIs, offering a kind of "third way" where SGEI-related principles are incorporated to the acquis, but through the terminology of "public service tasks" and the fiction of economic overriding reasons related to the general interest and "public service overriding reasons related to the general interest". Indeed, by calling public authorities' public service tasks "SGEI tasks", the Court would take the risk of forcing EU institutions to consolidate its case law on the basis of regulations in accordance with Article 14 TFEU. In openly political words, Sauter fears that to give direction to public services though a European Parliament and Council Regulation based on the SGEI provision in Article 14 TFEU "could degenerate into an open invitation to wild-eyed believers in state interventionism who favour public provision of everything, and more cynical supporters of cosy corporatist arrangements, to drive a battering ram into the delicately balanced edifice of the internal market, backfiring badly".[19] Although such concerns are probably shared by the CJEU, and may explain its avoidance of the term SGEI where it seems to be what is meant, this avoidance is nevertheless problematic for a clear understanding of EU constitutional law and also makes difficult to assess whether the Court's decisions are coherent and compatible with the normative stances established by the Treaties.

Nevertheless, the CJEU has made clear that Article 14 TFEU formulates a public service principle which has horizontal relevance in the Treaties, and in particular affects the substance of EU free movement and procurement law. Meanwhile, there is still much uncertainty regarding the exact meaning of this principle, and its articulation in the field of competition and state aid law with the public service principles stemming from Article 106(2) TFEU, which remains a major

[19] Sauter 2014, p. 179.

constitutional element in the Treaty framework on public services. Its specificity lies arguably in that (1) it reminds that there is a tension to be resolved between the EU general interest of market integration and other nonmarket interests and (2) it imposes the principles of transparency and proportionality on the process on defining SGEI tasks and taking measures ensuring their fulfilment. The combination of the principles stemming from Articles 14 and 106(2) TFEU is particularly important in the field of social services in the public sector of the Member States, which are normally highly regulated and subsidised and are in focus in part IV.

The principle of transparency allowing to control proportionality is embedded in the notion of "entrustment" in Article 106(2) TFEU and in the *Altmark* criteria, which has extended Member States' powers to finance SGEI tasks, but it does not give them carte blanche: *Altmark* submits Member States' use of these powers to strict transparency and proportionality requirements.[20] Yet, van de Gronden and Rusu observe that, by contrast with *Altmark*, the CJEU's case law in *BUPA*, *TV2* and *AG2R* adopts a relaxed approach regarding the requirement of entrustment in Article 106(2) TFEU and in the first *Altmark* criterion. Therefore, the message is not so clear, in particular given the GC's ruling in *CBI*, enjoining the Commission to examine more thoroughly the funding scheme of public hospitals, in particular the entrustment and the precision of the SGEI tasks compensated for.

Consequently, it appears that the EU legislator is left with quite some discretion regarding the enforcement of the principles of transparency and proportionality following from Article 106(2) TFEU, as it very much depends on the form and contents of the entrustment of SGEI tasks to undertakings in publicly funded welfare systems. While it has been submitted that the notion of "entrustment" lies outside the core of the notion of SGEI, it has a potential to be a key element in the EU *governance* of public services and may therefore have to be "rethought". The EU legislator is also left with a large discretion to catch the signal sent by the CJEU and apply the principle laid down Article 14 TFEU to its procurement rules. What it does with this discretion and why is the main subject of part III.

References

Azoulai L (2011) The 'Retained Powers' formula in the case law of the European court of justice: EU law as total law? Eur J Legal Stud 4(2)

Barnard C, De Baere G (2014) Towards a European social union: achievements and possibilities under the current EU constitutional framework. KU Leuven Euroforum

Davies G (2009) Article 86, The EC's economic approach to competition law, and the general interest. Eur Competition J August 2009

De Witte B et al (2010) Legislation after lisbon, new opportunities for the European parliament, EUI paper. http://www.eui.eu/Projects/EUDO/Documents/EUDO-LegislatingafterLisbon(SD).pdf

Fiedziuk NA (2013) Putting services of general economic interest up for tender: reflections on applicable EU rules. Common Market Law Rev 50:87–114

[20] This is underlined by van de Gronden and Rusu, in van de Gronden and Rusu 2013, p. 194.

Lenaerts K (2012) Defining the concept of "Services of General Interest" in light of the "Checks and Balances" set out in the EU treaties. Jurisprudencija/Jurisprudence 2012 19(4):1247–1267

Neergaard U (2008) Services of general (Economic) interest and the services directive. In: Nergaard U, Nielsen R, Roseberry L (eds) The services directive – consequences for the welfare state and the European social model. DJØF Publishing, Copenhagen

Sauter W (2014) Public services in EU law. Cambridge University Press, Cambridge

Szyszczak E (2009) Legal tools in the liberalization of welfare markets. In: Neergaard U, Nielsen R, Roseberry L (eds) Integrating welfare functions into EU Law – from Rome to Lisbon. DJØF Publishing, Copenhagen

Van de Gronden JW, Rusu CS (2013) The Altmark Update and Social services. In: Szyszczak E, van de Gronden JW (eds) Financing services of general economic interest, reform and modernization. T.M.C Asser Press, The Hague

Vedder H (2008) The Constitutionality of competition – EC internal market law and the fine line between markets, public interests and (self-)regulation in a changing constitutional setting. http://papers.ssrn.com/sol3/papers.cfm?abstract_id=1282035

Weiler JHH (2013) Epilogue: judging the judges – apology and critique. In: Adams M et al (eds) Judging Europe's judges: the legitimacy of the case law of the European court of justice. Hart Publishing, Oxford and Portland

Part III
The Cost of Loyalty, the Relationship Between EU Procurement and State Aid Legislation on Social Services and the Treaty Rules on SGEI, with a Case Study on Swedish Systems of Choice

Chapter 7
EU Legislation on Public Procurement and State Aid: What Is the Pressure on Member States to Enforce SGEI Principles in the Field of Social Services?

Abstract This chapter examines, with a special focus on social services, how the 2014 procurement directives and the Commission's 2011 SGEI Package relate to the Treaty principles and rules on services of general interest, including series of general economic interest and non-economic services of general interest. Part I sheds first light on the ambiguous relationship between the 2014 procurement directives and the SGEI framework in the Treaties. The analysis leads to conclude that the EU legislator thrives at maintaining an understanding of SGEI that is narrower than the CJEU's discreet but discernible understanding of SGEI as a broad concept of EU law. The chapter focuses secondly on the relationship between the SGEI state aid package and the SGEI framework in the Treaties. The analysis suggests that the EU legislator avoids forcing the Member States to formulate clearly the SGEI existing in their welfare systems. It concludes that although the package may be regarded as a significant step towards an EU approach to social services, its impact depends on whether its rules are applied loyally, which the package does not put pressure on the Member States to do. The chapter concludes that the Commission is presently not so preoccupied by the proportionality of public service compensation of social services. In particular, systems of choice and voucher systems are exempted from both the procurement directives and state aid notification. The de facto leeway consented for systems of choice for social services may come into conflict with the "Union's interest" that EU institutions and Member States show loyalty to the Treaty principles related to SGEIs, and to the state aid rules enforcing those principles. This legislative bias for systems of choice may be meant to support their development, which can be logical in the perspective of the SGI Quality Framework, pursuing the aim of facilitating cross-border trade of services.

C. Wehlander, *Services of General Economic Interest as a Constitutional Concept of EU Law*, Legal Issues of Services of General Interest,
DOI 10.1007/978-94-6265-117-3_7

Contents

This chapter examines the new procurement directives (adopted in 2014) and the latest Commission legislative package on SGEIs (adopted in 2011–2012, hereinafter the 2011 SGEI Package) with a focus on social services and in the light of two general questions:

- How do these rules relate to Article 14 TFEU?
- Do these rules put pressure on the Member States to identify SGEIs in their legal and administrative systems in order to put the public funding and the organisation of SSGIs in compliance with the 2011 SGEI Package?

There is no possibility here for an in-depth study, and the purpose is instead to shed some light on the legal-political process of harmonisation of EU market law on social services by giving more focused attention to specific questions regarding the new procurement directives and the 2011 SGEI Package.

Section 7.1 looks at the 2014 procurement directives, identifying their relation to the Treaty rules on SGEIs, first and foremost Article 14 TFEU, with the following questions in mind

- Do the new procurement directives mirror the CJEU's case law suggesting that procurement directives are covered by Article 14 TFEU and construe the concept as broadly as the CJEU's case law suggests?
- How do the new procurement directives relate to SGEIs in the field of social services and how explain that the new procurement directives do not use the notion of SGEI to justify the lighter regime for social services?
- How do the new procurement directives relate to the SGI Protocol and clarify what SGEIs and what NESGIs are?

The approach consists in reading the 2014 Procurement Directives at the surface level to identify their explicit references to SGEIs, but also in scrutinizing the textual elements denoting that the EU legislator had the Treaty provisions on SGEIs in mind when drafting the Directives. Therefore, some important novelties in the procurement directives are first outlined, to look then at the relationship between the procurement directives and the Treaty rules on SGEIs, and finally to "zoom in" on the particular regime for social services and its ambiguous connection to the Treaty rules on SGEIs.

Section 7.2 looks at the 2011 SGEI Package *in the perspective of social services*, with the following questions in focus

- Does this Package really clarify what constitutes an economic activity for the purpose of the state aid rules in the field of social services?
- Does this Package clarify what are SGEIs and is the Commission's approach legitimate in that respect?

Before the 2011 SGEI Package is examined in light of these questions, the regime for social services according to its predecessor of 2005 (hereinafter the "2005 SGEI Package") is first outlined, and second some cases in the Commission's state aid practice on social services are reviewed. The reason for this approach is to highlight that the application of the 2005 SGEI Package in the field of social services supposed that two important issues would be clarified: how to determine that the activity funded is economic, with what precision the SGEI task funded should be defined. The Commission's practice shows that its reasoning on these two questions is not so clear, is highly dependent on the CJEU's case law in the field of free movement, and in certain cases extremely time-consuming. As it seems, the Commission is engaged in a "dialogue" with the CJEU on those issues. In other words, when the Commission decentralises the control of the compliance of public funding of social services with its 2011 SGEI Package, it should know that it entrusts a *very* difficult task to the Member States.

In Sect. 7.3, the results are summed up and some conclusions are drawn in relation to the two general questions formulated at the beginning of this introduction.

In this chapter, the method is overall legal and the legal sources consist mainly of EU secondary law on procurement and state aid. As social services are in focus, the new Public Sector Directive, and the Commission Decision, which is part of the 2011 SGEI Package,[1] are predominant, but the legislative context of these texts is also relevant, in particular soft law in the 2011 SGEI Package which indicates the Commission's views on several important elements of its rules.[2] Some decisional

[1]Commission Decision 2012/21/EU on the application of Article 106(2) of the Treaty on the Functioning of the European Union to State aid in the form of public service compensation granted to certain undertakings entrusted with the operation of services of general economic interest [2012] OJ L7/3.

[2]Commission, "Communication on the application of the European Union State aid rules to compensation granted for the provision of services of general economic interest" 2012/C 8/02, p. 4–14.

practice of the Commission and of the EFTA Surveillance Authority (ESA) is also used to illustrate the approach taken by institutions which so far have been responsible to control state aid to social services, and in the analysis of these authorities' reasoning, a state aid decision of the EFTA-Court had also to be called in.

7.1 The 2014 Procurement Directives

The 2004 public procurement directives (hereinafter "the old public procurement directives"), expected to offer a flexible framework promoting efficient EU-wide competition and aiding the fight against corruption, were short-lived.[3] They were replaced less than ten years later by the new public procurement directives, which together with a revision of the rules on state aid to SGEIs, were presented by the Commission as one of the twelve levers meant to re-boost growth in Europe, in the context of economic crisis which followed the adoption of the Treaty of Lisbon 2007.[4] In fact, the Commission had many reasons to revise the directives. First, it had to address a years-long pressure from many stakeholders for simpler and more flexible procurement procedures, giving more possibilities to pursue environmental and social objectives. Second, it had long envisaged hard-law regulation of service concessions, which were only covered by the Treaties. Third, it was time to consolidate important case-law on in-house arrangements and public cooperation arrangements, and the Treaty-based procurement rules found applicable to social services.[5] Last but not least, the post-Lisbon Treaty framework on SGEIs had to be acknowledged and applied.

[3]Recitals 15, 16 and 43 of the 2004 Public Sector Directive.

[4]In response to the fear of a long-lasting economic crisis, the EU adopted the "Europe 2020 strategy" (Commission, "Europe 2020, A strategy for smart, sustainable and inclusive growth" (Communication) COM (2010) 2020). In its Conclusions of 24/25 March 2011, the European Council held that the Single Market had a key role to play to deliver growth and employment and promote competitiveness, and the Commission identified twelve levers in order to boost growth on the EU market, with a key action for each lever by the end of 2012, see Commission, "Single Market Act - Twelve levers to boost growth and strengthen confidence - Working together to create new growth" (Communication) SEC (2011) 467 final.

[5]In Case T-258/06 *Germany v Commission* [2010] ECR II-2027, the GC found inadmissible an action brought by Germany against the Commission's Interpretative Communication of 23 June 2006 on the Community law applicable to contract awards not or not fully subject to the provisions of the Public Procurement Directives. The General Court found that it did not contain new rules for the award of public contracts, in other words the rules formulated by the Communication did follow from the Treaties.

7.1.1 General Features

The 2014 Public Sector Directive and the 2004 Utilities Directive have been replaced by the 2014 Public Sector Directive and the 2014 Utilities Directive. The rules on works concessions have been moved to the 2014 Concessions Directive, which regulates both work and service concessions and covers both the public sector activities and utilities, subject to exceptions in the sector of water.

The Commission underlines that the new procurement directives address the policy requests of simplification and flexibility.[6] It is in particular emphasized that they introduce a higher threshold for sub-central authorities than central ones and a higher threshold for social, health and educational services than for other services, that they offer more flexibility to choose a procurement procedure which allows negotiations between contracting authorities and tenderers, and that they put emphasis on the possibility for individual contracting authorities to use procurement as a policy instrument and make choices related to environmental and social policy. These features are meant to achieve smart, sustainable and inclusive growth, and to increase the efficiency of public spending, facilitating in particular the participation of small and medium-sized enterprises (SMEs) in public procurement, and enabling procurers to make better use of public procurement in support of common societal goals.[7]

One novelty which has received much public appraisal is the reform concerning the choice of award criterion, implying that the sole criterion of "most economically advantageous tender" (MEAT, with a new meaning compared to the old procurement directives) has replaced the choice between lowest price and what was called MEAT in the old Directives. In the new regime, it is mandatory to identify the MEAT on the basis of a price or cost criterion, using a cost-effectiveness approach (one of those being the life-cycle costing approach regulated by Article 68), and it is voluntary to include the "best price-quality ratio" approach (a new term for what was called MEAT in the old Directives). Thus, while it is not the place here to analyse this aspect in any detail, it seems right to hold, as Bordalo Faustino did, that "in practice, the choice between awarding a public contract solely on the basis of price (or cost), or on the basis of a combination of the latter with quality, still applies". In her view, this novelty may be argued to encourage contracting authorities to procure in a more quality oriented way but in practice,

[6]See the information leaflet *New rules on public contracts and concessions simpler and more flexible*, published by the Commission and available per 31 December 2014 on its website at http://ec.europa.eu/internal_market/publications/docs/public-procurement-and-concessions_en.pdf.
See also the many references to simplification and flexibility in the preambles of the Directives, for instance Recital 42 in the 2014 Public Sector Directive. Another general feature highlighted by the Commission is the reinforcement of rules allowing to fight corruption.

[7]Recital 2 of the 2014 Public Sector Directive, Recital 4 of the 2014 Utilities Directive and Recitals 1 and 3 of the 2014 Concessions Directive.

contracting authorities may still decide that the lowest price is the most suitable criterion for the award of a particular contract.[8]

Two other important novelties are the Directives' codification of the exceptions for in-house arrangements and public-public cooperation arrangements established by the CJEU in case law, the removal of the divide between prioritized "A" and non-prioritized "B" services, and the introduction of a new legal category of "social and other specific services", to which a lighter regime applies. These elements are commented on in more detail below.

7.1.2 Explicit and Implicit Connections to the Treaty Principles on SGEI and NESGI

The Directives contain several explicit references to the Treaty provisions on SGEIs and NESGIs. The most central rule related to SGEIs appears to be the following provision, introduced in each of the 2014 Procurement Directives, and reading:

> This Directive does not affect the freedom of Member States to define, in conformity with Union law, what they consider to be services of general economic interest, how those services should be organised and financed, in compliance with the State aid rules, and what specific obligations they should be subject to.[9]

This provision, which has its focus on the freedom to *define* SGEI missions, asserts that the *Member States*' freedom to define what they consider to be SGEIs is not affected by the Directives, but that this definition must conform to EU law. There is no reference in the provision or in the recitals to what this conformity requires, but the very duty to conform to some – be it generous – constraint implies that the notion is regarded by the EU legislator as an EU notion. It may be wondered why the notion is not "defined" for the purpose of EU procurement law, considering that the EU legislator considered appropriate to define the notion for the purpose of the Services Directive. After all, if it is asserted solemnly that the

---

[8]Bordalo Faustino 2014, p. 125–126. As underlined by Bordino Faustino, the price or cost is now a mandatory element of the MEAT, according to Article 67(2) of the 2014 Public Sector Directive, but Member States may exclude or restrict the sole use of price or cost, which she considers to be in line with the *Sintesi* case law, see Case C-247/02 *Sintesi* [2004] ECR. I-9231. Imposing a price or cost element in the MEAT implies that a composition, where non-cost criteria are part of the MEAT *instead* of price, is not possible any longer except for the case where price or cost is fixed, which follows from Article 67(2) second paragraph of the Directive, providing that "[t]he cost element may also take the form of a fixed price or cost on the basis of which economic operators will compete on quality criteria only." Recital 93 clarifies that where national provisions determine the remuneration of certain services, it remains possible to assess value for money on the basis of other factors than solely the price or remuneration.

[9]Article 1(4) first sentence of the Public Sector Directive, Article 1(4) first sentence of the 2014 Utilities Directive, and Article 4(1) of the 2014 Concessions Directive.

Directive does not affect something, it seems legitimate to know what that can be, and which EU rules constrain Member States' definition of that "something".

The preamble provides some precision, explaining that the 2014 Procurement Directives do not prejudice the freedom of *national, regional and local authorities* to define, in conformity with Union law, services of general economic interest, their scope and the characteristics of the service to be provided, including any conditions regarding the quality of the service, in order to pursue their public policy objectives.[10] Together with these recitals, it seems possible to interpret the articles named above so that the Directives recognize a freedom to *define* SGEIs for both Member States (at legislative level) and for public authorities (at administrative level), a position that does not seem contradicted by the CJEU's case law related to the modes of entrustment of SGEI tasks. The possibility that SGEIs be defined at legislative or at administrative level is not explicitly formulated, and the recitals do not address issues such as the degree of precision in the definition of SGEI missions or tasks, or the type of entities are addressed by the SGEIs (undertakings, public authorities). Also, the recitals' wording suggests that, while *EU law* does not detract public authorities at national, regional and local level from defining SGEIs, it is not excluded that their freedom to do so may be restricted by national rules.

Further, it is stressed in recitals to the three new Directives that they "should be without prejudice of the power" of national, regional and local authorities to provide, commission and *finance* SGEIs, in accordance with Article 14 TFEU and the SGI Protocol.[11] As public authorities' prerogatives to *finance* SGEIs is not at all named in the SGI Protocol, the recognition of national, regional and local authorities' power to finance SGEIs in these recitals must be related to Article 14 TFEU. However, Article 14 TFEU has its focus on the *duty*, in particular for the Union, to *take care that SGEIs operate under economic and financial conditions enabling them to achieve their missions*. As made clear by *Altmark*, the Union's duty implies that the Member States may use their economic powers to *finance SGEIs*. But in the field of procurement law there is more to this duty for the EU legislator. While the very existence of public procurement procedures can certainly enhance competition and lead to savings in the public acquisition of SGEI-regulated services, their *design* is covered by Article 14 TFEU, because it can obviously affect the economic and financial conditions under which SGEIs operate. This is argued to be the implicit but essential motive for the important ruling in *Commission v Germany*.[12] Therefore, it is submitted that the recitals' wording side-steps the fact that under Article 14 TFEU, EU procurement rules must not simply respect Member States' power to *remunerate* SGEIs, they must strike the right balance regarding the degree of flexibility which contracting authorities dispose of for their SGEI missions to be achieved. The recitals underline also that none of the three Directives deals with the funding of SGEIs or with systems of aid granted by Member

[10] Recital 7 of the 2014 Public Sector Directive, Recital 9 of the 2014 Utilities Directive, and Recital 6 of the 2014 Concessions Directive.

[11] Recital 7 of the 2014 Public Sector Directive, Recital 9 of the 2014 Utilities Directive, and Recital 6 of the 2014 Concessions Directive.

[12] Case C-480/06 *Commission* v *Germany* [2009] ECR I-4747.

States, in particular in the social field, in accordance with Union rules on competition.[13] What is meant by "systems of aid granted by Member States, in particular in the social field, in accordance with Union rules on competition" is rather cryptic.

Several provisions address specifically the freedom to *organise* SGEIs. In this regard, Article 1(4) of the Public Sector Directive and Article 1(4) of the Utilities Directive contain the same rule, reading as follows

> Equally, this Directive does not affect the decision of public authorities whether, how and to what extent they wish to perform public functions themselves pursuant to Article 14 TFEU and Protocol No 26.

This provision gives visibility in EU legislation to a constitutional principle introduced by the Lisbon Treaty, that public authorities have a wide freedom to *provide* SGEIs. However, the discretion provided by Article 14 TFEU and the SGI Protocol is evoked in relation to public authorities' "public functions", an expression which is absent from both the Treaty provision and the SGI Protocol. It is hardly possible not to see that the EU legislator carefully avoids the terminology used in Article 14 TFEU and the SGI Protocol that impose principles in relation to "*SGEI missions*", and not in relation to "public functions".

Likewise, recitals in both the Public Sector Directive and the Utilities Directive emphasize that nothing in these Directives obliges Member States to contract out or externalise the provision of services that they wish to provide themselves or *to organise by means other than procurement within the meaning of these Directives*, but without connecting this organisational freedom to Article 14 TFEU and the SGI Protocol, and thus to SGEIs.[14] It is important to note that, in this formulation, what gives organisation freedom in the Public Sector and the Concessions Directives is not the SGEI-character of the service, but instead:

1. The EU legislator's recognition that public authorities may provide themselves services under their competence
2. The EU legislator's decision to define "procurement within the meaning of the Directives", thereby excluding – as will be seen with much support from Sweden – "situations where all operators fulfilling certain conditions are entitled to perform a given task, without any selectivity, such as customer choice and service voucher systems", which should not be understood as being procurement but simple authorisation schemes.[15]

---

[13]Ibid.

[14]Recital 5 of the 2014 Pubic Sector Directive and Recital 7 of the 2014 Utilities Directive.

[15]Recital 4 of the 2014 Public Sector Directive. In the Concessions Directive, it is held that this "situation" should not either be regarded as concession, see Recital 13, stating that "arrangements where all operators fulfilling certain conditions are entitled to perform a given task, without any selectivity, such as customer choice and service voucher systems, should not qualify as concessions, including those based on legal agreements between the public authority and the economic operators. Such systems are typically based on a decision by a public authority defining the transparent and non-discriminatory conditions on the continuous access of economic operators to the provision of specific services, such as social services, allowing customers to choose between such operators."

In this approach, every organisation of public services implying an externalisation falling within the broad concept of procurement in the meaning of the Directives, i.e. including concession contracts, is constrained by the EU procedural rules. In other words, EU procurement rules harmonise profoundly the principles and rules for an externalised organisation of public services, and evidently restrict public authorities' freedom to organise SGEIs. The clearest recognition of this fact lies arguably in the carving out of customer choice and service voucher systems from the definition of "procurement within the meaning of the Directives". Absent this legal-technical solution, this contract-based entrustment of tasks remunerated by the State would have had to comply with the procurement principles, in particular the principle of equal treatment, unless motivated by the principle of Article 14 TFEU.

If customer choice and service vouchers systems were covered by the notion of procurement, accommodating them under EU procurement rules would seem coherent with the principles on SGEIs enunciated in Article 1 of the SGI Protocol. To accommodate such systems by derogation from the principle of *equal treatment* would have to be justified as necessary to enable the achievement of SGEI missions in the meaning of Article 14 TFEU, whereby ensuring free choice would probably have to be claimed to constitute a "shared value" of SGEIs. Thus, if systems of choice or vouchers had been accommodated as procurement procedures on the basis of their SGEI missions (including the mission of "free choice"), the EU legislator would have been forced to acknowledge that harmonisation of procurement procedures affect the *organisation* of SGEIs before they are entrusted. It would arguably also force the EU legislator to explain why rules specifically enabling SGEI missions to be achieved, are harmonised through directives instead of regulations, as required by Article 14 TFEU. Lastly, it would arguably force the EU legislator to explain why the light procurement regimes is not more generally related to the SGEI-character of social services, and the contract-based entrustments not more clearly connected to the state aid rules.

In fact, the carving out of customer choice and service voucher systems from the scope of "procurement contract" in Recital 4 of the Public Sector Directive and of "service concession" in Recital 13 of the Concessions Directive, is ambiguous. In recitals touching on services to the person, it is stressed that Member States and/or public authorities remain free to organise social services in a way that does not entail the conclusion of concessions or public contracts, "for example through the mere financing of such services or by granting licences or authorisations to all economic operators meeting the conditions established beforehand by the contracting authority or contracting entity, without any limits or quotas". Such authorisation schemes can constitute the supply component of systems of service vouchers or customer choice, and therefore may be expected not to be unaffected by the new procurement directives. Yet, regarding social services, the Directives' recitals underline that the Member States' freedom to use such funding, authorisation or licensing systems is subject to *the condition* that such systems *ensure sufficient advertising* and comply with the principles of transparency and non-discrimination.[16] So after all, free choice or system voucher systems are perhaps regarded by the EU legislator as not "really outside" the scope of EU procurement law, unless the requirement of sufficient advertisement is simply regarded as following from EU administrative law.[17]

Public authorities' freedom to choose to perform their tasks themselves is also explicitly laid down as a principle in the Concessions Directive. However, by contrast with the Public Sector Directive and the Utilities Directive, this freedom is in the Concessions Directive not put in relation to Article 14 TFEU and the SGI Protocol, but instead *incorporated* as a part of a more general "principle of free administration by public authorities" formulated in Article 2(1), which reads

> This Directive recognises the principle of free administration by national, regional and local authorities in conformity with national and Union law. Those authorities are free to decide how best to manage the execution of works or the provision of services, to ensure in particular a high level of quality, safety and affordability, equal treatment and the promotion of universal access and of user rights in public services.
>
> Those authorities may choose to perform their public interest tasks with their own resources, or in cooperation with other authorities or to confer them upon economic operators.[18]

It appears as a remarkable step that the Concessions Directive introduces a principle of free administration, obviously transposing the Treaty principles on SGEIs and the "shared values" of SGEIs according to the SGI Protocol, but making the notion of SGEI invisible. This development is arguably worth scholarly attention.

Finally, it must be noted that provision is explicitly made that NESGIs "are not" or "should not be" covered by any of the 2014 Procurement Directives. In this regard, there is a notable difference between the assertive tone in the Utilities

---

[16]Recital 114 fourth paragraph of the Public Sector Directive, Recital 120 fourth paragraph of the 2014 Utilities Directive, and Recital 54 Directive of the 2014 Concessions Directive.

[17]Question 7 in the Questionnaire established as a platform for the FIDE Sessions on public procurement addressed the boundaries of EU procurement law and read: "Do the principles of non-discrimination/equal treatment and transparency (or rules derived therefrom) also apply to the selection of the beneficiary of unilateral administrative measures?" In his report on this question, Caranta held that "One can assume that non-discrimination, equal treatment and transparency are general principles potentially applicable to all instances where the State or any other public law entity disburses money or grant benefits or privileges (including the right to carry out an economic activity), on a selective basis, choosing among a number of market participants potentially exceeding the resources being distributed, such as for instance when exclusive rights are granted to a specific economic operator in connection with the provision of a SGEI". See Caranta R., 2014, p. 79–175.

[18]Article 2(1) of the 2014 Concessions Directive.

Directive[19] and the Concessions Directive,[20] and the more cautious approach in the Public Sector Directive, clarifying, although merely in a Recital, that "non-economic services of general interest *should not* fall within the scope of this Directive".[21] A first explanation for this asymmetry may be that, compared to the Public Sector Directive, activities covered by the Utility Directive are easier to categorise with certainty as economic SGIs, i.e. SGEIs. A second explanation may be that, while the Member States a priori retain powers to organise social services as non-economic SGI in their territory, the fact that a Member State allows service concessions for a specific type of social service will normally imply a degree of liberalisation that per se excludes the possibility for the service to be non-economic in that state.

Unsurprisingly, what is considered as NESGIs is very unclear in the 2014 procurement directives, which arguably constitutes a serious problem in a rule of law perspective. Recitals to the Public Sector Directive and the Concessions Directive "recall" that Member States are free to organise the provision of "compulsory social services or of other services such as postal services" as "services of general economic interest or as non-economic services of general interest or as a mixture thereof".[22] As these recitals also "recall" that this freedom is subject to compliance with the principles of the TFEU on equal treatment, non-discrimination, transparency and the free movement of persons, it seems that the Directives interpret NESGIs as services regulated and organised in a Member State in such a manner that their operation is not economic for the purpose of EU competition rules, even if this service, in theory or given its regulation in other Member States, *can be* economic and therefore is covered by EU free movement rules. Yet the examples named in these recitals shed very little light on which services are actually meant (what do "compulsory social services" and "other services such as postal services" have in common?) and there is no indication whatsoever in these recitals on the criteria which may be decisive for a service to be classified as SGEI or NESGI. This disastrous lack of legal certainty on what NESGIs actually are, may explain the introduction of recitals of the Public Sector Directive and the Utilities

[19]Article 1(6) of the 2014 Utilities Directive reads: "[t]he scope of this Directive shall not include non-economic services of general interest".

[20]Article 4(2) of the 2014 Concessions Directive reads: "[n]on-economic services of general interest shall fall outside the scope of this Directive".

[21]Recital 6 of the 2014 Public Sector Directive.

[22]Recital 6 of the 2014 Public Sector Directive and Recital 6 of the Concessions Directive. The word "recall" is strange in that context, given the fact that the case law on this issue is quite unclear, and that the only EU institution summing up and interpreting this case law is the Commission, in soft law documents.

Directive, stressing that the provision of services based on laws, regulations or employment contracts should not be covered by the Directives.[23]

As already mentioned, the exceptions for in-house arrangements and public-public cooperation arrangements have been codified in the new Public Sector Directive and the new Utilities Directive.[24] While this novelty is already subject to abundant scholarly attention, the purpose here is only to draw attention to elements betraying the EU legislator's awareness of the connection between these exceptions and the Treaty principles on SGEIs.[25] The conditions of application of the in-house exception have been extended compared to those established by the CJEU. The Directives allow direct private capital participation in the controlled legal person on the condition that it takes non-controlling and non-blocking forms, is required by national legislative provisions in conformity with the Treaties, and does not exert a decisive influence on the controlled legal person.[26] The conditions of application of the rule on cooperation between public authorities are also more "generous" in the Public Sector Directive than the conditions required by the CJEU in case law, as they do not preclude the participation of a private part.[27]

As underlined by Wiggen, the latter change is rather significant, not only as compared to the existing case law, but also to the Commission's proposal, and she explains that, "to soften the blow", the Commission's proposal to add an activity criterion similar to the in-house exemption has been retained, implying that the participating contracting authorities perform on the open market less than 20 % of the activities concerned by the cooperation.[28] In the legislative negotiation, concerns of an increased risk of competition distortion have had to be measured against a need of increased flexibility for mixed capital contracting authorities. The result tells us that "some argument" gave the upper hand to flexibility concerns, and it is argued here that the SGEI character of the missions pursued by the

[23]Recital 5 of the 2014 Public Sector Directive and Recital 7 of the 2014 Utilities Directive, which provide examples of services not covered because their provision is based on laws, regulations or employment contracts: regarding the public sector "certain administrative and government services such as executive and legislative services or the provision of certain services to the community, such as foreign affairs services or justice services or compulsory social security services" and regarding the utilities sector "in some Member States/…/the provision of certain services to the community, such as the supply of drinking water."

[24]"Public contracts between entities within the public sector" under Article 12 of the 2014 Public Sector Directive and "contracts between contracting authorities" under Article 28 of the 2014 Utilities Directive.

[25]See in particular Burgi 2014; Janssen 2014; Wiggen 2014; FIDE General Report on Public Procurement Law, 2014.

[26]Article 12(1)(c) of the 2014 Public Sector Directive and Article 28(1)(c) of the 2014 Utilities Directive.

[27]Recital 32 of the 2014 Public Sector Directive clarifies namely that "contracting authorities such as bodies governed by public law, that may have private capital participation, should be in a position to avail themselves of the exemption for horizontal cooperation".

[28]Article 12(4)(c) of the 2014 Public Sector Directive and Article 28(4)(c) of the 2014 Utilities Directive. See Wiggen 2014, *Directive 2014/24/EU: the new provision on co-operation in the public sector*, Public Procurement Law Review, 2014 Issue 3, p. 91.

cooperation may have been implicitly decisive, because it has constitutional support in Article 14 TFEU.

This is probably an explanation which the Commission would not easily agree on, given its implications, but there is an indicium that the concept of SGEI has been in the EU legislators' head when drafting the provision on cooperation between public authorities. The first condition required for the application of this exemption is namely in both Directives that

> [T]he contract establishes or implements a cooperation between the participating contracting authorities with the aim of ensuring that *public services* they have to perform are provided *with a view to achieving objectives they have in common*.[29]

This criterion is unmistakably close to the principle formulated in Article 14 TFEU, namely that conditions under which SGEIs operate must be designed in a manner which enables the missions pursued by the SGEI to be achieved. However, the notion of "public service task" in the first criterion formulated in *Commission v Germany* and *Lecce* is replaced in the Directives by the combination of the terms "public service" and "objectives", which tones down the idea contained in the notion of public service task, that the public authorities are under an obligation to achieve the same type of mission, instead of simply having a common "objective". It is submitted that, as every word of this provision must have been balanced on a gold weighing scale, the terminology difference is surely deliberate.[30]

In sum, the EU legislator, and principally the Commission, has registered the signal from the CJEU: Article 14 TFEU applies to EU procurement rules, but a cautious terminology is used in order to keep this acknowledgement as implicit as possible, so that the concept of SGEI cannot be understood as "too broad".

7.1.3 Lighter Procurement Regime for Social Services: Implicit Acknowledgement of Their SGEI Missions

A very important novelty in the 2014 procurement directives is the introduction of procedures for the procurement of social services and a number of other services, which belonged to the group of non-prioritized "B-services" in the old Directives. A simplified regime has however been considered appropriate for what is

---

[29] Article 12(4)(a) of the 2014 Public Sector Directive and Article 28(4)(a) of the 2014 Utilities Directive, emphasis added.

[30] It is important to note the difference between the notion of "public service" in these provisions and the notion of "public tasks" used in Article 1(6) of the 2014 Public Sector Directive establishes that "Agreements, decisions or other legal instruments that organise the transfer of powers and responsibilities for the performance of *public tasks* between contracting authorities or groupings of contracting authorities and do not provide for remuneration to be given for contractual performance, are considered to be a matter of internal organization of the Member State concerned and, as such, are not affected in any way by this Directive."

characterised in the Directives as "social and other specific services", with a higher threshold than other services (EUR 750 000 for public service contracts).[31] Under that threshold, such services are regarded as typically lacking cross-border interest, *unless there are concrete indications to the contrary*, and no EU rules apply. Above the thresholds, the EU rules imply that contracting authorities or entities awarding social service contracts or social service concessions must publicise *ex-ante* their intention to award contracts and publicise *ex post* contract award notices informing on the results of the procurement procedure.[32]

These minimal EU rules are accompanied by EU law "principles of awarding contracts", which the Member States must respect in determining their national procurement rules applicable to these services. These principles, formulated in the Recitals of the Concessions Directive,[33] are subject to specific provisions in the Public Sector Directive and the Utilities Directive, where they read as follows:

> Member States shall put in place national rules for the award of contracts subject to this Chapter in order to ensure contracting authorities comply with the principles of transparency and equal treatment of economic operators. Member States are free to determine the procedural rules applicable *as long as* such rules allow contracting authorities to take into account the specificities of the services in question.[34]

The freedom to determine procurement rules for social services is thus constrained by

(a) The principle of transparency
(b) The principle of equal treatment of economic operators
(c) A condition ("as long as") – or given the title of the provision rather meant as a principle – that contracting authorities must be enabled to take account of the *specificities* of the services in question.

---

[31] Articles 74 to 77 of the 2014 Public Sector Directive, Articles 91-94 of the 2014 Utilities Directive, Article 19 of the 2014 Concessions Directive. Article 4(d) of the 2014 Public Sector Directive, apply to a list of services found in Annex XIV of the Public sector Directive, Annex XVII of the Utilities Directive, and in Annex IV of the Concessions Directive.

[32] Article 75 of the 2014 Public Sector Directive, Article 92 of the 2014 Utilities Directive and Articles 19, 31(3) and 32 of the 2014 Concessions Directive.

[33] Recital 53 of the 2014 Concessions Directive, which reads: "An obligation to publish a prior information notice and a concession award notice of any concession with a value equal to or greater than the threshold established in this Directive is an adequate way to provide information to potential tenderers on business opportunities, as well as to provide information to all interested parties on the number and type of contracts awarded. Furthermore, Member States should put in place appropriate measures with reference to the award of concession contracts for those services, aimed at ensuring compliance with the principles of transparency and equal treatment of economic operators, while allowing contracting authorities and contracting entities to take into account the specificities of the services in question. Member States should ensure that contracting authorities and contracting entities are allowed to take into account the need to ensure innovation and, in accordance with Article 14 TFEU and Protocol No 26, a high level of quality, safety and affordability, equal treatment and the promotion of universal access and of users' rights."

[34] Article 76(1) of the 2014 Public Sector Directive and Article 93(1) of the 2014 Utilities Directive, emphasis added.

As national legislators may wonder which "specificities" are meant by the first paragraph of this provision, it appears that the second paragraph of these provisions is meant to provide some precision. This paragraph reads as follows:

> Member States *shall* ensure that contracting authorities *may take into account the need* to ensure *quality, continuity, accessibility, affordability, availability and comprehensiveness of the services, the specific needs of different categories of users, including disadvantaged and vulnerable groups, the involvement and empowerment of users and innovation.* Member States may also provide that the choice of the service provider shall be made on the basis of the tender presenting the best price-quality ratio, taking into account quality and sustainability criteria for social services.[35]

The relationship between the two paragraphs of this provision in the 2014 Procurement Directives is unsure, but it is easy to discern its connection to the Treaty principles on SGEIs, in particular the SGEI "shared values" in Article 1 of the SGI Protocol. As will be seen, this connection is itself eminently ambiguous.

The connection between the 2014 Procurement Directives and the Treaty principles on SGEIs and NESGIs is most explicit regarding social security services. The three Directives provide that they do not affect the way in which the Member States organise their social security systems.[36] This provision reflects evidently the CJEU's formula on retained powers, and even if less evidently, also the SGI Protocol. It is clearest in the Concessions Directive, where it is placed in Article 4 entitled "*freedom to define SGEIs*", together with another rule specifying that the Directive does not affect the freedom of Member States to define, *in conformity with Union law*, what they consider to be SGEIs, how those services should be organised and financed, in compliance with the State aid rules, and what specific obligations they should be subject to.[37]

It is also worth paying attention to a footnote (1) included in the Annexes listing social and other services covered by the Directives' lighter regimes. This footnote repeats the Recitals' stance that Member States are free to organise services as SGEIs or NESGIs or as "a mixture thereof", but also indicates that services referring to it are not covered by the Directives where they are organised as NESGIs. In these Annexes, compulsory social security services are however the only services referring to this footnote, and therefore it seems that they are the only ones for which the Directives *seriously* envisages the "very specific specificity" that they may be NESGIs, which is at odds with the assertion that Member States are "free to choose".

[35]Article 76(2) of the 2014 Public Sector Directive and Article 93(2) of the 2014 Utilities Directive. This is also stressed in Recital 53 of the 2014 Concessions Directive.

[36]Article 1(5) of the 2014 Public Sector Directive and of the 2014 Utilities Directive, Article 4(1) of the 2014 Concessions Directive. This is reinforced by recitals stating that the Directives should not affect the social security *legislation* of the Member States, see Recital 6 of the 2014 Public Sector Directive, Recital 8 of the 2014 Utilities Directive, and recital 7 of the 2014 Concessions Directive.

[37]Article 4(1) of the 2014 Concessions Directive.

Other social services, categorized "services to the person", and said to include "certain social, health and educational services", are addressed separately in the Directives' preambles. The specific regime applying to "services to the person" (but actually also to other "specific services") is motivated in recitals to the Directives by their provision in "a particular context that varies widely amongst Member States, due to different cultural traditions". "The importance of the cultural context and the sensitivity of these services" is explained to motivate that the Directives' rules "take account of the imperative"

- to give Member States a *wide discretion to organise* the choice of the service providers in the way *they* consider most appropriate
- to make sure that contracting authorities are able to apply specific quality criteria for the choice of service providers[38]

It is simply impossible not to interpret those recitals as an implicit acknowledgment that the principle formulated in Article 14 TFEU and interpreted by the SGI Protocol have constrained the EU legislator's approach and choices, in particular because in those recitals Member States are required *to take Article 14 TFEU and Protocol No 26 into account when determining the national procedures* to be used for the award of contracts for services to the person. Thus, the Member States are discreetly reminded that if there are SGEI missions in their legal systems, their achievement should not be obstructed by inappropriate national procurement rules, which denotes a perception that SGEI missions exist *before* they are entrusted through procurement. Meanwhile, the EU legislator avoids evoking SGEI missions as the rationale of *its own duty* to give Member States a wide discretion in the organisation of the choice of providers. Possible reasons for this avoidance have been submitted in Chap. 6.

Yet it should be stressed that the provision on contract awarding principles for social services in the 2014 procurement directives harmonise the conditions governing the procurement of social services, by referring to their "specificities" instead of their SGEI character, but "incorporating" SGEI elements in these "specificities". Indeed, if the provision on principles of awarding contracts in the Public Sector Directive is understood correctly, Article 76(2) indicates how Member States fulfil the principle in Article 76(1) and ensure that their procurement rules allow contracting authorities to take care of social services' "specificities". "Specificities" seem thus to correspond to service conditions that contracting authorities "need" to ensure. The Directives do not clarify who decides the "need" mentioned by Article 76(2) and in what form, but the open-ended locution "*need* to ensure" denotes a perception that contracting authorities have voluntary or compulsory social service missions to achieve (in other words, public service tasks imposed on public/contracting authorities by law or decided by public/contracting authorities in the frame of their competence).

[38]Recital 114 of the 2014 Public Sector Directive, Recital 120 of the 2014 Utilities Directive, and Recital 53 of the 2014 Concessions Directive.

Importantly, the specificities of social services enunciated in the Directives include not only the characteristics enumerated (non-exhaustively) in the SGI Protocol, but also (1) *including disadvantaged and vulnerable groups*, and (2) *the involvement and empowerment of users and innovation.* The latter specificities seem to promote a more residual welfare approach (the vulnerable and the disadvantaged, as in the Commission's understanding of social housing), or an approach favouring users' free choice of welfare services (through their "empowerment"). Thus, in requiring that contracting authorities are allowed to take into account social services' "specificities", the EU legislator invites the Member States to put in the balance not only their existing SGEI regulation, but also policy elements which are more compatible with a trade in social services.

It is also worth noting that, in taking Article 14 TFEU and Protocol No 26 into account, and according to the Public Sector Directive's and the Utilities Directive's recitals,

> Member States should also pursue the objectives of simplification and of alleviating the administrative burden for contracting authorities and economic operators; it should be clarified that so doing might also entail relying on rules applicable to service contracts not subject to the specific regime.[39]

If correctly understood, this may be a message that when taking Article 14 TFEU into account, in other words when establishing principles and conditions enabling SGEIs in the field of social services to achieve their missions, the Member States should keep in mind the principle of proportionality in the balance between the public service missions and the interest of opening the markets of social services to competition (a principle which in the Treaty framework on SGEIs seems inherent to Article 106(2) TFEU rather than to Article 14 TFEU). Also, regarding quality criteria for the choice of service providers, Member States are invited in these recitals to use the criteria set out in the voluntary European Quality Framework for Social Services, published by the Social Protection Committee Member States (SPC).[40] SPC being an EU advisory policy committee, its approach is to a large extent a *European* approach to social services.[41]

These elements – encouraging Member States to adopt procurement rules alleviating the administrative burden for contracting authorities and economic

[39] Recital 114 of the 2014 Public Sector Directive, Recital 120 of the 2014 Utilities Directive.

[40] A Voluntary European Quality Framework for Social Services, The Social Protection Committee, SPC/2010/10/8 final.

[41] The policy frame of the Voluntary European Quality Framework for Social Services builds in particular on arguments of growing financial constraints, cost-effectiveness, individual preferences, and growth potential. It holds in particular that "[a]s most social services are highly dependent on public funding, a consensus on the quality of social services in the present context when public authorities in the Member States are exposed to growing financial constraints will help policy-makers to prioritize investments that promote continuous development of both quality and cost-effectiveness of social service provision." (p. 1), that "the cross-border provision of social services, presently very limited but expected to grow, in particular in the area of long-term care, will call for a greater level of service comparability and transparency, as well as for new forms of protecting both users and workers" (p. 2) and that "[t]he service provision should empower users to define their personal needs and should aim to strengthen or maintain their capacities while retaining as much control as possible over their own lives." (p. 7).

operators, promoting the use of the European Quality Framework on social services, and adding to the criteria enumerated in the SGI Protocol other criteria for social services entrusted through procurement – are typically policy elements. They can certainly find support by the EU legislative instances, but it is striking that they are introduced through market harmonising EU directives, especially inasmuch as they may have an impact on the Member States' definition and organisation of SGEIs in the field of social services. Indeed, the EU legislator seems perfectly aware that Article 14 TFEU and the SGI Protocol cover EU – and national – procurement legislation, and the Member States are invited to adopt procurement rules which allow thc SGEIs contained in their own legal system to achieve their missions. However, it seems clear that in the field of social services, the EU legislator decided to "show them the way" outside the "SGEI frame".

While the Union is undeniably empowered to harmonize procurement rules on the basis of Article 114 TFEU, it has still very limited policy powers in the field of social services. As Article 9 TFEU may hardly justify that Union law imposes on the Member States to take account of the "specificities" of social services in their *national* procurement rules, the only provision able to give legitimacy to such a principle of awarding contracts appears to be Article 14 TFEU. However, acknowledging too explicitly that Article 14 TFEU is relevant for national procurement rules on social services is problematic because it means that it is a priori relevant for the EU rules and may pose the question of the legal basis of the EU procurement rules. It may also be problematic if it tends to cement SGEIs which EU institutions, in particular the Commission, may wish that Member States themselves liberalise.

In sum, the contract awarding principles imposed on the Member States in implementing the EU procurement rules related to social services show that the EU legislator acknowledges the applicability of Article 14 TFEU to EU procurement rules related to these services. It seems clear that concerns of market opening, but also of market integration have led the EU legislator to tone down the fact that the lighter regime is constitutionally justified by the SGEI-character of the services. In implementing the new Directives, Member States are not explicitly required to allow their contracting authorities to take account of social services' SGEI missions, but instead of social services' "specificities", which include more, and more market-friendly, service conditions than those enumerated in the SGI Protocol. This implies that, in the field of social services, the new procurement directives put a low pressure on the Member States to identify SGEIs in their systems. It also implies that EU procurement rules applying to social services do not focus on undistorted competition concerns.

7.2 The Commission's State Aid Rules on Public Service Compensation of Social Services

The Member States' freedom to give economic or financial support to undertakings in the internal market is restricted by the central state aid rule in Article 107(1) TFEU, providing that

> Save as otherwise provided in the Treaties, any aid granted by a Member State or through State resources in any form whatsoever which distorts or threatens to distort competition by favouring certain undertakings or the production of certain goods shall, in so far as it affects trade between Member States, be incompatible with the internal market.

The objective of this Treaty provision is to prevent trade between Member States being affected by advantages granted by the public authorities which distort or threaten to distort competition.[42] Given the CJEU's wide interpretation of the concept of undertaking, and the public turn of EU competition policy, this provision came in frontal collision course with the public funding of public service missions in national welfare systems, and in that way could paradoxically stand in the way of liberalising welfare systems by externalising provision. As a Treaty provision making public funding of social services a "persona non grata" on the internal market was at a certain stage of the development of EU law politically intolerable, the *Altmark* ruling has been welcome as a "deus ex machina" providing an EU market law test of this type of funding, and apparently useable in any field of activity. Its core is evidently the principle of proportionality, supported by the principle of transparency, and its enormous political dimension lies in the promotion of public procurement procedures as a privileged instrument to avoid over-compensation and ensure proportionality. Governance through contracts was offered as a way to escape the bureaucracy and incertitude of EU centralised state aid notification procedures.

The *Altmark* ruling was particularly welcome because the Treaties do not offer many instruments to solve the tension between public funding of social services and market interests. Baquero Cruz has aptly pointed at the limited functionality of the exemption rules in Article 107(2) and (3) TFEU in justifying aid to the provision of social services otherwise prohibited by Article 107(1) TFEU.[43] This explains that the

---

[42]See Case C-173/73 *Italy* v *Commission* 119741 ECR 709, para 26. Opinion of AG Léger of 19 March 2002 in Case C-280/00 *Altmark* [2003] ECR I-7747, para 77.

[43]Baquero-Cruz 2013, p. 296–300. Article 107(2)(a) TFEU, which allows aid having a social character granted to individual consumers, seems to be interpreted by the Commission as covering services. The provision is arguably of no use in case of qualified market failure, but may be of interest to address equity concerns on existing markets. In the latter case, Baquero Cruz holds that the provision can be used to finance provision of social services, but normally in combination with public service obligations and subject to tariff regulation. Article 107(3)(a) and (c) TFEU may allow to justify aid to providers of social services, but "to promote the economic development of areas where the standard of living is abnormally low or where there is serious underemployment" (Article 107(3)(a) TFEU, for instance employment and training aid) or "to facilitate the development of certain economic activities or of certain economic areas, where such aid does not adversely affect trading conditions to an extent contrary to the common interest" (Article 107(3)(c) TFEU, for instance regional aid schemes or rescue and restructuring aid schemes). Thus, under these exemptions, the aid's main concern must be to protect or create employment. Baquero Cruz noted that the Commission had approved on the basis of Article 17(3)(c) TFEU a Swedish aid scheme aimed at encouraging the construction of elderly housing in Northern Sweden. Indeed, in decision SA 33896 (2011/N), the Commission examined a scheme notified by Sweden, aimed at offering a financial incentive to property owners to construct special housing for elderly people, in the face of "a growing *demand*". The Commission raised no objections, finding the scheme compatible with the internal market as "aid to certain economic sectors" under Article 107(3)(c) TFEU, thereby accommodating the Swedish government's choice not to rely on Article 106(2) TFEU to motivate an aid scheme for elderly housing in a scarcely populated area.

Commission did not hesitate to use its powers pursuant to Article 106(3) TFEU and Article 108(3) TFEU, and build up on the basis of the CJEU's criteria in the *Altmark* ruling a first legislative package on the application of state aid granted to undertakings entrusted with the operation of SGEI. This first SGEI Package, known as the "post Altmark package" or "Monti package", and called here the "2005 SGEI Package", was replaced in 2011 by the 2011 SGEI Package, also known as "Almunia package".

7.2.1 Social Services in the 2005 SGEI Package

By building the 2005 SGEI Package on the basis of the *Altmark* ruling, the Commission's aim was to enhance the legal certainty for Member States' funding of public services. The Commission believed that many public service provision schemes did not fulfil the *Altmark* criteria, and that providers faced a risk of litigation on the legality of compensation payments received, as these payments had not been notified prior to implementation.[44] The 2005 SGEI Package consisted of three documents: a Decision (the "2005 SGEI Decision") specifying the conditions under which compensation would be compatible with Article 86(2) EC and not subject to the prior notification requirement of Article 88(3) EC, a Framework (the "2005 SGEI Framework") spelling out the conditions under which State aid could be found compatible with the common market pursuant to Article 86(2) EC, and the Transparency Directive.[45]

Both the 2005 SGEI Decision and the 2005 SGEI Framework distinguished between two basic alternatives allowing SGEI compensation to comply with the Treaty rules on state aid:

- In the first "Article 107(1) TFEU alternative", public funding fulfilling the four *Altmark* criteria was strictly limited to the amount needed to compensate an efficient operator, did not constitute state aid, and therefore did not have to be notified.
- In the second "Article 106(2) TFEU based alternative", a measure compensating undertakings for the costs of SGEI tasks but not fulfilling the fourth *Altmark* criterion (often called "the efficiency criterion") *could involve some distortion of competition* contrary to Article 107(1) TFEU but could be compatible with the Treaties, if *the distortion could be justified on the basis of Article 106(2) TFEU.*

[44]Commission, "Commission proposes new rules to increase legal certainty for services of general economic interest" (Press Release of 18 February 2004) IP/04/235, available at http://europa.eu/rapid/press-release_IP-04235_en.htm?locale=en.

[45]Commission Decision 2005/842/EC of 28 November 2005 on the application of Article 86(2) of the EC Treaty to State aid in the form of public service compensation granted to certain undertakings entrusted with the operation of services of general economic interest [2005] OJ L 312/67; Community framework 2005/C 297/04 for State aid in the form of public service compensation, [2005] OJ C 297/4; and Directive 80/723/EEC of 25 June 1980 on the transparency of financial relations between Member States and public undertakings as well as on financial transparency within certain undertakings, [1980] OJ L 195/35.

The 2005 SGEI Decision applied (1) to annual public service compensation of less than EUR 30 million to SGEI providers with a turnover of less than EUR 100 million per year, as an average over the two years preceding the assignment of the SGEI, (2) public service compensation of air and maritime links to islands and to ports and airports with limited amounts of passengers, and (3) to hospitals and social housing,[46] regardless of the aid amounts. Aid within that scope was exempted from notification on the following conditions (which did not have to be fulfilled if the aid was covered by the general de minimis rule):

(a) There must be an act of entrustment by way of one or more official acts, specifying the nature and duration of the public service obligations (PSO), the undertaking and the territory concerned, the nature of any special and exclusive rights involved, the parameters for compensation and a recoupment mechanism for overcompensation.
(b) Compensation must not exceed what is necessary to cover the costs incurred in discharging the public service obligations, taking into account the relevant receipts and a reasonable profit on any own capital necessary for discharging those obligations.
(c) Regular checks on overcompensation must be carried out, with an obligation for undertakings to repay any overcompensation received, and a possibility to carry forward to the next year overcompensation not exceeding 10 % of the amount of annual compensation.

As observed by Sauter, the 2005 SGEI Decision was in effect a Block Exemption, and the three conditions a-c above could be regarded as expressing the principle that aid must be justified by an objective task, necessary for fulfilling this task and proportional to the costs incurred for the task.[47] In substance, it seems that the alternative for Treaty compliance of PSO compensation designed by the Commission in its 2005 SGEI Decision, exempted the fourth criterion of efficiency of the "Article 107(1) TFEU alternative" in the *Altmark* ruling, but "in exchange" specified the first criterion in a manner that brought the substantial conditions in the "Article 106(2) TFEU alternative" much closer to public procurement's classical elements: a specification of what is funded, award criteria set in advance transparently, official documents (which may be a contract) objectifying the PSO arrangement, its "duration" and its conditions of operation for the specific

---

[46]The exemption concerned more precisely "hospitals providing medical care, including, where applicable, emergency services and ancillary services directly related to the main activities, notably in the field of research, and undertakings in charge of social housing providing housing for disadvantaged citizens or socially less advantaged groups, which due to solvability constraints are unable to obtain housing at market conditions", see Recital 16 in Commission Decision 2005/842/EC.

[47]Sauter 2014, p. 10. It may be interesting to note that, under point 167 of the state aid *IRIS-H* decision – NN54/2009, commented on in section 11.2.2.1 and 11.2.2.2 – the Commission gave a picture of how the material criteria of its 2005 SGEI Package relate to the conditions formulated in case law for public service compensation to comply with the proportionality principle in Article 106(2) TFEU.

provider(s). Seen in that perspective, the 2005 SGEI Decision was rather clearly initiating a process of material convergence between state aid rules and procurement rules for certain SGEIs, in particular for social services.

7.2.2 A First State Aid Package but Much Legal Uncertainty Emerging from the Commissions' Decision Practice on State Aid in the Field of Social Services

The Commission has taken relatively few state aid decisions related to public financing of social services. A number of them in the fields of health care insurance services, medical services, and education services are examined in this section, as they illustrate how difficult it is for the Commission to state in clear terms what makes an activity economic for the purpose of state aid rules. The second area of legal uncertainty follows from the Commission's approach in assessing the proportionality of public measures destined to secure the financing of SGEIs in the field of social services.

7.2.2.1 Determining Whether the Activity Is Economic for the Purpose of State Aid: The Commission's Practice

In the following, the Commission's approach in assessing whether the activity of the social service provider is economic is examined by sectors.

Health insurance schemes

In the "easy" *BUPA* case, there was no doubt at all that private medical insurers covered by the risk equalization scheme at issue conducted an economic activity. By contrast, the economic character of the activity at issue was less straightforward in the *Zorgverzekeringswet* case. Van de Gronden observes that in the Commission's reasoning, the decisive criterion to find that the Dutch insurance companies constituted undertakings was that were allowed to aim for-profit.[48] In his view, the Commission built on the CJEU's finding in *AOK* that profit-making should be regarded as a significant condition for applying the concept of undertaking. Unfortunately, the Commission Decision in *Zorgverzekeringswet* is only available in Dutch, a language that the author of this book does not understand.

However, while the profit-making character of the entities at issue in *AOK* was indeed relevant in that case, it was not to conclude that they were undertakings but to the contrary, to underline that, although these entities had to seek profit, they were not undertakings, because (1) they were required to seek profit by law and

[48]Commission Decision of 22 December 2005 on the introduction of a risk equalization system in the Dutch Health Insurance (Netherlands) in cases N541/2004 and N542/2004 – C (2005) 1329 final.

(2) they equalized their profits and thus profit-making had nothing to do with economic competition, in other words they did not operate on a market. Thus, contrary to van de Gronden's view, it is argued here that "profit" did not make any return in *AOK*, as it seems that the Court had never denied that, whilst for-profit is not a requisite for an entity to constitute an undertaking, for-profit can constitute an *indicium* that the entity's activity is economic.[49] Van de Gronden observes that the Commission gave also weight to the fact that the Dutch health insurance companies were able to influence the rates of the contributions and to determine the level of benefits granted to insured persons, a criterion of autonomy quite in line with the findings on the essential criteria used by the CJEU to determine the economic character of an activity in "difficult cases", and discussed in Chap. 2.

Recently, the Commission found that the Slovak compulsory health insurance system was non-economic in nature, so that the two state-owned health insurers (SZP and VZP) could not be considered as undertakings within the meaning of Article 107(1) of the Treaty.[50] According to Szyszczak, this conclusion is surprising, given that state-owned companies competed with private, for-profit health insurers. The Commission's view was that the competition and profit-orientation elements, consisting in a limited quality competition (with no price competition at all) and restrictions on the way profits could be made and used could not call into question the non-economic nature of the activities performed by health insurance companies in that system, given the latter's social, solidarity and regulatory features. Unsurprisingly, the Commission's decision is now under appeal to the General Court.[51]

Medical and hospital services

The *IRIS-hospitals* decision has already been discussed, as it was at issue in the *CBI* ruling discussed in Sect. 4.1.3.5. Let us rapidly remind ourselves here that the case concerned the complaint of two associations representing private hospitals against the Belgian State for alleged illegal and incompatible aid to the IRIS-hospitals in the Brussels region.[52] In the Brussels region, the IRIS-hospitals operated alongside with private hospitals, and both were publicly funded on the same basis, but the public IRIS-hospitals benefitted from additional financing measures related to specific missions which were not imposed on the private hospitals. In this decision, the Commission found that IRIS-hospitals constituted undertakings subject to the Treaty rules on state aid. It observed first that the hospital healthcare being almost free of charge in Belgium did not exclude that hospital care could

[49]Van de Gronden 2009, p. 13.

[50]Commission Decision of 15 October 2014 on the measures implemented by Slovak Republic for Spoločná zdravotná poisťovňa, a.s (SZP) and Všeobecná zdravotná poisťovňa, a.s (VZP) in case SA.23008 (C (2014) 7277 final), points 84 to 89. Szyszczak 2015, p. 682.

[51]Case T-216/15 *Dôvera zdravotná poist'ovňa v Commission*. The applicants claim that the Commission has committed errors of law and manifest errors of assessment in finding that SZP/VZP does not qualify as an undertaking.

[52]Commission Decision of 28 October 2009 on the public financing of Brussels public IRIS hospitals (Belgium), in case SA.19864 (2014/C) (ex NN54/2009).

also be provided for remuneration by private operators in that Member State. The Court referred to the comparative criterion applied in *Glöckner*, where it had found that providers of ambulance services for remuneration from users and on a market constituted undertakings, regardless of the fact that their public service obligations could render the service less competitive.

Thus, Sauter and van de Gronden have a point in holding that the decision *took into account* the argument of potential competition in accordance with *Glöckner*. However, it seems that the Commission did not regard the comparative criterion in *Glöckner* as sufficient, but instead found decisive that private entities de facto provided similar hospital care on the Belgian market. The Commission recalled namely that in *Smits and Peerbooms* the CJEU considered that for public hospitals, payments received from public authorities constituted remuneration, regardless of the fact that fees received from patients are very low or inexistent.[53] As clear from the French text, the Commission seemed to consider that *Smits and Peerbooms* gave support for its argument that public IRIS-hospitals were remunerated and pursued an economic activity, because private hospitals in Belgium provided similar services.[54] Yet in *Smits and Peerbooms*, the Court did not explicitly state that public hospitals conducted an economic activity under the scheme at issue *because private entities were allowed to provide the same service*, but instead that they could be seen as receiving remuneration when providing services *under the contractual arrangements* with the sickness funds. As argued in Chap. 2, the formulation in *Smits and Peerbooms* suggests that their margin of negotiation regarding the economic conditions for providing the service had relevance.

The Commission's approach in *IRIS-hospitals* shows how difficult it is to be sure about how the succinct paragraph in *Smits and Peerbooms* should be interpreted. The central question is whether, in the absence of formal contractual arrangements, the public character of an entity and the decisional autonomy it disposes of in relation to the public authorities funding it may have any relevance to determine whether its activity is economic. It seems that the Commission's answer to that question is "no", as in the *IRIS-H* decision, the funding of hospitals was largely based on statutory and administrative decisions which hospitals could

---

[53]Ibid, point 109.

[54]Ibid, points 108–109. The Commission's reasoning is worth quoting: "Sur base des arguments développés par la jurisprudence et rappelés ci-dessus, les financements que peuvent recevoir les H-IRIS par le biais de diverses allocations des autorités publiques centrales ou locales peuvent être analysés comme constituant la contrepartie économique des prestations hospitalières fournies, au même titre que les financements accordés par le biais des caisses maladies et autres organismes publics octroyant des fonds de manière similaire. Tel que mentionné par la Cour, le fait que par ailleurs le montant des paiements faits par les patients soit nul ou faible ne saurait altérer cette analyse (footnote omitted). *En l'espèce*, les activités principales des H-IRIS sont des activités hospitalières consistant dans la prestation de soins de santé médicaux, de services d'urgence et de services auxiliaires directement liés. Ces activités hospitalières prestées par les H-IRIS sont *également fournies par d'autres types d'organismes ou entités*, parmi lesquels des cliniques, des hôpitaux privés et d'autres centres spécialisés, *dont les hôpitaux privés plaignants*. *Dès lors*, ces activités hospitalières prestées par les H-IRIS doivent être considérées comme économiques (footnote omitted and emphasis added)."

apparently not influence.[55] In any case, having thus concluded that IRIS-hospitals conducted an economic activity, the Commission saw a need to "top-up" its argumentation on the more "orthodox" basis of competition cases *FENIN*, *FFSA* and *Albany*. As with AG Poiares Maduro in *FENIN*, the Commission made a distinction between the management of the national healthcare system, an activity which it regarded as including the exercise of powers typical of public authorities, and healthcare service provision. The latter could be regarded as economic in the case, in spite of solidarity elements, because private hospitals provided services similar – although perhaps not identical – to those provided by the public hospitals.[56]

In Hancher and Sauter's perception, "the Commission found that in view of established case law, the economic nature of the hospitals' activities was *without doubt*".[57] The footnote to this quote is worth particular attention, in light of the authors' assertion that the Commission "held no doubt". It is quite possible that the Commission held no "legal" doubt, as the footnote mentions rightly that the Commission referred to CJEU's competition case law – *Enirisorse, Höfner, and Pavlov* – reflecting its functional approach of the notion of undertaking. However, and interestingly, the footnote does not mention that the Commission also felt a need to refer rather extensively to *Smits and Peerbooms*, which shows its awareness that its decision was politically sensitive. The Commission's combined references to free movement and competition case law follows from the scarcity of rulings regarding the criteria of applicability of EU competition rules in the field of social services. Faced with a case dealing with services which are in the policy competence of the Member States, the Commission felt a need to ensure the full legitimacy of its decision. It did not simply apply the comparative test and the functional approach of *Höfner*, but also sought *legitimacy* support for its assessment in free movement case law. It did so by evoking the very elliptic obiter dictae in *Smits and Peerbooms*, which it unfortunately interpreted in a manner that is not unquestionable.

In any case, the Commission seems to share the view submitted in Chap. 2 that a service is not offered "on a market" unless it can be regarded as provided – not

[55]In the Belgian hospital system described in the IRIS-H decision, both public and private hospitals had mostly an identical public financing, in particular through payments from sickness and invalidity insurance funds (see points 28–30), and through budgets covering their running costs and decided by the Ministry of Social Affairs according to rates decided by law and laid down in ordinations (see points 33–40). Thus as a whole, in the Belgian system, it seems that public financing to any hospital was largely based on unilateral conditions set by the State rather than on "contractual arrangements". While private hospitals could express their decisional autonomy by seeking agreement, thereby establishing a kind of "non-contractual but bilateral arrangement" with public authorities, it is less clear whether the public hospitals had such an autonomy and whether their financing could come close to any "bilateral arrangement". Another thing is that the additional SGEI tasks for which public IRIS hospitals received compensation were entrusted through *conventions* with public bodies for social action (with some decisional autonomy on the part of these hospitals).

[56]Ibid, para 110.

[57]Hancher and Sauter 2013, p. 259–260, footnote omitted and emphasis added. In this paper, the authors conduct an in-depth discussion of the case.

"normally" but de facto – for remuneration. In fact, the Commission's decision in *IRIS-hospitals* gives support for the view that "for remuneration" in the field of free movement and "on the market" in the field of competition law mean substantially the same thing. The Commission's decision was annulled by the GC on the request of the association of private healthcare entities.[58] The GC considered namely that, in presence of serious difficulties in the examination of the case at issue, the Commission should have engaged a formal procedure in accordance with Article 108(2) TFEU. However, the GC confirmed the Commission's conclusion that the public IRIS-hospitals constituted undertakings.

Having underlined thc particular nature of hospital services, which motivates a flexible application of the *Altmark* ruling reflected in the 2005 SGEI Decision, the GC held firstly the hospital sector does not necessarily have such a competitive and commercial dimension.[59] Also, the GC recalled its finding in *FENIN* that when a national healthcare system is organised in accordance with the principle of solidarity, by its mode of financing and by providing services free of charge and on the basis of universal coverage, the bodies managing the system do not act as undertakings. The GC considered that this finding was taken into account in the Commission's decision, as it rightly made a distinction between the activity of "healthcare system management" conducted by public bodies exercising powers specific of public entities[60] and the activity consisting in the provision of healthcare services.[61] Importantly, the GC did not question the fact that the Commission had reached its conclusion through "crossover reasoning", i.e. by combining the CJEU's analytical elements in free movement case law and competition case law. Unfortunately, the GC did not seize this opportunity to give its view on whether in the field of social services, public operators' lack of autonomy in relation to the public authorities funding them may have any relevance for the economic character of their activity, or whether the fact that private entities may offer similar services also publicly funded, is wholly decisive.

It may lastly be mentioned that the Commission considered that a religious order providing healthcare and social services privately and non-profit, but at market prices and in competition with other private centres, performed an economic activity and therefore qualified as an undertaking pursuant to Article 107(1) TFEU.[62]

College and kindergarten services

In the *Prerov* decision, the Commission found that the city of Prerov's financial contribution to a college for tertiary education situated on its territory, destined to purchase educative equipment, did not constitute state aid in the meaning of

[58]Case T-137/10 *CBI* [decided on 7 November 2012, nyr].

[59]Ibid, paras 86–89.

[60]The link between the degree of solidarity in a system and the exercise of public authority in its management is not studied here.

[61]Case T-137/10 *CBI* [decided on 7 November 2012, nyr], para 91.

[62]Commission Decision of 10 December 2014 on rescue aid to PICFIC in A.S (Italy, health care services operator in the Region of Lazio in case SA.39426 (C(2014) 9255 final), point 24.

Article 87 EC (now Article 107 TFEU), on the basis of *two alternative grounds*.[63] First, the Commission argued that EU state aid rules did not apply because the college's activity was not economic, referring to definitions in competition case law: the *Höfner*'s definition of an undertaking, completed by the *Pavlov* definition of an economic activity as "the offer of goods or services on the market".[64] However, the Commission did not complete its argumentation on the basis of the *Poucet and Pistre* case law on activities fulfilling an exclusively social function, applied by the CJEU in the sectors of social security. Given the lack of case law on the applicability of EU competition rules to education, the Commission chose instead to refer to the Court's stance in *Humbel* that "courses taught in a technical institute which form part of the secondary education provided under the national education system cannot be regarded as services within the meaning of Article 59 of the EEC Treaty [now Article 56 TFEU], properly construed".[65]

This led the Commission to conclude that the college did not conduct any economic activity but "pursued an educational role of general interest activity" and acted "under the national education system", as it had been granted a state agreement to act as a tertiary technical education establishment and could not perform any other activity separable from this central activity.[66] Meanwhile, and although it is not so clear from the decision, it seems that the college was also financed by private funds. This would explain that the Commission referred to *Wirth*, where the Court of Justice has taken the view that courses provided in establishments financed essentially out of private funds, and which seek to make an economic profit, constitute services in the meaning of the Treaty. In *Prerov*, the Commission considered that the college did not seek to make profits, as possible profits had to be reinvested into the college's central activity. Under such circumstances, it found that its aim was not to offer a service for remuneration.[67]

Finally, the Commission stated that, even if the college's activity could be seen as economic, the aid granted had no effect on trade, given its relatively small amount (ca EUR 229 000), and the college's local dimension, teaching language, location and size. This shows that the Commission was uncertain about its argumentation to the purpose that the college's activity was non-economic. Also, by transposing the *Humbel* doctrine and the reasoning in *Wirth* in the field of EU competition law, the Commission appears to suppose the equivalence between the requirement that a service is provided for remuneration (economic activity for the purpose of free movement law) and the requirement that an entity offers services

[63]Commission Decision of 8 November 2006 on aid to the Přerov Logistics College (Czech Republic) in case NN54/2006 (C (2006) 5228).

[64]Ibid, point 14. It is not clear from the decision whether the Czech Republic had ever claimed that the college conducted a non-economic activity.

[65]Case 263/86 *Humbel* [1988] ECR I-5365, para 20.

[66]This consideration was important not only to regard the college as covered by the *Humbel* doctrine; it was also relevant to exclude a risk that public subsidization received for a non-economic activity could be used to distort competition in another economic activity.

[67]Ibid, point 16.

or goods on the market (economic activity for the purpose of EU competition law). On this background, interesting state aid cases decided by the EFTA Surveillance Authority (ESA) and by the EFTA-Court must be evoked here.

The *Barnehagers* decision was taken following a complaint by the Norwegian Association of Private Kindergartens against Norwegian rules on kindergartens' funding. It was established that, at the time of the complaint, municipalities could secure universal access at reasonable fees, either by running kindergarten services themselves or by giving financial support to non-municipal kindergartens. As a result, both municipal and non-municipal kindergartens were financed by a combination of parental payments and of public subsidies, one principle being equal treatment between municipal and non-municipal kindergartens.[68] The complaint alleged that financial features in the system, in particular the cost coverage principle, favoured municipal day-care centres, while the Norwegian State argued that this principle was precisely aimed at securing equal treatment of all kindergartens.[69] In its decision, the ESA adopted a strategy comparable to the Commission's in *Prerov*. It "piled up" alternative grounds motivating that the challenged statutory measures did not infringe EU state aid rules:

(a) The municipal kindergartens' activity was not economic
(b) The municipal kindergartens activity was economic but the Norwegian scheme did not constitute aid in the meaning of Article 107(1) TFEU as it did not affect trade and
(c) The Norwegian scheme included state aid, but kindergartens were entrusted services of general economic interest and the scheme was justified under Article 106(2) TFEU.

To reach the conclusion that the municipal kindergartens's activity was non-economic (ground (a) above), the ESA referred to many concepts and criteria developed in different parts of the CJEU's case law related to the applicability of free movement case law and competition case law to social services. The ESA, considering kindergarten as "pre-school education" part of the national education system, and referring to the Commission's *Prerov* decision, regarded the *Humbel* doctrine as relevant for assessing the applicability of EU state aid rules.[70] However, perhaps because it felt that this argument was weak, the ESA also referred to *Poucet and Pistre*, *Cisal* and *AOK Bundesverband*, and held that *municipal* kindergartens fulfilled an exclusively social function ("their duties towards their own populations in the social, cultural and

[68]See EFTA Surveillance Authority Decision No 39/07/COL on public financing of municipal day-care institutions in Norway, p. 5–6. The financing came from parental payments (up to 20 % of the cost of services) and public subsidies (50 % from the state channelled through the municipalities, and 30 % directly from the municipalities).

[69]Ibid, p. 7–8. The Norwegian State motivated the cost-coverage principle by cost variations between kindergartens caused by e.g. geographical cost differences, personnel education level, children with special needs, and held that granting a lump sum to all kindergartens would not fulfil the objective of equal treatment of all kindergartens.

[70]Ibid, p. 9.

educational fields") and were financed according to the principle of solidarity.[71] It was even brought up that in providing kindergarten services, municipalities exercised powers which are typically those of a public authority. On the basis of this pell-mell of arguments, the ESA concluded that "the tasks performed by the municipal kindergartens are of general interest, and not market-based."

The Association of private kindergartens appealed to the EFTA Court, referring to the comparative test in *Höfner* and the fact that it was itself an association of undertakings running kindergartens as an economic activity to argue that kindergartens constituted an economic activity in Norway.[72] The EFTA-Court dismissed the action, finding *doubtless* that the municipal kindergartens did not constitute undertakings.[73] It held that the comparative test alone was not decisive as what had to be assessed was "whether the Norwegian municipalities, when offering their kindergarten places, are providing a service as an economic activity or whether they are exercising their powers in order to fulfil their duties towards their population".[74] In this regard, the EFTA-Court took the view that "the reasoning of the ECJ in *Humbel*, which concerned the notion of "service" within the meaning of the fundamental freedoms, can be transposed to a State aid case such as the one at hand",[75] the question being whether the municipal kindergartens could be regarded as receiving remuneration for the kindergarten services they provided. Remuneration was absent in the activity of municipal kindergartens in Norway, said the EFTA-Court, because "[t]he parents' fee which constitutes only a fraction of the true costs of the service cannot be qualified as a quid pro quo vis-à-vis the municipal kindergartens, but only as a contribution to a system which is predominantly funded by the public purse. It is therefore clear that the Norwegian State, when establishing and maintaining a system where every child increases the costs incurred, is not seeking to engage in gainful activity but is fulfilling its duties towards its own population in the social, cultural and educational fields".[76]

---

[71]It was underlined that, according to Norwegian law, the municipal kindergartens' activity was entirely non-profit and that their financing was based on the principle of solidarity, as user fees were fixed, not proportional to the cost of the individual service and reduced for parents with more than one child and families with low income demonstrates the principle of solidarity. Ibid, p. 10–11.

[72]Case E-5/07 *Private Barnehagers*, Efta Court Report 2008, p. 62, para 79.

[73]Ibid, para 84.

[74]Ibid, para 80.

[75]Ibid, para 80.

[76]Ibid, para 83. Under para 82 the EFTA-Court had particularly emphasized that ca 80 % of the costs of municipal kindergartens were borne by the public purse there was no connection between the actual costs of the service provided and the fee paid by the parents whose child is attending the kindergarten the municipalities had a statutory duty to ensure that sufficient places for children below compulsory school age exist for their population kindergartens in Norway have important social, cultural, educational and pedagogical purposes. It may be recalled here that in *Commission v Italy*, the Court of Justice established that in the field of competition law, a distinction must be made between the State carrying on economic activities of an industrial or commercial nature by offering goods and services on the market on the one side and on the other side the State acting by exercising public powers. The EFTA-Court's finding implies a strong correlation between the fulfilment of the state's duties towards its own population and the exercise of public powers.

This ruling raises perplexity. First, the EFTA-Court did not see any need to discuss whether the municipalities' planning and financing activities as coordinators and financers for the supply of kindergarten to their population could be separable from their activity as providers of those services. The EFTA-Court did not either explain why, while it found free movement case law in the field of education relevant, it considered the *Poucet and Pistre* competition case law, invoked by the applicants in the case, and referred to by the ESA, irrelevant for its conclusion that municipalities did not pursue an economic activity. Most surprising is the EFTA-Court's statement that the ESA had not failed in not opening a formal investigation procedure because it did not need to entertain doubts on any of grounds (a-c) above.[77]

A good reason to doubt was namely the *Oslo kindergartens* decision, taken by the ESA some years earlier, where the issue was the municipality of Oslo's subsidies to real estate leasehold contracts granted to private undertakings in order to encourage them to establish and manage day-care facilities, thereby meeting the local *demand* and helping the municipality to fulfil its public service obligations.[78] The ESA concluded that the support scheme regarding the establishment of private day-care facilities did not constitute State aid within the meaning of Article 61 (1) of the EEA Agreement, as it considered that it had no effect on trade. In the *Oslo kindergartens* decision, the ESA *did not conduct any reasoning* on whether these kindergartens were part of the national education system or on the educational and social aspects of these activities; it simply acknowledged that support in the form of reduced annual leasehold was given to private day-care facility providers, giving them an advantage they would not have enjoyed in the normal course of *business*.[79] Thus, the ESA found that municipal kindergartens were not undertakings (2007, as part of the national system of pre-school education) but that kindergartens run by private entities but mostly financed by public resources were undertakings.[80] It is unknown to the author of this book whether public and private kindergartens at issue in these cases provided their services under different rules and/or within different systems of supply.[81]

---

[77]Ibid, para 84. The ESA's obligation to open a formal investigation procedure in case of doubts on a national measure's compatibility with state aid rules follows from Article 61(1) EEA, which corresponds to the Commission's obligation under Article 108(2) TFEU. The ESA held that there were several ways trade could potentially be affected. One was that the users of services from other EEA states would be more inclined to use the Norwegian service than the one in other EEA states. A second possible effect was that the support the municipal kindergartens receive would enable them to expand the scope of their services abroad. The third possible effect was that service providers from other Member States would be affected in their actual or potential operation in Norway. See Decision No 39/07/COL p. 12.

[78]291/03/COL EFTA Surveillance Authority decision of 18 December 2003 regarding the establishment of private day-care facilities on public sites with subsidized real estate leasehold fees in Oslo (Norway). Not mentioned in the 2013 SGEI Guide.

[79]Ibid, under Sect. 2.2.

[80]Indeed, it seems that private kindergartens allowed to provide for-profit, see Sect. 2.3 *in fine*.

[81]However, it seems that the rules on financing of public and private kindergartens at issue in the *Barnehagers* case were already in force in the *Oslo kindergartens* decision, as suggested in Sect. 2.5 in the latter decision.

On the same path, more recently, the Commission had to examine complaints lodged in 2008 against the privatization of schools, kindergartens and medical centres in the area of Stockholm. It was claimed that in the frame of a school privatization, the municipalities had sold key assets – in particular goodwill – under market price. More than three years later, the Commission sent a letter to the Swedish government informing on its decision to close the case administratively (i.e. without taking a formal decision to on the measures' compatibility with the Treaties).[82] Considering that the absence of effect on internal market and trade between Member States would a priori indicate that the measures described in the complaints would not constitute aid in the meaning of Article 107(1) TFEU, the Commission reserved itself the discretion to review the matters if new evidence arose. This "informal decision" reflects undeniably a view that education as provided by the operators at issue in the case is an economic activity for the purpose of state aid rules and more broadly of EU competition rules.

The picture emerging from the cases evoked in this section is that, when examining financing measures benefitting entities providing for-profit pre-school education (*Oslo day care centres*) and for-profit healthcare and school education (the Swedish privatization cases), neither the Commission nor the ESA refer to the *Humbel* doctrine. The economic character of the education or socio-educative activity is not questioned, but the measures examined are not considered as state aid in the meaning of Article 107(1) TFEU, because they are held not to affect trade. By contrast, when examining measures benefitting entities providing not-for-profit university education (*Prerov*) and pre-school education (*Barnehagers*), the Commission, the ESA and the EFTA-Court do refer to the *Humbel* doctrine to motivate that the entities at issue are not undertakings. In *Barnehagers*, the EFTA-Court royally ignores the criteria set in the *Poucet and Pistre* case law. However, in order to reach the conclusion that education provided by public entities is not economic, it seems that neither the Commission nor the ESA feel comfortable with relying exclusively on the *Humbel* doctrine to divert from the CJEU's functional approach of the notion of "economic activity" in the field of competition.

In sum, it appears that in the field of health insurance, the Commission finds possible to conduct its assessment on the basis of existing competition case law. By contrast, regarding medical and educational services, the state aid decisions evoked in this section show that the Commission and the ESA give relevance to the fact that the entities at issue may or not be considered as receiving "remuneration". This detour by a Treaty concept of free movement law is made necessary by the lack of CJEU cases for these social services, clarifying whether and how the solidarity elements in the entity's activity can limit the broad applicability of competition and state aid rules to social services, based on the functional approach of the notion of undertaking developed by the CJEU. In this approach the Commission does not seem to satisfy itself with the comparative test, but seeks to find out whether the social service *is* de facto *in the specific case* provided for remuneration.

---

[82]Letter to the Head of Section for Market and Competition Division at the Swedish Ministry of Enterprise, Energy and Communication, registered under reference COMP/H-2/BC – (2012)33624, dated 29.03.2012.

However, and importantly, the Commission seems to interpret the CJEU's stance in *Smits and Peerbooms* (the famous paragraph 58) as meaning that as soon as private operators offer services similar to those of the public operators, the latter's public funding should be seen as a *remuneration* for which they provide the service, and their activity should therefore be seen as economic for the purpose of state aid rules. For this social service, the lack of autonomy and the non-profit aim of the public entity are seen by the Commission as irrelevant for its qualification as an undertaking. In the field of education, it is striking to see that the Commission also takes a detour by free movement case law, but this time referring to *Humbel*, to establish whether the activity is economic. The result in that case is that the fact that the entity is part of the education system and not-for-profit is sufficient to declare that its activity fulfils exclusively a social function. For that social service, the non-profit aim is suddenly relevant for its qualification as an undertaking, which may explain that, in the Swedish case, the Commission could not deny the economic character of the activity of private for-profit schools.

7.2.2.2 Should the Aid's Assessment Be Economic or Jurisdictional? Some Insight in the Commission's Practice

As already mentioned in Sect. 4.1.3.5, de Vries and several other authors have underlined the considerable lack of clarity arising from the discrepancy between on the one side the Commission's legislative approach mirroring a detailed and strict assessment, in line with the economic approach promoted by its State aid Action Plan, and on the other side the more relaxed approach in the Commission Decision practice. In the still scarce decision practice of the Commission in the field of social services, we find the already evoked health care insurance systems cases *BUPA* (Irish private medical insurance system) and *Zorgverzekeringswet* (Dutch health care system) and the *IRIS-hospitals* case concerning public hospitals in Belgium Decisions.

The Commission's *BUPA* decision, taken in 2003 before the ECJ delivered its *Altmark* judgment, was based on its now overruled approach in *Ferring*.[83] The Commission found that the notified risk equalization system did not amount to aid in the meaning of Article 87(1) EC, or if it did, that it constituted public service compensation necessary to maintain the stability of a community rated health insurance market justified as compatible with the common market pursuant to Article 86(2) EC.[84]

The *Zorgverzekeringswet* decision was taken in 2005 and concerned a risk equalisation system under the Dutch Health Insurance Act.[85] As described by van de Gronden, the basic health care scheme in the Dutch health care system was

[83]Case C-53/00 *Ferring* [2001] ECR I-9067.

[84]Commission Decision of 13 March 2003 on a risk equalization scheme in the Irish health insurance market (Ireland) in case N 46/2003 – C (2003) 1322 final, points 60–61.

[85]Commission Decision of 22 December 2005 on the introduction of a risk equalization system in the Dutch Health Insurance (Netherlands) in cases N541/2004 and N542/2004 – C (2005) 1329 final. The Dutch Act is outlined in Hamilton 2005, p. 8ff.

managed in competition by private insurance companies allowed to aim for profit, and regarded as undertakings.[86] As the Dutch private insurers were submitted to a risk equalisation scheme managed by a state body, payments made in the frame of that scheme fell within the scope of the state aid rules. The Commission found that the Dutch risk equalisation scheme constituted aid in the meaning of Article 107(1) TFEU, considering that the fourth *Altmark* condition was not fulfilled as all insurance companies were entitled to a similar amount of compensation, whether or not they operated efficiently. Also, the Commission considered that the equalisation scheme could not compensate public service costs but rather aimed at neutralizing differences in risk profiles. Considering that it may be impossible for national health care authorities to set up general compensation schemes that take due account of the individual costs of efficient companies, Van de Gronden holds that a compensation scheme directed at an open group of operators should be expected to fail to meet the fourth *Altmark* condition.[87]

Nevertheless, the Commission considered that all health insurance companies were entrusted with SGEI tasks, although these tasks were not explicitly entrusted in a specific act of entrustment. The Commission interpreted Article 86(2) EC extensively, by deriving these tasks from general obligations imposed on the insurers by the Dutch Health Insurance Act (open enrolment, community rating, benefits granted to insured persons, and supervision mechanisms). According to van de Gronden, it was the first time this approach was used by an EU institution and came in strong contrast with the perception – dominant at the time – that SGEI tasks had to be entrusted by an explicit act.[88] However, van de Gronden also underlined that in finding the scheme compatible with the internal market on the basis of Article 106(2) TFEU, the Commission gave consideration to the fact that the Dutch scheme built mostly on *ex-ante* correction, leaving more room for competition by not compensating all costs. The lenient approach of the SGEI tasks' precision and entrustment mode was thus accompanied by a signal that *ex-ante* equalization is preferred, which in the future would constrain the Dutch government's options. It is easy to agree with van de Gronden that the case shows how, through the standstill provision, imposing notification of welfare financing schemes to the Commission before they can be put into operation, the Commission had the power to influence core elements of welfare systems.[89] Following a path suggested by this author, it is argued here that the Dutch health

---

[86]For a detailed analysis of this decision, see Van de Gronden 2009, p. 14–17.

[87]Van de Gronden 2009, p. 14–15.

[88]Ibid, p. 15.

[89]Ibid, p. 16. Van de Gronden held that, concerning health care systems, this is not necessarily unquestionable, as Article 152(5) EC stipulates that the organization and delivery of health care belong to the competences of the Member States. As a matter of fact, the Treaty of Lisbon makes more generally clearer that competences which have not been conferred on the EU remain by the Member States, which is the case in general for services to the person and to a large extent for education.

care system has not only been regulated by national public authorities, but also by the Commission.[90]

The insight of this power and the social importance of the schemes notified may also explain the Commission's approach in the *IRIS-H* decision.[91] As seen in the precedent section, the Commission had found that the public hospitals at issue constituted undertakings. It had to examine (1) the alleged absence of clear entrustment of hospital and non-hospital public service tasks, (2) the compensation of the IRIS-hospitals' deficit, (3) the alleged over-compensation of the public service obligations and lack of transparency in their financing mode and (4) the alleged cross-subvention of these hospitals' commercial activities.[92]

The Commission assessed first the Treaty compatibility of the funding measures in the light of the *Altmark* criteria ("Article 107(1) TFEU alternative") and found that the first *Altmark* criterion was fulfilled. With reference to the *BUPA* ruling and to Article 152(1) and (5) EC (now Article 168 (1) and (7) TFEU), the Commission underlined the wide freedom of the Member States to define SGEIs, and considered that both public and private hospitals were subject to a common body of public service obligations, and also that the public IRIS-hospitals were subject to additional and specific public service obligations: (1) an obligation of universal service for both emergency or non-emergency care, and (2) a duty to maintain a full range of hospital services at every location. Also, and unsurprisingly in light of the Commission's *Zorgverzekeringswet* decision, the Commission found the fourth *Altmark* criterion not fulfilled, considering that a compensation scheme granted to several operators, and based on average costs, could "mathematically" not exclude over-compensation, otherwise than for the average undertaking of reference.[93] As the fourth *Altmark* criterion was not fulfilled, the Commission did not assess the second and third *Altmark*

---

[90]Ibid, p. 15.

[91]Commission Decision of 28 October 2009 on the financing of public hospitals of the IRIS-network of the region Brussels-capitale (Belgium) in case NN54/2009 – C (2009) 8120 final. The *CBI* ruling is commented in Sect. 4.1.3.5 above.

[92]Ibid, points 1 and 9.

[93]Ibid, point 161. Hancher and Sauter underlined that in *IRIS-hospitals* the Commission considered that SGEI compensation granted to several undertakings and based on their average costs without requiring evidence of sound management would inevitably lead to overcompensation, and noted that at a later stage of the decision the Commission adopted what they considered to be the opposite view, namely that compensation based on average costs can lead to under-compensation; see Hancher and Sauter 2013, p. 263 and 264. In fact, it is argued here that the Commission's views are not illogical, as the point of departure is that compensation on the basis of average costs can involve *both* a risk of over-compensation and of under-compensation. In assessing the fulfilment of the fourth *Altmark* criterion, only the risk of over-compensation is relevant, while the risk of under-compensation may exist but needs not be mentioned at that stage. The risk of under-compensation is relevant as an issue when taking care that the conditions of operation enable the SGEI mission to be fulfilled, and may be invoked to justify an *ex post* measure allowing the SGEI mission to be ensured. The problem is of course that ex post measures do not allow much efficiency control, but do *ex-ante* compensation measures not have the same drawback, unless the tasks are précised, the parameters of compensation well adapted, and the efficiency control efficient? This emerges arguably from the Swedish case studied in Chap. 9.

criteria, but instead went over to assessing the funding measures under substantive compatibility following from Article 106(2) TFEU (the "Article 106(2) TFEU alternative" of compatibility).

The specific tasks imposed on the public IRIS-hospitals were related both to hospital and non-hospital services, the first covered by the 2005 SGEI Decision and the second by the 2005 SGEI Framework, and so the Commission referred in its decision to the "2005 SGEI Package", relying implicitly on the fact that the material requirements laid down in the two acts overlap to a large extent. Concerning the substantive condition related to the definition and the entrustment of the SGEI tasks, the Commission referred to its assessment of the first *Altmark* criterion. According to the Commission, the fact that the tasks were entrusted through different legal or administrative acts, or that certain elements, such as the territory covered by the SGEI tasks, derived from the applicable legal rules and in accordance with their purpose, did not put in question the existence of SGEI tasks.[94] Although the Commission asserted this approach to be settled practice, Hancher and Sauter underline that it is at odds with the 2005 SGEI Decision and the SGEI Framework, which require that the SGEI tasks are clearly defined and entrusted through an official act, in accordance with the principle of transparency.[95]

Concerning the control under Article 106(2) TFEU of the proportionality of the compensation for discharging an SGEI task, as established by an act of general application, the Commission referred to the following position taken by the GC in *BUPA*:

> [T]hat review is limited to ascertaining whether the compensation provided for is necessary in order for the SGEI in question to be capable of being performed in economically acceptable conditions (...), or whether, on the other hand, the measure in question is manifestly inappropriate by reference to the objective pursued (...)

The Commission recalled also that under Article 106(2) TFEU, public authorities may compensate SGEI providers up to 100 % of the net costs incurred plus a reasonable profit, irrespective of any consideration related to efficiency.[96] Hancher and Sauter have argued that, although this test may be undesirable from a perspective of competition, it is in line with the "balancing test" under Article 106(2) TFEU and with the 2005 SGEI Package.[97] However, as seen in Sect. 4.1.3.5, the GC annulled this decision, finding that the Commission should have initiated a formal procedure, as there were serious doubts regarding, first, the existence of a clearly defined mandate relating to the hospital and social public service missions specific to the IRIS hospitals, second, the existence of previously established compensation parameters and, third, the existence of procedures for avoiding

---

[94]Point 174.

[95]Hancher and Sauter 2013, p. 264.

[96]Point 199.

[97]Hancher and Sauter 2013, p. 267.

overcompensation in the funding of the public service missions. Also, there were also serious difficulties regarding the proportionality of the measures at issue.[98]

In sum, the Commission does not seem ready to systematically apply the fourth *Altmark* criterion as generously as the General Court did in *BUPA*, where the Court was satisfied that the equalisation system was regulated in a manner which excluded compensation of inefficiencies. This involves that the legality of funding depends on a "balance of interests" made under Article 106(2) TFEU. It is clear from the *Zorgverzekeringswet* and the *IRIS-H* decisions that this approach gives to the Commission a space of freedom in the exercise of its powers under Article 108(3) TFEU, which it may use differently depending on the cases at issue and its own policy agenda. It is also evident that the principles and rules it uses in this balance have a potential impact on the organisation and funding of social services in the Member States.

Seen in this perspective, the Commission's rules on state aid to SGEI must be seen as capable to harmonise social services on the basis of policy choices – in particular an economic approach of state aid. This harmonisation, initiated by the adoption of the 2005 SGEI Package, must be seen as imposed on the Commission itself, under the rule of law. It is therefore striking to find that, at odds with the material requirements in its 2005 SGEI Package that the act or acts of entrustment must specify, at least, the precise nature, scope and duration of the public service obligations imposed and the identity of the undertakings concerned,[99] the Commission, in practice, tends to accept a rather imprecise definition of SGEI tasks and very implicit modes of entrustment of SGEIs. This may be the main reason for the annulment of its *IRIS-H* decision by the General Court in *CBI*: the GC appears to expect the Commission to apply the principles and rules it has itself laid down.

7.2.3 Summing up on the Commission's Approach of State Aid Cases in the Field of Social Services

The Commission's practice examined in Sect. 7.2.2.1 shows that the Commission sees a necessity to combine references to competition case law and to free movement law when determining whether operators of social services in the field of medical care, health care insurance, education, and child-care constitute undertakings. The reason is submitted to be that the Court's functional approach in *Höfner* and the scarcity of the CJEU's case law on social services in the field of competition, clarifying the minimum criteria for the *Pavlov* definition of an economic activity ("an offer of goods or services on the market") to be fulfilled, does not offer sufficient legal certainty to apply state aid rules to public operators acting in

[98]Case T-137/10 *CBI* [decided on 7 November 2012, nyr], paras 308–309.

[99]See Recital 8 of Commission Decision 2005/842/EC and point 12 (a) and (b) of Community Framework 2005/C 297/04.

mixed systems. By using the test "provided for remuneration" instead of "offered on a market", the Commission shows that it sees those tests as equivalent. The problem is that it imports into competition law the "education exception" which characterizes the CJEU's case law on free movement, to the effect that the profit/not-for profit aims of the operator become relevant in competition, which is inconsistent with the case law of the Court. It is unsure whether the CJEU endorses all elements of the Commission's reasoning to determine the economic character of an activity. One thing is sure: given its approach, the Commission sends a signal that it may be easier for private operators to challenge the public funding of social services in Member States using mixed systems of social service supply.

Under such circumstances, the Commission's understanding of the application of state aid rules to SGEIs based on the *Altmark* ruling or on Article 106(2) TFEU, consolidated for the first time in its 2005 SGEI Package, becomes a prominent parameter for Member States in securing the legality of their welfare services' funding. The very adoption of this package signalled that the Commission decided to participate actively in the governance of social services in the Member States. It is therefore striking to find that, although the Commission's decisional practice implies that "the margins for public policy on public services in healthcare have been reduced", it is not only "flexible" as stressed by Sauter,[100] but in fact *more flexible than its own rules in the 2005 SGEI Package seem to allow.*

In a legal perspective, this "gap" may result from the lack of clear guidance from the CJEU on which impact the Treaty of Lisbon 2007/9 new constitutional framework should have on state aid rules applying to social services. The CJEU's approach is inconclusive, given the fact that the General Court adopted in *BUPA* and in *TV2/Denmark* an approach based on a lenient application of the *Altmark* criteria, but seemed to require a stricter approach from the Commission in *CBI*. Perhaps the Commission understood the GC's approach in *BUPA* as signalling that the post-Lisbon constitutional frame did not allow to apply an economic approach to the control of Member States financing of social services, and perhaps the meaning of *CBI* is to rectify this perception.

In a more political perspective, Sauter and Hancher claim that the Commission has taken an overly cautious approach by considering "all but the grossest violations of EU law out of bounds to intervention", especially in areas where the EU so far lacks what they call "extensive involvement" (some may call it "powers").[101] This caution is certainly related to the dialogue with the Member States and other stakeholders. In 2008, the Member States addressed their reports on the implementation of the Decision to the Commission, as required by the 2005 SGEI Package, and many Member States seized this occasion to give their views on the rules as a whole. Some of them referred to the Lisbon Treaty, and many to the difficulty to understand and apply the rules for public authorities in charge of social

[100] See 2014, p. 16, where Sauter adds that as a result conformity with EU norms is likely to increase.

[101] Hancher and Sauter 2013, p. 271.

services.[102] If anything, the *IRIS-H* case sheds light on the high complexity of the assessments required. The *IRIS* decision may have been an eye opener to the fact that a strict application and enforcement of the proportionality rule under Article 106(2) TFEU is extremely complex, time-consuming and administratively expensive, which can be quite problematic in case of litigation.

7.2.4 Some Important Issues Related to Social Services in the 2011 SGEI Package

The Commission presented its 2011 SGEI Package as an important instrument to address the economic crisis that broke out in 2008, stressing that it did not only make people across EU more dependent on "high quality public services", but that, as Member States were forced to reduce public budget deficits, there had to be a stronger focus on the economic efficiency of public spending and there was a "need to boost productivity across the board".[103] Thus, the 2011 SGEI Package appears as a more comprehensive and ostensibly more "EU policy-oriented" package than the 2005 SGEI Package.[104]

---

[102]Some Member States pointed at their efforts and costs to inform public authorities responsible for social services on these rules, and at their difficulty to assess whether the market for certain social services was purely local and whether in that case public funding would not be seen as aid. Some mentioned that local authorities tended to regard the very fact that an activity had to be organized on the basis of public funding as a sign that there was no "market" for it. Several Member States requested more emphasis on the CJEU's case law to the effect that social services are under certain conditions non-economic and therefore not covered by state aid rules, and emphasized that post Lisbon, the Commission had to consider how it would secure their discretion to organise and finance social services, considering that public procurement is not the only manner to secure the compliance of public service funding with EU state aid rules. Some reports also held that a single horizontal framework could not give sufficient precision on the way state aid rules could be complied with. It must be underlined that the views gathered here have been formulated in reports drafted in languages which the author of this study could most easily understand, i.e. from Germany, UK, France, and Sweden.

[103]Commission, "Reform of the EU State Aid Rules on Services of General Economic Interest" (Communication) COM (2011) 146 final, p. 4.

[104]The 2011 SGEI Package or "Almunia Package" consists of five instruments adopted by the European Commission between December 2011 and April 2012 for the modernization of SGEI rules: (1) Commission, "A Quality Framework for Services of General Interest in Europe" (Communication) COM(2011) 900 final (the "SGI Quality Framework") JO C/2012/102/35; (2) Commission Decision 2012/21/EU of 20 December 2011 on the application of Article 106(2) of the Treaty on the Functioning of the European Union to State aid in the form of public service compensation granted to certain undertakings entrusted with the operation of services of general economic interest (the "2011 SGEI Decision") [2012] OJ L7/3; (3) Commission, "Communication on the application of the European Union State aid rules to compensation granted for the provision of services of general economic interest" (the "2011 SGEI Communication") 2012/C 8/2; (4) Commission, "European Union framework for State aid in the form of public service compensation" (Communication) (the "2011 SGEI Framework") 2012/C

In a legal perspective, the 2011 SGEI Package has been adopted in a context where the importance of both procurement and state aid rules for the EU harmonisation of social services had become clear to most, but where very important issues had to be spelled out:

- The criteria determining that these services are economic
- The EU meaning of the concept of SGEI
- The state aid rules applying to social services.

According to the Commission, the Communication's aim is "to clarify the key concepts underlying the application of the State aid rules to public service compensation". Regarding the notion of "economic activity" for the purpose of the state aid rules, Buendia Sierra and Panero Rivas point particularly at points 12, 14, 13 and 37 of the Communication, which, in their view, displays some confusion between what constitutes an economic activity and the separate question of how the market is affected by the measure.[105] While their view is essentially shared here, the following remark may be added. Firstly, the Commission's explanations on this question reflect the casuistic approach of the CJEU; the Commission does not offer any systematic and pedagogical explanation of what the notions it uses—market, remuneration, competition—concretely mean and how they relate to each other. At the surface, the rule of law looks safe, but for the Member States to which this Communication is addressed, the notion of economic activity does not emerge as a concept understandable and workable by public authorities in the Member States. This is in particular so in light of the lack of clarity of the Commission's approach in its decision-making practice.

This is particularly problematic in a context where the control of state aid rules applicable to housing, hospitals and social services is decentralised. When the Commission states that "[w]hat is not a market activity today may turn into one in the future, and vice versa", it should clarify what can make this "vice versa" happen, as the Member States may legitimately be curious to know.[106] Regarding the notion of "economic activity", it is striking to observe that the Commission, in line with the analysis conducted in part I of this book, uses the notion of "provided for remuneration" as equivalent to "offered on a/the market", but does not explain *why* it considers these definitions of the notion of "economic activity" equivalent. In its decision practice, the Commission uses this equivalence to use free movement case law to fill in the lack of competition case law in the field of social service, but thereby also the oddity of the *Humbel* doctrine, with the result that for most social services the not-for-profit character of an entity's activity is irrelevant, while it magically becomes a relevant criterion in the field of school education.

Footnote 104 (continued)
8/03; and (5) Commission Regulation (EU) No 360/2012 of 25 April 2012 on the application of Articles 107 and 108 of the Treaty on the Functioning of the European Union to *de minimis* aid granted to undertakings providing services of general economic interest (the "SGEI de minimis Regulation") [2012] OJ L114/8.

[105]Point 12 of the Communication.

[106]See Buendia Sierra and Panero Rivas 2013, p. 134–135.

Regarding the meaning of the EU concept of SGEI, it is remarkable to find that the Commission spells out first that

> In the absence of specific Union rules defining the scope for the existence of an SGEI, Member States have a wide margin in defining a given service as an SGEI and *in granting compensation to the service provider*. The Commission's competence in this respect is limited to checking whether the Member State has made a manifest error when defining the service as an SGEI

and then considers that

> [i]t *would not be appropriate* to attach specific public service obligations to an activity which is already provided or can be provided satisfactorily and under conditions, such as price, objective quality characteristics, continuity and access to the service, consistent with the public interest, as defined by the State, by undertakings operating under normal market conditions. As for the question of whether a service can be provided by the market, the Commission's assessment is limited to checking whether the Member State has made a manifest error.

This stance is almost exactly repeated in the 2011 SGEI Framework, but this time the Commission *pronounces* that "Member States *cannot* attach specific public service obligations under such circumstances" (emphasis added).[107] It is submitted that this definition excludes that *public service tasks* may exist at the level of public authorities as SGEI missions which must be enabled to be achieved. Besides, unless the Commission clarifies that "conditions defined by the State" are SGIs, its stance may easily appear as a hopeless circular reasoning, where the national legislators are prevented from defining and imposing SGEI missions on public authorities in charge of supplying social services, and thereby make it *impossible for them to evaluate when the market fails*, i.e. when they must intervene on the market so that the SGI/SGEI missions can be achieved. In other words, this would mean that the market offer, even if based on public purchase, may not be affected by the way the legislator defines the service conditions regarded on the basis of ex ante decisions of what is *needed* by all and therefore may be publicly funded. As observed by Buendia Sierra, "the Commission is widening- or at least threatening to widen the traditional scope of the assessment of what constitutes a "true" SGEI".[108] The Commission's stance in the 2011 SGEI Framework leads Kavanagh to state that "if the service can be provided by the market at a price and level of access that are compatible with the public interest, it is *not* an SGEI".[109] He calls this a "reverse definition" of SGEI.

It is easy to see that understood in that manner (and Kavanagh is probably not alone in understanding it as so) the Commission's stance is at odds with the CJEU's (and the Commission's) recognition of the Member States' broad discretion to define SGEI missions, and thereby formulate what conditions of supply of social services they find appropriate in a policy perspective. How does the market know which conditions, "such as price, objective quality characteristics, continuity and access to the service", are "consistent with the public interest, as defined by

[107]Point 123 of the 2011 SGEI Framework.

[108]Buendia Sierra and Panero Rivas 2013, p. 136.

[109]Kavanagh 2013, p. 152.

the State", if this is not clear *ex-ante* in a transparent and clear definition of SGEI missions made by the legislator or by public authorities? The most problematic is perhaps not in that stance, but in the fact that it introduces ambiguously, through the notion of "public service obligations" which is so very close to the notion of SGEI that many hold them as synonyms, a *definition of SGEI* meant to govern *also* the Member States' discretion in the field of *social services*. This approach of discrete "small steps" towards an ever more restrictive definition of SGEIs, is arguably a constitutional issue. If the meaning of the EU concept of SGEI should ever be consolidated by any EU institution, it is submitted that it should be the EU legislator on the basis of Article 14 TFEU, and by no one else.

Regarding more specifically the fate of social services, the important step has been taken to include a number of them in the scope of the 2011 SGEI Decision, which exempts the Member States from the duty to notify their funding.[110] Article 2 provides that the social services exempted are SGEIs "meeting social needs as regards health and long term care, childcare, access to and reintegration into the labour market, social housing and the care and social inclusion of vulnerable groups". Van de Gronden and Rusu foresee that, as a result of the lack of definition of these services in the 2011 SGEI Decision, the Commission and the CJEU will be called upon to define these services, which eventually will lead to a European approach to important features of the social welfare states.[111]

To exempt from the duty of prior notification, the 2011 SGEI Decision imposes material conditions of transparency and proportionality which generally go further than the conditions provided by the 2005 SGEI Decision. First, the undertaking must be specifically entrusted with a public service obligation. The operation of the service of general economic interest must therefore be entrusted to the undertakings concerned by acts which may vary in form from one Member State to another, but which must include

(a) the content and duration of the public service obligations
(b) the undertaking and, where applicable, the territory concerned,
(c) the granting of any exclusive or special rights,
(d) a description of the compensation mechanism and the parameters for calculating, controlling and reviewing the compensation,
(e) the arrangements for avoiding and recovering any overcompensation and
(f) a reference to the Decision[112]

---

[110]At this stage in the development of the Treaties, another approach had arguably been difficult to justify in a subsidiarity perspective. It is stated under Recital 11 that "in the present economic conditions and at the current stage of development of the internal market", social services may require an amount of aid beyond the threshold of EUR 15 million to compensate for the public service costs, and thus that a large amount of compensation for social services does not necessarily produce a greater risk of distortions of competition.

[111]Van de Gronden and Rusu 2013, p. 213.

[112]Article 4 of Decision C (2011) 9380.

Importantly, the Decision applies only to public service obligations entrusted for a period not exceeding 10 years, unless the task implies a significant investment for the service provider, and needs to be amortized over a longer period in accordance with generally accepted accounting principles.[113]

Second, the amount of compensation must be limited to the costs of discharging the public service obligations and a reasonable rate of return. The eligible costs are all variable costs involved in providing the service, a proportionate contribution to fixed costs that are shared with other services, and necessary investment costs. The rate of return is determined with reference to the risk profile of the sector.[114] Third, the Member States must ensure that undertakings do not receive overcompensation. They must carry out regular checks on overcompensation, at least every 3 years during the period of entrustment and at the end of that period. Importantly, the undertakings concerned must commit to repayment of any overcompensation received.[115] Besides, the Decision requires that the Member States keep available, during the period of entrustment and for at least 10 years from the end of the period of entrustment, all the information necessary to determine whether the compensation granted is compatible with this Decision.[116]

For the state aid to be compatible with EU law, it is imperative that all these conditions are fulfilled, and thus it seems that the 2011 SGEI Package takes a decisive step towards an Europeanization of social services. Indeed, as observed by van de Gronden and Rusu, "significant bits and pieces" of a model for the delivery of social services are introduced by the Decision and they are certainly right in holding that "the path is paved for more binding EU measures in order to further build an EU model for social services".[117] However, it is submitted here that the perception of the 2011 SGEI Decision as a resolute step towards social services of quality, "with efficiency considerations and a certain degree of competition" is too simple.

A first issue, raised by Sanchez-Graells, is the tighter link in the Communication between procurement and state aid rules, which is relevant for the 2011 SGEI Decision.[118] In his view, the increased flexibility in the public procurement rules "frontally clashes with the assumption that they impose a tight procedure that works

---

[113]Article 2(2) of Decision C (2011) 9380. As an example of service where significant investments may be necessary, Recital 12 names social housing.

[114]Article 5 of Decision C (2011) 9380.

[115]Article 6(1) of Decision C (2011) 9380.

[116]This information must be available on request of the Commission, see Article 8 Decision C (2011) 9380.

[117]Van de Gronden and Rusu 2013, p. 214–215.

[118]2011 SGEI Communication, points 63–64: "The simplest way for public authorities to meet the fourth *Altmark* criterion is to conduct an open, transparent and non-discriminatory public procurement procedure in line with [Directive 2004/18 …] the conduct of such a public procurement procedure is often a mandatory requirement under existing Union rules. […] Also in cases where it is not a legal requirement, an open, transparent and non-discriminatory public procurement procedure is an appropriate method to compare different potential offers and set the compensation so as to exclude the presence of aid."

as a 'black box' and always ensures that the outcome is objective and excludes all possible economic advantages to the awardee of the contract". He believes that the feeble justification for the current position of the European Commission that compliance with EU public procurement rules excludes the risk of disguised State aid is in crisis.[119] In this respect, the Commission holds rather cryptically that for such systems "where it is not a legal requirement" to follow procurement procedures imposed by the 2014 procurement directives, "an open, transparent and non-discriminatory public procurement procedure" is an appropriate method to compare different potential offers and set the compensation so as to exclude the presence of aid.[120] One may wonder if this point addresses contracts under the thresholds or can also cover contract-based systems of choice, despite the fact, mentioned already, that voucher systems and systems of choice are (according to their recitals) exempted from the scope of the 2014 procurement directives.

Indeed, if procured contracts should be seen as an efficient alternative to otherwise complex and time consuming proportionality assessments, they should provide for transparent and equal competition. This supposes that the tasks are as clear and precise as possible. A very good reason for transparency and precision in the tasks' definition is not only operators' equal treatment, but at least as important should be the objective to secure access to quality services. Also, transparent and precise SGEI tasks are crucial for users and citizens to know what the publicly funded public service tasks are really meant to provide.

A second issue, underlined by Sauter, is the enforcement of the 2011 SGEI Package. Indeed, this is likely to be the very weak point of this emerging model, "as has always been the case for state aid and in the present context concerns in particular the services that will be covered by the new Decision".[121] This raises the question of which policy calculus may lead the Commission to formulate stricter material requirements for the definition, entrustment and control of SGEIs in the field of social services *and at the same time* decentralise the control of their enforcement to Member States, so far notoriously uninclined to respect these rules. In spite of the Commission's rhetoric of confidence in the loyalty of the Member States in performing this control, in practice decentralization gives the Member States considerable leeway not to fulfil their duty of loyalty towards EU law. Indeed, Baquero Cruz considers that such a move sacrifices "efficiency, sustainability and quality gains that a more vigorous enforcement of the State aid rules could bring to social services" as "there is almost nothing at the national level that can take care of distortions of competition with regard to those *seemingly* minor [social] services".[122]

[119]Sanchez-Graells 2013, p. 178.

[120]2011 SGEI Communication, point 64.

[121]Sauter 2012, p. 11. Sanchez-Graells agreed with this view, see Sanchez-Graells 2014, p. 3–4.

[122]Baquero-Cruz 2013, p. 309 and 310, emphasis and precision added.

7.3 Conclusions

The study conducted in this chapter gives ample evidence of the EU legislator's acknowledgement that EU procurement rules are covered by the principles in Article 14 TFEU and the SGI Protocol. The 2014 procurement directives reflect explicitly an awareness that EU procurement rules profoundly harmonise the principles and rules for the organisation of public services, and that their design must therefore respect the principle in Article 14 TFEU. This principle imposes on the EU legislator to take care that the procurement rules at least allow SGEIs to operate according to conditions, in particular financial and economic conditions, enabling them to achieve their missions. In this respect, and importantly, the 2014 procurement directives add to the SGI Protocol a stance that national, regional and local authorities have a wide freedom to *finance* SGEIs, which is indispensable for the very legitimacy of public procurement in many fields of activity.

In the new Public Sector Directive and the new Utilities Directive, the consolidation of the in-house and public-public cooperation exemptions is explicitly connected to Article 14 TFEU and the SGI Protocol, but in ambiguous terms. With respect to these Treaty provisions, public authorities are said to retain their power to decide if they want to perform *public functions* themselves. The notion of SGEI is also deafening silent in the provision of the new Concessions Directive laying down a "principle of free administration by public authorities", although this principle obviously transposes Treaty principles on SGEIs and the shared values of SGEIs in the SGI Protocol. The 2014 procurement directives convey an understanding of the concept of SGEI which is rather broad as relevant for the design of procurement rules, but not clearly acknowledging that the concept may cover *public service tasks devolved to contracting authorities*.

The lighter regime for social services is "officially" motivated in the 2014 procurement directives by the vague and politically malleable justification of their "specificities". However, the "principles of awarding contracts" for social services introduced in the Public Sector Directive and the Utilities Directive, oblige the Member States to allow their contracting authorities to take account of these "specificities", which are unofficially but evidently connected to "shared values" of SGEIs in the SGI Protocol and Article 14 TFEU. It is submitted that the only provision legitimising that the Union imposes such an obligation on the Member States is in fact Article 14 TFEU. It is also argued that by imposing this obligation, the Union fulfils its own duty to take care that SGEI missions can be achieved pursuant to Article 14 TFEU.

This leads to conclude that the 2014 procurement directives establish a principle of awarding contracts in the field of social services which is meant to enable the achievement of SGEI missions for the purpose of Article 14 TFEU, which does not fit with the rule in that provision that the Union and the Member States shall adopt regulations to establish such principles and rules. Confronted with the problem of legislating de facto on principles enabling SGEIs in the field of social services to fulfil their missions but on doing it on the "wrong" legal basis, the EU legislator chooses to "dilute" the notion of SGEI in the notion of "specificities". This dilution implies that, in the field of social services, the 2014 procurement directives put some pressure on the Member States to identify SGEIs in their systems, but do not force them to claim their existence to justify lighter procurement procedures, and what is more, invites them to include more, and more market-friendly, service conditions than those enumerated in the SGI Protocol.

By toning down that the lighter regime is necessary due to the existence of SGEI missions in the field of social services, the 2014 procurement directives prevent the conservation of "old SGEIs", and facilitate the Europeanisation of these services. At the same time, this approach weakens public procurement as a mode of entrustment preventing illegal state aid in the field of social services. As a consequence of this middle course approach ("un poco ma non troppo SGEIs"[123]) in the 2014 procurement directives, the proportionality of public funding of social services provided on the market depends heavily on which normative effect EU institutions give to Article 106(2) TFEU in applying state aid rules to social services. To render this instrument operative and legitimate, it is necessary for authorities in charge of their application that its basic concepts—in particular the notions of "economic activity" and "SGEI" are clarified.

Unfortunately, the 2014 procurement directives do not at all clarify what characterizes the difference between SGEIs and NESGIs, and the 2011 SGEI Package does not either deliver notable precision on the notion of "economic activity". The overview study of the Court's decision-making practice in the field of social services shows that it often has recourse to "cross-over reasoning" when determining the economic character of the activity at issue in a case, referring to competition case law and free movement case law in the same case. This approach seems to reflect well the conclusions in Chap. 2 that the two locutions "provided for remuneration" (free movement) and "offered on a/the market" (competition) are equivalent in the CJEU's case law, and in that sense it is argued that "crossing-over reasoning" is not a priori incorrect.

Nevertheless, the problem with the Commission's cross-over reasoning is that it is not explained, and that is not coherent with its view that the notion of "economic activity" may correspond to two different sets of criteria in the fields of free movement and of competition.[124] Another problem with the Commission's "cross-over reasoning" is that it transposes the oddity of the *Humbel* ruling from the field

---

[123]"Some SGEI but not too much SGEI" would be the translation of this metaphor inspired by instructions in Italian accompanying many musical scores.

[124]Regarding this issue, it is important to note that the Commission has issued a draft Notice on the notion of aid, where it anew tries to charter "what is an economic activity for the purpose of state aid rules" in different fields of activity. The Commission writes: "In the absence of a definition of economic activity in the Treaties, the case-law appears to follow different criteria for the application of internal market rules and for the application of competition law (Case C-519/04 P *Meca-Medina* [2006] ECR I-6991, para 30–33; Case C-350/07 *Kattner Stahlbau* [2009] ECR I-1513, paras 66, 72, 74 and 75; Opinion of Advocate General Poiares Maduro in Case C-205/03 P *FENIN* [2006] ECR I-6295, paras 50–51.)" Communication from the Commission, Draft Commission Notice on the notion of State aid pursuant to Article 107(1) TFEU, para 16. The inconsistency of the Commission's

of free movement law to the field of competition law, which increases the inconsistency of the criteria determining that an activity is economic in the meaning of competition law. In other words, the Commission does not give "the keys to the castle" to national authorities to which it has delegated the responsibility to control that public funding of many social services complies with EU state aid rules. And in the field of school education, it may be argued that the Commission gives the wrong keys.

In the consultation on the Commission's draft notice on the notion of "aid", it is argued by certain stakeholders that the Commission should more systematically refer to the case law of the CJEU rather than to its own decisions. A problem is however that with the CJEU's reluctance to articulate the notion of "economic activity", there is less reason for the Commission to turn to the Court for guidance and more reasons to fall under the pressure of many interest groups.[125] Due to the Court's understandable reluctance to spell explicitly and clearly how the EU concept of SGEI under Article 14 TFEU may be understood, the Commission gets also more leeway to formulate its own views on this concept, and has done so in the 2011 SGEI Package, where it professes a restrictive understanding of what the Member States may define as SGEI missions. This initiative is particularly problematic in a context where this view is not legitimated by the co-decision procedure. It is submitted that if the concept of SGEI should be restricted, it should at least be decided by the EU legislator on the basis of Article 14 TFEU. This argument seems to get support from Sauter, who considers that adopting state aid rules based on Article 108(3) TFEU is the most effective method to harmonize the regime applying to SGEIs, but reckons that legitimacy concerns may eventually force the Commission to propose a regulation based on Article 14 TFEU.[126]

Footnote 124 (continued)
view that the notion of economic activity may be dual with its own decision-making practice has been noted by King's College in London in its comments on the draft notice in the following terms: "Para 16 is rather ambiguous, as it does not explain to what extent the interpretation of Court of the notion of economy/non-economic activities in the context of internal market, competition and State aid is different. Further explanations are needed in this regard—or alternatively the paragraph should be deleted altogether. This is especially so as many footnotes in Sect. 2 of the draft Notice, refer interchangeably to internal market/competition case law suggesting an identical application."
Comments on the Draft Commission Notice on the notion of State aid pursuant to Article 107(1) TFEU from Centre of European Law, King's College London, available at http://ec.europa.eu/competition/consultations/2014_state_aid_notion/index_en.html, point 3.7.

[125]The final version of the Commission Notice on the notion of state aid, which was planned to be adopted in the second quarter of 2014, has not yet been adopted. In December 2014, Commissioner Vestager declared: "[a]s for the Communication on the Notion of Aid, the one piece of the SAM which has not yet been adopted, I have decided to take a moment for reflection at the start of my mandate. This document is too important for us to rush into a decision. But once I have had the chance to better assess where the limits of State aid control are, I intend to propose a Communication to the College for adoption."/…/ Speech at High Level Forum of Member States by Margrethe Vestager, Commissioner for Competition, 18 December 2014 available at http://ec.europa.eu/commission/20142019/vestager/announcements/speech-high-level-forum-member-states-margrethe-vestager-commissionercompetition-18-december-2014_en.

[126]Sauter 2014, p. 179.

Under such circumstances, where the two key concepts of "economic activity" and "SGEIs" are still so easy to litigate on, the decentralisation of state aid control in the field of social services becomes an issue. Fiedziuk observes that traditionally, "decentralisation of State aid control has been regarded as a controversial topic due to the high potential for political bias in decision-making on the national level in this field".[127] If one adds to this the Commission's rather lenient approach of what may be regarded as "clear and precise SGEI tasks", the risk of non-transparent and overcompensated public service tasks in the field of social services is arguably non-negligible, especially when many Member States wish to render this activity field more attractive to private operators. This risk is particularly high if the Member States are expected to rely on the guidance provided by the Draft Notice on the Notion of State Aid. In this draft Notice, Sanchez-Graells observes that the Commission blurs the boundaries of the notion of State aid at a conceptual level through an exemption for "purely local interventions", which creates uncertainty as to the limits and scope of application of the rules applicable to SGEI support and, "muddles the legal framework applicable to sponsorship of local public services".[128]

Decentralisation may be seen as a manner for the Commission to "focus on the important state aid issues", and let distortions of competition in the sensitive social services be dealt with by national authorities. It is however argued here that if decentralisation of state aid control leads to devitalise the principle of proportionality inherent to Article 106(2) TFEU in the public funding of social services, this may be detrimental for EU citizens' access to well-defined and reliable social rights. Indeed, the essence of the principle that the right of access to SGEIs must be respected when EU law is applied may be argued to be that there are clearly defined SGEI-tasks, which are transparent not only for authorities, but also for the citizens concerned, especially when the trend goes towards market control by users in that area of activity. If public funding of SGEI tasks is not subject to proportionality requirements, the tasks do not have to be precise. The more diffuse the tasks, the more the principle of "access to SGEIs" loses substance.

In sum, the legislation underpinning the Commission's "Quality Framework for SGIs" denotes much ambivalence to the emergence of SGEI as a "new" Treaty concept capable of structuring principles and rules in a process of Europeanisation of public services. The Commission and the EU legislator seem aware that the integration and growth of social service markets must show a certain degree of loyalty to the Treaty rules on SGIs, in particular on SGEIs, to be legitimate. At the same time, there are many signs that the EU legislator avoids tying up the procurement and state aid rules too clearly and functionally to the explicit or de facto existence of SGEIs in the Member States. In the field of social services, the EU procurement rules seem to show the way out from "welfare state SGEIs" towards lighter "market SGEIs" closer

[127]Fiedziuk 2013, p. 18.

[128]Sanchez-Graells 2015, p. 17. The treatment of local public services is also considered by Szyszczak as a significant aspect of the Draft Notice on the Notion of State Aid, see Szyszczak E., 2015, p. 681.

to the concept of universal service obligations. The Member States are invited to include in the shared values of SGEIs such values as "the specific needs of different categories of users, including disadvantaged and vulnerable groups", "the involvement and empowerment of users" and "innovation". These words rather promote (1) the acquisition with public funds of social services which are more differentiated according to "groups" where the disadvantaged are specified as a particular group, and (2) the rationalisation of production methods.

In this discourse, systems of choice and voucher systems fit well, and the fact that such systems have been exempted from the new procurement directives may be taken as a token that they are politically welcome at EU level. Seen in that perspective, the choice to decentralise the control of state aid rules applying to social services to the Member States can arguably not be seen in the simplistic light of a Commission victim of centrifugal forces, but rather of a European political development that receives support from a majority of governments in the Member States. If lighter "market SGIs" should develop on the financial platform of "welfare SGEIs", this can only be made by the Member States themselves, and to achieve this shift, they may need some leeway from a loyal application of the rules governing state aid to social services elaborated at EU level. Indeed, for Member States engaged in the marketization of social services, identifying the SGEI missions and tasks justifying the public financing hypothesis of market-based social services and applying the EU rules related to their externalization, may hamper the development of social service markets, and the case of Sweden, studied in Chaps. 8 and 9, appears to verify this.

References

Baquero-Cruz J (2013) Social services of general interest and the state aid rules. In: Neergaard U et al (eds) Social services of general interest in the EU. T.M.C. Asser Press, The Hague

Bordalo Faustino P (2014) Award criteria in the new EU directive on public procurement. Public procurement law review, pp 125–126

Buendia Sierra JL, Panero Rivas JM (2013) The almunia package: state aid and services of general economic interest. In: Szyszczak E, van de Gronden JW (eds) Financing services of general economic interest—reform and modernisation. T.M.C. Asser Press, The Hague

Burgi M (2014) Contracting authorities, in-house services and public authorities cooperation. In: Lichère F, Caranta R, Treumer S (eds) Modernizing public procurement: the new directive. DJØF Pusblishing, Copenhagen

Caranta R (2014) FIDE general report on public procurement law: limitations, opportunities and paradoxes. In: Neergaard U, Jacqueson C, Skovgaard Ølykke G (eds) The XXVI FIDE Congress in Copenhagen, 2014, Congress Publications, vol 3. DJØF Publishing, Copenhagen, pp 79–175. Accessed 31 December 2015 at http://www.aanbestedingsrecht.org/project/userfiles/Fide_rapport_2014.pdf

Fiedziuk NA (2013) Services of general economic interest in EU law: the role of the 'public service' exception in the light of recent developments in EU law. Wolf Legal Publishers, Oisterwijk

Hamilton GJ (2005) A new Private Universal Health Insurance in the Netherland. In: den Exter A (ed) Competitive Social Health Insurance Yearbook 2004. Erasmus University Press, Rotterdam

Hancher L, Sauter W (2013) This won't hurt a bit: the commission's approach to services of general economic interest and state aid to hospitals. In: Szyszczak E, van de Gronden JW (eds) Financing services of general economic interest—reform and modernization. T.M.C. Asser Press, The Hague

Janssen WA (2014) The institutionalised and non-institutionalised exemptions from EU public procurement Law: towards a more Coherent approach? Utrecht Law Review, vol 10, Issue 5. URN:NBN:NL:UI:10-1-115852

Kavanagh J (2013) Financing services of general interest: the European Commission's economic tests. In: Szyszczak E, van de Gronden JW (eds) Financing services of general economic interest—reform and modernization. T.M.C. Asser Press, The Hague

Sanchez-Graells A (2013) The Commission's modernisation agenda for procurement and SGEI. In: Szyszczak E, van de Gronden JW (eds) Financing services of general economic interest, reform and modernization. T.M.C. Asser Press, The Hague

Sanchez-Graells A (2014) Enforcement of state aid rules for services of general economic interest before public procurement review bodies and courts. The Competition Law Rev 10(1):3–34

Sanchez-Graells A (2015) Digging itself out of the hole? A critical assessment of the European Commission's attempt to revitalise state aid enforcement after the crisis. J Antitrust Enforcement, Forthcoming. 5 May, 2015 http://ssrn.com/abstract=2602798

Sauter W (2012) The commission's new SGEI package: the rules for state aid and the compensation of services of general economic interest. TILEC Discussion Paper No. 2012-018, http://ssrn.com/abstract=2044680

Sauter W (2014) The criterion of advantage in state aid: Altmark and services of general economic interest. TILEC Discussion Paper 2014-015, http://ssrn.com/abstract=2426230

Szyszczak E (2015) Services of general economic interest and state measures affecting competition. J Eur Competition Law Pract 6(9)

Van de Gronden JW (2009) Financing health care in EU law: do the European state aid rules write out an effective prescription for integrating competition law with health care? December 2009, vol 6, Issue 1, pp 5–29

Van de Gronden JW, Rusu CS (2013) The Altmark update and social services. In: Szyszczak E, van de Gronden JW (eds) Financing services of general economic interest, reform and modernization. T.M.C. Asser Press, The Hague

Wiggen J (2014) Directive 2014/24/EU: the new provision on co-operation in the public sector. Public Procurement Law Rev 3:83–93

Chapter 8
Social Services Under the Competence of Swedish Local and Regional Authorities: SGEI?

Abstract This chapter places the case study on Swedish systems of choice for social services, discussed in Chap. 9, in its broader legal context. It examines in particular whether Swedish public and competition law governing activities under the competence of local and regional authorities is conceptually apt to "receive" EU state aid rules applying to social services, and allows relating the cases studied in Chap. 9 to the broader question of the decentralised and increasingly individualised model of welfare services in Sweden.

Contents

C. Wehlander, *Services of General Economic Interest as a Constitutional Concept of EU Law*, Legal Issues of Services of General Interest,
DOI 10.1007/978-94-6265-117-3_8

The EU policy framed in the SGI Quality Framework, and the recently revised procurement and state aid rules applying to social services, suppose and require that public authorities in the Member States are able to assess (1) whether a social service, as provided in a specific regulatory context, is economic, and (2) whether it is attached to SGEIs. Given the lack of clear guidance from EU institutions on these two issues, this is a tricky mission, but arguably not a mission impossible. Sweden is an interesting case to look at closer, because in that Member State, many social services may be provided by both public and private operators in systems of choice, under public regulation and with public financing. In other words, the probability that these operators provide a service of general interest in the frame of an economic activity, is very high. However, as already mentioned, the Swedish legislator has so far avoided characterizing their statutory and contractual obligations as SGEI tasks, which suggests that EU principles and rules on SGEIs are perceived as problematic, not so much in a legal perspective, but rather in a policy perspective.

Before examining in Chap. 9 two specific systems of choice in Sweden, and the issues arising from the necessity to bring the rules they build on in compliance with EU competition and state aid principles related to market-based social services, the purpose of the present chapter is to provide a legal introduction to the case-study of elderly-care and school education in Swedish systems of choice. More to the point, the purpose of this chapter is (1) to evaluate whether social services in the Swedish public sector may generally be seen as SGIs and generally regarded as provided in the frame of an economic activity, and (2) to provide a legal background on local and regional authorities' wide competence in the field of social services, necessary for a better understanding of the analysis of two specific social services in systems of choice in Chap. 9, and to draw more general conclusions in Chap. 10. The focus is on social services under LRAs' competence, because the large majority of social services in the public sector have been devoluted to local and regional authorities, which have extensive possibilities to intervene in their organisation and financing.

Section 8.1 sets to evaluate whether social services under LRAs' competence may be taken to constitute services of general interest in the meaning of the SGI Protocol., and thus are "important" in EU law and EU policy. As the notion of SGI is even "less defined" in EU law than the notion of SGEI, the approach chosen is to track the criterion of "general interest" *in Swedish statutory and constitutional law* governing LRAs' competence for social services. This is logical, because the question is whether social services under LRAs' competence constitute "*Swedish* SGIs". In this part, a first premise is that the notion of "general interest" in services of general interest must have both a political meaning and a legal substance, even if this meaning and substance can certainly evolve with time. A second premise is that the principles of public action in the Swedish constitution are relevant to interpret the criterion of "general interest" founding LRAs' competence.

Section 8.2 evaluates at an overall level whether Swedish systems for the provision of social services under LRAs' competence are organized in a manner implying that the regulatory and statutory measures related to these services are covered by EU free movement and competition rules. Some light is also shed on the fact that several concepts determining the applicability of Swedish horizontal rules governing LRAs' competence to act on the market are construed in a manner that hardly reflects the market-character of social services in the Swedish public sector, and makes difficult to assess which measures and entities in the field of social services may be subject to EU market rules.

In this chapter, horizontal and sector law applicable to social services under LRA's competence is interpreted with the support of preparatory works, jurisprudence and doctrine, in accordance with the Swedish legal method. Section 8.1, a number of Swedish constitutional provisions related to public authorities' missions are examined, in particular those related to social rights, because they are relevant to apprehend the "essence" of the notion of "general interest" which is decisive to delineate LRAs' competence in Swedish law. To consider constitutional provisions formulating the objectives and missions of Swedish public authorities as relevant for interpretation open-ended Swedish legal concepts is unusual in Swedish practice. For the purpose of the question addressed by Sect. 8.1, it is however argued that the EU legal method, allowing to rely on "constitutional" objectives as principles guiding the interpretation of imprecise EU law concepts and provisions, may influence the "traditional" Swedish legal method.

Some terminology indications must also be given for the purpose of this chapter. Both local and regional authorities exist in Sweden, and are in the following generally referred to as "LRAs".[1] The terms "local authorities" and "regional authorities" are used instead when the issue examined is more directly related to the competence attributed to the local or regional levels of government. The terms "municipal entities" and "LRA-owned entities" are used synonymously in the meaning of entities which are "in-house" in the meaning of EU procurement law, in other words, either parts of LRAs' own administration producing services, or companies which they wholly own, and control, either alone or together with other LRAs.

8.1 Do Social Services Under LRAs' Competence Constitute SGI?

This section assesses whether social services under LRAs' competence may be regarded as SGIs in the meaning of the SGI Protocol. To this purpose, Sect. 8.1.1 introduces the notion of "general interest" as a fundamental ground for LRAs'

[1]See Chapter 1 Article 7 of the Instrument of Government. In Sweden, "local authorities" exist at two levels, local and regional, called municipalities and county councils, or alternatively "primary and secondary municipalities". 290 primary municipalities and 18 county councils. The Swedish constitution consists of four fundamental laws: the Instrument of Government, the Act of Succession, the Freedom of the Press Act and the Fundamental Law on Freedom of Expression. The principles governing specifically the powers and missions of local and regional authorities are laid down in Chapter 14 of the Instrument of Government.

powers in Swedish law, delineating their general competence together with several other principles and conditions. Section 8.1.2 outlines briefly the general (voluntary) and the special (mandatory) competence of LRAs in the field of social services. Section 8.1.3 explores the meaning of the criterion of "general interest" founding LRAs' competence, in the interpretative frame of Swedish constitutional provisions. Based on this analysis, Sect. 8.1.4 proposes an answer to the question addressed by this section.

8.1.1 General Interest Central for LRAs' Competence in the Local Government Act

LRAs' *general* competence is laid down in the following provision of the Swedish Local Government Act:

> Municipalities and county councils may themselves attend to matters of general interest which are connected with the area of the municipality or county council or with their members and which are not to be attended to solely by the state, another municipality, another county council or some other body.[2]

On the basis of this provision, a local or regional authority may decide to take *voluntary* responsibility and on that basis intervene in a given sector. Whatever their precise object, measures taken on the basis of the general competence must be in the general interest of the municipality or its members. As will be seen in Sect. 8.1.3, this provision is in line with the principle that LRAs are responsible for matters of public interest laid down in the Swedish Instrument of Government (Sw: *Regeringformen*), which is one of the four fundamental laws constituting the Swedish constitution.[3]

Several principles and rules limit LRAs' discretion when adopting measures in the frame of their competence. Thus, a local or regional authority's measures must be connected to its area or its members, and may not impede on the competence of other LRAs (the so called "localization principle"). Also, LRAs must treat their members equally, unless objective reasons allow otherwise, and may not take retroactive decisions which are detrimental to their members, unless there are very strong grounds for doing so (the so called "equality principle" and "non-retroactivity principle").[4] The requirement of a "general interest" does not mean that quantitatively significant needs must exist, but is instead assessed on the basis of whether

[2]Chapter 2 Section 1 of the Local Government Act (Sw: Kommunallagen (1991:900).

[3]The Swedish constitution consists of four fundamental laws: the Instrument of Government (Sw: Regeringsform (1974:152), the Act of Succession (Sw: Successionsordning (1810:0926)), the Freedom of the Press Act (Tryckfrihetsförordning (1949:105)), and the Fundamental Law on Freedom of Expression (Sw: Yttrandefrihetsgrundlag (1991:1469)).

[4]Chapter 2 Sections 2 and 3 of the Local Government Act.

it is appropriate, rational, reasonable, etc. that a local or regional authority attends to the matter in question. Unless provided for by specific law, LRAs may not support individuals, as such assistance as a general rule does not constitute a general interest.[5] These principles of localisation, equality and non-retroactivity, apply both to LRAs' general and mandatory competence, unless exemption from their application is provided by law.

LRAs may conduct commercial activities, as confirmed by the following provision:

> Municipalities and county councils may engage in commercial activity if it is conducted without a view to profit and is essentially concerned with providing communal amenities or services for the members of the municipality or county council.[6]

Thus, while a large portion of commercial activity is regarded in Swedish law as normally reserved to private undertakings, LRAs may traditionally engage in certain commercial activities such as waste management, energy, housing, sporting facilities, transport, harbours, airports, and parking places.[7] Where provided by LRAs, these services are to a large extent funded by fees and it cannot be excluded that they generate profits. However, as is clear from the provision above, LRAs' aim with conducting the activity must essentially be to provide their own members with certain facilities or services, and may in principle not be to seek profit (the so called "principle of non-speculation").

A number of principles govern how LRAs may organise, provide and finance activities and services in the frame of their competence. They may deliver services under their competence through their own administration, but they have also statutory powers to transfer the management of their activities to private legal or natural persons, through municipal companies or through external providers in the frame of contracts.[8] In the exercise of this power they must nevertheless respect the following rules. Activities which according to law or decree must be conducted by a municipal administration, and activities which include the exercise of authority, may not be transferred to private legal or natural persons unless provided for by special law.[9] Also, a local or regional authority which decides to transfer the

---

[5]Report of the commission of inquiry on the Local Government Act "Kommunallagskommittén" SOU 1947:53, s. 68.

[6]Chapter 2 Section 7 of the Local Government Act.

[7]This discretion was consolidated in 1991 and is provided in Chapter 2 Section 7 of the Local Government Act. A complication is which activities may be seen as commercial for the purpose of the Local Government Act., an issue examined under Sect. 8.2.2. Commercial activities regarded as in principle reserved to the private sector are commonly known in Swedish law practice as "the genuine business sector".

[8]Chapter 3 Section 16 first paragraph of the Local Government Act.

[9]Chapter 3 Section 16 second paragraph of the Local Government Act.

management of one of its activities to a limited company it wholly or partly owns, must keep control over the purpose and the major decisions of this company.[10]

LRAs may finance their tasks through taxes, but they may also levy charges for services and facilities.[11] However, for services or utilities which they are under an obligation to provide, they may not charge fees unless this is expressly prescribed.[12] Importantly, the general principle established by the Local Government Act is that they may not charge more than the cost of the services or utilities which they provide (the "prime cost principle").[13]

LRAs have a constitutional right to levy taxes. They are under a duty to respect budget balance rules[14] and must act—within their administrations and at the level of their companies—according to good economic management.[15] In particular, they must take care that their funds generate a good return and are administered with adequate security.[16] The principle of good economic management sets a general objective for municipal action, and it was not meant by the legislator that a municipal measure can be challenged simply on the basis of this principle. However it is not excluded that it can be invoked against measures which diverge extremely from what can be seen as good economic management.[17] Also, LRAs' powers to grant financial aid to undertakings is also strictly circumscribed. They may take measures, including aid, for the general promotion of enterprise in their municipality, but not grant aid to individual undertakings unless "there are very strong grounds for doing so".[18]

As is the case for the localization principle, the equality principle and the non-retroactivity principle, the economic principles governing LRAs' action as providers (not-for-profit, prime-cost) have been consolidated in the Local Government

[10]Chapter 3 Sections 17–18 of the Local Government Act. Regarding a company that it wholly owns, a local or regional authority must in particular take care that the company activity's purpose and the authority's competence justifying this activity are explicitly stated in the articles of association.

[11]It is well established in Swedish case law that a local or regional authority may decide to partly or wholly tax finance services or facilities for which there are no statutory charging principles (the so called "deficit-principle"). For references to this case law, see Lindquist 2011, pp. 177–178.

[12]Chapter 8 Section 3b of the Local Government Act. As will be seen, such prescription is made in several laws concerning social services.

[13]Chapter 8 Section 3c of the Local Government Act.

[14]Chapter 8 Sectin 5a of the Local Government Act. Very simplified, a year's negative result must be resorbed under the three following years.

[15]Chapter 8 Section 1 of the Local Government Act provides that "municipalities and county councils shall exercise good economic management in their activities and in activities conducted by the agency of other legal entities."

[16]Chapter 8 Section 2 of the Local Government Act.

[17]See decision of the administrative court in Malmö of 26 June 2013, case nr.13858-10. For instance, this principle imposes on local authorities to strive to get the best possible price when selling municipal property.

[18]Chapter 2 Section 8 of the Local Government Act.

Act. Although they are still approached as "general principles", several of them, in particular the prime cost principle, are growingly seen as problematic in sectors where private operators provide the same service as LRA-owned entities, which is now the general case in Sweden. A "market operator principle" has therefore been introduced in several laws, regulating activities where LRAs may act as providers on the basis of their general competence. The "market operator principle" obliges LRAs to derogate from the prime cost principle but also from the not-for-profit principle, regardless of whether the activity is conducted in administrative form or through private law companies.[19] Also, in accordance with the Act on Certain Municipal Competence (Sw: *lag (2009:47) om vissa kommunala befogenheter*), which extends LRAs' powers in the frame of their general competence, LRAs may also provide collective transportation, ambulance transport, office industrial buildings and service sector premises, on the condition that they do so in accordance with the "market operator principle", and thus by derogation from the principles of not-for-profit and prime-cost.[20] In certain sectors, they may also derogate from the equality principle and from the localization principle.[21]

Thus, the very principle that LRAs may conduct such commercial activities has so far not been challenged as such. Indeed, the general interest motivating LRAs' measures must be connected to their municipality, but it is often linked to general interests founding social or environmental policies set at global, European or national level. Such policies build a *non-binding political expectation*—by international bodies, national authorities, their voters, or varied interest groups—that LRAs will loyally endorse and implement them in the frame of their competence. LRAs are thus expected to efficiently contribute, *if appropriate as providers*, to the achievement of environmental goals (often connected to measurable standards defined at national, EU or international level), social goals (cohesion and social peace, access to housing, employment, minimum living standard) and economic goals (good infrastructure for growth, welfare efficiency through competition, regional development, public finances in balance).

Both the Local Government Act and the Instrument of Government mention that LRAs' powers and obligations follow also from special law.[22] Indeed, a large

---

[19]Government Bill on LRAs' competence, *Kommunala kompetensfrågor* m.m., proposition 2008/09:21, p. 58.

[20]See Section 3 of the Act on Certain Municipal Competence (in Sw: *Lag (2009:47) om vissa kommunala befogenheter*). On the basis of this Act, LRAs may also provide tourism infrastructures, export expertise on municipal administration, etc.

[21]In some traditional municipal sectors, LRAs acting as providers are not only obliged to act business like but may also derogate from the localization principle laid down in the Act on Local Government. This is for instance the case according to Chapter 7 Sections 1 and 2 in the Swedish Act on Electricity (in Sw: *Ellag (1997:857)*), Section 39 of the Distance Heating Act (in Sw: *Fvärrvärmelag (2008:263)*) or Section 57 of the Public Water Services Act (in Sw: *Lag (2006:412) om allmänna vattentjänster*). The reason for this exception is often of technical nature.

[22]Chapter 2 Section 4 Local Government Act.

amount of Acts regulating activities in the public sector establish what is called LRAs' "special competence" or "mandatory competence", and in fact impose on LRAs obligations to ensure access to certain services or infrastructures under conditions determined by law. In these sector laws, LRAs are not only required to conduct planning and supervisory activities, in particular physical planning and certain environmental control of certain industrial and commercial activities). They also have to *ensure the supply* of public services and facilities as education, healthcare, social services as well as limited social security, emergency services, library, collective transport, water and waste management. In other words, sector-specific Swedish frameworks in social and environmental fields impose on LRAs a *legal obligation to fulfil tasks of general interest*.

In as much as the principles governing LRAs' general competence in the Local Government Act come into conflict with provisions in sector laws governing their mandatory competence, the latter prevail as *lex specialis*. As a result of the cohabitation of old "general principles" in the Local Government Act and of many exemptions in special law, LRAs' margin of discretion as operators has been limited: they must in all the more fields behave as market economy market investors and at the same time in the general interest of their members or of their territory, a circle which can be tricky to square.[23]

8.1.2 LRAs' General and Special Competence for Social Services

Based on their *general* competence, *local* authorities may conduct commercial activities, most notably in the fields of housing and ambulance transport. Concerning housing, LRAs' discretion to act as providers on the market on the basis of their general competence has been and is still of paramount importance. In that sector, it is important to be aware of the distinction between housing measures based on local authorities' voluntary respectively local authorities' mandatory

[23]Cyndecka holds that "being profit-motivated or pursuing economic objectives is the fundamental characteristic of a behavior that is typical of private market operators" but that "the state is by no means precluded from pursuing [non-economic objectives] when acting as a private investor would", as in particular, "a public investor does not need to be guided by profitability in the short term. It may be so also in a medium or long term while pursuing a structural policy, either general or sectoral". See Cyndecka 2015, p. 319. To argue that a long-term profitability may comply with the market economy investor principle (MEIP) appears to be a convenient way to "square the circle", and prevent that public authorities' decisions to invest for instance in housing in geographic areas where profitability is inexistent, and where a private investor would not invest a penny, are challenged on the ground that they are incompatible with the MEIP imposed on their behaviour. Another manner to address the problem, arguably more solid legally, is to admit that in case for-profit is required from public investors as a general rule, market failure may necessitate a derogation from the MEIP under Article 106(2) TFEU.

competence. Local authorities' general competence allows them to voluntary decide to *provide* housing, in particular rental housing, in the general interest of their municipality or of their members. By contrast, they have a mandatory competence to supply housing, under certain conditions, to elderly persons and to disabled persons. Regarding ambulance transport, it may be noted that securing the supply of such services is a mandatory competence of *regional* authorities, not of local authorities, but that the latter may offer ambulance transport services to regional authorities—in the frame of procurement procedures—and thereby must respect the market operator principle which allows that they derogate from the localization principle and in fact prohibits that they apply the prime cost principle.

The most important part of LRAs' competence in the field of social services is however based on *special* legislation. According to several framework laws, LRAs have thus a *mandatory* competence for a broad range of social services. In the field of health care, most of the responsibility for securing the supply of services is assigned to regional authorities. [24] Local authorities have also been attributed mandatory missions in the field of health care, but they must also secure the supply of childcare,[25] elderly care,[26] support for disabled persons,[27] preschools, primary and secondary education,[28] emergency services and emergency preparedness, economic support for their members in temporary need, specific forms of housing to several groups of persons in particular special elderly housing,[29] family support services[30] and housing support in ordinary housing.[31]

---

[24]These missions are mainly regulated by the Health and Medical Services Act (Sw: *Hälso- och sjukvårdslag (1982:763)*), but also for instance by other acts such as the Act on Care of Addicts under certain circumstances (Sw: *lag (1988:870) om vård av missbrukare i vissa fall*); the Act on Involuntary Commitment (Sw: *lag (1991:1128) om psykiatrisk tvångsvård*); the Act on Forensic Psychiatry (Sw: *lag (1991:1129) om rättspsykiatrisk vård*).

[25]These missions are generally regulated by the Social Services Act (Sw: *Socialtjäntlag (2001:453)*) but also by other pieces of legislation, for instance, for children in problematic family or social situation, the Act on Care of certain Young Persons (Sw: *Lag (1990:52) med särskilda bestämmelser om vård av unga*).

[26]The task consists in supplying assistance at home to elderly persons in need of it, see Chapter 5 Section 5 first paragraph in the Social Services Act.

[27]This task is subject to provisions in the Social Services Act, named above, but also in other legislation such as the Act on support and service to persons with disabilities (Sw: *lag (1993:387) om stöd och service till vissa funktionshindrade*).

[28]Education Act (Sw: *Skollag (2010:800)*).

[29]This task consists in setting up special housing for elderly persons in need of special care, see Chapter 5 Section 5 second paragraph in the Social Services Act.

[30]Chapter 5 Section 3 in the Social Service. The main task within this social service is to contribute to solving conflicts and problems in family and couple relations through therapeutic conversation.

[31]To persons living in their own ordinary housing who need support because of handicap or addiction problems.

In this decentralized model, and based on the principle of self-government, LRAs have a margin of discretion in fulfilling their missions. Their tasks in the field of social services are regulated through framework laws, in particular the Health and Medical Services Act and the Social Services Act. This type of legislation does not confer enforceable rights, but puts instead on local or regional authorities obligations to secure that their members have access to subsidized social services according to their need. In other words, the individual situation is decisive for the service received.[32]

LRAs' missions based on their general competence and on their mandatory competence in special laws are fundamentally related to the duties of public authorities—at national, regional or local level—laid down in Chapter 1 Section 2 of the Instrument of Government.

8.1.3 Public Authorities' Duty to Secure and Promote Social Rights: A "Principle" of Swedish Constitutional Law

In the frame of the latest constitutional reform which came into force in 2010, the foundational principles on local and regional authorities have been completed and gathered in a specific chapter (Chapter 14) on local authorities in the Instrument of Government (IG). One of the modified provisions gives a general definition of LRAs' competence:

> The local authorities are responsible for local and regional matters of public interest on the principle of local self-government. More detailed rules on this are laid down in law. By the same principle, the local authorities are also responsible for other matters laid down in law.[33]

This provision's primary aim was to clarify that the principle of local self-government applies to LRAs' general *and* mandatory competence. However, it constitutionalises at the same time the fact that LRAs' responsibility for "matters of public interest" consists both of voluntary tasks under their general competence, and mandatory tasks under their competence in special law. It is important to note that the term "public" is used in the English version of the Instrument of Government accessible on the site of the Swedish government, as a translation of the Swedish word "allmän". However, the Swedish word "allmän" is also routinely translated by the English word "general". Hence, the English version can arguably also be "matters of *general* interest". As already mentioned, to finance their activities and tasks of general interest, LRAs' economic powers include a right to levy tax, which is constitutionally enshrined.[34]

---

[32]Whether the public authorities or the individuals themselves may evaluate this need is another question.

[33]Chapter 14 Article 2 of the Instrument of Government.

[34]Chapter 2 Section 5 of the Local Government Act, referring to Chapter 14 Section 4 Instrument of Government.

While the notion of "general interest" in Chapter 14 Section 2 IG is open-ended, its constitutional substance must arguably be interpreted in the light of the very first provisions of the Instrument of Government, spelling the fundamental principles, values and objectives which govern public power in Swedish law. In particular, Chapter 1 Article 2 IG reads as follows:

> Public power shall be exercised with respect for the equal worth of all and the liberty and dignity of the individual.
>
> The personal, economic and cultural welfare of the individual shall be fundamental aims of public activity. In particular, the public institutions shall secure the right to employment, housing and education, and shall promote social care and social security, as well as favourable conditions for good health. The public institutions shall promote sustainable development leading to a good environment for present and future generations.
>
> The public institutions shall promote the ideals of democracy as guidelines in all sectors of society and protect the private and family lives of the individual. The public institutions shall promote the opportunity for all to attain participation and equality in society and for the rights of the child to be safeguarded. The public institutions shall combat discrimination of persons on grounds of gender, colour, national or ethnic origin, linguistic or religious affiliation, functional disability, sexual orientation, age or other circumstance affecting the individual.
>
> The opportunities of the Sami people and ethnic, linguistic and religious minorities to preserve and develop a cultural and social life of their own shall be promoted.[35]

Introduced in 1976 in the Instrument of Government adopted in 1974, this provision, put forward by the commission of inquiry on fundamental freedoms and rights, is the result of a political compromise.[36] In short, it may be seen as the condition which socio-democrats put for introducing in the Swedish constitution a specific chapter on fundamental rights and freedoms and a provision on judicial review which reinforced the rule of law in Sweden but could also restrict parliamentary powers.[37]

Importantly, although the Instrument of Government has been reformed several times, this "political" provision stands relatively unchanged since more than 40 years in the very first chapter of the Swedish constitution.[38] It is provided in the

---

[35]Chapter 1 Article 2 Instrument of Government.

[36]A commission of inquiry was set up directly after the adoption of a new Instrument of Government to examine in detail the constitutional status of fundamental freedoms and rights. It was this commission that proposed the introduction of the provision under in Chapter 1 Section 2 of the Instrument of Government, see report of the commission of inquiry on fundamental rights "Medborgerliga fri- och rättigheter—Regeringsformen" SOU 1975:75.

[37]For a very detailed account of the political and legal debates underpinning the preparatory works that eventually led to the introduction of the provision in Chapter 1 Section 2 of the Swedish Instrument of Government, see Lind 2009, pp. 52–76.

[38]The following modifications were introduced through the latest broad modification of the Instrument of Government, in force since 2010: under para 2 "secure the right to health" was replaced by "promote favourable conditions for good health", in para 4 a specific duty to promote the opportunity "for the rights of the child to be safeguarded" was introduced, in para 5 the Sami people is specifically named.

second paragraph that public authorities have a "duty to secure" a number of social rights, but Lind observes that the status of social rights has so far been neither analysed nor problematized in the Swedish constitutional process.[39] Nevertheless, a point of departure of the commission of inquiry which proposed the introduction of the provision was that, in addition to classical fundamental freedoms and rights destined essentially to protect an individual *against* the state, some countries had included in their constitution "social rights" destined essentially to protect an individual *with the help* of the state. The commission of inquiry on fundamental freedoms and rights found natural to establish rights to employment, education, health care and social care in the Swedish constitution etc., as in its view they expressed both a modern society's care for the individual person, and principles of great importance for individual welfare.[40] Having emphasized the role of fundamental freedoms and rights for democracy, the commission of inquiry found obvious that a certain material standard of life for individual persons was necessary for a democratic government, and therefore that certain social and economic rights were necessary, or at least very important in order to give citizens a possibility to take part in the political work and an interest in maintaining democracy. In this sense, promoting welfare was regarded as constituting a part of political democracy.[41]

However, it was repeatedly emphasized by the commission of inquiry on fundamental freedoms and rights that the provision in Chapter 1 Article 2 IG is not a legal rule formulating what public powers *must* do, but instead a declaration of objectives formulating what public powers *ought to* do.[42] Consequently, whether public powers fulfil these objectives can only be submitted to a political control and not to a legal control. As the duty to treat individuals as equals, the social rights laid down in Chapter 1 Section 2 IG may be understood as a *principle* directed to the legislator which, in the commission of inquiry's view, should not be absent from a constitution. Hence, neither this principle nor the social rights written down in the Swedish constitution are per se binding on the state, which is understandable given the life expectancy of a constitution and the variation of political and economic conditions which may be expected in a democratic state.[43]

---

[39]Lind shows that the preparatory works and proposals discussing this provision only give a summary analysis of its practical significance. See Lind 2009, p. 76.

[40]Report of the commission of inquiry on fundamental rights "Medborgerliga fri- och rättigheter—Regeringsformen" SOU 1975:75, p. 163.

[41]Ibid.

[42]Even socio-democrats, who drove forward the adoption of this constitutional provision, were against binding rules both on positive and negative rights. Their view was that it could freeze political reforms, and that the establishment of a minimum level in the Swedish constitution would not give a correct picture of further developments in that field. See Lind 2009, p. 73.

[43]Back in 1978, Petrén went further and held that *no law* can guarantee a right to good care, employment, housing etc., a statement which may be questioned, in particular in the light of the Swedish Act on support and service to persons with disabilities (Sw: *lag (1993:387) om stöd och service till vissa funktionshindrade*), which gives disabled persons an opposable right to assistance and support allowing them to a good standard of life. See Petrén 1978, p. 29.

Petrén, who observed and deplored that the Swedish judiciary had at that time no tradition to take the constitution seriously and control its application, expressed doubts as to whether it was in principle right to lay down in a democratic constitution meant to be valid over a long period of time certain "political objectives rather limited in time".[44] At any rate, in 2003, the protection of the environment and of the rights of minorities were added to Chapter 1 Section 2 IG. The government Bill which proposed this modification held that this constitutional provision, although it does not confer any personal rights, may be legally relevant in the interpretation of diverse statutory rules.[45]

But is it really so that the provision in Chapter 1 Section 2 IG has no legal meaning at all and mostly fulfils a "psychological" function, by mobilizing the public opinion to defend social rights?[46] The answer seems clearly to be "no". In fact, the commission of inquiry on fundamental freedoms and rights explained that this provision, spelling the fundamental values of Swedish democracy profoundly anchored in the Swedish society, may be regarded as a *substantial* equivalent to Chapter 1 Section 1 IG establishing that Swedish democracy is founded on free formation of opinion and universal and equal suffrage, and realized through (a) a representative and parliamentary form of government and (b) local self-government.[47] And if there is, as suggested by the commission of inquiry, normative"substance" to Chapter 1 Section 2 IG, it is submitted here that it is a tangible expression of what may be regarded as "matters of general interest", in particular such "matters of general interest" which LRAs may attend. In other words, it is submitted that the objectives and missions enunciated in Chapter 1 Section 2 IG, in particular the duty to secure social rights, constitute general interests explicitly promoted by Swedish constitutional law.

The perception that certain social services are of general interest in the sense that securing access to such services legitimates public powers, is clear for instance from the government Bill on the 2010 reform of the framework for municipal housing companies. Reminding that local authorities, in accordance with the Local Government Act, may voluntarily engage in activities in the general interest of their territory or their members, the government underlined that Chapter 1 Section 2 IG can be seen as expressing the *importance* of housing and that public powers must support access to housing.[48] The "importance" of housing for individual welfare implies that securing access to this service is in the general interest and motivates that LRAs have powers, on the basis of their general competence, to voluntary

[44]Petrén 1978, pp. 30–31.

[45]Government Bill on certain modifications to the Instrument of government, *Ändringar i regeringsformen—samarbetet i EU m.m.*, proposition 2001/02:72, pp. 15–16.

[46]Such a psychological effect was envisaged in the report of the commission of inquiry on fundamental rights "Medborgerliga fri- och rättigheter—Regeringsformen" SOU 1975:75, p. 13.

[47]Report of the commission of inquiry on fundamental freedoms and rights "Medborgerliga fri- och rättigheter—Regeringsformen" SOU 1975:75, pp. 183–184.

[48]Government Bill on municipal housing companies, *Allmännyttiga kommunala bostadsaktiebolag och reformerade hyressättningsregler*, proposition 2009/10:185, pp. 12–13.

engage in providing rental housing on the market. Likewise, the “importance” of other objectives in Chapter 1 Section 2 IG, often connected to social or environmental policies at global, European or national level, creates an already mentioned political expectation that LRAs will voluntarily intervene in certain economic sectors not or not fully harmonized at national or EU level.

Regarding LRAs’ responsibility for “other matters laid down in law”—their mandatory tasks—it is not specified in Chapter 14 Section 2 IG quoted above whether they also must be of general interest. Nevertheless it seems clear that such “other matters”—tasks and powers defined by the national legislator—must also be in the general interest as they are defined in sector laws constituting *lex specialis* to the Local Government Act, and fundamentally legitimated by the principles enumerated in Chapter 1 Section 2 IG.[49] And thus, services for which LRAs are responsible for on the basis of their mandatory competence are in the general interest, though *not specifically* of their own territory or of their own members.

On this background, it may be questioned whether Sweden’s membership in the EU can affect Swedish public authorities’ fundamental missions in accordance with Chapter 1 Section 2 IG. Since 2010, Sweden’s membership in the EU is mentioned in the introductory chapter on the basic principles in Chapter 1 Article 10 IG, reading as follows

> Sweden is a member of the European Union. Sweden also participates in international cooperation within the framework of the United Nations and the Council of Europe, and in other contexts.

By introducing this provision, the objective was to signal clearly to the Constitution’s readers that Sweden plays an active role in extensive international cooperation that has a major impact on Swedish society, the EU membership being Sweden’s most significant area of cooperation.

As a consequence of this “small revolutionary step”,[50] Sweden’s EU membership is constitutionalised, which is explicitly meant by the Swedish legislator to draw attention to the political and legal consequences on the Swedish society following from the fact of EU membership. What is less clear is whether, by constitutionalising EU membership, the Swedish legislator intended to increase the dignity of EU objectives, compared to values and principles in Swedish law. In other words, does the new provision in Chapter 1 Section 10 IG per se imply that the Swedish State has a stronger duty of loyalty to EU values and objectives than to

[49]This is particularly clear from Chapter 3 Section 2 Para 2 in the Swedish Act on Social Services laying down that “the Social board must in the frame of its activity promote the individual’s right to labour, housing and education.”

[50]See the report of the commission of inquiry on the reform of the constitution “En reformerad grundlag” SOU 2008:125 del 1, pp. 47–48. Bergström has described the introduction of this provision as a “small revolutionary step”, because it gives constitutional status to the Sweden’s membership in the EU. Bergström 2009, p. 204; see also the Comments from the Swedish Institute for European Political Studies (Sieps) on the report of the commission of inquiry on the reform of the Swedish constitution “En reformerad grundlag” SOU 2008:125, Dnr 16/2009, http://www.sieps.se/sites/default/files/Remissvar_sou2008_125.pdf, accessed 27 February 2015.

Swedish constitutional values and objectives? As evoked by Wenander, there is a debate between legal scholars believing that certain provisions in the Swedish constitution should be seen as simply descriptive of a political agreement, and other legal scholars considering that constitutional provisions must be regarded as having *as such* normative substance. Wenander, clearly part of the latter group, considers that what is legally interesting is to assess which legal meaning a provision consolidating this political compromise may be taken to have.[51]

While Wenander's view is shared here, it goes beyond the frame of this study to analyse in depth the normative strength of EU objectives and values in Swedish law. However, it is argued that nothing—even the fact that EU law has precedence over national law in case of conflict—seems to support a priori that the duty to respect EU objectives and fundamental freedoms has a *higher* normative dignity in Swedish law than the duty to promote Swedish values and social rights laid down in the Swedish constitution, in particular in policy fields where the principles of Chapter 1 Section 2 IG are directly relevant for Swedish legislation. What may have happened with the constitutionalisation of Sweden's EU membership is that the two normative sets in Chapter 1 IG—public authorities' loyalty to the values and social rights enumerated in Section 2 and public authorities' loyalty to the values and rights implicitly following from EU membership—are more openly "on par" than before. Thus, a paradox can be that by constitutionalising EU membership as a "political fact", the Swedish legislator has also reminded the "political fact" in Chapter 1 Section 2 IG, the latter being at least as constitutional as the former and certainly not less democratically anchored. As a result, if the values and principles for public action formulated in Chapter 1 Section 2 IG have some normative value in Swedish law, they have been given *more* visibility by the implicit reference to EU values and objectives in Chapter 1 Section 10 IG.

It is important to keep in mind that the EU legal system and the Swedish legal system base public authorities' action on separate institutional grounds. By contrast with Union institutions, Swedish public authorities have no constitutional mission to establish an internal market, including a system ensuring that competition is not distorted. The constitutional missions of Swedish public authorities, including the State, are laid down in the Instrument of Government (IG) and consist primarily in securing societal objectives and social rights. Consequently, the legitimacy of legal frameworks decided by the Swedish state's parliamentary representatives and defining LRAs' powers and obligations in certain environmental or social fields of activity, depends on their coherence with the fundamental objectives and missions of public powers enunciated under Chapter 1 Article 2 of the Instrument of Government. The Swedish welfare frameworks found their fundamental legitimacy on the public powers' constitutional welfare missions and objectives, in particular the mission to secure social rights, in the respect of the equal worth of all and the liberty and dignity of the individual. In other words, it may be doubted that constitutionalising

[51]Wenander 2011, p. 549, and his references to legal scholars' positions in this debate, under footnote 68.

Sweden's EU membership has the effect to transform the Swedish constitution into an economic constitution. It is namely difficult to imagine why constitutionalising EU membership can restrict the political freedom of the Swedish legislator—and beyond the Swedish citizens—more than the constitutionalisation of public missions decided by these citizens, even if it was a long time ago. Another thing is that this double loyalty to Swedish constitutional missions and EU constitutional missions, requires that the Swedish legislator thinks—literally—twice.

8.1.4 Preliminary Conclusion

On the background of the Swedish constitutional and statutory rules outlined in Sects. 8.1.1 to 8.1.3, it is submitted that social services under LRAs' competence constitute services of general interest in the meaning of EU law. The duty for public authorities to secure social rights does not per se found individual opposable rights, but must instead be seen as a normative principle, connected by the Swedish legislator to the notion of "social contract" and explicitly meant by the Swedish legislator to contribute to social cohesion.[52] The social rights formulated in Chapter 1 Section 2 IG constitute a frame for legislative work and administrative decision-making which is primarily addressed to the legislator. By placing certain social rights under LRAs' mandatory competence, the legislator must primarily fulfil *its own* duty as public power to promote access to these rights. The Swedish legislator must *also*, in the exercise of its legislative power related to LRAs' responsibility, respect the equal worth of all and the liberty and dignity of the individual.

8.2 Are Social Services Within LRAs' Competence Covered by EU Law on Free Movement and Competition (Including State Aid)?

As services of general interest, social services within LRAs' competence may be subject to EU competition and state aid rules, depending on how they are regulated in Swedish law. This section outlines therefore first how these social services may be

[52]In the government Bill on the Social Services Act, it was recalled that some form of legal regulation giving individuals a right to livelihood support has existed since the 18th century, with the Enlightenment's idea that the state has welfare duties towards its citizens, this "membership" implying rights but also duties. It also underlined that the notion of "social rights" had been used as a legislative instrument to build up the welfare state, by expressing the need of distributing society's resources and as an instrument to solve conflicts between the interests of individual and of public authorities. See government Bill on the Social Services Act, *Ny socialtjänstlag m.m.*, proposition 2000/01:80, p. 81. The goal of cohesion is confirmed by the existence of a compensation system equalizing LRAs' economic resources and allowing them to supply their members with equivalent standards of welfare services.

organised in Sweden. In the second part of this section, an attempt is made to show how a number of concepts delineating the applicability of horizontal Swedish competition and aid rules to LRAs' activity as operators and financiers of social services contribute to delay the acknowledgement of the economic character of many social services under LRAs' competence, and of the necessity to comply with EU market rules, in particular state aid rules. In the last part, a general assessment of the economic character of social services within LRAs' is conducted, before the question is approached in more depth and precision in the frame of the case studies in Chap. 9.

8.2.1 Organisation of Social Services Under LRA's Competence with a Focus on Systems of Choice

Regarding most social services within their mandatory competence, LRAs may decide whether the service will be provided in-house or by private entities. In fact, as a result of the legal and political developments in Sweden, most tax-funded social services are today provided by both public and private operators, known as "mixed systems". When the service is provided by external entities, the Swedish rules on procurement procedures must normally apply. The Swedish procurement rules implement the EU procurement directives, but they also include autonomous rules concerning in particular the procurement of social services and services under the directives' threshold values, for which they put stricter procedure requirements on contracting authorities than the directives.[53] Instead of these procurement procedures, LRAs may also choose to open for competition social services covered by the Act on Systems of Choice (LOV). LRAs' *freedom* to use LOV-based systems is subject to two important exceptions. First, regional authorities are under a statutory obligation to organise publicly funded primary care so that all their members can choose provider within the whole authority's territory, and thereby to apply LOV.[54] Second, there is an extensive system of free choice in the field of school education, but this system is not covered by LOV.

In LOV-based systems, individual users may choose among providers which are part to the system.[55] LRAs having introduced LOV-based systems of choice

---

[53]The only general exception from the obligation to apply the procedures provided for by the Swedish procurement rules is for low-value contracts, i.e. contracts with a value of less than 28 % of the threshold values.

[54]Section 5 paras 2 and 4 of the Health and Medical Services Act.

[55]Chapter 1 Section 1 second paragraph of the Act on Systems of Choice (Sw: *lag (2008:962) om valfrihetssystem*, LOV) entered into force 1st January 2009. This provision clarifies also that the contracting authority does not need to apply the same system of choice within all services affected. The Act does not only cover social services under LRAs' competence. The Swedish Public Employment Service may apply the Act when procuring services within its labour-market activities, and since 1 May 2010, establishment of systems of choice is mandatory for some of its activities focusing on recently arrived immigrants. The Swedish Competition Authority has been given the task to supervise the establishment of systems of choice.

have often their own entities as providers in the system, in which case users have access to a choice of private and public providers, for profit or not-for-profit. For the user who does not choose a supplier, the contracting authority must provide a no-choice alternative. A contracting authority that has decided to establish or change a system of choice must publish the relevant tender documents on the national website set up for the purpose, and it must continuously request applications.[56] All applicants satisfying the requirements referred to in the contract notice and tender documents must be approved and may conclude a contract with the contracting authority.[57] While operators admitted to participate in the system must fulfil the basic obligations imposed on the activity by Swedish legislation (including administrative rules), the local or regional authority may impose its own additional requirements as a condition to provide within its system of free choice, in particular on service quality.

It is important to note that providers allowed to participate in LOV-based system do not compete on price, but are meant instead to compete on quality. Interestingly, this crucial element is not provided for by the Act itself, but instead by its preparatory works.[58] In the preparatory works, it is also stipulated that the tender documents must give information on the economic compensation for a service unit, which for given tasks must be the same for all providers.[59] The compensation rates set by the contracting authority must be specified in the contract documents, and the amount ultimately paid by the authority to a service provider depends on the amount of users which have chosen this provider.

Subject to EU and Swedish autonomous procurement rules, local and regional authorities may cooperate to fulfil their missions in the field of social services through public law and private law instruments. In the field of health care and social services, they may form local federations or cooperate through common boards.[60] They may also cooperate through contracts,[61] although normally not regarding tasks involving the exercise of public authority. Since 1991 LRAs may conduct certain tasks in the form of private law entities. As a result, LRAs have incorporated many of their activities, even in the field of social services.

[56]The national website is www.valfrihetswebben.se.

[57]In that sense, these systems are "open". A provider may be excluded pursuant to Chapter 7 Section 1 of the Act.

[58]See the government Bill on the Act on Systems of Choice, *Lag om valfrihetssystem*, proposition 2008/09:29, p. 80.

[59]Ibid.

[60]In the field of health care and social services, common boards are generally subject to provisions in the Local Government Act, and may be used to take care of services listed in the Act on common board in the field of health care and social services (Sw: *lag (2003:192) om gemensam nämnd inom vård- och omsorgsområdet*).

[61]See Chapter 2 Section 5 of the Social Services Act and Section 3 para 3 of the Act on Health and Medical Services.

LRAs may fund with tax most social services to the person under their competence, but they may (and do) finance charge fees in accordance with rules in special laws on for instance health care and on social services. In systems of choice, such fees must not be confused with the compensation paid to private operators to which a local or authority entrusts a social service.

8.2.2 Lack of Visibility in Swedish Law of Social Services' Economic Character for the Purpose of EU Law

The existence and rapid development in Sweden of markets for publicly funded social services, including school education, is the result of a policy sustained by the Swedish liberal government in place between 2006 and 2014, and embraced by many local and regional authorities. Studies and reports on the development of private for-profit activity in publicly funded social services show what is known in international business contexts, namely that this sector has been an attractive business sector in Sweden over the last decade.[62] The present existence of such social services markets, where a number of bigger companies active in Sweden also conduct their activity in other Member States, is undeniable, regardless of the uncertainty which the change of Swedish government in September 2014 implies for future developments. On this background, it is remarkable that the economic character of social services, in particular for the purpose of EU law, is still so unclear in Swedish law. The main concepts delineating the scope of application of the Swedish rules governing LRAs' intervention as financiers, organisers or operators of welfare services, are spread in several horizontal Swedish Acts, the Local Government Act (LGA), the Procurement Acts, and the Competition Act. These concepts are all in some sense related to the notion of "economic activity" in EU law, but their meaning, generally explained in relatively old preparatory works, has not yet been updated to the reality of Swedish welfare activities.

As already mentioned, a local or regional authority may pursuant to Chapter 2 Section 7 LGA engage in so called "commercial activity", but not with a view to profit, as it must instead be essentially concerned with providing services or facilities of general interest to its members. The meaning of the term "commercial activity" in this provision is neither clear from LGA's text, nor from its preparatory

[62]See for instance the report of Grant Thornton Sweden AB on the development of the markets for health care and care in Sweden "Den privata vård- och omsorgsmarknaden ur ett finansiellt perspektiv—Hur mår den privata vård- och omsorgsmarknaden i Sverige?" November 2012, accessed 27 February 2015 at http://www.grantthornton.se/Global/Dokument/Publikationer/Rapporter/2012/V%C3%A5rdstudie%202012.pdf, The existence of these markets is not only well-known in Sweden, but in fact has been the main subject of the national elections in September 2014, with a focus on the profits made by some operators (four private companies made together a profit of 590 million kronor for 2013, according to an article of Jan Almgren, "Flera välfärdsjättar återinvesterar vinsterna" *Svenska Dagbladet Näringsliv* (Stockholm, 9 October 2014).

works. In the Bill on LGA, the government explained that the use of the term "commercial" in the provision's text played a role in delineating LRAs' competence. It was underlined that there was no clear legal distinction between "the municipal sector" and "the commercial sector", but that LRAs may only exceptionally conduct commercial activities considered as being reserved to private undertaking (generally called in Swedish law "the genuine commercial sector"). Consequently, although LRAs may conduct certain activities normally provided by commercial operators, for instance energy supply and transport service, the government held necessary to prohibit as a main rule a profit motive in LRAs' "commercial activity", to reinforce that it is the criterion of "general interest" which founds LRAs' competence in such cases.[63] It is very clear (and broadly consensual in the legal practice) that the term "commercial activity" in Chapter 2 Section 7 LGA was not meant to cover social services when the provision was introduced in the Local Government Act.[64] Hence, this provision conveys the perception that social services are not "commercial activities", and thus gives no visibility that social services as organised under Swedish law, may constitute an economic activity in the meaning of EU free movement and competition law.

It has also been mentioned that LRAs are forbidden to grant aid to "individual enterprise" according to Chapter 2 Section 8 para 2 LGA.[65] Indén has observed that the main difficulty in applying this provision—obviously related to the prohibition of state aid in Article 107(1) TFEU—is the lack of precision of the notion of "individual enterprise".[66] What is sure is that the provision does not cover LRA-owned entities. As a result, the notion of "individual enterprise" in this provision is not equivalent to the notion of undertaking for the purpose of EU competition and state aid law, and consequently the scope of this provision is not equivalent to the scope of the state aid provision in Article 107(1) TFEU.[67] In the preparatory

[63]Government Bill on a new Local Government Act, *En ny kommunallag*, proposition 1990/91:117, pp. 32–33.

[64]In fact, if the term "commercial activity" in Chapter 2 Section 7 LGA was understood as covering social services, the point of departure expressed in the government Bill to the Local Government Act of 1991, regarding LRAs' engagement in business sectors as a matter of exception, would place LRAs' mandatory competence for social services in the category of "exception", which from a political and constitutional point of view would probably be problematic. The Swedish legislator would have the tricky task to explain how a competence directly connected to the constitutional mission of public authorities to promote social rights can be allowed "by exception".

[65]This provision was also introduced in the Local Government Act in 1991 but regarded as consolidating case law, see Lindquist 2011, p. 363.

[66]Indén 2008, pp. 50–51.

[67]This was brought to the Swedish government's attention by the report put forward by the law firm Öberg and Associés (hereafter the "Öberg report") on the request of the committee of inquiry on LRAs' competence, and included in the report of the commission of inquiry on LRAs' competence "Kommunal kompetens i utveckling" SOU 2007:72, and entitled "Opinion on the relation between Chapter 2 Section 8 LGA and EC state aid rules" (Sw: *Utlåtende avseende förhållandet mellan 2 kap. 8 § kommunallagen och EG:s statsstödsregler*). The committee proposed not to adapt the provision in Chapter 2 Section 8 § LGA to EU law, based on a view that the Swedish aid prohibition is more restrictive than the state aid rules in EU law, a view that is questionable, but not discussed here.

works, the notion of "individual enterprise" in Chapter 2 Section 8 para 2 LGA is said to mean only the "genuine commercial sector".[68]

The following case law sheds light on the fact that this "genuine commercial sector" can include the provision of publicly funded social services. Indeed, the Swedish Supreme Administrative Court had in the *Stockholm elderly care* case no doubt that a private operator of publicly funded elderly care which had taken over the activity of a municipal entity was an "individual enterprise" in the meaning of this provision Chapter 2 Section 8 para 2 LGA. On that basis, the Court found that it had received individual aid prohibited by this provision, as it had acquired the municipal entity's assets under market-price in the frame of the spin-off procedure.[69] The Supreme Administrative Court's approach, implying that social services are not per se excluded from the scope of the aid prohibition in LGA, was also adopted in two earlier cases in the Swedish administrative courts of appeal.[70] These two cases—the *Tibble gymnasium* case[71] and the *Sollentuna schools and pre-schools* case[72]—are particularly interesting because the courts' decisions are clearly based on the view that the operators of the private schools and preschools at issue in the cases constituted "individual enterprises", and thus were part of the "genuine commercial sector".

These cases call for some observations. First, the Swedish courts found so evident that the private providers of publicly funded social services at issue constituted individual "enterprises", that they did not even mention it. Second, it is interesting to note that the administrative courts of appeal chose not to examine whether the aid at issue also infringed Article 107(1) TFEU, although the applicants had raised this ground in both cases (at least in first instance in the *Sollentuna schools and pre-schools case* and in appeal in the *Tibble gymnasium* case). Third, the *Stockholm elderly care* case implies logically that, as covered by Chapter 2 Sector 8 para 2 LGA, the social service of elderly care, although placed under LRAs' mandatory competence, is seen as belonging to the "genuine commercial sector".

Although the judgments of the administrative courts of appeal do not set precedent, they signal that providers of school education in the national education

[68]Report of the commission of inquiry on LRAs' competence "Kommunal kompetens i utveckling" SOU 2007:72, p. 68 and the Öberg report, p. 5.

[69]In particular, the private operator had only been charged for equipment, and not for the municipal entity's goodwill, see the judgment of the Supreme Administrative Court, RÅ 2010 ref. 100 (Stockholm kommun).

[70]It is important to underline that while judgments from the Supreme Administrative Court set precedent in Swedish law, judgments from the administrative courts of appeal do not, and are merely "indicative".

[71]Judgment of the Administrative Court of Appeal, Kammarrätten i Stockholm, KR nr 584-08 (Täby kommun).

[72]Judgment of the Administrative Court of Appeal, Kammarrätten i Stockholm, KR nr 3801-09 (Sollentuna kommun).

system probably also must be regarded as belonging to the "genuine commercial sector", at least in Sweden. As LRA-owned entities are not covered by the notion of "individual enterprise" in Chapter 2 Section 8 para 2 LGA, this brings about a situation where publicly funded social services belong to the "genuine commercial sector" when provided by private operators and not when provided by LRA-owned entities, a legal political result which defies common sense and arguably needs be addressed by the Swedish legislator.[73] At any rate, the aid prohibition in Chapter 2 Section 8 para 2 LGA does not give visibility to the fact that EU competition and state aid rules may cover LRA-owned entities (within or outside their administration), provided the latter offer services or goods on the market and thereby conduct an economic activity in the meaning of EU law.

It is also interesting to note that the Swedish legislator decided not to introduce in the Swedish Public Sector Procurement Act[74] the term "economic operator" used in the Public Sector Directive to cover both contractors, suppliers and service providers, but instead the term "provider" (Sw: "*leverantör*"). In the Swedish Act's Bill, this choice was based on the argument that the term "provider" has so far been broadly used in Sweden and should be kept, although it is now generally held that Swedish law should adopt a terminology similar to EU procurement directives, in order to facilitate their implementation and the interpretation of decisions taken by the CJEU.[75] This choice makes "invisible" the fact that LRA-owned entities (even within their administration) may tender in certain fields of activity such as emergency transport, thereby constituting "economic operators" in the meaning of procurement law, and offering services on a market.

Lastly, the notion of "LRAs' sales activity" in the Competition Act must be named in this non-exhaustive review of concepts which in Swedish law delineate LRAs' intervention in economic activities. Its scope is not defined clearly—neither in the Act's text nor in its preparatory works, and therefore it is uncertain whether LRAs' own operation of social services may be seen as such "sales activity", or whether LRAs' measures as operators in the field social services may be subject to EU competition and state aid rules. The provisions of the Competition Act on LRAs' sales activities are explained and commented in more detail in Sect. 9.1.2.

In sum, the economic character for the purpose of EU competition and state law of activities under LRAs' competence—in particular social services—is so far quite invisible in Swedish law. The conceptual situation outlined above is not only problematic in a Swedish perspective, given its lack of coherence and connection to the economic reality. Its effect is also arguably that the applicability of EU rules on state aid and competition to social services is not signalled in central Swedish

[73]A solution might be to stop using the expression "genuine commercial sector", which nowadays appears to be a source of incoherence.

[74]Sw: Lag (2007:1091) om offentlig upphandling.

[75]Government Bill on new procurement Acts in the public sector and in the utilities sector, *Ny lagstiftning om offentlig upphandling och upphandling inom områdena vatten, energi, transporter och posttjänster*, proposition 2006/07:128, p. 147.

Acts, and not either the possible necessity to rely on the existence of SGEI missions and tasks to justify certain measures in the field of social services, in particular public funding.

8.3 Conclusions

Based on the Swedish constitutional and statutory rules, it is submitted that social services under LRAs' competence may be regarded as services of general interest in the meaning of the SGI Protocol.

It is also submitted that a considerable part of the Swedish legislation pertaining to social services to the person under LRAs' competence must with certainty be seen as economic regulation constrained by EU market law, because this regulation is related to activities which *can be* economic, to services *normally* provided for remuneration in the meaning of Article 57 TFEU. This is due to the fact that economic operators in Sweden may and do provide them in exchange for remuneration, either wholly from public authorities, or from public authorities and users in combination. As a consequence, and in accordance with *Freskot*, Swedish law affecting social services such as elderly care at home, primary care must respect the fundamental freedoms related to these activities. Also, EU competition law *can be relevant* for Swedish law on these social services, because they fulfil the comparative test in *Höfner*. They are not necessarily, and have not always been, provided by public bodies. As will be seen in more detail in Chap. 9, this is now also true of school education.

Another question is whether the different categories of operators providing different social services under different types of Swedish schemes must be regarded as undertakings conducting an economic activity in the meaning of EU law. This question, and the question of whether social services under LRAs' competence are de facto SGEIs, must be answered on a case by case basis, as a preliminary step to analyse the compatibility of Swedish rules with EU competition law (including state aid law). As concluded under part I, the economic character of a service provided by an operator under a specific scheme may be determined *equivalently* by asking whether the operator offers this service on the/a market or by asking whether the operator *actually* provides the service for remuneration.

There is some judicial evidence that social services under LRAs' competence should in many cases be regarded as economic activities. The cases in Swedish courts concerning the privatization of Swedish schools and health care entities show that they have come within the radar of Swedish rules on public aid. Also, in its assessment of the complaints brought against the privatization of a number of Swedish municipal health care and school units, the Commission has signalled rather clearly that it regarded the private providers of primary care and school education at issue in the cases as undertakings a priori not excluded from EU state aid rules. Moreover, the necessity of assessing the market character of social services in public systems has become all the more obvious in the light of the *IRIS-H* case.

References

Bergström CF (2009) Grundlagsutredningen och EU. Europarättslig Tidskrift nr 2/2009

Cyndecka MA (2015) The applicability and application of the market economy investor principle. University of Bergen, Norway

Indén T (2008) Kommunen som konkurrent, Kommunalrättsliga befogenheter och konkurrensrättsliga begränsningar. Skrifter från juridiska institutionen vid Umeå universitet, Iustus Förlag, Uppsala

Lind A (2009) Sociala rättigheter I förändring – en konstitutionell studie. Uppsala universitet

Lindquist U (2011) Kommunala befogenheter. Norstedts Juridik, Stockholm

Petrén G (1978) Vägen till en svensk rättighetskatalog, in Skrifter till minne av Halvar G.F. Sundberg. Institutet for offentlig och internationell rätt, Stockholm

Wenander H (2011) En princip om internationell öppenhet – 1 kap. 10 § regeringsformen och socialförsäkringsrätten. Förvaltningsrättslig Tidskrift, Särtryck ur häfte 3/2011

Chapter 9
Compatibility Between EU Secondary Law on SGEIs and Systems of Choice in Swedish Law: The Cases of Elderly Care and School Education

Abstract This chapter examines the compatibility with the SGEI state aid rules of two Swedish systems of choice for social services, namely elderly home care and school education. It looks first into the regulation, organisation and public funding of elderly home care in Swedish contract-based systems of choice. These systems, based on a procurement model that promotes competition but not based on price, fall outside the 2014 directives' definition of procurement and their present design does not appear to fit the concept of SGEI addressed by the regulatory model of the Commission's state aid rules. Second, this chapter examines school education in Swedish authorisation-based systems of choice. Whilst for-profit provision of school education is allowed in the public system, the Swedish legislator is reluctant to acknowledge the economic character of its social services and has argued, not so convincingly, that systems of choice fulfil the fourth *Altmark* criterion, which indicates that EU state aid rules applying to SG(E)Is under Article 106(2) TFEU are perceived as problematic for the systems' design and the policy pursued. This chapter draws some conclusions on the relationship between the lack of clear SGEI tasks and issues of service quality, service continuity, under-compensation and over-compensation, which have occurred in these fields, and on how EU procurement and state aid rules applicable to SGEIs would probably have been fatal for Swedish systems of choice, had it not been for the leeway which these systems enjoy in the recently adopted EU legislation.

C. Wehlander, *Services of General Economic Interest as a Constitutional Concept of EU Law*, Legal Issues of Services of General Interest,
DOI 10.1007/978-94-6265-117-3_9

Contents

The purpose of this chapter is to examine how EU rules on state aid and procurement may affect the Swedish systems of choice for social services within LRAs' competence. More to the point, the question is whether these systems are regulated and used in compliance with EU law on state aid and procurement, and if not, whether this may explain the Swedish legislator's avoidance of the notion of SGEI in this field. The approach is selective as only two social services are in focus, both under the compulsory competence of local authorities, and both examined in the frame of systems of choice.

The case of elderly home care in LOV-based systems is examined in Sect. 9.1. It must be recalled here that local authorities *may* supply elderly home care in a LOV-based system of choice. They may also use other models to ensure access to that service, in particular they may provide the service themselves or procure the service under the Public Sector Act. Section 9.2 studies systems of choice in the field of school education. Local authorities have an obligation to supply school education in this organization model, and do not have much influence on which private school operators are established on their territory. The approach consists in examining these two types of systems of choice in the light of the following questions

- Are operators providing these services in systems of choice to be regarded as undertakings in the meaning of EU competition and state aid law?
- Are these services *de facto* subject to SGEI regulation in Sweden?
- Does their public funding comply with EU state aid rules applying to the compensation of public service obligations imposed on undertakings entrusted with SGEI tasks?

Section 9.3 sums up and discusses the findings for each service studied.

In this chapter the focus is on valid law, and the method is therefore overall dogmatic, using in relevant parts the traditional Swedish (Scandinavian) legal method, and an EU legal method where EU market law need be interpreted. The necessity to rely on certain economic facts in order to conduct the reasoning on the applicability of EU state aid rules to social services in Swedish systems of choice, has led to refer to some of the many reports and studies on different aspects of systems of choice for social services published since the mid-2000s. These documents, chosen on criteria of relevance to the question studied, reliability, and probable objectivity, include academic research reports on the process of marketization of social services, reports by well-established organisations and firms, providing economic data on the market for the social services studied, or on the models of compensation used by local authorities, surveys on the quality of social services supplied in systems of choice, and finally institutional reports. This material is important to evaluate whether, and why, an explicit characterisation of the Swedish rules on social services as SGEIs may have been perceived as problematic in the process of liberalisation of these services.

9.1 Elderly Home Care Provided Under the Act on Systems of Choice (LOV)

Introduced under the 1950s, Swedish public elderly care has been provided on a universal basis, and has thus consisted of comprehensive, publicly financed and high quality services available to all citizens according to their needs rather than their ability to pay.[1] Demographic, political and economic developments have led to a situation where elderly care is nowadays mostly provided at home, with the proportion of persons above 80 years of age in the group getting most home care (25 hours a week or more) increasing steadily, and a very small proportion of elderly persons living in nursing homes. While coverage has declined in Sweden

[1]Characteristic for a universal model is normally that the same services are directed at, and also used by, all social groups. See the research report of the Nordic Research Network on Marketisation in Eldercare, 2013, "Marketisation in Nordic eldercare: a research report on legislation, oversight, extent and consequences" (hereinafter, the "2013 Eldercare Marketisation Report"), Meagher G. and Szebehely M. (eds.), Department of Social Work, Stockholm University, p. 24.

regarding both home care and nursing homes, Sweden is still one of the world's most generous countries when it comes to spending on eldercare, as users pay only a small fraction of the cost (5–6 %).[2]

9.1.1 Regulation

All forms of elderly care – at home or in nursing homes – are regulated by the Social Services Act 2001,[3] which is a typical "goal-oriented" framework covering many other social services. This Act does not confer any right to specific services but instead a basic right for any person at any stage of life, who is unable to ensure his/her needs, to claim assistance for his/her maintenance and everyday life from the local authority's social board. This assistance must secure that the person has a decent standard of living and be organised in a manner promoting an autonomous life.[4] However, local authorities have a wide margin to decide elderly care's specific objectives, budgets, and mode of supply. This explains the large variation regarding the services offered and their organisation among local authorities.[5]

In particular, the type of services which local authorities must make available to elderly persons in need of assistance is not specified in statutory rules. Generally, local authorities include in the assistance to elderly persons both cleaning, washing, shopping and catering services, but also more personal services such as personal assistance for hygiene, shower, dressing/undressing and eating, as well as safety alarm, and in some municipalities, accompanying services and replacement of relatives are also available. Publicly funded elderly home care is initiated formally by a request from the elderly person, and provided on the basis of an administrative decision précising the services he/she is entitled to, on the basis of an evaluation of his/her needs.[6]

Service provision may be entrusted by local authorities through contract to natural or legal persons, including other local authorities.[7] In 2013, 132 out of 290 local authorities had introduced systems of choice for elderly home care based on

---

[2]See the report of the Stockholm Gerontology Research Centre, Hjalmarson I., 2014, "Vem ska bestämma i hemtjänsten?", Rapporter/Stiftelsen Stockholms läns Äldrecentrum 2014:2, p. 11.

[3]Sw: *Socialtjänstlag* (2001:453).

[4]Chapter 4 Section 1 of the Social Services Act.

[5]See the "2013 Elderly Care Marketisation Report", Meagher G. and Szebehely M. (eds.), Department of Social Work, Stockholm University, p. 24.

[6]The local authority board in charge of elderly care is composed of elected representatives, see Chapter 4 Section 1 of the Local Government Act. On delegation, see Chapter 6 Section 33 of the Local Government Act.

[7]Chapter 2 Section 5 of the Social Services Act. Tasks which are related with the exercise of official authority may not be entrusted to other legal or natural persons on the basis of this provision.

the Act on Freedom of Choice (hereinafter LOV).[8] In such LOV-based systems, an elderly person must receive information from the administrator about the system when informed about the administrative decision entitling to assistance. The person can choose any contracted provider, which is then commissioned by the administrator, and there is also a no-choice alternative. A care plan is then set up, normally together with the person concerned, including the provision of a given amount of specific services (in hours). The provider chosen will be remunerated at flat rates in accordance with the compensation model chosen by the local authority. This compensation must, as already mentioned, be distinguished from fees paid by users to the local authority, in accordance with rules outlined below.

9.1.2 Applicability of Swedish Competition Rules to Elderly Home Care Services in LOV-Based Systems: The Conflict-Solving Rule

There is no doubt that private providers of social services in LOV-based systems are seen by the Swedish legislator as conducting an economic activity. In Swedish law, public funding in LOV-based systems is addressed as an issue of competition neutrality rather than as an issue of undistorted competition between all providers, and thus the preparatory works of the Act on Systems of Choice emphasize that the funding conditions should be equal between private and LRA-owned providers.[9] The difficulty to ensure neutral competition is acknowledged, in particular because the local authority, as *public authority*, is ultimately responsible to secure that the service is actually provided and therefore must have access to additional capacity, in particular in acute situations.[10] By contrast, the preparatory works are ambiguous on whether LRA-owned entities constitute undertakings when they participate in systems of choice.[11] The Bill on LOV underlines that elderly care entities which

[8]Act on Systems of Choice in the Public Sector (Sw: *Lag om Valfrihetssystem (2008:962)*). Report of the Swedish Association of Local Authorities and Regions (SALAR) on quality requirements in systems of choice for elderly home care, 2014, "Kvalitetskrav i valfrihetssystem – en analys av förfrågningsunderlag för hemtjänst", http://webbutik.skl.se/bilder/artiklar/pdf/978-91-7585-100-6.pdf?issuusl=ignore, accessed 27 February 2015, p. 9.

[9]Government Bill on the Act on Systems of Choice, *Lag om valfrihetssystem*, proposition 2008/09:29, p. 22.

[10]Ibid., p. 62. As another example of this difficulty, the bill names that as employers, LRAs are bound by collective agreements giving their employees working conditions which can differ from those granted by private employers, and in particular local authorities may grant a right to work full-time.

[11]In LOV's preparatory works, LRA-owned entities are referred to as "own management" (Sw: *egen regi*), but it is clear that entities regarded as part of LRAs' own management can be either entities in the own administration or LRA-owned private law entities.

are part of the municipal administration cannot be entrusted their tasks on the basis of contracts, but that they must be given the same conditions as external operators.[12] The Bill characterizes the local authority's decision on compensation model as *primarily political*, but adds that competition rules apply to that decision, and refers thereby to the "conflict solving rule" (Sw: *konfliktslösningsregeln*), without explaining why and how this rule could be relevant for that decision.[13]

The conflict-solving rule, in force since 2010, aims at preventing anti-competitive "sales activities" carried out by public authorities – or by a legal person under their direct or indirect dominant influence – in competition with private undertakings. Accordingly, the District Court of Stockholm may forbid that a local or regional authority conducts anti-competitive "sales activities" or adopts certain anti-competitive conducts, for instance cross-subsidization and price-dumping.[14] The Bill names activities such as fitness centres, plants, broadband, and property maintenance, but does not exclude the applicability of the rule to other activities, although it underlines that LRAs' competence is not affected. The Bill explains also that the provision applies to national, regional or local authorities conducting activities as "undertakings", defined in the Act as a legal or natural person which conducts an activity of economic or commercial nature.[15] It is underlined that the notion of "undertaking" excludes elements consisting in the exercise of public authority, but that the notion of economic activity has the same wide meaning as in EU law, i.e. can be for-profit or not, and be conducted by a public entity, but only consists in *selling* goods, services and other facilities.[16]

The District Court may not prohibit (1) public authorities' conduct that is justifiable on public interest grounds and (2) activities carried out by local or regional authorities which comply with law. These exemptions necessitate an analysis and proportionality test that is complex and has to be clarified through case law.[17] As it first affirms that public authorities may not distort or restrict competition when acting as providers on the market, but admits that such distortions and restrictions must be accepted if necessary by regard to the general interest, the conflict solving rule is obviously related to the balancing rule in Article 106(2) TFEU.[18] It differs,

[12]See government Bill on the Act on Systems of Choice, *Lag om valfrihetssystem*, proposition 2008/09:29, p. 90.

[13]Ibid. When the governent Bill on LOV was put forward, the conflict solving rule was not yet in force in the Swedish Competition Act.

[14]The main rule is laid down in Chapter 3 Section 27 of the Swedish Competition Act (Sw: *Konkurrenslagen (2008:579)*, but is completed by Sections 28–32 in the same chapter. The District Court of Stockholm is the first instance civil court in Sweden.

[15]Chapter 1 Section 5 of the Competition Act.

[16]Government Bill on conflict solving for public sales activities on the market, *Konfliktlösning vid offentlig säljverksamhet på marknaden m.m.*, proposition 2008/09:231, p. 34.

[17]Ibid., p. 37–40. This complexity has been emphasized in the legislative process and underlined by Hedelin 2010, p. 225.

[18]On the elements of similarity between the conflict-solving rule and Article 106 TFEU, see Hedelin 2010.

however, from the EU balancing rule, in particular because it only covers economic activity conducted by LRA-owned entities, whereas Article 106(2) TFEU covers any undertaking entrusted SGEI tasks, private or public. Besides, the exemptions from the conflict solving rule are not clearly related to the SGEI exemption and consequently not either to EU competition rules applicable to SGEIs.

Given this lack of connection to the EU notion of SGEI, the application of the conflict solving rule may perhaps get unexpected effects.[19] It is explained that the rule should not lead to prohibit the conduct of a local or regional authority (or entities under their control) which is a direct or an inevitable effect of legislation, but that such conduct *cannot be justifiable on public grounds if it breaches against law*.[20] As will be seen in the next section – LRA-owned entities seem to act as undertakings in many fields under their competence, and the legality of LRAs' decisions vis-à-vis these entities can also depend on their compliance with EU state aid law. One may wonder whether the Civil Court of Stockholm may prohibit anti-competitive measures which cannot be justified on the basis of Article 106(2) TFEU, an eventuality which has not been openly envisaged by the Swedish legislator.[21]

On this background, the "ambiguous connection" evoked above may be understood as follows. When a local or regional authority decides on a model of compensation for a social service in free choice, it may (and arguably should) have a political ambition to ensure a social service's continuity and quality, but it must also beware of the risk to thereby distort competition, as it might infringe the conflict solving rule. This confirms, albeit discreetly, the view that the conflict solving rule may be claimed to apply to LRAs' definition and funding of social services under their competence. It also suggests that LRA-owned entities in systems of choice are, in fact, regarded as undertakings by the Swedish government.

9.1.3 Applicability of EU State Aid Rules to Elderly Home Care Services in LOV-Based Systems

The government Bill on LOV drew attention on the importance of not overcompensating the services supplied in free choice systems, as this could involve that providers receive an advantage which may be regarded as incompatible with EU

[19]Hedelin 2010, p. 246.

[20]Government Bill on conflict solving for public sales activities on the market, *Konfliktlösning vid offentlig säljverksamhet på marknaden m.m.*, proposition 2008/09:231, p. 34.

[21]The risks of the uncalculated effects which the conflict-solving rule may have on LRAs' competence have been evoked in the legislative debate, see the report of the Swedish parliament's constitutional committee conflict solving for public sales activities on the market "Konfliktlösning vid offentlig säljverksamhet på marknaden" 2009/10:NU8, p. 11–13.

state aid rules.[22] However, this perception is arguably not settled, as a commission of inquiry on certain activities within LRAs' competence held as late as 2007 that

> On the background of EU law as expressed in particular in the Services Directive and the law on transparency (sic), it may be presumed that services subject to a high degree of public financing are not covered by the notion of market, as they often are so called non-economic services such as school, social service or culture. If goods or services are tax-funded, the consumer does not directly pay for the service, and thus they cannot either be regarded as provided on a market. Therefore the fact that the activity is financed by tax should also be relevant for a notion of market in relation with the application of the prime-cost principle.[23]

Given the complexity of the CJEU's case law and the political sensitivity of the matter, this uncertainty on the applicability of EU market rules to social services is certainly not specific for Sweden, but it is problematic in particular because the Commission trusts the Member States to control the correct application of EU competition and state aid rules in that field, and because an incorrect interpretation of EU law on SGEIs risks being detrimental to the respect of certain social rights.

Under the contractual arrangements provided for by LOV, it must be held as certain that private operators offering elderly home care services – regardless of whether they are for-profit or not – offer services on the publicly funded markets for elderly care, and consequently conduct an economic activity in the meaning of EU law. They act autonomously, and doubtlessly perceive payments from public authorities as compensation for the services delivered, a remuneration in the meaning of free movement law.[24] In LOV-based systems, private operators are evidently undertakings in the meaning of EU competition and state aid rules.

Whether LRA-owned entities providing elderly home care in LOV-based systems conduct an economic activity in the meaning of EU law may seem less straightforward, but the element of competition in the system seems decisive. As users can choose *any* provider in the system, *all* providers – even LRA-owned

[22]See government Bill on the Act on Systems of Choice, *Lag om valfrihetssystem*, proposition 2008/09:29, p. 81. For instance, evoking the general funding of health care provided by regional authorities' own entities, and the fact that these entities may conduct both commercial activities and tasks related to the exercise of public authority, the government Bill on mandatory systems of choice for primary healthcare recommended that the activity which is in competition with private operators be organised as a separate production entity in the administration or that its costs be subject to a separate accountancy, in order to prevent cross-subsidization and competition distortions. The government considered that the principles for separate accountancy of financial compensation to undertakings entrusted with services of general *economic* interest laid down in the EU framework on the application of state aid rules to SGEI may be guiding, even for funding below the thresholds set by this framework. See government Bill on the obligation for regional authorities to introduce free choice of primary care under LOV, *Vårdval i primärvården*, proposition 2008/09:74, p. 44.

[23]See the report of the commission of inquiry on LRAs' competence "Kommunal kompetens i utveckling" SOU 2007:72, p. 113 and 116.

[24]In other words, they are in a situation similar to the situation of hospitals analysed by the CJEU in Case C-157/99 *Smits and Peerbooms* [2001] ECR I-05473, para 58.

providers are in competition on the market for elderly home care. Under such circumstances, and on the background of the CJEU's case law studied in chap. 2,[25] there is not either much doubt that even LRA-owned entities conduct an economic activity in the meaning of EU competition and state aid law. Hence, it is submitted that a local authority must be regarded as an undertaking in the meaning of the state aid rules, inasmuch as it provides elderly home care through its own entities in a system of choice, independently of the fact that it has itself decided to set up this system and manages it, and in spite of the solidarity elements in the system which must now be examined.

9.1.4 Does Elderly Home Care Include SGEI Missions?

According to the Social Services Act, the objective of public elderly care is that elderly persons can live in dignity and well-being. Local authorities have much discretion regarding how this objective should be pursued, but they must supply elderly care covering citizens' needs.[26]

At a general level, the local authority's board in charge of elderly care must in principle act so that elderly persons can live and dwell in safe conditions and have an active and meaningful existence together with other people, but the board – and the local authority itself – have also substantial duties. The board must take care that elderly persons have good housing and must supply to those in need of it, assistance and help at home and other services that it has decided to give them access to. It must know well the living conditions of elderly persons in the local authority's area, inform them on which social service is available for them in the municipality, and give them as much as possible choice regarding when and how they receive assistance services at home. The local authority must plan its measures in the field of elderly care, in particular cooperate with the regional authority (that has a broad mandatory competence regarding health care services) and with other organisations. It must set up special housing for elderly persons in need of special assistance, and take care that personnel able to speak Finnish, Meänkieli or Samish is available where necessary for elderly care.[27]

At an individual level, the local authority must ensure that each elderly person has *access* to the assistance and support he/she may need for his/her livelihood. The assistance provided must ensure that the person has a reasonable living standard, and be organised in a way that strengthens the possibility to live an autonomous life, but this statutory obligation does not give an elderly person any right to specific services.[28] When evaluating an elderly person's need of assistance, the

[25]Beginning with Case 118/85 *Commission v Italy* [1987] ECR 2599.

[26]Government Bill on the Social Services Act, *Ny socialtjänstlag m.m*, proposition 2000/01:80, p. 83.

[27]Chapter 5 Sections 4–6 of the Social Services Act. Meänkieli is an official minority language in Sweden.

[28]Chapter 4 Section 1 of the Social Services Act.

local authority may not consider his/her economic means but may charge fees which must be related to income, and neither exceed the local authority's prime cost for the service nor exceed certain thresholds.[29] Also, the fees charged may not deprive the person from a minimum amount covering his/her personal needs and other normal life costs, and not either imply an unreasonable deterioration of the economic situation of the person's wife/husband/cohabitee.[30] Fees do not vary depending on which entity provides the services, as they are paid to the local authority and not to the provider. In accordance with the so called "quality paragraph", assistance provided on the basis of the Social Services Act must be of good quality. However, what "good quality" requires in substance is imprecise, as it is only prescribed that social services must be provided by personnel with appropriate qualification and experience and that the activity's quality must be developed and secured systematically and continuously.[31]

It may thus be concluded that the Social Services Act 2001 imposes on local authorities a public service task to secure access to elderly home care assistance of good quality for any person in *need* of it, which is binding on them in two ways. First, individual persons seeking elderly care may appeal in administrative courts against the local authority's decision related to his/her request for home care assistance.[32] Second, every local authority has the *ultimate* task to secure that persons residing in their territory receive the support and assistance which they need, although the local authority's task does not restrict the obligations incumbent on other principals.[33]

This statutory task is the specific expression of a general principle, reaffirmed recently by the Swedish legislator, that LRAs remain mandators (Sw: *huvudmän*) of all their activities regardless of who operates the service.[34] This principle is

[29]Chapter 8 Section 2 para 2 of the Social Services Act. In August 2013, the maximum fee was SEK 1,780 per month, corresponding to approximately €205. Municipalities may set the fees up to the national maximum threshold and up to the actual cost for providing services. For those with small amounts of help the fees can vary considerably between the Swedish municipalities, from SEK 77 to SEK 435 per hour.

[30]Chapter 8 Section 6 of the Social Services Act. This minimum amount (Sw: *förbehållsbelopp*) takes account of the person's life minimum costs and housing costs separately. The minimum life costs cover normal costs for food, clothes, shoes, hygiene, daily newspaper, telephone, radio- and TV-fees, home insurance, open health care, dental care, household electricity, consumer goods, transport, furniture, household effects and medicine.

[31]Chapter 3 Section 3 of the Social services Act. A commission of inquiry on care assistants proposed to introduce a law on the professional qualification of care assistants, based on a three-year secondary school programme or a validation from the employer. It did not lead to any government Bill as it was feared, in particular by the Swedish Better Regulation Council, to increase undertakings' administrative costs for instance for staff planning, learning and validating. It was also criticised because employers' validation of experience could lead to an extremely heterogeneous quality standard. See the report of the commission of inquiry on care assistants "I den äldres tjänst Äldreassistent – ett framtidsyrke" SOU 2008:126.

[32]Chapter 16 Section 3 of the Social Services Act.

[33]Chapter 2 Section 1 of the Social Services Act.

[34]Government Bill on private operators in municipal activities, *Privata utförare i kommunal verksamhet*, proposition 2013/14:118, p. 34.

considered important to ensure democratic control, good quality and rule of law in LRAs' activity. It has also been reaffirmed that the principle is valid even when LRAs have a statutory obligation to introduce systems of choice.[35] LRAs' mandatorship implies that they have the general *political* responsibility for the activity under their competence, by which is meant that they must first decide the activities' objectives, volume and quality, and second control and follow up the activity.[36] The extent of this responsibility may vary depending on the activity's importance for the local or regional authority's members, the municipal fees charged for it, or the tax resources invested in the activity.[37] When an activity is entrusted to private operators through contracts, LRAs must control and follow up the activity, ensure through those contracts that they receive information allowing the public to get insight in the activity. The authority's council must establish for each mandate period a programme with objectives and guidelines for private operators, indicating how they are followed up, but also how the respect of legal rules governing the activity is followed up, and how public information on the activity is ensured.[38]

The government Bill on LOV-based systems underlines that they build on the principle that the contracting authority is responsible to secure that the services are supplied to the users or the inhabitants and that this responsibility implies in substance also that the tender documents and contracts must include requirements ensuring that private operators fulfil the levels of quality wished by the local or regional authority.[39] Therefore, LRAs cannot acquit themselves of their responsibility by referring to insufficient or inadequate contract requirements.

In light of the above, it is submitted that local authorities have under the Social Services Act a public service task, which may be seen as an SGEI mission in the meaning of Article 14 TFEU, to secure for any person in *need* of it, access to elderly home care assistance of good quality, at an affordable cost.[40] When they choose to organise the SGEI in LOV-based systems, this mission implies that *SGEI tasks* entrusted to *providers* must be defined and financed adequately, that the local authority has a reserve capacity covering the "no choice alternative" and sudden

[35]Ibid., p. 37. In the report which led to this Bill, the commission of inquiry held that LRAs' responsibility was indirectly clear from a provision in Chapter 6 Section 7 LGA, requiring that LRAs' boards' control that the activity is conducted satisfactorily, even when it has been externalized. Interestingly, the commission's proposal to introduce a provision explicitly reminding that LRAs remain responsible of activities which they externalize, was not approved by the government and therefore finally not introduced in law. See report of the commission of inquiry on private operators "Privata utförare – kontroll och insyn" SOU 2013:53, p. 102–103.

[36]Ibid., p. 38.

[37]Ibid., p. 39.

[38]Chapter 3 Sections 19, 19a and 19b of the Local Government Act.

[39]Government Bill on the Act on Systems of Choice, *Lag om valfrihetssystem*, proposition 2008/09:29, p. 137.

[40]This task is comparable to the public service task at issue in Case C-480/06 *Commission v Germany* [2009] ECR I-4747.

disruptions in the system, and that it delivers an infrastructure – including IT-systems – allowing to administrate the system in relation to users and providers.

9.1.5 Risk of State Aid Under Article 107(1) TFEU

LOV-based systems provide for a flat-rate compensation without any price competition, and therefore, as already mentioned, both the commission of inquiry on LOV and the government saw risks of state aid.

In a LOV-based system, providers are remunerated by local authorities, covered by the notion of "state" in Article 107(1) TFEU. The compensation is selective as it is only directed to services such as cleaning, washing, catering, and personal assistance. Also, there is cross-border trade for such services, as some larger companies conduct elderly home care in Sweden and other Nordic countries.[41] Competition distortions may arise firstly because private providers of elderly home care may offer additional services to users willing to "top" the assistance services which they are entitled to by administrative decision of their local authority. Many of those services are since 2007 subject to tax reduction for domestic services, and it is easier for providers in LOV-based systems of elderly home care to offer such subsidised extra services to elderly persons having chosen them.[42] Second, and more importantly, some of the large elderly home care companies are owned by holding companies conducting other activities and in particular other social services, such as elderly housing, health care services and for some even school education services. Risks of cross-subsidization are not negligible.

As the general de minimis exemption is not applicable, the question is whether LOV-based payments to elderly care providers complies with EU law on the basis of their SGEI tasks, which can be the case if the public service compensation fulfils the four cumulative *Altmark* criteria, and consequently does not constitute aid in the meaning of Article 107(1) TFEU: (1) the SGEI task must exist and be clearly defined, (2) the parameters of compensation must be defined *ex-ante*, be objective and transparent, (3) there must be a system to prevent and avoid

[41]Attendo AB conducts elderly care in Sweden, Finland, Norway and Denmark. Aleris AB conducts elderly care in Sweden, Norway and Denmark, but as it seems elderly home care only in Sweden and Denmark. In February 2014, Attendo had about 3, 4 % and Aleris about 1 % of the total volume of elderly home care provision in Sweden, see presentation of Mats Bergman and Henrik Jordahl "Goda år på ålderns höst?" Available at http://www.sns.se/sites/default/files/2014-02-21_bergman_jordahl.pdf.

[42]This tax reduction was originally allowed for cleaning, maintenance and washing (Sw: *Rengöring, Underhåll och Tvätt)*, and is known in Swedish as the "RUT-avdrag". It was introduced in Swedish law in 2007. See the Act on the functioning of tax reduction for household work (Sw: *Lag (2009:194) om förfarandet vid skattereduktion för hushållsarbete*) referring to Section 67 of the Act on income tax (Sw: *Inkomstskattelagen* (1999:1229)).

over-compensation, and (4) if the task is not entrusted through procurement, the compensation must be calculated on the basis of the costs incurred by a well-run undertaking able to meet the necessary public service requirements.

When it pointed at the risk of state aid, the commission of inquiry considered that setting the amounts paid to providers on the basis of the costs of LRA-owned entities would fulfil the fourth *Altmark* criterion and exclude aid. Thus, it acknowledged implicitly the existence of SGEIs in social services covered by LOV, but awkwardly did not assess whether the other *Altmark* criteria were fulfilled by the scheme. In any case, it is very doubtful that municipal entities may be considered as the "typical and well run undertaking" of the fourth *Altmark* criterion. That municipal entities are regarded as undertakings in the meaning of EU competition law seems correct, but for the municipal entity to be held as "typical" and "efficient", its service tasks must be clearly defined *and* "typical", so that its costs constitute an acceptable market benchmark in the meaning of the fourth *Altmark* criterion. This is not only doubtful but also somewhat ironic, as it contradicts the legislator's declaration in LOV's Bill that inviting external providers to compete with LRAs' own entities leads to increase quality and efficiency in this field of activity.[43]

This approach has been followed by local authorities introducing LOV-based systems, but the Swedish Agency for Public Management has described the analysis of municipal providers' costs as a very challenging task.[44] It found that the task of calculating LRA-owned entities' costs in order to establish reasonable economic conditions for operators had led local authorities to be more aware of the costs incurred for providing elderly home care, which in turn has led them to assess more critically the way their own administration had organised the service so far, and to realize that the time and assistance granted to a person in the administrative decision must be distinguished from the time actually provided to the user by operators.[45] Also, in a pilot study aimed at testing a method for determining if external care providers and the municipalities' own providers are given equal financial conditions to compete within systems of choice for home care services, the Swedish Competition Authority found that the tasks were not clearly defined in

[43]As underlined by the government Bill on LOV, the County Administrative Boards had seen deficiencies in LRAs' quality work in several fields of activity, see government Bill on the Act on Systems of Choice, *Lag om valfrihetssystem*, proposition 2008/09:29, p. 18 and 70. In Sweden, the County Administrative Board is the representative of the Government in the region and the coordinating body for State activities in the county.

[44]This is in particular because there were originally no separate accounts for municipal entities, and because their activity is financed through yearly allocations. Report of the Swedish Agency for Public Management on the effect of LOV on the development of costs and efficiency in LRAs' activities, "Lagen om valfrihetssystem. Hur påverkar den kostnader och effektivitet i kommunerna?", Statskontorets slutrapport 2012:15, p. 32 and 34–36.

[45]Ibid., p. 37 and 74.

two of the three local authorities studied.[46] Also, SALAR found a large variation of the compensation amounts across local authorities[47] and published a guide addressed to local authorities using the costs of the municipal elderly home care provider as a benchmark, in which it highlighted the fact that many local authorities did not follow up how much time was actually spent with elderly persons.[48]

The above leads to submit that, while municipal entities may be well run, they cannot be a priori held to constitute typical well-run undertakings in the meaning of the fourth *Altmark* criterion. Besides, it must be emphasized that a comparison with the municipal entity' costs was only *recommended* by the commission of inquiry which proposed LOV, and not imposed on local authorities by the Act nor otherwise. Also, the Swedish Competition Authority underlined that it can be difficult to achieve neutral competition between private operators and LRAs' own operators, because the contracting authority bears the primary obligation to ensure that users receive the services which they are entitled to.[49] This implies that LRA-owned entities may bear additional public service obligations, for instance to provide service to users in remote areas of the authority's territory, or to users whose operator suddenly ceases to provide.

Although the fourth *Altmark* criterion could hardly be argued to be fulfilled on the basis of the comparison with a well-run municipal entity, the Swedish State declared in its report on the application of the 2005 SGEI Decision that public funding in LOV-based schemes was no aid.[50] If its point of departure was that participants to these

---

[46]Report of a pilot study conducted by the Swedish Competition Authority on neutral competition in local authorities' systems of choice "Konkurrens på likvärdiga villkor i kommunernas valfrihetssystem Pilotstudie i tre kommuner med valfrihetssystem inom hemtjänsten" Rapport 2013:8, p. 7–8, accessed 27 February 2015 at http://www.kkv.se/globalassets/aktuellt/nyheter/konkurrens-pa-likvardiga-i-kommunernas-valfrihetsssytem.pdf.

[47]In 2014, SALAR found that the compensation amount per hour varied between SEK 228 and SEK 512 per hour, se SALAR statistics on elderly home care at http://skl.se/demokratiledning styrning/driftformervalfrihet/valfrihetssystemersattningssystem/ersattningssystem/ersattnings systemsocialtjanst/ersattningssystemhemtjanst.1064.html

[48]"Koll på hemtjänsten? En handledning för analys av kommunens hemtjänstkostnader", A guide to conduct the analysis of the costs of the municipal elderly home care provider, published by SALAR and rådet för främjande av kommunala analyser, 2013, http://www.rpg.org.se/static/sv/882/images/Koll%20pa%20hemtjanst.pdf, p. 16.

[49]Guide of the Swedish Competition Authority on LOV, *Lagen om valfrihetssystem– en introduktion*, available at http://www.konkurrensverket.se/globalassets/publikationer/informationsmaterial/lagen-om-valfrihetssystem-en-introduktion.pdf, p. 10.

[50]In Sweden's report on the application of the 2005 SGEI Decision, it is stated (own translation) that: "as a large part of the services are not of economic nature, state aid rules are held not to apply. These are services consisting in the exercise of public authority and services normally not offered on a market as primary education, certain cultural activity etc. There are also services which are compensated so that the so called *Altmark* criteria are fulfilled. Such compensation does normally not constitute state aid." See Sweden's report on the application of the 2005 SGEI Decision "Rapport om genomförandet av kommissionens beslut av den 28 november 2005 om tillämpningen av artikel 86(2) EG-fördraget på statligt stöd i form av ersättning för offentliga tjänster som beviljas visa företag som fått i uppdrag att tillhandhålla tjänster av allmänt ekonomiskt intresse" N2008/5126, p. 2–3, accessed 27 February 2015 at http://ec.europa.eu/competition/consultations/2010_sgei/se_sv.pdf.

systems are undertakings in the meaning of EU competition law, this assertion had to be based on a view that the fourth *Altmark* criterion was fulfilled because the tasks were procured. In fact, although LOV uses to a large extent the concepts of procurement law and is perceived in Sweden as a procurement regime, LOV-based contracts have no defined volume, no total contract-value, and in general no specified contract duration. The government's view was that LOV-based contracts had to comply with the EU principles on free movement, but that they were not covered by EU procurement directives because they constituted service concessions.[51]

Now that the Concessions Directive has been adopted, it appears that LOV-based contracts do not fit with the definition of service concessions, but as it seems not either with the definition of public contracts, following from Directive recitals which the Swedish government makes no secret of having pushed forward in the process on the Directives' adoption.[52] As a result, LOV-based systems cannot be argued to exclude aid if the tasks are not seen as "procured", but simply compensated on the basis of a flat-rate based system. As aid is not excluded, the compatibility of public funding of elderly home care should be assessed on the basis of Article 106(2) TFEU and under 2011 SGEI Package.

[51]Government Bill on the Act on Systems of Choice, *Lag om valfrihetssystem*, proposition 2008/09:29, s. 52 and 55–57. This view was held by the government despite the fact that the services were not remunerated by users, and because providers bear not only the normal commercial risks of conducting the activity at issue, but also bear an important economic risk in the transaction, as they are dependent on whether users choose them instead of competitors. This view has been challenged by legal scholars, see Sundstrand 2012.

[52]The Swedish Ministry for Social Affairs explains how it pushed forward these recitals in order to ensure that LOV would not be affected by the new procurement directives, in *Färdplan för den offentliga upphandlingen*. S2014:22, Socialdepartementet, available at http://www.regeringen.se/content/1/c6/24/62/40/2bddbc31.pdf, p. 5. In fact, it appears from the 2013 SGEI Guide that Sweden's position had already won the Commission's support, see point 4.2.17: "The competent public authority may, for example, establish in advance the conditions for provision of a social service and, after sufficient advertising and in accordance with the principles of transparency and non-discrimination, grant licences or authorizations to all providers meeting these conditions. Such a system does not specify any limits or quotas concerning the number of service providers; all those meeting the conditions can participate. Providers which have obtained a licence/authorization must provide the service at the request of the user, who will thus have the choice of several providers, at a price set beforehand by the public authority." The system described in the 2013 SGEI Guide is strikingly similar to LOV. While the EU legislator has decided to characterize a system such as LOV as an authorization or a license scheme in the meaning of EU free movement law, it cannot be excluded that, if consulted on the matter, the CJEU would take a different line. It is namely challenging to reconcile the concept of authorization with LOV-based contracts, under which services are provided against public remuneration.

9.1.6 Compliance of Elderly Home Care in LOV-Systems with the 2011 SGEI Package

The Regulation on de minimis aid to undertakings providing SGEI is not applicable, because there are large companies in that field, and because aid is not calculated precisely *ex-ante*.[53] Aid to undertakings providing elderly home care in LOV-based systems must instead be examined in the light of the 2011 SGEI Decision.[54] Under the Decision, LOV-based systems for the supply of publicly funded social services – including elderly home care, and regardless of the aid amount – do not have to be notified to the Commission, but substantive conditions must be fulfilled for these systems to comply with EU law. In LOV-based systems, public service obligations are entrusted to private providers through contracts in which local authorities have a wide discretion to decide the service requirements. Local authorities have also a wide discretion to design the compensation mechanism. So far, Swedish national law – including administrative rules – does not draw local authorities' attention to the fact that their compensation mechanism for elderly home care under LOV *must* comply with the conditions set by the Decision, already outlined above in Sect. 7.2.3.

As a result, many local authorities may breach the 2011 SGEI Decision's requirements on their compensation mechanism, and risk that their compensation system be challenged, as they are not made aware that:

- Contracts for elderly home care must refer to the 2011 SGEI Decision.
- The public service obligations compensated must be *ex-ante* clearly defined.
- LOV-based contracts for elderly home care *must* be limited to 10 years for their system to be compatible with the Decision (it is doubtful whether the costs of elderly home care, essentially related to wages and transport, may be considered as necessitating a longer amortising period). It is only stated in LOV's *preparatory works* that the tender documents must include information on the contract period.[55]
- The compensation mechanisms *must* ensure compensation proportionality, which in particular supposes that there are not only arrangements to avoid overcompensation but also to *recover* over-compensation.
- There is an *obligation* on the Swedish State, and on local authorities, to ensure that undertakings do not receive overcompensation (with checks at least every 3 years during the period of entrustment and at the end of that period).

---

[53]Commission Regulation (EU) No 360/2012 of 25 April 2012 on the application of Articles 107 and 108 of the Treaty on the Functioning of the European Union to *de minimis* aid granted to undertakings providing services of general economic interest, OJ L114/8.

[54]See Recital 11 and Article 2(1) (c) of Commission Decision 2012/21/EU of 20 December 2011 on the application of Article 106(2) of the Treaty on the Functioning of the European Union to State aid in the form of public service compensation granted to certain undertakings entrusted with the operation of services of general economic interest [2012] OJ L7/3.

[55]Government Bill on the Act on Systems of Choice, *Lag om valfrihetssystem*, proposition 2008/09:29, p. 71.

- There is an *obligation* on the Swedish State, and on local authorities, to require that the undertakings concerned must commit to repayment of any overcompensation received.

The principle of sincere cooperation implies that it is the Swedish State's duty to take any appropriate measures, general or particular, to ensure that public authorities in Sweden fulfil obligations arising out of EU primary and secondary law. A cornerstone of this duty is to ensure that public service compensation in the frame of LOV-based systems fulfils the first *Altmark* criterion which is also the first condition set by the 2011 SGEI Decision: the SGEI tasks must be clearly defined and transparently entrusted. In law, this duty exists as soon as competition distortions which can arise from aid to elderly home care providers can have an effect on trade. The Commission has taken a number of decisions considering that certain activities had a purely local impact and therefore did not affect trade between Member States, but the CJEU's position appears generally to be that an aid measure's effect on trade does not depend on the local or regional character of the services supplied or on the scale of the field of activity concerned.[56]

The Commission observed in March 2011 that there is a progressive development of a "real" internal market in health services, as "a relatively small, but growing, number of companies deliver health care in more than one country in Europe".[57] As to other social services, the Commission deemed that they are mainly provided at local level by small operators entrusted by the public authorities, but that in some fields, large service providers are present with subsidiaries in several Member States.[58] Under such circumstances, and in particular because large companies provide different social services on the market and can cross-subsidise, it is argued that by infringing the 2011 SGEI Decision's requirements, aid to elderly care providers may affect trade.

9.1.7 Definition of Public Service Tasks and Compensation Mechanisms in LOV-Based Systems for Elderly Home Care: Some Important Issues

To comply with the Treaties, public funding of undertakings entrusted with SGEIs must be limited to what is necessary to cover the net costs incurred in discharging

[56]Case C-172/03 *Wolfgang Heiser v Finanzamt Innsbruck* [2005] ECR I-01627, para 33: "The second condition for the application of Article 92(1) of the Treaty, namely that the aid must be capable of affecting trade between Member States, does not therefore depend on the local or regional character of the services supplied or on the scale of the field of activity concerned. Also, see Case C-280/00 *Altmark* [2003] ECR I-7747, para 82.

[57]Commission, "The Application of EU state aid rules on Services of General Economic Interest since 2005 and the Outcome of the Public Consultation" SEC(2011) 397, p. 26–27.

[58]Ibid., p. 28.

the public service obligations, including a reasonable profit.[59] This proportionality constraint implies that (1) the public service obligations must be defined clearly and precisely, (2) the parameters used to calculate, control and review the compensation are known *ex ante* and (3) arrangements exist to avoid and recover any over-compensation. In the following, an attempt is made to assess whether local authorities' systems of choice for elderly home care fulfil these conditions.

Regarding condition (1), it must be noted that LOV does not lay any specific requirements on operators, an approach which the legislator has motivated by the variety of activities covered by the Act.[60] Instead, requirements on operators are meant to follow from the LOV-based contract, which firstly implies that the operator fulfils the obligations following from Swedish sector law. The obligation following from the Social Services Act is that the provider must provide elderly home care of "good quality", characterised in the Act only by two criteria formulated in very general terms: the service should be delivered by qualified personnel and the operator should have a quality management system. In 2011, the Swedish National Board of Health and Welfare was mandated to give more precision to this "quality condition", and adopted administrative rules requiring that operators use such quality management systems to plan, steer, control, assess and improve the activity.[61] These administrative rules are binding on operators, and if correctly fulfilled, they certainly involve costs which may be compensated for. However, they are difficult to see per se as "public service obligations".

In LOV-based systems, local authorities are free to add more specific requirements in the tender documents, but the government Bill lays much emphasis on the fact that these requirements must comply with EU principles of non-discrimination, transparency, equal treatment, proportionality and mutual recognition. As an example of *possible* contract requirement, the Bill mentions an obligation for the provider to serve any person choosing this provider, which shows that there is *no statutory universal service obligation* on elderly home care providers.[62] In general, the Bill on LOV underlines that contracts should contain requirements that are precise enough for LRAs to ensure the service quality, but warns that too many and

---

[59]Article 5(1) of Decision 2012/21/EU.

[60]Government Bill on the Act on Systems of Choice, *Lag om valfrihetssystem* proposition 2008/09:29, p. 71.

[61]See Chapter 3 Section 1 of the General rules and recommendations on management systems for systematic quality work of the Swedish National Board of Health and Welfare (Sw: *Ledningssystem för systematiskt kvalitetsarbete Socialstyrelsens föreskrifter och allmänna råd* SOSFS 2011:9), adopted on the basis of Chapter 8 Section 5 of the Social Services Ordinance, Sw: *Socialtjänstförordningen* (2001:937). Operators must inform on how the tasks related to systematic and continuous quality control and development are assigned in the activity, continuously analyse which events may affect the activity's quality, have a self-monitoring which allows securing quality, take and inquire on complaints on the activity's quality, and fulfil the incident reporting obligation set by law (Chapter 5). They must also document this quality work (Chapter 7 Section 1).

[62]Government Bill on the Act on Systems of Choice, *Lag om valfrihetssystem*, proposition 2008/09:29, p. 71–72.

too specific requirements can hinder the establishment of potential operators.[63] In the Bill, quality is primarily expected to be secured by users' possibility to "exit" from poor-quality provision, although it is admitted that quality cannot be left to users' responsibility.[64]

The question is therefore how clearly public service obligations local authorities are in practice defined by contracts. The Swedish association of local and regional authorities (SALAR) published in 2014 a report on contract requirements in LOV-based systems, in which it distinguished between structure requirements, process requirements, and result requirements.[65] It found that process requirements dominate hugely (88 %) and are often abstract and difficult to follow up, for instance "the user must get as much to say as possible."[66] It also found that about half of the requirements were impossible to follow up, 44 % possible to follow up but impossible to measure, and only 7 % possible to follow up and measurable. As several other studies on the subject, SALAR's report pointed to the difficulty of formulating workable quality requirements.[67] Nevertheless, it showed that a large majority of the requirements in LOV-based contracts did not allow assessing whether the requirements were fulfilled, and not either terminating the contract for

---

[63]Ibid., p. 73.

[64]Ibid. The government foresees that it will take many years until quality criteria could be unanimously accepted by all parts involved.

[65]Study of the Swedish Association of Local Authorities and Regions (SALAR) on quality requirements in systems of choice "Kvalitetskrav I valfrihetssystem". Taking as a point of departure Avis Donabedians model for different quality measurement, the requirements found were divided between (1) "structure requirements" related to which resources are invested in the activity, for instance personnel amount and qualification, (2) "process requirements" related to how the service is organised and conducted in practice, and (3) "result requirements" as for instance users' satisfaction and good health condition. In this model it is expected that structural quality can increase the development of good quality on the process which in turn can lead to good results. Structure requirements stood for 12 % and result requirements for 1 % of all requirements, see p. 16 and 29. SALAR's report came in a context of "demands for stricter regulation and more quality control /.../heard from many corners – from the government, the political opposition and from organisations representing private providers as well as users and older people in general". See the "2013 Elderly Care Marketisation Report", p. 74. The issue of which constraints should be imposed on private operators of welfare systems has been intensely debated in Sweden during the latest years.

[66]Another example of abstract requirement was "in delivering home care the provider must have an activating working method and attitude".

[67]Ibid., p. 32. In particular, SALAR's report questions whether it is at all possible to impose requirements that are possible to follow up, as there are few objective quality standards (compared for instance to health care) and as individual users can have different perceptions of what service quality is. It also suggests that certain requirements are signals to providers on what the local or regional authority considers as valuable and important in the service, and need not be possible to follow up. Finally it recommends to place requirements in tender documents in a larger perspective, where other instruments can support quality control, for instance interviews with users and providers, inspections or questionnaires.

non-fulfilment of the quality expected.[68] In other words, public service obligations compensated in LOV-based elderly home care are generally not clearly defined.

Regarding requirement (2), i.e. *ex-ante* parameters of compensation, it has already been mentioned that in LOV-based systems, local authorities are free to choose the model of compensation, but it is a tricky task and central public agencies provide guidance. In practice, data gathered by SALAR show that local authorities build up their compensation model on the basis of the municipal entities' costs. In most models, elderly home care providers are compensated on a time parameter, generally per hour provided, and some local authorities differentiate their payment per hour depending for instance on whether the service area is urban or sparsely populated, or on the type of task.[69] Some local authorities differentiate between private providers and municipal providers (the latter having an obligation to serve users in the whole territory of the local authority). Some local authorities invest in user satisfaction surveys and pay a bonus to operators obtaining high scores on a parameter of good treatment.

The picture emerging from these reports is that service time is so far the totally dominating compensation parameter. Other quality requirements may be found in tender documents or in contracts, but a minority of these requirements are clear enough to be followed up, most of which cannot be measured and therefore are not used as compensation parameters. Under such circumstances, it is submitted that the proportionality of compensation is in general not ensured by the compensation models themselves, as they stand today. The conclusions drawn by SALAR on the basis of these data converge with studies which have led the National Board of Health and Welfare to find that LOV procedures to set up requirements and follow up care services must be defined more clearly to ensure that the services delivered are of good quality.

Finally, regarding requirement (3), i.e. the existence of mechanisms preventing and avoiding over-compensation, it seems that local authorities have grown aware that the time spent with users can differ from the time they pay to providers, and some local authorities require registration of the time performed, either manually by the personnel, by telephone or by electronic means. However, a general mechanism allowing to recover over-compensation *ex post* does, according to what was found in this research, not exist for LOV-based contracts.

---

[68]Ibid., p. 30. One example of requirement which can be followed up but is not measurable is "there must be a contact personnel function". One example of specific and clear "result requirement" is: "in average, there must be a maximum of 10 persons helping a customer entitled to daily assistance under a 14-days period."

[69]According to SALAR's data, only a third of local authorities supplying elderly home care in LOV systems reported in 2013 the time effectively spent with users. It varies between 44 and 82 percent of the working time and is in average 65 percent of the working time. SALAR's data on compensation models for 2013, accessed 27 February at http://www.skl.se/demokratiledningstyrning/driftformervalfrihet/valfrihetssystemersattningssystem/ersattningssystem/ersattningssystemsocialtjanst/ersattningssystemhemtjanst.1064.html.

Certain measures have been taken to analyse the performance of elderly care provision in a context where about half of Swedish local authorities have introduced free-choice systems for elderly home care. At national level, systems have been set up to monitor users' feeling of quality and cost efficiency, for instance "Open comparisons of eldercare services", an initiative commissioned by the government and developed by the Swedish Association of Local Authorities and Regions together with the National Board of Health and Welfare.[70] For elderly home care, the quality parameters used in Open comparisons are (1) fall frequency and (2) customer satisfaction index (CSI).[71] These surveys fulfil a political and a national governance role, but they focus on the performance of private providers *globally compared to* public providers, not on the performance of individual providers.

Surveys on customer index satisfaction at the level of local authorities are commissioned by some local authorities themselves, in certain cases in connection to a bonus payment for providers showing good results in these surveys.[72] Such surveys may be perceived as a local authority's manner to follow up how providers deliver the assistance which users have been entitled to, as they remain ultimately responsible for quality results of their free choice systems, in spite of the expectation that users' choice "naturally" breeds quality. According to the Nation Board of Health and Welfare, it is unclear to which extent local authorities fulfil this obligation, as there are hardly any studies on that question.[73]

In any case, such initiatives do not measure the proportionality of public service compensation, and do not ensure that local authorities' entrustment and compensation of elderly home care complies with EU state aid rules. It is submitted that as a whole, LOV-based systems elderly home care, in the frame of the present regulation, do neither avoid nor *systematically* prevent over-compensation.

---

[70]Open Comparisons for eldercare are published in two ways: the web-based *Äldreguiden* (the Elderly Guide) and the printed and the web-based publication *Öppna jämförelser - Vård och omsorg och äldre (Open Comparisons – Eldercare).* The system of Opens Comparisons for eldercare is outlined in the "2013 Elderly Care Marketisation Report", p. 39–42. According to this report, the focus of this system on measuring results and efficiency is conform to the New Public Management approach.

[71]The Swedish Board of Public Administration (Sw: *Statskontoret*) uses these two quality criteria, although it underlines that "quality" is subjective. It observes that in the satisfaction surveys carried out in the frame of the national projects of open comparisons, satisfaction does not necessarily mirror the appreciation of the specific service received but can also express the fact that users appreciate the possibility to choose provider. See report on LOV's effect on LRAs' costs and efficiency "Lagen om valfrihetssystem – Hur påverkar den kostnader och effektivitet i kommunerna?", Statskontorets rapport 2012:15, p. 49–50.

[72]This activity is also growing in the sector of welfare services, in Sweden Demoskop AB is one of the main providers.

[73]Report of the National Board of Health and Welfare, 2012, "Kommunal eller enskild regi, spelar det någon roll? – en jämförelse av utförare av vård och omsorg om äldre", p. 56, accessed 27 February 2015 at http://www.socialstyrelsen.se/Lists/Artikelkatalog/Attachments/18732/2012-5-30.pdf.

An efficiency driven compensation model without clear and measurable *ex-ante* quality obligations may be regarded as a manner for local authorities to both close their budgets and avoid over-compensation, but it raises serious issues. While it does not exclude overcompensation of "bad quality providers", it threatens the existence of "good quality providers" (private or LRA-owned), and it puts at risk offer diversity in particular through market foreclosure. While over compensation risks infringing EU state aid rules, undercompensating is not consistent with Article 14 TFEU requiring that Member States take care that SGEIs in the frame of their competence are governed by principles and rules allowing them to achieve their missions.

These risks have been evoked in the Bill on LOV.[74] In the absence of clear public service obligations in *ex-ante* measurable qualitative terms, the co-existence of LOV-based schemes allowing providers to offer extra services and "increase their operation and reach a higher profitability",[75] with the Swedish tax-reduction scheme for household services (the so called "RUT" scheme),[76] can lead to cross-subsidisation and over-compensation of services actually covered by the LOV-based contracts. In the absence of clearly defined quality standards for SGEI-compensated services, the combination of the LOV-based schemes and the RUT tax scheme blur providers' public funding to the point where it becomes very difficult to know what the SGEI task exactly is and what local authorities' funding exactly covers. This may perhaps not be so detrimental to certain objectives of LOV-based systems, such as the promotion of women entrepreneurship, of small undertakings in the public sector, and of more attractive conditions generally to

[74]Government Bill on the Act on Systems of Choice, *Lag om valfrihetssystem*, proposition 2008/09:29, p. 81. To identify under-compensation, the Bill suggests to check test whether LRAs' own entities, even when they have rationalized their activity and increased its cost-efficiency, cannot produce elderly home care at the same level of compensation as private providers. If they do not, it may constitute a sign that compensation is too low, although it may be due to the fact that LRA-entities may have additional costs due to LRAs' ultimate responsibility for all users.

[75]Government Bill on the Act on Systems of Choice, *Lag om valfrihetssystem*, proposition 2008/09:29, p. 123.

[76]Many of those extra services (Sw: *tilläggstjänster*) are covered by a tax reduction scheme introduced in 2007, entitling taxpayers to deduct 50 % of the price of household services (in Swedish this legislation is often called "RUT").[1364] Persons entitled to elderly home care by administrative decision can thus order more hours or more services from the same provider chosen in the frame of the LOV-based system. It is difficult for the local authority to know whether this "private order" in fact corresponds to needs which should be covered by an increase of the assistance time granted by the administrative decision. By under-compensating the LOV-based services, local authorities may indirectly give an advantage to RUT-based services, which may be cheaper than LOV-based fees for the user, and better remunerated – although also heavily tax-subsidized – for providers. In such situations, providers lack interest in informing the local authority on the increased needs of users, but get eventually "overcompensated". This problem of "interaction" between LOV and RUT is evoked in several reports, for instance in the report of the National Board for Health and Welfare, 2012 *Vad efterfrågar kommuner?*, referred above, p. 13.

operate in the field of public social services.[77] However, this combination tends arguably to blur users' understanding of what their "social SGEI-based right" includes, and where their consumer rights begin, and renders very uncertain their capacity to defend these rights effectively. At a more general policy level, the real contribution of solidarity funding to equity-based services becomes very difficult to assess, and public authorities' *legal accountability* for quality social services diminishes.

9.2 School Education in the Swedish System of Choice

"Sweden has a history of adopting original education policies. In 1842, in order to improve equity, Sweden became the first country to establish compulsory schooling laws. Exactly 150 years later, Sweden became the second country – after Chile – to adopt a nationwide education voucher system."[78] This quote from Shafik points to the originality of the Swedish education policy, especially in a European context, as it is very similar to the neoliberal school voucher system promoted by economist Milton Friedman's in the 1950's.[79] This development may involve state aid and free movement issues, as providers of school education in the Swedish national system may probably be regarded as undertakings entrusted with SGEI tasks in the meaning of Article 106(2) TFEU. The Swedish education system comprises activities from preschool to university courses, but the focus in this part is on education covered by the Swedish Education Act.

9.2.1 School Education in Swedish Law: A Right and an Obligation

The Swedish constitution imposes on public institutions a particular duty to secure the right to education.[80] Moreover, the constitution also guarantees all children

[77]These objectives are also promoted by LOV, see government Bill on the Act on Systems of Choice, *Lag om valfrihetssystem*, proposition 2008/09:29, p. 18–19.

[78]Shafiq and Myers 2014, p. 113.

[79]Friedman described his school model in the following words: "Governments could require a minimum level of education which they could finance by giving parents vouchers redeemable for a specified maximum sum per child per year if spent on "approved" educational services. Parents would then be free to spend this sum and any additional sum on purchasing educational services from an "approved" institution of their own choice. The educational services could be rendered by private enterprises operated for profit, or by non-profit institutions of various kinds. The role of the government would be limited to assuring that the schools met certain minimum standards such as the inclusion of a minimum common content in their programs, much as it now inspects restaurants to assure that they maintain minimum sanitary standards." Friedman 1962, p. 89.

[80]Chapter 1 Section 2 of the Instrument of Government.

subject to statutory compulsory school attendance, the right to a free of charge elementary education in the national school system.[81] This implies that there is no unrestricted right for individuals to education in upper secondary education and university, which means that the state may impose conditions on pupils, for instance conditions of eligibility and aptitude, to have access to non-compulsory education, and also impose conditions related to available places.[82] These education rights, of which the "right to free of charge education connected to compulsory school attendance" is evidently the strongest, are reaffirmed in the Education Act, where it is also provided that the obligation to attend school is imposed on children between 7 and 16 living in Sweden, and that "certain rights" to school education exist even outside the scope of compulsory education.[83]

All children – regardless of their place of residence, social situation and economic situation – must be given equal access to education in the Swedish public school system, subject to certain restrictions in the Education Act.[84] This "right to equal access", arguably founded of the constitutional value of equal worth of all, is applicable throughout the national school system, at pre-school, compulsory and upper secondary levels, and regardless of whether pupils/students attend a school in the municipality of residence, in another municipality or an independent school.[85] In practice, this implies for instance that in compulsory school and upper secondary education, teaching material, school meals, health services and under certain conditions school transport are free of charge.[86]

9.2.2 Regulation and Organisation of the School System in Sweden: General Features

The main principles and rules for the organisation of the Swedish school system, in particular the goals and guidelines for the education to be provided, are set by the Education Act. The education system consists mainly of ground school education (compulsory for children aged 7 to 16) and of upper secondary education. At present, upper secondary education is voluntary, but a vast majority of ground

[81] Chapter 2 Section 18 of the Instrument of Government.

[82] This was reaffirmed by a commission of inquiry on independent schools "Friskolorna i samhället", SOU 2013:56, p. 54–55.

[83] Chapter 7 Section 3 of the Education Act (Sw.: *Skollagen (2010:800)).*

[84] Chapter 1 Section 8 of the Education Act.

[85] See Chapter 7 Section 3 of the Education Act. The value of equal worth for all is enshrined in Chapter 1 Sect. 2 first paragraph of the Instrument of Government.

[86] See Chapter 9 Section 8, Chapter 10 Section 10 and Chapter 15 Section 17 of the Education Act.

school pupils enrol directly in upper secondary school, which consists of three-year programs offering basic eligibility for students to continue studies at the post-secondary level. Upper secondary education consists of 'national programs', alongside with specially designed and individual study programs, and four-year programs for the learning disabled. On a voluntary basis, six years old children may also attend a one-year preschool class. The national school system includes also kindergartens, adult education, education for adults with learning disabilities, Swedish courses for migrants and after-school centres completing education in pre-school and compulsory classes.[87]

Both publicly owned schools (hereinafter called "municipal schools") or privately owned schools (hereinafter called "independent schools") are allowed to participate to the system, and have a certain degree of discretion to allocate resources and organise activities so that pupils attain the national goals. This freedom has been restricted in the new Education Act which came into force in July 2011. As a result, the methods used and the results to be achieved are now subject to more detailed rules and supervision at central level.[88] The system of choice in the field of education implies that pupils have a rather extensive freedom to choose provider of pre-school, compulsory and upper secondary education.

To have access to public funding, independent schools must have received an authorization from the Schools Inspectorate. Authorization entitles independent schools to receive a fixed amount of compensation per child/pupil (Sw: *skolpeng*) from every municipality where a child enrolled in that school resides, and importantly, independent schools may be for-profit.

These features in the Swedish school system result mainly from two legislative reforms, in 1991 the decentralisation to local authorities of the responsibility for school education by a social-democrat government, and in 1992 the introduction of a system of free choice by a market liberal government.[89] Since these reforms, and owing to consecutive legislative reforms and measures promoting the privatisation of municipal schools, the number of independent schools has increased considerably in the course of the latest 10 years, leading the percentage of children enrolled in these schools to increase steadily.

---

[87]See Chapter 1 Section 1 of the Education Act.

[88]The National Agency for Education (Sw.: *Skolverket*) is responsible for following up and evaluating the school system. The Schools Inspectorate (Sw.: *Statens Skolinspektion*) is the central Swedish agency responsible for supervising schools and ensuring that municipal and independent schools follow existing laws and regulations.

[89]The new political majority elected in 1991 promoted the development of independent schools as vectors of competition, cost efficiency and free choice in the field of education. Before the 1992 reform, independent schools could be publicly funded if they were considered beneficial to complement the municipal schools, typically in terms of alternative pedagogical methods.

9.2.3 *Are Swedish Schools Covered by Swedish and EU Law on Competition, Including State Aid?*

The fact that school education has developed into a business activity in Sweden is hard to deny, as clear from the following figures. By 2010, more than 15 per cent of ground schools and 48 per cent of upper secondary schools were independent schools in Sweden. Today, independent ground schools operate in about 210 of the 290 municipalities, mostly the urbanized areas of south and middle Sweden and in particular in the Greater Stockholm. In 2013, 85 percent of the pupils in independent upper secondary schools were enrolled in schools owned by for-profit limited companies, the corresponding proportion for compulsory elementary schools being of 66 percent.[90] For school year 2011/12, 207 000 pupils attended an independent school (54 per cent of them in compulsory elementary school and 46 per cent in upper secondary school).[91] That same year, about 11 per cent of all pupils at compulsory level and 22 per cent of all students at upper secondary level were enrolled in independent schools.[92]

Although a larger proportion of independent schools are elementary schools, independent upper secondary schools have relatively the "strongest position".[93] Most independent schools are situated in the largest Swedish cities, and the largest number of authorisations go to the biggest ten companies on the market. So far, the Swedish market for independent schools has been characterized by a rather steady growth, and by trends of consolidation (one fourth of the pupils attending independent schools are enrolled in one of the ten biggest independent school companies) and of incorporation (one fourth of the principals are part of a concern).[94] It is interesting to note that most recently, the private equity firm EQT has announced its plans to sell – with a market listing as a leading option – the Swedish education company Academedia, the largest education company in Sweden with over 90,000 children and adults enrolled in education programmes.[95]

---

[90]Report of the National Agency for Education on private actors in preschool and school education, "Privata aktörer inom förskola och skola - En nationell kartläggning av enskilda huvudmän och ägare", Skolverkets rapport 410 (2014), Stockholm: Frizes, p. 59.

[91]Report of the commission of inquiry on independent schools, "Friskolorna i samhället" SOU 2013:56, p. 76.

[92]Report of the National Agency for Education "Enskilda huvudmän och skolmarknadens ägarstrukturer", Skolverkets aktuella analyser 2012, Stockholm: Fritzes.

[93]Report of the commission of inquiry on independent schools, "Friskolorna i samhället" SOU 2013:56, p. 76.

[94]Ibid., p. 26 and 29.

[95]Academedia has reported a revenue of 6.4 billion Swedish crowns ($759 million) for the fiscal year 2013/14. This move may indicate that returns from investment in that sector are perceived as uncertain in the future.

During the latest years, the number of authorizations to open independent schools has decreased.[96] Spin-offs have also become rare.[97] These trends can be related to demographic and market data but they must also be seen in the context of the present intense debate on the liberalization of social services in Sweden. Among the topics of this debate, we find bankruptcies affecting the continuity of pupils' education, tax planning of independent schools owners, the drop of Swedish pupils' results in PISA studies since 2000, and signs of growing segregation.[98] Business analysts perceive the public debate as mostly centred on the for-profit issue, and underline that this is the main worry for operators in that sector. Their perception is that the development of a market sector in the field of education may be irreversible, for financial and legal reasons.[99]

It has been mentioned above (Sect. 8.2.2) that in the *Tibble gymnasium* and the *Sollentuna schools and pre-schools* cases,[100] the Swedish Supreme Administrative Court found that local authorities which closed municipal schools and sold their assets under market price to private operators starting independent schools at their place, infringed the Swedish administrative rule prohibiting that local authorities grant aid to individual undertakings.[101] As already underlined, these judgments are

---

[96]As a result, actors applying for an authorization cannot show that they will have a sufficient number of pupils to operate satisfactorily. According to the Swedish Schools Inspectorate there may be several factors for the decreasing interest in opening an independent school: stricter requirements on operators have been introduced in the Education Act, an uncertain state of the market, the political debate on independent schools, and decreasing pupils groups. See report of the Swedish Schools Inspectorate to the Swedish government "Årsredovisning 2012", published 2013-02-19, available at http://www.skolinspektionen.se/Documents/publikationssok/regeringsrapporter/arsredovisningar/skolinspektionen-arsredovisning-2012.pdf

[97]Planning becomes a difficult exercise in a dynamic market with free choice for users. Demographic aspects, like the decrease of the number of pupils, can necessitate consolidation but also cooperation between municipal schools to secure quality and continuity.

[98]In 2009, the gap between the best and worst Swedish students was larger than the OECD average, and while there was still less difference between good and bad schools than in many OECD countries, the gap in Sweden was in 2009 twice as wide as in 2000. See PISA 2009 results: What Students Know and Can Do – Student Performance in Reading, Mathematics and Science, Vol. 1, available at http://www.oecd.org/pisa/pisaproducts/48852548.pdf.

[99]See report of Grant Thornton Sweden AB on the development of the markets for health care and care in Sweden, Den privata vård- och omsorgsmarknaden ur ett finansiellt perspektiv - Hur mår den privata vård- och omsorgsmarknaden i Sverige? November 2012, available at http://www.grantthornton.se/Global/Dokument/Publikationer/Rapporter/2012/V%C3%A5rdstudie%202012.pdf, p. 12. Interviewed on the subject of political proposals to prohibit for-profit in the sector of publicly funded welfare services, professor Lars Henriksson has expressed doubts as to whether provisions requiring that from a certain date in the future, independent schools are driven in a specific legal form and not for profit, can be reconciled with constitutional rights enjoyed by existing companies, regardless of the activity pursued. See Kristina Lagerström and Johan Zachrisson Winberg, "Grundlagen skyddar skolbolagens vinster" *Sveriges Television* (8 September 2014), accessed 27 February 2015 at http://www.svt.se/nyheter/sverige/grundlagen-skyddar-valfardsvinsterna.

[100]Judgments of the administrative courts of appeal: Kammarrätten i Stockholm KR nr 584-08 (Täby kommun) and Kammarrätten i Stockholm KR nr 3801-09 (Sollentuna kommun).

[101]Chapter 2 Section 8 para 2 of the Local Government Act.

not binding on other courts, but they mirror the perfect lack of doubts of Swedish courts on the commercial character of the independent schools at issue in those cases, which were in both cases limited companies for profit.

Another question is whether local authorities, whose municipal schools directly compete with independent schools on pupils' enrolment, may be seen as exercising "sales activities" in the meaning of Chapter 3 Section 27 of the Swedish Competition Act. Given the uncertainty of the notion of "sales activities" in that provision, this is perhaps not excluded, but let us leave this question unanswered, and focus instead on whether independent schools in Sweden constitute undertakings in the meaning of EU competition (including state aid) rules. This question has already been answered elsewhere, but the main elements of the reasoning are rapidly recapitulated here.[102]

The relevant question, in accordance with the definition in *Höfner*, is whether independent schools conduct an economic activity, which, as established by the CJEU in *Pavlov*, consists in "offering services or goods on the market.[103] It has been shown in part I (Chap. 2) that the meaning of the notion of "economic activity" appears to be unitary in EU market law, which involves that determining whether a service is offered on a/the market gives the same result as determining whether a service is provided for remuneration. It has also be seen in Sect. 7.2.2.1 that this understanding explains that the Commission commonly applies a "cross-over reasoning" in state aid cases, assessing whether a service in a specific situation is "provided for remuneration" to find out whether it is "offered on a/the market" by the entity at issue. If this approach is used in the case of independent schools in Sweden, they are unmistakably to be regarded as undertakings.

The simple reason is that the amount per pupil enrolled which they receive from local authorities constitutes *for them* the consideration for the service in question. Not only does this consideration correspond to costs which they envisage to incur to provide the service, but it is also agreed by them when they apply for an authorization to open an independent school in a specific area which they consider appropriate. Independent schools are not bound to the national system by contract, and their strategic decisions are not subject to a strict State control. They operate on the basis of their own interest, even if this interest in some cases can be more "socially responsible" than simply aimed at maximizing profits. Although they have been formally integrated in the Swedish system of education, and therefore are constrained by public service obligations, they organise their activity autonomously, in particular regarding crucial financial decisions, which may imply considerable risks for them but even more for their users, as was the case in June 2013 when one of the largest operators of independent schools in Sweden went bankrupt.[104]

---

[102]Madell and Wehlander 2013, p. 487–493.

[103]Case C-41/90 *Höfner and Elser* [1991] ECR I-1979 and Joined Cases C-180/98 to C-184/98 *Pavlov* [2000] ECR I-6451.

[104]The John Bauer concern of independent upper secondary schools was sold 2008 to the Danish private equity firm Axcel.

In other words, it does simply not seem arguable to apply the *Humbel* formula to them and hold that their activity is not a service provided for remuneration because "*the State, in establishing and maintaining the system, is not seeking to engage in gainful activity but is fulfilling its duties towards its own population*". The situation of independent schools is comparable to the situation in *Jundt*, where courses occasionally provided by a German teacher at a French university in exchange for allowances, i.e. not for nothing, were regarded by the CJEU as a service, although these courses were not paid by students but by the university (and thus indirectly, by the French State).[105] Education provided by independent schools constitutes a service provided for remuneration, offered on the Swedish quasi-market of school education. Let us therefore conclude that they constitute undertakings in the meaning of the Treaty rules on competition (and state aid).

Another perhaps even more burning issue is whether municipal schools in competition with the independent schools, should also be regarded as undertakings. Their "raison d'être" may be rightly perceived by themselves as being exclusively to fulfil the duties of local authorities towards their population. However, in the functional approach of the CJEU, this circumstance – i.e. their social objective – is a priori not relevant. Given the fact that they are in competition with market operators (competing for pupils), it seems quite probable that they should also be regarded as undertakings. To be sure, this is some revolution, be it quiet.

9.2.4 Financing of Schools in Free Choice System: Risk of State Aid?

Independent schools must cover their costs with the voucher received from local authorities for each pupil enrolled, and may not charge fees from their users. This voucher consists of a basic voucher, plus an additional voucher for each pupil/student in need of extensive support or entitled to native language lessons.[106] The basic voucher's amount, set for each calendar year by every local authority on the basis of the municipality's budget, is meant to cover a determined set of costs such as teaching material, wages, pupils' healthcare, meals, facilities and VAT. This amount varies between local authorities and is also different for different programmes, but it must correspond to the average costs per child/student for an

[105]Case C-281/06 *Jundt* [2007] ECR I-12231.

[106]The principles for determining the vouchers granted to independent schools are set by governmental decrees (when this is written, these decrees include in particular *Skolförorningen (2011:185)* for elementary schools, and *Gymnasieförordningen (2010:2039)* for upper secondary schools).

equivalent municipal school unit and programme.[107] The Swedish legislator has emphasized that the "principle on equal conditions" must not only govern children's access to the public education system, but also the economic conditions of school operators, as a condition for a real freedom of choice.[108]

Hence, a central objective in Swedish law on school education is to ensure that independent schools have the same economic conditions as municipal schools. In a pedagogical perspective, as independent schools are now a part of the public system, the preparatory works underline that they must serve the same national objectives as municipal schools, and therefore must operate under equivalent conditions, so that school education has an equivalent content and high quality everywhere in Sweden, secures good skills and paves the way for life-long learning. Meanwhile, it has also been repeatedly emphasized that equivalence should not mean uniformity, as schools must be allowed pedagogical freedom, and to develop their own profile.[109] The Bill on the new Education Act in force since 2011 expressed an ambition to achieve a balance between pedagogical freedom and creativity – which made independent schools attractive to their users and legitimate to support with public funding in the first place – and a level of convergence between municipal and independent schools securing quality, equal chances and legal security.[110]

As a result, there is today more homogeneity in the public service obligations imposed on municipal and independent schools, but there are no detailed rules on how vouchers should be used for each of the posts they are meant to cover. Thus, independent schools are free to organise teaching in a specific school, as long as "quality is high enough to enable the objectives set for education to be achieved".[111] This space of freedom can serve pedagogical and organisational innovation, but opens also for overcompensation in a system where remuneration per service unit is fixed, and thus risks of state aid arise if the condition of trade effect is fulfilled.

In this respect it is important to mention here the "independent schools committee", appointed to establish a broad political platform on the question of independent schools, in particular the conditions for spin-offs, in a context of growing

---

[107]An independent school is not obliged to enrol or keep a pupil in need of extensive support or of native language lessons, if the municipality has not granted the additional voucher for this pupil. The municipality is not either obliged to grant the additional voucher in case this causes particular organisational or financial problems.

[108]Government Bill on state funding on equal conditions, *Offentliga bidrag på lika villkor*, proposition 2008/09:171, p. 25.

[109]Ibid.

[110]See government Bill on the new Education Act, *Den nya skollagen - för kunskap, valfrihet och trygghet*, proposition 2009/2010:165, p. 206. An earlier report of the commission of inquiry on an Education Act for quality and equality "Skollag för kvalitet och likvärdighet" SOU 2002:121, had already expressed the view that municipal and independent schools to the largest possible should be submitted to the same regulation.

[111]Report of the commission of inquiry on independent schools "Friskolorna i samhället" SOU 2013:56, p. 62 (own translation).

concern about Swedish pupils' worsening performance and turbulent debate on issues such as operators' profits and "grades' inflation".[112] In their report, issued in 2013, the political parties gathered in the committee did not agree on the cause of these problems, in particular on whether decentralisation of school education or for-profit actors in the public school system were to blame. Nevertheless, six of these parties agreed to propose modifications in the Education Act in order to make clear that "the possibility to make profit in that sector is always coupled to requirements on good quality".[113]

A point of departure for the independent schools committee was that its proposals would not preclude independent schools from being for-profit. Its report emphasized that school operators must achieve a surplus in order to secure their long-term financial stability and invest in the activity, and that schools organised in limited companies must primarily seek profit, and may distribute dividends.[114] The report took the view that in spite of these market-mechanisms, the school system was not a genuine market, because children and their families can choose education but do not pay for it, because the community financing public education has own preferences on its definition, and because the price of the service is set through political decisions and not through an agreement between the provider and the recipient.

However, referring to the Commission's decision to close the Swedish complaints on school spin-offs, the independent schools committee remarked that the Commission had not stated that state aid rules do not apply to measures such as schools' spin-offs.[115] The committee concluded that "the legal situation was clear", that there was no possibility to sell municipal assets under market price, and that "an assessment must be made in each individual case".[116] It is easy to see that the report did perhaps not consider pupils are real consumers (although amusingly, the report explained that in the Swedish education system, resources are

---

[112]Ibid., p. 43. In appointing this committee, the government gave its view that the independent schools' reform has been a success which *raised interest in other countries*, but expressed a concern that private operators should pay a market price when taking over the activity of municipal schools, and that it was necessary to provide more information on independent schools for pupils, families and other stakeholders to assess their quality. See the mission of inquiry of the commission (Sw: *Kommittédirektiv 2011:68*), in the report of the commission of inquiry on independent schools "Friskolorna i samhället" SOU 2013:56, p. 374–375.

[113]Ibid., own translation. The six parties were De nya moderaterna, Folkpartiet, Centerpartiet and Kristdemokratern (the four parties which together have governed Sweden between 2006 and 2014 under the name "Alliansen"), Social-demokraterna and Miljöpartiet. An even more recent report of the commission of inquiry on the Swedish school system "Staten får inte abdikera" (SOU 2014:5), concluded that the problems affecting Swedish education are related to the decentralisation of the responsibility for school education to local authorities.

[114]Ibid., p. 79–80.

[115]Report of the commission of inquiry on independent schools "Friskolorna i samhället" SOU 2013:56, p. 283.

[116]Ibid., own translation.

allocated on the basis of a "*customer* choice model"[117]), but did consider independent schools as real undertakings. The independent schools committee described namely the public funding of independent schools, under the principle of equal conditions, in the following terms:

> The funding is therefore not related to the costs actually incurred by the school for providing the service. The funding is not either related to the education's quality, even if a certain level of quality is required to be authorized as principal and to offer education in an independent school./…/Schools cannot compete through price, because they are funded by the State on the basis of flat rates. They can instead compete by raising quality and by adapting education to the requests of pupils and their families. However, for this competition to promote quality, the consumer must be able to make rational choices based on facts.[118]

If we sum up the independent schools committee's observations, the situation is rather clear: independent schools' activity is surely economic in the meaning of EU state aid law, but there is no competition on price, public funding is not related to the costs incurred and not either to the quality of the education provided. Under such circumstances, the risk of over-compensation is patent, one indication being the profit levels of some actors in that sector, although the committee found out that there was no statistics available on profits for undertakings conducting elementary school education and upper secondary school education.[119] This lack of statistics may be related to the fact that the government has never used its legal mandate to adopt provisions requiring from independent school principals to submit an economic account of their activity, with an objective to increase the control and the transparency of their use of public resources.[120]

Depending on how clearly and precisely independent schools' public service tasks are formulated and followed up, the risk that flat rate vouchers lead to overcompensate certain operators must clearly be envisaged, in particular because they know their costs best. However, to constitute state aid in the meaning of Article 107(1) TFEU, public funding must not only provide or risk providing selective advantages to undertakings, it must also affect trade between the Member States. For medium and large firms on the Swedish market, it seems clear that the amounts perceived in their school education activities exceeds the general de minimis threshold and the SGEI de minimis threshold, and thus effect on trade cannot

---

[117]Ibid., p. 86.

[118]Ibid., p. 87 and 90, own translation.

[119]Ibid., p. 83.

[120]This mandate follows from Chapter 29 Section 25 of the Education Act. The committee pointed to the fact that no provisions have been adopted on the basis of this delegation, see the report of the commission of inquiry, "Friskolorna i samhället" SOU 2013:56, p. 140.

a priori be excluded.[121] An effect on trade could be argued to be lacking, as education markets may be described as in principle local, given the fact that pupils must normally attend a school not too far away from their place of residence.

However, school education services can also be subject to international trade, especially if the service is connected to an "education concept" that may be sold to public or private school owners in other countries. This seems to be the approach of some large school concerns established in Sweden. For instance, Kunskapsskolan Education, owned to a large part by the Magnora group, is the owner and developer of the "KED program", described by the company as a "proven concept for personalized education".[122] Kunskapsskolan explains that its goal is "to establish, operate and develop schools where every student is recognized as a unique individual with the ability, ambition and support to learn and grow beyond what she or he thought possible".[123] The company informs on its joint venture since 2013 with investors in Saudi Arabia to build schools on a Saudi version of the KED Program, its collaboration since 2014 with a Dutch company to offer Dutch schools consulting services and/or the possibility to introduce the whole KED Program, and since 2012 its opening of "academies" in the UK. Academedia, owned by the Swedish private equity firm EQT, is the largest company for independent schools in Sweden, but runs also pre-schools and adult education, both in Sweden and Norway.[124] Academedia's CEO declared recently that the voucher system, in an export perspective, can allow a rapid expansion of kindergartens in Europe and sees strong possibilities to export Swedish companies' service model.[125]

Such examples show not only that school education is already to some extent an international business activity, but also that companies conducting school education and integrated in larger business corporations, can easily cross-subsidize

[121]The de minimis amount is of EUR 200 000 over any period of three fiscal years pursuant to Article 3(2) of Commission Regulation (EU) No 1407/2013 of 18 December 2013 on the application of Articles 107 and 108 of the Treaty on the Functioning of the European Union to de minimis aid [2013] OJ L352/1, and of EUR 500 000 over any period of three fiscal years pursuant to Article 2(2) of Commission Regulation (EU) No 360/2012 of 25 April 2012 on the application of Articles 107 and 108 of the Treaty on the Functioning of the European Union to de minimis aid granted to undertakings providing services of general economic interest [2012] OJ L114/8.

[122]When this is written, Magnora owns a large part of Kunskapsskolan, as well as a communication consultancy firm (Kreab Gavin Anderson), a company for market and opinion research consultancies (Demoskop), and a company for elderly care and housing (Silver life).

[123]Kunskapsskolan explains that its founding idea is "that successful learning must be personalized and based on each student´s individual strengths, weaknesses, previous educational experiences and goals. This task demands a tailor-made education on an individual level. We take on the burden of conceptualizing and standardizing materials, tools and systems, thereby freeing the schools to customize and personalize the students´ education. When the resources of learning — time, curricula, syllabuses, premises and working tools — are geared to support the same educational concept and if these resources are designed from the best proven practices, optimal conditions are created for schools to succeed in the task of focusing on each individual."

[124]Academedia owns also one of Norway's largest provider of kindergartens, Espira.

[125]See article of Karin Grundberg Wolodarski, "Skoljättarna ökar vinsterna" *Dagens Industri* (Stockholm, 12 March 2014).

other activities subject to trade within and outside the EU, unless the proportionality of their compensation for school education services is secured. Hence, it is submitted that risks of state aid may exist, and therefore the question is whether the amounts received from local authorities may be seen as public service compensation for SGEI tasks entrusted to independent schools under Article 106(2) TFEU.[126]

9.2.5 *Municipal and Independent Schools' Public Service Tasks: SGEI Tasks?*

In this section, the purpose is simply to give a summarized and non-exhaustive account of tasks imposed on school operators. The point of departure is that principles and missions are set for the national school system as a whole,[127] but that public and private school operators are individually responsible for the compliance of their education activities with Swedish law.[128] Both municipal and independent schools must be open without distinction to all pupils entitled to education in preschool, compulsory school and upper secondary school.[129] However, an independent school does not have to enrol a child with special educational needs if this would cause serious economic or organisational difficulties for the school. Conversely, the local authority is not obliged to compensate a free school that enrols such children. Whereas instruction may not be confessional, independent schools may include confessional education, on a non-compulsory basis for the children enrolled.

Pupils must have access to qualified teachers, learning support, and objective and comprehensive instruction, regardless of which operator is managing the school unit.[130] As a general rule curricula are decided at central level and must be followed by all local operators – public or private – of compulsory schools.[131] National programs in upper secondary schools are likewise established at central level and as a general rule must be followed by all operators. All operators are

[126] For an overview of the structure of several large school concerns in Sweden, see a report of the National Education Agency on independent schools and the school market ownership structure, *Enskilda huvudmän och skolmarknadens ägarstrukturer*, Skolverkets aktuella analyser 2012, p. 36–41.

[127] Chapter 1 Section 4–5 of the Education Act.

[128] Chapter 2 Section 8 of the Education Act.

[129] See Chapter 9 Section 17, Chapter 10 Sections 25 and 35, Chapter 11 Sections 25 and 34, Chapter 16 Sections 42–48, Chapter 18 Sections 8–9 of the Education Act.

[130] See the preparatory works to the Education Act, Government Bill on the new Education Act, *Den nya skollagen - för kunskap, valfrihet och trygghet*, proposition 2009/10:165, p. 206.

[131] Chapter 10 Section 8 of the Education Act.

subject to an obligation to secure that the facilities are appropriate for education purposes, that pupils and students have access to certain health care services, to a school library, and at relevant level to student- and professional counselling. Also, all operators must secure that their teachers have opportunities to skills development.

The overall amount of teaching hours in elementary and upper secondary school is regulated by the Education Act, and teaching at elementary school may not be provided on Saturdays, Sundays and holidays.[132] Although upper secondary schools have a certain freedom to allocate teaching hours to different courses, provisions on the number of teaching hours which pupils have a right to are laid down in the Decree on elementary school (Sw: *Skolförordningen* (2011:185) and the Decree on upper secondary school education (Sw: *Gymnasieförordningen* (2010:2039).

Some specific obligations rest upon the municipal schools, as particular instruments for the local authorities to fulfil their duties towards their inhabitants. Local authorities must in particular ensure that all pupils entitled to compulsory education have access to education in ground school (operated by public or private bodies) and that all students entitled to upper secondary education have access to the national upper secondary education programs.[133] By contrast, private operators are not entrusted with continuity obligations. They may offer a limited number of upper secondary education programs and may close down a school unit for economic reasons, which in practice happens in case of bankruptcy. Furthermore, a number of exception rules offer more flexibility to independent schools under certain conditions.

The sum of these obligations seems to go further than simply imposing certain rules of authorization, of functioning or of control on all operators, as the Education Act instead defines service conditions of universality, quality, and adaptation to users' needs, which the GC considered in *BUPA* as characteristic of an SGEI.[134] If the public funding of independent schools is considered justified by the SGEI character of their task, it would appear that their public service obligations are defined in law, principally the Education Act, and that law is also the official document whereby the tasks are entrusted to them, a form of entrustment that was found compatible with the Treaties by the GC in *BUPA*.[135]

---

[132]Chapter 7 Section 17 of the Education Act. Chapter 16 Section 18.

[133]Chapter 10 Section 24 and Chapter 16 Section 42 of the Education Act.

[134]Case T-289/03 *BUPA* [2008] ECR II-81, para 182. See above Sect. 9.2.3. The GC considered that the obligations at issue restricted the commercial freedom of the insurers to an extent going considerably beyond ordinary conditions of authorisation to exercise an activity in a specific sector.

[135]Ibid., para 179.

9.2.6 Does School Education Provided in Free Choice Comply with the 2011 SGEI Package?

As school education is still axiomatically claimed to be a non-economic activity if it is conducted in the frame of a national school system, the Commission has not found useful to mention education among the social services covered by the 2011 SGEI Decision, which implies that Swedish law imposing on local authorities to compensate public service obligations imposed by the State on undertakings providing education in the Swedish school system would have to be notified to the Commission, plausibly on the basis of the 2011 SGEI Framework.

This is where problems appear, as the 2011 SGEI Framework requires that the act or acts of entrustment of SGEI tasks include in particular the content and duration of the public service obligations (point 16 (a)), the description of the compensation mechanism and the parameters for calculating, monitoring and reviewing the compensation (point 16 (d)), and the arrangements for avoiding and recovering any overcompensation (point 16 (e)). Also, the duration of the period of entrustment should be justified by reference to objective criteria such as the need to amortise non-transferable fixed assets, and in principle, should not exceed the period required for the depreciation of the most significant assets required to provide the SGEI (point 17).

It is obvious that the system of free choice for school education does not fulfil these conditions, in particular because no duration is provided for the authorizations granted to independent schools, and as no arrangements exist for recovering any overcompensation. Some would say that the 2011 SGEI Framework requirements, meant to balance market interests and public service interests, seem almost incapable to accommodate the specificities of a social service as characterized by needs of continuity, equal treatment, and "objective" quality as school education, and that it may be a sure sign that school education, *a fortiori* if it is compulsory and wholly tax funded, *should* perhaps not be economic. But facts are hard here: the activity *is* economic in Sweden.

In contrast with this book, the Swedish State has not yet questioned whether the system of free choice for school education is compatible with EU state aid rules, in other words whether it is "legal". However, the Swedish State is struggling to find an appropriate balance between the many interests it has attached to school education, and the following proposals have been agreed to by six political parties in the parliamentary committee on independent schools evoked above:

- Assessment of principal's suitability in terms of conduct and economic diligence
- Assessment of owners' suitability and long-term engagement
- Consultation with local authority before establishment
- Protection of whistle-blowers for workers in independent schools
- Transparent information on independent schools, in particular on their economy
- Sanctions in case of serious deficiencies.[136]

[136]Report of the Commission of inquiry on independent schools "Friskolorna i samhället" SOU 2013:56, p. 287.

One of the most arduous issues is how secure school education's continuity, in a sector where limited companies dominate, and where private equity firms own several of the largest independent school companies. In order to prevent frequent changes of ownership and to secure independent schools' quality, the committee on independent schools considered appropriate to verify owners' intention to conduct the activity on a long-term basis. The Swedish government proposed to introduce several provisions ensuring some control of owners' "seriousness", and these provisions have recently entered into force.[137] Also, a commission of inquiry was appointed 2012 to examine which conditions should be imposed on owners and operators of welfare service companies in Sweden.[138]

To pursue this objective is easier said than done. The independent schools committee underlined that, for administrative efficiency motives, the Schools Inspectorate should not have to examine in detail each change of ownership in an independent school company leading a new owner to gain a decisive influence on the company's activity. The difficulty seems to lie in finding a legal instrument capable of imposing a commitment from private operators, in order to secure school education' critical need of *continuity*, *stability* and *planning*, in the interest of young citizens, their family, and public authorities responsible for securing access – *equal* access conditions – to school education.

The Swedish authorization-based system for free choice school education is particularly advantageous for private owners of independent schools, as they can at any time withdraw from the provision of school education without incurring particular sanctions, and also because the public authorities funding their activity have no clear powers on their establishment (independent schools are only required to engage a *consultation* with the local authority before they establish). The new procurement directives do not impose any procedure leading to their funding by local authorities, carving out from the notion of procurement both:

- "situations where all operators fulfilling certain conditions are entitled to perform a given task, without any selectivity, such as customer choice and service voucher systems" which "should not be understood as being procurement but simple authorisation schemes".[139]
- "acts such as authorisations or licences, whereby the Member State or a public authority thereof establishes the conditions for the exercise of an economic activity, including a condition to carry out a given operation, granted, normally, on request of the economic operator and not on the initiative of the contracting authority or the contracting entity and where the economic operator remains free to withdraw from the provision of works or services", which "should not qualify as concessions".[140]

[137]Modifications of the Education Act entered into force in July 2015, Government Bill on condition for independent schools, *Villkor för fristående skolor m.m.*, proposition 2013/14:112.

[138]Report of the commission of inquiry on requirements on private actors providing welfare services "Krav på privata aktörer i välfärden" SOU 2015:7 (Ägarprövningsutredningen).

[139]Recital 4 of the 2014 Public Sector Directive.

[140]Recital 14 of the 2014 Concessions Directive.

In other words, EU *procurement* legislation does not impose *any* procedure for the entrustment of wholly tax-funded SGEIs tasks in the systems of choice, allowing to introduce some competition between providers by imposing a contract-based continuity obligation, be it a long-time concession contract, and preventing over-compensation by precluding that operators withdraw too easily from their publicly funded task. This is even more so if school education provided by independent schools is not even characterized as a service in the meaning of the Treaties, on the weak argument that it is provided in the frame of a national school system.

9.2.7 A Very Inconvenient Question: Has School Education in Public Systems Become a Service Within the Meaning of Article 57 TFEU?

It has been argued in Sect. 13.1.2.3 that the compensation received for each pupil enrolled in an independent school is perceived by this school as remuneration for the service provided, and logically, this implies that school education as provided in such schemes constitutes an activity that *is* economic in Sweden, a service entitled to free movement in accordance with Article 56 TFEU. An important issue is whether the fact that this type of service *is de facto* provided for remuneration in *one* Member State implies automatically that it may be considered as *normally* provided for remuneration and therefore a service in the meaning of Article 57 TFEU.

As seen in chap. 2, the CJEU's approach to this question appears to be "once a service, always a service", in other words Member States where the provision of a service is not economic due to regulatory restrictions will have to adapt their regulation to the fact that in other Member States, operators may provide a similar service for remuneration, related to fundamental freedom protected by Article 56 TFEU. This is because the existence, be it in other Member States, of economic operators of this activity proves that this activity, for instance a service, *can be* economic, *can be* provided for remuneration, and may considered as *normally* provided for remuneration in the meaning of Article 57 TFEU. So the answer to the inconvenient question is probably "yes".

Interestingly, Davies raised this issue more than a decade ago, considering that "the use of the duty of the State [made by the CJEU] as a magic bullet to stop Article 49 [now Article 56 TFEU] is an oddity of *Humbel* and *Wirth*, rather than an authentic legal rule".[141] Asking when payment from a State body can be remuneration/consideration, Davies saw three structural differences in the welfare arrangements in the fields of school education respectively health care. In his view the health care situation was characterized by a stronger link recipient-payer and

[141] Davies 2002, p. 32.

identifiable payments for specific services, while in the education case payments seemed more internal, as payer and provider were part of the same system. He concluded that, *Humbel* notwithstanding, the most convincing element determining that the service is provided for remuneration is the separateness of the paying and providing institutions, the element of "free will" and wrote:

> If a Member State introduced a voucher education system, where students (or parents) were issued vouchers which they could use at either State or private schools, which would then return the voucher to the State for payment, this would introduce that market, free will element.[142]

Thus, writing at a time (2002) when no Member State allowed publicly funded school education to be for-profit, Davies suggested already that "education should fall under Article 49" adding that "of course public policy might well allow national restrictions to be maintained".[143] The situation in Sweden is that, not only do pupils and their families have a right to freely choose school, but private schools have a right to receive payment per pupil enrolled from public authorities (a well identified payment for the specific service), and to have another objective than the State with their activity (in most cases seek profit). Under such circumstances, *Humbel* gives simply no argument to claim that school education is not a service in the meaning of the Treaties.

In the field of school education, where pupils' cross-border mobility can be expected to be very low, and where school education, which is a very integrated service extremely determined by national public law rules as well as by local human and material resources, it may seem difficult to let the specific national school education service cross border, and so the fact that school education may be regarded as a service, at least in its definition in Sweden, is perhaps not a big issue for other Member States from a regulatory point of view.

However, as explained above, Swedish school education companies have established in other Member States. In Member States which do not allow for-profit education, these companies can instead offer and sell their pedagogical concepts on the market, for instance Magnora in the Netherlands.[144] Under such circumstances, it is not unimaginable that education companies at a certain stage of their development find opportune to claim that their right to establishment should not be restricted by the national rules of the Member States where they have exercised this right, for instance by national rules reserving public funding to private not-for-profit operators. If they claimed this right judicially, Member States wishing to

---

[142]Ibid., p. 33–35.

[143]Ibid., p. 35 footnote 24, where Davies delivered this conclusion after making the following remark: "[t]he voucher system is difficult to distinguish from the current situation in the Netherlands, where both private and State universities and schools exist, and receive funding from the State for each student they take. There may be no vouchers that pass through hands, but the system is essentially the same."

[144]This appears to be the case of Kunskapsskolan in the Netherlands, clearly, and perhaps in UK, less clearly, as the financing terms of "sponsors" for academies in UK is not easy to understand for outsiders.

uphold that rule would probably have to rely on the CJEU's approach of "judicial subsidiarity" in *Sodemare* which, contrary to what several legal scholars expected, has not been reversed but rather confirmed by the Court in *San Lorenzo*.[145]

Such developments should arguably be anticipated, given the political interest existing in certain Member States for the model experimented in Sweden, and the democratic importance of the governance of school education. An important question is which legal arguments Member States would be able to rely on in order to claim their powers to regulate the conditions which must be fulfilled by school operators in their publicly funded system, for instance a not-for-profit condition. Would their system be regarded as involving SGEI tasks for operators or would it be considered as a NESGI? Could they successfully claim their view that cohesion and education quality might be adversely affected by the introduction of profit motives in school provision?

9.3 Conclusions

Findings related to elderly home care in the Swedish LOV-based systems of choice

It has been found that elderly home care in LOV-based systems of choice constitutes an economic activity and that its public funding of can affect trade. Although the Swedish market for elderly home care is local on the demand side, and characterised by the presence of many SMEs, it comprises also large companies offering their services both in Sweden and in other Member States, and which often belong to company groups conducting other activities in the field of social services or in other fields. The analysis of elderly home care in LOV-based systems of choice has shown that LOV-based systems for elderly home care do not, in the present state of Swedish and EU law, comply with the *Altmark* criteria, in particular the fourth criterion, as

- LOV does not seem to constitute procurement in the meaning of EU procurement directives, and as
- Municipal entities do not constitute benchmarks in the meaning of the fourth *Altmark* criterion.

[145]Case C-113/13 *San Lorenzo* [decided on 11 December 2014, nyr], para 50. For a critical discussion on the Court's reasoning in *Sodemare*, see for instance Hancher and Sauter 2009, p. 20. For a discussion on their view that the Court's approach was "perhaps naïve", see Wehlander 2015, p. 82–83, arguing that it may instead be understood as a manifestation of the Court' loyalty to the Treaties, implying that it lets democracy withhold substantive economic powers in social sectors, where the Court knows that its case law has abolished any possibility for the Member States to claim a nucleus of national sovereignty.

LOV-based systems for elderly home care do not either comply with the 2011 SGEI Decision which applies to this social service as LOV

- Does not impose explicitly that local authorities refer to the SGEI Decision in their contracts,
- Does not impose on local authorities to define the tasks compensated precisely to ensure that providers are on equal terms,
- Does not limit the duration of the contracts with providers under 10 years, - Does not provide for a mechanism preventing or avoiding over-compensation.

If correct, this finding may explain the Swedish State's reluctance to explicitly characterise the public funding of elderly home care as a compensation of SGEI tasks, as it would have highlighted the applicability of EU state aid rules under Article 106(2) TFEU and rendered very difficult to rapidly develop LOV-based markets for a social service such as elderly home care.

To limit the risk of distorting competition arising from funding elderly home care, public authorities should define clearly and precisely their public service obligations, but this can perhaps involve higher provision costs and also reduce the number of operators in the system. If local authorities refrain from imposing precise public service tasks in LOV-based systems, and pay the same amount to all operators, they infringe the principle of undistorted competition. It may be tempting to argue that a derogation from this principle is necessary to serve the "general interest that users may choose among many different market operators". But is a "broad market choice" what is meant by the SGEI values of "high level of quality, safety and user rights" in the SGI Protocol?

Arguably not, and therefore the legal issue of imprecise SGEI tasks should be related to the policy issue of service quality. To define clear quality criteria *ex ante* in elderly home care is frequently claimed to be very difficult, in particular because users know best what is good for them, but it is arguably *possible* to define *ex ante* non-discriminatory and proportional quality requirements – including time spent with users – which can be followed up and measured, and which *any* user would like if allowed to choose. The vagueness of elderly home care providers' tasks has become a central policy issue in Sweden, but it is arguably also a legislative issue, as it seems that local authorities' discretion under LOV can affect the proportionality of the compensation paid (an EU competition law issue), and the equal treatment of users by allowing a heterogeneous service quality (a Swedish administrative law issue).

In the Swedish decentralised model of elderly home care, local authorities have undeniably a statutory public service task to supply elderly home care of good quality to all of their inhabitants in need of such care, but this task is formulated in very general terms in the Social Services Act, in fact rather as a universal service obligation, and leaves them with a wide discretion to define operators' SGEI tasks. Unless they receive clear instructions from the legislator, the risk is patent that they do "the wrong thing" and define the public service obligations attached to the services which they finance vaguely, especially

- If the Swedish legislator lays emphasis on the risk that requirements are not proportional and infringe EU free movement law
- If the Swedish legislator insists that two specific requirements may limit the number of operators in the system
- If the Swedish legislator puts them under budget balance constraints.

This is where a broad understanding of the notion of "SGEI" in Article 14 TFEU, which seems to be the CJEU's understanding, becomes valuable in a normative perspective. Article 14 TFEU supposes that the SGEI missions exist *before* they are entrusted, as the reference allowing Member States to determine the principles and conditions enabling these missions to be achieved. By imposing a universal service obligations of elderly home care on local authorities, it is submitted that the Swedish legislator defines an SGEI mission in the meaning of Article 14 TFEU, but unless the objective of this mission is clear, it is doubtful whether the SGEI tasks entrusted to undertakings will be precise. A factor explaining the lack of clear public service requirement in LOV-based elderly home care is arguably that LOV, as already mentioned, has many policy objectives, not only to supply "good quality" elderly home care, but also to promote women entrepreneurship, small undertakings in the public sector, and attractive conditions to operate in the field of public social services.

If the substantial conditions imposed by the 2011 SGEI Decision were loyally considered as a normative point of departure in LOV-based elderly home care systems, the public service tasks would have to be defined with more precision, which would arguably allow to address competition concerns and quality – and continuity – concerns at the same time. This would be valuable because elderly home care is delivered in many homes, and is particularly difficult to ensure through elderly people's market control.

Findings related to school education in the Swedish authorisation-based systems of choice

The analysis of the Swedish system of choice for primary and upper-secondary school education shows that in that system, operators conduct an economic activity. It is submitted that both private and public operators in the system constitute undertakings for the purpose of EU competition law. While this argument has already been made elsewhere,[146] it has also been found here that the public funding of school education can affect trade and is constrained by EU state aid rules, given the risks of cross-subsidisation and the presence in the Swedish school market of companies offering school education services in several Member States and in third countries. It has also been submitted that the statutory obligations imposed on school operators constitute public service obligations and that private and public school undertakings may be seen as undertakings entrusted with SGEI tasks in the meaning of Article 106(2) TFEU.

If it is admitted that Article 107(1) TFEU applies to the public financing of large companies conducting both for-profit school education in Sweden and other educational and social services in other Member States, a logical conclusion

[146] Madell and Wehlander 2013, p. 471–495.

should be that this public financing should be compatible with the EU state aid rules on SGEIs, which primarily aim at limiting competition distortions caused by the existence of public service missions imposed of some or all operators on a market. It seems arguable that a loyal application of these rules would allow addressing both competition and quality concerns.

A loyal application of the 2011 SGEI Framework covering school education in Sweden would namely imply that a duration for the entrustment of operators' SGEI-tasks *must* be clear in the act or acts entrusting these tasks. As the possibility to ensure continuity in the service provision of school education has become a very delicate issue in Sweden, it seems that a loyal application of EU rules on SGEIs may, for once, be welcome by the Swedish legislator. It seems easier to control private school operators' performance in terms of continuity by introducing a statutory condition of explicit and proportional duration for the education task entrusted and publicly funded, than by trying to control the motives and conditions of school operators' ownership.[147]

References

Davies G (2002) Welfare as a service. Legal Issues Econ Integr 29(1):27–40

Friedman M (1962) The role of government in education, chapter 6 in capitalism and freedom: University of Chicago Press, Chicago. The chapter is based on an article that appeared 1955. In: Robert A. Solo (ed) Economics and the public interest, Rutgers University Press, New Brunswick, NJ

Hancher L, Sauter W (2009) One foot in the grave or one step beyond? from Sodemare to DocMorris: the EU's freedom of establishment case law concerning healthcare. http://ssrn.com/abstract=1429315, Accessed 31 Dec 2015

Hedelin J (2010) De nya svenska reglerna om konkurrensbegränsande offentlig verksamhet – en spegel av reglerna om tjänster av allmänt ekonomiskt intresse? In: Madell T, Bekkedal T, Neergaard U (eds) Den nordiska välfärden och marknaden: Nordiska erfarenheter av tjänster av allmänt intresse i en EU-rättslig kontext. Iustus förlag, Uppsala

Madell T, Wehlander C (2013) SSGIs in Sweden: with a special emphasis on education. In: Neergaard U et al (eds) Social services of general interest in the EU. T.M.C Asser Press, The Hague

Shafiq MN, Myers JP (2014) Educational vouchers and social cohesion: a statistical analysis of student civic attitudes in Sweden 1999–2009. Am J Educ 121(1):111–136

Sundstrand A (2012) Offentlig upphandling - primärrättens reglering av offentliga kontrakt. Stockholms universitet

Wehlander C (2015) Who is afraid of SGEI – services of general economic interest in EU law with a special study on swedish systems of choice. Skrifter från Juridiska Institutionen i Umeå, Nr. 32, Umeå

[147]This is the regulatory alternative which has been studied by the committee of enquiry on requirements on private actors providing welfare services "Krav på privata aktörer i välfärden" ("Ägarpröningsutredningen") SOU 2015:7, already evoked above.

Chapter 10
Conclusions of Part III: EU Market Governance of Social Services a Democratic Issue

Abstract This Chapter draws conclusions on part III and pulls together these strands with the results of parts I and II set out in Chaps. 2 and 6 in order to propose answers to the research questions of the book formulated in Chap. 1. It proposes a short final reflection on the Europeanisation of social services from a democracy perspective.

Contents

Based on the findings in Chaps. 7 to 9, this final chapter answers the sub-question addressed by part III, namely

> What place does the EU legislator give to the Treaty principles on SGEIs in EU legislation harmonizing the market for social services and how can it affect the liberalization of these services in the Member States?

Thus, Sect. 10.1 concludes on how EU legislation adopted under the SGI Quality Framework and harmonizing the market for social services is connected to the Treaty principles on SGEIs, and Sect. 10.2 concludes on whether a loyal application of the Treaty rules on SGEIs can affect the liberalization of social services in the Member States.

C. Wehlander, *Services of General Economic Interest as a Constitutional Concept of EU Law*, Legal Issues of Services of General Interest,
DOI 10.1007/978-94-6265-117-3_10

These conclusions allow proposing an answer to main research question of the book, which should be recalled here

> Is it possible to understand SGEI as a constitutional EU concept relevant throughout the EU Treaties, and can a transparent and loyal enforcement of the Treaty principles attached to SGEIs restrict the Member States' discretion to liberalize social services and the expansion of a European market for social services?

Indeed, Sect. 10.3 concludes on concerns shared by the Commission and certain Member States that the development of market-based public services – in particular for social services – be hampered if the SGEI-regulation affecting them at EU or national level is too apparent in legislation. The evidence of these concerns is confirmed by fresh evidence – the Commission Communication on public procurement rules connected to the asylum crisis deepening in Europe. Finally, the last section points at the democracy issue in the process of Europeanisation of social services.

10.1 What Place Does the EU Legislator Give to the Treaty Principles on SGEI in EU Legislation Harmonizing the Market for Social Services?

While the applicability of Article 106(2) TFEU to procurement has long been debated, and problematic given this provision's wording, the analysis in Chap. 7 has shown that the EU legislator recognises that EU procurement rules can *in principle* affect the possibility to fulfil SGEI missions, and are therefore covered by Article 14 TFEU and the SGI Protocol. It has been found that in the 2014 Public Sector Directive and the 2014 Utilities Directive, the derogations for in-house and public-public cooperation are *in fact* approached as "conditions enabling SGEI missions to be achieved" in the meaning of Article 14 TFEU. Also, the "principle of free administration" in the 2014 Concessions Directive transposes arguably the SGEI principles in Article 14 TFEU and the SGI Protocol.

In the field of social services, the new public procurement directives impose a duty for the Member States to allow their contracting authorities to take account of social services' "specificities". It has been submitted that this duty is obviously related to the principles in Article 14 TFEU and the SGI Protocol and can only be legitimated by the Treaty principle in Article 14 TFEU.

Thus, the new procurement directives recognise that pursuant to Article 14 TFEU, the Union and the Member States must adapt their procurement rules to the existence of SGEIs in the national systems, but the new procurement directives have not overtly been adopted "with regard of Article 14 TFEU".

This ambiguous presence of Article 14 TFEU in the new procurement directives reflects the Commission's arbitration of the debate on whether legislation based on Article 14 TFEU should be adopted.[1] Indeed, former commissioner

[1]Maxian Rusche gives insight on this political debate, which has divided both the EU Parliament and the Member States, see Maxian Rusche 2013, pp. 107–109.

Barnier has stated that he had relied on Article 14 and the SGI Protocol each time he could between 2010 and 2014, in order to "modify earlier attitudes", the most important thing being in his view to take inspiration from Article 14 TFEU and the SGI Protocol, and "take steps forward".[2] His declaration suggests that the Commission's decision to infuse the new procurement directives with normative elements from Article 14 TFEU and the SGI Protocol was *political*. However, it is argued here the Commission could *in law* not propose new procurement directives without at least acknowledging the normative relevance of these provisions for procurement rules at EU and national level.

Given the CJEU's use of the criterion "public service task" in *Commission v Germany* – the Commission could consolidate the case law on in-house and public cooperation without putting into words that contracting authorities' "public service tasks" may be seen as SGEI *missions* in the meaning of Article 14 TFEU. At the same time, the Commission could not deny that contracting authorities' "public service tasks" *may be seen* as SGEI *missions* in the meaning of Article 14 TFEU. This emerges rather evidently from the stance that the Public Sector Directive and the Concessions Directive do "not affect the decision of public authorities whether, how and to what extent they wish to perform *public functions* themselves pursuant to Article 14 TFEU and Protocol No 26".[3]

Another conclusion is that introducing procurement rules for social services over a certain threshold could not happen without taking into account that SGEI missions de facto exist in that field. In fact, by limiting these rules to a duty of prior notice of contracts seems actually to confirm that the Commission saw a need, pursuant to Article 14 TFEU, to strike *ex-ante* a balance between the EU interest of free movement and competition and the SGEI missions usually pursued by contracting authorities in the field of social services. Yet in the 2014 procurement directives, the principle that Member States must allow contracting authorities to ensure quality, safety, affordability, user rights etc. in their procurement

[2]Asked why the Commission had not adopted legislation on basic banking services on the basis of Article 14 TFEU, as it first intended to, former commissioner Michel Barnier answered: "In the past three and a half years, I have used every occasion to refer to this Article, and to the values in Protocol 26, in order to change attitudes developed in the past. I believe that we have succeeded with this in the fields of state aid, public procurement, concessions, and access to essential services, with our proposal on basic bank account which corresponds to an essential need. We have promoted other developments in that area, such as social entrepreneurship. What is important is that the text is proposed, finally we have reached our objective through the internal market [legal ground], and in my view the most important is to be pragmatic. There might still be some reluctance to use these new Articles, this is changing, and the most important is that we take inspiration from them. That we take steps forward." (Own translation from interview of Michel Barnier, former Commissioner for Internal Market and Services by Sophie Mosca, "Remettre les services publics au coeur du projet européen", Europolitics, Hiver 2013–2014, Hors série, available at http://www.philippejuvin.fr/wp-content/uploads/2014/01/D13113-Europolitics-HS-FR-4.pdf, p. 24.

[3]Article 1(4) of the 2014 Public Sector Directive and Article 1(4) of the 2014 Utilities Directive.

does not refer to SGEI missions, but to a "need to ensure" these results, given the "specificities" of social services. Social services' "specificities" and the "need to ensure" them are very vague terms, which do not explicitly indicate that national procurement rules should enable contracting authorities to achieve *their* public service tasks, often defined in law.

In fact, the EU legislator was not free to take inspiration from Article 14 TFEU and the SGI Protocol in the new procurement directives, but had to respect their principles. A *political* choice has been made to refer to these provisions in a generally vague and cautious manner, which is arguably due to the risks of acknowledging the *application* of these provisions too openly. One risk was that the concept of SGEI may be understood "too broadly". Another risk must have been that relating the mild procurement regime to the SGEI character of social services would raise the issue of which legal basis should have been chosen, which could have jeopardised the broad revision of EU procurement rules so many stakeholders wanted.

However, by "diluting" the notion of SGEI missions in the vague notion of "public functions" and the SGEI missions of social services in the notions of "needs" and "specificities", it can seem that contracting authorities may freely decide how they organise, commission and provide social services. Yet, their decisions *must* be guided by their constitutional, statutory or administrative missions, which constitute the benchmark of the "needs" to ensure. The new procurement directives do not deny these missions, but clearly invite the Member States to transform "communitarian SGEIs" into lighter "market SGEIs" which are closer to the concept of universal service obligations and facilitate the Europeanisation of these services.[4] Thus, the Member States are invited to procure social services in a manner which differentiates "categories of users" and specifically "the disadvantaged and vulnerable groups", and promotes innovation.

In this approach, the principle that the Union must take care that the principles and conditions under which SGEIs operate allow them to achieve their missions, is actually used to introduce *new* EU principles for social services, going beyond those enumerated exhaustively in the third paragraph of Article 1 in the SGI

[4]The term "communitarian" is borrowed from Davies. By "communitarian reasons" Davies pointed at "subtle, non-quantitative, subjective, unprovable motives" for designing welfare systems which go beyond the goal of ensuring the most effective treatment and teaching right now. He considered that governments can have legitimate reasons to structure their systems in a manner that may restrict change and individual freedom, and therefore competition, in particular the will to ensure that the system is stable, enjoys support, and can go on developing and surviving, that it contributes to a society's cohesion and identity. In his view, "[g]overnments concerned about the quality of life of their citizens – which might be influenced by trust in society, social division and the criminal and social costs it brings, and the perception and actual pursuit of equality – must look at welfare institutions in context, and consider the contribution they make beyond the concrete services they provide". Thus "communitarian reasons" cannot easily "be expressed in terms of the narrowly functional requirements to provide the highest-quality services at the lowest cost to all customers now" and are "well expressed in terms of social capital". See Davies 2010, p. 114, referring to Rothstein 2001, *Social capital in the social democratic welfare state*, (2001) 29 Politics and Society 207.

Protocol. These additional principles – such as "including disadvantaged and vulnerable groups" and "the involvement and empowerment of users and innovation" – reflect the "residual" and market-friendly approach of welfare services which the Commission has generally promoted, in particular in the field of housing. It is highly questionable whether the missions of social services financed by citizens in the Member States should be redefined under the pressure of EU directives on procurement. It seems neither compatible with the value of democracy which the Union and the Member States must loyally respect, nor with Article 14 TFEU imposing on the Union and the Member States to establish such principles through *regulations*.

By their evident lack of concern with undistorted competition, the light rules for the procurement of social services have a clear potential to weaken public procurement as a mode of entrustment preventing illegal state aid in this field, depending on how the notion of "aid" will be defined by the Commission. Also, systems of choice and vouchers systems have been excluded from the definition of procurement for the purpose of the new procurement directives. It may be noted that this exemption is only made in the recitals, and does not evoke the elements of agreement and pecuniary interest which may characterise such systems. Thus, the normative strength of Article 106(2) TFEU, and the proportionality of public funding of social services – be it through procurement, systems of choice, or vouchers systems – depends heavily on the design of state aid rules applicable to social services under Article 107(1) TFEU or under Article 106(2) TFEU.

A crucial feature in the design of state aid rules applicable to social services is that the control of their application has been devolved to the Member States, which calls for precise guidance from the Commission. In this respect, the short study of particular relevant parts of the 2011 SGEI Package, and of the Commission's decision-making practice, has led to the following findings.

First, it has been found that the Commission does not provide sure and clear guidance on the criteria allowing to determine the economic character of social services funded with public resources, although it is primordial for a correct application of these rules by the Member States. While the Commission had announced clarifications on that issue, the draft Notice on the notion of aid has not yet been adopted when this is written, two years after the end of the consultation. At any rate, the Commission takes in the draft Notice a rather casuistic approach to determine whether the activity at issue is economic, instead of presenting the decisive criteria in a coherent system. The draft Notice tends to refer to the Commission's own decision-making practice, where the economic character of an activity has at several occasions been determined with the support of both competition case law and free movement case law. This "cross-over reasoning" appears to build on a view that "provided for remuneration" is equivalent to "offered on a/the market", which is in line with the results of the study conducted in part I (Chap. 2). However, the "why" of this approach is not explained by the Commission in soft law, is at odd with its view that there may be two sets of criteria for the notion of economic activity (one in the field of free movement, the other in the field of competition and state aid), and moreover has the major drawback of importing the oddity of the *Humbel* doctrine into the field of state aid law.

Second, the Commission has asserted that Member States cannot attach specific public service obligations to an activity which is already provided or can be provided satisfactorily by undertakings operating under normal market conditions and under conditions, such as price, objective quality characteristics, continuity and access to the service, consistent with the public interest as defined by the State.[5] It has been submitted that the Commission's stance causes confusion in a field that was not in need of it, as it seems to imply that national legislators may not define SGEI missions, for instance in the field of social services, allowing them to evaluate whether and how the market offer can achieve the missions defined, and to intervene on the market so that the SGI/SGEI missions can be achieved. While some scholars seem to support the Commission's understanding, this narrow "reversed definition" is problematic in several respects.[6] Although some Commission decisions may suggest otherwise, it follows from the case law studied in chapter 4 that, to borrow Schweitzer's words, Article 106(2) TFEU "acknowledges that a political choice to intervene into the market may be legitimate irrespective of a finding of a "market failure" in a narrow economic sense", and "respects the Member States' political decision to pursue redistributive policies in the provision of essential services and to pursue citizenship values over and beyond the mere protection of user rights".[7]

Indeed, the Commission's narrow definition is also at odds with the findings summarised in Chap. 6 that, largely as a result of the impossibility for Member States to withdraw public services within their competence from EU market law, SGEI emerges from the EU Treaties and the CJEU's case law as a broad concept of EU constitutional law, whose core is not limited by the notion of entrustment, and which is therefore able to encompass public service tasks incumbent on public authorities, as clearest in *Commission v Germany*.[8] Last but not least, it is certainly not coherent with the affirmation made in Article 1(4) of the Public Sector Directive that "this Directive does not affect the decision of public authorities whether, how and to what extent they wish to *perform public functions themselves*

[5]Point 123 of the 2011 SGEI Framework.

[6]In a paper of 2008, Sauter held namely that: "the concept of market failure (and/or government failure) is a logical starting point when defining the scope of SGEI and universal service obligations" as "it is only in those cases that the services concerned are not already provided to the requisite standard by the market (and/or by public authorities) that market parties must be entrusted with the provision of particular services in the public interest." See Sauter 2008, pp. 17–18. In a later paper of 2014, Sauter concluded that the concept of SGEI is still developing. He found a new emphasis on the requirements of universality and market failure, and considered that this "tandem" of equity and efficiency is likely to further increase the relevance of what he calls "this ever-expanding exception". Sauter 2014, p. 18.

[7]Schweitzer 2011, p. 59, footnotes omitted. Schweitzer refers to an Opinion prepared by the State Aid Group of EAGCP of 29 June 2006, "Services of General Economic Interest", 1 and 2–3, and to Prosser's view that there are three different rationales for regulation, in principle all covered by Article 106(2) TFEU: economic principles, individual rights, and social solidarity, in Prosser 2006, pp. 364–365.

[8]Case C-480/06 *Commission v. Germany* [2009] ECR I-4747.

pursuant to Article 14 TFEU and Protocol No 26". In fact, it is difficult to understand why the Commission chooses to launch a cross-sectoral definition of what Member States may characterise as SGEI, encompassing even social services where redistribution policies can be an expression of democratic choices.

Third, it appears that the relation of the rules on social services in the 2011 SGEI Package with the Treaty provisions on SGEIs is somewhat unclear. Undeniably, the 2011 SGEI Decision, which exempts public funding of social housing, hospital health care and now a wide range of social services from the duty of notification, requires that substantial conditions are fulfilled, and thus shapes an "EU model for social services" endorsing efficiency and a certain degree of competition.[9] Meanwhile, the Member States must now assess themselves whether the conditions are fulfilled case by case, and are certainly expected to seek guidance in the Commission's own decision-making practice. And in fact, the Commission's practice does not seem to require precise public service obligations. The risk of such leniency is that over-compensation of public service obligations is not really sanctioned, and consequently that Article 106(2) TFEU is "devitalised" as an exception rule. It can be argued that, even if compensation *has been paid* on the basis of vaguely defined tasks, Article 36 EUCFR implies that EU law must not endanger the right of access to SGEIs, which could be the case if operators unexpectedly must pay back over-compensation. On the other hand, allowing unreasonably vague public service obligations does not serve efficiency and may lead to quality issues. Besides, it has been submitted that unclear public service obligations do not allow to delineate what user rights include and does not allow to enforce them efficiently.

Considered on this background, letting Member States assess the compatibility of their organisation and funding of social services with EU principles and conditions governing state aid to social services, is thought provoking. While it seems defendable on reasons of administrative economy, and to give Member States time to adapt to the emerging "EU model for social services", it also seems to overestimate the possibility to apply these rules correctly on the basis of the guidance provided by the Commission. The record of Member States' application of state aid rules applying to social services is very low and cannot be expected to be much better in the future, unless the Member States receive pedagogic, precise and concise guidance, in particular because the rules can affect the policies promoted by their systems.

The Commission is certainly aware that its guidance on the criteria determining that an activity is economic and on the degree of precision in defining public service obligations is still uncertain. The Commission is certainly also aware that its 2011 SGEI Package comprises both legislation adopted in the frame of its powers and soft law documents where its interpretation of EU law, in particular of the EU concept of SGEI, may be affected by political preferences. It could therefore well

[9]Van de Gronden and Rusu 2013, pp. 214–215.

be so that the Commission does not expect that Member States loyally apply these rules, but instead enter an "incubation phase", under which its vision of an EU harmonisation of social services gains acceptance at national level and is discussed, although not in the brutal light of a too democratic debate.[10]

10.2 Can EU Rules on Procurement and State Aid Applying to Social Services Affect Their Liberalisation in the Member States?

This question has been approached through the case study of social services in systems of choice in Sweden. Although this question has not particularly been highlighted in Chap. 9, it must be noted here that neither LOV-based elderly home care systems nor school education systems seem *prima facie* covered by the 2014 procurement directives, under the condition that they constitute systems of choice exempted from these directives. As a result, these directives do a priori not affect this mode of organisation of social services in Sweden. Another thing is that these systems must comply with EU free movement rules, an issue which is outside the scope of this study.

It has been found in Chap. 9 that social services under the competence of Swedish local and regional authorities (LRAs) constitute services in the meaning of the Treaties. They are *normally* provided for remuneration (and thus services in the meaning of Article 57 TFEU) and are not necessarily provided by public entities (and thus fulfil the comparative criterion in *Höfner*). It has also been found that social services in local and regional authorities' competence may certainly be regarded as services of general interest. This does not necessarily imply that the activity conducted by entities providing social services conduct an economic activity subject to state aid rules, as this question must be examined case by case.

Regarding elderly home care in LOV-based systems of choice and school education in systems of choice, it has been found that both private and municipal entities conduct an economic activity and constitute undertakings in the meaning of EU competition and state aid rules, a fact which is not visible in Swedish national rules and preparatory works on LRAs' aid to economic operators and on LRAs' sales activities. Taking as a plausible point of departure that public funding of elderly home care in Sweden can affect trade, due to the presence of large

[10]European commissioner for Competition Margrethe Vestager has however addressed the following message to the Member States: "To balance that change, your commitment was to take greater responsibility for ensuring compliance. /…/ I would like to propose a strategic approach to how we can work together." Speech at High Level Forum of Member States by Margrethe Vestager, Commissioner for Competition, Brussels 18 December 2014, available at. http://ec.europa.eu/commission/2014-2019/vestager/announcements/speech-high-level-forummember-states-margrethe-vestager-commissioner-competition-18-december-2014_en.

companies offering both elderly home care and other services both in Sweden and in other Member States, it has been found that LOV-based systems for elderly home care do not to comply with the fourth *Altmark* criterion. To be compatible with the Treaties, public service compensation received by providers in the system must therefore fulfil the criteria in the 2011 SGEI Decision, which is not the case, and had not either been under the 2005 SGEI Framework which had applied to these systems before the 2011 SGEI Decision came into force. Had these legal facts been established, which depends to a large extent on whether an effect on trade becomes plausible, it seems that LOV would have had to be modified, and required the definition of precise public service obligations, as well as mechanisms preventing and avoiding over-compensation. Such requirements had probably reduced profit opportunities and rendered the activity less attractive for private operators, which had affected the development of this market in Sweden.

Regarding systems of choice for school education, where both municipal and independent schools may operate, and where many operators are for-profit, including larger groups conducting this activity in Sweden but also selling educational services in other Member States and in third countries, it has been argued that public service compensation can affect trade. If and when this condition is fulfilled, it is covered by the 2011 SGEI Framework, which in particular requires that the duration of operators' SGEI-tasks is set by the act or acts entrusting these task, a condition that makes less attractive for private equity firms to invest on the Swedish school market, and can affect market development.

Although it seems that the Commission does not put particular pressure on the Member States to assess whether the 2011 SGEI Decision applies to social services which they fund and how they ensure compliance, there are good reasons to examine this issue. One is evidently to ensure the legality of the systems, and thereby secure the social rights which they uphold. Another is the interesting question of whether EU rules on state aid applying to elderly home care in LOV-based systems and to school education in the Swedish systems of choice may have a positive role to play in the governance of these public services in Sweden.

Some of the problems arising in systems of choice have been evoked in Chap. 9. In LOV-based systems of elderly home care, there are issues related to the proportionality of public service compensation, and also of service quality, in particular concerning the time actually spent with elderly persons. Regarding school education, there is presently an intense debate on the Swedish systems of choice, given the decline in pupils' performance and the growing differences between schools in terms of achievement.[11] A particularly burning issue is the continuity of

[11] To name but a few of the studies conducted on the Swedish system of education, a recent OECD analyses the decline in student performance and the growing differences in achievement between schools in Sweden, on the background of the decentralised model, the importance to school choice, and the presence of many corporate providers to enter the education market, see Blanchenay P., Burns T. and Köster F., 2014, *Shifting Responsibilities—20 Years of Education Devolution in Sweden: A Governing Complex Education Systems Case Study, OECD Education Working Papers,* No. 104, Paris: OECD Publishing, DOI: http://dx.doi.org/10.1787/5jz2jg1rqrd7-en, p. 37.

service provision, as nothing so far obliges private operators fulfil to commit to a duration of the tasks for which they receive public funding. Such problems should certainly be addressed because these systems of choice have been presented by both right and left parties governing in Sweden as "here to stay".[12]

It has been argued in Chap. 9 that quality issues in systems of choice for elderly home care, may be related to the vagueness of providers' tasks, and to the legislator's insistence on designing requirements capable of attracting a large amount of operators. Elderly care is delivered to many vulnerable elderly persons in Sweden, and its quality is therefore difficult to ensure through market control. It is not excluded that if the substantial conditions imposed by the 2011 SGEI Decision were loyally considered as a normative point of departure in LOV-based elderly home care systems, the public service tasks would have to be defined with more precision, which may allow to address competition concerns and quality concerns at the same time. It has also been argued in Chap. 9 that continuity in market-based school education may be easier to achieve by introducing a statutory condition of explicit and proportional duration for the education task entrusted and publicly funded, than by trying to control the motives and conditions of school operators' ownership.[13]

If applied loyally to these systems, the SGEI rules may perhaps contribute to solve some of these issues. Indeed, both under the *Altmark* criteria and under the 2011 SGEI Package, clearly and precisely defined public service obligations constitute a point of departure in the assessment of compensation proportionality. Also, applying the 2011 SGEI Framework to the public funding of schools in systems of choice would imply that the duration of the task entrusted is set in the act of entrustment and justified by reference to objective criteria such as the need and the costs of continuity in service provision. Besides, linking systems of choice to

Footnote 11 (continued)

Böhlmark and Lindahl have found that the Swedish system of school choice appears to generate positive results, but see a risk that it may increase school segregation and affect pupils' equal chances, see Böhlmark and Lindahl 2012, "Friskolereformens långsiktiga effekter på utbildningsresultat" (En: *Long-term effects of the free schools reform on education results*), SNS Analys nr 7 (2012), available at http://www.sns.se/sites/default/files/sns_analys_nr_7.pdf, p. 10. Vlachos recalls that school choice is popular and does not deny that competition may have positive effects, but points at performance, segregation and continuity issues and calls for debate on how regulation, control and sanction instruments could limit the system's adverse effects. See Vlachos J., 2011, *Friskolor i förändring* (En: *Developments in free schools*) in Konkurrensens konsekvenser – Vad händer med svensk välfärd? (En: *The effects of competition – What happens with Swedish welfare?*), Laura Hartman (ed.), Stockholm: SNS Förlag, p. 107.

[12]The independent schools committee of inquiry's conclusions were that "independent schools are here to stay", as the possibility to choose school is important both for pupils and for the development of education. (p. 287).

[13]This is the regulatory alternative which has been studied by the committee of enquiry on requirements on private actors providing welfare services "Krav på privata aktörer i välfärden" ("Ägarpröningsutredningen", En: *obligations on private operators providing welfare services*), SOU 2015:7, already evoked above.

EU rules on the public funding of SGEIs would arguably also imply a duty for the Swedish legislator's as well as local authorities', to ensure under Article 14 TFEU that the conditions of SGEIs' operation, in particular financial and economic, enable them achieve their missions. Given the public service task – arguably an SGEI mission in the meaning of Article 14 TFEU – to ensure access to social service of good quality in the Swedish Social Services Act, this may lead the issue of under-compensation to receive more attention in the design of LOV-based elderly home care systems.

EU state aid rules on SGEIs are not argued here to constitute a panacea for a good governance of social services, and these EU rules are not only dynamic but should also be subject to democratic scrutiny. However, as already emphasized, in a context where local authorities responsible for social services have to address an array of societal objectives and must achieve their statutory missions under budget discipline, the explicit SGEI characterization of a service may bring more focus on the "core mission". In market-based systems of choice, the obligation to explicitly characterise publicly funded service provision as SGEI tasks may constitute an instrument of democracy, by obliging the legislator to be more explicit on what missions public authorities exactly have.

More precise missions, in particular concerning the quality levels ensured, may force public authorities to design more clearly the public service obligations which they fund, thereby preventing that citizens funding the system and individuals entitled to use it bear a disproportionate societal and individual risk of poor delivery. Indeed, many would agree with Davies that in the field of social services "it [is] hard for a customer to truly judge the quality of what he receives".[14] Thus, in a report commissioned by the Swedish Competition Authority, Spagnolo held that a customer choice model should not create special problems public service provision if added to a well-designed procurement strategy, but can lead to very poor outcomes if introduced *instead* of a well-designed strategy for the selection and management of contractors. The reason in his view is that the role of a skilled public procurer cannot be delegated to uninformed customers, generally unwilling to collect information, compare performance, and switch suppliers, which firms are well aware of.[15]

In this respect, it is interesting to note that, although Sweden has so far been reluctant to explicitly characterise social services as SGEIs, the Swedish Competition Authority considered in a report of 2009 that

> Also aid not comprised by the EU's state aid rules can have a tangible competition-distorting effect in markets in Sweden. Consequently there is a need for a national set of rules to handle aid which, in this manner, ends up outside the EU's state aid rules. There are at

[14]Davies adds wittingly that "[h]ospitals simply wanting to come high in customer satisfaction rankings would probably do better to teach their staff to smile a lot and provide free tea than invest in the latest treatments and advances. An analogous statement could be made of education, see Davies 2010, p. 113.

[15]Report of Giancarlo Spagnolo commissioned by the Swedish Competition Authority "Open Issues in Public Procurement", pp. 20–21, footnotes omitted, accessed 27 February 2015 at. http://www.konkurrensverket.se/globalassets/publikationer/uppdragsforskning/open-issues-in-publicprocurement.pdf.

present no national rules with which to deal efficiently with public subsidies. /…/ National state aid rules should, however, according to the Swedish Competition Authority comprise all aid given from the public, consequently also the municipal sector.[16]

10.3 Political Concerns that the Treaty Principles on SGEI May Hinder the Development of Social Service Markets

This study has amply shown that SGEI must be regarded as a constitutional EU concept relevant throughout the EU Treaties. The expansion of EU market law led to it, the Treaty provisions suggest it, the CJEU's case law confirms it, and the 2014 procurement directives acknowledge it.

Yet it is clear that the CJEU approaches the concept with much caution. In the context of the post-Lisbon Treaties, the Court's challenge is to find a politically acceptable understanding of the concept, neither too restrictive nor too broad. It has been shown that by using the notions of overriding reason related to the general interest, "public service obligations", and "public service tasks" the Court has so far been able to suggest its understanding of SGEI as a broad constitutional concept without being too explicit. The use of alternative notions has allowed the Court to apply the Treaty market rules to public services with a varying degree of political empowerment and market empowerment, thereby avoiding that characterising a regulation or a measure as constituting an SGEI becomes a trump argument for any derogation from the market freedoms.

Unfortunately, this bifurcated approach involves that the CJEU's understanding of the EU concept of SGEI is still obscure, even if this study has proposed some interpretations of its case law and argued that the Court approaches SGEI as an EU concept. At the same time, the Court withholds margins of decisional freedom by delineating the criteria of applicability of free movement and competition case by case, which makes it difficult to see the "system", even if this study has also tried to identify it.[17] The price of these approaches is that in the field of public services, the Court's case law does not emerge as firm and assessable, and rather far from the ideal formulated by Pescatore that "the structure of the European Community and its law form a system, that is to say, a structured, organised and finalised whole. The Community thus benefits from the resources and the dynamics of the system."[18]

[16]Report of the Swedish Competition Authority "Action for Better Competition", report 2009:4, pp. 104–105, accessed 27 February 2015 at. http://www.kkv.se/globalassets/english/publications-and-decisions/action-forbetter-competition.pdf.

[17]Baquero Cruz: "It is at least true that our knowledge tends towards forming a system. Without this tendency – the tendency towards finding a meaningful connection between the various particulars – reality falls apart." Baquero Cruz 2002, p. 5.

[18]Pescatore 1974, p. 41.

Under such circumstances, the EU legislator may look away and develop its own "system" for the application of EU market law to public services, now also social services, were EU law is more obviously political. Thus, it is important to see that in engaging the process of EU harmonisation of social services, the Commission makes reference to the Treaty rules on SGEIs, but keeps Article 14 TFEU and the SGI Protocol at a cautious distance. The pragmatic approach consists in not proposing legislation on the basis of Article 14 TFEU, but to take sufficient "inspiration" from Article 14 and the SGI Protocol to render harmonisation acceptable, thereby avoiding very carefully to force Member States to render their SGEIs explicit, arguably so that they are not tied up to present models and can liberalise them.

Most recently, the Commission gave renewed evidence of its *political* concern to avoid invoking SGEIs in the field of procurement law. In its Communication on the public procurement rules in connection with the asylum crisis in Europe,[19] the Commission evokes the Union's "numerous challenges due to a sudden, steeply increased influx of asylum seekers", and points at the "negotiated procedure without prior publication" as a last-resort procurement procedure to allow public authorities to ensure access to housing, supplies and services for asylum seekers, "in a simple, speedy and non-bureaucratic manner". It is underlined that all the criteria imposed to use this exceptional procedure must be met, in particular the occurrence of an "extreme urgency making compliance with general deadlines impossible". Regarding the *reason* of this urgency, the Commission states that the Member States "*have to* satisfy adequately and speedily the most immediate needs of the asylum seekers". Yet, instead of acknowledging that the Member States have a public service task to meet the needs of asylum seekers in accordance with international conventions and principles – an SGEI mission – the Commission evokes cautiously a "*need* to provide for [asylum seekers] needs" which "cannot reasonably be doubted".[20] In the name of legal certainty, it would be simpler to say that Article 14 TFEU imposes on the EU and the Member States a duty to secure that EU procurement rules do not obstruct the achievement of the SGEI mission based on international law commitments.

As to the Swedish legislator's choice not to characterise social services as SGEIs, the two cases studies have shown rather clearly the complications which the application of EU state aid rules on SGEIs may imply for a rapid and large scale development of systems of choice. Therefore, the Swedish State's reluctance to explicitly point at the SGEI-missions connected to activities belonging to the Swedish public sector, is not simply an ideological reaction against a concept which may conserve the welfare state, but is explained more convincingly by the Swedish State's ambitions to develop the private consumption of social services in Sweden and to promote Swedish companies' export of social services.

---

[19]Commission, Communication from the Commission to the European Parliament and the Council on Public Procurement rules in connection with the current asylum crisis, COM (2015) 454 final, published on 9 September 2015.

[20]Ibid, p. 8, emphasis and precision added. In particular, Article 14 of the Universal Declaration of Human Rights states that "everyone has the right to seek and to enjoy in other countries asylum from persecution".

In the field of school education, things are particularly complicated. Admitting that school education is an economic activity in Sweden implies that the activity *can be* economic, which makes school education a good candidate to become a "service in the meaning of Article 57 TFEU". Politically, acknowledging this legal-economic fact may render the Swedish welfare liberalisation hugely unpopular in some Member States. No EU institution would like to announce such news, even if EU is not ancient Greece and messengers of bad news are not killed on the spot.

The answer to the main research question is thus that indeed, a transparent and loyal enforcement of the Treaty principles attached to SGEIs is, by different institutions and at different levels of governance, feared to restrict the Member States' discretion to liberalize social services and the expansion of a European market for social services. "Old SGEIs" existing de facto in the legislation of many Member States are good to have, as they support welfare systems as we still know them. If the principle of proportionality inherent to Article 106(2) TFEU should remain vital, they ought to be formulated, in particular because it is necessary for a loyal application of the 2011 SGEI Package. Yet their explicit formulation can tie Member States to welfare commitments and modes which restrict a differentiated demand of social services, may restrict profit opportunities in this field of activity, and render liberalisation more difficult.

10.4 A Democratic Issue

The Commission has taken the bold step to engage EU into the governance of social services through the EU harmonisation of EU procurement and state aid law, in the frame of a policy alluringly entitled "A Quality Framework for Services of General Interest in Europe". The Union is now in the front line of the governance of social services, and if we believe Nettesheim, this may threaten its legitimacy.[21] To be sure, this SGI Quality Framework has been presented as an answer to Europe's economic crisis, but it comes also in the context of Union requirements of budget discipline controlled by EU institutions on the basis of a legislative armada,[22] and of controversial austerity programmes imposed by the Union on certain Member States of the Eurozone.[23]

[21]"As long as EU limited itself to imposing market discipline on the Member States, it was not only strong politically but also legitimate from the perspective of its objective and mission of economic efficiency. By becoming the guardian of the European social virtue it ventures into a dangerous and extremely politicized territory; this weakens it and threatens its very legitimacy" (own translation from French), Nettesheim 2008, p. 637.

[22]By this expression is meant the impressive amount of new legislation adopted since 2011, including in particular the so called "Six Pack" and the Treaty on Stability, Co-ordination and Governance (TSCG) signed on 2 March 2012 by 25 Member States.

[23]Scharpf fears that these austerity programmes "create the conditions for anti-European political mobilization from the extremes of the political spectrum", and in the worst case undermine democracy in EU member states as well as endanger European integration itself. Scharpf 2011, p. 38.

The democracy issue is patent: social services are now under pressure not only of EU economic control, but now also of EU market rules, without any debate on what the "EU model for social services" may become in this process. There are probably visions underpinning the frameworks, but citizens are not invited to know what they are, and even less to discuss them. Is there for instance a positive bias for "lighter procurement" and systems of choice? Is there a policy preference for residual models of welfare services, differentiating between disadvantaged groups and more well-off groups of users, as some wording in the Public Sector Directive suggests?

To initiate an EU governance of social services, the Union communicates with EU citizens and their representatives through two voluminous and highly technical legal Packages mixing binding rules and political recommendations in legal text. Unless the governments having voted the new procurement directives and discreetly endorsed the 2011 SGEI Package inform their parliaments on the meaning of these acts, and unless these parliaments perceive this new reality, translate it into intelligible language, and inform their voters on the state of the art, EU citizens will have no idea of which laws govern the social services financed with their tax.

The scholarly response to these developments vary, and thus Baquero Cruz is concerned that EU legislation on SGIs may show a market bias,[24] while Davies is confident that "[t]he liberalization of welfare can be understood as a statement or suggestion that Europe is politically mature".[25] Scharpf is convinced that "a European social market economy cannot come about, and social market economies at the national level will be destroyed, unless the politically uncontrolled dynamics of (negative) "Integration through Law" can be contained."[26]

The concern here is one of democracy.[27] EU institutions and national governments take a considerable risk if they allow EU law to be used as an instrument pre-empting a debate on the Europeanisation of social services, as "given any plausible model of democracy, citizens need a rough idea of how public policy is

[24]Baquero-Cruz 2013, p. 290.

[25]"The liberalization of welfare can be understood as a statement or suggestion that Europe is politically mature, and no longer needs closed institutions to maintain its social cohesion—it can now have the best of both worlds, of freedom and solidarity. /.../ The fear that it evokes may then be understood as a fear of ourselves, that we are in fact not ready for freedom – perhaps given the chance we will rush off and be selfish and abandon the weak to their fate. To use the European's (unjustified) stereotype of the United States; are we just Americans waiting to be released, or do we really have rooted European social values?" Davies 2010, p. 121.

[26]Scharpf 2009, p. 30.

[27]In his speech on the "State of the Union 2012", former president Barroso appealed to European democracy in grand words. Taking the view that the economic interdependency of the Member States requires a stronger economic policy co-operation, former president Barroso said: "I would like to see the development of a European public space, where European issues are discussed and debated from a European standpoint. We cannot continue trying to solve European problems just with national solutions. This debate has to take place in our societies and among our citizens."

produced."[28] This kind of empowerment is the necessary foundation of a politically mature European democracy. Who knows, EU citizens may be able to understand the EU domino games that shape their lives and the destinies of their children.

References

Baquero Cruz J (2002) Between competition and free movement: the economic constitutional law of the European Community. Hart Publishing, Oxford and Portland

Baquero-Cruz J (2013) Social services of general interest and the state aid rules. In: Neergaard U et al (eds) Social services of General Interest in the EU. T.M.C Asser Press, The Hague

Böhlmark A, Lindahl M (2012) Friskolereformens långsiktiga effekter på utbildningsresultat, SNS Analys nr 7 (2012). Accessed 31 Dec 2015 at http://www.sns.se/sites/default/files/sns_analys_nr_7.pdf

Davies G (2010) The price of letting courts value solidarity: the judicial role in liberalizing welfare. In: Ross M, Borgmann-Prebil Y (eds) Promoting solidarity in the European Union. Oxford University Press, Oxford

Maxian Rusche T (2013) The Almunia package: legal constraints, policy procedures, and political choices. In: Szyszczak E, van de Gronden JW (eds) Financing services of general interest, reform and modernization. T.M.C Asser Press, The Hague

Nettesheim M (2008) Les services d'intérêt général en droit communaturaire entre libre concurence et état social, Revue Internationale de Droit Comparé 3-2008

Pescatore P (1974) The law of integration emergence of a new phenomenon in international relations, based on the experience of the European communities. A. W. Sitjhoff, Leiden

Rothstein B (2001) Social capital in the social democratic welfare state. Polit Soc 29:207–241

Sauter W (2008) Services of general economic interest and universal service in EU Law. http://ssrn.com/abstract=1136105

Sauter W (2014) The criterion of advantage in state aid: Altmark and services of general economic interest. TILEC discussion paper 2014-015, http://ssrn.com/abstract=2426230

Scharpf FW (2009) The double asymmetry of European integration or: why the EU cannot be a social market economy max planck institute for the study of societies. MPIfG Working Paper 09/12

Scharpf FW (2011) Monetary union, financial crisis, and the preemption of democracy. Max Planck Institute for the study of societies, LEQS paper 36, http://ssrn.com/abstract=1852316

Schweitzer H (2011) Services of general economic interest: European law's impact on the role of markets and of member states. In: Cremona M (ed) Market integration and public services in the European Union. Oxford University Press, Oxford

Van de Gronden JW, Rusu CS (2013) The Altmark update and social services. In: Szyszczak E, van de Gronden JW (eds) Financing services of general economic interest, reform and modernization. T.M.C Asser Press, The Hague

[28]Lindvall and Rothstein 2006, p. 49.

Cases and Decisions

CJEU - Court of Justice

10/71 *Ministère public luxembourgeois v Madeleine Muller, Veuve J.P. Hein and others (Port of Mertert)* [1971] ECR 723

127/73 *BRT II* [1974] ECR 318

155/73 *Giuseppe Sacchi* [1974] ECR 409

9/74 *Donato Casagrande v Landeshauptstadt München* [1974] ECR 773

59/75 *Pubblico Ministero* v *Manghera* [1976] ECR 91

152/82 *Sandro Forcheri and his wife Marisa Forcheri, née Marino, v Belgian State and ASBL Institut Supérieur de Sciences Humaines Appliquées - Ecole Ouvrière Supérieure* [1983] ECR I-2323

238/82 *Duphar BV and others v The Netherlands State (Duphar)* [1984] ECR I-00523

72/83 *Campus Oil Limited and others v Minister for Industry and Energy and others (Campus Oil)* [1984] ECR 2727

293/83 *Gravier v. City of Liège* [1985] ECR I-593

118/85 *Commission* v *Italy* [1987] ECR 2599

352/85 *Bond van Adverteerders and Others* ECR [1988] p. I-2085

263/86 *Belgian State v René Humbel and Marie-Thérèse Edel (Humbel)* [1988] ECR I-5365

C-5/88 *Hubert Wachauf v Bundesamt für Ernährung und Forstwirtschaft* [1989] ECR 02609

C-202/88 *France v Commission* [1991] ECR I-1223

C-347/88 *Commission* v *Greece* [1990] ECR 1-4747

C-221/89 *R. v Secretary of State for Transport, ex parte Factortame (Factortame II)* [1991] ECR I-3905

C-260/89 *Elliniki Radiophonia Tiléorassi AE and Panellinia Omospondia Syllogon Prossopikou v Dimotiki Etairia Pliroforissis and Sotirios Kouvelas and Nicolaos Avdellas and others (ERT)* [1991] ECR I-2925

C-41/90 *Klaus Höfner and Fritz Elser v Macrotron GmbH (Höfner)* [1991] ECR I-1979

C. Wehlander, *Services of General Economic Interest as a Constitutional Concept of EU Law*, Legal Issues of Services of General Interest,
DOI 10.1007/978-94-6265-117-3

C-179/90 *Merci Convenzionali Porto di Genova SpA v. Siderurgica Gabrielli SpA* [1991] ECR I-05889

C-159/91 and C-160/91 *Poucet and Pistre* [1993] ECR I-00637

C-320/91 *Criminal proceedings against Paul Corbeau (Corbeau)* [1993] ECR 1-2563

C-19/92 *Dieter Kraus v Land Baden-Württemberg (Kraus)* [1993] ECR I-1663

C-364/92 *SAT Fluggesellschaft v Eurocontrol* [1994] ECR I-43

C-393/92 *Gemeente Almelo and Others v Energibedrijf Ijsselmij NV (Almelo)* [1994] ECR I-1477

Case C-279/93, *Finanzamt Köln-Altstadt v Roland Schumacker* [1995] ECR I-225

C-55/94 *Gebhard v. Consiglio dell'Ordine degli Avvocati e Procuratori di Milano* [1995] ECR I-4165

C-157/94 *Commission v Netherlands* [1997] ECR I-05699

C-158/94 *Commission v Italy* [1997] ECR I-5789

C-159/94 *Commission v France* [1997] ECR I-5815

C-70/95 *Sodemare SA, Anni Azzurri Holding SpA and Anni Azzurri Rezzato Srl v Regione Lombardia (Sodemare)* [1997] ECR I-3395

C-120/95 *Decker* [1998] ECR I-1831

C-242/95 *GT-Link A/S v De Danske Statsbaner (DSB) (GT-Link)* [1997] ECR I-4449

C-343/95 *Diego Cali & Figli Srl v. Servizi Ecologi Porto di Genova (Diego Cali)* [1997] ECR I-1547

C-35/96 *Commission* v *Italy* [1998] ECR I-3851

C-55/96 *Job Centre coop. arl.* [1997] ECR I-7119

C-67/96 *Albany International BV v Stichting Bedrijfspensioenfonds Textielindustrie (Albany)* [1999] ECR I-5751

C-158/96 *Raymond Kohll v Union des Caisses de Maladie* [1998] ECR I-1931

C-203/96 *Chemische Afvalstoffen Dusseldorp BV and Others v Minister van Volkshuisvesting, Ruimtelijke Ordening en Milieubeheer (Dusseldorp)* [1998] ECR I-4075

C-266/96 *Corsica Ferries France SA v Gruppo Antichi Ormeggiatori del porto di Genova Coop. arl, Gruppo Ormeggiatori del Golfo di La Spezia Coop. arl and Ministero dei Trasporti e della Navigazione (Corsica Ferries)* [1998] ECR I-3949

C-107/98 *Teckal Srl v Comune di Viano and Azienda Gas-Acqua Consorziale (AGAC) di Reggio Emilia (Teckal)* [1999] ECR I-8121

C-180/98 to 184/98 *Pavel Pavlov and Others v Stichting Pensioenfonds Medische Specialisten (Pavlov)* [2000] ECR I-6451

C-209/98 *Entreprenørforeningens Affalds/Miljøsektion (FFAD) v Københavns Kommune (Pavlov)* [2000] ECR I-3743

C-324/98 *Telaustria Verlags GmbH and Telefonadress GmbH v Telekom Austria AG, joined party: Herold Business Data AG (Telaustria)* [2000] ECR I-10793

C-157/99 *B.S.M. Geraets-Smits v Stichting Ziekenfonds VGZ and H.T.M. Peerbooms v Stichting CZ Groep Zorgverzekeringen (Smits and Peerbooms)* [2001] ECR I-5473

C-184/99 *Rudy Grzelczyk mot Centre public d'aide sociale d'Ottignies-Louvain-la-Neuve* [2001] ECR I-6193

C-205/99 *Asociación Profesional de Empresas Navieras de Líneas Regulares (Analir) and Others v Administración General del Estadonalir* [2001] ECR I-1271

C-268/99 *Aldona Malgorzata Jany and Othersand Staatssecretaris van Justitie (Jany)* [2001] ECR I-8615

C-309/99 *J. C. J. Wouters, J. W. Savelbergh and Price Waterhouse Belastingadviseurs BV v Algemene Raad van de Nederlandse Orde van Advocaten, intervener: Raad van de Balies van de Europese Gemeenschap (Wouters)* [2002] ECR I-1577

C-385/99 *V.G. Müller-Fauré v Onderlinge Waarborgmaatschappij OZ Zorgverzekeringen UA and E.E.M. van Riet v Onderlinge Waarborgmaatschappij ZAO Zorgverzekeringen (Müller-Fauré and van Riet)* [2003] ECR I-4509

C-475/99 *Ambulanz Glöckner v Landkreis Südwestpfalz* [2001] ECR I-8089

C-53/00 *Ferring SA v Agence centrale des organismes de sécurité sociale (ACOSS) (Ferring)* [2001] ECR I-9067

C-355/00 *Freskot AE v. Elliniko Dimosio* [2003] ECR I-5263

C-34/01 to C-38/01 *Enirisorse SpA v Ministero delle Finanze* [2003] ECR I-14243

C-264/01, C-306/01, C-354/01 and C-355/01 *AOK Bundesverband* [2004] ECR I-2493

C-422/01 *Försäkringsaktiebolaget Skandia (publ) and Ola Ramstedt v Riksskatteverket (Skandia)* [2003] ECR I-6817

C-496/01 *Commission v France (French laboratories)* [2004] ECR I-2351

C-247/02 *Sintesi SpA v Autorità per la Vigilanza sui Lavori Pubblici* [2004] ECR I-9215

C-438/02 *Criminal proceedings against Krister Hanner* [2005] ECR I-04551

C-147/03 *Commission* v *Austria* [2005] ECR I-5969

C-172/03 *Wolfgang Heiser v Finanzamt Innsbruck* [2005] ECR I-1627

C-205/03 P *Federación Española de Empresas de Tecnología Sanitaria (FENIN) v Commission of the European Communities (FENIN v. Commission)* [2006] ECR I-6295

C-209/03 *The Queen (on the application of Dany Bidar) v. London Borough of Ealing, Secretary of State for Education and Skills (Bidar)* [2005] ECR I-2119

C-451/03 *Servizi Ausiliari Dottori Commercialisti Srl v Giuseppe Calafiori* [2006] ECR I-2941

C-458/03 *Parking Brixen GmbH v Gemeinde Brixen and Stadtwerke Brixen AG (Parking Brixen)* [2005] ECR I-8585

C-532/03 *Commission v Ireland* [2007] ECR I-11353

C-372/04 *Yvonne Watts v Bedford Primary Care Trust, Secretary o State for Health (Watts)* [2006] ECR I-4325

C-410/04 *Associazione Nazionale Autotrasporto Viaggiatori (ANAV) v Comune di Bari and AMTAB Servizio SpA (ANAV)* [2006] ECR I-3303

C-519/04 P *David Meca-Medina and Igor Majcen v Commission (Meca-Medina)* [2006] ECR I-6991

C-76/05 *Herbert Schwarz and Marga Gootjes-Schwarz v Finanzamt Bergisch Gladbach (Schwarz)* [2007] ECR I- 6849

C-318/05 *Commission v Germany* [2007] ECR I-6957

C-444/05 *Stamatelaki* [2007] ECR I-3185

C-250/06 *United Pan-Europe Communications Belgium SA and Others v Belgian State (UPC)* [2007] ECR I-11135

C-281/06 *Hans-Dieter Jundt and Hedwig Jundt v Finanzamt Offenburg (Jundt)* [2007] ECR I-12231

C-480/06 *Commission* v *Germany* [2009] ECR I-4747

C-49/07 *Motosykletistiki Omospondia NPID (MOTOE) v. Elliniko Dimosio (MOTOE)* [2008] ECR I-4863

C-141/07 *Commission v Germany (German hospitals pharmacies)* [2008] ECR I-6935

C-169/07 *Hartlauer Handelsgesellschaft mbH v Wiener Landesregierung and Oberösterreichische Landesregierung (Hartlauer)* [2009] ECR I-1721

C-171/07 and C-172/07 *Apothekerkammer des Saarlandes and Others (C-171/07) and Helga Neumann-Seiwert (C-172/07) v Saarland and Ministerium für Justiz, Gesundheit und Soziales (Apothekerkammer des Saarlandes)* [2009] ECR I-4171

C-324/07 *Coditel Brabant SA v Commune d'Uccle and Région de Bruxelles-Capitale (Coditel Brabant)* [2008] ECR I-8457

C-350/07 *Kattner Stahlbau GmbH v Maschinenbau- und Metall-Berufsgenossenschaft (Kattner Stahlbau)* [2009] ECR I-1513

C-567/07 *Minister voor Wonen, Wijken en Integratie v Woningstichting Sint Servatius (Sint Servatius)* [2009] ECR I-9021

C-160/08 *Commission v Germany* [2010] ECR I-03713

C-265/08 *Federutility m.fl. v Autorità per l'energia elettrica e il gas (Federutility)* [2010] ECR I-3377

C-515/08 *Criminal proceedings against Vítor Manuel dos Santos Palhota and Others* (CJEU 7 October 2010)

C-437/09 *AG2R Prévoyance v Beaudout Père et Fils SARL (AG2R)* [2011] ECR I-973

C-242/10 *Enel Produzione SpA v Autorità per l'energia elettrica e il gas (Enel)* [2011] ECR I-13665

C-544/10 *Deutsches Weintor eG v Land Rheinland-Pfalz (Weintor)* [decided on 6 September 2012, nyr]

C-159/11 *Azienda Sanitaria Locale di Lecce and Università del Salento v Ordine degli Ingegneri della Provincia di Lecce and Others (Lecce)* [decided on 19 December 2012, nyr]

C-197/11 and C-203/11 *Eric Libert, Christian Van Eycken, Max Bleeckx, Syndicat national des propriétaires et copropriétaires ASBL, Olivier de Clippele v Gouvernement flamand (Libert)* [decided on 8 May 2013, nyr]

Case C-113/13 *Azienda sanitaria locale n. 5 «Spezzino» and Others v San Lorenzo Soc. coop. sociale and Croce Verde Cogema cooperativa sociale Onlus (Spezzino)* [decided on 11 December 2014, nyr]

CJEU - General Court

T-17/02 *Fred Olsen* v *Commission* [2005] ECR II-2031

T-289/03 *British United Provident Association Ltd (BUPA), BUPA Insurance Ltd and BUPA Ireland Ltd v Commission of the European Communities (BUPA)* [2008] ECR II-81

T-388/03 *Deutsche Post and DHL International v Commission (DHL)* [2009] ECR II-199

T-442/03 *SIC v Commission* [2008] ECR II-1161

T-309/04, T-317/04, T-329/04 and T-336/04, *TV 2/Danmark A/S and Others v Commission* [2008] ECR II-293

T-354/05 *TF1* v *Commission* [2009] ECR II-471

T-258/06 *Germany v Commission* [2010] ECR II-2027

T-87/09 *Andersen* v *Commission* [2009] ECR II-225

T-137/10 *Coordination bruxelloise d'institutions sociales et de santé (CBI) v Commission (CBI)* [decided on 7 November 2012, nyr]

Commission State Aid Decisions

Commission Decision of 13 March 2003 on a risk equalisation scheme in the Irish health insurance market (Ireland) in case N46/2003 – C (2003)1322 final

Commission Decision of 22 December 2005 on the introduction of a risk equalisation system in the Dutch Health Insurance (Netherlands) in cases N 541/2004 and N542/2004 – C (2005)1329 final

Commission Decision of 8 November 2006 on aid to the Přerov Logistics College (Czech Republic) in case NN54/2006 (C (2006) 5228)

Commission Decision of 2 July 2009 on nature conservation areas (Germany) in case NN8/2009 – C (2009)5080 final

Commission Decision of 28 October 2009 on the public financing of Brussels public IRIS hospitals (Belgium) in case SA.19864 (ex NN54/2009) – 2014/C

Commission Decision of 20 April 2011 on subsidies for nature management (Netherlands) in case SA.31494 (ex N376/2010) – C (2011)2631 final

Commission Decision of 13 July 2011 on a subsidy scheme for acquisition of land for nature conservation (Netherlands) in case SA.31243 (ex N308/2010) – C (2011)4945 final

EFTA Court

E-5/07 *Private Barnehagers Landsforbund v EFTA Surveillance Authority*, Efta Court Report 2008, p. 62

EFTA Surveillance Authority Decisions

No 291/03/COL EFTA Surveillance Authority decision of 18 December 2003 regarding the establishment of private day-care facilities on public sites with subsidized real estate leasehold fees in Oslo (Norway)

No 39/07/COL EFTA Surveillance Authority Decision on public financing of municipal day-care institutions in Norway

Swedish Courts Decisions

Judgment of the Administrative Court of Appeal, Kammarrätten i Stockholm, KR nr 584-08 (Täby kommun)

Judgment of the Administrative Court of Appeal, Kammarrätten i Stockholm, KR nr 3801-09 (Sollentuna kommun)

Bibliography

Arrowsmith S (2005) The law of public and utilities procurement, 2nd edn. Sweet and Maxwell, London

Arrowsmith S (2014) The law of public and utilities procurement: regulation in the EU and UK, 3rd edn. Sweet and Maxwell, London

Arrowsmith S et al (2011) EU public procurement law: an introduction. Arrowsmith S (ed) Asia Link Europe Aid

Azoulai L (2011) The 'retained powers' formula in the case law of the European Court of Justice: EU law as total law? Eur J Legal Stud 4(2)

Baquero Cruz J (2002) Between competition and free movement: the economic constitutional law of the european community. Hart Publishing, Oxford and Portland

Baquero-Cruz J (2005) Beyond competition: services of general interest and European Community Law. In: De Búrca G (ed) EU law and the welfare state. Oxford University Press, Oxford

Baquero-Cruz J (2011) The case law of the European Court of Justice. In: van de Gronden JW et al (eds) Health care and EU law. T.M.C. Asser Press, The Hague

Baquero-Cruz J (2013) Social services of general interest and the state aid rules. In: Neergaard U et al (eds) Social services of General Interest in the EU. T.M.C Asser Press, The Hague

Barnard C, De Baere G (2014) Towards a European Social Union: achievements and possibilities under the current EU constitutional framework. KU Leuven Euroforum

Bauby P (2011) From Rome to Lisbon: SGIs in primary law, in developments. In: Szyszczak E et al (eds) Services of general interest. T.M.C Asser Press, The Hague

Bauby P (2013) Unity and diversity of SSGIs in the European Union. In: Neergaard U et al (eds) Social services of general interest in the EU. T.M.C Asser Press, The Hague

Bekkedal T (2011) Article 106 TFEU is dead. Long live Article 106! In: Szyszczak E et al (eds) Developments in services of general interest. T.M.C. Asser Press, The Hague

Bergström CF (2009) Grundlagsutredningen och EU. Europarättslig Tidskrift nr 2/2009

Bernitz U (2009) Europarättens genomslag i svensk rätt – var står vi idag? Juridisk tidskrift, nr 3 2009/10

Bertola G, Hettne J, Scharpf FW, Tarschys D (2011) Är EU en social marknadsekonomi, Sociala Europa – en antologi, Svenska Institutet for Europapolitiska Studier (SIEPS) 2011: 2op

Bovis CH (2006) Developing public procurement regulation: jurisprudence and its influence on law making. Common Mark Law Rev 2:461–495

Bovis CH (2012) Public procurement in the EU: jurisprudence and conceptual directions. Common Mark Law Rev 1:247–289

Buendia Sierra JL (1999) Exclusive rights and State Monopolies under EC law. Oxford University Press, Oxford

C. Wehlander, *Services of General Economic Interest as a Constitutional Concept of EU Law*, Legal Issues of Services of General Interest,
DOI 10.1007/978-94-6265-117-3

Buendia Sierra JL (2008) Finding the right balance: state aid and services of general economic interest. In: EC state aid law: Liber Amicorum Francisco Santaolalla. Kluwer, Alphen aan den Rijn

Buendia Sierra JL, Panero Rivas JM (2013) The almunia package: state aid and services of general economic interest. In: Szyszczak E, van de Gronden JW (eds) Financing services of general economic interest—reform and modernisation. T.M.C Asser Press, The Hague

Buendia Sierra JL, Smulders B (2008) The limited role of the "refined economic approach" in achieving the objectives of state aid control: time for some realism. In: EC state aid law: Liber Amicorum Francisco Santaolalla. Kluwer, Alphen aan den Rijn

Burgi M (2014) Contracting authorities, in-house services and public authorities cooperation. In: Lichère F, Caranta R, Treumer S (eds) Modernizing public procurement: the new directive. DJØF Publishing, Copenhagen

Böhlmark A, Lindahl M (2012) Friskolereformens långsiktiga effekter på utbildningsresultat, SNS Analys nr 7 (2012). Accessed 31 Dec 2015 at http://www.sns.se/sites/default/files/sns_analys_nr_7.pdf

Caranta R (2014) FIDE general report on public procurement law: limitations, opportunities and paradoxes. In: Neergaard U, Jacqueson C, Skovgaard Ølykke G (eds) The XXVI FIDE Congress in Copenhagen, 2014, Congress Publications, vol 3. DJØF Publishing, Copenhagen, pp 79–175. Accessed 31 Dec 2015 at http://www.aanbestedingsrecht.org/project/userfiles/Fide_rapport_2014.pdf.

Chérot JY (2003) Le droit communautaire de la concurrence fonde-t-il un ordre concurrentiel - Essai sur la notion d'entreprise et d'activité économique dans la jurisprudence de la Cour. In: L'ordre concurrentiel: mélanges en l'honneur d'A. Pirovano. Frison-Roche, Paris

Craig P, De Búrca G (2008) EU law text, cases and materials, 4th edn. Oxford University Press, Oxford

Cyndecka MA (2015) The applicability and application of the market economy investor principle. University of Bergen, Norway

Damjanovic D (2013) The EU market rules as social market rules: why the EU can be a social market economy. Common Mark Law Rev 6:1685–1717

Damjanovic D, de Witte B (2009) Welfare integration through EU law: the overall picture in the light of the Lisbon Treaty. In: Neergaard U, Nielsen R, Roseberry L (eds) Integrating welfare functions into EU law—from Rome to Lisbon. DJØF Publishing, Copenhagen

Dann P (2006) Thoughts on a methodology of European constitutional law. German Law J 06(11)

Davies G (2002) Welfare as a Service. Legal Issues Econ Integr 29(1):27–40

Davies G (2006a) Subsidiarity: the wrong idea, in the wrong place, at the wrong time. 43 C.M.L.Rev. 63, p 63

Davies G (2006b) The process and side-effects of harmonisation of European welfare states. Jean Monnet working paper 02/06

Davies G (2009a) Article 86, The EC's economic approach to competition law, and the general interest. Eur Compet J

Davies G (2009) What does Article 86 actually do? In: Krajewski M, Neergaard U, van de Gronden JW (eds) The changing legal framework for services of general interest in Europe. T.M.C Asser Press, The Hague

Davies G (2010) The price of letting courts value solidarity: the judicial role in liberalizing welfare. In: Ross M, Borgmann-Prebil Y (eds) Promoting solidarity in the European Union. Oxford University Press, Oxford

Davies J, Szyszczak E (2011) Universal service obligations: fulfilling new generations of services of general economic interest. In: Szyszczak E et al (eds) Developments in services of general interest. T.M.C Asser Press, The Hague

De Cecco F (2013) State aid and the European economic constitution. Hart Publishing, Oxford and Portland

De Vries SA (2011a) BUPA: a healthy case, in the light of a changing constitutional setting in Europe? In: van de Gronden JW et al (eds) Health Care and EU Law. T.M.C Asser Press, The Hague

De Vries SA (2011b) Services of general economic interest in the interplay between public and private in europa after Lisbon: the search for more coherence. Europarättslig Tidskrift Nr 3(2011):462–482

De Vries SA (2013) The protection of fundamental rights within Europe's internal market after Lisbon—an endeavour for more harmony. In: de Vries S, Bernitz U, Weatherill S (eds) The protection of fundamental rights in the EU after Lisbon. Hart Publishing, Oxford

De Witte B et al (2010) Legislation after Lisbon, New opportunities for the European Parliament, EUI paper. Accessed 31 Dec 2015 at http://www.eui.eu/Projects/EUDO/Documents/EUDO-LegislatingafterLisbon(SD).pdf

Delors J (1986) The single act and Europe: a moment of truth. Office for Official Publications of the European Communities, Luxembourg

Dougan M (2009) The spatial restructuring of national welfare states: the contribution of union citizenship and the relevance of the treaty of Lisbon. In: Neergaard U, Nielsen R, Roseberry L (eds) Integrating welfare functions into EU law. DJØF Publishing, Copenhagen

Dougan M (2013) The bubble that burst: exploring the legitimacy of the case law on the free movement of union citizens. In: Adams M et al (eds) Judging Europe's judges: the legitimacy of the case law of the European Court of Justice. Hart Publishing, Portland

Due O (1998) The impact of the Amsterdam Treaty upon the Court of Justice. Fordham Int Law J 22(6) (Article 4)

Duguit L (1923) Traité de droit constitutionnel, tome 2. Sirey, Paris

Durkheim E (1893) De la division du travail: Etude sur l'Organisation des Sociétés Supérieures, Livre I-III Division of labor in society: a study of the Organisation of Advanced Societies, 1997, Halls WD (trans), Coser LA (introd). Free Press, New York

Durkheim E (2002) Moral Education, Courier Dover Publications

Edwardsson E (2003) Konkurrenslagen och konkurrensbegränsande offentliga regleringar. Uppsala universitet

Ehlerman CD (1987) The internal market following the single European Act. Common Mark Law Rev 24(3):361–409

Enchelmaier S (2011) Always at your service (within limits): the ECJ's case law on article 56 TFEU. Eur Law Rev 2011:36

Fiedziuk NA (2013a) Putting services of general economic interest up for tender: reflections on applicable EU rules. Common Mark Law Rev 50:87–114

Fiedziuk NA (2013b) Services of general economic interest in EU law: the role of the 'public service' exception in the light of recent developments in EU law. Wolf Legal Publishers, Oisterwijk

Foster N (2008) EU law directions. Oxford University Press, Oxford

Freedland M (1998) Law, public services, and citizenship—new domains, new regime, in public services and citizenship. In: Freedland M, Sciarra S (eds) European law. Public and labour law perspectives. Clarendon Press, Oxford

Friedman F (1955) The role of government in education. In: Solo R (ed) Economics and the public interest. Rutgers University Press, New Brunswick

Gerard D (2010) EU competition policy after Lisbon: time for a review of the "state action doctrine"? Accessed 31 December 2015 at http://dx.doi.org/10.2139/ssrn.1533842

Gerber DJ (1994) The transformation of European Community competition law. Harvard Univ Law J 35(1)

Gideon A (2012) Higher education institutions and EU competition law. Compet Law Rev 8(2):169–184

Groussot X, Pech L, Peturson GT (2011) The scope of application of fundamental rights on member states action: in search of certainty in EU adjudication. Eric Stein working paper 1/2011

Habermas J (2013) Democracy, solidarity and the European crisis. Lecture delivered by Professor Jürgen Habermas on 26 Apr 2013 in Leuven. Accessed 10 Sept 2013 at http://www.kuleuven.be/communicatie/evenementen/evenementen/jurgen-habermas/democracy-solidarity-and-the-european-crisis

Hamilton GJ (2005) A new private universal health insurance in the Netherland. In: den Exter A (ed) Competitive social health insurance yearbook 2004. Erasmus University Press, Rotterdam

Hancher L, Sauter W (2009) One foot in the grave or one step beyond? From Sodemare to DocMorris: the EU's freedom of establishment case law concerning healthcare. Accessed 31 Dec 2015 at http://ssrn.com/abstract=1429315

Hancher L, Sauter W (2013) This won't hurt a bit: the Commission's approach to services of general economic interest and state aid to hospitals. In: Szyszczak E, van de Gronden JW (eds) Financing services of general economic interest—reform and modernization. T.M.C Asser Press, The Hague

Hatzopoulos V (2011) The concept of "economic activity" in the EU Treaty: from ideological dead-ends to workable judicial concepts. Research papers in law 06/2011, College of Europe

Hatzopoulos V (2012) Regulating services in the European Union. Oxford University Press, Oxford

Hedelin J (2010) De nya svenska reglerna om konkurrensbegränsande offentlig verksamhet – en spegel av reglerna om tjänster av allmänt ekonomiskt intresse? In: Madell T, Bekkedal T, Neergaard U (eds) Den nordiska välfärden och marknaden: Nordiska erfarenheter av tjänster av allmänt intresse i en EU-rättslig kontext. Iustus förlag, Uppsala

Heide-Jørgensen C (2013) Private distortions of competition and SSGIs. In: Neergaard U et al (eds) Social services of general interest in the EU. T.M.C. Asser Press, The Hague

Hettne J (2008) Rättsprinciper som styrmedel – Allmänna rättsprinciper i EU:s domstol. Norstedts Juridik, Stockholm

Hirschman AO (1970) Exit, voice, and loyalty: responses to decline in firms, organisations, and states. Harvard University Press, Cambridge

Hordijk P, Meulenbelt M (2005) A bridge too far: why the European Commission's attempts to construct an obligation to tender outside the scope of the Public Procurement directives should be dismissed. Publ Procure Law Rev 123

Idot L (2003) La notion d'entreprise en droit de la concurrence, révélateur de l'ordre concurrentiel in L'ordre concurrentiel: mélanges en l'honneur d'A. Pirovano, Frison-Roche, Paris

Indén T (2008) Kommunen som konkurrent, Kommunalrättsliga befogenheter och konkurrensrättsliga begränsningar, Skrifter från juridiska institutionen vid Umeå universitet. Iustus Förlag, Uppsala

Jääskinen N (2011) The New Rules on SGEI. EStAL 4/2011

Jacobs FG (2001) Human rights in the European Union: the role of the court of justice. Eur Law Rev 2001(26):331–341

Jacqué JP, Weiler JHH (1990) On the road to European Union—a new judicial architecture: an agenda for the intergovernmental conference. Common Mark Law Rev 27(2):185–207

Janssen WA (2014) The institutionalised and non-institutionalised exemptions from EU public procurement law: towards a more coherent approach? Utrecht Law Rev 10(5), URN:NBN:NL:UI:10-1-115852

Joerges C, Rödl F (2004) "Social market economy" as Europe's social model. EUI working paper law 2004/8. European University Institute, Florence

Karayigit M (2010) A new type of exemption from the EU rules on public procurement established: "in thy neighbour's house" provision of public interest tasks. Publ Procure Law Rev 6(2010): 183–198

Kavanagh J (2013) Financing services of general interest: the European Commission's economic tests. In: Szyszczak E, van de Gronden JW (eds) Financing services of general economic interest—reform and modernization. T.M.C Asser Press, The Hague

Kennedy D (2006) Three globalizations of law & legal thought. In: Trubek D, Santos A (eds) The new law and economic development, a critical appraisal. Cambridge University Press, Cambridge

Krajewski M (2009) Conclusion. In: Krajewski M et al (eds) The changing legal framework for services of general interest in Europe: between competition and solidarity. T.M.C Asser Press, The Hague

Kunzlik P (2012–2013) Neoliberalism and the European Public procurement regime. In: Barnard C et al (eds) Cambridge yearbook of European legal studies, vol 15, pp 283–356

Lenaerts K (1990) Constitutionalism and the many faces of federalism. Am J Comp Law 38:205–220

Lenaerts K (2012) Defining the concept of "services of general interest" in light of the "checks and balances" set out in the EU Treaties. Jurisprudencija/Jurisprudence 19(4):1247–1267

Lind A (2009) Sociala rättigheter I förändring – en konstitutionell studie. Uppsala universitet

Lindholm J (2008) Idrottens särart och EU:s konkurrensrätt. Europarättslig tidskrift 4:914933

Lindquist U (2011) Kommunala befogenheter. Norstedts Juridik, Stockholm

Lindvall J, Rothstein B (2006) Sweden: the fall of the strong state. Scand Polit Stud 29(1)

Madell T (2011) Tjänster av allmänt intresse – ett svenskt perspektiv. SIEPS 2011:8, Svenska Institutet för europapolitiska studier, Stockholm

Madell T, Wehlander C (2013) SSGIs in Sweden: with a special emphasis on education. In: Neergaard U et al (eds) Social services of general interest in the EU. T.M.C Asser Press, The Hague

McDougall G, Roberts AS (2009) Commercializing air traffic control: have the reforms worked? Can Publ Adm 51(1):45–69. Accessed 31 Dec 2015 at Suffolk University Law School Research Paper No. 09-11

Merola M (2011) Conclusions of the conference on the reform of state aid rules on services of general economic interest from the 2005 Monti-Kroes Package to the 2011 Almunia Reform, College of Europe, Bruges, 30 September 2011. Accessed 31 Dec 2015 at https://www.coleurope.eu/content/gclc/documents/GCLC%20%20SGEI%20Conference%20Booklet.pdf

Micklitz HW (2010) Failure or ideological preconceptions – thoughts on two grand projects: the European constitution and the European civil code. EUI working papers law 2010/04. European University Institute, Florence

Mitchel de S-O-l'E. Lasser (2004) Judicial deliberations – a comparative analysis of judicial transparency and legitimacy. Oxford University Press, Oxford

Naundrup Olesen K (2011) Formål af almen interesse som element i EU-retten. In: Madell T, Bekkedal T, Neergaard U (eds) Den nordiska välfärden och marknaden: Nordiska erfarenheter av tjänster av allmänt intresse i en EU-rättslig kontext. Iustus förlag, Uppsala

Neergaard U (2008) Services of General (Economic) Interest and the Services Directive. In: Nergaard U, Nielsen R, Roseberry L (eds) The Services Directive – consequences for the welfare state and the European social model. DJØF Publishing, Copenhagen

Neergaard U (2009) Services of general economic interest: the nature of the beast. In: Krajewski M et al (eds) The changing legal framework for services of general interest in Europe: between competition and solidarity. T.M.C. Asser Press, The Hague

Neergaard U (2013) The concept of SSGI and the asymmetries between free movement and competition law. In: Neergaard et al (eds) Social services of general interest in the EU. T.M.C. Asser Press, The Hague

Neergaard U, Nielsen R (2010) Blurring boundaries: from the Danish welfare state to the European social model? Accessed 31 Dec 2015 at http://ssrn.com/abstract=1618758S

Nettesheim M (2008) Les services d'intérêt général en droit communautaire entre libre concurrence et état social, Revue Internationale de Droit Comparé 3-2008

Nicolaides P (2014) State aid uncovered: a critical analysis of developments in state aid 2014. Lexxion, Berlin

Nielsen R (2010) Scandinavian legal realism and EU Law, in the role of courts. In: Neergaard U, Nielsen R, Roseberry L (eds) Developing a European social model—theoretical and methodological perspectives. DJØF Publishing, Copenhagen

Odudu O (2009) Economic Activity as a Limit to EU Law. In: Barnard C, Odudu O (eds) The outer limits of European Union Law. Hart Publishing, Oxford

Ølykke GS (2011) The definition of a "contract" under Article 106 TFEU. In: Szyszczak E et al (eds) Developments services of general interest. T.M.C. Asser Press, The Hague

Pernice I (2009) The Treaty of Lisbon: multilevel constitutionalism in action. Walter Hallstein Institut für Europäisches Verfassungsrecht, Paper 2/09. Humboldt-Universität, Berlin

Pescatore P (1974) The law of integration emergence of a new phenomenon in international relations, based on the experience of the European communities. A. W. Sitjhoff, Leiden

Petrén G (1978) Vägen till en svensk rättighetskatalog, in Skrifter till minne av Halvar G.F. Sundberg. Institutet for offentlig och internationell rätt, Stockholm

Piernas Lopez JJ (2010) The notion of State aid and regulation in the EEU: drawing the shape of a moving target. Cuadernos de Derecho Transnacional 2(2)

Prosser T (2005) Competition law and public services: from single market to citizenship rights? Eur Publ Law 11(4)

Prosser T (2005) The limits of competition law: markets and public services. Oxford University Press, Oxford

Prosser T (2006) Regulation and social solidarity. J Law Soc 33:364–387

Reichel J (2011) European legal method from a Swedish perspective. In: Neergaard U, Nielsen R, Roseberry L (eds) European legal method—paradoxes and revitalisation. DJØF Publishing, Copenhagen

Rodrigues S (2009) Towards a general EC framework instrument related to SGEI? In: Krajewski M, Neergaard U, van de Gronden JW (eds) The changing legal framework for services of general interest in Europe, between competition and solidarity. T.M.C Asser Press, The Hague

Ross M (2000) Article 16 E.C. and services of general interest: from derogation to obligation? Eur Law Rev 25(1):22–38

Ross M (2007) Promoting solidarity: from public services to a European model of competition? Common Mark Law Rev 44(4):1057–1080

Ross M (2009) A healthy approach to services of general economic interest? The BUPA judgment of the Court of First Instance. Eur Law Rev 127–140

Rossi LS (2008) How fundamental are fundamental principles? Primacy and fundamental rights after Lisbon. Oxford J Yearbook Eur Law 27(1):65–87

Roth WH (2011) The importance of the instruments provided for in the treaties for developing a European legal method. In: Neergaard U, Nielsen R, Roseberry L (eds) European legal method – paradoxes and revitalisation. DJØF Publishing, Copenhagen

Rothstein B (2001) Social capital in the social democratic welfare state. Polit Soc 29:207–241

Rott P (2009) The user-provider relationship: informed choice and user protection through private law. In: Krajewski M, Neergaard U, van de Gronden JW (eds) The changing legal framework for services of general interest in Europe, between competition and solidarity. T.M.C Asser Press, The Hague

Rusche TM (2013) The almunia package: legal constraints, policy procedures, and political choices. In: Szyszczak E, van de Gronden JW (eds) Financing services of general interest, reform and modernization. T.M.C Asser Press, The Hague

Sanchez-Graells A (2011) Public procurement and the EU competition rules. Hart Publishing, Oxford

Sanchez-Graells A (2013) The Commission's modernisation agenda for procurement and SGEI. In: Szyszczak E, van de Gronden JW (eds) Financing services of general economic interest, reform and modernization. T.M.C Asser Press, The Hague

Sanchez-Graells A (2014) Enforcement of state aid rules for services of general economic interest before public procurement review bodies and courts. Compet Law Rev 10(1):3–34

Sanchez-Graells A (2015) Digging itself out of the hole? A critical assessment of the European Commission's attempt to revitalise state aid enforcement after the crisis, 5 May 2015. J Antitrust Enforcement (Forthcoming). Accessed 15 Jan 2016 at http://ssrn.com/abstract=2602798

Sauter W (2008) Services of General economic interest and universal service in EU law. Accessed 15 Jan 2016 at http://ssrn.com/abstract=1136105

Sauter W (2014) Public Services in EU Law. Cambridge University Press, Cambridge UK

Sauter W (2014) The criterion of advantage in state aid: Altmark and services of general economic interest. TILEC Discussion Paper 2014-015. Accessed 15 Jan 2016 at http://ssrn.com/abstract=2426230

Sauter W, Schepel H (2007) "State" and "market" in the competition and free movement case law of the EU courts. TILEC Discussion Paper 2007-024. Accessed 15 Jan 2016 at http://ssrn.com/abstract=1010075

Sauter W, van de Gronden JW (2010) Taking the temperature: a survey of the EU law on competition and state aid in the healthcare sector. TILEC Discussion Paper 2010-038. Accessed 15 Jan 2016 at http://ssrn.com/abstract=1702832

Scharpf FW (2009) The double asymmetry of European integration or: why the EU cannot be a social market economy Max Planck Institute for the study of societies. MPIfG Working Paper 09/12

Scharpf FW (2011) Monetary Union, financial crisis, and the preemption of democracy. Max Planck Institute for the Study of Societies, LEQS Paper 36. Accessed 15 Jan 2016 at http://ssrn.com/abstract=1852316

Schweitzer H (2007) Competition law and public policy: reconsidering an uneasy relationship. The example of Art. 81. EUI Working Papers Law 2007/30. European University Institute, Florence

Schweitzer H (2011) Services of general economic interest: European law's impact on the role of markets and of member states. In: Cremona M (ed) Market integration and public services in the European Union. Oxford University Press, Oxford

Semmelmann C (2010) The European Union's economic constitution under the Lisbon Treaty: soul-searching among lawyers shifts the focus to procedure. ELRev 35:516–541

Shafiq MN, Myers JP (2014) Educational vouchers and social cohesion: a statistical analysis of student civic attitudes in Sweden 1999–2009. Am J Educ 121(1):111–136

Snell J (2008) Freedom to provide services in the case law and in the services directive: problems, solutions, and institutions. In: Neergaard U, Nielsen R, Roseberry L (eds) The Services Directive—consequences for the welfare state and the European social model. DJØF Publishing, Copenhagen

Spaventa E (2007) Free movement of persons in the European Union: barriers to movement in their constitutional context. Kluwer, Alphen aan den Rijn

Steinicke M (2011) In house-kontrakter eller administrative aftaler. In: Madell T, Bekkedal T, Neergaard U (eds) Den nordiska välfärden och marknaden – Nordiska erfarenheter av tjänster av allmänt intresse i en EU-rättslig Kontext. Iustus Förlag, Uppsala

Stergiou HM (2008) The increasing influence of primary EU law and EU public procurement law: must a concession to provide services of general economic interest be tendered? In: van de Gronden JW (ed) EU and WTO law on services: limits to the realization of general interest policies within the services market. Kluwer, Alphen aan den Rijn

Szyszczak E (2004) Financing services of general interest. Mod Law Rev 67(6):982–992

Szyszczak E (2007) The regulation of the State in competitive markets in the EU. Hart Publishing, Oxford

Szyszczak E (2009) Legal tools in the liberalization of welfare markets. In: Neergaard U, Nielsen R, Roseberry L (eds) Integrating welfare functions into EU law—from Rome to Lisbon. DJØF Publishing, Copenhagen

Szyszczak E (2013) Soft Law and Safe Havens. In: Neergaard et al. (eds.) Social Services of General Interest in the EU. T.M.C. Asser Press, The Hague

Szyszczak E (2014) *Article 36: access to services of general economic interest. In:* Peers, Steve et al (eds) The EU charter of fundamental rights: a commentary. CH Beck Hart Nomos, Oxford, pp 969–982

Szyszczak E (2015) Services of general economic interest and state measures affecting competition. J Eur Compet Law Pract 6(9)

Treumer S, Werlauff E (2003) The leverage principle: secondary law as a lever for the development of primary community law. Eur Law Rev 28(1):124

Tridimas T (1999) The general principles of EU law. Oxford University Press, Oxford

Tuori K (2002) Critical legal positivism. Ashgate, Aldershot

Van de Gronden JW (2009) The Services Directive and SG(E)I. In: Krajewski M, Neergaard U, van de Gronden JW (eds) The changing legal framework for services of general interest in Europe. T.M.C Asser Press, The Hague

Van de Gronden JW (2009a) Cross-border health care in the EU and the Organisation of the National Health Care systems of the Member States: the dynamics resulting from the European Court of Justice's decisions on free movement and competition law. Wis Int Law J 26:705–760

Van de Gronden JW (2009b) Financing health care in EU law: do the European state aid rules write out an effective prescription for integrating competition law with health care? CompLRev 6(1):5–29

Van de Gronden JW (2011) The treaty provisions on competition and health care. In: Van de Gronden JW et al (eds) Health care and EU law. T.M.C. Asser Press, The Hague

Van de Gronden JW (2013a) Transnational competition law and public services. In: Hermann C, Krajewski M, Terhechte JP (eds) European yearbook of international economic law. Springer, Heidelberg, pp 109–146

Van de Gronden JW (2013b) Free movement of services and the right of establishment: does EU internal market law transform the provision of SSGI? In: Neergaard et al (eds) Social services of general interest in the EU. T.M.C. Asser Press, The Hague

Van de Gronden JW, Rusu CS (2013) The Altmark update and social services. In: Szyszczak E, van de Gronden JW (eds) Financing services of general economic interest, reform and modernization. T.M.C Asser Press, The Hague

Vedder H (2008) The constitutionality of competition—EC internal market law and the fine line between markets, public interests and (self-)regulation in a changing constitutional setting. Accessed 15 Jan 2016 at http://papers.ssrn.com/sol3/papers.cfm?abstract_id=1282035

Vlachos J (2011) Friskolor i förändring in Konkurrensens konsekvenser – Vad händer med svensk välfärd? Laura Hartman (ed). SNS Förlag, Stockholm

Von Bogdandy A (2010) Founding principles of EU law: a theoretical and doctrinal sketch. Eur Law J 16(2)

Weatherill S (1995) Law and integration in the European Union. Clarendon Press, Oxford

Wehlander C (2015) Who is afraid of SGEI—services of general economic interest in EU law with a special study on Swedish systems of choice. Skrifter från Juridiska Institutionen i Umeå, Nr. 32, Umeå

Weiler JHH (1991) The transformation of Europe. Yale Law J 100(8):2403–2483

Weiler JHH (2001) Federalism and constitutionalism: Europe's sonderweg. In: Nicolaidis K, Howse R (eds) The federal vision: legitimacy and levels of governance in the US and the EU. Oxford University Press, Oxford

Weiler JHH (2005) Mutual recognition, functional equivalence and harmonization in the evolution of the European Common Market and the WTO. In: Kostoris F, Schioppa P (eds) The principle of mutual recognition in the European integration process. Palgrave Macmillan, Basingstoke

Weiler JHH (2013) Epilogue: judging the judges – apology and critique. In: Adams M et al (eds) Judging Europe's judges: the legitimacy of the case law of the European Court of Justice. Hart Publishing, Oxford

Wenander H (2011) En princip om internationell öppenhet – 1 kap. 10 § regeringsformen och socialförsäkringsrätten. Förvaltningsrättslig Tidskrift, Särtryck ur häfte 3/2011

Wernicke S (2009) Taking stock: the EU Institutions and SGEI. In: Krajewski M, Neergaard U, van de Gronden JW (eds) The changing legal framework for services of general interest in Europe. T.M.C Asser Press, The Hague

Wiggen J (2011) Public procurement rules and cooperation between public sector entities: the limits of the in-house doctrine under EU procurement law. Publ Procure Law Rev 2011(20):157–172

Wiggen J (2014) Directive 2014/24/EU: the new provision on co-operation in the public sector. Publ Procure Law Rev 2014(3):83–93

Winterstein A (1999) Nailing the jellyfish: social security and competition law. ECLR 1999(6):324–333

Wipfelder HJ (1986) Die verfassungsrechtliche Kodifizierung sozialer Grundrechte. Zeitschrift für Rechtspolitik 1986(19):140–149

Index

C. Wehlander, *Services of General Economic Interest as a Constitutional Concept of EU Law*, Legal Issues of Services of General Interest,
DOI 10.1007/978-94-6265-117-3

T

U

V

W

MIX
Papier aus verantwortungsvollen Quellen
Paper from responsible sources
FSC® C105338

If you have any concerns about our products,
you can contact us on
ProductSafety@springernature.com

In case Publisher is established outside the EU,
the EU authorized representative is:
Springer Nature Customer Service Center GmbH
Europaplatz 3, 69115 Heidelberg, Germany

Printed by Libri Plureos GmbH
in Hamburg, Germany